CLASSICAL MYTHOLOGY & MORE

A READER WORKBOOK

MARIANTHE COLAKIS AND MARY JOAN MASELLO

Bolchazy-Carducci Publishers, Inc.
Mundelein, Illinois USA

General Editor
Vicki Wine

Contributing Editors
LeaAnn A. Osburn
Laurie Haight Keenan

Cover Design
Adam Phillip Velez

Cartography
The Ohio University Cartographic Center

Classical Mythology and More
A Reader Workbook

Marianthe Colakis and Mary Joan Masello

Bolchazy-Carducci Publishers, Inc.
1570 Baskin Road
Mundelein, IL 60069 USA
www.bolchazy.com

Printed in the United States of America
2016
by United Graphics

ISBN 978-0-86516-573-1

Contents

Publisher's Preface . . . vii

Preface . . . ix

Acknowledgements . . . xi

1. **The Muses** . . . 1

2. **The Creation of the World and the Earliest Deities** . . . 9

3. **The Olympian Deities, Part I: The Children of Cronus and Rhea** . . . 19
   Zeus (Jupiter or Jove), Hera (Juno), Poseidon (Neptune), Demeter (Ceres) and Persephone (Proserpina), Hades (Pluto), Hestia (Vesta)

4. **The Olympian Deities, Part II: The Children of Zeus** . . . 39
   Athena (Minerva), Apollo (Apollo, Phoebus Apollo) and Artemis (Diana), Aphrodite (Venus), Hermes (Mercury), Ares (Mars), Hephaestus (Vulcan), Dionysus (Bacchus, Liber)

5. **Other Deities** . . . 69
   Asclepius (Aesculapius), Eileithyia, Eos, Eris, Ganymede, Hebe, Hecate, Helius, Hypnos, Janus, Nemesis, Nike, Pan, Selene

6. **The Gods in Love** . . . 83
   Zeus and Io, Eros (Cupid) and Psyche, Apollo and Daphne, Zeus and Callisto, Aphrodite and Adonis, Aphrodite and Anchises, Zeus and Europa

7. **Daring Adventurers** . . . 107
   Phaethon, Bellerophon, Daedalus and Icarus

8. **Perseus** . . . 123

9. **Heracles (Hercules)** . . . 135
   Birth and early life; The twelve labors; Heracles' deeds after his labors, his death, and his apotheosis

10. **Jason and the Argonauts** . . . 153

11. **Theseus** . . . 171

12. **Victims of Olympian Wrath** . . . 189
    Prometheus, Arachne, Niobe, Meleager, Actaeon, Erysichthon

13. **The House of Atreus** 207

14. **Thebes and Oedipus** 229

15. **Mortal Love and Metamorphosis** 249
Narcissus and Echo; Pyramus and Thisbe; Tereus, Procne, and Philomela; Philemon and Baucis; Orpheus and Eurydice; Pygmalion and his statue; Atalanta and Hippomenes; Ceyx and Alcyone

16. **The House of Troy and the Trojan War** 277

17. **Odysseus** 309
Telemachus' search for information and Odysseus' arrival at Phaeacia, The travels of Odysseus, Odysseus' return to Ithaca and revenge on the suitors, Odysseus' later history

18. **Aeneas** 343

19. **The Kings of Rome** 377

Appendix A: Deities Chart 403

Appendix B: Genealogical Charts 405

1. The Muses (Ancestry of Orpheus) 405
2. Descendants of Chaos 405
3. Descendants of Uranus and Gaea 406
4. Descendants of Cronus and Rhea 406
5. Wives and Descendants of Zeus 407
6. Ancestry and Select Descendants of Apollo 408
7. Descendants of Nyx (Night) 408
8. Descendants of Gaea and Pontus 409
9. Descendants of Hyperion the Titan 410
10. Ancestry of Phaethon 410
11. Descendants of Agenor of Sidon 411
12. Descendants of Zeus and Danae 412
13. Family of Jason 412
14. Family of Theseus 413
15. Minoan Descendants of Europa 413
16. House of Atreus 414
17. Descendants of Cadmus, House of Thebes, and Descendants of Oedipus 415

18. House of Troy: Descendants of Priam 414
19. Family of Achilles 416
20. Family of Odysseus (Ulysses) 417
21. Family of Heracles (Hercules) 417
22. Ancestry and Family of Romulus; Kings of Rome 418
23. Sabine, Latin, and Etruscan Kings of Rome and the First Consuls. 419

Appendix C: Chapter-by-Chapter Glossary of Names and Pronunciation Guide . . 421

Bibliography 433

Credits 439

Index 441

LIST OF MAPS

A Possible Route for the Voyage of Jason and the Argonauts 154
A Possible Route for the Voyage of Odysseus from Troy to Ithaca 310
A Possible Route of Aeneas 344
Italy in the Time of the Kings 378
Rome: the Seven Hills and the Tiber River 380

Publisher's Preface

As a former teacher of mythology at the university level and one who discovered relatively late in life how powerful and life-enhancing myths can be, I am pleased to be able to offer *Classical Mythology and More* as a starting point for the study of mythology for middle- and high-school students and their teachers. I know from my own experience how myths can enlighten at the same time that they entertain, can lead to a fruitful and humanizing questioning of our learned or preconceived notions and fondly held beliefs.

Myths are more than just delightful and provocative stories. Myths speak the truth through their fantastic plot details, and (to paraphrase John 8:32) this truth can make us more free. Pondering the myths of the Greeks and Romans found in this book, and later perhaps going beyond the Western tradition and delving into the study of comparative mythology, can lead to the liberation of "demythologization." We will find ourselves reconsidering, perhaps even reformulating, our beliefs and values in light of the beliefs and values of other cultures. Myths of different cultures can further help us recognize and develop a greater appreciation for what unites us despite our varying beliefs and values: the significant truths about the human psyche.

Plato's Socrates said it best, "The unexamined life is not worth living." Myth is, I believe, one of many portals into an examined—and more worthwhile—life.

LADISLAUS J. BOLCHAZY

Preface

On August 24, 2006, a headline, quite literally of astronomical proportions, spun across television screens and web-news sites world-wide: the former ninth planet, Pluto, had been demoted to the status of a "dwarf planet" by a vote of an international assembly of astronomers meeting in Prague. Then came the news that there were several other heavenly bodies waiting in the wings that, by the new definition of "dwarf planet," would now fall into this new celestial category: Ceres, Charon, UB313 (nicknamed "Xena" for the pseudo-mythological, eponymous TV character)—these would be joining Pluto as "dwarfs."

Alas, poor Pluto, we knew you well—like your namesake Olympian of old, cast down from lofty Olympus to lowly Hades, now banished from the solar system to "dwarfdom"! To hear these Greco-Roman mythological names tripping off the tongues of anchorpersons, consultants, and other "talking heads" on the morning talk shows reassured us mortals once again, that yes, the Olympians really still do rule heaven and earth! Most assuredly, as well, bad things can happen to good gods, good mortals, and good planets whenever mortals dare, or Olympians deign, to "mess with" one another.

We set out to write a mythology workbook that would help middle school, junior high, and early high school students and their Language Arts, English, or Classics teachers discover the excitement and modern relevance of the mythological world of the ancient Greeks and Romans. Our vision was to provide in each chapter of *Classical Mythology and More* a fresh retelling of selected myths followed by activities that would provide many opportunities for creativity and further reflection; these are the "More" of the book's title: review sections that reinforce the learning of key names, places, and concepts; "Words" sections to serve for English vocabulary enrichment; "Musings" sections to suggest ideas for reflection, research, writing, and class activities; and "How 'Bout That?" sections designed to link mythology with contemporary issues, science, trivia, recipes, and popular culture—music, art, poetry, drama, and sports.

We began by using the primary ancient mythological sources: Homer, Hesiod, *Homeric Hymns,* Pindar, Aeschylus, Sophocles, Euripides, Apollonius of Rhodes, Apollodorus, Vergil, Ovid, and a few others. Our first goal was to retain the dynamism of the stories in the original Greek and Latin texts and make them more accessible by paraphrasing them in modern English, in as colloquial and informal a style as possible, while still keeping them appropriate for classroom use. We have kept our own embellishments and editorial comments on the tales to a minimum. At the same time, we hope that we have succeeded in showing how and why these tales continue to be influential in Western culture. The ancient sources for each myth have been referenced alongside chapter and section titles for those wanting to consult the stories in the original languages.

It must be acknowledged here that, although many of the Greco-Roman myths are a delight and a joy to read and ponder, there are several that contain very difficult subject matter, especially where a younger readership is concerned. Should these pivotal stories have been glossed over or omitted for an audience of this age? (In earlier generations, authors tended to excise or euphemize sections of texts deemed too grisly or salacious, sometimes leaving students confused and scratching their heads over exactly what was going on in that story!) In the end, we have tried to choose a middle way for this generation of students: stories such as the castration of Uranus, the incest of Oedipus, and the cannibalization of Pelops are neither "sugar-coated" nor sensationalized in this workbook but retold simply, albeit accurately. As always, *teachers need to thoroughly prepare themselves, their students, and their administrators both in teaching these myths and in moderating student and parent reaction and discussion*. Teachers also need to make very prudent and reasoned judgments, in consultation with colleagues, administrations, and so on, as necessary, about the appropriateness of particular myths for particular classes, taking into account students' ages, levels of development, and all other important factors. It is *always* wise policy to keep parents and administrators informed about curriculum selections.

Over five hundred photos, illustrations, and images, including many of canonical masterpieces, enhance the text and provide the optical palatability expected as a birthright by this generation of visual learners. Readers' aids abound in the form of sidebars and text boxes that highlight and briefly summarize essential information and accentuate definitions of literary terms. The book also includes several maps, genealogical tables, a pronunciation glossary, and bibliography for further reading.

Because the Internet has become such an important—if not *the* primary—source for information gathering and research in contemporary schools and the culture at large, we have provided addresses throughout the book for various websites. We were scrupulous in rechecking the accuracy of website names and web addresses right up to the time of publication of this workbook. *A caution and a disclaimer*, however: due to the inherent ephemeral nature of information found on the World Wide Web, websites are about as reliable in the long term as smoke signals were for folks in the not-too-distant past: critically informative in one minute but lost in the ether the next! We will update web addresses, of course, with each reprinting of the book, but must count on our users' own web searching capabilities to locate appropriate substitutes for invalid addresses in the interim.

As for the perpetually thorny issue of the spelling of mythological names, we have used the Latinized spelling of Greek names throughout, though we used Latin names in the chapters about Aeneas and the Roman myths. We realize that Latin students will be more comfortable with the Latin names they have already learned in class, but we also know that students will inevitably run across the Greek names in other reading. Since the Romans used Greek names, learning the Greek names helps to remind us that, in the end, these are Greek myths told and retold in Romanized versions throughout many generations. Teachers can still choose the spellings and pronunciations they prefer, with explanation to the students that they will be encountering significant variation in spelling of mythological names both inside and outside of this workbook.

Finally, we would like to mention the translation of the invocation to the Muses from Hesiod's *Theogony* found at the beginning of this workbook. It is our own, written for, and mindful of, all the wonderful young students of this generation, truly our Muses, who inspire the writing of this book. We aim, in this workbook, to engage young people of this current age, who might understandably include among their daily preoccupations "soft complexions" or "nimble feet," and who have, as well, some curiosity about whom these denizens of Helicon and Olympus might be! We have consulted both the wonderful translations of Norman O. Brown's and Hugh G. Evelyn-White's *Theogony* for our effort here and to both we are certainly indebted.

MARIANTHE COLAKIS
MARY JOAN MASELLO

Acknowledgments

This book would not have been possible without the encouragement, advice, and support of dear colleagues and family: Elisa Denja who connected me to this project and Rickie Crown who so generously mentored me in so many ways at Baker Demonstration School; Bolchazy-Carducci Editors Vicki Wine, Laurie Haight Keenan, and LeaAnn Osburn who so equably shepherded this effort into a coherent whole. To Dan, Chris, Tim, and James Masello, special thanks for all their technological assistance and critical advice from the teen perspective; most of all, thanks to my husband, my humorous and bearded muse, Steve Masello.

Mary Joan Masello

Chapter One
The Muses

General Source:

Hesiod *Theogony* 1–115, 1018–1022

Invocation to the Muses

Let us begin singing this song of the Muses of Mount Helicon
Who dance with delicate feet around a violet-blue spring
At the altar of the almighty son of Cronus.
After bathing their soft complexions . . .
They perform beautiful, charming dances.
They move with nimble feet on the high summits of Mount Helicon. . . .
From there, they set out at night, hidden within a deep mist.
Stepping in a line of dancing, they send forth their lovely voices
When they sing of Zeus the aegis-bearer and Queen Hera
Of the golden sandals.

Hesiod *Theogony* 1–12

The Muses dancing with Apollo

Introduction to the Muses and Hesiod

Let *us* begin this book of Greek and Roman mythology with the poetic verses above. They were written by Hesiod, an ancient Greek poet and shepherd who lived near Mount Helicon in Greece. Hesiod tells us that the Muses called upon him, inspiring him to begin his song-poem, *Theogony,* which tells the Greek version of the creation of the world. Hesiod wanted inspiration in telling how the Greek gods, goddesses, and human beings came to be. Hesiod's address to the Muses in this way is called an invocation.

An *invocation* is the "calling upon" of a god, goddess, or supernatural being by an author to help to inspire the author in composing a poem, a written work, or a song.

Definition of the Muses

The ancient Greeks considered the Muses to be the patrons of choral music, choral dancing, poetry, and literature. Centuries after Hesiod lived, during the late days of the Roman Empire, the Romans assigned each Muse by name a special "job" as patroness of a specific art. In fact, a Muse was thought to be a personification of a particular one of the arts, based upon the meaning of each Muse's Greek name.

> ***Personification* is a figure of speech in which inanimate (non-living) things, ideas, or objects are given human qualities or a human form.**

Homer personifies the Muses.

In the opening lines of the epic poems *Iliad* and *Odyssey,* the Greek poet Homer calls upon a Muse to inspire him as he tells the story of the Trojan War. Homer personifies the idea of "inspiration" as a goddess who can supply him with the right turn of phrase and enough suspense to tell a good, gripping tale!

Muse with lyre

"*Sing, goddess,* of Achilles' wrath. . . ." (*Iliad* 1.1)

"*O Muse, tell* me about the wily man. . . ." (*Odyssey* 1.1)

Hesiod's first encounter with the Muses

Hesiod describes his first encounter with the Muses in this way: "One day they taught me glorious song while I was shepherding my lambs near Mount Helicon. The Muses, daughters of Zeus, said to me, 'We know how to say many false things as though they were true, but we also know how to speak the truth when we want to.' And they gave me some laurel, and breathed into me a divine voice to sing of things that have been and things that will be" (*Theogony* 22–28).

Birth of the Muses

Hesiod also tells the story of the Muses' birth. Their mother, Mnemosyne (Greek for "memory"), spent nine nights with Zeus in Pieria, and later gave birth to nine daughters. (See GENEALOGICAL CHART 1 in Appendix B.) They went to their father's home on Mount Olympus, singing sweetly all the way as the earth echoed their songs, and beautiful music rose beneath their feet.

The nature of the Muses

The Muses sang and danced at the banquets on Mount Olympus, often led by Apollo. Those inspired by the Muses were considered very wise and fortunate, capable of settling the worst quarrels or healing the deepest sorrows. Yet, the Muses could also be cruel if they were challenged. Homer tells us that the poet Thamyris, who dared to compete against the Muses, lost both his sight and his gift of song (*Iliad* 2.594).

The Nine Muses and Their Attributes
(according to later Roman writers)

Names of the Muses	Meaning of Each Name	Assignment of Art
Calliope	"Beautiful Voice"	Epic Poetry
Clio	"Celebrate"	History
Erato	"Lovely"	Lyre; Lyric Poetry
Euterpe	"Delight"	Flute (wind instruments)
Melpomene	"Choir"	Tragedy
Polyhymnia	"Many Songs"	Sacred Hymns
Terpsichore	"Delight in Dancing"	Dance
Thalia	"Comedy"	Comedy
Urania	"Heavenly"	Astronomy

Which Muse is which in the above picture? What clues in the picture can help you to determine this?

A. Review Exercises

MATCHING! Match the phrase in the left-hand column with the correct word from the right-hand column. Write the letter in the space provided. Keep in mind that there are more words than available phrases!

1.	____	One of the Muses' homes, near Olympia where Zeus encountered Mnemosyne	a.	Muses
2.	____	Father of the Muses	b.	Memory (Mnemosyne)
3.	____	Invoked at the beginning and end of epic poems	c.	Poet
4.	____	Mother of the Muses	d.	Nine
5.	____	Most exalted of the Muses whose name means "beautiful voice"	e.	Helicon
6.	____	The Muse of dance	f.	Apollo
7.	____	One who receives from the Muses laurel and the gift of inspiration	g.	Calliope
8.	____	The number of Muses	h.	Seven
9.	____	Birthplace of the Muses	i.	Hermes
10.	____	Deity who, with the Muses, leads song and dancing on Olympus	j.	Pieria
			k.	Zeus
			l.	Terpsichore

Frank Sinatra • **Come Dance with Me** • 1959

Go to this website for complete lyrics to the song:
http://www.azlyrics.com/lyrics/franksinatra/comedancewithme.html

In "Come Dance with Me," to which Muse does Frank Sinatra refer? To what activity with that Muse is he looking forward?

B. MUSINGS

1. To which of the Muses would *you* turn for creative inspiration? Which one most appeals to you? Why?

2. The National Gallery in London has a mosaic completed in 1933 titled *The Awakening of the Muses.* It features famous writers and actors of the time shown as Muses. If you were making such a mosaic, whom would you depict as each of the nine Muses? Why?

3. In the downtown section of the city of New Orleans, Louisiana, there are nine parallel streets named after the Muses: Calliope Street, Terpsichore Street, and so on. Why do you think city planners chose those names in that particular city? Do you know of any reference to the Muses in any public art or public space in your town, city, or state?

4. What is a "mnemonic" device? Which goddess gets her name from the word from which "mnemonic" comes? Why?

5. In 1959, archaeological excavations just south of the city of Pompeii, Italy, at a complex building, perhaps a seaside resort hotel or a business headquarters, revealed a series of *triclinia,* dining halls. Triclinium A is known as the "Triclinium of the Muses" because the figures of Apollo and eight of the Muses adorn the red walls of the room. A very small representation of this mosaic by Russian-born artist Boris Anrep (1885–1969) may be seen at the National Gallery of London's website: http://www.nationalgallery.org.uk/plan/faq/facts/mosaics.htm or consult the book, *Boris Anrep: The National Gallery Mosaics* by Lois Oliver (The National Gallery Company, 2004). This building, along with the city of Pompeii and three other cities at the base of Mount Vesuvius, was buried as a result of the volcanic explosion and lava flow on the day of August 24, 79 CE. Locate photos of the Triclinium of the Muses to see how these goddesses were used among the popular motifs in ancient Italy. A good source is the book *Domus: Wall Painting in the Roman House* by Donatella Mazzoleni and Umberto Papalardo (Los Angeles: Getty Publications, 2004), pages 320–321.

6. At the beginning of their works, poets Hesiod and Homer call upon the Muses with an invocation. When might an invocation be used in present times? (Think about public ceremonies, religious services, celebrations, memorials, etc.)

   ____

   ____

7. The mother of the Muses was named Mnemosyne, "memory." Memory is yet another example of *personification.* As a matter of fact, the whole story of Zeus' union with Mnemosyne to produce the Muses is all a personification, a figure of speech used by the ancient Greeks to explain where inspiration comes from. Here's another way of looking at this idea:

   Zeus (Creative Divine Power) + Mnemosyne (Memory) = The Muses (Inspiration)

   In your own words, write a definition of personification: ______________________

   ____

8. What is being personified in each of these selections? Which descriptive words create the personification?

All downtown wore a new, woolly-white blanket this morning; the snow had made this shabby, old man with all his creaking skyscrapers and clogged arteries a fresh, exuberant youth again, at least for a little while. ____________________

____

Joy somersaulted through the halls of our school last Tuesday. Riding piggyback on a latecomer to math class, she slid off and leaped from chair to desk around the room to proclaim that the Cubs had won and had made the playoffs! ____________________

____

C. Words, Words, Words

The Daily Muse
News you can use

Have you ever noticed how really tricky words can be? Here's an example: there are three words below that all contain the syllable "**mus(e).**" At first look, you might think all these words are related, but they're not!

Two of the following words come from the *noun* "muse," that is, from the Greek name-word given to the nine daughters of Zeus and Mnemosyne.

One of the words that follows, however, comes from a very different word, the *verb* "muse," from an old French verb *muser,* meaning something like "to stare into space." This verb is defined in the box below.

- Circle the two words that you believe are derived from the *noun* "muse."
- Put in a square the word that you believe comes from the *verb* "muse."

MUSIC

AMUSE

MUSEUM

VERB **MUSE**	**Meaning:** To reflect, consider, ponder, wonder (often used with *upon, on,* or *over*)
Sample: Teenagers **muse** upon their future careers. Will they be race car drivers? Paleontologists? Basketball players? Computer graphics specialists? Other?	When you have time to **muse** about your future plans, what are some of the careers you think you'd like to pursue?

In the example that follows, do you suppose that the word "bemused" comes from the *noun* "muse," or the *verb* "muse"?

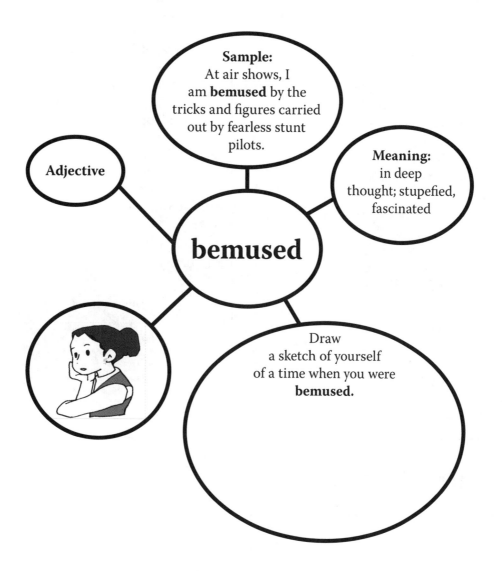

bemused

Sample:
At air shows, I am **bemused** by the tricks and figures carried out by fearless stunt pilots.

Meaning:
in deep thought; stupefied, fascinated

Adjective

Draw a sketch of yourself of a time when you were **bemused.**

D. How 'Bout That?

Clio

Every year, the Clio Awards are given to the best advertisements of the year. Why do you think this award was named for the Muse of History? Which ads that you see today do you think merit a Clio?

Terpsichore

"Let's Terpsichore (pronounced terp' si - kor *in vernacular American dialects) around the floor!"*

From around the middle years of the 19th century, dance clubs and societies were popular in the United States, especially in the South. They were often called "Terpsichore Societies."

Terpsichore Rap

Is Swing your "thing"?
Do you boogy on down?
Break dance? Hip-hop?
Live on line dance?
Cha-cha, Rhumba?
Like to Limbo?

Ballet or toe dance?
So much romance!
Twist and shout?
Turn inside-out?

A-MUSE yourself!

Calliope

Do you remember the last time you went to the circus or carnival? Did you hear carnival music played upon a calliope?

A calliope is a musical instrument fitted with steam whistles that are played from a keyboard.

At the Fourth of July Parade in Evanston, Illinois, a red calliope leads off the festivities, tootling old-time melodies and chugging off steam from its whistles. Good, old-fashioned MUSE-ic!!!

E. Who's Who?

- For the ancestry of Orpheus (son of Calliope), see GENEALOGICAL CHART 1.

Chapter Two

The Creation of the World and the Earliest Deities

General Sources:
Hesiod *Theogony*
Ovid *Metamorphoses* 1.5–176

The primordial gods and the Titans

What did the Muses inspire Hesiod to sing of first? They told him how the first gods and the world came to be. First of all Chaos was born, then Gaea (Earth) and the dark underworld of Tartarus, then Eros (Love). (See Genealogical Chart 2.) Night was born from Chaos; then Night gave birth to Day. Gaea bore Uranus, or Sky, to be her equal and to provide a home for the gods. With Uranus she bore the Cyclopes, who later made the thunderbolts for Zeus. They were like the other gods in all ways, except that they had only one eye in the middle of their foreheads. She also bore the Titans, including Oceanus, Iapetus, Rhea, Themis, and Mnemosyne. (See Genealogical Chart 3.) Her youngest Titan son, however, was the wiliest and most terrible of her children. His name was Cronus, and he hated his father from the beginning.

Gaea's monstrous children

Gaea also gave birth to monsters. Three of her sons, Cottus, Briareus, and Gyes (the "Hundred-handed Ones"), each had a hundred hands and fifty heads. Their father hated them and hid them in a secret part of Gaea when they were born. He never let them see the light and was very pleased with what he had done. Gaea groaned within and plotted revenge. She created the element of flint and formed a sickle out of it. Then she gathered all her children to her and said, "We should punish your father for what he has done." Everyone trembled in fear, except Cronus. He said, "I will do the deed you want, Mother." Gaea was delighted. She gave him the sickle, hid him in an ambush, and told him what she wanted him to do.

Rhea and Cronus

Cronus overthrows Uranus.

That night, as Uranus came to Gaea, Cronus emerged from his hiding place and castrated his father with the sickle. From the blood of Uranus, Gaea bore the Erinyes, or Furies, the race of Giants, and the Nymphs. (See Genealogical Chart 4.) Cronus threw Uranus' genitals into the sea. They floated a long time, and white foam spread around them. From this foam grew a beautiful goddess, Aphrodite.

Representation of *The Birth of Venus*, 1482, by Sandro Botticelli (1446–1510), Uffizi Gallery, Florence, Italy

We will see Eros, Aphrodite, and the Erinyes playing important roles in other myths. Many other beings were born from these early divinities, and they will be mentioned in later chapters. Let us pick up the story of Cronus and his wife, Rhea.

Cronus swallows his children.

Cronus had learned from his parents that one of his children would one day overthrow him, as he had overthrown his own father. He therefore kept close watch, and when his children were born, he swallowed them, devouring the first five: Hestia, Demeter, Hera, Hades, and Poseidon. When she was about to deliver her sixth child, Zeus, Rhea could stand no more and asked Gaea and Uranus for help. They sent her to Crete, and when Zeus was born, Gaea took him and hid him in a remote cave. She then wrapped a huge stone in a blanket and gave it to Cronus. He gulped it down, unaware that his youngest son was still alive and growing stronger by the day.

The goat Amalthea nurses infant Zeus.

Later authors have added details about Zeus' babyhood in the cave. They say that he was fed by bees and nursed on the milk of a goat named Amalthea. Her horns were magical, filled with ambrosia and nectar, the food and drink of the gods. When one of these horns was broken off, it was magically filled with fruits to feed the young god. The Latin name for this horn, *cornu copiae,* or "horn of plenty," remains a symbol of abundance.

Cornucopia

Cronus disgorges his children.

When Zeus was fully grown, Gaea tricked Cronus into disgorging all of the children that he had swallowed. The first thing he vomited up was the stone that he had swallowed. In ancient times, this stone was exhibited at the shrine of Delphi, Greece, and was looked upon as a sign and a wonder by the people who saw it. Zeus then released his other brothers whom Cronus had buried, the Hundred-handed Ones and the Cyclopes, who in gratitude gave him power over thunder and lightning. Together they all made war upon Cronus and banished him.

Although Cronus does not appear again in mythology, his name has been confused with the Greek word for time, *chronos,* and thus associated with Chronus, the personification of time, who emerged from the primeval Chaos. Perhaps this false etymology is in part responsible for the characterization of Old Father Time, an old man with a scythe and an hourglass who symbolizes the passing of the old year.

Father Time

The Four Ages according to Ovid

The Roman poet Ovid shows us Cronus (whom the Romans called Saturn) in a different way. He was the god of the Golden Age, a time when people did not need laws and courts in order to treat one another well. Trees had not yet been cut down to make boats that would visit other places. There were no military fortifications, trumpets, swords, helmets, or soldiers. Earth brought forth fruits and grains with no labor on the part of people. There were rivers of milk and honey, and sweet nectar dripped from the trees. It was always springtime.

When Zeus took over, the Silver Age came in. He added the four seasons, and people first built houses for themselves. Nature's shelters were no longer enough. Agriculture began then also, and oxen had to struggle to pull the plows.

Then the Bronze Age came, when people became aggressive and quick to seize weapons, although they were not entirely evil yet. That was left for the Iron Age, a time when modesty and goodness fled from the earth, and all sorts of trickery, violence, and greed took their place. People sailed to parts unknown, the land was marked off by boundaries, and precious metals hidden deep within the earth were pried out. No one was safe. Even family members plotted death for one another.

A. REVIEW EXERCISES

MATCHING! Match the phrase in the left-hand column with the correct word from the right-hand column. Write the letter in the space provided.

1.	____	The goat that fed Zeus	a.	Saturn
2.	____	The Roman name for Cronus	b.	Tartarus
3.	____	The age when all evil was let loose	c.	Ambrosia
4.	____	Manufacturers of Zeus' thunderbolts	d.	Bronze Age
5.	____	The age when rivers of milk and honey flowed	e.	Crete
6.	____	The dark underworld, one of the first creations	f.	Cyclopes
7.	____	The sky god and mate of Gaea	g.	Iron Age
8.	____	The place where the stone disgorged by Cronus was displayed	h.	Cornucopia
9.	____	The food of the gods	i.	Amalthea
10.	____	The age when seasons were introduced	j.	Uranus
11.	____	The time when humans became aggressive and started wars	k.	Delphi
12.	____	A symbol of abundance	l.	Silver Age
13.	____	The birthplace of Zeus	m.	Golden Age

B. MUSINGS

1. What details in these myths shocked you? Why do you think Greek mythology has so much violence?

2. Ovid depicts a world that began as perfect, then steadily worsened. Do you believe that this is true?

CRETE

The king of the gods, Zeus, spent his early childhood on the lovely island of Crete. Look for this island on a map.

C. Words, Words, Words

The Daily Muse
News you can use

The same Greek word that gave **Chronus** (the personification of time, commonly confused with Cronus) his name has given us a couple of words to use:

- A **chronometer** is a very precise timepiece or clock.
- A **chronology** is the arrangement of events in sequence by the time in which they occurred.

1. Can you place these **chronometers** in **chronological** order, that is, in order by the time when they were invented, beginning with the oldest?

a.

b.

c.

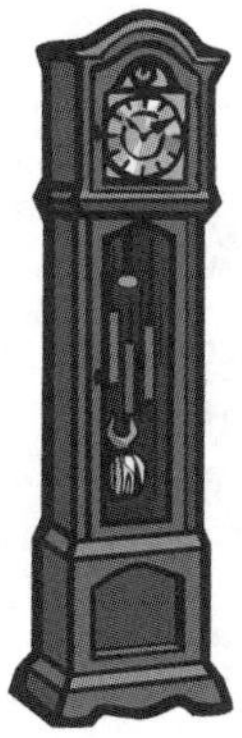

d.

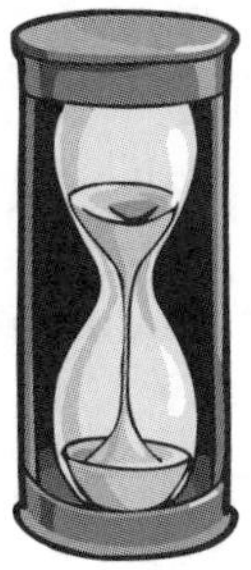

e.

Your answer: 1._____, 2._____, 3._____, 4._____, 5._____

2. Poor Peter Rabbit has a **chronic** illness. Circle the answer that best describes unfortunate Peter Rabbit's condition.
    a. Temporary
    b. Painful
    c. Prolonged
    d. None of the above

3. A **chronicle** gives a **chronological** story or record of events in a history. Perhaps you have heard of the books of *Chronicles* in the Bible or read the series of books by C. S. Lewis, *The Chronicles of Narnia.* Can you list any other **chronicles** you have read or read about?____________________

4. My dad likes to golf with his **cronies** on weekend afternoons. Circle the answer that best describes my dad's companions.
    a. Loyal employees
    b. Longtime friends
    c. Business partners
    d. Capable workers

5. Answer the following questions about these words: **chronometer, chronicle, chronology, chronic.**
    a. Which of these words is a different part of speech than the others?__________
    b. Which part of speech is it?____________________
    c. What part of speech are all the other words?_______________

D. How 'Bout That?

Ambrosia

Did you know that Ambrosia is also a dessert? Here is a recipe you may want to make: Mix together 1 cup each coconut, canned pineapple chunks (save juice), orange sections (fresh or canned), and vanilla yogurt. Stir in 1 cup miniature marshmallows and the reserved juice.

Bon appetit!

Titans and ships

Three sister ships of the White Star Line were launched in 1910, 1912, and 1914. They were not only the largest ships, but the largest vehicles of any kind ever built up to that time. The owners of the White Star Line hoped that these ships would be *godlike* in size, speed, and luxurious accommodations, so they bestowed on two of the ships mythological names.

One of these sister ships met a disastrous fate of *mythic* proportions during the night of April 14–15, 1912, on its maiden voyage from Southampton, England, to New York. The name of this ship, as you may have guessed, was the *Titanic.* Knowing what you do about the Titan gods, can you see any irony in the fate of the *Titanic?*

***Irony* is the discrepancy between what is intended or supposed and what actually occurs.**

The second sister ship of the three, named for a Titan god and nicknamed "Old Reliable," had a long sailing career and helped the Allies to win World War I by safely transporting 7,000 soldiers at a time back and forth across the Atlantic. The third sister ship was used as a hospital ship.

Extra challenge: Can you guess or research the names of the two sister ships of the *Titanic*?
(Hint: Their names all have the same ending "-ic.")

(*See bottom of page for answers!)

Titans and chemistry

The German chemist Martin Heinrich Klaproth (1743–1817) discovered several of the basic materials from the earth known in chemistry as *elements.* He discovered uranium in 1789 and rediscovered and named the element titanium in 1796, five years after it had been discovered by William Gregor. Research the chemical properties of these elements and try to deduce why Professor Klaproth gave them these mythological names.

(*The three sister ocean liners were ***Titanic, Olympic,*** and ***Britannic.***)

Titans and the planets

Which of the planets are named for Titan gods? Research the discovery of these planets. Why were they given these names?

____

____

____

____

Saturn and its moon, Titan: the Cassini-Huygens Probe

The United States Space Agency (NASA) is studying Titan, a moon of the planet Saturn. To learn more about this mission and to see a picture of Titan that's simply out of this world, visit this website: http://www.nineplanets.org/titan.html.

REMEMBER THE TITANS

Have you ever noticed how many sports teams are called the "Titans"?

Perhaps the most famous in the United States is the NFL Tennessee Titans.

If you have time, watch the 2000 movie *Remember the Titans.* This film tells the story of a losing, small town football team that overcomes discrimination and adversity. The coach, played by Denzel Washington, references the Titans of myth and challenges his football team to emulate the Titan gods' power.

Discuss

Do you think the football team portrayed in the movie is appropriately named? Why? Why not?

If you had the power to name your school's team after a mythological character, place, or episode, which would you choose? Why?

Cyclopean walls

In the old Greek city of Mycenae, the stones in the city walls are so immense, it seems that only giants could have set them in place. This type of wall, made of gigantic boulders and using no mortar or cement to hold the blocks in place, is called a Cyclopean wall, named for the one-eyed race of giants, the Cyclopes, some of the monstrous children of Cronus and Rhea. The monumental entrance gate to the city of Mycenae is called the Lion Gate for its famous, headless lions sculpture. You will read more about Mycenae in chapters 13 and 16.

Cyclopean walls at Mycenae

E. Who's Who?

- For descendants of Chaos, see Genealogical Chart 2.
- For descendants of Uranus, see Genealogical Chart 3.
- For descendants of Cronus, see Genealogical Chart 4.

Chapter Three

The Olympian Deities, Part I: The Children of Cronus and Rhea

General Sources:
Homer *Iliad*
Hesiod *Theogony*

Cronus and Rhea had six Olympian children: Zeus, Poseidon, Hades, Demeter, Hera, and Hestia. (See GENEALOGICAL CHART 4.) They all lived on Mount Olympus (except for Hades, who lived in the Underworld). This snow-capped mountain between Macedonia and Thessaly is the highest mountain in Greece and was considered sacred by the ancients. No one dared to climb it in antiquity; not until 1913 did a team of Greek and Swiss climbers reach its summit.

Mount Olympus, thought by the ancient Greeks to be the home of the gods, lies roughly on the border between the Greek regions of Thessaly and Macedonia, about 48 miles south from the modern city of Thessaloniki. At 9,570 feet, it is the tallest mountain in Greece.

Zeus (Jupiter or Jove)

Parents: Cronus and Rhea

Dominion: Sky, weather, especially thunderstorms and winds

Favorite Places: Olympus, Dodona, Crete

Symbols: Thunderbolt, eagle, aegis (goatskin shield), oak tree

Archetype (characteristics of personality): Ambitious, decisive, competitive; "networker"

Literary Source:
Hesiod *Theogony* 886*ff.*

Zeus was both the youngest and the oldest of the brothers who were sons of Cronus and Rhea. He became the undisputed king of the gods. Although he appears comical in many stories, he was a symbol of order and justice to the ancient Greeks. In art, he appears as a dignified, bearded man, often holding a thunderbolt. The thunderbolts were gifts given to him by his gigantic brothers the Cyclopes, after he had freed them from Tartarus, the most dismal part of the Underworld. Cronus had hurled his giant children, the Cyclopes, into Tartarus as a punishment. Homer often describes Zeus in an epithet as "aegis-bearing." The aegis was a shield or breastplate symbolic of Zeus' royal power, made from the goatskin of his nurse, Amalthea. The eagle and the oak tree were sacred to him.

An *epithet* is an adjective or phrase that describes some quality, characteristic, or the nature of a person or thing. Some epithets from Greek mythology are "aegis-bearing" Zeus, "swift-footed" Achilles, "white-armed" Helen, and the "wine-dark" sea.

Zeus' first wife was Metis, one of the daughters of Oceanus. The strange story of their marriage and its end is discussed in "Athena" (Chapter 4). Zeus' subsequent wives bore him many children, including the Fates, the Graces, and the Muses. Demeter gave him Persephone, and the Titan goddess Leto gave birth to Apollo and Artemis.

Zeus was a powerful god, but there were forces even he could not control. Like all the gods, he was bound by oaths sworn by the Styx, a river in the Underworld. He also never overruled the Fates, even when he very much wanted to save mortals that he especially loved.

Hera (Juno)

Parents: Cronus and Rhea

Dominion: Marriage, fertility

Favorite Place: Argos

Symbols: Crown, scepter, cow, peacock, pomegranate

Archetype: Traditional, marriage-minded; fierce opponent of any threat to family

Literary Source:
Homer *Iliad* 15.18–22

Zeus is generally associated with his last wife, Hera. She was also Zeus' sister, a child of Cronus and Rhea. She appears in art as a lovely and dignified queen, and the Greeks worshipped her as the protector of marriage.

Hera's beauty is denoted with the epithet "cow-eyed" (perhaps like the modern "doe-eyed"), and she is associated with the peacock (see the story about Io in Chapter 7). Many myths show her as cruel and jealous, holding a grudge against heroes and against mortal women whom Zeus loved. Her marriage to Zeus is a difficult one, and we have many tales of their quarrels. In Homer's *Iliad*, she tricks Zeus into lying down with her and falling asleep in order to stop him from helping the Trojan army. When he wakes, he is outraged and reminds Hera of what he can do to her: "Don't you remember when I hung you on high and put two anvils around your feet and tied two unbreakable golden chains to your hands, and you hung in the air and the clouds? The gods were outraged, but they could not release you" (15.18–22).

Pomegranate bush and flower, dear to goddess Hera and symbol of fertility. Cutaway shows seed-filled fruit.

Poseidon (Neptune)

Parents: Cronus and Rhea

Dominion: Sea, earthquakes, horses

Favorite Place: Sounion

Symbols: Trident (three-pronged spear), horse

Archetype: Emotionally intense, impulsive; can be angry and vengeful and troubled by sense of inferiority

Literary Sources:
Homer *Odyssey* 4.365*ff.*
Ovid *Metamorphoses* 6.75*ff.*

Zeus' brother Poseidon was the god of the sea, a protector of those who sailed. Homer often gives him the epithet of "earthshaker," which suggests that the Greeks may also have thought of him as an earth-god. In art, he is generally indistinguishable from Zeus, except that he carries a three-pronged spear called a trident. He is also the god of horses, and has the epithet of "hippios" or "horsey one." The Greeks, who must have felt the earth shake as horses stampeded across it, found it natural to associate a horse-god with earthquakes.

Poseidon had a wife, Amphitrite, about whom little is known. She bore him a son, Triton, who was the original "merman": human from the waist up and having a fish's tail. Another of Poseidon's company was Proteus, who tended Poseidon's seals. He could foretell the future, but he was difficult to find and hold on to. The only way to catch him was to sneak up and grab him when he took an afternoon nap in a cave, surrounded by his seals. If caught, he would transform himself into all sorts of wild animals and even into fire and streams of water trying to escape. But if the seeker held on, Proteus would return to his normal shape and answer.

Various myths show Poseidon as vengeful and bad-tempered. He delayed the homecoming of the hero Odysseus because Odysseus had blinded his son, the Cyclops Polyphemus. He competed with the goddess Athena to become the patron god of Athens. He struck a rock on the Acropolis with his trident, and a spring of salt water poured out. (According to Ovid, however, his gift was a wild horse.) Athena then presented an olive tree, and the Athenians judged her gift the more useful. In anger, Poseidon flooded the plain around Athens.

Demeter and Persephone

Demeter (Ceres) and Persephone (Proserpina)

Demeter (Ceres)

Parents: Cronus and Rhea

Dominion: Crops, motherhood

Favorite place: Eleusis

Symbols: Stalk of wheat, torch

Archetype: Motherly, nurturing, deeply spiritual

Persephone (Proserpina)

Parents: Zeus and Demeter

Dominion: The Underworld

Favorite Place: Eleusis

Symbols: Torches, sheaf of grain

Archetype: Compliant, girlish

Literary Source:
Homeric Hymn to Demeter (2)

Hades abducts Persephone.

Demeter "of the beautiful braids" controlled the fertility of the land. She is closely associated with her daughter, Persephone, also known as "the maiden." The best-known myth about them explains the change in the seasons. The story is that Persephone was playing one day with the daughters of Oceanus, gathering all sorts of flowers. At Zeus' request, Gaea caused a special bloom to spring up: a sweet-smelling marvel, from whose roots a hundred flowers sprang. As Persephone reached out to grasp it, the earth gaped open and Hades, the lord of the dead, sprang out upon her. He carried her away in his golden chariot drawn by immortal horses. She screamed, but no one heard her except Hecate, an earth-goddess, and Helius, the sun-god.

Demeter searches for Persephone.

When Demeter discovered her daughter was missing, she sped like a wild bird over land and sea with a torch in each hand, looking for her child. But no one told her anything. For nine days she wandered in this way. On the tenth day, Hecate came up to her with a torch in hand and said, "Demeter, I heard your daughter cry out, but I did not see who it was that carried her away." Together the goddesses went to Helius, and Demeter said, "Helius, if I have ever cheered your heart, please help me. I heard my daughter's screams, but I did not see her. If you saw her with your light, tell me which god or mortal man carried her off."

Helius replied, "Queen Demeter, I will tell you the truth. Zeus is responsible. He gave her to his brother Hades to be his wife. Hades took her in his chariot down to his gloomy kingdom. But, Goddess, stop your loud lamentation. You should not hold on to useless anger this way. Hades, the Ruler of Many, is a worthy husband for your child, as he received one-third of the world when the lots were first drawn."

Hades seizes Persephone.

Demeter comes to Eleusis.

Demeter was even more grief-stricken when she heard this. She was so angry with Zeus that she withdrew from Mount Olympus and wandered the lands. She put off her divine beauty and turned herself into an old woman, a rich man's nanny, or housekeeper. Finally, she came to Eleusis, to the property of Celeus, a wise leader of the land. She sat down by a shady well, still deep in her grief. There the daughters of Celeus found her when they came to draw water. They asked her, "Ma'am, who are you? Why are you here so far from the city? There are many women in the households there who would welcome you."

Demeter (Doso) seeks employment.

Demeter answered, "My name is Doso. I come from Crete, and I sailed from there—not because I wanted to, but because pirates captured me and took me from my home. When they stopped at Thoricus and went out onto the shore to eat, I escaped from them. I wandered until I came here, and I don't know what land this is or what people are in it. May the gods bless you with husbands and children, and tell me if anyone here has work for a woman my age. I can nurse a baby, or keep house, or teach women their tasks."

The girls said, "There are many important men here who would be pleased to have you. But please wait here until we go home and tell our mother, Metaneira, about you. She has a newborn son, and if you can take care of him, our mother will richly honor you."

Demeter becomes baby Demophon's nurse.

The girls ran home and told their mother about the old woman. Metaneira told them, "She's hired; hurry back and tell her." Eagerly they ran down the path, energetic as fawns in springtime, their hair streaming about their shoulders. They found the sad, old woman where they had left her, and they led her to their father's house. As Demeter reached the threshold, she filled the doorway with her heavenly glow. Metaneira was in awe, and offered Demeter her place on the couch. Demeter refused it and would not sit down until one of Metaneira's daughters, Iambe, offered her a stool to sit on. Demeter sat down and remained there silent and sorrowful for a long time, still missing her daughter.

But Iambe cheered her up, telling Demeter jokes until she smiled and laughed again. Then Metaneira offered her a cup of red wine, but Demeter said it was not lawful for her to drink it. Instead, she asked for a drink of meal, water, and mint. Metaneira gave it to her and said, "Greetings, lady! I think you *are* a lady. You have such grace and dignity. We all have our burdens to bear from the gods, and since you have come here, you will have what I can offer. If you can take care of this newborn son, an unexpected blessing in my old age, and bring him to young manhood, I will reward you well."

Demeter tries to make Demophon immortal.

The Eleusinians build a temple to Demeter.

Demeter answered, "I will gladly nurse this boy and make sure no harm comes to him." She took the child in her divine hands, and his mother rejoiced. Thus Demeter became the nurse of Demophon, as the boy was called. She anointed him with ambrosia every day as if he were the child of a god. He grew faster than his years. But at night, she would secretly place him in the fire, intending to burn off his mortality and make him divine. She would have succeeded, but one night Metaneira saw her. She screamed, "Oh, Demophon, this strange woman is burning you to death! What a grief for me!" Demeter was furious at Metaneira's meddling. She snatched the child out of the fire and threw him to the ground. To Metaneira she exclaimed, "You fool! I could have made your son immortal and given him everlasting honor, but now he cannot escape the Fates. Still, I will give him glory, since he lay on my knees and slept in my arms. I am Demeter! Let the Eleusinians build me a temple and altar, and I will teach you my rites so that you can win my favor back."

When the goddess had said this, she shed the guise of an old woman, and stood in all her divine beauty and fragrance. The house was filled with brightness like lightning. Then she left. Metaneira was so stunned she did not even pick up her baby from the ground. His sisters heard his wailing and tried to comfort him, but he kept crying because he missed the special touch of Demeter.

Demeter mourning Persephone

Demeter grieves, creating famine on earth.

The next morning, Metaneira's husband, King Celeus, summoned the people to an assembly and ordered them to begin work immediately on Demeter's temple. In a short time the temple was finished and the people returned home. Demeter sat in it apart from all the other gods, still wasting with longing for her daughter. She caused a dreadful year of famine to come upon the earth. The seeds were planted, the oxen drew the plow, but nothing grew. The entire human race would have died, but Zeus saw what was happening. He sent all of the gods, one after the other, and they offered her all sorts of gifts and whatever honors she wanted. But Demeter rejected all their pleas, and vowed that she would never return to Olympus or let the crops grow until she saw Persephone again.

Zeus orders Hades to free Persephone.

Demeter would not be moved, so Zeus decided to approach Hades instead. He sent Hermes into the Underworld to persuade Hades to release Persephone. Carrying out his orders, Hermes said, "King Hades, Zeus has ordered me to bring Persephone back to her mother. If Demeter does not end her anger soon, she will destroy the human race by keeping seeds hidden beneath the earth. If humans perish, it means the end of honors for us."

Persephone holding a wheat sheaf with Hades

Hades smiled grimly and said to Persephone, "Go back to your mother now, Persephone, but think of me fondly too. Cheer up! I am a good husband for you. I am Zeus' brother, after all. While you live here, you will be a great queen and have more honors than any of the gods. Those who fail to perform the proper rites and give appropriate gifts will be punished forever."

When he said this, Persephone was filled with joy and leaped up. But before she left, Hades gave her pomegranate seeds to eat. He prepared his golden chariot, Persephone mounted it, and Hermes drove her through the air across the waters, plains, and mountains until they came to Demeter's temple at Eleusis. The reunited mother and daughter embraced enthusiastically, but Demeter was filled with sudden uneasiness. "Persephone, did you eat anything while you were below? If you did not, you can stay with me all year, but if you did, you must return to Hades for a third of the year."

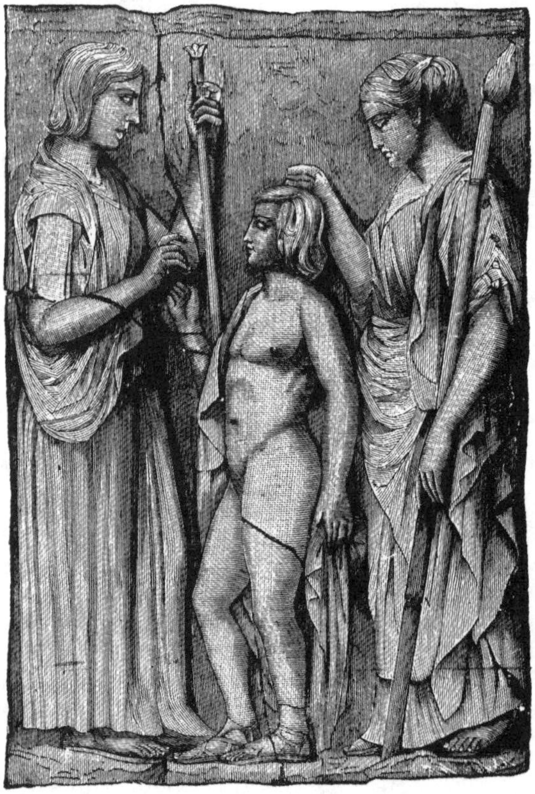
Demeter hands Triptolemus a sheaf of wheat as Persephone, holding a torch, crowns him.

Persephone lives one-third of the year with Hades, two-thirds with Demeter.

Persephone told her mother all that had happened to her. Then Zeus sent down Rhea to offer Demeter whatever honors she chose among the gods. He agreed that Persephone needed to spend a third of the year with Hades, but would live with her mother the rest of the time. And the land was once more waving with stalks of wheat and ears of corn, as Demeter let the crops grow again.

Eleusinian mysteries

Demeter also taught Triptolemus, either another name for Demophon or Demophon's brother, along with other leaders of her sacred town, Eleusis, her mysteries. The Eleusinian mysteries were secret rituals that were practiced for hundreds of years. It was forbidden to reveal the secrets of these rituals, but the Greeks—and later, the Romans—believed they would confer great benefits after death.

A myth may serve many purposes, and the same myth may be interpreted in different ways. For example, the myth of Demeter and Persephone can be seen as an aetiological myth, or a pre-scientific explanation for natural events, in this case the change in the seasons. It may also be understood as a charter myth, or a myth that gives authority to the customs of a society (why the Greeks celebrated the Eleusinian mysteries). Myths may also dramatize a psychological truth. The same story of Demeter is a powerful depiction of "empty nest syndrome," a mother's depression after her child grows up and leaves home.

When a myth has been composed to explain a practice, custom, tradition, or a natural phenomenon whose actual origin is either unknown or not scientifically understood, it is called an *aetiological* myth. The word "aetiological" comes from the Greek word *aetios,* meaning "cause."

A *charter myth* provides a story that explains or endorses certain customs, rites, or rituals practiced by a particular culture.

A myth that reveals enduring truths about the human psyche ("soul") may be said to dramatize a *psychological* truth.

Hades (Pluto)

Parents: Cronus and Rhea

Dominion: The Underworld

Favorite Place: The Underworld

Symbol: Magical helmet of invisibility, bident (2-pronged staff), chariot

Archetype: Dark, secret, imaginative; can become depressed

Literary Sources:
Odyssey 11
Vergil *Aeneid* 6
Apollodorus 1.5.1–3

Hades played an important role in the tale of Demeter and Persephone. Elsewhere, we encounter him mainly in tales in which a hero or heroine enters the Underworld. His name in Greek means "unseen" and he had a cap that made him invisible. The Greeks preferred not to speak his name, fearing that it would catch his attention and bring him to them. Today, we also prefer words such as "passed on" and "gone to a better place" in place of direct references to death. However, it would be a mistake to think of Hades as evil or as comparable with the Christian Satan. He was a good husband to Persephone, and the great musician Orpheus acknowledges that even in the Underworld, there may be love: "This god [Love] is well known in the lands above; I doubt whether he is known here [in the Underworld] as well, but I suppose that he is. If the old story is true, Love has joined the two of you [Hades and Persephone] also" (Ovid *Metamorphoses* 10.26–29). As the Roman Pluto, he is also a god of wealth, especially the mineral wealth buried under the earth.

The ancient Greeks had no consistent view of life after death. The earliest account of the Underworld, in Homer's *Odyssey,* shows very little to look forward to. The ghosts dwell on an island at the edge of the world in a shadowy state, without thoughts or feelings. They are not able to recognize Odysseus and speak with him until they drink blood. There is little by way of reward or punishment.

Charon, the ferryman who carries souls of the dead across the River Styx, receives some passengers.

Later authors worked out a more specific geography of the Underworld. According to Vergil and others, souls were accompanied to the bank of the River Styx by Hermes. There they were met by a dirty and surly ferryman named Charon, who demanded payment to row them across the river and into the Underworld. Anyone who did not have the money was doomed to wait at the riverbank forever. For this reason, people were buried with a coin in the mouth.

All newcomers had to pass by the three-headed dog, Cerberus. He left them alone on their way in but would turn vicious if any tried to escape. They were then judged. Most were neither rewarded nor punished but simply allowed to flit about, without substance. They drank from the River Lethe, the river of forgetfulness, which erased their memories of their earthly lives. A few of those especially dear to the gods were sent to the Elysian Fields, a paradise of eternally perfect weather, balmy ocean breezes, and fragrant flowers.

Tantalus, Sisyphus, and Ixion in Tartarus

Famous sinners: Sisyphus, Tantalus, Ixion

Punishment was reserved for relatively few who had committed especially heinous crimes. They were sent to Tartarus, and the punishments of a few great sinners have gripped the imagination for centuries. Here are their stories:

Sisyphus was a great trickster. When Death came to claim him, Sisyphus placed strong bonds upon him and took him prisoner. Ares, the god of war, freed Death, who did not like the notion that no one would ever again die. When Death came for Sisyphus again, Sisyphus left instructions to his wife that he not be buried. When he arrived in the Underworld, he told Persephone, "I don't belong here because I was never buried. Just let me go and haunt that no-good wife of mine and make her bury me, and I promise I'll be right back." Persephone let him go, but when he did not return as promised, she had to send Hermes to drag him back. As a punishment for wasting the gods' time this way, Sisyphus was sentenced to push a boulder up a hill. As soon as he reached the top, the boulder rolled back, forcing Sisyphus to start over.

Persephone, Sisyphus, and Hades

Tantalus stands in water with fruit above his head forever.

Tantalus was once a friend of the gods; he was on close enough terms with them to invite them to a banquet. His main course was horrible: it was the flesh of his son Pelops! Tantalus believed that he could trick the gods into eating human flesh without realizing it. They were undeceived and refused to eat, except for Demeter, who was distracted by her grief for Persephone and ate a piece of Pelops' shoulder. The gods restored Pelops to life and gave him an ivory shoulder to replace the missing one. They then punished Tantalus by placing him in the Underworld in a cool lake, with branches laden with fruit waving overhead. Whenever he bent down to drink, the water withdrew until he was left with only dust in his mouth. Whenever he reached for a piece of fruit, the wind lifted the branches out of reach.

Ixion fell in love with Hera. Zeus decided to give him his heart's desire without making his wife unfaithful to him, so he gave Ixion a dummy Hera made out of clouds. He cautioned Ixion not to boast about being with Hera, but Ixion could not resist. As a punishment, he was bound to an eternally spinning wheel of fire.

Ixion on the wheel in a vase painting. Hermes, lower left, and Hephaestus, lower right, observe.

The daughters of Danaus, known as the Danaids, were fifty sisters betrothed by their father to fifty brothers. They did not want to be married, so they all made a pact to kill their husbands on their wedding night. One of the sisters took pity on her mate and spared him, but the rest carried out the bloody plan. They were sentenced to fill eternally leaky pitchers.

The name Danaides or Danaids is a *patronymic,* a proper name derived from a father's name or paternal ancestor's name. The use of patronymics in naming both daughters and sons was quite common in both ancient Greece and in ancient Rome as well as in many, if not most, ancient cultures. Patronymics appear frequently in several modern cultures as well. Names like O'Brien ("son of Brian"), Fitzpatrick ("son of Patrick"), Thorsen ("son of Thor"), MacDougal ("son of Douglas") are all examples of surnames that were originally patronymics. The feminine equivalent of a patronymic is a *matronymic,* though matronymics were not used by the ancient Greeks and Romans.

Hestia (Vesta)

Parents: Cronus and Rhea

Dominion: The home

Favorite Place: Rome (as Vesta)

Symbol: Hearth fire

Archetype: Home-loving, unassuming

Literary Source:
Homeric Hymn to Aphrodite (5)

The goddess Hestia appears in fewer myths than any other divinity. This does not mean that she was insignificant to the Greeks and Romans, however. According to the *Homeric Hymn to Aphrodite*, she was the first-born child of Cronus and Rhea and the last to be disgorged from her father's belly. Both Poseidon and Apollo wanted to marry her, but she swore upon Zeus' head that she would never marry. So Zeus gave her great honors instead of marriage, and proclaimed that the center of the household would be sacred to her. It was also thought that she was the first to discover how to build houses, and because of this almost all Greeks had a shrine to her in every home. She received the first and the last offering at each banquet.

Vestal Virgins tend the sacred fire in the temple of Vesta in Rome.

The Romans had an important cult of Vesta, presided over by six priestesses known as Vestal Virgins. The Vestal Virgins, girls from freeborn (non-slave) families, spent thirty years in service to the goddess. Their chief function was to preserve the eternal fire in the shrine of Vesta, but they also kept wills and participated in various religious ceremonies. Vestal Virgins were also empowered to pardon criminals who pleaded to them for mercy. If, however, one of them allowed the sacred fire to go out or lost her virginity, she was punished by being buried alive.

A. Review Exercises

1. **CHRONOLOGY COUNTS!** Place the following events in chronological order. Use the numbers 1–5, with 1 as the first event and 5 as the last event in the sequence. Write the number in the space provided.

a. Demeter and Persephone

____ Demeter roams aimlessly over the earth.

____ A large crack opens up the earth through which Hades emerges in his chariot.

____ Persephone plucks flowers with her friends.

____ Zeus sends Hermes to the Underworld to persuade Hades to free Persephone.

____ Persephone joins her mother for the majority of the year.

b. Tantalus

____ The gods restore Pelops to life and give him an ivory shoulder.

____ Tantalus serves his son, Pelops, as the main course at dinner.

____ Tantalus is punished with eternal hunger and thirst.

____ Demeter absent-mindedly ingests a portion of Pelops' shoulder.

____ Tantalus invites the gods to a banquet.

c. Sisyphus

____ Ares frees Death.

____ Sisyphus tells Persephone, "I was never buried. I don't belong here. Let me go."

____ Death comes to claim Sisyphus.

____ Sisyphus is sentenced to push a boulder uphill eternally.

____ Sisyphus takes Death prisoner.

2. **WHO AM I?** Fill in the blank with the name of the mythological person or figure indicated. Answers may be used more than once.

   a. I am queen of the gods. Because my eyes are brown and beautiful, "cow-eyed" is my epithet. _______________

   b. I mourn my daughter in winter, but rejoice with her in spring and summer. _______________

   c. The first daughter of Cronus and Rhea, I am honored by a shrine near the hearth in nearly every Greek home. _______________

   d. I use my thunderbolt to enforce my position of supremacy. _______________

   e. I am the goddess of home and hearth and receive the first and last offerings at banquets. _______________

   f. Although I was mortal, I couldn't help but fall in love with Hera, so I am eternally punished on the wheel. _______________

   g. I'm the grumpy, nasty ferryman who transports souls across the river leading to the Underworld. _______________

   h. My barking is especially fearsome because I bark with three heads. _______________

   i. I am Persephone's husband in the Underworld. _______________

   j. I overthrew Cronus, freed my siblings, and became the king. _______________

   k. I am the sea-goddess who married Poseidon. _______________

   l. In Rome, a dedicated group of women perpetually tended my sacred fire. _______________

   m. I am the "merman" child of Poseidon and Amphitrite. _______________

   n. In the Underworld, I live in a pool but can never drink. _______________

   o. As an infant I was nursed by a she-goat on the island Crete. _______________

   p. I called myself "Doso" when I came to the house of Metaneira. _______________

   q. I tried to trick Death but was punished for it. _______________

   r. I'm a slippery fellow who's hard to catch or hang onto because I can transform myself at will into any shape, size, creature, or object. _______________

B. Musings

1. In the city of Chicago, there are at least two statues of the goddess Ceres (Demeter). One can be found on Columbus Drive near the Art Institute; the other sits atop the Chicago Board of Trade. Why would the city of Chicago in particular choose to honor Ceres by placing her statue in two prominent places in the city? Are there any Olympians adorning your hometown? Why?

2. In old movies, you can sometimes catch a British actor saying, "By Jove!" What does that mean, and why is he or she saying such a thing?

3. In the last chapter, we read about ships like the *Titanic* and *Olympic*. Can you find the names of any ships named for Olympians? Under the flag of what country does each one sail?

4. The Greek village of Eleusis was sacred to Demeter. It's not far from Athens. (Look on a map to see how close Eleusis is to Athens.) The Athenians built there a temple to Demeter and celebrated religious rites called the "Eleusinian Mysteries." Research the Eleusinian Mysteries and share what you learn with your class.

5. The third-largest asteroid in the solar system is named Vesta. Research in your school library to find a picture and more information. Share with your class. Why is it so named?

C. Words, Words, Words

The Daily Muse

News you can use

Hades and the Underworld have both chilled and heated up the English language with some of these HARROWING words. Which of these words do you recognize? These words come from the names of mythological figures or places.

1. Rate your knowledge of these words. Write what you guess the meaning of a word might be; then check it out in your favorite dictionary!

Word	I KNOW this word	I THINK I know this word	I have HEARD this word	NO WAY! I never saw/heard this word	Guess	Definition
lethal						
protean						
tantalizing						
stygian						
lethargic						

2. Each sentence below contains one of the words given in the table above. Circle the letter of each sentence in which you believe the italicized vocabulary word is used correctly. If you believe an italicized word is incorrectly used, tell why you think so.

   a. On a torrid summer afternoon, what could be more **tantalizing** than an ice-cold lemonade?

   b. The U.S. Government Food Pyramid suggests that we should try to eat three to four servings of **protean** every day.

   c. The **stygian** brightness of the beach in the afternoon made me reach for my sunglasses.

   d. Ingesting a drug prescribed for a person other than yourself can have **lethal** consequences.

   e. After staying up too late last night, I have felt **lethargic** all day long.

D. How 'Bout That?

Epithets

Using epithets or labels for the gods and mythological figures made a lot of sense to ancient storytellers. It was perhaps a way for the storyteller himself to remember, in the midst of a long narrative like the *Iliad,* let's say, the characteristics of the person he was talking about. In a time before TV, it was also a great way for a storyteller or bard like Homer to draw a "word picture" of some attribute of the mythological figure for his listener!

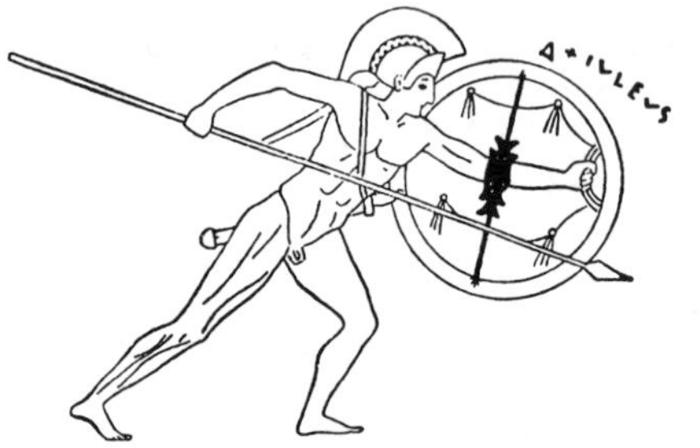

Swift-footed Achilles

White-armed Helen

Creating colorful epithets

In the space below, insert a favorite picture of yourself. Caption the photo by inserting an epithet (appropriate, please and thank you!) that describes you well and write it in the space below the photo.

Now, it's your turn to create an epithet! For each option below, write an appropriate epithet in the space provided. (PG rated, please!)

- Your best friend ________________________
- One of your family members ________________________
- Your least favorite performer ________________________
- Your pet ________________________
- Your musical instrument or favorite hobby ________________________

Vesta and advertising

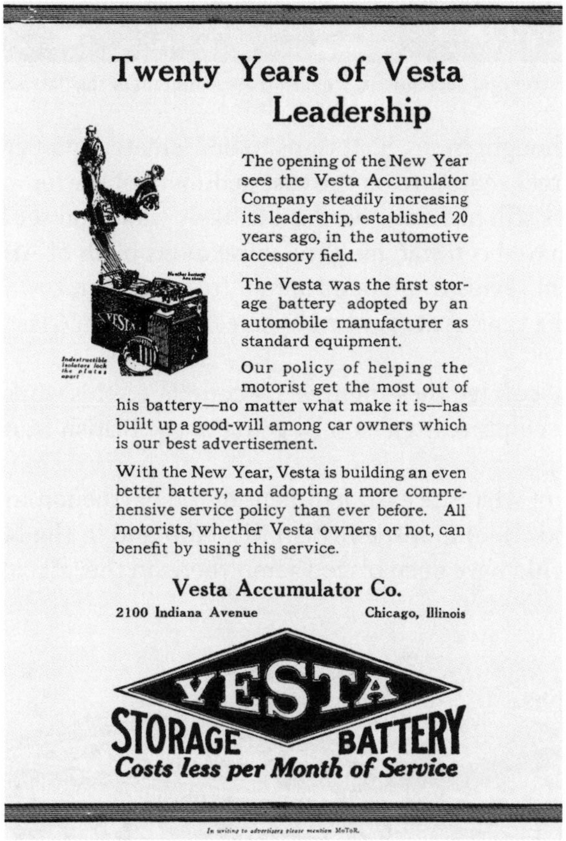

Here's a vintage advertisement from the 1920s for a car battery. Why do you suppose it was called the "Vesta"?

Can you think of any companies or products that use the name of a god or goddess in their name or title? Why would they choose such a name?

Demeter, Persephone, and the Parthenon

Demeter and Persephone, from the east pediment of the Parthenon

This sculpture fragment is thought by art historians to be Demeter and Persephone. It is part of the remains of what was once a larger sculpture on the east pediment of the temple of Athena, the Parthenon of Athens. If these sculptures still had their heads, it is likely we would see them turned to the right, as we view them. They would have been watching the miraculous birth of Athena from the head of Zeus. Notice that Persephone's arm seems to be pointing up to the center, toward Athena. Notice also that both are wearing a *peplos,* the typical dress worn by Greek women in Classical times.

The Greek artist Phidias sculpted these figures. He completed this work sometime between 447 and 432 BCE. You could see this sculpture in person by going to the British Museum in London!

Here's an artist's sketch of what the east pediment of the Parthenon might have looked like, based on the sculptural remains now found in the British Museum and in the National Museum of Athens. The sculpture seen above would have been placed somewhere on the left side of the triangle (pediment) above the columns.

E. WHO'S WHO?

- For Cronus' descendants, see GENEALOGICAL CHART 4.

Chapter 4

The Olympian Deities, Part II: The Children of Zeus

General Sources:
Homer *Iliad*
Hesiod *Theogony*

Zeus was the father of a great number of children by his various wives and lovers. His divine Olympian children were Athena, Apollo, Artemis, Hermes, Ares, Hephaestus, and Dionysus. (See Genealogical Chart 5.)

Athena (Minerva)

Parents: Zeus (and Metis)

Dominion: The arts and crafts, wisdom, training, taming horses

Favorite Place: Athens

Symbols: Helmet, spear and shield, aegis decorated with the head of the Gorgon Medusa, thunderbolt, owl, olive tree

Archetype: Intelligent, creative; identifies with males

Literary Sources:
Hesiod *Theogony* 886–898
Homeric Hymn to Athena (28)

I now sing of Pallas Athena, that famous goddess, bright-eyed, keen-minded, and strong-hearted, pure and powerful virgin. Zeus himself, the wise one, gave birth to her from his sacred head. She emerged, dressed in war-armor, all shining and golden; each one of the immortal gods was awestricken as they observed the birth. As she leaped out from the immortal head of aegis-bearing Zeus, she brandished her pointed spear. High Olympus quaked mightily at the sight of the flashing-eyed goddess. Earth groaned and the ocean's deep waves churned and boiled . . . when the virgin Pallas Athena lifted the godly armor from her immortal shoulders; Zeus, the wise one, was overjoyed.

Homeric Hymn to Athena (28) 1–16

The passage above tells the marvelous story of the birth of the goddess Athena. It is found in the *Homeric Hymm to Athena,* and is narrated by a Greek poet whose name is unknown to us, but who lived about the same time as Homer. The poet Hesiod elaborates on how this most unusual birth came about. Zeus had taken the Titan goddess Metis, the wisest of all the gods then living, as his first wife. The name "Metis" means "common sense" or "practical wisdom."

Soon Zeus and Metis conceived a child. Just as Metis was about to give birth, Zeus was given a prophecy from his grandparents, Uranus and Gaea. The prophecy foretold that Metis would bear two children. Her second child would overthrow his royal father, Zeus, just as Zeus had overthrown *his* own father, Cronus, and in turn, Cronus had overthrown *his* father, Uranus. Fearing that this prophecy would come to pass, Zeus subverted this outcome by tricking Metis so that she would not give birth in the usual way.

Zeus swallows pregnant Metis.

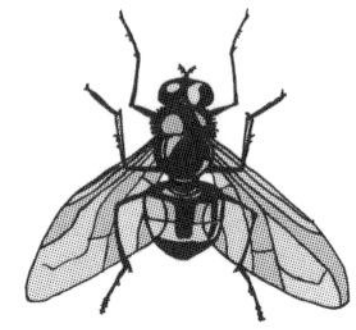

Metis had the power to magically transform herself at will into any thing, animal, shape, or figure. Zeus began to tease her, "Show me some of your famous tricks! I'll bet you can't change yourself into roaring fire, can you?" In the blink of an eye, Metis became a blazing, mighty fire. Zeus then challenged her, "That's an easy trick. Any god can do that! I doubt that you could turn yourself into a swift-running mountain stream, could you?" Metis, again rising to the challenge, immediately became a rushing river of sparkling water. Zeus continued to taunt her so that she quickly morphed into the shapes of a boar, a snake, and last of all, a small insect, perhaps a housefly. Suddenly, Zeus swallowed the insect, which was, of course, his goddess-wife, Metis, pregnant with Athena! Metis stayed inside Zeus, continuing to advise him and dispense common sense and right judgment that Zeus so needed as king of the gods and humans.

The birth of Athena from the head of Zeus

Shortly after swallowing Metis, Zeus developed a throbbing migraine headache. Clutching his mighty head, he moaned and groaned and finally thundered, "Somebody, help me!" One of the gods (some say it was Hephaestus, others, Prometheus) rushed to help him by splitting open Zeus' godly head with an axe. To the shock of all the heavenly deities, out leaped the bright-flashing, grey-eyed goddess Athena, fully armored, brandishing her spear! She became Zeus' favorite child, because it was from his head that she was born. Athena is also sometimes called Pallas Athena. (See GENEALOGICAL CHART 5.)

Because Metis remained inside Zeus' body, the prophecy that a son would later be born to them never was fulfilled. So Zeus remained the king of gods and men.

Birth of Athena from the head of Zeus (center), attended by Hermes with winged sandal and Apollo with lyre on the left, and Eileithyia and Ares on the right

The story of Athena's birth is amazing and fantastic! Her unusual birth, the characters involved, and the events leading up to her birth are, in every way, symbolic. Scholars have shown that Zeus' headache, the loud noise, the shaking of the earth, the flashing of Athena's eyes at her birth, are the ancients' way of trying to give some accounting of the reasons for the natural phenomena of thunderstorms and violent weather. Because ancient people had little scientific understanding of these atmospheric and climatic phenomena, they could only attribute the vagaries of storm, wind, and weather to the whims and moods of the gods, in this case, to mighty Zeus.

Archaic bronze statue of Athena

Let's examine Athena's birth in a different way. Zeus chose Metis, who was the wisest of all the Titan gods, to be his first wife. As king of the gods, Zeus needed knowledge of good and evil, or wisdom, so that he could make right judgments and rule well. Zeus swallowed Metis (wisdom) and she stayed within him, advising him and giving him good counsel. The story of the swallowing of Metis by Zeus can also be seen as a literary device called allegory.

Athena holding Nike, the goddess of victory. Note the Gorgon Medusa on her breastplate.

***Allegory* is a symbolic representation in words or pictures of a story that both parallels and illustrates a deeper sense, meaning, or idea.**

Athena was the protector of cities for the Greeks, and patron of Athens. In the fifth century BCE, in relief and gratitude after defeating their archenemies, the Persians, in the Persian Wars, the people of the city-state of Athens built and dedicated a perfectly beautiful temple to Athena. The temple was erected on the highest part of Athens' Acropolis. This temple, called the Parthenon, in honor of one of Athena's titles, *Parthenos,* which means "virgin" or "maiden," commands the summit of the Acropolis down to this day. In the summer religious festival of ancient Athens, a procession of young maidens and all the citizens of Athens marched through the city and up the Acropolis to honor Athena in her temple, the Parthenon. Inside, an exquisite statue of Athena, made of ivory and gold, was an object of special devotion. Specially chosen maidens clothed Athena's statue in a new, beautifully fashioned dress called a *peplos.* (See examples of a *peplos* in the image at left and on page 38.)

Apollo (Apollo, Phoebus Apollo) and Artemis (Diana)

Apollo (Apollo, Phoebus Apollo)

Parents: Zeus and Leto

Dominion: Music, poetry, healing, the woods, medicine, grazing animals, herds

Favorite Places: Delphi, Parnassus, Delos

Symbols: Sun, silver or golden bow and arrows, laurel tree, dolphin

Archetype: artistic, rational, orderly; "favorite son"; can be arrogant

Artemis (Diana)

Parents: Zeus and Leto

Dominion: Hunters and hunting, young children, youth

Favorite Places: Woods and forests

Symbols: Moon, silver bow, deer, stag, dog

Archetype: Athletic, fond of nature and animals, close to other females; can be violent

Literary Sources:
Hesiod *Theogony* 920
Homeric Hymns to Apollo (3) and *to Artemis* (27)

Leto and Zeus, the lord of the aegis, mingled together. . . .
She gave birth to twins, the most beautiful of children
Of all those descended from Uranus—Apollo and Artemis.

Hesiod *Theogony* 918–920

Hera tries to prevent the birth of Leto's twins.

In these few words, Hesiod recounts the birth of these most important Olympians of the younger generation. One of Zeus' many loves was the goddess Leto, yet another of the Titan goddesses. The goddess Hera was insanely and irrationally jealous of the lovely and gentle Leto of the golden tresses. When Hera heard the news that Leto was to bear twin children, she tried to prevent the births. Hera forbade any land upon which the sun shone to receive Leto for her childbirth. Leto flew all over the earth, desperately searching for any suitable place at all.

The serpent Python terrorizes Leto.

Even worse, Hera allowed Leto's enemy, the monster Python, to chase and pursue her as she searched in vain for safety. Python was a huge, coiling she-snake that guarded the site of the oracle at Pytho on Mount Parnassus in Phocis. Python hated Leto because the oracle had foretold that a child of Leto's would kill her. Zeus protected those whom he loved, so he ordered his brother Poseidon to see that Leto escaped from the monstrous Python. The god of the sea, Poseidon, calmed the waves as Leto, resting on the wings of the south wind, flew across the seas to Delos.

Leto finds sanctuary on the island of Delos.

Another of the Homeric Hymns, the *Hymn to Apollo* (3), tells how Leto finally found a safe refuge for the birth of her children: "Leto, in labor, approached so many places, hoping that one would make a home for her children. But all the lands shook with fear, and not one dared to receive her. Finally, Leto came to the island Delos, and asked for sanctuary. Delos rejoiced and answered: 'Leto, most famous daughter of Coeus, I will receive your offspring with joy'" (45–65).

In gratitude, Leto swore in return that Delos would become a sacred place. Delos was a very small, insignificant island in the Aegean Sea, midway between mainland Greece and the Greek settlements in the eastern Mediterranean and Asia Minor. It would be a sanctuary to her future son, the god Apollo.

Leto gives birth to Artemis, then Apollo.

The *Hymn to Apollo* (3) observes that all of the great and lesser goddesses except Hera came to help Leto give birth. Leto labored for nine days and nine nights and finally gave birth to two beautiful children. The firstborn was a girl, Artemis, who astonished all the other goddesses by proceeding to help her mother give birth to her twin brother! The exquisite boy was called Apollo, and also known as Phoebus, meaning "the one who shines bright" (90–122).

Immediately, Leto's sister, the Titan goddess Themis, offered the babies nectar and ambrosia to drink and eat. To the amazement of all the goddesses present for the birth, the baby Apollo jumped up and sang out: "Let the lyre and curving silver bow be mine. I will prophesy to mortal humans the unmistakable will of Zeus, my father" (*Hymn to Apollo* [3] 131–132).

Apollo and Artemis slay Python.

Just a few days after they were born, Artemis and Apollo, already fully grown thanks to the nourishing nectar and ambrosia, set off to take vengeance on Python, the she-snake that had stalked and terrified Leto when she frantically searched for a place to give birth. When the twin gods found Python lurking in the shadows of Mount Parnassus, they killed it with a shower of their silver arrows. Apollo cried out that now that Python was dead, the oracle belonged to him. He changed the name of the place to Delphi. There, he would prophesy the will of his father, Zeus, to humans (*Hymn to Apollo* [3] 277–494).

Apollo and Artemis

The Oracle of Apollo and the Pythian Games

The priestess of Apollo at Delphi was known as Pythia, recalling the name of Python, the giant snake slain by the god. Athletic games to honor Apollo, titled the Pythian Games, were held at Delphi every four years, just as the Olympic Games were held near Mount Olympus to honor Zeus in a separate, four-year cycle.

In another of the Homeric Hymns, the *Hymn to Artemis* (27) 1–15, the author celebrates the daughter of Leto:

> *I sing of Artemis of the golden arrow, pure hunting-maiden, who takes delight in her arrows and takes down the stag, the only sister of Apollo of the golden sword. Roaming over shaded hill and wind-blown heights and finding joy in the hunt, she draws her bow, all silver-made, and shoots her fateful arrows. . . . When the huntress . . . has unstrung her curved bow and goes to the mighty dwelling of her beloved brother, Phoebus Apollo, in the fertile land of Delphi, she oversees the graceful dancing of the Muses and Graces. Exquisitely-robed, she leads the dancing.*

In art, we are accustomed to seeing Apollo as the ideal young man, strong, active, and perfectly proportioned. He usually carries his lyre, his bow, or both. He is sometimes crowned with a circlet of laurel leaves, from the tree sacred to him. His expression is almost always calm, reflective, and moderate.

Apollo with lyre and his sister, Artemis, stand near an altar. Representation of detail of an Attic red-figure vase painting.

Aphrodite (Venus)

Parents: Zeus and Dione (according to Homer) or born from Cronus' severed sexual member (according to Hesiod)

Dominion: Love and beauty

Favorite Places: Cyprus, Corinth, Cythera

Symbols: Rose, dove

Archetype: Emotionally open, appreciative of beauty and luxury; can be vain

Literary Sources:
Homeric Hymns to Aphrodite 5, 6
Homer *Iliad* 5

According to the opening lines of the *Homeric Hymn to Aphrodite* (5), this goddess "stirs up sweet desire in the gods and tames the tribes of mortal men and all the birds and beasts and creatures of the sea." Homer often refers to her as "radiant" and "gold-wreathed" Aphrodite. There are only three she cannot move: Hestia, Athena, and Artemis. Even the mighty Zeus time and again proves unable to resist her power and falls in love with mortal women. Her name means "one born from the foam."

In the version of the birth of Aphrodite that you read in a previous chapter, she is the daughter of Cronus. Homer, on the other hand, says that Aphrodite was the daughter of Zeus and Dione, who was either one of the Titan goddesses or a daughter of Oceanus. Dione's name presents the feminine parallel of Zeus'.

Aphrodite played an important divine role in causing the Trojan War. She offered Paris the golden apple, and time and again she intervened in the war to save both Paris and her son Aeneas during some of the worst fighting of the war when their lives were threatened.

In addition to Ares, Aphrodite had numerous other lovers, some of whom we will meet in a later chapter. With these lovers, she had several children, the best known of whom is Eros, or Cupid.

Eros

Hermes (Mercury)

Parents: Zeus and Maia

Dominion: Liars, thieves, travelers, merchants and commerce; domesticated herds (cattle, sheep), dogs, boars, lions; weights and measures; pipers; guiding dead souls in transit to the Underworld

Favorite Places: Roads

Symbols: *Caduceus* or wand, winged sandals, winged traveler's helmet (*petasus*), lyre, syrinx (shepherd's pipes)

Archetype: Mischievous, fun-loving, communicative with all; trickster

Literary Sources:
Hesiod *Theogony* 935–940
Homeric Hymn to Hermes (4)

One of the many goddesses whom Zeus loved was Maia, a daughter of Atlas. According to Hesiod, their child was "noble Hermes, the herald of the gods." The *Homeric Hymn to Hermes* (4), speculated to be written around 600 BCE, is a long poem, one of the longest of the Homeric Hymns. The anonymous author tells a charming story of an adorable baby who is precocious, thieving, clever, funny—a miniature and loveable rascal! Here is the story:

Maia gives birth to Hermes, an infant prodigy.

Shy Maia, the beautiful-haired one, lived in a shadowy cave on Mount Cyllene in Arcadia. After Zeus found and fell in love with her, she brought forth a child who was devious, irresistibly clever, a thief, a cattle-driver, a dream-guide, a night-spy, a door-watcher, whose accomplishments were soon to be the talk of all the immortal gods! He was born as the sun rose in the morning. By noon, he was plucking the strings of a lyre he had made himself, and by evening he had stolen the cattle of Apollo, his look-alike half brother!

Hermes turns a tortoise into a lyre.

Bored in his infant cradle, he rolled out looking for some fun. Before long, he spied a tortoise ambling along near the entrance to the cave where he was born. Hermes spoke to the tortoise, "Hey you there, how sweet you are! Where did you get that speckled shell? Come here, I'll bring you inside and I'll make something useful out of you." So he seized up the tortoise and scooped out its insides. With a gray iron knife, he cut down some reeds and extended them across and through the tortoise shell. Over it all, he stretched some ox-hide, making a bridge and two arms. Last, he stretched seven strings of sheep gut across, affixing them to the bridge. When he finished, he picked up the lovely toy and tried to pluck at its strings. The delicate sounds that resulted when he plucked the strings enchanted him; he began to sing a baby song to accompany his own playing.

Lyre

Hermes steals the cattle of Apollo.

After the hard work of inventing and building the lyre, the baby Hermes was hungry for meat, so he wandered off to find some. Just as the sun was setting, he arrived at the mountains of Pieria where the immortal cattle of the Olympian gods were accustomed to graze. Hermes rounded up fifty of these cattle for himself. Smart enough to realize that they would be missed and that he could get into serious trouble, he devised a trick to outwit the godly shepherd and cattle-owner, who happened also to be his half brother, Apollo.

From oak saplings and twigs of myrtle and tamarisk, he fashioned a pair of sandals for himself that would prevent his feet from leaving any tracks. He then began to drive the cattle *backwards*, while he himself marched straight ahead, their faces facing him as they took their backward steps. He drove them all through the night under the cover of darkness. In that way, the tracks left by the cattle appeared to be moving forward, but *going in the direction from which they had come.*

Hermes bribes an old man to keep quiet.

No one witnessed the baby cattle-thief and his new-found herd except an old man who was digging trenches in his vineyard. Hermes spoke to the old man, "Hey, Pops, you with the hunchback! I'll make sure these vines of yours have plenty of grapes for making lots of great wine, if you just listen up. These cattle here—you didn't see nothing, right! If you keep your trap shut nice and tight, everything will be OK, got it?" Too astonished to reply, the old man said nothing. So Hermes toddled blithely off. At last, the youngster arrived at the river Alphaeus near his home on Mount Cyllene. There, he fed and watered the loud-groaning cattle who were thirsty and starving after their backwards, nocturnal march.

Hermes invents fire by friction.

While the cows were busy grazing, clever little Hermes collected sticks and kindling and devoted himself to mastering a new accomplishment: learning to start a fire! He grasped a stick of laurel in his tiny hand and rubbed it against another piece of wood. A hot tongue of fire jumped up! As young as he was, Hermes had invented a method of making fire using the friction of two pieces of wood.

Hermes slaughters and sacrifices two cattle.

Still full of energy, the infant Hermes dragged two enormous horned cattle to the fire, where he slaughtered and roasted them, dividing the meat into twelve equal portions as a sacrifice to the twelve Olympian gods, including a portion for himself, of course! But, even though he was weak with hunger, he resisted eating any of the meat, because he was an immortal and the meat was meant only for sacrifice. Now that he had done all that he needed to do, he tossed away the trick sandals into the river Alphaeus, doused the fire, and hid the bones and ashes of the sacrificed cows in the sand. The two cattle skins, however, he left stretched out on a rock where they were to remain forever.

To evade Apollo, Hermes feigns sleep.

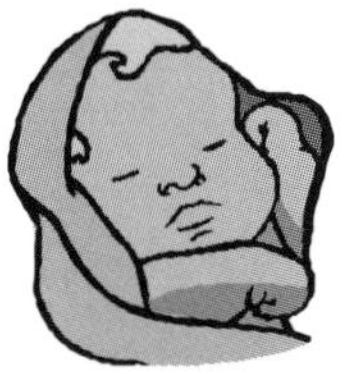

Sleepy after the adventures of the past day and night, Hermes returned home to his cradle, cuddled into his baby blanket, and tucked the tortoise-shell lyre in by his side. But Maia was an anxious mother who realized that her little son was a mischief-maker: "You little scamp, where in the world have you been? And in the middle of the night! I must think that Apollo will drag you, all tied-up, right out this door, or else—you're doomed to be a hoodlum, a thief, and a cheat!"

Maia suspects Hermes has been into mischief.

Hermes, in all innocence, lisped: "Mama, how can you accuse me this way? Me? A helpless tiny babe, who never disobeys or does anything naughty? Me, a shy, little infant, worried about his mother's disapproval? Mama, look, I'll take care of you. Let's get out of this old place, this dark, scary cave. Let's move to where we belong—with the gods, to the good life, where there's plenty of food and wealth! I want fame just like Apollo's got fame! And if my father Zeus doesn't recognize me as his son, well then, I'll just make a name for myself—as the Prince of Robbers! And if Apollo comes looking for me, well, I'll just break into his big, gorgeous house at Pytho and steal some beautiful tripods, some gold and shiny iron pots, and his clothing—lots of it. You can watch me. Yes, you can!"

Apollo searches for his missing cattle.

It didn't take long at all for Apollo to discover his missing cattle. Furious, he set off to collar young Hermes. Whom should he find along the way but the old man to whom Hermes had spoken the day before? "Old man, I'm here from Pieria looking for my cows—a herd of them. Tell me, have you seen them?" The old man hesitated: "My friend, it's awful hard to r'member everythin' ye sees in a day. So many folks passin' along dis-here road! But, come to t'ink on't, I reckon I *mebbe did* see a youngun wit' a stick, goin' down dis-here road wid' some cows. Funny t'ing is—he's a-walkin' dem cows backways, wi' der heads facin' 'im as he goes 'long."

Apollo continued on down the road; he noticed the odd-looking tracks and, a little way ahead, observed a circling eagle—his father Zeus' bird. This omen revealed to him that the thief was a child of Zeus! Apollo soon reached the cave where Maia and baby Hermes lived and, in a rage, he stormed over the threshold. When Hermes sensed that Apollo had entered the cave, he sank deeper into his blankets and pretended to be sound asleep, clutching the lyre like a security blanket.

Apollo confronts Hermes.

Apollo crashed through the cave dwelling, flinging open every door and closet, shouting and looking for the thief and his cattle. He came upon the tiny cradle containing little Hermes, took one look, and wasn't fooled for a minute. He launched right in: "You child in that cradle of yours, tell me where you put my cattle and be quick, or you and I are going to fight and it won't be pretty. I'll get my hands on you and I'll hurl you down to the depths of Tartarus; neither your mother nor your father will rescue you back up here to the daylight, but you'll wander forever under the earth as the leader of the little people."

Hermes denies the cattle theft.

Clever little Hermes was ready for this tirade. He nonchalantly replied to his half brother, "Son of Leto, why are you speaking so roughly to me? Are you looking for your cattle? I haven't seen a thing. I don't know anything about them. Do I look like a cattle thief? Like a strong man? No way! I'm only interested in baby things: sleeping, nursing at my mother's breast, and cuddling in my blankets. Don't even think of mentioning this to anyone. The gods would be incredulous to think that a newborn baby like me could bring cattle all the way here. No one would ever believe you. I was just born yesterday and my tender little feet could never walk over that rocky ground. If you want, I'll swear an oath by my father's head that I'm not guilty and that I'm hearing about this for the first time." After this speech, Hermes lifted his eyebrows and began to whistle an innocent tune.

This performance melted Apollo's anger and in spite of himself, he began to chuckle. "You magnificent little liar; I'll bet that you've already deprived many a poor homeowner of his possessions by breaking and entering, without so much as a peep from you. And that's just the beginning of your career. Come on, get up, you little rogue! From now on you will be known as the Prince of Robbers." Then, once again, they fell to arguing with one another over the cattle. In the end, they decided to let Zeus, high up on the summit of Olympus, settle the quarrel.

Apollo and Hermes take their dispute to Zeus.

When he had heard each one of his quarreling sons tell his side of the story, Zeus laughed out loud at the absurdity of his infant son as a cattle thief, but ordered his sons to work together to find the remaining cattle. Setting off toward Pylos together, Hermes led Apollo to the cave where the cattle were hidden. Apollo was about to reclaim the cattle when he discovered the two skins of his sacrificed cows, which only rekindled his fury. Hermes, reluctant to give up his booty of cattle, had one more plan up his sleeve. He drew out the tortoise-shell lyre and began to play it and sing along. It was the first time Apollo had heard such lovely sounds! He was beguiled and entranced by the beauty of the melody. Apollo pleaded with his little half-brother to teach him how to play this amazing instrument. If Hermes would give him the secret of how to play and sing in such a way, he, Apollo, would give him marvelous gifts in return.

Hermes gives Apollo the lyre and creates the syrinx.

Considering this, Hermes answered that he would teach him all about the lyre that very day. Because Apollo's heart was set on having the instrument, Hermes would give it to him as a gift. Apollo lived up to his word, rewarding his brother with the care of his cattle herds and bestowing on him his own precious, shining whip, which was exactly what Hermes wanted. Zeus, pleased and proud of their agreement, made them the closest of brothers and closest of friends. Because Apollo took over the playing of the lyre, clever Hermes made a new instrument for himself, a syrinx, that is, shepherd's pipes, whose sound can be heard from afar.

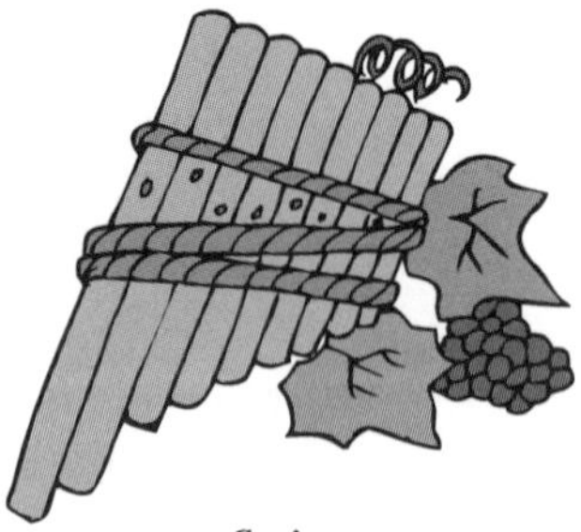

Syrinx

Hermes

Cretan coin showing Hermes wearing the *petasus,* the Greek traveler's hat

In art, Hermes appears as a handsome and masculine boy in his late teens, a younger version of Apollo, some might say. Statues of Hermes could be found in all the gymnasiums of the Greco-Roman world. He often was shown with wings either on his sandals, his legs, or his feet, wearing a winged *petasus,* the Greek traveler's hat, and carrying a herald's staff or a *caduceus,* lyre, or syrinx. In Book 5 (44–49) of the *Odyssey,* Homer paints a charming portrait of Hermes who has just been ordered by Zeus to bring a message to the nymph Calypso:

The Argus-slaying guide (Hermes) . . .
Directly, then, tied handsome sandals, godly and golden, to his feet.
They carried him on gusts of wind over water and land without end.
He wiggled his wand to charm human eyes to sleep
Or wake the sleepy-eyed, as he wished.

Hermes was known by a host of other Homeric epithets, some of which were "the way-finder," "slayer of Argus," and "he of the golden wand."

Ares (Mars)

Parents: Zeus and Hera

Dominion: War

Favorite Places: Thebes, Thrace

Symbols: Helmet, sword, shield, spear

Archetype: Angry and violent, intensely competitive

Literary Sources:
Homer *Iliad* 5
Hesiod *Theogony* 921–923, 934–937

Ares, the god of war, was the least loved and most despised of all the Greek gods. The Greeks associated him with senseless destruction and the utter foolishness of battle. If Athena represented wisdom, calculated strategy, and right judgment in the midst of conflict, Ares stood as her opposite: one who engages in reckless passion, vengeance, the horror of bloodshed, uncontrolled chaos, the worst in human—or godly—nature. Ares was also a marriage-wrecker and disloyal brother: he was the lover of his brother's wife, Aphrodite. Most of the ancient writers chose not to say very much about Ares. Hesiod simply says that last of all, Zeus married Hera to bear him children and that she gave birth to Ares, and to his sisters Hebe and Eileithyia.

Homer is the poet who shows Ares at his worst, engaging in the acts of violent death and destruction with which he is associated forever after. In *Iliad* 5, Homer calls him "scourge of men, blood-lusting, fortress-smasher, maniac, double-dealing, butcher" among numerous other negative epithets. Ares takes the Trojan side in the war between the Greeks and Trojans, even though Zeus had forbidden any of the gods to participate in the war.

Diomedes wounds Ares in the Trojan War.

Early in the war, one of the Greek heroes, Diomedes, under the guidance of Athena, wounded Ares. When Ares realized he was hurt, he shrieked as loud as nine or ten thousand fighting men. Whimpering with self-pity, he rushed off to show the bloody wound to his father. Disgusted by his cowardly son's behavior, Zeus showed no sympathy.

In another encounter, Athena faced off against her brother, knocking him over with a well-aimed rock. Homer says that Ares' body stretched out over seven acres! The Greeks, both the soldiers in the Trojan War and the listeners to the tale in generations after, were only too happy to see Ares laid low once more.

Hephaestus entraps Ares and Aphrodite.

Homer tells another tale of Ares in which he is made a laughing-stock. In *Iliad* 8, the poet Demodocus recounts the story of how Ares stole away Aphrodite, the wife of Hephaestus, Ares' own brother. Helius (the Sun) came to tell Hephaestus that he had seen Ares and Aphrodite together. Hephaestus went to his forge to plot his revenge. He made a very fine metallic net that he suspended over his and Aphrodite's bed, fastening it invisibly to chains for a trap set on the bedposts. When Ares and Aphrodite later got into the bed, the net and chains descended, shackling them, and preventing them from escaping.

After Hephaestus discovered them tangled in his trap, he shouted out for Zeus and all the other gods to come have a look at the two caught in adultery. Curious at being so abruptly called to Hephaestus' house, the gods saw how Ares and Aphrodite were so ridiculously bound up together, and they burst into peals of laughter. They were delighted to see the humiliation of arrogant Ares, the swiftest of gods, caught by Hephaestus, the lame but intelligent and clever god.

In art, Ares is represented as girded for war with helmet, shield, and sword.

Ares girded for war in his chariot

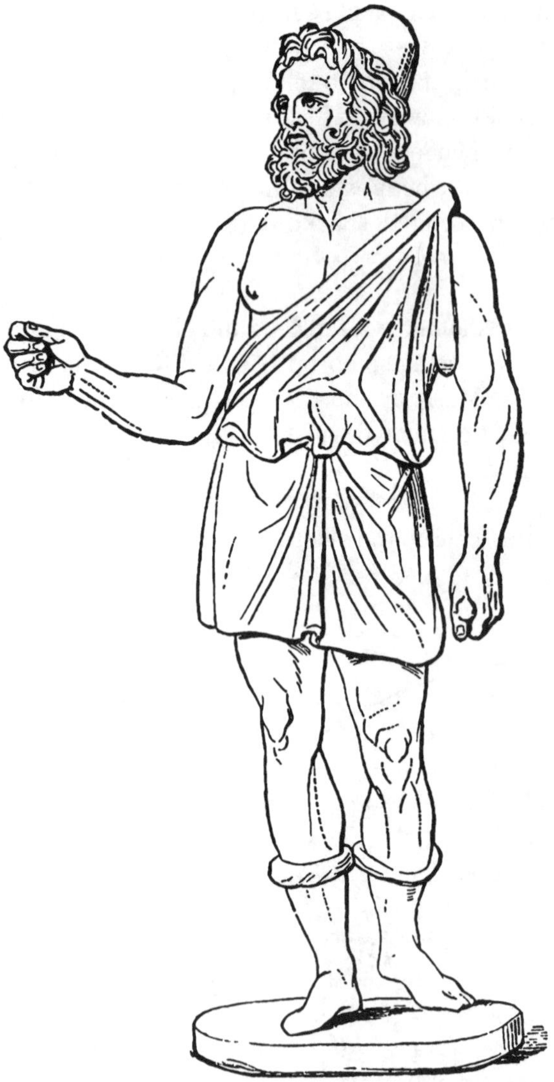

Hephaestus (Vulcan)

Parents: Zeus and Hera or Hera alone

Dominion: Smithing and crafts of the forge, metalworkers, artisans

Favorite Places: Lemnos, Mount Etna in Sicily, other volcanoes in the Mediterranean region

Symbols: Hammer and anvil

Archetype: Earthy, gentle, creative, kindly, even when mocked or wounded

Literary Sources:
Homer *Iliad* 1
Hesiod *Theogony* 927–929

In Hesiod's *Theogony,* Hephaestus was a child born to Hera alone. Hera was jealous when she saw Zeus give birth to Athena from his head. So she conceived her own child, "more skilled at crafts than any other child of the heavens," without any help at all from Zeus. Homer tells us that when Hera saw this newborn son for the first time, she was dismayed to find that he was lame, deformed by a clubfoot. In her rage and disappointment, she flung the poor infant from Mount Olympus. He fell for a full day, landing in the arms of the sea-goddess Thetis. Thetis and Eurynome adopted and raised Hephaestus for nine years in an underwater cave.

Hephaestus was thrown down to earth a second time by his father, Zeus, after he sided with his mother in a dispute. Again, he fell for an entire day until he crashed on the island of Lemnos. Later, Hephaestus was forgiven by Zeus and returned to Olympus.

In ancient societies, able-bodied young men became soldiers and farmers; people with physical disabilities had to fend for themselves as best they could in other occupations. Blacksmithing and metalworking were some of the occupations that might offer a livelihood to persons whose disabled legs and or feet made them unfit for war or agriculture. Hephaestus' lameness led him to the occupation of a craftsman, armorer, and jeweler to the gods and heroes. Hephaestus fashioned the exquisitely wrought armor Achilles wore at Troy.

Dionysus (Bacchus, Liber)

Parents: Zeus and Semele

Dominion: The vine, wine

Favorite Places: Asia Minor, Thebes

Symbols: Wine cup; vine leaves; thyrsus (a staff topped with a pine cone); many wild animals, especially panther, lion, tiger, leopard, dolphin, and snake

Archetype: Moody, mystical, friendly to women, passionate; may develop substance abuse problems

Literary Sources:
Homeric Hymn to Dionysus (7)
Euripides *Bacchae*
Ovid *Metamorphoses* 3.256–315

"Loud-crying" Dionysus is generally seen as a latecomer among the Olympian gods. Some say that the modest Hestia gave up her seat in the divine assembly of the Olympians for him. Dionysus was born as the result of an affair between Zeus and a human woman, Semele. Like many of Zeus' lovers, Semele would become a victim of Hera's jealousy. The Roman poet Ovid tells the story in his poem *Metamorphoses.* Hera (Juno) had heard this news most unwelcome to her ears: Zeus (Jupiter) had fallen in love again with a mortal woman, Semele, daughter of King Cadmus of Thebes.

Hera plots the destruction of Semele, Zeus' beloved.

Dionysus, Semele's son, is born from Zeus' thigh.

At first, Hera started to give her tongue a good workout in preparation to curse Semele in person. Then, remembering that her previous tirades of cursing against her rivals had proven ineffective, she decided that Semele should be destroyed. Disguised as an old woman, Hera went to the pregnant Semele and told her, "If Zeus loves you so much, tell him to show himself to you in all his divine glory!" When Semele made the request, Zeus tried desperately to persuade her to change her mind, as he had sworn by the Styx to give her anything she wanted. But she insisted. Zeus duly dressed himself in his full splendor, although he made it a point to use only his lesser thunderbolts. However much he attempted to downplay and cover his glory, the sight of him was too much for Semele and she was burned to death. Zeus did manage to rescue her baby and hid it in his thigh until it was ready to be born.

Semele, at right, embraces her young son, Dionysus, while Apollo, holding an olive branch, looks on. A satyr plays a flute, at left. Etruscan mirror from Vulci, Italy.

Dionysus spent his childhood raised by nymphs, and most of his followers were women. He caused these women, known as maenads or bacchantes, to go into ecstatic states in which they would become supernaturally strong and have other miraculous powers. In some of Dionysus' myths, the maenads frighten men in authority who see them as a threat to order and decency. One such man—or rather, boy—was Dionysus' own teenage cousin, Pentheus, who was ruling over Thebes.

Dionysus and Pentheus

Mortal Pentheus confronts his cousin, Dionysus.

As a punishment for refusing to worship him, Dionysus caused the women of Thebes, including Pentheus' aunts and his mother, Agave (the sister of Semele, Dionysus' mother), to go mad and take to the woods, dancing and reveling. Pentheus ordered the women to be rounded up and thrown into jail and the "new god" to be brought to him in chains. As he stood face to face with Dionysus, disguised as a youthful follower of the god, Pentheus thought the stranger's long hair and soft white skin were too unmanly. "First I'll cut off your hair, then I'll take away your wand, then I'll lock you up in my dungeons!" he threatened. "Go ahead," said Dionysus calmly. "The god himself will release me when I call on him." As Pentheus led Dionysus away, under guard, the god began to work his magic. First he deceived Pentheus' sight and made him believe a bull was the god. Dionysus stood by quietly as he watched Pentheus, streaming with sweat and chewing his lips, tying up the animal. Next Dionysus lit a sudden flame on his mother Semele's tomb, and laughed as Pentheus ran here and there, yelling, "Fire! Fire! Get water!" Finally Dionysus caused a big earthquake, and sent Pentheus' palace toppling to the ground. The women whom Pentheus had imprisoned immediately escaped back to the woods.

Pentheus learns of the strange behavior of the maenads.

Pentheus was in a rage at the escape of his prisoner and the women when a herdsman came to him. "I wanna tell ya about what I saw, but I'm skeered o' yer royal temper," he said. "Tell your story, don't be afraid," replied Pentheus. The herdsman answered: "A while ago, while the sun was risin', we were drivin' our cattle up the hills. Suddenly I saw all these women in three groups. Yer ma, Agave, was headin' up one and yer aunts the other two. They were sleepin'—but they didn't look like a bunch o' drunks. All peaceful and relaxed they was, until yer mother yelled, "Wake up!" when she heard our cattle mooin'. They all jumped up at once an' let their hair down an' pulled up fawnskins that had slipped off their shoulders an' tied them 'round their waists. All this time there were snakes lickin' their faces, an' some nursed fawns er wolf cubs like babies.

Pentheus' mother, Agave, leads the frenzied maenads.

"One woman hit her thyrsus against a rock an' a spring a' water gushed out! Another one hit her stick on the ground an' out came wine! Another scratched the ground an' milk bubbled up! If you could'a seen them, you'd be shoutin', 'Praise Dionysus!' We kept askin' each other, 'Do you believe this! Did you see that!' Then one guy who'd been hangin' around the city folks said, 'Hey, why don't we bring in Agave—the king will like that!' We said OK an' we hid in the bushes, waitin'. Then Agave shouted to the others, 'They're hunting for us! Rally 'round me! Wands out!' We ran fer our lives, but they fell on our cattle. They rassled bulls t' the ground an' tore 'em to pieces with their bare hands! Then they ran across the plain an' looted all the houses they found. They carried ever'thin' on their shoulders without droppin' a thin', an' they carried fire on their heads without burnin' a curl! The menfolk grabbed their weapons, but their javelins didn't draw a drop o' blood! The women routed the men with these—*sticks!*"

Two maenads hold the thyrsus, and two play musical instruments associated with Dionysus: a goatskin drum and pipes. The figure second from right wears a goatskin.

Pentheus is tricked into putting on women's clothing.

As the herdsman finished his tale, Pentheus was even more determined to punish Dionysus and his women. The thought that women could defeat men infuriated him! The disguised Dionysus came to him once more and begged him to change his course. "Never!" exclaimed Pentheus.

"Would you like to see the women in the hills?" asked Dionysus.

Dionysus disguised as a maenad

"Yes! I'd pay a lot to see them!" was Pentheus' surprising reply.

"Very well, I'll guide you, but you can't let them see you as you are. You'll have to be disguised as one of them—in a dress, with a fawnskin."

Pentheus grumbled at this, but he eventually agreed. Under the god's influence, he threw himself wholeheartedly into his feminine disguise. "How do I look? Like my mother or my aunt?" he asked, sashaying about in his dress.

"Exactly like them! Soon you'll be coming home in your mother's arms!" the god said slyly as he led the young king off to the hills.

When they reached Mount Cithaeron, Dionysus bent back a tall pine tree and let Pentheus climb into it. As soon as it reached its full height, the god called to the bacchants, "Look! There's the man who ridiculed you and me! Punish him!" The women all rushed to surround the tree. At first they tried throwing stones and branches, but could not reach Pentheus.

Agave and the maenads dismember Pentheus.

Then Agave cried, "Surround the tree! Uproot it!" The women did so, using their supernatural strength. Poor Pentheus plummeted down into the hands of the maddened women who did not recognize him. "Stop, Mother! Don't kill your own son!" he screamed. But Agave, together with her sisters, attacked him in a frenzy until his body was torn to pieces. When she later came to her senses, Pentheus' severed head was in her hands. She screamed with horror and remorse, but the god had taken his revenge.

Agave, with thyrsus, in a Dionysiac frenzy, holding the head of her son, Pentheus

Pentheus and other humans were sometimes slow to recognize the god Dionysus. Dionysus could appear in disguise, or he might present himself in a strange way that veiled his true identity. In the *Homeric Hymn to Dionysus*, there is a memorable story of another such epiphany of the god and the dire consequences that result when humans are too ignorant or are too blind to recognize an epiphany.

An *epiphany* is a revelation or manifestation of a deity to a human. An epiphany can also occur when a human experiences a sudden or profound insight into the essence or nature of a deity.

Dionysus and the Pirates

Pirates take Dionysus prisoner.

Dionysus stood on a headland of the sea, looking like the picture of handsome young manhood. His glossy, dark hair waved in the wind; around his strong shoulders he had flung a purple robe. A pirate ship was sailing on the sea nearby. Seeing the young man on the headland, the pirates made straight toward him, seized him, and forced him into their ship, foolishly thinking he was the son of a rich king. They tried to tie him up, but the restraints would not hold him; the chains and ropes fell from his hands as soon as they had been fastened. The mysterious young man put up no active resistance, merely sitting and smiling mysteriously, his dark eyes shining.

The helmsman recognizes Dionysus as a god.

Suddenly, the helmsman of the ship understood that this was a god; he raged at his fellow pirates: "Madmen! Which of the gods is this you've taken aboard? Zeus? Apollo of the silver bow? Poseidon? Come on, let him go, set him free upon the shore this instant! Don't touch him in case he gets mad and stirs up the winds and storms!"

The captain disregarded his helmsman, ordering the crew to hoist the sails and move off into the open sea. He said: "As for this man—don't worry! We'll look after him. I'd guess he's headed to Egypt or Cyprus or to the Hyperboreans. Eventually, he'll tell us who his friends and brothers are and where his wealth is." Just as soon as the crew had hoisted sail upon mast, and the wind began to fill the sails, eerie things began to happen.

Grapevines grow on the mast of the ship.

Sweet-smelling wine began to flow through the decks of the dark ship. All the crewmen were struck dumb with astonishment. Then a grapevine started to grow rapidly from the topsail, rich clusters of grapes hanging thickly upon it. Up and down the mast, an ivy vine sprouted and twisted round and round, blossoming with flowers and berries. At these signs, the crew mutinied against the captain and begged the helmsman to sail the ship back to land in order to return the young man to shore. But in the meantime, the god had transformed himself into a lion, roaring loudly. He also made a bellowing, threatening, and shaggy bear to appear on the deck.

Dionysus lounges in a grapevine-bedecked ship. He has transformed the ship's sailors into dolphins. Representation from painting on Attic black-figure kylix.

Dionysus becomes a lion and destroys the pirates.

The frantic crew rushed to the stern, crowding around the helmsman, who was the only one insightful enough to have recognized the god from the beginning. Suddenly, the lion seized and ate the captain of the ship. Terror overtook the sailors now when they saw the fate of the captain; one and all they jumped overboard into the sea. As they jumped, the god turned them into dolphins. Dionysus, however, spared the helmsman, who had recognized him, and then vociferously shouted out his true identity, "I am loud-crying Dionysus, whom Semele, daughter of Cadmus, bore in union with Zeus."

These are just a few of the epithets of the god, Dionysus:

God of joy! **God of wine!** **Splendid son of Zeus!**
Blossom-bringer! **Fruit-bringer!** **Abundance of life!**
Bull-horned! **Loud-crying!**

A. Review Exercises

1. **EPITHETS FOR EVERY GOD!** Homer and other writers gave titles or epithets to each of the gods. In the exercise below, write the name of the appropriate god or goddess next to each epithet. (Each epithet is mentioned somewhere in Chapters 3 and 4 of this book. Many of the gods have several epithets, as you will see below.)

Part I

Apollo	**Artemis**	**Demeter**	**Leto**	**Hera**	**Zeus**
Poseidon	**Dionysus**	**Ares**	**Hades**	**Athena**	**Hermes**

____________ Cloud-gathering

____________ Of the tasseled-tresses

____________ White-armed

____________ Neat-ankled

____________ Delighting in arrows

____________ Slayer of Argus

____________ The earth-shaker

____________ Far-shooting

____________ Loud-crying

____________ Golden-helmeted

____________ Grey-eyed / bright-eyed

____________ Dark lord of the dead

PART II

Hephaestus	**Leto**	**Hermes**	**Athena**	**Zeus**	**Hades**
Demeter	**Phoebus**	**Persephone**	**Aphrodite**	**Hera**	**Ares**

___________ Of the strong arms

___________ Gold-wreathed

___________ Battle-stirring

___________ Aegis-bearing

___________ The way-finder

___________ Long-haired

___________ The Great Goddess

___________ Lord of all beneath the earth

___________ The maiden

___________ Man-destroying

___________ Fair-haired

___________ Cow-eyed

2. **MULTIPLE CHOICE!** For each sentence below, circle the number of the answer that best answers the question or completes the statement.

a. What were feminine followers of Dionysus called?

1. Muses
2. Graces
3. Maenads
4. Eumenides

b. Hermes used these to trick Apollo.

1. Sticks
2. Sandals
3. Peacocks
4. Tortoise shells

c. Hephaestus trapped these two gods in a net.

1. Apollo and Hermes
2. Aphrodite and Ares
3. Zeus and Hera
4. Artemis and Apollo

d. Some myths say Aphrodite is the daughter of Cronus. Which god is also said to be Aphrodite's father?

1. Uranus
2. Atlas
3. Zeus
4. Chaos

e. This creature hounded poor Leto as she searched for a place to give birth.

1. Argus
2. Python
3. Tantalus
4. Cerberus

f. Thunder and lightening shook earth and sky at the birth of this god or goddess.

1. Apollo
2. Ares
3. Aphrodite
4. Athena

g. Who was the offspring of Zeus and fire-consumed Semele?

1. Pentheus
2. Prometheus
3. Ixion
4. Dionysus

h. He eternally pushes a boulder up a steep hill in Hades.

1. Sisyphus
2. Ixion
3. Cerberus
4. Tantalus

i. This god or goddess is the only one other than Zeus who wears the *aegis.*

1. Aphrodite
2. Athena
3. Hera
4. Ares

j. Hermes stole these from Apollo.

1. Lyres
2. Sandals
3. Cattle
4. Pipes

k. Whom did Zeus swallow?

1. Semele
2. Athena
3. Dionysus
4. Metis

l. The sea-god Poseidon rules the waters along with his spouse. What is her name?

1. Amphitrite
2. Aphrodite
3. Tethys
4. Thetis

m. The story of Demeter and Persephone explains which of the following?

1. The weather
2. Mother Nature
3. The seasons
4. Geology

n. Why did Maia live in a cave with her son Hermes?

1. She wished to protect her delicate skin.
2. She wished to protect Hermes from Hera.
3. She was shy.
4. Zeus ordered her to remain there.

o. Ixion, a mortal, dared to fall in love with this goddess and so was eternally punished.

1. Hera
2. Demeter
3. Hestia
4. Aphrodite

p. Which one is not found in Tartarus?

1. Amalthea
2. Sisyphus
3. Tantalus
4. Ixion

q. Python was slain by the arrows of Artemis and Apollo. What sort of creature was it?

1. A bull
2. A snake
3. A tortoise
4. A fly

r. The small island of Delos gave refuge to this goddess as she was about to give birth.

1. Maia
2. Leto
3. Metis
4. Themis

s. This woman did not recognize her own son, Pentheus, whom she killed while under the influence of Dionysus.

1. Metaneira
2. Semele
3. Agave
4. Persephone

t. This god was twice hurled from Olympus to earth.

1. Hades
2. Hephaestus
3. Ares
4. Poseidon

B. Musings

1. In the earlier chapter on the Muses, you saw that the ancient poets used personification to express certain abstract ideas: Mnemosyne, the mother of the Muses, was the personification of the idea of "memory." Which character(s) introduced in this chapter personify an abstract idea? What ideas are personified?

2. Can you think of any other myths, nursery rhymes, songs, poems, or fairy tales in which a character swallows someone or something? Describe what happens. Does the particular rhyme, story, tale, or poem you are thinking of contain personification, allegory, or another literary figure?

3. Another example of allegory is the medieval idea of the search for the Holy Grail. The Grail symbolizes the quest for inner wisdom or spirituality. Can you think of any other examples of allegory in other myths? In books you have read? In movies you have seen? Briefly describe one example of such a story or film and tell how it is allegorical.

4. Draw a cartoon, paint a picture, or make a clay sculpture of one or all of the following:
   - Metis transforming herself into water and/or fire, a boar, a lion, an insect, etc.
   - Zeus swallowing Metis, pregnant with Athena
   - Zeus' splitting headache
   - The birth of Athena

5. Athena was said to have been Zeus' favorite child. Zeus loved her mother, Metis, and he also needed her very much, keeping her within his head. What does this myth reveal to you about Greek priorities and values?

6. Theater was one of the favorite entertainments for the Greeks and Romans. An essential part of an actor's costume was the mask worn to represent a god or hero. Make a mask of your favorite Olympian or Titan. Use a brown grocery-store paper bag and cut openings for eyes, nose, and/or mouth. To decorate the mask, use construction paper, beads, feathers, paint, markers, fabric, or cloth. Fashion hair from paper, yarn, string, pompons, shredded newspaper, or other materials at hand. On a day designated by your teacher, wear your mask to class. Be prepared to tell a brief story, in three to five sentences, about the deity depicted in your mask using a first-person narrative. See if your classmates can guess your identity. For example, "I was born on the Aegean Isle of Delos, far from Mount Olympus. I killed the Python that terrified my mother. I took over the oracle on Mount Parnassus. I am the lord of music and carry the lyre. The Pythian Games were held in my honor. What is my name? Who am I?"

7. Besides the Olympic games, held every four years at Olympia to honor Zeus, the ancient Greeks celebrated games to honor Apollo. These games, held at Delphi on Mount Parnassus, were called the Pythian games. Research the Pythian games. How were they similar to or different from the Olympic games?

8. The ancient site of Delphi on Mount Parnassus is one of the most spectacular places in Greece. Why did so many Greeks and people from other nations throughout the ancient world travel there?

9. The sayings of Apollo were especially loved and revered by the people of ancient Greece. Two of these sayings or proverbs were "Know thyself" and "Nothing in excess." Choose one of these sayings and draw a picture, find a photograph, or construct a themed collage to illustrate this idea. Then write a paragraph explaining what you have illustrated and attach it to the paper.

10. Locate Delos, the birthplace of Apollo and Artemis, on a detailed map of Greece and the eastern Mediterranean, or Aegean, Sea. Now locate Delphi. Where is Delphi in relation to Delos? To Athens? To Mount Olympus?

11. Where is Lemnos? Where is Mount Etna? What natural geographical feature of both these islands might make them sacred to Hephaestus (Vulcan)?

12. How do the myths of Hephaestus (Vulcan) and Ares (Mars) reflect Greco-Roman ideas about ability/disability? What were the prejudices and limitations encountered by people with disabilities in Greek and Roman societies? How have these attitudes changed or not changed in contemporary society?

13. How many deities can you identify from their icons in this depiction of a council of the gods?

C. Words, Words, Words

The Daily Muse

News you can use

Wouldn't the Olympian gods be astonished to know that we are using words referring to their names or attributes, two or three millennia after Homer, Hesiod, Ovid, and the other ancient Greeks and Romans? Here are six utterly "divine" words, many of which you probably are familiar with:

aegis, volcano, vulcanize, martial, jovial, plutocrat

________ ________ ________ ________ ________ ________

1. Which god(s) is associated with each of the words given above? Write the god's name beneath each vocabulary word in the designated space.

2. In the table below, using the six words written in boldface above, list familiar words on the left and unfamiliar words on the right:

I know these words and I can sketch them here:	These are new words for me:

3. Match each of these "Olympian" words in the left-hand column with an appropriate synonymous word or phrase from the right-hand column. Write the letter in the space provided.

1.	____	Aegis	a.	Hardened/strengthened by fire
2.	____	Jovial	b.	Protection
3.	____	Martial	c.	Wealthy ruler
4.	____	Plutocrat	d.	A mountain formed from lava and escaped gas
5.	____	Volcano	e.	War-like
6.	____	Vulcanized	f.	Jolly

Athena wearing the *aegis*

4. Discuss: Do you suppose that there are any **plutocrats** living in contemporary times? Has there ever been a government that could be described as a **plutocracy**?

5. Draw a picture here of any useful item that you know has been **vulcanized.**

D. How 'Bout That?

The museum of the goddess Athena

There is an online museum devoted to the Goddess Athena that shows just about every picture, drawing, painting, photograph, cartoon, or other visual representation of Athena that possibly exists! Visit it at: http://www.goddess-athena.org/Museum/Paintings/Arachne/Athena_Arachne_Barbier_x.htm

Freaky flora and fauna

Have a look at just a few of the plants and creatures whose names reflect mythological figures we have met in the last two chapters. The Latin name (scientific nomenclature or taxonomic classification) is given below each picture. Can you research to find the common English name of each one?

Agave americana

Dionaea muscipula

Zeus faber

How in the world did these plants and this fish get their names? Explain:

Extra credit!

Find as many pictures as you can of other creepy creatures from nature that have been named for an Olympian god or goddess. Place and paste them in the space below (or better yet, draw a sketch!).

Venus and love songs

It seems as though every generation has its own Venus love songs! Here are a few you might hear on your local "Oldies" radio station. Do you know any of these? Compare the lyrics of these songs and point out the characteristics of Venus each brings out:

- "Venus" sung by Frankie Avalon (1959):
  www.oldielyrics.com/lyrics/frankie_avalon/venus.html
- To see and hear Frankie Avalon performing "Venus," visit this *YouTube* site:
  https://www.youtube.com/watch?v=fakpqLDEQAo
- "Venus in Blue Jeans": (a recording with still photos)
  https://www.youtube.com/watch?v=Knq_BY6xpbQ
- "Venus in Blue Jeans" sung by Jimmy Clanton (1962):
  http://www.songlyrics.com/jimmy-clanton/venus-in-blue-jeans-lyrics/
- "Venus" sung by Shocking Blue (1969):
  www.oldielyrics.com/lyrics/shocking_blue/venus.html

- To watch and hear Shocking Blue with Mariska Veres performing "Venus," visit either or both these two *YouTube* links:
  www.youtube.com/watch?v=U2DBcbZc3ck or
  www.youtube.com/watch?v=RpQL4SKq7JY
- "Venus and Mars/Rock Show" sung by Paul McCartney and Wings (1975):
  http://www.metrolyrics.com/venus-and-marsrock-show-lyrics-paul-mccartney.html

Cupid and love songs

Cupid has also had popular songs written and sung about him. How true to his character in the ancient myths are these two?

- "Cupid" sung by Sam Cooke (1961):
  www.metrolyrics.com/cupid-lyrics-sam-cooke.html

- "Stupid Cupid" sung by Connie Francis (1958); re-recorded by Mandy Moore (2001):
  http://homepage.ntlworld.com/gary.hart/lyricsf/francis.html

Who named the planets?

Who on earth decided to name the planets after the gods? Which is the only planet *not* named for one of the Greek or Roman gods? Research the answers to these questions. The following website, where you can type in your questions, operated by Cornell University Department of Astronomy is a great place to start:

- http://curious.astro.cornell.edu/

E. Who's Who?

- For Zeus' descendants and wives, see Genealogical Chart 5.

Chapter Five
OTHER DEITIES

General Source:

Hesiod *Theogony*

Aside from the great Olympian gods whom you met in the two previous chapters, there are several other lesser gods and a few highly favored humans, some of whom were taken to Olympus. The names and attributes of many of these have proven influential. Sometimes they play a crucial role in several well-known myths.

Asclepius

Asclepius (Aesculapius): The god of healing was one of the only two Greek gods born a mortal and deified after death (the other was Heracles). His father was Apollo; his mother was the mortal woman Coronis. Although Apollo loved Coronis and she was pregnant with his child, she planned to marry a mortal man, reasoning that Apollo would abandon her once her beauty faded. A crow saw Coronis with her mortal lover and told Apollo, who in his anger turned the crow black (it had previously been white). He sent his sister Artemis to kill Coronis, but he saved her baby, who was later educated in the art of medicine by a wise centaur. When Asclepius grew up, fame of his skill spread all over.

Asclepius had several children; his daugher Hygeia was the personification of health. Another daughter was Panacea, or "cure-all." His two sons served in the Trojan War as both warriors and physicians. Asclepius unfortunately carried his healing powers too far; when he began to resurrect the dead, Zeus struck him with a thunderbolt. (See GENEALOGICAL CHART 6.)

Hygeia

As you might imagine, Asclepius was one of the most popular of the gods. In art, he is depicted carrying a staff with a snake coiled around it; a staff entwined with snakes is still one of the symbols of the medical profession. You saw Hermes holding this staff, also called a *caduceus,* in the last chapter.

Eileithyia (also **Ilythia):** one of two daughters of Zeus and Hera, also sister of Ares. (See GENEALOGICAL CHART 5.) She was the goddess of childbirth. Homer refers to the Eileithyiae, goddesses of childbirth as plural. She is an aspect of Hera herself, who was patroness of all phases of a woman's life, including childbirth. Hera prevented Eileithyia from attending the childbirth of Leto's twins, delaying the birth of Apollo and Artemis.

Eos (Dawn, Aurora) driving her chariot

Eos: the goddess of Dawn, known to the Romans as Aurora. (See GENEALOGICAL CHART 9.) Homer calls her "rosy-fingered" and "saffron-robed," from the colors of the dawn sky. She is generally depicted in art as winged. She had several love affairs with mortal men, the most notable being with a man named Tithonus. She loved him so much that she begged Zeus to give him immortality, which he did, but unfortunately Eos forgot to ask for him to have eternal youth also. Poor Tithonus grew older and older; eventually he was transformed into a grasshopper.

Eris: the goddess of Strife, sister and companion of Ares. (See GENEALOGICAL CHART 7.) Her most crucial role in myth is as the instigator of the judgment of Paris and thus of the Trojan War. This will be fully discussed in a later chapter. In his *Works and Days*, however, Hesiod speaks of Eris as twofold, both good and bad (11–24). The bad Eris fosters war and conflict; the good one represents healthy competition.

Representation of *The Judgement of Paris*, 1633–1635, by Peter Paul Rubens (1577–1640). Eris appears flying above the scene with a snake in her right hand and a torch in her left. Hermes is behind the tree. Paris, the shepherd with his crook, judges among Hera with her peacock, Aphrodite accompanied by Eros (Cupid), and Athena with her *aegis* decorated with the Gorgon Medusa.

Ganymede: the most handsome of all mortals, according to Homer, who says that the gods spirited him up to Olympus to serve as the cupbearer to Zeus. (See Genealogical Chart 18.) Other authors say Zeus appeared as an eagle who carried off Ganymede himself. The eagle (Aquila) and Ganymede (Aquarius, "the water-bearer") appear next to each other in the sky as heavenly constellations.

Aquarius the Constellation

Ganymede with Zeus as an eagle

Hebe: the cupbearer to the gods. She poured nectar for all the Olympians until Zeus brought the mortal Ganymede to Olympus. Hebe was daughter of Zeus and Hera, and sister of Ares and Hephaestus. (See Genealogical Chart 5.) When Heracles was taken up to Olympus, Hebe became his wife. Her name means "youth." As such, Hebe has the power to rejuvenate.

Hebe

Hecate

Hecate: a goddess of sorcery and magic, although first mentioned without any sinister associations by Hesiod, who praises her as a powerful goddess and source of many blessings. (See Genealogical Chart 8.) Hecate, as we saw above, helped Demeter in her search for Persephone, and later became Persephone's attendant. Her closeness with the queen of the Underworld led to her association with magic, witchcraft, ghosts, and the night. She was worshipped at crossroads, especially where three roads met. Statues such as the one in the picture at left were common throughout the countryside, where travelers often left votive offerings. In ancient art, she is often shown having three faces or three bodies. In Shakespeare's *Macbeth*, she makes an appearance to direct the three witches.

Helius: the sun-god, known as Sol to the Romans. He was the brother of Eos. He had several famous children and grandchildren, including Aeetes, Pasiphae, Circe, Augeas, Phaethon, and Medea. (See GENEALOGICAL CHART 9.) You will meet all of these characters in subsequent chapters. His ability to see everything made him the first to see Hades' abduction of Persephone (as we saw in chapter 3) and Ares' love affair with Aphrodite (covered in chapter 6).

Helius

The Greek island of Rhodes was an important center of his worship. Every year, the inhabitants of Rhodes threw into the sea a chariot and four horses to replace the ones that had been working every day for the previous year. The Colossus of Rhodes, a giant statue of Helius at the entrance to Rhodes' harbor, was one of the seven wonders of the ancient world.

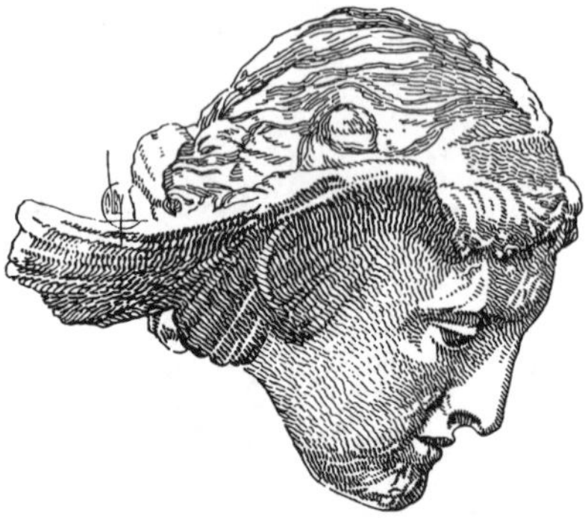

Hypnos (Somnus)

Hypnos: the spirit of sleep, called Somnus by the Romans. He is the twin brother of death, known as Thanatos, or Mors by the Romans. (See GENEALOGICAL CHART 7.) Hypnos plays an important role in Book 14 of the *Iliad,* when Hera bribes him into lulling Zeus to sleep so that the Greeks can gain the upper hand over the Trojans. Hypnos' son was Morpheus, the god of dreams. The drug morphine derives its name from him.

Iris: the personification of the rainbow, seen as the link between the divine and human worlds. (See GENEALOGICAL CHART 8.) She takes the role of messenger of the gods in the *Iliad,* although elsewhere this part is taken by Hermes. She sometimes acts as cupbearer to the gods. Iris is a popular figure in Greek art, where she is shown as winged. Her name survives as the name of the flower and as the colored part of the human eye.

Iris flower

Janus

Janus: one of the few Roman deities with no exact Greek counterpart. He was the guardian of doorways and gates and the god of beginnings and endings. The gates to his temple in Rome were open during wartime and closed during peacetime. He is usually represented with two faces, looking simultaneously forwards and backwards. The month of January is named for him, as it is a time to look back at the old year and ahead to the new.

Nemesis: the goddess of retribution. (See Genealogical Chart 7.) If anyone violated the moral order or did anything to excess, those affected thereby could call upon Nemesis for revenge. The Greek author Apollodorus records the tale (3.10.7) that she was the true mother of the beautiful Helen of Troy. Perhaps the tradition came about because of all the grief Helen caused.

Nemesis

The Nike of Samothrace, Louvre, Paris

Nike: the goddess of victory. (See Genealogical Chart 8.) She is closely associated with Pallas Athena. On the Acropolis at Athens, Nike was the personification of victory under the aegis of Athena. The most famous representation of her from antiquity is the Nike of Samothrace, also known as "La Victoire de Samothrace," one of the greatest treasures of the Louvre Museum in Paris.

Pan: a god of shepherds and flocks. His birth in the northern Greek region of Arcadia is recorded in the *Homeric Hymn to Pan* (19). Hermes fell in love with a shepherd's daughter, and for her sake spent his time tending her father's sheep. She later bore him an unusual child: a bearded baby with two horns and the feet of a goat! His nurse ran away from him in fear, but Hermes wrapped him in a rabbit's hide and took him to Mount Olympus.

The gods found the strange-looking baby delightful, and called him "Pan" (Greek for "all") because he delighted all their hearts. Pan could generally be found in the wild countryside or in the lonely stretches of mountains, playing upon the pipes he had created. According to Ovid (*Metamorphoses* 1.689–713), he fell in love with a nymph named Syrinx, but she ran away from him. She fled to a river, where she prayed to the other nymphs to transform her. Just as Pan reached for her, he found himself clutching a bunch of marsh reeds instead of his beloved's body. He sighed with disappointment; as the air blew through the reeds, Pan was struck by the sound. He cut the reeds into different lengths and produced the first set of panpipes.

Pan with syrinx (panpipes)

Pan had a more sinister side. He could produce a feeling of overwhelming terror in travelers crossing through the lonely places where he lived. We know this feeling as "panic," and it is named for him.

Selene: the Moon, known to the Romans as Luna. She was the sister of Helius and Eos. Like them, she was thought to drive a chariot through the sky to light the world. The best-known myth about her connects her with a shepherd boy, Endymion. She put him into an eternal sleep that preserved his youth and beauty, and watched him in his sleep every night. She was later identified with Artemis.

***Selene and Endymion*, 1630, by Nicolas Poussin (1594–1665), Institute of the Arts, Detroit, Michigan**

A. Review Exercise

MULTIPLE CHOICE! For each sentence below, circle the letter of the word/phrase that best answers the question or completes the statement.

1. Which of these pairs were children of Night?

   a. Hypnos and Thanatos   b. Selene and Endymion
   c. Pan and Syrinx   d. Asclepius and Hygeia

2. A doctor might have this god's symbol in his office.

   a. Erebus   b. Asclepius
   c. Hebe   d. Hypnos

3. What is another name for the moon goddess, Selene?

   a. Iris b. Eos (Aurora)
   c. Luna d. Syrinx

4. Who is the rainbow goddess?

   a. Hecate b. Iris
   c. Hebe d. Eileithyia

5. Which of these was born a mortal?

   a. Hebe b. Ganymede
   c. Endymion d. Pan

6. These two served nectar to the gods on Olympus.

   a. Pan and Hebe b. Iris and Ganymede
   c. Hebe and Ganymede d. Aurora and Hebe

7. Women who were about to give birth were assisted by this goddess, the daughter of Hera.

   a. Eileithyia b. Hebe
   c. Iris d. Eos (Aurora)

8. Along with Ares and Hephaestus, these were the children of Zeus and Hera.

   a. Hebe and Eileithyia b. Eos and Hebe
   c. Iris and Selene d. Eileithyia and Hecate

9. Statues of the goddess Hecate usually had this number of bodies and/or heads.

   a. Two b. Three
   c. Four d. Five

10. The sun-god, Helius, was the model for which of the seven ancient wonders?

    a. The Pharos of Alexandria b. The Colossus of Rhodes
    c. The Mausoleum of Halicarnassus d. The Hanging Gardens of Babylon

11. This goddess drives her beautifully colored chariot across the sky at dawn.

    a. Eos (Aurora) b. Selene
    c. Hecate d. Eileithyia

12. This is the two-faced Roman god who looks back to the old year and forward to the new year.

    a. Pan b. Janus
    c. Helius d. Asclepius

13. Who is the goddess associated with strife, discord, or disagreement?

    a. Hebe b. Iris
    c. Eris d. Eos (Aurora)

14. This is the goddess whose name means "youth" and who has the power to rejuvenate.
    a. Eileithyia   b. Hebe
    c. Eris   d. Eos (Aurora)

15. Which goddess punished humans for excess and demanded retribution or vengeance for crimes committed?
    a. Nemesis   b. Hebe
    c. Eris   d. Eileithyia

16. Which goddess accompanies Athena in victory?
    a. Nemesis   b. Iris
    c. Nike   d. Hygeia

17. Which two daughters of Asclepius are associated with health and cures?
    a. Eris and Hebe   b. Hygeia and Nemesis
    c. Hygeia and Panacea   d. Eris and Panacea

18. This mythological figure was ultimately responsible for the Trojan War.
    a. Thetis   b. Eris
    c. Nemesis   d. Hecate

19. Statues of this goddess often stood near a crossroads; she was the goddess of magic and sorcery.
    a. Nemesis   b. Hebe
    c. Hecate   d. Hera

20. This ugly baby had a beard, two horns, and goat's feet.
    a. Eris   b. Pan
    c. Hecate   d. Hephaestus

21. Syrinx was the name given to which of the following?
    a. Panpipes   b. The goddess of the undergrowth
    c. The moon goddess   d. The wand carried by Hermes

22. This unfortunate mortal, beloved of Eos (Aurora), was granted immortality but not eternal youth.
    a. Ganymede   b. Pan
    c. Endymion   d. Tithonus

23. Pan pursued this poor nymph through the woods.
    a. Hebe   b. Europa
    c. Syrinx   d. Nike

24. If you had difficulty sleeping, you might call upon this god.
    a. Somnus
    b. Pan
    c. Thanatos
    d. Ganymede

25. The positive side of this goddess was that she fostered healthy competition.
    a. Nemesis
    b. Eris
    c. Hebe
    d. Eos (Aurora)

B. MUSINGS

1. Have you ever noticed that certain products carry the name of a deity or mythological figure? What are some of these products? Can you find an advertisement or brand label for a product named for a god or goddess? Here is a vintage advertisement capitalizing on the name of Apollo to sell a product. Why do you think it made sense to use Apollo's name for this product?

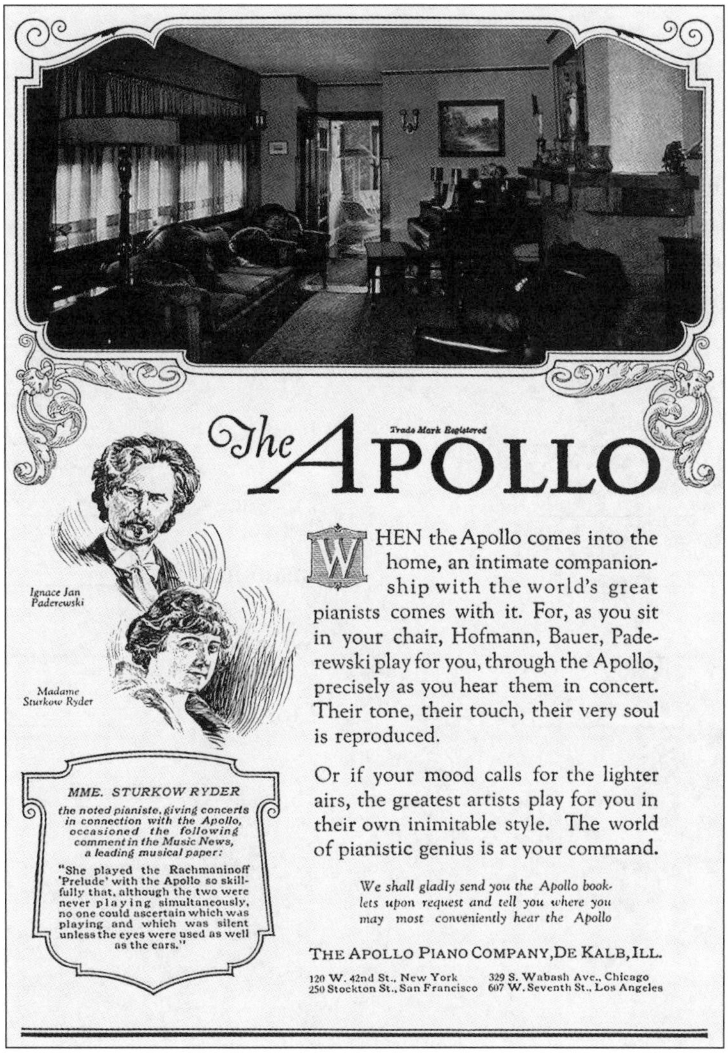

2. What are the aurora borealis and the aurora australis? Why do they have the same name as the Roman goddess of Dawn?

3. The author Edmund Wilson titled his novel, based on observation and personal detail, *Memoirs of Hecate County.* Based on what you read about Hecate above, what sort of memories would you expect the book to contain?

4. The Roman name for the moon-goddess, Luna, simply means "moon." This Latin word has given us the word "lunacy" (insanity). What connection did the ancients create between madness and the moon? Are there any survivals of this connection, and if so, where?

C. Words, Words, Words

The Daily Muse

News you can use

1. Mythological figures in this chapter who played minor roles were mighty enough to end up as *major* players in our own English language. Can you identify the figure, god, or goddess whose name is hidden within each of these words? Write the name in the space provided. (Some names will appear more than once!)

Morphine	__________	Hypnosis	__________
Somnolent	__________	Panic	__________
Nemesis	__________	Lunatic	__________
Iridescent	__________	Insomnia	__________
Somnambulist	__________	Syringe	__________
Hygiene	__________	Mortal	__________

2. Using the selection of words below, choose the one that best fits the meaning of each given phrase. Write your answer in the space provided.

Morphine	**Hypnosis**	**Somnolent**	**Panic**	**Syringe**	**Hygiene**
Nemesis	**Lunatic**	**Iridescent**	**Insomnia**	**Somnambulist**	**Mortal**

______________ A sleepwalker

______________ Displaying a rainbow of shimmering colors, as do butterfly wings

______________ A tube-shaped instrument used to inject medicine or fluids into the body

______________ A powerful drug extracted from opium used as an anesthetic or sedative

______________ Insane; one thought to be deranged by association with a phase of the moon (archaic)

______________ A being who is subject to death; deadly, fatal

______________ One who inflicts vengeance; an avenger; a rival, as in sports

______________ Sleepy, drowsy; inducing sleep or a sleepy state

______________ A sudden state of terror, sometimes affecting several people simultaneously

______________ Sleeplessness; inability to sleep

______________ A sleeplike condition induced by power of suggestion

______________ Disease prevention by use of healthful practice such as cleanliness

3. **PANIC!** Use your own words to write your own definition of the word **panic:**

____

____

4. **DREAMS AND SLEEP.** Below are vocabulary words containing the same root words visible in the names of the Greek (and Latin) god **Hypnos (Somnus).** Circle the picture in each picture pair that better fits or illustrates the word.

Somnambulist

Insomnia

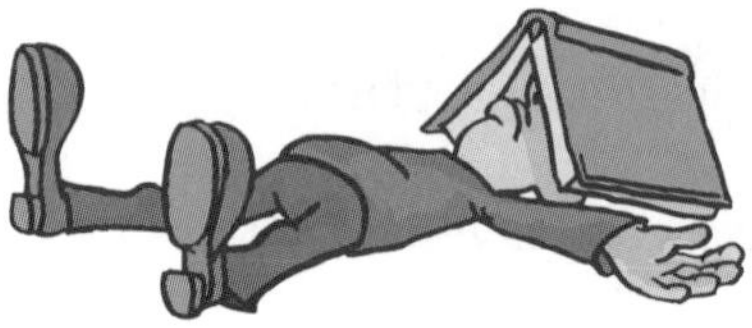

Somnolent

Hypnosis

D. How 'Bout That?

Nike

Which deity appears *most* frequently in classical art? It just might be **Nike**! No wonder—she *was* **Victory** personified. Here are just a few examples of artistic representations of Nike from different periods by various artists. Which do you find most appealing? Write or tell why. To learn more about these Nikes, research them on the Internet or in the library.

Nike fastening her sandal, from the relief parapet of the temple of Athena Nike, ca. 415–410 BCE, Acropolis Museum, Athens

***Nike of Olympia* by Paionios of Mende (Chalcidice), ca. 421 BCE, Archaeological Museum, Olympia, Greece**

***Nike of Delos* by Archermos of Chios, ca. 550 BCE, National Museum, Athens**

Nike driving quadriga. Detail of Athenian red-figure vase painting, 5th century BCE.

The *Nike of Paionios* was the official symbol of the 2004 Olympic Games at Athens.

Nemesis

Harry Potter's nemesis is Lord Voldemort. A nemesis can be a figure of retribution and vengeance or simply an archrival. A sports team might have a nemesis, a rival with which the team frequently contends and who is tough to beat! Who is the archrival of your school's sports teams? Would you consider them your school's nemesis or vice versa?

Calling all Trekkies! Did you know that there is a Star Trek film, released in 2002, entitled *Nemesis?* Can you think of another well-known nemesis from literature or from the movies?

The Hon. East India Company's Steamer 'Nemesis' and the Boats of the Sulphur, Calliope, Larne, and Starling, Destroying the Chinese War Junks in Anson's Bay, January 7, 1841, **by G. W. Terry (artist) and George Great Back (engraver)**

The *Nemesis* was the first steam-powered warship to be used in action by Britain. It is the large vessel on the left side of the picture. Notice that it has the large humps in the center to accommodate the paddlewheel that powered the steam. It also has masts and rigging for sailing the ship, if needed. Because the ship did not need to be dependent on winds and tides, it was a formidable and terrifying new weapon. It was used primarily in the rivers and estuaries of southern China during the First Opium War. Why do you suppose that it was christened with the name *Nemesis?* Which one of the other ships named in the title of the engraving is also named for a mythological figure?

Chapter Six

The Gods in Love

General Sources:
Hesiod *Theogony*
Ovid *Metamorphoses*

Zeus and Io

Literary Source: Ovid *Metamorphoses* 1.568–750

Inachus mourns his lost daughter, Io.

In Thessaly, Greece, there was a valley called "Tempe." Steep woods ascended on either side of the valley, and it was well watered by several rivers. One of these was the river Inachus that originated deep within a mountain cave. It used to flow over rocky ledges and out into the sea. However, Ovid tells in *Metamorphoses* that the abundant river Inachus dried up. For Inachus was wretched, lamenting his beloved lost daughter, Io. Inachus remained pooled within his mountain cave, adding a stream of his own tears to stagnant waters. Despite all his efforts, Inachus couldn't find Io anywhere; he feared she had met a fate worse than death.

Zeus in the form of a cloud steals a kiss from the beautiful river nymph Io. Representation of *Jupiter* and *Io*, 1532, by Antonio Allegri da Correggio, Kunsthistorisches Museum, Vienna, Austria.

Zeus kidnaps Io.

A god had indeed seen poor Io as she was returning from the river Inachus. The god was none other than Zeus, who accosted her, "O maiden, you are worthy of Zeus' love. Come into these shady woods, out of the heat of the noonday sun. If you are frightened of coming toward the hidden lairs of wild animals, don't worry—a god will protect you. No ordinary god, not at all; I am he who holds the mighty scepter of the heavens and hurls the thunderbolt! Oh no, don't run away from me!" But Io had already started to flee. Zeus enveloped the whole region in a thick mist, caught Io as she fled, and made love to her.

Zeus changes Io to a heifer and gives her to Hera.

Meanwhile, Hera happened to be looking down from heaven toward her beloved land of Argos. She was surprised to see thick mists covering the region, especially at that time of the day. Suspicious, she looked all around for her divine husband and didn't see him. Quickly, she flew down to earth and made the clouds disappear. In order to escape Hera's notice, Zeus instantly changed Io into a beautiful cow. Hera gazed upon the cow and couldn't help admiring her. She asked whose cow she was and where had she come from, as if she didn't know. Zeus lied, claiming the cow had sprung from the earth. Hera asked that he give her the heifer as a gift. What to do? Zeus knew it would be a very cruel fate indeed to turn Io over to Hera; not to give her over would make him suspect in Hera's eyes. So, reluctantly, he gave the cow to Hera.

Hera orders 100-eyed Argus to guard the heifer, Io.

Triumphant for the moment, but still suspicious of Zeus, Hera handed the heifer over to Argus of the one hundred eyes for safekeeping. Argus served as Io's guard and watchman. Argus' eyes were set all around and about his head, and they took turns sleeping, two at a time, so that at any given time, the other ninety-eight eyes were awake and watchful. Even when Argus' back was facing Io, he could still see her. He let her graze in the daytime; after sunset, he humiliated her by placing a halter round her neck to prevent her getting away. Instead of a soft bed, she slept upon the ground, sometimes even in the mud. She tried to extend her arms to Argus to implore him for mercy, but she couldn't because she no longer had arms that would stretch forth. She tried to call out to Argus, but she could only low, "Moooo." She terrorized herself with the sound.

Not recognizing his daughter, Inachus feeds the heifer.

One day, she came pasturing to the very banks of her father Inachus' stream, where she had frolicked as a girl. Looking into the waters at her reflection, she was horrified to see her wide-open mouth and the horns on her head. Neither her father nor her naiad sisters recognized her. But she followed her father and sisters around and let them touch and pet her. Inachus held out to her some grass he had picked; she licked his hand, trying in vain to kiss it. She could not hold back her tears.

Argus, Io (note horns), and Hermes with pipes

The heifer reveals her true identity to Inachus.

If she had been able to speak, she would have told the story of what had happened to her. Instead, she traced words in the dust with her hoof, revealing to her father the sad story of how she had been transformed into a heifer. "O, I am an unhappy wretch," cried out her father when he understood. "Can you really be the beloved daughter I have looked for over all the earth? The grief of not finding you was easier to bear than the grief of finding you like this! I had been looking for a suitable husband for you; I looked forward to becoming a grandfather. Now, I must find a mate for you from the herd, and my grandchildren will be cattle!" Hundred-eyed Argus then dragged Io from her father's embrace and drove her to a distant pasture. He settled himself on a nearby mountain where he could watch over her from all sides.

Hermes slays Argus in the presence of Zeus. Io, the heifer, stands behind Argus.

Zeus orders Hermes to kill Io's guard, Argus.

In the meantime, Zeus could no longer bear to watch Io's sufferings. He summoned his son Hermes, bidding him to get rid of Argus. Hermes put on his winged sandals, seized his sleep-inducing wand, covered his hair with his traveling cap, and flew down to earth. Removing his sandals and cap, keeping only his wand, and playing his shepherd's pipes, he entranced Argus with his music, and by telling him a bedtime story. After putting up a tremendous struggle to stay awake, Argus' hundred eyes closed one by one until at last he was fast asleep. Using a curved sword, Hermes quickly cut off Argus' head, sending it tumbling off the mountain cliff.

Hera puts Argus' eyes on the peacock's feathers.

Hera scooped up Argus' hundred eyes and placed them like jewels on the tail feathers of the peacock, her favorite bird. Then, choked with anger, Hera sent a Fury (some say a gadfly) to drive Io mad and chase her all over the earth. Poor Io ran here, there, and everywhere, panic-stricken. Finally, she reached the Nile River in Egypt, where she staggered in agony upon the riverbank. Seeing this pitiable sight, Zeus begged Hera for mercy. "Put aside all fear for the future; she will never be a cause of sorrow to you again." Relenting at last, Hera allowed Io to return to her former self. The Egyptians worshipped Io as the goddess Isis. Io had a son, Epaphus, who was said to have been the offspring of Zeus. (See GENEALOGICAL CHART 5.)

Hera snatches up the eyes of Argus and places them on the tail feathers of her favorite bird, the peacock.

Isis-Io and Horus-Epaphus

Eros and Psyche

Literary Source: Apuleius *Metamorphoses* 4.28–6.24

Mortals flock to gaze upon the beautiful but unhappy Psyche.

Once upon a time there were a king and queen who had three daughters. They were all beautiful, but the beauty of the youngest, Psyche, was beyond description. So outstanding was her loveliness that people came from miles around to look at her, and they swore she was the goddess Aphrodite on earth. In fact, they preferred to worship her and neglected the great shrines of Aphrodite. "We can see Psyche, but nobody has ever seen Aphrodite!" they reasoned.

***Cupid and Psyche*, 1798, by François Gérard (1770–1837), Louvre, Paris**

Aphrodite enlists Eros to help her punish Psyche.

As Aphrodite's temples fell into disrepair and her ceremonies were ignored, the goddess was outraged. "I can't believe that I, the source of all life and nature, must share honors with a *mortal!* But I'll fix her! I'll make her wish she had never been beautiful!" She summoned her son Eros to her, kissed him, and said, "Dearest son, your mother needs you to uphold her honor. I want you to use your arrows to make Psyche fall in love with the lowest, most despised being in the entire world! Make sure she has no equal in misery!" Satisfied that she had thus eliminated her rival, she departed to some of her favorite beaches, accompanied by an entourage of sea nymphs.

Meanwhile, Psyche's beauty did not bring her joy. Everyone admired and worshipped her, but no one dared to speak with her. Her older sisters were married, but no one sought Psyche's hand in marriage. Troubled, her father consulted the Delphic oracle to find out whether Psyche would ever be married. He received a frightening response. "O King, place the girl on a high cliff dressed for her funeral. Your son-in-law will not be human, but a savage monster that flies over the earth and devastates all with fire and iron! Even Zeus and the other gods and the creatures of the Underworld are terrified of him!"

An oracle tells Psyche's father to leave her on top of a cliff.

The king told his wife the sad news. They mourned for several days, but they had to obey the oracle. Psyche's wedding procession was turned into a funeral; she was led to the cliff accompanied by dirges instead of marriage songs. "Why are you crying now?" she asked her parents. "You should have grieved back when everyone was worshipping me and calling me Aphrodite!" At last they all went away, extinguishing the torches with their tears, and left Psyche on the cliff alone to face the unknown.

Zephyr carries Psyche to her new palace home.

What happened next was most unexpected. Psyche was slowly lifted off the cliff by Zephyr, the gentle west wind. He carried her down the slope and laid her tenderly in the soft grass of the valley below. There, her fears eased, Psyche went to sleep. When she awoke refreshed and calm, she saw a grove planted with tall trees, and in its midst a royal palace, built not by human hands but by divine art. It was a dwelling fit for a god, with high ceilings carved in ivory, supported on golden columns, with its walls covered in silver carvings of animals. Even the floors were made of precious stones cut into tiny pieces. Psyche approached the palace, attracted by its beauty, and slowly began to explore it. She was amazed that there were no chains, locks, or guards protecting this rich place. As she gazed in delight, a voice without a body said, "Welcome to your new home! All this belongs to you. You may go to your room and rest, or have a bath. We whose voices you hear are your servants, and we will prepare a feast for you when you are ready."

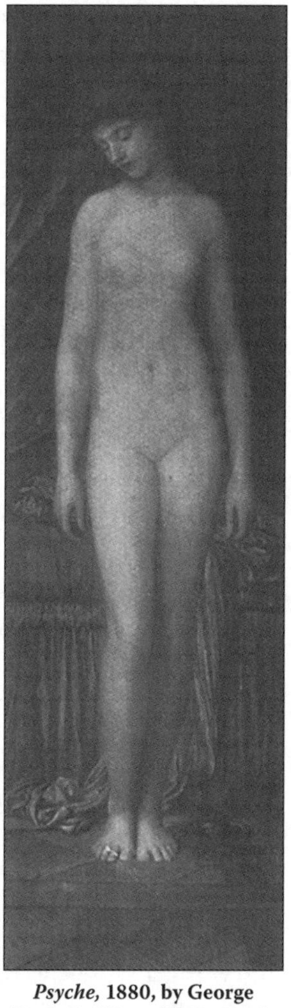

***Psyche*, 1880, by George Frederic Watts (1817–1904), the Tate Gallery, London**

Eros, unseen by Psyche, makes love to her.

Psyche did as the voice suggested. After she napped and bathed, she saw near her a table set for dinner. She reclined, and immediately trays came out filled with delicious food and wine. After she ate, someone invisible played an invisible lyre, and then an invisible choir sang. When it was time for bed, Psyche went back to her room and waited nervously. Eros, unseen by Psyche, came to her in the night and made love to her.

Eros warns lonely Psyche to beware of her sisters.

Thus Psyche lived for many months. Meanwhile, her parents and sisters mourned incessantly. Eros realized this and feared for the time when Psyche would want to see them again. He warned, "My dearest Psyche, your sisters will soon come to the cliff where they last saw you. If you hear them, do not listen! Do not even look at them! If you do, you will ruin everything for us!"

Psyche promised to obey, but she spent the entire next day weeping. She felt so lonely without any human contact, and she missed her sisters. When Eros came that night, he found her still in tears. "Psyche, is this how you keep your promise to me? All right, go ahead and let them visit, but if they try to tell you that you should try to see me, don't listen!"

Psyche answered, "Thank you so much! I would rather die than let anything come between us. I love you; I couldn't love you more if you were Eros himself! Please tell Zephyr to bring them here tomorrow!" Eros agreed reluctantly, and left in the morning as usual.

Psyche's sisters come for a visit.

By now, Psyche's sisters had found the cliff, and stood there lamenting. Psyche called out, "Don't cry! Here I am! I'm not dead! Soon you can see me for yourselves!" She called for Zephyr to bring the sisters down, and he did. They hugged and kissed and wept for joy at their reunion. Psyche then took them into the splendid house, showed them its riches, and let them hear the voices of the invisible servants. Surrounded by their sister's luxury, they began to feel envy. One of them began to bombard Psyche with questions about her husband. Who was he and what was he like? Psyche remembered Eros' warning, and said, "He's young and handsome, just beginning to have a beard. He spends most of his time out hunting." She was afraid to say more. She gave her sisters presents of gold and jeweled necklaces and quickly summoned Zephyr to take them home.

As they journeyed, the sisters began to complain to each other. "It's so unfair!" said one. "What did she ever do to deserve all those jewels and gold and rich clothes? You'd think she was going to be a goddess, the way she acted with those invisible servants! Why does she have everything, while I'm married to a short bald man older than my father?"

The other sister answered, "That's right! I have to put up with a husband all hunched over with arthritis! I have to rub all those smelly ointments on him! I feel more like a nurse than a wife. Did you see how arrogant Psyche was? When she was done showing off her wealth, she threw us a few little trinkets and couldn't wait to be rid of us! Here's what we'll do: Let's not tell anyone that we've seen Psyche. We'll hide what she gave us, go back to our poor but respectable homes, and think about ways to punish her pride."

Eros renews his warnings; he reveals Psyche's pregnancy to her.

They agreed upon this. Meanwhile, Eros renewed his warnings. "You are in very serious danger, Psyche! Your sisters are hatching a plan to persuade you to see my face! If you must see them again, tell them nothing about me! You are now carrying my child, who will be a god if you keep our secret but mortal if you give it away."

Psyche renewed her promise to Eros and rejoiced at the thought of becoming a mother. But she insisted upon seeing her sisters a second time. When Zephyr had brought them to the palace as before, they pretended to be joyful at the news of Psyche's pregnancy. But they also renewed their questions about Psyche's husband. Psyche forgot her earlier story and said, "He's a middle-aged merchant who travels a lot."

The sisters realized that Psyche had never even seen her husband. They said, "You poor thing, you don't realize what danger you're in! Several people who live around here have said they've seen a huge poisonous snake coming this way in the evening and swimming in the brook. Don't you remember Apollo's oracle saying that you were destined to marry a savage monster? He's just biding his time, fattening you up, and then he's going to eat you and your baby too! Is that what you want, or are you going to listen to your sisters who love you?"

Psyche's sisters urge her to look at her husband and kill him.

Poor Psyche was filled with terror and forgot her husband's warnings. "You're right! I've never seen his face. He must be a beast! Why else would he keep telling me that I mustn't ever try to see him? What do I do now?"

The sisters said, "Tonight, take a knife and hide it under your pillow. Hide a lamp under a pot. Then, when he falls asleep, take out the lamp and cut his head off. We'll be waiting to escort you out of here, with all these treasures of course. Then we'll marry you off to a human being!"

When they had left, Psyche was torn apart by her conflicting feelings. How could she kill her husband? But at the same time, she was terrified of the monster she thought he was. She decided to do what her sisters had suggested. As soon as Eros fell asleep that night, she gathered all her courage, seized her knife, and raised the lamp.

Psyche, with knife and lamp, regards the sleeping Eros.

Psyche uses a lamp to look at her husband and sees Eros, who abandons her as punishment.

What she saw was no monster, but a beautiful god, the gentlest and sweetest "beast" of all. She stared in amazement at his fair skin, soft curls, rosy cheeks, and the wings fluttering gently on his back. Ashamed at what she had been planning to do, she lowered her knife and began to kiss him passionately. But a drop of boiling oil fell out of her lamp and onto the sleeping god's shoulder. He awoke in pain from his wound. Horrified at seeing his beloved standing over him with a knife, he pushed her away and took off from the house without a word. Psyche hung on to him until she could hang on no more. He flew up into the branch of a cypress tree and scolded Psyche: "Is this what I disobeyed my mother for? She wanted me to make you fall in love with some lowlife! But I was hit by my own arrow and I fell in love with you and gave you everything, and what do I get for it? You thought I was a monster and came at me with a knife! I warned you not to listen to your sisters! They'll get the punishment they deserve—but your only punishment is losing me." And he flew off into the sky.

Psyche takes revenge on her sisters.

Psyche thought of a way to take revenge upon her sisters. She went to one of them and said, "Remember your advice to me—take a knife and stab my 'monster' husband in his sleep? Well, I had the knife all ready, but when I looked at him by the lamplight, guess what I saw! Eros himself! He was angry and said he didn't want me any more, but he asked for you!" The sister believed this; she ran immediately to the cliff and shouted, "Here I am, Eros, a wife worthy of you! Carry me away, Zephyr!" But the wind was not there, and she fell from the cliff to her death. Psyche told the same story to her other sister, who died the same way.

Aphrodite learns of Eros' love affair with Psyche.

Meanwhile, Eros was lying in his mother's house, still nursing his wound. Aphrodite was still enjoying her seaside vacation when a garrulous seagull brought her the news about him.

"So, he's got a girlfriend, has he? Who is she?"

"I'm not sure. . . . I think her name was . . . Psyche," answered the bird.

Aphrodite immediately flew home and scolded her son, "What is this? I gave you an order and you made a fool of me! I can always have another son and turn over your bow and arrows to him, you know!" She then went to Zeus and persuaded him to let Hermes make a public proclamation for Psyche's capture.

Psyche searches for Eros.

While Eros was ill, Psyche searched for him incessantly. She went to a temple of Demeter, then to one of Hera, and they both told her the same thing: "You poor thing, I'd like to help you, but I don't want to offend Aphrodite. You had better go to her yourself and beg for her mercy."

Aphrodite punishes Psyche with three daunting tasks.

Psyche reasoned, "Whatever Aphrodite does, it can't be any worse than living without Eros." She let Hermes lead her to Aphrodite, who beat her and then sneered at her, "So you've finally decided to come see the husband that you've nearly killed! You're not so beautiful anymore. Maybe you can win your husband back by being a hard worker." She led Psyche to an enormous heap of mixed grains, and said, "Sort all these out by nightfall!" Psyche was in despair, but an ant saw her and took pity on her. He said to his fellows, "Come on, men! Let's sort out these grains!" And they did. Aphrodite, however, was not impressed. "You must have had help," was all she said. She threw Psyche a crust of dry bread for her supper and went away.

The next day, Aphrodite ordered Psyche to go to a river bank where sheep with golden wool grazed, and to bring back some of the wool. This time, a reed whispered to her, "Don't try to go near those sheep! They have sharp horns and teeth! Wait until noon when they lie down to rest, and then gather the wool from the bushes and the tree branches." And so Psyche accomplished her second task.

Aphrodite was still not satisfied. She next led Psyche to the top of a high mountain and showed her a stream that ultimately led to the Underworld. "Fill this jar with water from that stream!" she commanded. Psyche looked down into the steep valley and was filled with despair. The very waters seemed to murmur, "Go away. You'll die. Beware!" This time it was Zeus' eagle that showed up to help Psyche. He took the jar in his beak, flew down to the stream, filled the jar, and returned it to Psyche.

By now, Aphrodite was determined to be rid of Psyche for good. As her final task, she commanded, "I want you to go down to the Underworld and ask Persephone to fill this box with some of her beauty. Tell her that I've lost some of mine while nursing my sick son back to health."

Psyche had no idea how to find her way to the Underworld, so she climbed a high tower and prepared to throw herself off. Suddenly the tower itself came to life and spoke: "No, not that way! You'll get in, all right, but you won't be able to get out! What you need to do is take a coin to pay the ferryman Charon and some drugged cake to put the guard dog Cerberus to sleep. Above all, don't look in the box that Persephone gives you!"

Psyche descends to the Underworld and meets Persephone.

Psyche carried out the tower's instructions. Persephone received her kindly and filled up the box willingly. But on her way back, Psyche thought, "I must look terrible after all these hard tasks! I need to look my best if I want to win Eros back. Aphrodite will never miss a little of the beauty in this box if I take it for myself!" She opened the box, but there was no beauty inside it. Instead, Psyche was enveloped by the sleep of the Underworld.

***Cupid Revives Psyche*, 1787, by Antonio Canova (1757–1822), Louvre, Paris**

Eros revives Psyche; Hermes gives her ambrosia to drink.

Eros and Psyche, now immortal, marry on Olympus.

By now, Eros had recovered from his wound. Longing to see Psyche again, he flew out on wings refreshed by their long rest and found her lying in her deathlike sleep. He gathered the clouds of sleep, put them back in the box, and awakened Psyche by a gentle touch of his arrow. "Once again, you nearly ruined everything by your curiosity!" he scolded, but there was no anger in his words. He bade Psyche complete her task while he flew off to Zeus and asked him to approve his marriage to Psyche. Zeus agreed, and Aphrodite finally conceded. After all, she reasoned, her son needed to settle down! Hermes brought Psyche back to Olympus, where she was given a drink of ambrosia to make her immortal. Eros and Psyche's marriage was celebrated with a glorious feast. In time, Psyche delivered a daughter, and her name was Pleasure.

Representation of *Psyche Received into Olympus*, 1524, by Polidoro Caldara da Caravaggio (1496–1543), Louvre, Paris

This tale is more than a love story. It has often been interpreted as an allegory, a story whose surface meaning contains a deeper, often symbolic meaning, as we have seen in a previous chapter. Psyche is the Greek word for "soul," and her adventures may be seen as the journey of a soul from happy innocence to mature fulfillment through suffering. Moreover, since Eros represents love or sexual desire, the allegory also shows the human soul in search of divine love. In art, souls were often depicted as winged beings; thus Psyche is sometimes depicted in art with the wings of a butterfly. Fairies were later depicted in the same way.

Apollo and Daphne

Literary Source: Ovid *Metamorphoses* 1.438–567

Apollo disparages Eros' use of bows and arrows.

Among the monstrous creatures that Gaea bore was a snake named Python, huge enough to cover the side of a mountain. Although Apollo had never previously hunted anything except deer and wild goats, he shot Python until his quiver was nearly empty and killed the enormous serpent. Apollo was immensely proud of himself for this mighty deed, when he happened to spot Eros drawing a string on his own bow. "You silly boy, what business do you have with men's weapons?" he said. "Be happy lighting the fires of love with your torches, and leave the bow and arrow to me!"

Eros, offended, takes revenge on Apollo with his arrows.

Eros replied, "Your arrows may hit everything else, but mine will hit you!" With that, he flew off to the peak of Mount Parnassus, and there he drew two arrows: one arrow of love and one arrow of indifference to love. The love arrow was made of gold and had a sharp, glittering point; he shot this one at Apollo. The arrow of indifference was made of lead and had a blunt point. Eros fixed this one in the heart of Daphne, the daughter of the river god Peneus.

At once Apollo was madly in love, but Daphne rejected all suitors, preferring to hunt wild beasts in the woods like her favorite goddess, Artemis. Often her father said to her, "When are you getting married? I want to see grandchildren!" But Daphne answered, "Please, Father, promise me you'll let me stay unmarried forever. Artemis' father, Zeus, made that promise to her!" Daphne's father reluctantly agreed, but Apollo was not so easily put off. He gazed at her longingly, admiring what he could see of her and wondering what her loose and windblown hair would look like if it were styled. Soon he was no longer content to look and began to run after her. She ran away, swifter than a breeze. "Wait!" he called after her. "Don't run so fast! The ground is rough! You could fall or scratch your legs on the brambles! I'll run more slowly if you will! At least ask me who I am! You must be running away because you think I'm some common shepherd! My father is Zeus! I rule over Delphi and Claros and Tenedos and the realm of Patara! I can reveal whatever is and has been and will be, and the lyre makes music through me. My arrows are the surest in the world, except for that one arrow of Eros' that made me fall in love with you. The art of medicine is my discovery, but none of my herbs can cure my lovesickness!"

***Apollo and Daphne*, 1622–25, by Gianlorenzo Bernini (1598–1680), Villa Borghese Gallery, Rome**

Daphne runs away from Apollo.

He would have said more, but Daphne kept running. Apollo wasted no more time on words, but pursued at top speed. He was like a hound that spots a rabbit in an open field and chases her, again and again almost catching her with his sharp fangs as he snaps at her heels.

Caught by Apollo, Daphne prays for deliverance.

Daphne knew she could not keep running forever; her strength was gone at last. She looked at her father's waters and cried, "O father, help! Change my body! Take away my beauty!" She had barely finished speaking when her limbs grew numb. Her sides were covered with bark. Her hair was now leaves; her arms, branches. Her feet, only now so swift, were fastened to the ground in roots. Only her beauty remained.

Daphne is changed to a laurel tree.

Although Daphne was transformed into a laurel tree, Apollo still loved her. He placed his hand on the trunk and felt her heart still beating under the bark. He embraced the branches as if they were human limbs and kissed the wood. The wood still shrank away from his kisses. The god cried, "Since you won't be my wife, you will be my tree! I will weave your leaves into my hair, my lyre, and my quiver! Someday triumphant Roman generals will crown their heads with you! Just as I am forever young, so too will be the beauty of your leaves!" The laurel waved her branches, and her treetop seemed to nod, "Yes."

Zeus and Callisto

Literary Source: Ovid *Metamorphoses* 2.401–530

Zeus, disguised as Artemis, approaches to seduce Callisto.

When once in Arcadia, Zeus chanced upon a nymph named Callisto, who was devoted to Artemis. He immediately felt the fire of love. As she sat alone in the forest, resting from a strenuous morning of hunting, Zeus thought, "My wife will never find out about this. Even if she does, her insults will be worth it!" At once he disguised himself as Artemis and approached Callisto. "Hello, my favorite nymph! Where have you been hunting today?" Callisto stood up and answered, "Hello, my goddess, greater to me than Zeus—I don't care if he hears me say that!" Zeus was amused at her words and embraced her, abandoning his disguise. Callisto struggled as hard as she could, but she was no match for Zeus.

***Diana and the Nymph Callisto*, 1759, by Francois Boucher (1703–1770), the Nelson-Atkins Museum of Art, Kansas City, Missouri**

Artemis drives away Callisto, now expecting Zeus' child.

After Zeus went back to the sky, Callisto retraced her steps out of the forest, nearly forgetting to take her bow and arrows back with her. Just then Artemis came over the slopes of a nearby hill, brandishing the animals she had caught. At first Callisto ran away, thinking this was Zeus in disguise again, but when she saw the other nymphs with Artemis, she was reassured and joined them. Yet it was hard for her to keep her shame at what had happened from showing in her face. She walked with downcast eyes, not beside the goddess, as she had done before. If Artemis had not been so inexperienced, she could have guessed her friend's secret. She found out nine months later, on a hot day. The group had come to a cool grove through which a stream flowed. Artemis dipped her feet into the water and said, "There's no one around to see us. Let's undress and have a swim!" Callisto tried to make excuses not to join the rest, but they coaxed her until her pregnant belly was in plain sight. As she stood terrified, trying in vain to cover herself, Artemis cried, "Go away! You pollute this sacred grove!"

***Diana Dismissing Callisto* by Giovanni Costetti (1878–1949)**

Hera changes Callisto, after she gives birth to Arcas, to a bear.

Hera had known for a long time about Callisto, but she put off her revenge until a fitting time. After Callisto delivered a son named Arcas (see GENEALOGICAL CHART 5), Hera sneered, "You *would* have to have a baby and show the world how my husband hurt me and disgraced himself! But I'll take away that beauty you're so proud of and that Zeus likes so much!" With that, she grabbed Callisto by the hair and threw her to the ground. As the poor nymph stretched out her hands to beg for mercy, her arms became covered with shaggy black hair; her hands changed into clawed feet; the mouth that Zeus had loved was now huge and ugly. Her power of speech was taken away so that she could not pray to him; her voice was now a harsh growl. Only her thoughts and feelings remained human. She who had been a huntress now fled in terror from hunters. She feared the other bears, forgetting that she was one. She was even afraid of the wolves, although her father, Lycaon, ran with them.

Zeus transforms Callisto and Arcas into constellations.

Her son, Arcas, grew up unaware of her fate. One day when he was fifteen, he happened upon her while he was hunting, spreading his nets in the Arcadian woods. She stared as if she recognized him. He shrank back from her gaze, and when she tried to approach him, he raised his spear to her. He was about to pierce her with his weapon when Zeus intervened. The god caught them both up in a whirlwind and set them in the heavens as neighboring stars. We know them as the Great Bear and the Little Bear (Ursa Major and Ursa Minor).

Aphrodite and Adonis

Literary Source: Ovid *Metamorphoses* 10.518–739

Aphrodite falls in love with a young hunter, Adonis.

In a previous chapter, you read that Aphrodite had many lovers. She had at least two great mortal lovers, Adonis, whose story is told here, and Anchises, whose tale is told in the next episode. Eros was responsible for Aphrodite's love for Adonis. While he was kissing his mother, quiver on shoulder, he happened to graze her with one of his arrows. Aphrodite pushed him away, but the scratch was deeper than she thought. Having fallen victim to the power of Eros' arrow, Aphrodite couldn't help falling in love with the handsome Adonis when she saw him. She abandoned all her favorite cities and even Mount Olympus to be with him.

Aphrodite finds Adonis lying dead in his own blood, and transforms his blood into the anemone flower.

Although she had never been a lover of the great outdoors, she went with him over mountain ridges and through the woods, hunting hares and deer. She avoided the dangerous animals, however, and urged her beloved to stay away from boars, lions, wolves, and bears. But he would not take her advice. His hounds chased a boar from its hiding place, and as the beast was rushing from the woods, Adonis hit him with his spear. The boar shook off the missile and chased Adonis, now full of fear and running for his life. It sank its tusk deep into the young man's body. Aphrodite heard his groans as she was riding through the air on her chariot borne by white swans. She rode immediately to his side, only to find him lying lifeless in his own blood. "My Adonis! I couldn't save you, but I will make sure the world remembers you," she said. She sprinkled his blood with nectar, and within the hour a blood-red flower sprang up from it. The flower was the anemone, whose name is derived from the Greek for "wind." The bloom is beautiful but short lived, as the winds for which it is named easily shake off the fragile petals.

Anemone

Anemone is also known as Wind-flower or Pasque-flower, blossoming in early spring. Its colors range from white to shades of red, pink, and violet. It is said that the red-petaled varieties of anemone come from Adonis' blood and the white-petaled flowers derive from the tears of Aphrodite.

Aphrodite and Anchises

Literary Source: *Homeric Hymn to Aphrodite* (5)

Zeus causes Aphrodite to fall in love with Anchises, a mortal.

One day Zeus decided, "Why should Aphrodite make fools of us gods by constantly matching us up with mortals? Let her see how it feels to love a mortal, for a change!" He therefore made her fall in love with a handsome Trojan youth named Anchises. She spotted him tending cattle on the slopes of Mount Ida, and was filled with desire for him. She went to her temple in Cyprus, where the Graces anointed her with sweet-smelling oil, and she dressed herself in her richest clothes. Then she hurried to Troy and Mount Ida. As she went, wolves, lions, bears, and leopards followed her and fawned on her. She was glad to see them and filled them with the urge to mate. When she came to Anchises' house, she found him alone, playing thrillingly upon the lyre. She stood before him looking like a young mortal woman. However, as he gazed at her and took in her golden robes brighter than fire, her brooches and necklaces and earrings in the form of flowers, he realized this was no ordinary girl! He said, "Hello! Are you Artemis, or Leto, or Aphrodite, or Athena, or maybe one of the Graces or Nymphs? I'll make you an altar on a mountain and sacrifice there all year! Please be good to me! Make me famous among the Trojans and give me strong offspring and let me live long and happily!"

Aphrodite proposes marriage to Anchises.

Aphrodite responded coyly. "Oh, Anchises, why do you call me a goddess? I'm just a mortal girl from Phrygia. I know your language because a Trojan nanny brought me up. Hermes found me while I was doing Artemis' dances with my friends, and he carried me off a long, long way. He told me that I was to be the wife of Anchises and give him a son. Please, introduce me to your family and send a messenger to my parents to bring you bridal gifts. Marry me!"

Anchises was in love, and said, "If what you've told me is true, I would love to marry you. You are as beautiful as a goddess, and I would gladly die after loving you!" He took her by the hand and led her to his couch. Then he, a mortal man, made love to an immortal goddess, not knowing what he did.

***Venus and Anchises*, 1890, by Sir William Blake Richmond (1842–1921), National Museums Liverpool, Liverpool, UK**

The epiphany of Aphrodite to Anchises

Near the end of the workday, Aphrodite poured sleep upon Anchises and returned to her goddess form. Then she roused her lover from sleep and said, "Up, sleepyhead! Do I look the same now as I did before?" He awoke instantly, and when he saw the true form of the "girl from Phrygia," he was terrified. He turned away and hid his face with his cloak, saying, "I knew you were divine as soon as I saw you. Don't hurt me, please!"

Aphrodite prophesies the birth of their son, Aeneas.

Aphrodite answered, "Don't worry, I won't hurt you and neither will any of the other gods. You will have a son named Aeneas, and he will be a great ruler. I'll have him raised by nymphs and I'll bring him back in about five years for you to see. You will be very proud of him. But don't tell anybody about us. If anyone asks, say that his mother is one of the nymphs from these parts. If you are foolish enough to boast that you were with Aphrodite, Zeus will strike you with a thunderbolt!"

Another story says that Anchises did boast of his brief romance with Aphrodite one day when he was drunk, and Zeus' thunderbolt crippled him. The next we see him, in Vergil's *Aeneid,* Aeneas is carrying him out of the burning city of Troy on his shoulders.

Anchises, carried by his son Aeneas, the Trojan hero of the *Aeneid*. Aeneas holds the hand of his young son, Ascanius.

Zeus and Europa

Literary Sources: Moschus *Europa*, Ovid *Metamorphoses* 2.836–875

The Phoenician ancestry of Europa

Once again, Zeus had fallen in love. This time, the girl he loved lived at the eastern edge of the Mediterranean, in the land that the ancients called Phoenicia (modern Lebanon) in Asia Minor. At that time, one of the principal cities of that region was Sidon. King Agenor (a descendant of Io and her son, Epaphus) ruled Phoenicia, including Sidon. Agenor and his wife Telephassa had a son named Cadmus (whom we shall meet later), and a daughter named Europa, who would become the object of Zeus' affection. (See Genealogical Chart 11.)

Europa's dream of the struggle between two continents

A little-known poet named Moschus wrote a "mini-epic" poem of 166 lines in Greek called *Europa* around the year 150 BCE. In this poem, the Sidonian princess Europa had a dream one night in which two continents, each in the form of a woman, argued and struggled over who was to claim Europa as her own. One of the continents was Asia, the other continent was not named. Asia argued that she had the stronger right to possessing Europa, for the girl was born in her continent. The other unnamed continent countered by declaring that Zeus would give Europa to her in the near future.

Zeus falls in love with Europa.

Meantime, Zeus gazed down at Earth from Olympus and caught sight of the lovely daughter of Agenor. At that moment, Aphrodite passed by with her little son, Eros, who shot one of his tiny but potent arrows into Zeus' heart. Zeus instantly fell in love with Europa! Fortunately, Hera was nowhere around. Once again, Zeus planned to get the girl by changing his godly form to a different shape in order to deceive her.

Zeus descends to Europa as a white bull and carries her away to Crete.

Europa, on Zeus, the bull

In Ovid's *Metamorphoses*, Zeus commanded his son Hermes to drive down from a hillside to the seashore a herd of cattle belonging to King Agenor of Sidon. Europa and her young friends were accustomed to play and gather flowers at that spot at the seashore. Putting aside his thunderbolt and godly appearance, Zeus took on the form of a white bull whose horns were perfectly shaped, more beautiful than pearls. The bull's unusual color, perfection of form, mild expression, and peaceful, friendly demeanor attracted Europa. Because he was a bull, however, she hesitated to touch him. After a little while, it became clear that the bull was not going to be aggressive and Europa came closer, offering him some flowers. Zeus (in his bull disguise) was overjoyed at her approach and began to lick her hands. In reality, of course, it was Zeus covering her hands with kisses. He could hardly contain his passion and he began to leap about playfully in the grass. At length, he prostrated his snow-white body in the sand along the shore at Europa's feet. Bit by bit, Europa came closer and bent down to stroke his chest. The bull even let her wind garlands of flowers through and around his beautiful horns. Finally, Europa sat down on his back, unaware that she was seated on the back of the king of the gods. At that moment, the bull rose up. The beast, massive though he was, soared out over the open ocean. Europa's light garments rippled in the breezes as trembling, she clung to the bull in flight.

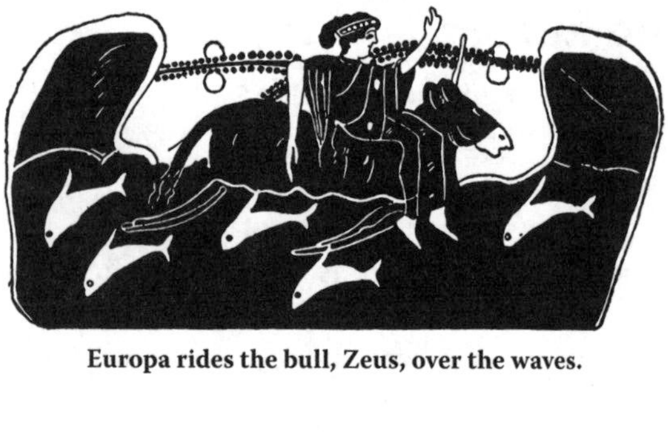

Europa rides the bull, Zeus, over the waves.

A noisy and colorful parade of sea-gods, dolphin-riding Nereids, Tritons, and Poseidon himself rose up out of the sea, Moschus tells us, accompanying Europa and the bull-Zeus with great fanfare and blowing of horns and conch shells. Europa knew then that this must be some great god on whose back she was traveling. She spoke to the bull-god, begging him to have pity on her and set her down in some remote place. Zeus the bull answered, congratulating her for guessing his identity. He reassured her of his great love for her, then gently placed her down on his very own beloved island of Crete. This was the very spot in which Gaea had sheltered him from Cronus at the time of Zeus' birth.

Triton blowing on the conch shell

Europa bears Zeus three sons.

Zeus prophesied to Europa that she would bear him great sons who would hold power over all who dwelt on earth. Europa's sons did indeed become famous potentates. They were Minos, Rhadamanthys, and Sarpedon. (See Genealogical Charts 5 and 15.) King Minos would rule over Crete. Minos and his brothers Rhadamanthys and Sarpedon would become judges in the Underworld as reward for having lived just lives on Earth. Europa's name continues on, of course, as the name of the nameless continent in her dream!

A. Review Exercise

MULTIPLE CHOICE! For each sentence below, circle the letter of the answer that best answers the question or completes the statement.

1. If a man were described as a "true Adonis," which of the following would *not* be true?
   a. He would be good-looking. b. He would be middle-aged.
   c. He would be attractive to Aphrodite. d. He might be a hunter.

2. Which is Argus' most remarkable feature?
   a. Ears b. Head
   c. Fur d. Eyes

3. Who transformed Io into a cow?
   a. Hera b. Argus
   c. Hermes d. Zeus

4. Which of the following disguises or tricks did Zeus *not* use when trying to entrap his human lovers or deceive his wife, Hera?
   a. A thick mist b. A bull
   c. The shape of Artemis d. Argus

5. Zeus transformed Callisto and her son Arcas into which of the following?
   a. Flowers b. Trees
   c. Constellations d. Rivers

6. Phoenicia is the ancient name for which of the following?
   a. Crete b. Israel
   c. Africa d. Lebanon

7. If you were to go to the zoo, on which animal might you see the eyes of Argus?
   a. A bear b. A cow
   c. A peacock d. A horse

8. Which island was most beloved to Zeus?
   a. Aegina b. Rhodes
   c. Crete d. Delos

9. What is the title of Ovid's book about myths of transformation?
   a. *Theogony* b. *Metamorphoses*
   c. *Odyssey* d. *Aeneid*

10. Who was the divine lover of Io, Callisto, and Europa?

a. Apollo b. Hermes
c. Zeus d. Phaethon

11. Which of the following young women survived an ordeal devised by Hera and was worshipped in Egypt as Isis?

a. Callisto b. Io
c. Europa d. Aphrodite

12. Libya was a name used interchangeably for which country?

a. Africa b. Egypt
c. Lebanon d. Lycia

13. Where is Crete in relation to mainland Greece?

a. North b. South
c. East d. West

14. Who is Europa's father?

a. Agenor b. Inachus
c. Zeus d. Cadmus

15. Where would you most likely find the Nereids and Tritons?

a. In the skies b. In the forests
c. In the seas d. In homes

16. The girl whom Apollo loved became which of the following?

a. A cow b. A peacock
c. A tree d. A bear

17. Ursa Major: Ursa Minor : : Big Bear : which of the following?

a. Brown bear b. Black bear
c. Large bear d. Little bear

18. Where is Arcadia?

a. Greece b. Phoenicia
c. Crete d. Africa

19. In matters of love, who is more powerful than Zeus himself?

a. The son of Hera b. The son of Io
c. The son of Artemis d. The son of Aphrodite

20. Which of these deities never married or fell in love?

a. Aphrodite b. Artemis
c. Hephaestus d. Apollo

B. MUSINGS

1. Most of the stories in this chapter were taken from the *Metamorphoses* by Ovid. *Metamorphoses* is a Greek word that literally means "changes of forms" or "transformations." Almost every tale Ovid tells in the *Metamorphoses* explains how various mythological figures were changed or transformed into creatures, trees and flowers, constellations, or other natural phenomena. So, for example, Ovid offers the story of Apollo and Daphne not only as a love story, but also to give a fanciful origin of the laurel tree, which is ubiquitous in Greece, Italy, and throughout the lands and islands of the Mediterranean region. List some other transformations that take place in the stories of this chapter. Who is transformed? What do they become?

2. Branches of the laurel tree, so dear to Apollo, were woven into wreaths to crown the victors in the Olympian games, the winners of theatrical competitions or political contests, and triumphant military leaders. In the United States, laurel leaves (botanical name, *Laurus nobilis*) are known as "bay leaves" and are often dried as herbs. Since ancient times, they have been used to flavor soups and stews. Look in your kitchen herb and spice shelf for bay (laurel). Take one or two leaves, crumble them, and inhale the aroma!

   Note:
   The mountain laurel shrub in the United States was named after the bay laurel tree because it reminded the early North American settlers of the small Mediterranean bush they were familiar with, but it is from a different family (*Kalmia latifolia*) and its leaves are poisonous.

3. What tests must Psyche undergo before she and Eros can live "happily ever after"? What cultural values or rules of morality are revealed through these tests?

4. The tale of Psyche as told in this book is recounted from Psyche's point of view. Retell the story from the point of view of a different character or characters: Aphrodite, Psyche's sisters, or Eros.

5. C. S. Lewis' *Till We Have Faces: A Myth Retold* presents the myth of Eros and Psyche from another character's point of view. How does Lewis' version of the story differ from the way Apuleius told the story, which you read in this chapter?

6. Some aspects of the Eros and Psyche tale should remind you of the story of "Beauty and the Beast." What are they? What are the differences in the two plots?

7. The planet Jupiter has many moons. For whom are these moons named? Which are the "Galilean Moons"?

8. Where in the world?

   - Use a good map or atlas to find Thessaly, Greece, the home of Io and her father, Inachus.

   - Now, look for Argos, Greece. Where is Argos in relation to Thessaly? How does the topography (features of the landscape) differ between Thessaly and Argos? Estimate the distance Zeus carried Io away in the thick mist, using the map's mile/kilometer legend. (You may give an answer in either miles or kilometers.)

- Next, locate Arcadia. Tell where in Greece Arcadia is located. Why do you suppose that Arcadia has always been a poetic code word for a perfect pastoral location or paradise? In what way does Zeus favor Arcadia? Why?

9. Choose one of the myths included in this chapter. If you were a Hollywood director, which actors would you choose to play the chief characters in the myth you've chosen? Write a short essay explaining your choices. Be prepared to defend your choices in a discussion with your classmates.

C. Words, Words, Words

The Daily Muse

News you can use

PSYCHE: The Greek word ***psyche*** means "soul," or "mind." It has come into our language, both as a word in itself and as a combining form in other words. The terms **psychology**, **psychiatrist**, and **metempsychosis** are just three of the several words using this root.

Find and list three other words that include the word **"psyche"** as a root word, a prefix, or a suffix. Write a short definition for each in the space provided below.

1. ______________________________

2. ______________________________

3. ______________________________

"I'm so psyched!"

In this sentence, the word "psyched" is a colloquialism.

A *colloquialism* is a term used in informal conversation, but not generally accepted as proper usage in formal use. Expressions that are colloquialisms sometimes eventually become accepted in formal, standard usage.

D. How 'Bout That?

Jupiter and the Galilean moons

Source: National Aeronautics and Space Administration

In 2003, Jupiter and its four Galilean Moons were clearly visible in the night sky. The moons of Jupiter were also a subject of research for Harry Potter and his friends, Hermione and Ron, in *Harry Potter and the Order of the Phoenix.* Check it out at the following website: http://science.nasa.gov/headlines/y2003/02jul_harrypotter.htm.

Adonis

You can find the lyrics of "Sweet Adonis" by Carole King and David Palmer at this link:

- http://lyricsdepot.com/carole-king/sweet-adonis.html

Venus and Adonis, 1921, woodcut by Roger Grillion for an illustrated copy of a poem of the same name by William Shakespeare

E. Who's Who?

- For Zeus' descendants and wives, see Genealogical Chart 5.
- For Agenor of Sidon's descendants, see Genealogical Chart 11.
- For Europa's Minoan descendants, see Genealogical Charts 5 and 15.

Chapter Seven
Daring Adventurers

General Sources:

Homer *Iliad*
Hesiod *Theogony*
Pindar *Olympian Odes*
Ovid *Metamorphoses*

Phaethon

Literary Source: Ovid *Metamorphoses* 1.200–227, 2.1–238

Phaethon and Epaphus are friends.

Epaphus was the son of Zeus and Io, and grandson of Inachus. He had a friend named Phaethon, who was near his age. Phaethon bragged that his father was none other than Helius, also known as Phoebus, the Sun. (See Genealogical Chart 10.) Epaphus grew tired of hearing his friend boasting all the time and one day burst out, "You're out of your mind to believe everything your mother tells you. Your head is all puffed up with your notions of who your father really is!" Phaethon blushed with shame. Seething with fury and humiliation, barely able to suppress his anger, Phaethon stormed off.

Phaethon confronts his mother, Clymene.

Phaethon confronted his mother, Clymene, and told her about Epaphus' insulting taunt. Then he hugged her and asked her to show him by some sign who his father really was. Clymene was moved by her son's prayers and by the grave insult to herself. She flung out her arms and gazed skyward toward Helius' light. She cried out, "My son, I swear to you by the radiance of Helius, which you now look upon, that from him you have been sprung. It is not hard to find your father's home; the place where he rises borders our own land. If you are so worried, go and get answers from him yourself." Phaethon jumped up enthusiastically and immediately set out, quickly crossing over the continents until he came to the place where his father rose each morning.

Phaethon meets his father, Helius.

Phaethon was dazzled by Helius' palace with its lofty columns and exquisite craftsmanship of gold, bronze, silver, and ivory. He followed the steep path that led to his father's dwelling, and immediately came face to face with his father. Phaethon was forced to stand back a bit because the luminous rays of the sun were too strong for his mortal eyes. Helius sat on his throne, cloaked in purple, brilliant with glittering emeralds. His attendants, equally spaced apart, surrounded him: Day, Month, Year, Century, and the Hours. Spring wore her flowering crown; Summer wore nothing but a garland of ripe grain. Grape-stained Autumn was also there, as was frosty Winter with his old, white locks.

"Phaethon was dazzled by Helius' palace with its lofty columns . . . ."

Helius offers to grant Phaethon a wish.

Helius, whose eyes watch over all things, saw young Phaethon and asked why he had come to his palace. Phaethon answered, "O Light for All the Peoples of the World, O Phoebus, my father, if indeed you give me the right to use that name, if Clymene does not hide her shame beneath false pretenses, give me proof that you are my father!" Helius took off his bright crown, which shot forth rays of light. He embraced his son and said, "You are indeed my worthy son. Clymene has told the truth about your origin. Now, so that you do not doubt me, ask whatever gift you wish and I will bestow it upon you."

Helius enthroned

Helius regrets his rash promise.

He had scarcely finished speaking when the boy answered, "Oh Father, please, let me drive your chariot and winged horses—just for one day!" Instantly, his father regretted that he had foolishly made such a rash promise. "Son, forgive me, I spoke too soon—that's the one thing I cannot give you. Do not forget: you are just a mortal, human boy. You are asking me for something that I cannot grant even to the gods themselves. Not even thunderbolt-hurling Zeus could steer this chariot of mine!"

Helius gravely warns Phaethon of danger.

Helius driving his chariot

Helius continued to explain. "When my horses first set out at dawn, they can hardly mount up, straining upwards along the steep and arduous way. The summits of the highest heavens tower up to incredible heights. If I momentarily happen to glance down at the sea or lands from those dizzying heights, even I can't help quaking and my heart races with anxiety. The way down is much worse with its swift and precipitous decline, requiring the surest and steadiest of drivers. Moreover, the rapid, whirling motion of the spinning universe brings on sudden dizziness, overcoming anyone except me alone, as I plow through the heavens in a direction opposite to the spinning of the earth.

The perils of the constellations

"Imagine that you have been given that chariot," Helius went on to say. "What would you do with it? Would you be able to hold fast in it against the spinning poles so that their revolving axes would not carry you away? No! And you would face these other dangers among the heavenly constellations:

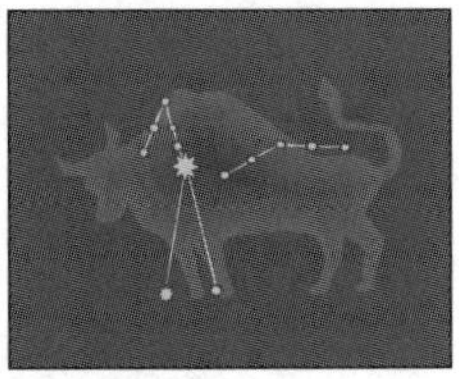

- the Horned Bull (Taurus)

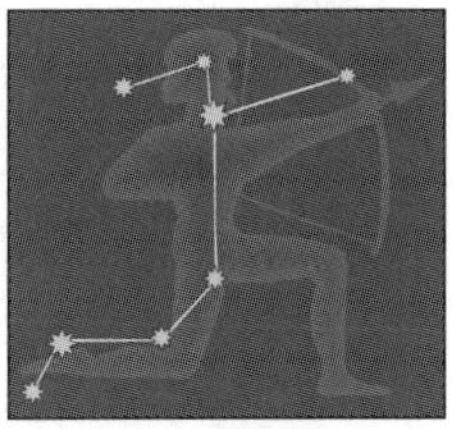

- the Haemonian Archer (Sagittarius)

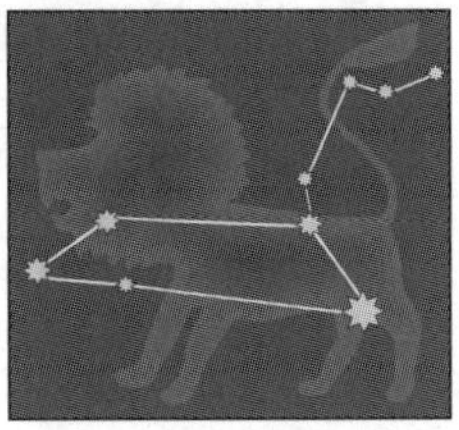

- the Savage Lion (Leo)

- the Crab (Cancer)

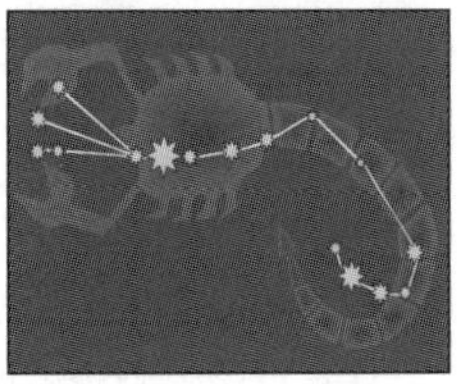

- and the Scorpion (Scorpio)

curving his wild arms in a long arc while the Crab swings out with his arm in the other direction. And what about my spirited horses? They breathe out fire from nose and mouth. I can scarcely manage them myself."

"Ah, child, beware in case I have granted you a deadly gift! Change your wish while there is still time! You have arrived here asking for a sign that I'm your father. Here's a sure sign: I give you all the proof you need by the way in which I fear for your life. I have a father's unselfish concern for your welfare. Come on, look all around, see all that is in this rich world and choose some other good thing. I will deny you nothing! I beg you not to ask of me this one request, which is not an honor and privilege, but instead, a dreadful punishment!"

Despite the warnings, Phaethon chooses to drive the chariot.

Phaethon stubbornly disregarded his father's pleas and warning. Helius, putting off the moment as long as possible, finally led the boy to his chariot. A spectacular vehicle, it was the magnificent handiwork of Hephaestus, with golden wheels and silver spokes. It was encrusted with chrysolites and other gems that reflected the sparkling brilliance of Helius' rays. Phaethon gaped with open-mouthed wonder at the sight of so beautiful a car. In the meantime, Aurora, goddess of dawn, began to open her lovely purple gates and rose-tinted courts. The stars dispersed; the Light-Bearer, the morning star Lucifer, last to appear in his heavenly post, went off. It was time.

Then Helius commanded the goddess Hours to yoke his horses. He put on Phaethon's face a sacred ointment as protection against the hot flames. With a profound sigh, he gave a last piece of fatherly advice: "If, at least, you can obey your father's warning, spare the lash and use the reins more strongly. The horses will go forward of their own will; the harder task will be to hold them back. Follow the course of my tracks in the skies—you'll see them. Don't wander too high off course or the heavens will burn; don't go too low or the earth will be scorched. Stay between the writhing Serpent on the right and the Altar of Heaven on the left. Hold tight to the wheel! I leave the rest to Good Fortune who will help you and guide you better than you can yourself."

Phaethon sets out but quickly loses control.

Phaethon mounted the light chariot, rejoiced to take up the reins from his unwilling father, and thanked him for the gift. The horses exploded forward, pulling a lighter than accustomed weight, for Phaethon's weight was in no way equal to his father's. To the horses, it felt as if no one was driving. They ran wild, jumping off the well-worn track. Phaethon felt the first prick of alarm; he didn't know the course, and even if he did, he was already having trouble handling the reins. Phaethon glanced down from high heaven and grew pale, his knees shook with fear, and darkness covered his eyes. Why had he questioned who his father really was? Why had he asked to drive his father's horses? Confused and panicked, he couldn't decide whether to hold on to the reins or drop them.

Phaethon driving Helius' chariot.

Hurtling along, he became more terrified as the long, curving arms of the Scorpion seemed to reach down to grab him. Overcome by his fear, he dropped the reins and then the horses truly broke loose. Nothing stopped them as they impulsively reared up against the stars, then plunged down toward Earth, scorching clouds and setting the lands afire. Large, walled cities perished; all the woods of the high mountains soon caught fire. Phaethon saw the earth burning in every direction. He could no longer endure the furnace-like heat, and the deep smoke prevented him from seeing where they were headed. He was finally at the mercy of the swift horses.

Phaethon's blazing chariot scorches the earth.

The intense heat dried up Northern Africa and made it a desert. The terror-stricken Nile River fled to the outer limit of earth; the River hid its head and it still lies hidden. Its seven mouths lay empty, filled with silt. Even the great rivers of the West, the Rhone, the Po, and the Tiber dried up. Mountains that had been covered by the sea sprang up. The god of the sea, Poseidon, tried three times to lift his arms and face from the waters of Ocean; three times he gave up, unable to stand the dreadful heat.

Earth is all in flames.

Even Mother Earth, into whose very bowels all the rivers of earth had receded, lifted up her face, shielding it with her hand, and cried out to Zeus for mercy. She prayed for herself, for Poseidon, and even for the skies and heavens that were in danger of falling:

"Look! Atlas himself strains and is scarcely able to hold up the white-hot world upon his shoulders. If the seas, the lands, and the palaces of heaven perish, we will be thrown together into primordial chaos. Mighty Zeus, snatch from the flames whatever still remains, and think of the safety of the universe!" Then Earth retreated into herself.

Zeus hurls a thunderbolt to stop the chariot.

Hearing the cry of Mother Earth, all-powerful Zeus intervened. He called upon the gods, and especially Helius, who had handed over the chariot, to give witness to what he would do. He called out that unless he should help, all the universe would be destroyed. Zeus thundered. With his right hand, he flung a three-fold thunderbolt at the chariot and Phaethon, extinguishing fires with fire.

The death of Phaethon

Flames reddened Phaethon's hair, and he was cast headlong from the chariot. He fell to his death in a long arc through the sky, just like a star that seems to fall, yet does not truly fall. The naiads of a western land provided a tomb for his remains, still smoking from Zeus' triple thunderbolt. On his tombstone they inscribed this little epitaph:

SON of mighty Father SUN
Here lies young, noble
PHAETHON,
Chariot Driver, Devastator.
He held not the well-worn course,
But rashly dared with cart and horse.

Phaethon falls from the heavens.

Storytellers and mythmakers in almost all ancient cultures composed fanciful stories such as the myth of Helius, Phaethon, and the fiery chariot to attempt to explain these awesome and incomprehensible movements in the universe. The myth of Helius and Phaethon explains the aetiology (cause) of the sun's rising, just as the myth of Demeter and Persephone (see Chapter 3) explains the natural phenomenon of the seasons of the year.

At the time of Ovid and other mythographers, there was limited scientific knowledge, and therefore very limited understanding of certain natural phenomena. We take this understanding for granted, but the question "Why does the sun rise every day in the east and set each evening in the west?" was certainly an enigma to all the ancients. It was only in the late Middle Ages and Renaissance that astronomers like Copernicus and Galileo discovered the scientific explanation of this phenomenon, proving that the earth revolved around the sun, not the sun around the earth! Even then, their discoveries were suspect and it was several more centuries before scientific explanation of the movement of the sun, the planets, and earth came to be understood and accepted.

Bellerophon

Literary Sources: Homer *Iliad* 6.155–240; Pindar *Olympian Odes* 13.64–91

Bellerophon, descendant of Sisyphus of Corinth

Like Phaethon, Bellerophon forgot that he was a mere mortal. He dared to be godlike and fly up to Mount Olympus; he was punished for this daring attempt. Bellerophon was born in the important Greek city of Corinth, which lies on the narrow isthmus of land between Attica, the region ruled by Athens, and the Peloponnesus, controlled in those early times by the city of Mycenae and later by Sparta. Some say that Bellerophon was a child of the god Poseidon, others that he was the son of King Glaucus of Corinth and a descendant of the unfortunate Sisyphus, whom you met in Chapter 3. Homer tells us his story.

Bellerophon kills his brother and is exiled to Tiryns.

Bellerophon killed one of his brothers in a mysterious accident. According to Greek custom, a murderer must be exiled from his hometown and cannot return until purified. Therefore, Bellerophon was exiled from Corinth and sought refuge in Tiryns, a city close to Mycenae and controlled by the Mycenaeans. Bellerophon begged the king of Tiryns, Proetus, for the purifications of a murderer required by law. Proetus agreed to perform the necessary ablutions and welcomed Bellerophon to stay at his court. In the ancient world, hospitality to strangers was one of the most important and revered customary laws.

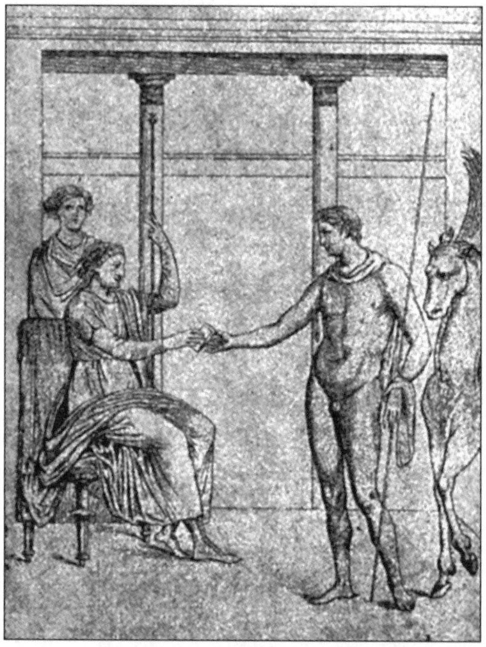

Departure of Bellerophon from Tiryns. Anteia stands behind enthroned King Proetus, who bids farewell to the hero and Pegasus. Mural painting from Pompeii, Italy.

King Proetus' wife accuses Bellerophon.

Proetus' wife, Anteia (some say her name was Sthenoboea), caught sight of handsome Bellerophon and fell deeply in love with him. She tried to get him to return her love, but Bellerophon refused. Outraged by his rejection, Anteia went to Proetus and accused Bellerophon of making improper advances to her. King Proetus wanted to kill Bellerophon instantly, but the law of hospitality forbade a host from harming a guest so long as the guest remained under the host's roof.

Proetus directs Iobates to kill Bellerophon, and so Iobates sends Bellerophon to kill the Chimera.

Proetus devised a sinister plan. He gave Bellerophon a stone tablet on which certain symbols were scratched, and ordered Bellerophon to carry the tablet to Anteia's father (his father-in-law), Iobates, king of Lycia in Anatolia. With this task, Proetus was setting Bellerophon up to be killed, for this "letter" contained a sign language that said "murder the carrier of this tablet." In other words, Iobates was being asked to murder the very person who handed over the tablet! Iobates read the message and gazed upon the handsome young man standing before him. He hesitated to kill Bellerophon, for he feared to break the customary laws of hospitality to a stranger. He, too, thought of a plan by which someone else could dispose of Bellerophon. He directed Bellerophon to seek out and kill a monster called the Chimera that had been menacing the people of his kingdom.

Chimera: lion-goat-dragon creature

The Chimera, Hesiod tells us, was a hideous monster that "breathed forth irresistible fire, a creature unspeakable, huge, swift-footed, and hard-hearted. She had the three heads of a fierce-eyed lion, of a she-goat, and of a cruel dragon-serpent." Homer describes her a bit differently, claiming that her head and face were a lion, her hindquarters a dragon, and her middle a goat. Both Homer and Hesiod agree that she "erupted in a flaming furnace of fiery force" (Hesiod *Theogony* 319–324; Homer *Iliad* 6.181–182). The Chimera inherited her hideousness, as she was part of a line of monsters stretching back to Tartarus, the monstrous personification of the Underworld itself. Her grandfather was Typhon, a fire-eating giant, and her grandmother, Echidna, a half-woman/half-snake. Her mother, the Lernean Hydra, was a multi-headed water snake later killed by Heracles (see Chapter 9). From each parent she inherited some of the gruesome characteristics that made her the horrible hybrid she was!

Chimera

Typhon in sculpture group from the east pediment of the Parthenon, British Museum, London

The Greek poet Pindar picks up the thread of the story here: Poseidon appeared to give Bellerophon a winged horse, Pegasus. Pegasus was the offspring of the Gorgon Medusa, whom we shall meet later in the next chapter.

Bellerophon meets the winged horse, Pegasus.

The beautiful and spirited horse stood close by the Corinthian spring of Hippocrene, the "horse fountain." As soon as Bellerophon approached him, Pegasus restlessly pawed the ground, neighed, and reared up. Each time Bellerophon tried to get near the winged horse, Pegasus skittered and shied away.

Exhausted by his efforts, Bellerophon fell asleep on the ground. Athena appeared to him in a dream, handing him a golden bridle. "Get up, take this charm to calm the steed, and sacrifice a white bull to the horse-tamer, Poseidon," she urged. Bellerophon leaped up and quickly caught Pegasus by placing the golden bridle into the horse's mouth. After carrying out the proper sacrifice, he immediately mounted and the winged horse straightaway rose up into the sky carrying the armored hero.

Bellerophon with Pegasus

In this way, Pegasus helped Bellerophon slay the grim, fire-breathing monster, Chimera. Bellerophon then went on to fight a warrior tribe of men, the Solymi, and the Amazons, a warrior tribe composed of women.

Finally, Iobates tried to ambush Bellerophon using the finest warriors from his kingdom. These, too, Bellerophon easily dispatched. At last, Iobates conceded that Bellerophon was a man whom the gods loved, too powerful to be outdone by any mere king like himself. He offered him his daughter, Philonoë, in marriage as well as half his kingdom. They had three children: Isander, Hippolochus, and Laodamia.

Bellerophon, overcome by his pride, meets a sad fate.

Unfortunately, Bellerophon's story did not end "happily ever after." Homer says that the day soon came when even the gods hated Bellerophon. It seems that he was overcome with hubris (a Greek word meaning "excessive pride") over his accomplishments, and tried to ride his winged steed up to the realm of the gods. Angered by this bold action, Zeus caused Pegasus to hurl Bellerophon down to earth; Bellerophon ended his days as a lonely fugitive, wandering far from wherever humans lived.

***Hubris* is the expression of excessive pride or over-confidence that often leads humans to defy the gods. The ancients believed that acts of hubris, especially by heroes, were inevitably severely punished by the gods.**

Daedalus and Icarus

Literary Source: Ovid *Metamorphoses* 8.183–259

Daedalus is exiled to King Minos' Crete, where he designs the Labyrinth to enclose the Minotaur.

Once upon a time, there was a clever architect and inventor named Daedalus. His nephew Talus was also his apprentice. Daedalus feared that Talus would surpass him, so he tried to kill Talus by throwing him off the Acropolis. However, Athena saved Talus by turning him into a partridge. Daedalus was sentenced to exile on the island of Crete and forced to work for King Minos.

Ancient disk with representation of the Cretan labyrinth

During his exile, Daedalus had a son named Icarus by one of the king's slave women. He worked hard for the royal family and designed the famous Labyrinth to house the Minotaur. You will learn more about these stories in a later chapter.

Minotaur

Daedalus fashions wings to escape Minos and Crete.

Daedalus longed to return to his native Athens, but Minos controlled all the land and sea routes. "I know! We will travel by air! That's the one area Minos does not possess!" thought Daedalus. So he constructed wings for himself and Icarus, arranging the feathers in order from smallest to largest and binding them together with wax. As he worked, Icarus kept hindering his father's work, playing with the feathers and poking the wax with his fingers. At last, however, the wings were ready. Daedalus tested them on himself first, hovering briefly above the ground, and then fitted his son's wings onto him. As he did so, he gave Icarus instructions for the upcoming flight.

Daedalus warns Icarus to take care when flying.

"Now remember, Icarus, fly midway between the earth and the sky. If you fly too low, moisture from the sea will weigh you down. If you fly too high, the sun will melt the wax off your wings. Stay close to me!"

Daedalus fashions one wing as Icarus models another.

Daedalus' heart was already heavy with foreboding. His hands trembled as he placed the wings on Icarus, and his elderly cheeks were wet with tears. He gave his son a last kiss, and they were off! As they flew, shepherds and fishermen stopped working and watched them in amazement, thinking, "These must be gods!"

Icarus flies too close to the sun.

The pair had completed about three-quarters of their journey when Icarus, emboldened by the joy of flight, flew higher and higher. As his father had warned, the sun melted off the wax. Before Icarus knew it, he was flapping bare arms and plummeting into the sea, calling his father's name for the last time as the waves covered him.

Icarus plunges into the sea.

"Icarus! Icarus! Where are you?" called Daedalus. Too late, he saw the feathers floating on the surface of the sea. He retrieved the body from the sea, cursing his invention, and buried his son as soon as he reached land. The sea where Icarus had fallen was thereafter called the Icarian Sea, and the island where Daedalus buried him was named Icaria.

At top, Icarus falls into the sea at left as Daedalus watches on the right. In the lower portion, Daedalus buries Icarus. Woodcut, 16th century, by Peter Brueghel the Elder.

A. REVIEW EXERCISES

1. **CHRONOLOGY COUNTS!** Place the following events in chronological order. Use the numbers 1–5, with 1 as the first event and 5 as the last event in the sequence. Write the number in the space provided.

   a. **Phaethon**

   ____ Phaethon tumbles to earth.

   ____ Phaethon confronts his mother, Clymene, about his paternity.

   ____ Phaethon encounters the constellations.

   ____ Helius welcomes Phaethon and promises him the gift of his choice.

   ____ Aurora (Dawn) opens her purple gates to welcome the day.

   b. **Bellerophon**

   ____ Bellerophon flees from Corinth to the court of Proetus at Tiryns.

   ____ Bellerophon slays the Chimera.

   ____ Zeus punishes Bellerophon by causing Pegasus to throw him off.

   ____ Bellerophon fights the Solymi and the Amazons.

   ____ Proetus of Tiryns sends Bellerophon to Iobates of Lycia, hoping to kill him.

2. Imagine that you are either Daedalus or Icarus and retell the story of his daring adventure from the first person point of view. Write your story in four or five sentences using the space below.

____

____

____

____

____

____

____

____

____

B. Musings

1. How is personification used in the myth of Phaethon?

2. What are the constellations that Ovid refers to in the myths of Phaethon? Where are they located in the night sky? Where can you see the Morning Star (Lucifer) in the sky at dawn?

3. Using a map of Greece and the Aegean, locate the places named in the myth of Bellerophon: Corinth, Tiryns, Argos (all in the Peloponnese). Can you identify the name of the modern country in which ancient Anatolia was located?

Napoleon was held on the H.M.S. *Bellerophon,* anchored at Plymouth, England, before his imprisonment at St. Helena. Each evening he appeared at 6 p.m. on deck so the local people could come view the defeated former emperor.

4. Can you think of any way in which Napoleon might have resembled the mythological figure of Bellerophon? Is there any irony in the fact that the ship that held Napoleon as prisoner was called *Bellerophon*?

5. The myth of Daedalus and Icarus shows that technology can be useful but also potentially destructive. Consult newspapers and magazines for evidence of the "double-edged sword" of technology in our daily lives.

6. What personality characteristics do Phaethon, Bellerophon, and Icarus share? Which do you find appealing? Which not?

7. Ovid wrote a beautiful and moving epitaph to honor the memory of the daring adventurer Phaethon. Write an original epitaph for a person you admire in the space below.

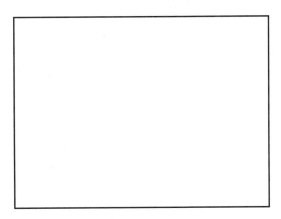

C. Words, Words, Words

The Daily Muse

News you can use

1. One of the constellations that Phaethon encountered in his heavenly journey was **Leo** (that's Latin for "lion"). The Latin word *leo* gives us a wonderful, descriptive adjective **"leonine,"** meaning "lion-like" or "resembling a lion."

   a. You could say that the man pictured below on the right has a "leonine head." How so?

***Leo* (lion)**

Leonine

   b. Can you think of an actor or an acquaintance of yours who has a leonine appearance?

2. a. As you know, Daedalus was the architect of the first labyrinth. The Greek word *labyrinthos* gives us another delightfully descriptive adjective: **labyrinthine.**

The new employee was confused by the **labyrinthine** layout of the office.

b. Describe the problem of the man in the picture at the right using the word **labyrinthine:**

c. Can you deduce and write down the meaning of the suffix **–ine** in the words **leonine** and **labyrinthine?**

The meaning of **–ine** is: ______________________________

List as many English words as you can think of that end in the suffix **–ine:**

3. **Eeek!!!** After watching your favorite, just-released horror flick, have you ever let your imagination trick you into thinking you've just seen a monstrous, scary vision? The fire-breathing, she-monster **Chimera** (also **Chimaera**) gave us the English word **chimera** that neatly describes that precise experience! In the space below, write a VIVID (USE THRILLER-CHILLER ADJECTIVES AND VERBS) summary (two to three sentences) of your most memorable experience of your very own, personal **chimera.**

The phaeton

Did you know that Phaethon gave his name to a vehicle commonly used in the nineteenth century? The drawing below shows a **phaeton**, a light, open, four-wheeled carriage usually drawn by a pair of horses. Where, when, and how do you think this vehicle might have been used? How does it resemble a chariot? Write your answer in the box below.

D. How 'Bout That?

Daedalus

1. A quick online search under "Daedalus" reveals that the following are named for him:

    - A bookstore
    - The journal of the American Academy of Arts and Sciences
    - A project to design human-powered aircraft that can fly the distance of 115 kilometers (71 miles calculated as the distance of Daedalus and Icarus' flight)
    - A system of acoustic instrument amplifiers
    - A manufacturer of wheelchair accessible workstations and desks
    - A program that allows one to create and solve mazes

    What others can you find?

    Why do you think all of these were named Daedalus? Create a word map of the qualities associated with Daedalus and his myth and with the above products/services.

2. Imagine you are the president of "Daedalus, Inc." What sort of company is it? Create a mission statement and a description of what your company has to offer and to whom.

Daedalus, flying. Marble relief from Florence's Campanile. Museo dell'Opera del Duomo, Florence, Italy.

3. Have you read *Harry Potter and the Sorcerer's Stone*, the first Harry Potter book by J. K. Rowling? You may remember that when Harry first visits The Leaky Cauldron shop, he meets an eccentric wizard named "Dedalus Diggle"!

Chimera and biology

 +  = **geep???**

The word **chimera** is used in a branch of biology called zoology to describe a single organism which contains tissues from two or more different genetic sources. This combination can occur either naturally by cell mutation or in a laboratory environment by implantation in an embryo. In 1984, researchers produced a "geep" chimera by mixing the cells of a goat and a sheep.

Chimera and the computer

Chimera has been a popular name for multimedia and hypermedia applications for computers (because of the "mixing" of heterogeneous media types within a program). At least two different Web browsers and a hypermedia program have been named **Chimera** over the last fifteen years; look at http://www.cgl.ucsf.edu/chimera/ and http://portal.acm.org/citation.cfm?id=192783 for examples.

Chimera and Broadway

In the popular Broadway musical *The 25th Annual Putnam County Spelling Bee* by William Finn, the word "chimerical" prompts the musical number titled "I Love You Song."

E. Who's Who

- For Phaethon's ancestry, see Genealogical Chart 10.

Chapter Eight
PERSEUS

General Sources:
Pindar *Pythian Odes* 10 and 12
Apollodorus *Library* 2.4.1–5
Horace *Odes* 3.16
Ovid *Metamorphoses* 4.604–803, 5.1–249

Zeus visits the imprisoned Danae, and Perseus is born.

Acrisius exiles Danae and Perseus.

Perseus was a descendant of Io, the beloved of Zeus who had been transformed into a cow. Like many heroes, he was conceived under unusual circumstances. His grandfather Acrisius had received word from the Delphic oracle that the child of his daughter, Danae, would grow up to kill him. (See GENEALOGICAL CHART 12.) To prevent her from having children, Acrisius imprisoned Danae in a tower of bronze with doors of oak always guarded by watch dogs. But the crafty Zeus entered her prison by transforming himself into a shower of gold. Their child was Perseus, and Danae hid him from her father until the noise he made gave him away. Acrisius therefore enclosed both mother and baby in a chest and threw them into the sea.

Danae, Eros, and Zeus as a shower of gold

Acrisius places Danae and Perseus in the chest.

The Greek poet Simonides wrote a lovely poem of Danae's thoughts as she lay tossed about the stormy sea with her infant in her arms:

Taking Perseus in her circle of arms,
she said, "My child,
what trouble I have!
But you sleep and dream,
like the infant you are,
suspended in this dark blue, starry night,
prisoner of joyless, bronze-studded wood.
The sea that towers overhead
on the passing wave
and the groaning wind
do not alarm you,
lying with your pretty face swaddled in purple.
But if this danger were danger to you,
you would lend your delicate ear to my words.
Sleep, child,
and let the sea and its infinite evil sleep."

Simonides *Poem* 543.6–22

The chest floated to the island of Seriphus, where it was found by a fisherman named Dictys. He rescued Danae and Perseus, and Perseus grew to manhood in his home.

Perseus volunteers to obtain Medusa's head.

Dictys had a brother, Polydectes, who was the king of the island. This king had fallen in love with Danae, who continually refused him. One day Polydectes invited all the leading men of the island to a banquet, where he demanded that each man give him the gift of a horse. "A horse! I can get you the head of Medusa!" boasted Perseus. "Good, why don't you?" retorted Polydectes, who thought he stood a better chance with Danae once her son was out of the way.

Hermes and Athena help Perseus.

Medusa was one of three sisters known as Gorgons. Their hair was wreathed in snakes, and they had great tusks like wild boars', hands of brass, and golden wings. They were so terrifying to see that all who looked on them turned to stone. Perseus was already regretting his words. How could he possibly kill Medusa when he could not even look at her without losing his life? He wandered off in despair to a lonely part of the island, where Hermes and Athena found him. "We will help you, Perseus," they told him. "First, you must go to the Gorgons' sisters, the Graeae. They can guide you to the nymphs who will tell you what you need next, but you have to force them into giving you information. The Graeae have only one eye and one tooth that they share among themselves. Snatch them away and don't give them back until the sisters tell you what you want to know!"

The Gorgon Medusa

The nymphs give Perseus three objects.

Heartened by their advice, Perseus sped off to the Graeae. Their name, which they were given because they were old from their birth, means "Gray Ones." Perseus was easily able to grab their one eye and their one tooth. "Give them back at once!" the old women demanded. "First tell me, where are these nymphs I need to find!" retorted Perseus.

The Graeae reluctantly told him. From the nymphs Perseus received three objects: a cap of invisibility (borrowed from Hades), a pair of winged sandals that enabled him to fly, and a sack in which to store Medusa's severed head. Hermes then gave Perseus a sword, and he was off to seek Medusa.

According to Pindar's version of the legend, the Gorgons lived in the land of the Hyperboreans. This was a country in the far north (the name means "beyond the north") and was envisioned by the poet as a land of perfect bliss whose people spent their time feasting, playing music, singing, and dancing. Neither disease nor old age had any place in their holy nation. When Perseus slew Medusa, it was their first contact with death, as she was the only mortal Gorgon (her sisters Stheno and Euryale were immortal).

***Perseus with the Head of Medusa*, ca. 1800, by Antonio Canova (1757–1822), Vatican Museums, Vatican City, Italy**

Perseus decapitates Medusa; Pegasus springs forth.

When Perseus came upon the Gorgons, they were sleeping. Athena guided Perseus' hand, and he avoided Medusa's petrifying gaze by not looking directly at her but only at her reflection in his shield. When he had decapitated her, he placed Medusa's head in his sack and flew away, leaving her sisters lamenting for her. From Medusa's blood sprang the flying horse Pegasus. According to Ovid, when this magic horse's hoof struck Mount Helicon, the fountain named Hippocrene (or "horse's fountain") sprang up. This fountain was believed to have powers of creative inspiration and was associated in antiquity with the Muses, about whom you read in chapter 1.

Cassiopeia

Poseidon punishes Cassiopeia for her foolish boast.

On his way back with Medusa's head, Perseus had another adventure involving Andromeda, a princess of the Ethiopians. Andromeda's mother, Cassiopeia, had foolishly boasted that she was more beautiful than the sea nymphs called Nereids. As a punishment for her act of hubris, Poseidon sent a sea monster (sometimes called Cetus) to ravage the land.

Andromeda is chained to a rock to appease Poseidon.

Andromeda's father, Cepheus, consulted the oracle of Zeus to find out how to be rid of the creature. He received a horrifying response: Poseidon would be appeased only by the sacrifice of Andromeda to the monster! Chained to a rock, Andromeda awaited her doom. As Perseus flew past the rock, he fell in love with the beautiful princess and made a bargain with her father: if he, Perseus, killed the monster, he could have Andromeda as his bride. Both Cepheus and Andromeda were pleased with this. Perseus killed the monster and released Andromeda. He also got rid of a rival suitor for Andromeda's hand, Phineus, by showing the Gorgon's head to him. Phineus froze into a statue of a man cowering in fear, which served as a permanent reminder to everyone of his less-than-admirable end.

Perseus kills monstrous Cetus and frees Andromeda.

Perseus frees Andromeda.

Perseus used Medusa's power two more times before he returned to Seriphus. When Atlas refused him hospitality, Perseus turned him into stone. His head and body became a mountain range (the Atlas Mountains) and his hair the forests of the mountains. According to Ovid, Medusa was also responsible for the first coral formations in the sea. As Perseus rinsed the dirt and blood of battle off his hands by the seashore, he laid Medusa's head on a bed of sea plants. The grasses, previously soft and pliant, became hard. It is said that coral still grows hard on contact with air because of this.

When Perseus and Andromeda returned to Seriphus, Perseus displayed Medusa's head to the evil Polydectes and his followers. He then installed the kindly Dictys as king. His task done, he returned the magical objects to Hermes and Athena. Throughout the history of art, Hermes is represented wearing the cap and winged sandals. We also see Medusa's head in the middle of Athena's shield as an apotropaic object.

An *apotropaic* object is one that was believed to have power to turn away evil influences or bad luck.

***Perseus*, 1545–1554, by Benvenuto Cellini, Loggia dei Lanzi, Florence, Italy**

Fulfilling the prophecy, Perseus kills Acrisius.

As for Perseus' grandfather Acrisius, he received the death at his grandson's hand that he had tried so hard to avoid. When Perseus was competing in athletic games in the city of Larisa in Thessaly (northern Greece), he accidentally struck his grandfather with a discus and killed him.

Perseus founds Mycenae and a kingly line.

Despite this bloody deed, Perseus went on to even more honors. He founded the city of Mycenae, where he was worshipped as a hero. The sons of Perseus and Andromeda became kings also. From them descended Heracles and Eurystheus, whom you will meet in the next chapter.

A. Review Exercises

1. **MATCHING!** Match the word in the left-hand column with the correct phrase from the right-hand column. Write the letter in the space provided. Keep in mind that there are more phrases than available names!

1. ____	Heracles	a.	Mother of Perseus
2. ____	Graeae	b.	Famous descendant of Perseus
3. ____	Cepheus	c.	Sea monster
4. ____	Hippocrene	d.	Danae's suitor
5. ____	Hyperboreans	e.	Andromeda's mother
6. ____	Dictys	f.	The one who sent Perseus to seek Medusa
7. ____	Cetus	g.	The ones who shared one eye and one tooth
8. ____	Cassiopeia	h.	Fisherman who saved Perseus and his mother
9. ____	Polydectes	i.	Andromeda's father
10. ____	Acrisius	j.	People who lived in an ideal world
		k.	Fountain created by Pegasus
		l.	Perseus' grandfather

2. **DID YOU NOTICE . . . ?** Review the definition of an aetiological myth (see page 27). Name three natural features whose origin is explained in the myth of Perseus. Give your answers in the space below.

a. ______________________________

b. ______________________________

c. ______________________________

B. Musings

1. Perseus is known as a hero. He slays a monster and harnesses her power in different ways. What are some of the ways in which he uses Medusa's ability for constructive purposes? Does he ever use her for destructive purposes? What are some things in the world around us that can be used both for good and for evil?

2. Locate representations of Medusa from early Greek art (eighth to fifth centuries BCE), from later Greek art (around the fourth century BCE), and from the Renaissance (fifteenth to sixteenth centuries CE). How does the portrayal of the Gorgon change over time? Look, for example, at her facial features and expression, the depiction of her hair, and the extent of the artist's sympathy for her.

3. The best-known film version of the Perseus myth is the 1981 *Clash of the Titans*. View it and list the ways in which it changes the myth as described above. Why do you think the filmmakers took these liberties with the story? *Clash of the Titans* was remade in 2010 as a 3-D movie. Its sequel, *Wrath of the Titans*, was released in 2012.

4. Rick Riordan's series *Percy Jackson and the Olympians* features a young hero named for Perseus. In these books and the follow up series, *Heroes of Olympus*, the ancient Greek gods and monsters come to America! Read these books to see how many mythological references you can spot.

5. One of the most interesting recent developments in Perseus' myth is the use of Medusa as a symbol for women's anger, power, and creative energy. Read the excerpt from the following poem titled "Eve Meets Medusa" by Michelene Wandor, a British poet and playwright. What attitudes towards the myth come through?

Eve Meets Medusa

Medusa. Sit down. Take
the weight off your snakes. We have
a lot in common. Snakes, I mean.

Tell me, can you really turn men
to stone with a look? Do you
think, if I had a perm—
maybe not.

Don't you think
Perseus was
a bit of a coward? Not even
to look you in the face . . .

it's a good mask; you must
feel safe and loving

behind it

you must feel very powerful

tell me, what conditioner do you use?

Medusa

C. Words, Words, Words

The Daily Muse

News you can use

You've seen how mythological heroes were a favorite source for naming stars and constellations. The Andromeda galaxy (spiral nebula) and the constellations Cassiopeia and Perseus are three whose names come from important mythological figures in this chapter. Let's take a closer look at some words that have some real "star power."

aster = the ancient Greek word for "star"

In fact, the English word "star" comes from the same Indo-European root word (ster) as ***aster*** and the Latin (Roman) word for "star," ***stella.*** ("Indo-European" is the name of a prehistoric language or languages, thought to have been the ancestor tongue of a family of languages including ancient Greek, Latin, Sanskrit, and many others.)

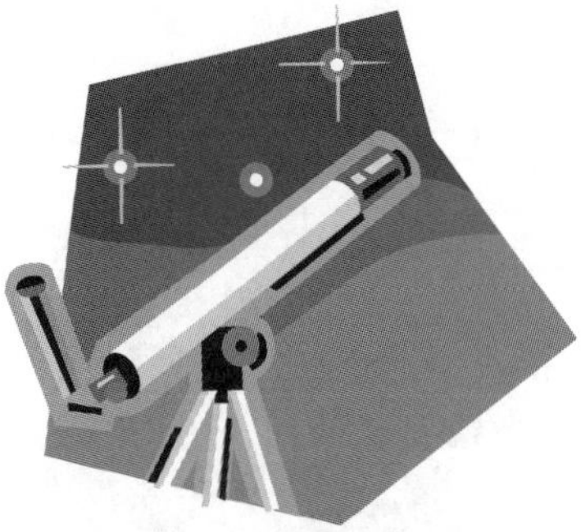

So, **astronomy** is the scientific study of the stars, planets, heavenly bodies, and physical universe beyond the earth. It comes from the Greek words for "star" (*aster*) and "law" (*nomos*).

Astrology, on the other hand, is the study of the positions and alignments of the stars and planets, with the object of predicting the influence of these heavenly bodies on human affairs. It comes from the Greek words for "star" (*aster*) and "word" (*logos*). It is considered a "pseudo" (that's Greek again, folks, for "false"!) science.

- Which of these two would be likely taught as a major course of study in a college or university? ______________________
- Which of these two might be practiced by the person pictured at left? ______________________

An **asteroid** refers to a starlike heavenly body.

stella = the Latin (Roman) word for "star"

A **con<u>stella</u>tion** is a grouping of stars that form a recognizable pattern. There are 88 named constellations or stellar groups; most are named from mythology. Can you list the names of at least six constellations?

1. ________________ 2. ________________ 3. ________________

4. ________________ 5. ________________ 6. ________________

What's an **asterism?** Is it (circle one) the *same as,* or *different from,* a **constellation?**

Galaxy (spiral nebula) Andromeda

NASA currently defines a **galaxy** as "A system of about 100 billion stars. Our Sun is a member of the Milky Way Galaxy, . . . There are billions of galaxies in the observable universe." (http://antwrp.gsfc.nasa.gov/apod/lib/glossary.html).

The word **galaxy** comes from the Greek word *gala* for "milk." The phrase "milky circle" from the Latin *galaxias* (from the Greek *γαλαξίας*) or *kyklos galaktikos* was used to describe how our galaxy looks. What is the name of our galaxy in which Earth is located? ________________ (Hint: There's a candy bar with the same name!)

A **nebula** gets its name from the Latin word for "cloud." It is used to describe a mass of interstellar dust or gas, or both. It is sometimes mistakenly confused with the word "galaxy." To learn more about the different types of **nebulae,** visit this website: http://astro.nineplanets.org/twn/types.html.

Here is yet one more "starry" word derived from the name of Andromeda's father, **Cepheus,** who figures in this chapter:

A **Cepheid,** "a pulsating variable star" according to NASA's definition, alternately brightens and dims according to a regular schedule (http://antwrp.gsfc.nasa.gov/apod/lib/glossary.html). It got its name because the first one was found in the constellation **Cepheus.** You may have to download one of the following free video players to see this demonstration if your computer does not have video player software installed: Real Player, Time MPEG, or Adobe Flash. Follow links on website as listed.

The constellation Andromeda

To see a very cool, animated view of a pulsating **Cepheid,** visit the Hubblesite website: http://hubblesite.org/newscenter/newsdesk/archive/releases/1994/49/video/.

Wordplay

From the **constellation** of "star-powered words" given below, choose one that best fits each written phrase or statement. Write your answer in the space provided.

galax

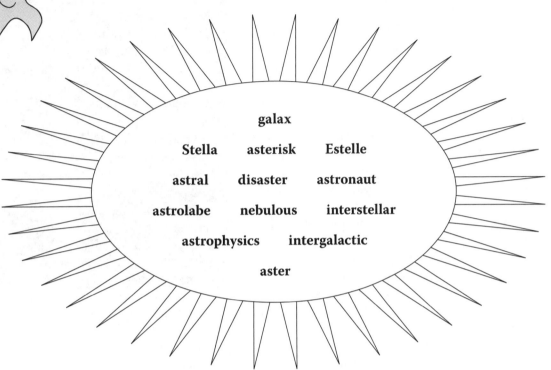

Stella **asterisk** **Estelle**

astral **disaster** **astronaut**

astrolabe **nebulous** **interstellar**

astrophysics **intergalactic**

aster

1. ____________ A daisylike flower whose colors range from white to mauve and pink.
2. ____________ A girl's name derived from the Latin word for "star."
3. ____________ Another girl's name from the Latin word for "star."
4. ____________ A star-shaped printing mark used to call attention to a footnote or a reference.
5. ____________ A plant with milky-white clusters of flowers and glossy, evergreen leaves.
6. ____________ A "star-sailor" who navigates through the universe in a spaceship.
7. ____________ A branch of astronomy that studies the physics of stellar phenomena.
8. ____________ Between or among galaxies.
9. ____________ Between or among stars.
10. ____________ A device used during the Middle Ages to determine the altitude of stars and the sun.
11. ____________ An "ill-starred" occurrence, that is, an event that causes, or is the result of, damage, failure, or destruction.
12. ____________ Resembling or pertaining to stars.

D. How 'Bout That?

As mentioned above, the science of astronomy has come down to us from the ancient Near East and Egypt and through ancient Greece. The constellations were named by the ancients and given a description recognized everywhere. Thus we continue to use ancient myth even as our ever-developing technology brings us new information about the universe.

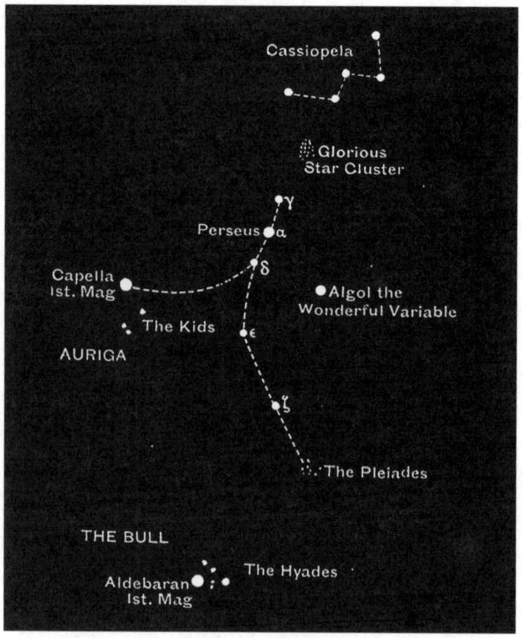

Perseus, Cassiopeia, Algol, the Pleiades, and other neighboring stars in the winter sky of the northern hemisphere

Perseus, the Hero, is a northern constellation that can sometimes be seen in winter skies in the northern hemisphere. The most unusual star in this constellation is the second brightest. This is sometimes called Algol, Arabic for "the ghoul" or "the demon." Its more benign name is Beta Persei (beta being the second letter of the Greek alphabet). The star was considered demonic by the ancients because it appeared to blink every now and then, losing its light temporarily. We now know that Algol is periodically eclipsed by another star. But the ancients, who knew no other stars that behaved like this, invested it with demonic powers and identified it with the eye or the head of Medusa.

The constellation Andromeda

The constellation Cassiopeia

Andromeda, the Princess, lies due west of the constellation of Perseus. She may be imagined as lying on her side, chained to her rock.

Immediately to the north of Andromeda is the constellation named for her mother, **Cassiopeia**, the Queen. The five stars of Cassiopeia form the shape of a "W" or an "M," depending on the time and place when viewed. The constellation is sometimes called the "Celestial M" or "Celestial W." It is always visible in mid-northern latitudes, since it is circumpolar, circling Polaris (the North Star). Cassiopeia was cast into the heavens by Poseidon as a punishment for her vanity. Sometimes she appears to be sitting in a chair, and the constellation is also known as "Cassiopeia's chair." When viewed at other times, she appears to be hanging upside down. So, half the time she is right side up, half the time upside down.

To the west of Cassiopeia we may find **Cepheus,** the King. The five stars that comprise this constellation look like a child's drawing of a house with a steep roof, but they were imagined as representing Cepheus with arms outstretched, begging for mercy from Poseidon.

Even the sea monster **Cetus** can be found in the sky. He gave his name to the fourth largest constellation that stretches out along the equator. His name is Latin for "whale" or "sea monster."

To learn more about these constellations and view photos of the Great Andromeda Galaxy, visit the website of the American Association of Amateur Astronomers: http://www.astromax.org/arp/arp1002.htm.

Medusa and Mother Nature

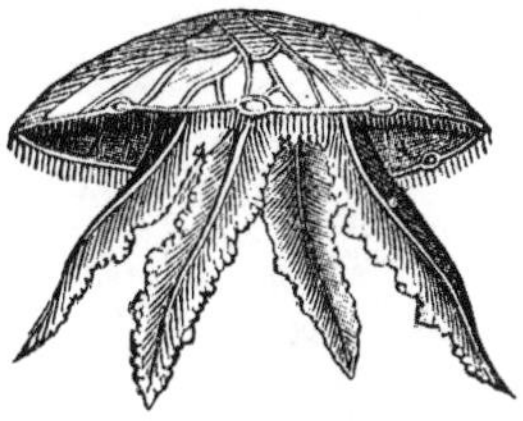

Medusa jellyfish

Did you know that a medusa is also a jellyfish with an umbrella-shaped body and stinging tentacles? How do you think this creature received its name?

RIDDLE ME: What is the favorite cheese of the Gorgons?*

Medusa's Favorite Gorgonzola Tortellini

Celebrate the victory of Perseus over the Gorgons with this delicious recipe.

1½ pounds fresh tortellini pasta (meat, cheese, or spinach)
1½ cups homemade chicken broth or low-sodium canned broth
2½ cups heavy cream (or half milk, half cream)
¾ pound gorgonzola cheese, crumbled
¼ teaspoon nutmeg
½ cup parmesan cheese
3 tablespoons minced parsley
Salt and freshly ground pepper, to taste

Heat chicken broth in medium saucepan and bring to a boil. Stir in cream, gorgonzola cheese crumbles, and nutmeg. Keep stirring constantly until the cheese has melted into the sauce. Reduce heat to very low simmer. Meanwhile, cook tortellini according to manufacturer's directions and drain. Return tortellini to pot and add gorgonzola sauce and parmesan cheese. Ladle gorgonzola tortellini into individual serving bowls or plates. Sprinkle each bowl or plate with some of the minced parsley. Enjoy with crusty bread and a salad! Serves 4–6.

E. WHO'S WHO?

- For Zeus and Danae's descendants, see GENEALOGICAL CHART 12.

*The favorite cheese of the Gorgons is *gorgonzola* of course!

Chapter Nine
HERACLES (HERCULES)

General Sources:

Pindar *Nemean Odes* 1
Sophocles *Trachiniae*
Euripides *Alcestis*
Theocritus *Idyl* 25
Xenophon *Memorabilia* 2.1.21–34
Plautus *Amphitryon*
Apollodorus *Library* 2.4.7–2.7.7
Vergil *Aeneid* 8.184–279

Birth and Early Life

The most popular of all the Greek heroes is Heracles, best known by the Latin form of his name, Hercules. There are many tales about him, and his character has shown amazing adaptability—from comic buffoon to tragic hero, from cartoon character to savior of souls from death.

The parentage of Heracles

As for Perseus and other heroes, unusual circumstances surrounded Heracles' birth. Zeus fell in love with Heracles' mother, Alcmena of Thebes. While Alcmena's husband, Amphitryon, was away, Zeus came to Alcmena disguised as Amphitryon and stayed with her for a night, which he expanded to three times its usual length. When Amphitryon came home, he also lay with his wife and she conceived Heracles' twin brother, Iphicles. (See Genealogical Charts 12 and 21.)

Hera attempts to prevent Alcmena from giving birth.

As she often did, Hera sought revenge upon Zeus' lover. On the day that Heracles was due to be born, Zeus foolishly boasted: "Today the goddess of childbirth Eileithyia will bring into the world a man of my blood who will rule over everyone living around him!" Hera outwitted Zeus by hastening the birth of Heracles' cousin, Eurystheus, and ordering Eileithyia to delay the birth of Heracles and his brother.

Baby Heracles strangles two snakes sent by Hera.

Eileithyia accomplished this by sitting outside Alcmena's door with her hands clasped around her knees. As Alcmena struggled through the long labor, her maid broke the spell by rushing from the house crying, "It's a boy!" Eileithyia was so shocked that she jumped up and unclasped her hands. Thus Alcmena was able to give birth, but Eileithyia turned the poor maid into a weasel. However, Hera was not through yet. She had not prevented the infant's birth, but she thought she could kill him instantly. She sent a pair of snakes after him. The newborn Heracles then fought the first battle of his life. He gripped the snakes in his hands and strangled them to death. Alcmena leaped out of her bed to protect her infants; Amphitryon and the Theban leaders quickly seized their weapons and rushed into the room. They were not needed; the baby had already saved the day! Astounded at the might of his son, Amphitryon summoned the seer Tiresias, who foretold that Heracles would fight many wild beasts and lawless men but would ultimately receive his reward with a place on Mount Olympus.

Heracles is exiled to Thebes for killing Linus.

As Heracles grew up, he learned chariot driving, wrestling, archery, and music. He was a fast learner in all of these skills, except music. In fact, he killed his teacher, Linus, by striking him with his lyre. As punishment for this homicide, Heracles was sent away to the Theban pastures on the outlying mountains. Here he made himself very useful: he killed a lion that was preying on the cattle, and he led the Theban army against a people who were forcing the Thebans to pay tribute. The king of Thebes therefore gave Heracles his daughter Megara as a reward, and Heracles had three children by her. (See GENEALOGICAL CHART 21 for Heracles and his wives.)

Tiresias the seer

Heracles marries Megara, then kills her and their children.

Some time later, Hera attacked Heracles again. This time, she sent a fit of madness upon him, and in its clutches he killed Megara and the children. When he recovered his sanity, he went to the oracle of Delphi in search of purification. Here he was told that he must serve his cousin Eurystheus for twelve years.

The Greek historian Xenophon in his study

Xenophon's version of the reason for Heracles' labors

The historian Xenophon told a different story of how Heracles undertook his labors. When he was on the verge of manhood, he went to a quiet place and began to meditate on how he would live his life. Suddenly two women of great stature approached him. One was proper-looking and dignified, slim, and dressed in a white robe. The other was plump, wearing a revealing dress and heavy makeup. She often looked around to see if anyone was admiring her.

This latter woman rushed up to Heracles and said, "Heracles, I see you're wondering which path to take in your life. If you come with me, your life will be so easy and pleasant! Your only problem will be deciding which pleasures to enjoy, and how you can have them with no labor and no cost to yourself!"

When Heracles heard this, he asked, "What is your name, ma'am?"

She answered, "My friends call me Happiness, but my enemies call me Vice."

The other woman then spoke up. "Heracles, my name is Virtue. I am here to tell you that you have the ability to become a doer of great deeds. But I won't lie to you; blessings never come easily. If you want the favor of the gods, you must worship the gods. If you want friends, you must help others. If you want honors from Greece, you must benefit Greece."

Vice said, "Do you see how long and hard the road she's describing is? Wouldn't you rather have a short and easy path to happiness?"

Heracles undertakes 12 labors in service to his cousin, Eurystheus.

Virtue responded, "There is no happiness in taking things you haven't earned! What kind of a life is that—eating and drinking before you're hungry and thirsty, needing the softest covers before you can sleep? You'll never know the joy of hearing your name praised, of looking proudly at a job you've done well, of having good people as your companions! Join me, and you'll be remembered with glory forever!"

Heracles decided to follow Virtue's difficult way, and willingly served Eurystheus for the good of humankind.

Hereupon he took up his famous Twelve Labors. The first six take place in the Peloponnese. The second six take the hero to increasingly distant parts of the world and ultimately into the Underworld.

The Twelve Labors (and other deeds performed during the Labors)

1. **The Nemean Lion.** Heracles was required to bring the hide of this animal to Eurystheus. Theocritus says that the lion could not be wounded, so Heracles had to club it to death. He then used its own claws to skin it, and thereafter wore its hide as a trophy. We can usually identify Heracles in art by his club and lion's skin.

Heracles wrestles the Nemean lion.

2. **The Lernaean Hydra.** This serpent had nine heads, one of which was mortal. Each time Heracles cut a head off, two grew in its place. The Hydra was also accompanied by a huge crab, which Hera had sent. Heracles killed the crab and then, helped by his nephew Iolaus, dealt with the Hydra. Each time Heracles cut off one of the heads, Iolaus burned the stump so that the head could not grow back. Heracles then buried the immortal head under a huge rock. Heracles dipped his arrows in the Hydra's venom, an act that would be instrumental in his own death.

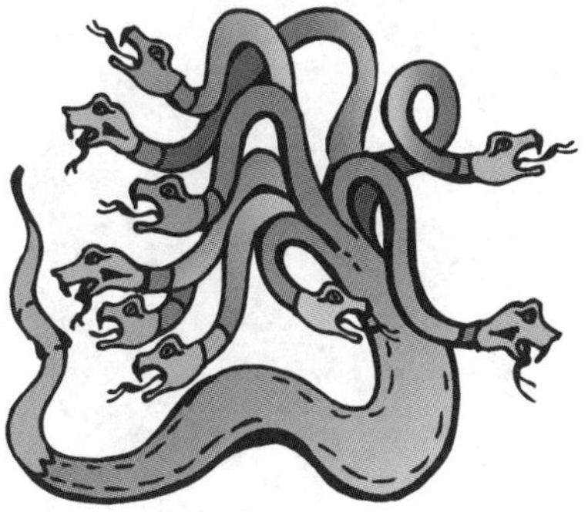

The Hydra

3. **The Cerynean Deer.** This golden-horned animal was sacred to Artemis and could not be harmed without incurring the goddess' wrath. Heracles pursued it for a whole year before he finally caught up to it. On the way back to Eurystheus, he met Artemis, who demanded the animal's release. Heracles did so, blaming his cousin for the theft.

4. **The Erymanthian Boar.** This animal had ravaged the land around Mount Erymanthus. Heracles chased the boar out if its hiding place into some deep snow and trapped it. He brought it back to Eurystheus, who was so terrified by the animal that he cowered in a large jar.

5. **The Augean Stables.** Augeas, the king of Elis, owned vast herds of cattle. Their stables had never been cleaned out, and Heracles was commanded to do this. He accomplished this deed by diverting two rivers so that they flowed through the stables.

   After this labor, Heracles was said to have instituted the Olympian Games. He was believed to have paced out the stadium himself, and to have fetched from the land of the Hyperboreans the first olive tree to be planted on the site. The winners in the games received crowns of olive leaves.

6. **The Stymphalian Birds.** Heracles was required to shoot these creatures, which had feathers that they shot like iron. He brought them out of hiding with a pair of castanets that Athena had given to him; he then shot the birds with his arrows.

7. **The Cretan Bull.** This bull was ravaging the land of Crete; you will learn more about it when you read about Theseus. Heracles caught it and brought it back to Eurystheus, who turned it loose. Eventually, Theseus sacrificed it on the plains of Marathon.

Heracles encounters Artemis.

Heracles returns to show off the Erymanthian Boar while Eurystheus cowers in a bronze vessel.

Heracles wrestles with the Cretan Bull.

8. **The Horses of Diomedes.** Diomedes was a Thracian king who owned a herd of horses that fed on human flesh. Heracles got possession of them and fed them the flesh of their master. He then sailed back home with the horses, where Eurystheus set them free and dedicated them to Hera.

Heracles visits his friend Admetus.

During his journey to Thrace, however, Heracles won one of his famous victories over Death. He stopped off at the home of his friend Admetus. Admetus had previously employed Apollo (in a disguise), who had been forced to work as a shepherd for him as an act of atonement. Admetus had treated the god well. When Apollo learned that Admetus was fated to die soon, he managed (with a bribe of some wine) to receive a concession in his friend's behalf from the usually implacable Fates: They would let him live if he could find someone willing to die in his place. No one, including Admetus' elderly parents, was willing to make the sacrifice—until his young wife, Alcestis, volunteered. Shortly before Heracles arrived at Admetus' palace, Death had come for Alcestis. When Heracles found his friend looking tearful, he asked why.

Admetus hides the death of his wife, Alcestis, from Heracles.

"I had to bury a . . . member of my household," said Admetus, making it sound as if he were burying a servant and not his wife.

"I'm sorry I came at such a bad time. I could go stay someplace else," offered Heracles.

"I won't hear of it. You're staying right here." Admetus instructed one of his servants to house Heracles, to give him plenty to eat and drink, and to make sure the guest was not disturbed by sounds of mourning.

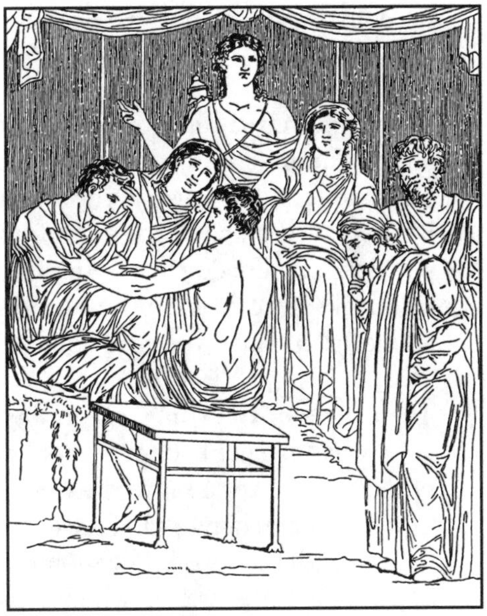
Heracles returns Alcestis to Admetus.

Admetus' servant unwittingly reveals Alcestis' death.

Heracles ate and drank abundantly, aware only that everyone in the household was sunk in gloom.

"Why is everyone so sad when there's company in the house?" he asked the servant drunkenly. "Look, everybody dies, so wipe off that frown and join me in a drink!"

"I can't join your party at a time like this!" the shocked servant exclaimed.

"Why not? It's not as if you lost Admetus or Alcestis!"

"Didn't Admetus tell you that his wife died?"

"You mean . . . how could you let me make a fool of myself like that? Where did they take her body?"

Heracles wrestles Death and restores Alcestis to Admetus.

The servant told him, and Heracles vowed, "I'll bring her back to my friend. What a wonderful host he was, not wanting to burden me with his troubles!"

He immediately set out to Alcestis' burial site, where he saw Death carrying her away. He wrestled with Death and forced him to release Alcestis, whom he then returned to Admetus.

9. **The Belt of Hippolyta.** Hippolyta was queen of the Amazons, a fierce tribe of warlike women generally believed to live in the northernmost limits of the known world. These women raised only their female children, and they cut off their right breasts so that they could throw the javelin more easily (they kept their left breasts for nursing purposes).

An Amazon

Heracles was ordered to take the queen's belt, given to her by Ares for her superior military prowess, because Eurystheus' daughter wanted it. Heracles assembled a small band of volunteers and sailed off. When he reached the Amazons' land, Hippolyta received him kindly and promised to give him the belt. But Hera, disguising herself as an Amazon, stirred up the warrior women by shouting, "Strangers are kidnapping your queen! Take up your weapons and fight!" When Heracles saw them in arms, he slew the queen and took her belt. He and his men fought off the rest of the Amazons and sailed away.

While returning from this labor, Heracles stopped off at Troy. He there rescued a princess named Hesione, who was about to be fed to a sea monster. The monster had come from Poseidon, who had sent it in anger at the king of Troy, Laomedon. Poseidon and Apollo, disguised as common laborers, had helped Laomedon build the walls of Troy. When they finished, Laomedon refused to pay them. Laomedon also refused to pay Heracles his reward for rescuing Hesione; Heracles therefore sacked the city, deposed Laomedon, and put Priam on the throne. You will hear much more about Priam when you read about the Trojan War.

10. **The Cattle of Geryon.** Geryon was a triple-bodied monster who tended a herd of cattle that Heracles was to bring back to Eurystheus. The monster lived on an island named Erythia, at the edge of the known world far to the west. To reach Erythia, Heracles received help from Helius, who gave him his golden cup to sail across the ocean. On the island, he killed Geryon and sailed back toward Greece with the cattle. As a monument to his journey, he set up the Pillars of Heracles on either side of the Strait of Gibraltar, which separates Spain from Morocco in northern Africa.

He also passed through Italy on his journey home. Here he encountered a son of Hephaestus named Cacus, a fire-breathing monster who lived in a cave on the Aventine Hill (which would one day be part of Rome). Cacus stole some of Geryon's cattle and (as Hermes had done) led them backwards into his cave, so that their footprints appeared to lead away from the cave. Bewildered, Heracles was about to give up searching for them when a timely "moo" from the cave alerted him. Heracles broke into the cave, strangled Cacus, and retrieved the stolen cattle. Ever since then, the Greek Heracles was worshipped in Italy as Hercules. He was the only one of the Greek heroes to be worshipped by the Romans.

Atlas carrying the world

11. **The Apples of the Hesperides.** The Hesperides were three daughters of Night who lived far away in the West and tended a tree which grew golden apples. This tree was guarded by a hundred-mouthed dragon named Ladon. Heracles first had to find out the location of the tree from the sea-god Nereus, who had the power to transform himself into many different shapes. Nereus tried all of his shape-shifting wiles, but Heracles held him firm. "Do not try to pluck the apples yourself," advised Nereus at last. "Get Atlas to do it." Atlas, you recall, was the Titan who carried the world on his shoulders. He was happy to fetch the apples and shift the burden of carrying the world to Heracles. In fact, he volunteered to take the apples back to Eurystheus himself. "Please do," said Heracles. "Just hold the world a little longer while I get a cushion for my shoulders. I'll be right back, I promise!" The foolish Titan agreed, and Heracles hurried back to Greece with the apples. Eurystheus later returned the apples to the garden because they were too holy to keep.

Heracles, left, struggles with Antaeus, right.

Heracles defeated another enemy on this journey to the garden. This was a giant son of Poseidon and Gaea named Antaeus, who lived in the African land of Libya. Antaeus forced all who came to his kingdom to wrestle with him, and he used their skulls to build a temple to his father when he had killed them. When Heracles was wrestling him, he noticed that the giant seemed stronger after he had been thrown on the ground. Figuring out that the source of Antaeus' strength was the earth, Heracles held him overhead until he weakened and died.

12. **The Capture of Cerberus**. The final labor was to fetch Cerberus, the three-headed dog that guarded the Underworld. Hades was surprisingly agreeable about letting Heracles "borrow" his dog, asking only that Heracles not use violence against the beast. Heracles wrestled with Cerberus, brought him back to Eurystheus, and then returned him to the Underworld.

Heracles frees Theseus from Hades and meets Meleager.

While he was in the Underworld, Heracles released the Athenian hero Theseus, who was being kept there as a prisoner by Hades (you will learn why in a later chapter). He also met Meleager, an encounter that later led (indirectly) to his death. Meleager told him the sad story of his premature death and also mentioned that Heracles might be an appropriate husband for his sister, Deianira.

Heracles, wearing the lion skin, accompanied by Athena and Hermes, subdues Cerberus at right with Persephone. Greek vase painting.

Heracles' Deeds after His Labors, His Death, and His Apotheosis

After Heracles had completed his labors, Eurystheus released him from slavery. He was now free to seek a new wife. He had heard about a princess named Iole, whose father, Eurytus, had offered her hand in marriage to any man who could defeat his four sons and himself in an archery contest. Heracles easily won this contest, but Eurytus refused to hand over Iole. "You killed your first wife and children, you cheated by using magic arrows, and you worked as a slave for Eurystheus! Get out!" he shouted at Heracles. Heracles left but vowed revenge.

Heracles kills Eurytus' son, Iphitus, in rage.

Sometime after Heracles left, some of Eurytus' horses went missing. Eurytus' eldest son, Iphitus, went out to search for them. He tracked them to the city of Tiryns, where Heracles was staying. Heracles promised to help him and offered him hospitality, but soon recognized that Iphitus suspected him of the theft. He also remembered his humiliating treatment at the hands of Iphitus' father.

He led Iphitus to the highest tower of the city and demanded, "Look around! Do you see your horses anywhere?"

"No," answered Iphitus.

"Then you've accused me falsely!" exclaimed Heracles. At that moment a fit of insane rage hit him and he threw Iphitus off the tower to his death.

Heracles seeks purification.

When Heracles realized what he had done, he went to the oracle of Delphi to ask for purification. The priestess there received him coldly, however. "I have nothing to say to people who murder their guests!" she exclaimed. Heracles responded by sacking the sanctuary and trying to steal the tripod on which the priestess was sitting. Apollo appeared, and he and Heracles engaged in a tug-of-war until Zeus intervened. The priestess relented and told Heracles, "To be purified you must be sold as a slave and serve for three years. The money from your sale will be given to Eurytus."

Queen Omphale of Lydia purchases Heracles as a slave.

Heracles' purchaser was Omphale, the queen of Lydia. He served her for the required three years. The term of service was humiliating; she had him dress in feminine clothes and do women's tasks, while she took his club and wore his lion's skin. There are statues of her dressed in Heracles' characteristic clothes.

Heracles does women's work of weaving.

Heracles marries Deianira, kills a servant, goes into exile again.

When his enslavement to Omphale ended, Heracles, still without a wife, remembered what Meleager had said to him in the Underworld about his sister, Deianira. Heracles found her and defeated a river-god for her hand in marriage. Their marriage was happy until one day, while Heracles was feasting with his father-in-law, a young servant accidentally splashed Heracles' feet while pouring water on his hands. Heracles, in another fit of rage, killed the boy with one blow. In his shame, he left for exile along with his wife and their small son, Hyllus.

Heracles kills Nessus, who, dying, gives Deianira some of his blood.

They were about to cross a flooded river, when they were met by a centaur named Nessus, who volunteered to ferry them across for a fee. Heracles placed his wife and baby on the centaur's back, deciding that he would swim the river. Suddenly, he heard his wife screaming that the centaur was trying to attack her! He shot Nessus with one of his poisoned arrows. The dying centaur then whispered to Deianira, "Take some of the blood from my wound! If Heracles ever stops loving you, smear it on his clothing, and it will act as a love charm to make him love you again!" Deianira believed him and did as he said.

Nessus, the centaur, offers to Heracles to ferry Deianira and their baby son, Hyllus, across a river.

Heracles kidnaps Iole; Deianira puts Nessus' blood on a robe.

The family settled down in the Greek city of Trachis, but Heracles still remembered Iole and how her father had cheated him of her. He therefore gathered an army and sacked her city. He killed her father and her surviving brothers and took her captive. When Deianira heard of this rival that Heracles was bringing home, she was consumed by jealousy. She decided to use Nessus' "love charm" on a new robe, which she gave to a herald who had come to announce that Heracles had defeated his foes and wanted a fresh garment in which to sacrifice.

Heracles is burned by the poisonous blood on the robe.

Heracles put on the robe without suspecting anything. As soon as his body warmed the garment, however, he felt an extremely painful burning all over his body. The centaur's blood combined with the Hydra's venom acted as a powerful poison. When he tried to pull the garment off, it clung to him, so that he could not remove it without tearing his skin. When Deianira learned what had happened, she was so overcome by remorse that she hanged herself.

Philoctetes helps Heracles to build his own funeral pyre.

Heracles, realizing that he was dying, resolved to hasten his death. He ordered his son to help him up Mount Oeta, the highest peak in Trachis. He then built his own funeral pyre, spread out his lion's skin like a blanket, and lay down on it. He commanded his companions to light the pyre, but none had the heart to. At last, a nearby shepherd named Philoctetes carried out Heracles' orders. In gratitude, Heracles turned over his bow and arrows to Philoctetes.

The apotheosis of Heracles and marriage with Hebe

As the flames rose up to heaven, the chariot of Zeus descended and lifted Heracles to the sky. Thunderbolts fell and destroyed the pyre. The mortal part of Heracles had been burned off. Athena took him by the hand and escorted him into the splendid halls of Olympus. Hera gave up her grudge at last and welcomed him, giving him her daughter, Hebe, as his wife.

Thus Heracles received the glorious reward that Virtue had promised him in his youth: immortality and a place among the immortals.

An *apotheosis* is the transformation of a human, a mortal, into an immortal god.

At top center, Hebe is seated. Heracles stands to the left of her with his club. Zeus and Hera are to the left of Heracles. Lower right, Dionysus with his thyrsus steers a panther-driven chariot.

A. Review Exercises

1. **WHO AM I?** From the word bank given below, select the name that best fits the person described in each of the phrases following the word bank. Fill in the blank with the name that best matches the description. One name will be used twice.

Hercules	**Alcmena**	**Zeus**	**Eileithyia**
Amphitryon	**Iphicles**	**Eurystheus**	**Hera**
Tiresias	**Linus**	**Iolaus**	**Megara**

a. ______________ Heracles' nephew, who proved invaluable in assisting with the destruction of the Hydra; he cauterized each stump with a torch.

b. ______________ The blind seer who foretold Heracles' struggles with human and beast and prophesied his eventual welcome to Mount Olympus

c. ______________ She tried twice to prevent Heracles' birth.

d. ______________ Stepfather to Heracles

e. ______________ Goddess of childbirth, ordered to delay the birth of Heracles

f. ______________ Heracles' mother

g. ______________ The Roman name for Heracles

h. ______________ Heracles' fraternal twin

i. ______________ Heracles killed this teacher of his by hurling a lyre at him.

j. ______________ Although Amphitryon appeared to be father to Heracles, this one was his actual father.

k. ______________ Her jealousy over her spouse's infidelity caused her to plague Alcmena and Heracles.

l. ______________ The king of Thebes' daughter who became the first wife of Heracles

m. ______________ Cousin to Heracles and the one whom Heracles served for twelve years

2. **MATCHING!** Match the name in the left-hand column with the correct phrase from the right-hand column. Write the letter in the space provided. There are more phrases than available names!

1.	____	Hippolyta	a.	Giant who drew strength from the earth
2.	____	Philoctetes	b.	Heracles' son
3.	____	Xenophon	c.	Owner of man-eating horses
4.	____	Iole	d.	Woman brought back from death by Heracles
5.	____	Cacus	e.	Wife responsible for Heracles' death
6.	____	Alcmena	f.	Princess loved and later captured by Heracles
7.	____	Diomedes	g.	Inheritor of Heracles' bow and arrows
8.	____	Antaeus	h.	Philosopher who narrates the tale of Heracles' choice
9.	____	Megara	i.	Amazon queen
10.	____	Alcestis	j.	Heracles' mother
			k.	Fire-breather killed by Heracles in Italy
			l.	Killed by Heracles in a fit of madness

B. Musings

1. Create a contemporary version of Heracles' twelve labors, in which he deals with "monsters" and other problems of today.

2. Watch the 1997 Disney cartoon "Hercules." Which aspects of the myth are kept, and which are changed? Why do you think some aspects of the myth are changed?

3. Heracles made regular appearances on the small screen in the 1990s, first in several TV movies and then in a series titled *Hercules: The Legendary Journeys.* Try to obtain a video or DVD of this series for viewing. Cite examples in which (a) the storyline is close to the ancient myths of Heracles; (b) the storyline is taken from Greek myths but not those of Heracles; (c) there are characters from the traditional Heracles myths but their roles in the modern tales are different; (d) the creators of the series place the hero in situations that have no equivalent in the ancient myths.

4. What do you think accounts for the popularity of the Heracles character through the ages? Kevin Sorbo, who played the title role in the television series *Hercules: The Legendary Journeys,* sees the hero as accessible and appealing because he isn't invulnerable. He can be injured, make mistakes, laugh at himself, yet still risk his life for others' benefit. (From *Hercules X-Posed: The Unauthorized Biography of Kevin Sorbo and His On-Screen Character* by Ted Edwards, Prima Publishing 1998, p. 8.)

C. Words, Words, Words

The Daily Muse

News you can use

Several words and phrases associated with Heracles/Hercules have become **metaphors**.

> **A *metaphor* is a comparison that does not use words and phrases such as "like" or "just as."**

Something that has many parts may be referred to as **hydra-headed**. Draw a picture in the space below and then describe in a sentence or two your idea of one of these:

- A hydra-headed organization
- A hydra-headed problem

Any filthy place can be described as **Augean stables**. To **clean the Augean stables** is to put something extremely disorganized into a state of order. Where do you see Augean stables around you?

Draw or paste an appropriate picture of your idea of an **Amazon** in the oval space to the right.

A misfortune from which there is no escape, or a "gift" that harms the recipient, is a **shirt of Nessus**.

- Cite an example of a shirt of Nessus, either from your reading or personal experience.

Someone forced to choose between what is easy and what is right has to make a **choice of Hercules**. Give an example of this, either from your reading or personal experience.

The hero's Roman name has given us several words:

1. Something **herculean** requires great strength or effort. Can you name a job that might be described as a "herculean task?" ______________________________

____

2. Any man of great strength or size can be called a **Hercules**. Name a contemporary or classic film star who could be described as a Hercules; give a reason why: ______________________________

____

D. How 'Bout That?

Heracles and music

Heracles wasn't much of a music student—check out the fate of his poor music teacher, Linus! But he still has a strong influence on musicians. There are many contemporary tunes about the hero Hercules.

Heracles (or Hercules) may be the only hero whose name appears in the titles of two very different songs. Compare and contrast the aspects of Heracles' character brought out in each of these:

- "Little Hercules" sung by Trisha Yearwood (1996); by Craig Carothers
  http://www.azlyrics.com/lyrics/trishayearwood/littlehercules.html
- To view a photograph of Elton John and hear him performing "Hercules," visit this *YouTube* link:
  www.youtube.com/watch?v=fZxiw-dhlIY

An English singer, born Reginald Kenneth Dwight in 1947, took the stage name Elton Hercules John, and went on to become an international star. In 1998, he was knighted by Queen Elizabeth II and is now Sir Elton John.

What does "Hercules" mean in each of these songs? ______________________________

____

____

____

Costume party?

To see a photo of Omphale dressed as Heracles, go to this website for the Vatican Museum: http:// www.christusrex.org/www1/vaticano/GP-Profano.html. Scroll down to "Statue of Omphale."

Heracles and Mother Nature

Did you know?
One of the largest rhinoceros beetles lives in South America and is called the Hercules beetle.

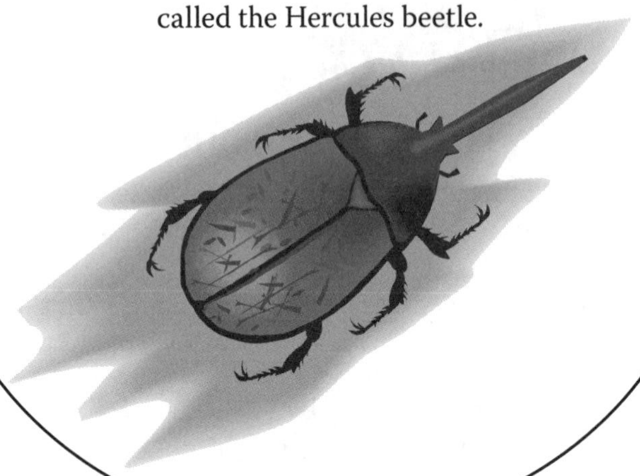

Hercules' club is the name of several prickly shrubs and small trees found in the United States.

To see beautiful color photo examples of two different Hercules' clubs and to learn more about this fascinating tree (*Zanthoxylum clava-herculis*) and shrub (*Aralia spinosa),* visit these websites:

Aralia spinosa

Tree: *Zanthoxylum clava-herculis*
- http://www.eattheweeds.com/hercules-club-speak-softly-but/

Bush or shrub: *Aralia spinosa*
- http://plants.usda.gov/core/profile?symbol=arsp2

- Why is the Hercules' club tree (*Zanthoxylum clava-herculis*) also called "toothache tree"?
- How did Hercules' club (*Zanthoxylum clava-herculis*) also get the name "tingle-tongue"?
- Where does the name "Hercules' club" come from?
- The Hercules' club bush (*Aralia spinosa*) is also called "devil's walking stick." Why?

Hercules is a constellation whose stars form the shape of a large, crouching man. Several of the animals he defeated—Hydra (the Water Snake), Cancer (the Crab, which accompanied the Hydra), Leo (the [Nemean] Lion) and Draco (the Dragon)—are also constellations (see page 109).

The constellation Hercules

E. WHO'S WHO?

- For Zeus and Danae's descendants, see GENEALOGICAL CHART 12.
- For Heracles' family, see GENEALOGICAL CHART 21.

Chapter Ten

Jason and the Argonauts

General Sources:

Pindar *Pythian Odes* 4
Euripides *Medea*
Apollonius Rhodius *Argonautica*
Ovid *Metamorphoses* 7.262–349

***Jason*, 1803, by Bertel Thorvaldsen (1770–1844), Thorvaldsens Museum, Copenhagen, Denmark**

The legend of Jason is a bit different from the other hero myths in that the victories do not belong solely to one man occasionally helped by the gods or by faceless companions. Instead, there is a cast of heroes, many of whom contribute his or her distinctive talent at some point in the adventure.

A golden ram carries Phrixus and Helle across the sea.

Jason and the Argonauts are usually associated with the Golden Fleece, which itself had an interesting history. It was once a golden ram that had carried two children, Phrixus and Helle, across the sea to help them escape from an evil stepmother. Helle, unfortunately, fell into the strait separating Europe from Asia Minor and drowned. Ever since then, the strait was known as the Hellespont. (*Pontus* means "sea.") Phrixus continued alone to the city of Colchis on the Black Sea and there sacrificed the ram. The king of Colchis hung the ram's gold fleece on a tree and set a never-sleeping dragon to guard it.

Jason is raised by Chiron, the centaur.

Like many heroes' adventures, Jason's story begins with an oracle. His uncle, Pelias, had deposed Jason's father, Aeson, from the throne of Iolcus (a city in northern Greece) and driven Jason and his parents into exile. (See Genealogical Chart 13.) For his protection, Jason was sent to be raised and educated by the wise centaur Chiron. Meanwhile, Pelias received a peculiar oracle: "Beware of the man wearing one sandal!"

The Golden Fleece hanging on a tree, guarded by a dragon

Chiron

A Possible Route for the Voyage of Jason and the Argonauts

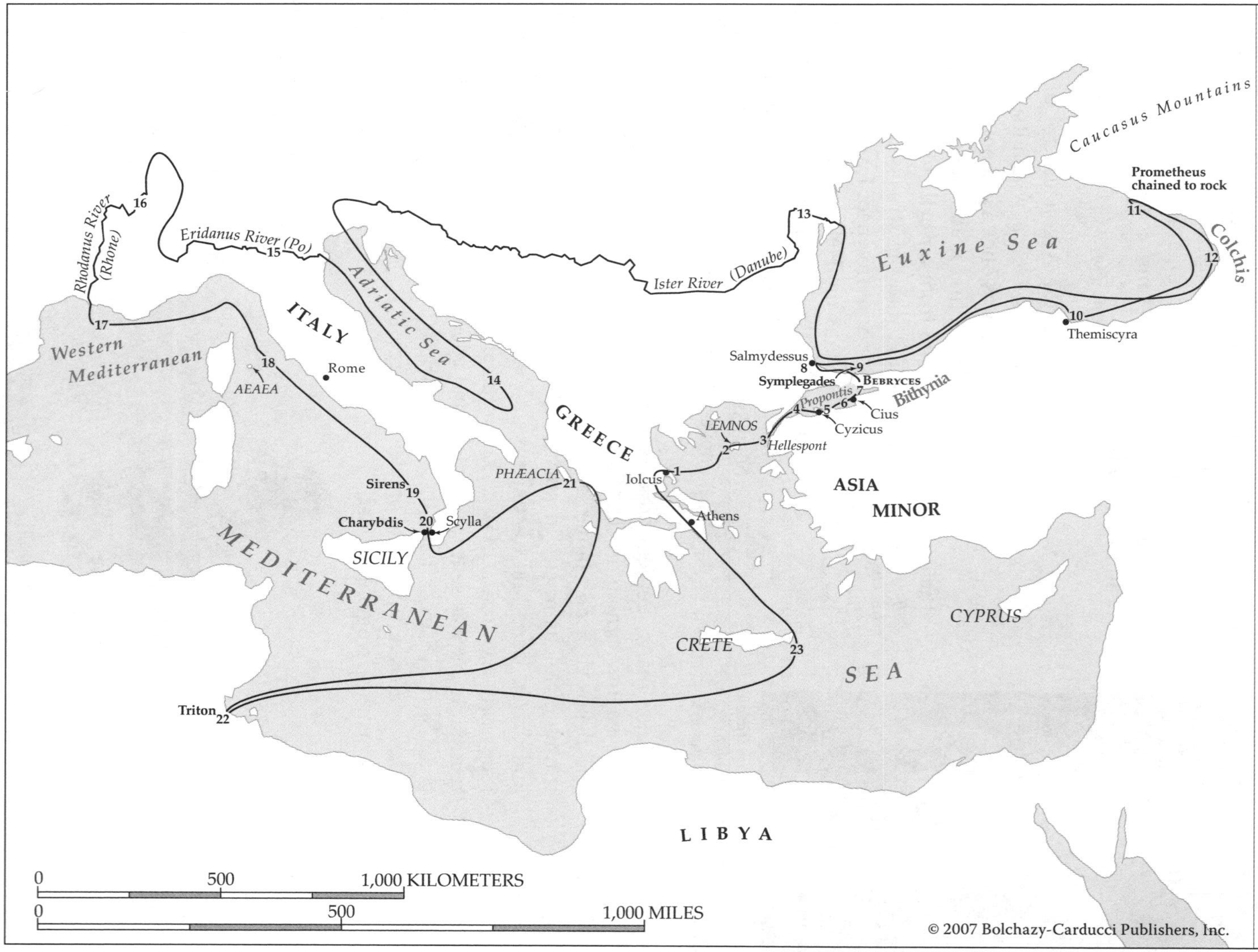

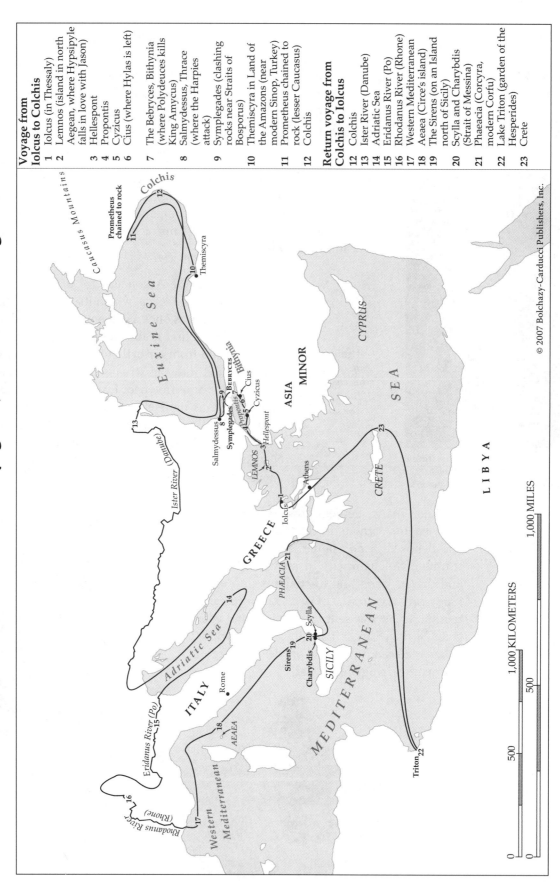

Voyage from Iolcus to Colchis

1 Iolcus (in Thessaly)
2 Lemnos (island in north Aegean, where Hypsipyle falls in love with Jason)
3 Hellespont
4 Propontis
5 Cyzicus
6 Cius (where Hylas is left)
7 The Bebryces, Bithynia (where Polydeuces kills King Amycus)
8 Salmydessus, Thrace (where the Harpies attack)
9 Symplegades (clashing rocks near Straits of Bosporus)
10 Themiscyra in Land of the Amazons (near modern Sinop, Turkey)
11 Prometheus chained to rock (lesser Caucasus)
12 Colchis

Return voyage from Colchis to Iolcus

12 Colchis
13 Ister River (Danube)
14 Adriatic Sea
15 Eridanus River (Po)
16 Rhodanus River (Rhone)
17 Western Mediterranean
18 Aeaea (Circe's island)
19 The Sirens (on an Island north of Sicily)
20 Scylla and Charybdis (Strait of Messina)
21 Phaeacia (Corcyra, modern Corfu)
22 Lake Triton (garden of the Hesperides)
23 Crete

Jason returns to Iolcus; Hera helps Jason reclaim the throne.

When Jason was twenty years old, he was ready to reclaim the throne for his father. He was journeying back to Iolcus, and had to cross a swollen river. An old woman stood beside the river. "Can I help you across, ma'am?" asked Jason. The old woman nodded and let Jason carry her. As they proceeded across the river, Jason lost one of his sandals in its muddy bed. The old woman had been Hera in disguise; she was thereafter friendly to Jason and hostile to Pelias because he had failed to sacrifice to her.

As soon as Pelias saw the young man in one sandal, he recognized the danger to himself. "Tell me, young man," he said to Jason, "if an oracle had told you that you were destined to be killed by . . . well, let's say Mr. X . . . , what would you do?" Jason replied, "I would send Mr. X off to get the Golden Fleece."

Jason assembles a crew of famous heroes for the ship Argo.

Representation of a terracotta relief sculpture in which Argus builds the *Argo* under Athena's direction

Pelias commanded Jason to do exactly that, saying that the ghost of Phrixus had come to him in a dream and begged him to bring the Golden Fleece back to Greece. Pelias was hoping that Jason would be lost at sea or slain by barbarians. Jason thereupon assembled a large group of heroes (fifty is the generally accepted number), who are referred to as Argonauts. The Argo was Jason's ship, built by the skilled shipman Argus under the direction of Athena. Its brilliant design included a plank of oak that could speak! Among the most prominent Argonauts were the great musician Orpheus, the twin brothers of Helen of Troy named Castor and Polydeuces (Pollux), and the mighty Heracles himself. There were others whose sons would become prominent warriors in the Trojan War: Peleus (father of Achilles), Telamon (father of Ajax the Greater), and Oileus (father of Ajax the Lesser). Many of them had special powers: Castor was a great horseman and Polydeuces a first-rate boxer; Lynceus could see under the earth; Zetes and Calais were the sons of the North Wind and could fly.

The Argonauts meet Hypsipyle on the isle of women, Lemnos.

After leaving Iolcus, the Argonauts sailed to the island of Lemnos. Here they found only women. The women had been punished by Aphrodite for neglecting their worship by being cursed with a bad smell. Their husbands therefore turned to other women, and the wives in revenge killed all the men. The women of Lemnos therefore received the Argonauts gladly (the smell had disappeared by this time), and the men stayed for a year. Jason was particularly beloved by the island's queen, Hypsipyle.

They then moved on to the Propontis and landed at Cyzicus, which was ruled by a young king of the same name. The Argonauts were received hospitably, and Heracles killed some of the giants that were menacing the area. Unfortunately, when the Argonauts sailed from there, contrary winds drove them back to land. The people mistook them for pirates, and the disoriented Argonauts did not recognize that these were their recent hosts. A battle broke out, and Cyzicus was killed. The Argonauts joined in the mourning for the king (who was a recent bridegroom) and set sail again.

Hylas and the Nymphs, 1896, by John William Waterhouse (1849–1917), Manchester Art Gallery, England

The Argonauts abandon Hylas, Heracles' friend.

At their next stop, the Argonauts lost Heracles. They stopped on the island of Cius so that Heracles could replace a broken oar. While Heracles' young servant and companion, Hylas, was filling a pitcher at a pool, the nymphs of the pool fell in love with him and dragged him into the water to live with them. Heracles was distraught and ran through the woods bellowing for Hylas. He refused to sail on without his friend, and the Argonauts reluctantly left him behind.

As the Argonauts passed into the Euxine (now the Black Sea), they came across a tribe in Bithynia (now Turkey) whose king, Amycus, compelled all strangers to fight with him. Polydeuces fought the hitherto undefeated king and killed him.

The Harpies harass the seer Phineus.

Their next stop was on the shore of Thrace where a seer named Phineus lived. Apollo had granted him the gift of divination, but he had not respected the gods in using his art. Zeus therefore granted him long life but took away his eyesight. People who sought Phineus' advice always brought him gifts, but Zeus made sure that Phineus took no enjoyment from them. As soon as Phineus stretched out his hands to take any food, creatures named Harpies, who were half-bird, half-woman, came and snatched it away, leaving behind a horrible stench.

The Harpies in Inferno by Armando Spadini (1883–1925), created for the Alinari Edition (Florence, 1902–1903) of Dante Alighieri's *La Divina Commedia*. Dante included numerous classical allusions to Greek and Roman mythology in his depiction of Hell, Italian "Inferno."

Sometimes the Harpies took all the food; sometimes they left just enough to keep Phineus from starving to death and ending his misery. Yet Zeus had told Phineus that strangers would one day come to release him from the Harpies. When he heard the voyagers arriving, he struggled up from his bed and shuffled to the door, tapping his way with a stick, weak from hunger and old age. He nearly collapsed from joy as he realized that these travelers would be his salvation, and begged them, "Help me!" The Argonauts, especially the sons of the North Wind, took pity on him and promised to help.

The Argonauts attack the Harpies.

The Argonauts help free Phineus from the Harpies.

They laid out a feast, and as soon as the old man touched the food, the Harpies came screeching down and gobbled up the food, left their unbearable odor behind, and sped off over the sea, still screaming. Calais and Zetes flew off after them with their swords drawn, ready to kill. As they were about to overtake the creatures, Iris appeared and said, "It is not ordained for you to kill these hounds of Zeus, but I swear by the River Styx that they will never bother Phineus again!" So the two turned back; meanwhile, the rest of the crew helped Phineus to bathe and let him enjoy his first full meal in years.

Grateful Phineus warns the Argonauts about the Symplegades.

As they feasted late into the night, Phineus told them about the dangers they could expect during the remainder of their journey, particularly one: the Clashing Rocks, or Symplegades. "No ship has ever passed through them successfully! Do not trust in your own strength, but respect the will of the gods. Before you attempt to sail through, send a dove as an omen to you. If it flies safely through the rocks, then you also will pass through. But if the dove perishes, you must turn back." He described the other lands and peoples they would encounter, and concluded cryptically, "The success of your venture depends much on Aphrodite."

The Argonauts sailed off the next morning, leaving the grateful old man. When they reached the Clashing Rocks, they did as Phineus had ordered and released the dove. They watched anxiously as it narrowly missed being smashed. A few of its tail feathers were clipped off by the rocks, yet it darted away to loud cheers from the Argonauts. "Row hard! The rocks are parting again!" shouted the helmsman. They exerted all their strength in a panic as the rocks loomed on either side of them. The tidal waves kept tossing them and they could not row clear of the Symplegades, until Athena held back one rock with her left hand and pushed the *Argo* with her might. The vessel sped through as swiftly as an arrow, yet the rocks sheared off some of its stern. From then on, the Symplegades fused together and smashed no more ships, as the gods had decreed they would as soon as one ship passed them successfully.

The Argonauts pass by Prometheus and arrive in Colchis.

The Argonauts passed the rest of their journey smoothly; although they skimmed the coast of the Amazons' territory and caught a glimpse of the eagle that was tormenting Prometheus, they did not land. They reached the land of Colchis by nightfall and hid among the reed beds, discussing how best to approach Aeetes, the king. Hera and Athena had seen them land, and they went to a private room together to discuss how best to help Jason.

Prometheus and the eagle

Hera and Athena scheme to help the Argonauts.

Hera spoke first. "Athena, can you think of any tricks that will let them get the Golden Fleece? I don't think they'll be able to talk Aeetes into giving it up voluntarily."

Athena answered, "I've been giving it a lot of thought, but haven't yet hit upon the perfect plan."

Roman copy of Athena Lemnia, Staatliche Museum, Dresden.

They pondered in silence, until Hera exclaimed, "I know! We can ask Aphrodite to have Eros hit Aeetes' daughter Medea with one of his arrows! If Medea helps Jason, I'm sure he can get the fleece!"

The scheme pleased Athena, but she added, "You'll have to do the talking to Aphrodite. I don't know a thing about these desires."

The goddesses found Aphrodite in her room, combing her long hair. She smiled ironically as they entered, and said, "Hello, dear ladies, what's the occasion? You don't come to visit here very often!"

Hera replied, "We need to talk with you about a serious matter. We're very worried about the Argonauts, especially Jason. I've wanted to help him ever since he carried me across the river when I was disguised as an old woman, and to make Pelias pay for his outrage against me."

Aphrodite said gently, "Of course, I'd be glad to help any way I can."

Hera explained what she wanted, and Aphrodite exclaimed, "My Eros is so naughty, I don't know if I can get him to obey me. Sometimes I want to smash his bow and arrows in public! But I'll do my best."

Aphrodite bribes Eros for help in the goddesses' scheme.

The goddesses shook hands on this, and Aphrodite went to search for Eros. She found him in Zeus' orchard, playing dice with Ganymede and gloating over his victory. Chucking her son under the chin, she addressed him sharply: "Were you cheating again? Listen—I need you to do something for me, and if you do it, I'll give you a beautiful blue and golden ball that once belonged to Zeus himself!"

Eros hugged her close and said, "Can I have it *now*, Mommy?" She answered, "I swear I won't cheat you of it! Just shoot one of your arrows into Aeetes' daughter Medea."

Jason plans to ask King Aeetes of Colchis for his help.

Eros sped off. Meanwhile, Jason addressed the Argonauts: "Here is my plan. Let's ask Aeetes nicely for the fleece first. Words often accomplish goals better than force."

The crew agreed, and Jason set out to the palace accompanied by a few select men. People gathered around from all over at the arrival of the strangers, and ushered them to Aeetes' throne room. When the king asked them what their purpose was, Jason answered mildly, "Do not worry that we've come to attack your city. I am here at the demand of an arrogant king for the Golden Fleece. If you show favor to us, I'll make sure your glory spreads throughout Greece."

Aeetes tests the Argonauts and plans to kill them.

Aeetes wondered whether or not to slaughter the strangers at once, but decided on another course of action. "I'll give you the fleece once I've tested you to see if you're worthy of it. I have here, out at pasture on the field of Ares, two bronze-footed bulls that can breathe fire. Every day I yoke them and drive them over four acres, all the time sowing a dragon's teeth. These grow instantly and bring forth armored men. I slaughter these men at once with my spear as they crowd around me. If you can do this, the fleece is yours."

Jason was distressed and fearful of the ordeal to come, but nonetheless, he retorted, "I accept the challenge!" However, he was right to be apprehensive. Despite his moderate words, Aeetes was thinking, "Once the bulls have torn this fool to bits, I'll set fire to his ship, crew and all!"

The Argonauts urge Jason to get Medea's help.

Fortunately for Jason, Eros was crouching unseen at his feet. The love-god let one of his arrows fly at Medea, and she was filled with desire for Jason. She was torn between loyalty to her father and love for the young hero. At the same time, the crew urged Jason, "Aeetes' daughter is said to be skilled in magic. If you can win her over, victory will be yours. Remember that Phineus said our success depended on Aphrodite!" The Argonauts decided to approach Medea through her sister, Chalciope, who happened to be the mother of their shipbuilder Argus.

Love-struck Medea's dream and Chalciope's advice

Medea's sleep was full of strange dreams that night. She dreamed that Jason was undertaking the task not to obtain the Golden Fleece, but to win her as a bride. Then she dreamed *she* was the one yoking the bulls and plowing the field. She awoke shaking with fear that the strangers' arrival would lead to great trouble. She sought her sister's advice, and Chalciope told her what Argus and the others had said. "Jason will be waiting for you at dawn in Hecate's temple," she added.

Medea prepares a charm and meets Jason.

After long hesitation, Medea resolved to help Jason. While her servants prepared the wagon to take her to the temple, Medea took out a special ointment known as the "Promethean charm" because it came from a plant that had sprung from the first blood that Prometheus had shed. Whoever smeared it on his body after offering prayer and sacrifice to Hecate would be invulnerable to fire and sword for that day.

When Jason saw Medea at the temple, he addressed her with flattering words: "Don't be afraid, you can trust me and speak freely! I can't win this contest without your help. Ariadne once helped Theseus in a similar ordeal, and she now has a crown in heaven. The gods will honor you too if you rescue this great crew, and I think you will, because you look like a sweet and friendly person."

Hecate, the three-faced goddess

Medea at last spoke with great effort: "Listen carefully, this is what you must do . . ." and she told him in detail how to use her magic ointment and accomplish his task. "When you have the fleece and you return home, wherever your home is, please remember me," she concluded tearfully.

"I'll do better than that—I'll take you with me," promised Jason. "Everyone will honor and respect you and treat you like a goddess!"

They parted soon after, and Medea went back to the palace troubled at the enormity of the treason she had committed. Aeetes handed over the dragon's teeth to Jason's messengers as Jason performed his prayers and sacrifices to Hecate.

Jason yokes the bulls and sows the dragon's teeth.

At last all was ready for the task. The bulls burst forth from their underground cave, snorting fire. The Argonauts shuddered, but Jason stood firm. The beasts engulfed the hero in a fireball, but Medea's magic ointment saved him. He seized the bulls one at a time and brought them under the yoke. Then he took the helmet full of dragon's teeth and moved across the field, scattering the "seeds" and using his spear to goad the bulls. Late in the afternoon, the plowing was finished, and Jason released the bulls. He had no sooner finished a drink of water than armed men sprang up all over the field. Remembering Medea's advice, Jason lifted up an enormous boulder and threw it into their midst. Mad for slaughter, the warriors sprang at each other, and fell like trees in a hurricane. Jason charged and killed the rest, and the furrows filled with blood. As the sun went down, Jason's task was accomplished.

Medea's treason is revealed and she flees, helping Jason retrieve the Golden Fleece, and getting his promise of marriage.

Aeetes spent the night plotting with his warriors how he could bring disaster on the heroes. By now he realized that nothing had happened without his daughter's knowledge. Medea fled, panic-stricken, to the riverbank where the heroes were celebrating. She knelt at Jason's feet, and cried, "Get me out of here! My father knows everything! Let's escape in the ship before he can harness his horses. I'll get you the Golden Fleece after I've put the dragon guarding it to sleep, but please don't forget your promises to me!"

Jason answered, "May Zeus and Hera, goddess of marriage, be my witnesses that you will be my wife as soon as our voyage is over and we're back in Greece!"

He took her by the hand, led her onto his ship, and followed her directions to the sacred grove where the fleece was. The dragon was aware of their approach and hissed horribly, scaring people for miles around. But Medea held it down as it writhed, all the time calling on Sleep to charm the creature and praying to Persephone for success. As the dragon relaxed its enormous coils, Medea dripped a sleeping charm into its eyes and at last it lay unconscious. Then Jason reached onto the oak tree and brought down the Golden Fleece.

Jason retrieves the Golden Fleece while Medea holds back the dragon with a sleeping charm.

The Argonauts set sail, pursued by Absyrtus, Medea's brother.

Dawn was breaking when they arrived back at the ship. The Argonauts were all eager to touch the fleece, but Jason commanded, "Set sail for home!" They cast off, but Aeetes and his soldiers, including Medea's brother, Absyrtus, pursued them.

Jason kills Absyrtus.

Their route home took them up the Ister River, now called the Danube. Finding that their way southward was blocked by the Colchians and by natives friendly to Absyrtus, Jason and Medea formed a desperate plan. Medea enticed Absyrtus to meet her at night in a temple of Artemis, alleging that the strangers had forced her to steal the fleece and go with them. What she really wanted, she said, was to form a plan with her brother to recapture the fleece and return home. When Absyrtus arrived, Jason sprang forth from a hiding place and killed him. Then he cut up his body and scattered the pieces on the sea, knowing that the Colchians would delay their pursuit to collect the remains for proper burial.

The speaking plank of the *Argo* then found its voice and warned, "You have angered Zeus. You will not escape a lengthy journey and numerous storms unless you seek purification from Circe for the ruthless murder of Absyrtus." Circe was Medea's aunt, another powerful witch. You will read about her encounter with Odysseus in Chapter 17.

Circe

Circe had a premonition that trouble lay ahead, for she had just had a nightmare in which the walls of her house ran with blood and her stores of magic herbs were on fire. But she greeted her guests as graciously as she could, surrounded by an entourage of grotesque beasts that wore one another's limbs. She guessed at once that Jason and Medea were suppliants guilty of murder; she performed the ritual cleansing but ordered Jason and Medea to leave. "I won't harm you. But, Medea, take your stranger and get out of my house. I won't approve of your plans or your flight from home!" Medea wept at this, and quivered in fear. The witch who had fearlessly faced a dragon had to be led out, with her husband holding her hand.

After seeking purification from Circe, Jason and Medea marry in Phaeacia.

They sailed past other dangers that were later to menace Odysseus, such as Scylla and Charybdis and the Sirens. The latter were bird-women with beautiful voices, whose singing lured sailors to crash on the rocks. Fortunately, the great musician Orpheus was able to sing well enough to drown out the Sirens' song, and the Argonauts sailed past them without damage. In the land of the Phaeacians, Jason and Medea were married. From here they were driven southward past the garden of the Hesperides, where they saw the dragon lately killed by Heracles.

Scylla crushing her human victims in the whirlpool

The Argonauts sail past the Sirens while Orpheus drowns out their charming singing.

Medea helps the Argonauts to slay Talus, a bronze giant, at Crete.

Their final adventure on the voyage involved a bronze giant named Talus who guarded the island of Crete. He kept strangers from landing by throwing rocks at their ships. His only vulnerable spot lay beneath one tendon of the ankle. Here was a vein of blood covered by a thin membrane. As the heroes prepared to back off from the island, Medea said, "I can master him, even if he is made of bronze. He was never intended to be immortal. Keep the ship out of reach of his rocks and wait." Then she wrapped herself in a dark cloak, called upon the Furies three times, and bewitched the bronze man. As he was heaving the boulders, he cut his ankle against a sharp point of rock, and the stream of life poured from him. He fell like a towering pine cut down by lumberjacks.

Death of Talus. Castor and Polydeuces are on horseback. Poseidon, crowned, and his spouse, Amphitrite, are to the right of Castor. Medea stands to the left.

Back in Iolcus, Jason hands over the Golden Fleece to Pelias.

At last they arrived back in Iolcus, where Jason handed over the fleece to Pelias. At this time, Jason's father, Aeson, was close to death from old age. Medea formed a clever plan to help him and at the same time take revenge upon Pelias. She created a rejuvenating bath by heating a huge cauldron into which she placed magic herbs. Jason brought out his father, and Medea ordered all to leave. She cut Aeson's throat to let out all his old blood, and he drank in her magic potion through his wounds and through his mouth. Instantly, his gray hair turned black again, his pallor disappeared, his withered limbs filled out, and his wrinkles vanished. Forty years fell away at once!

Medea restores youth to Jason's father, Aeson.

Medea with the daughters of Pelias prepares the cauldron.

Medea takes revenge upon Pelias on behalf of Jason.

Medea then went to Pelias' daughters and offered to do the same for their father. To overcome their skepticism, she commanded, "Bring me the oldest ram you have!" They did, and she cut it up and placed the pieces in the magic bath. Soon they heard a thin bleat from the cauldron, and a frisky lamb leaped out. The daughters stood amazed, and Medea urged, "So then, why do you hesitate? Draw your swords! Let his old blood out, so that I can fill his veins with new blood! Your father's life is in your hands. Do your duty if you love him and end his old age with your weapons!" They went to their father's bed and turning their heads away in fear, reluctantly did what Medea said.

Medea rejuvenates the ram.

Pelias tried to rise; he groaned, "What are you doing, daughters?" At last the deed was done, and they laid him in the cauldron. But Medea, who had placed useless herbs in there, was already gone. They wept in horror; the only daughter to escape guilt was Alcestis, the woman who would later offer to sacrifice her life for her husband's (see the eighth labor of Heracles). She had refused to participate in the scheme.

In exile at Corinth, Jason's infidelity with Glauce outrages Medea.

Jason and Medea went into exile in the city of Corinth for their role in Pelias' death. They lived there for several years, and Medea bore Jason two sons. Yet, Jason divorced Medea, intending to marry Glauce, the daughter of King Creon of Corinth. Outraged, Medea reminded him of how she had repeatedly saved his and his crew's lives, abandoning her own home and family in the process. "Where am I supposed to go now? Back home? To Pelias'daughters? How can you let your children be beggars in exile, along with the woman who saved your life?" Jason was not impressed, and retorted, "Aphrodite saved my life. Besides, I gave you as much as you gave me. I made you famous! Who would have heard of you if I hadn't brought you to Greece? As for the children, they will live with Glauce and me and I can give them everything. If you love us, why doesn't this make you happy?"

Medea secures refuge for herself, and a day's leave to take revenge on Jason.

Medea was not without resources, however. She arranged with King Aegeus of Athens to give her shelter. She persuaded Creon to allow her to stay in Corinth one more day, despite his misgivings. "What could I possibly do in one day?" she coaxed. "After all, I'm only a weak woman and you're a great and powerful king." Summoning Jason back to her, she pretended that she had changed her mind. "You were right and I was wrong to be angry at your new marriage. In fact, let our children deliver a wedding present from me to Glauce: a beautifully-woven dress and a gold crown. When she sees how cute and nice the boys are, she'll love them like a mother."

Medea's gift, a poisoned robe, kills Glauce.

"All right. I'm glad you've come to your senses," said Jason. The dress and the crown, however, were covered in the same sort of poison that had caused so much agony to Heracles. Glauce received them with pleasure and smiled fondly at the children, as Medea had hoped. She tried on the new clothes at once, admiring herself in the rich garments from every angle. Then suddenly her smile faded; she grew pale and staggered. The crown on her head burst into flame, and the dress was burning her flesh. She tried to shake the crown off, but it only blazed more fiercely. All fled in terror except her father, Creon, who was enveloped by the fire as he tried to douse it.

Medea murders the children born to Jason and herself.

Medea was still not finished exacting her revenge. She steeled herself to a hideous deed that would cause Jason the worst pain of all. Because Jason wanted to create a dynasty, she would deprive him of his only means to that end: his children! As the children returned from delivering the fatal gift, Medea said to herself, "For this one day, forget their sweet faces! Forget you're their mother! Do it!"

Jason returned just in time to see Medea standing in a chariot yoked to a team of dragons, the bodies of their children at her feet. "Medea, how could you? You've caused terrible pain for yourself as well as me!"

"At least you can't make light of my grief now!"

"Please, let me hold them one last time!"

Medea receives asylum in Athens; Jason dies without glory.

"No! I'll bury them myself in Hera's temple and then I will receive asylum from Aegeus in Athens. As for you, you'll die without glory, as is right—you'll be struck on the head by a rotting piece of your own ship!"

She flew off, leaving Jason a broken man. We will see in the next chapter how she fared in Athens. There is scarcely any information of her subsequent life and death otherwise.

Jason and Medea. The serpent-dragon guarding the Golden Fleece looms over Jason.

A. Review Exercises

MATCHING! Match the name in the left-hand column with the correct description from the right-hand column. Write the letter in the space provided. Keep in mind that there are more descriptions than names!

1. ____ Phineus
2. ____ Circe
3. ____ Pelias
4. ____ Hylas
5. ____ Glauce
6. ____ Talus
7. ____ Aeetes
8. ____ Hypsipyle
9. ____ Orpheus
10. ____ Symplegades

a. Jason's wicked uncle
b. Queen of Lemnos who loved Jason
c. Bronze giant with one vulnerable spot
d. Heracles' friend left behind on Cius
e. Famous musician who was an Argonaut
f. Blind prophet aided by Argonauts
g. Princess of Corinth courted by Jason
h. Medea's aunt
i. Clashing rocks
j. King of Corinth
k. Medea's father

B. Musings

1. The legend of Jason appeared on film in two notable versions: as a film in 1963 and as a television miniseries in 2000 (both titled *Jason and the Argonauts*). Both are available in DVD format. Compare and contrast the two versions with regard to the depiction of characters and episodes.

2. Robert Graves' 1945 novel *Hercules, My Shipmate* is an account of the voyage of Jason from a sailor's viewpoint. If you can locate a copy, read it and show what Graves retains from the ancient sources and what he adds or deletes. Pay particular attention to the author's view of the gods, and of the roles of men and women.

3. Imagine that you are a divorce lawyer for either Jason or Medea. How would you convince a judge that your client is the best choice for custody of the children?

4. An antihero is a main character who is obviously lacking in heroic qualities. Jason has sometimes been considered an antihero. Do you agree? Why or why not?

5. "Hell hath no fury like a woman scorned." This well-known proverb adapted from the English playwright William Congreve is frequently used as a description of the tragedy of Medea, who was abandoned by Jason when he took a new lover, Glauce. Several great playwrights, beginning with the Greek tragedian Euripides, of fifth-century BCE Athens, explored this powerful tale of love, betrayal, and vengeance in the theater. Other dramatists who wrote about Medea were the first-century CE Roman Seneca and Pierre Corneille, a seventeenth-century French writer. In the twentieth century, the Frenchman Jean Anouilh wrote the play *Medea* (1946), and the Italian Pier Paolo Pasolini wrote and directed the film *Medea* (1969). Research both the playwright and the filmmaker and, if it is possible for you to read the play and watch the film, compare their interpretations.

   Do you empathize with Medea? Is her extreme anger justified? Who is (are) the guilty party(-ies)? Who bears primary responsibility for the sad events?

C. Words, Words, Words

The Daily Muse

News you can use

Several English words, both familiar and unfamiliar, come from the same word the Argonauts used for their name. For example:

- The "Argonaut" was a sailor on the *Argo* (*nautes* is the Greek word for "sailor"). Many years later, the early NASA space program coined the word **astronaut**, or "star sailor." In the Soviet or Russian space program, the equivalent is a **cosmonaut** (*cosmos* is the Greek word for "universe" or "order").
- A **nautilus** is a type of shellfish that was believed to have a membrane that served as a sail.

A nautilus

- Anything relating to ships or sailing is **nautical**.
- The all-too-familiar experience of **nausea** originally referred to seasickness but came to refer to the same feeling from other causes as well.

D. How 'Bout That?

1. The constellation of Aries (the Ram) has been identified with the ram that carried Phrixus and Helle and whose skin later became the Golden Fleece. To find this constellation in the night sky, go to this website for instructions for viewing this constellation in the night sky and a diagram: http://www.constellation-guide.com/constellation-list/aries-constellation/.

2. The large constellation Argo (Navis) is made up of four smaller constellations: Vela (the Sail), Carina (the Keel), Puppis (the Stern) and Pyxis (the Compass).

   During the second century CE, the Greek astronomer Ptolemy identified and named forty-eight separate constellations, one of which was a huge constellation, visible only in the southern hemisphere, that he called "Argo Navis," that is, "the Ship, Argo." In the sixteenth and seventeenth centuries, astronomers studying the night sky identified some forty additional constellations. An eighteenth century scholar, Nicolas Lacaille, in 1763, thought it made more sense to divide the too-large Argo Navis into four separate constellations. Astronomers now recognize eighty-eight official constellations. For a list of these constellations, visit this site: http://www.iau.org/public/constellations/.

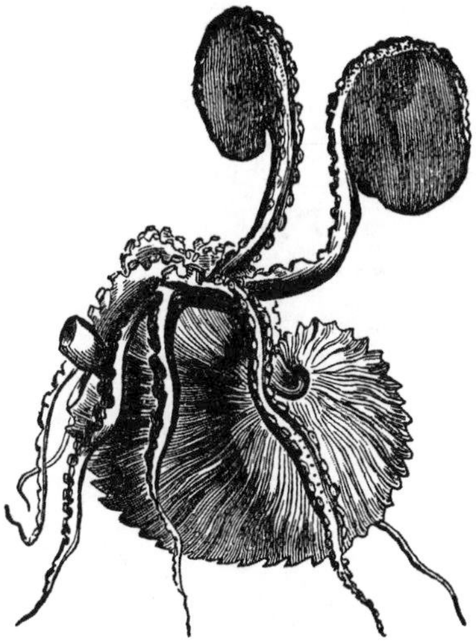

An argonaut (paper nautilus)

3. A relative of the octopus, sometimes called the paper nautilus because its shell is as thin as paper, is also known as an argonaut (from the genus Argonauta). The largest species is named *Argonauta argo.* Compare the paper nautilus with the nautilus (sometimes called a chambered nautilus) described above in C.

4. Nautilus is also the name of a line of beds. Do you think this is a good or bad choice of name for such a product? Why?

5. The scientific nomenclature for the snake pictured at the right is *Pelias berus* of the genus *Vipera.* It is the common European adder. Why might *Pelias* be a suitable name for this creature?

E. Who's Who?

- For Jason's family, see Genealogical Chart 13.

Chapter Eleven
THESEUS

General Sources:
Bacchylides *Odes*
Catullus *Carmina* 64.50–264
Ovid *Metamorphoses* 8.6–173
Plutarch *Life of Theseus*

Theseus' mother, Aethra, caresses her son's face.

Theseus was the most renowned of the Athenian heroes, although he was born in Troezen, some distance from Athens. His father, Aegeus, had stopped there on a journey from Delphi to Athens, and fell in love with a young woman named Aethra. (See GENEALOGICAL CHART 14.)

Before he continued on to Delphi, he left a sword and a pair of shoes under a huge boulder. Suspecting that she was pregnant, he instructed Aethra, "If you have a boy, when he grows up and is able to move the stone aside and remove the things I put there, send him to me in Athens. But tell him to keep his journey a secret as much as possible."

Aethra gives birth to Theseus in Troezen.

When Aethra gave birth, she named her son Theseus, which some believe came from the Greek word for "place," because of the tokens Aegeus had placed under the boulder. Theseus' grandfather spread the story that Theseus' true father was Poseidon, because the people of Troezen honored that god above all.

Theseus sets out toward his father in Athens.

Theseus grew up to be quick, strong, and intelligent. When his mother led him to the stone and told him about Aegeus, he moved the obstacle without difficulty. His mother and grandfather urged him to journey to Athens by sea, because the overland route was beset by robbers and murderers. But Theseus had heard about the noble deeds of Heracles, and wanted to prove his noble birth by similar feats. So he set out with a plan: he would do injury to nobody, but he would repel and take revenge upon any who attacked him.

Aegeus gives Aethra his sword.

Shortly afterwards, he slew a bandit named Periphetes, sometimes called Corynetes or "Club-bearer." Theseus took the bandit's club and made it his trademark, as Heracles had used the Nemean Lion's skin.

Passing further along the Isthmus of the Peloponnese, he slew Sinis, the Bender of Pines. Sinis would tie passersby to a pine tree he had bent over, and laugh as they flew to their deaths when he released the tree. Theseus overcame him and killed him using his own method.

Theseus kills Sinis.

Theseus believed that a hero should also fight dangerous, wild animals. He went out of his way to encounter and kill the savage Crommyonian sow, named Phaea after the woman who bred her. Some claim that she was not an animal at all but a vicious female robber, who was dubbed "Sow" because of her dirty ways.

Another dangerous man was Sciron, who stood at the edge of a cliff. He not only robbed travelers but out of sheer insolence would stretch out his feet and command his victims to wash them. When they did this, he would kick them over the cliff. At the bottom, his enormous pet turtle would devour them. Theseus killed this man in the same way Sciron had killed others.

Theseus slays Sinis, Phaea, Sciron, and Procrustes.

Going further on, Theseus killed Procrustes, who owned a bed that he forced travelers to lie on. If they were too short for the bed, he stretched them out so that they died from the injury; if they were too tall, he would lop off the protruding parts. (Some have also alleged that he had two beds, one large and one small, to ensure that no one would ever fit exactly.)

Theseus reveals his identity to Aegeus.

When he arrived in Athens, Theseus went to the palace as a stranger; he decided not to reveal himself to Aegeus just yet, but let his father find him out. At this time, Medea was living with Aegeus. In exchange for protection from Jason, she had promised Aegeus that she would make him capable of begetting children. She feared that Theseus would somehow damage her plans, and persuaded Aegeus to kill the stranger with poison at that night's banquet. When the meat was on the table, Theseus drew his sword as if he were going to carve with it. Aegeus recognized the sword at once and overturned the cup of poison. The next day, he presented his son to the citizens of Athens, who had heard tales of his deeds and received him gladly.

Theseus kills the Cretan bull and honors Hecale.

Longing for more action, Theseus left Athens shortly afterwards to fight with the bull that Heracles had previously brought from Crete (see chapter 9). On his way, a poor old woman named Hecale gave him hospitality. When he returned to her house after capturing the bull, he found she had died. He therefore declared special honors to commemorate her. (You will read other stories of humble people rewarded for unknowingly offering hospitality to the powerful.) As for the bull, Theseus paraded it alive in triumph through the city, and later sacrificed it to Apollo.

The sacrifice of fourteen Athenian youths to the Minotaur

Soon afterwards, the Athenians had to pay their third tribute to Crete. This duty had been imposed upon Athens more than twenty-five years before, when the son of King Minos of Crete, named Androgeus, had been treacherously murdered in Athens. The gods had sent pestilence and famine upon the land until the Athenians appeased Minos. Minos demanded that they send him seven young men and seven young women every nine years. These fourteen youths were then sent into the Labyrinth, the huge maze that Daedalus had constructed, and killed by the Minotaur. This was a half-human, half-bull offspring of Minos' wife, Pasiphae, and the Cretan Bull, which Heracles had fought. (See GENEALOGICAL CHART 15.) The penalty would be cancelled, however, if the Minotaur were ever killed. On the two previous occasions, the Athenians had sent their youth in a ship with black sails, convinced that they were going to certain destruction.

Theseus vows to kill the Minotaur.

This time, however, Theseus volunteered to go on the journey, confident that he could master the Minotaur. Aegeus gave the ship's pilot another sail, a white one, ordering him that if he returned with Theseus alive, to hoist the white sail, but otherwise to sail with the black one. Theseus also received this advice from the Delphic oracle before he set out: "Make Aphrodite your guide!"

Pasiphae and the Cretan Bull

One version of this tale, narrated by the Greek poet Bacchylides, has Minos himself going to Athens to supervise the selection of the fourteen young Athenians and returning with them in the black-sailed ship. On the voyage back to Crete, he began to molest one of the young Athenian women.

Theseus intervened, saying, "Minos, this is wrong! Stop it! It's true you are the son of a god, but so am I! Restrain yourself, or have the gods decide which of the two of us is right!"

Minos was angry, and he cried out, "Father Zeus, if I am truly your son, send forth a lightning bolt as a sign!" At that moment, an affirming bolt of lightning lit up the sky. Then Minos turned to Theseus and sneered, "You claim that Poseidon is your father. If so, you should be able to bring back this ring from the depths of the ocean!" He then threw a ring into the sea. Not intimidated, Theseus leaped overboard. At once, dolphins appeared to escort the hero to the sea-god's palace. Poseidon and Amphitrite received him and gave him a purple cloak and a garland of roses, as well as the ring. All were astonished as Theseus reboarded the ship, not even wet!

Poseidon and Amphitrite in their sea chariot. Triton, on the left, blows a conch shell, and, on the right, a Nereid rides a sea monster.

Ariadne helps Theseus kill the Minotaur.

When they reached Crete, Theseus and the others were herded towards the dark tunnels of the Labyrinth. But just before Theseus entered, Ariadne, the daughter of Minos and Pasiphae, slipped him a ball of yarn. "Tie one end of this to the entrance and unwind it as you go, so you can find your way out again!" she instructed. She had fallen in love with Theseus, as Medea had fallen in love with Jason.

Theseus slays the Minotaur.

Theseus did as she advised. As he reached the center of the maze, he found the Minotaur asleep and fell upon the monster with his bare hands. He crushed the life out of the creature, like an oak tree falling and crushing all beneath it. As the Minotaur gave his head a final toss, Theseus dashed out of the maze along with the other thirteen Athenians. After boring holes in the ships of the Cretans' navy to keep them from pursuing, the Athenians set sail for home, taking Ariadne with them.

Theseus abandons Ariadne at Naxos.

On the way home, Theseus deserted Ariadne on the island of Naxos. There are different versions as to why he did this. Some relate that he had not abandoned her intentionally, but had set her on shore to let her recover from seasickness, and a violent wind had carried him unexpectedly back out to sea. Another story is that the god Dionysus had fallen in love with Ariadne himself, and commanded Theseus in a dream to leave her for him.

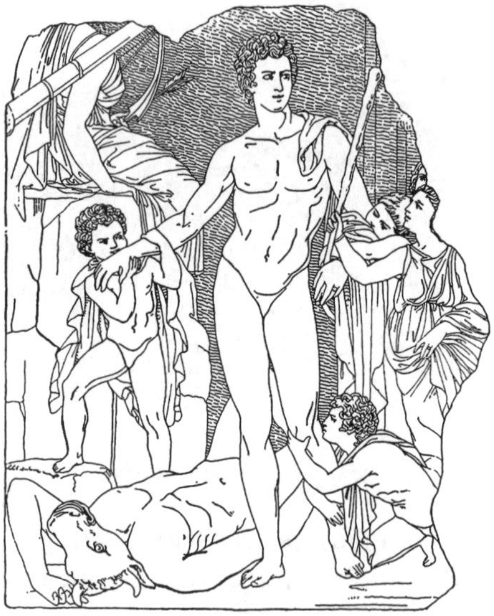

Theseus receives thanks for killing the Minotaur. Representation of Pompeiian wall painting.

Ariadne, abandoned at Naxos with only Eros as a companion, watches Theseus sail away.

The Roman poets Catullus and Ovid both wrote poems from Ariadne's point of view, as she awoke on a strange island to see her lover's boat just a receding dot on the horizon. Ariadne cries out to Theseus in this portion of Catullus' poem:

You cannot deny that you were tossing
in the middle of the whirlpool of death
when I saved you, and I decided to lose
my brother rather than to fail you in
your hour of crisis, you cheat.
As thanks for all this I shall be given
over to the wild beasts to be torn apart, as carrion to the birds,
nor will I have a mound heaped over me
with earth thrown upon me when I am dead.
What lioness gave birth to you under a lonely rock?
What sea conceived you and vomited
you out of its foaming waters?

Catullus *Carmina* 64.149–55, trans. John Godwin

Ariadne, center right, and Dionysus (Bacchus), center left, with priests, satyrs, and maenads

Dionysus marries Ariadne.

Shortly afterwards, however, Dionysus arrived with his retinue of maenads and satyrs, all beating drums and crashing cymbals, followed by the god himself on a chariot with golden reins, drawn by tigers. Ariadne was too afraid even to run, but the god said to her, "Don't be afraid! I will be more faithful than Theseus! I can give you the heavens!" Dionysus leaped down from the chariot and took her in his arms, and his followers sang a wedding song.

After his departure from Naxos, Theseus went to Delos and created a dance that became traditional there. The Greeks called it the Crane Dance; its movements were believed to imitate the windings of the Labyrinth. Some claim he also originated games in Delos, the first to award a palm as a prize to the victors.

Theseus forgets to change sails; Aegeus throws himself into the sea.

Unfortunately, Theseus was so caught up in the celebrations that he forgot to change the sails from black to white. Aegeus saw the black sails approaching and in despair threw himself off a rock into the sea that was thereafter called the Aegean Sea.

Theseus founds the Isthmian games and shelters Oedipus.

As king, Theseus was responsible for many reforms. He set up a centralized government and annexed the surrounding *demes* or towns. He is credited with writing a constitution for Athens and with organizing the people into three classes (nobles, farmers, and craftsmen). He also is said to have founded the Isthmian Games, ancient athletic contests much like the Olympian Games (which Theseus' role model Heracles founded). Athens became a place where outcasts could find refuge. Theseus comforted Heracles and brought him to Athens when Heracles was suffering remorse from killing his family. He also sheltered the aged and disgraced Oedipus, whose story you will read in chapter 14.

Theseus marries the Amazon Hippolyta and fathers Hippolytus.

Theseus also joined Heracles in his expedition to the Amazons. On this journey he seized an Amazon as a bride (her name is given as either Antiope or Hippolyta), and she bore him a son named Hippolytus. The Amazons attacked Athens in revenge, and Theseus' wife was killed in the battle. The defeat of the Amazons by the Athenians often turns up in Greek art to illustrate the triumph of civilization over barbarism.

Lapith and centaur. Representation of a metope from the Parthenon, Athens.

The battle of the Lapiths and the centaurs

Another "civilization vs. barbarism" battle that is common in Greek art concerns the battle of the Lapiths with the centaurs. The Lapiths were the people of Peirithous, a king of Thessaly in northern Greece. Theseus and Peirithous were originally enemies, when Peirithous led a cattle raid on Attica (the territory around Athens). But they later became close friends and had several adventures together. When Theseus was a guest at Peirithous' wedding, some of his friend's more unruly relatives, the centaurs, became drunk and tried to carry off the bride and other women present. The centaurs were swiftly routed by the Lapiths and the Athenians.

Theseus kidnaps Helen and accompanies Heracles to the Underworld.

A less successful adventure began when Theseus and Peirithous decided they both wanted daughters of Zeus as brides. Theseus chose Helen (who later gained fame as Helen of Troy). The two kidnapped her and sheltered her in Attica with Theseus' mother, Aethra. Peirithous' prospective bride proved more of a challenge; she was Persephone, the queen of the Underworld. Hades invited his two "guests" to sit in chairs, which they did. Unfortunately, the chairs contained invisible bonds that held the sitters immovable. Theseus was not released until Heracles came on his journey to the Underworld. Heracles pulled Theseus off the chair, but he was stuck so firmly that half of his posterior remained behind. Peirithous never did obtain release, and the Roman poet Horace mentions his sad fate to show that even the greatest heroes cannot always save their friends from death.

Peirithous in the Underworld, harassed by one of the Erinyes

Theseus marries Phaedra, Ariadne's sister.

Theseus' last wife was Phaedra, the younger sister of Ariadne. She was a devoted and faithful wife until she met her downfall because her stepson Hippolytus refused to worship Aphrodite. Hippolytus preferred to hunt in the woods in the company of the chaste Artemis. In retaliation, Aphrodite caused Phaedra to fall in love with Hippolytus. The modest wife was horrified at the passion she felt, and decided to die by starving herself to death, telling no one what was troubling her. At last, though, Phaedra's nurse pulled the truth out of her. Although shocked at first, the old woman advised her mistress to make her feelings known to Hippolytus. "Zeus himself yielded to the power of Aphrodite! Are you trying to be superior to the gods?" she argued. "Let me use a love charm I know about to heal your pain!"

Phaedra falls in love with Hippolytus, who rejects her.

Despite her misgivings, Phaedra allowed the nurse to have her way. Without Phaedra's knowledge, the nurse told Hippolytus about his stepmother's desire for him. Hippolytus not only rejected Phaedra but launched into a brutal tirade on the evils of women: "Zeus, why couldn't you just have us bring gold to your temples and buy our children, so we wouldn't need women? Women are nothing but trouble—the smarter they are, the more they scheme! Their own fathers pay dowries to be rid of them! As for you, old woman, only my piety keeps me from killing you! I want to wash out my ears to clean away your filthy words!"

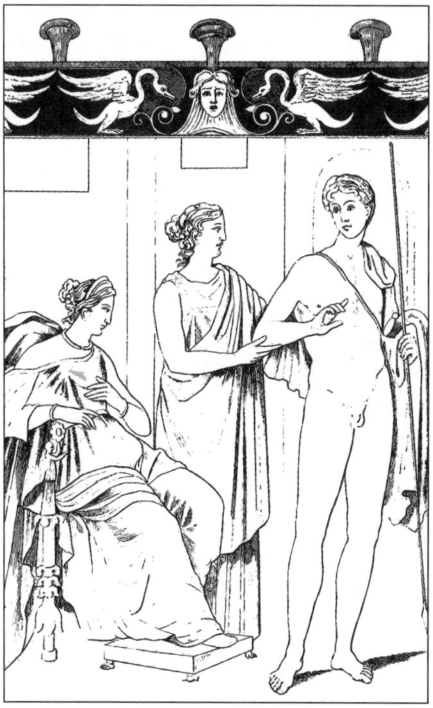

Phaedra, seated left, and Hippolytus. Phaedra's nurse is at center.

Determined to avenge her shame, Phaedra hanged herself, but left a note saying that Hippolytus had violated her. When Theseus returned home and found his dead wife and the note, he did not even wait to hear Hippolytus' side of the story. He commanded his son to leave the city at once. As the young man departed, Theseus called upon Poseidon: "You promised once to grant me three wishes. Here is one: May Hippolytus not live out this day!"

Hippolytus is driven into the sea.

The sea-god heard Theseus' prayer. As Hippolytus rode in his chariot along the seashore, waves as high as mountains arose. Suddenly a bull emerged from them and charged towards Hippolytus' chariot. The panicked horses ran wild and crashed the chariot on the rocks, dragging the driver until he was near death. As the dying Hippolytus was carried back to Athens, Artemis appeared to Theseus. "Your son was innocent, Theseus. Don't let him die disgraced because of what Aphrodite did." She told him the whole story. Hippolytus lived just long enough to forgive his father and die in his arms.

The death of Hippolytus and the end of Theseus

Theseus' life ended without glory. He was driven out of Athens by a coup, and he went into exile on the island of Scyrus. A local king named Lycomedes pretended to offer him hospitality but treacherously shoved him off a cliff. (You will meet Lycomedes of Scyrus again in chapter 17.) In historical times, however, Theseus was restored to honor. During the Persian Wars (492–449 BCE) Cimon, the leader of the Athenians, was told by the Delphic oracle to bring the bones of Theseus back to Athens. On Scyrus, he saw an eagle clawing at the ground. He dug there and found the bones of a large man buried with a spearhead and sword. He loaded these onto his ship and brought them to Athens. In the same war at the Battle of Marathon in 490 BCE, soldiers claimed to have seen the ancient hero fighting beside them, waving his powerful club.

A. Review Exercises

1. **MATCHING!** Match the name in the left-hand column with the correct description from the right-hand column. Write the letter in the space provided.

1.	____	Pasiphae	a.	The "pine bender"
2.	____	Hippolytus	b.	Theseus' friend and companion
3.	____	Sinis	c.	Princess who gave ball of yarn to Theseus
4.	____	Minos	d.	Old woman who offered Theseus hospitality
5.	____	Phaedra	e.	Mother of the Minotaur
6.	____	Sciron	f.	Amazon lover of Theseus
7.	____	Aethra	g.	The one who made people lie down on a bed and either stretched or cut them
8.	____	Peirithous	h.	Son of Theseus and an Amazon
9.	____	Hecale	i.	King of Crete
10.	____	Antiope	j.	The one who forced travelers to wash his feet, then kicked them over a cliff
11.	____	Ariadne	k.	Theseus' mother
12.	____	Procrustes	l.	One who fell in love with her stepson

2. **MULTIPLE CHOICE!** For each sentence below, circle the number of the answer that best answers the question or completes the statement.

a. Aegeus handed over to Aethra these items that she was to pass on to their unborn child as symbols of his royal blood.

1. Sandals
2. Swords
3. A sword and shoes
4. A sword and a lion's skin

b. Where did Aegeus place these items?

1. In the labyrinth
2. In a cave
3. Under a rock
4. In a box under his palace

c. Where is Theseus' birthplace, Troezen, located?

1. In the Peloponnesus
2. Between Athens and Delphi
3. In Asia Minor
4. On the island of Delos

d. To whom did Theseus' maternal grandfather in Troezen attribute the paternity of his son?

1. Heracles
2. Aegeus
3. Poseidon
4. Zeus

e. This hero was Theseus' inspiration as he set out on the road from Troezen to Athens.

1. Jason
2. Perseus
3. Heracles
4. Bellerophon

f. What was Theseus' "trademark," the item he always carried with him, taken from Periphetes after he conquered him?

1. A sword
2. A lion's skin
3. A traveler's hat
4. A club

g. Aegeus instructed his son, Theseus, to carry out this action if he successfully defeated the monstrous Minotaur.

1. Change the color of his sails
2. Change the color of his ship
3. Change the color of his clothing
4. Change the color of his hair

h. Who were the parents of the Minotaur?

1. King Minos and Pasiphae
2. King Minos and Ariadne
3. Pasiphae and the Cretan bull
4. King Minos and Antiope

i. Which of these characters whom Theseus encountered was the son of Zeus?

1. Sinis
2. Sciron
3. Procrustes
4. Minos

j. If you were tired from traveling and looking for a motel in ancient Greece, whose inn would you be most likely to avoid because of the uncomfortable bed?

1. Aegeus
2. Sinis
3. Procrustes
4. Minos

k. Which of the following statements applies to both Ariadne and Medea?

1. Each endangered her own life to help a hero.
2. Each fell in love with a hero.
3. Each was abandoned by the hero.
4. All of the above

l. After being left on the island of Naxos, what did Ariadne do?

1. She killed herself.
2. She became a shepherdess.
3. She was discovered by Dionysus.
4. She fell asleep forever.

Ariadne sleeping

m. How many Athenian maidens and youths were sent as tribute to the Minotaur in Crete?

1. Ten of each
2. Seven of each
3. Fourteen of each
4. Three of each

n. Heracles is said to have founded the Olympic Games. Which games is Theseus said to have founded?

1. Delphic
2. Corinthian
3. Isthmian
4. Nemean

o. Theseus' third wife, Phaedra, was whose sister?

1. Antiope
2. Pasiphae
3. Ariadne
4. Aethra

p. Which of Theseus' wives fell helplessly in love with Theseus' son, Hippolytus?

1. Ariadne
2. Hippolyta
3. Antiope
4. Phaedra

q. Theseus kidnapped this daughter of Zeus before she married Menelaus or went to Troy.

1. Clytemnestra
2. Athena
3. Helen
4. Artemis

r. This body of water was named for a relative of Theseus.

1. The Gulf of Corinth
2. The Cretan Sea
3. The Aegean Sea
4. The Mediterranean Sea

s. This person freed Theseus from a sticky seat in Hades, but was unable to save Theseus' pal, Peirithous.

1. Persephone
2. Helen
3. Heracles
4. Ariadne

t. Which of these goddesses, feeling rejected by him, punished Hippolytus?

1. Hera
2. Aphrodite
3. Artemis
4. Athena

B. MUSINGS

1. The story of Theseus and the Minotaur has been turned into a fabulous 25-minute-long musical, *Theseus and the Minotaur*, by Audrey Snyder and Kathleen Black. Why not get your class involved in performing this delightful, humorous retelling of the myth? Go to this website for more information or to obtain a copy of the score and a CD: http://www.jwpepper.com/3297088.item#.VPuAYPnF-So

2. As with the legend of Perseus and Medusa, the monster in the Theseus legend, the Minotaur, has captured the imagination almost more than the hero. Cutting-edge artists of the early twentieth century titled a journal of their ideas *Minotaure*. Pablo Picasso is one of several artists who were inspired by the Minotaur in their work. Why do you think the Minotaur and his story were so significant for these artists?

3. In some contemporary adaptations of the Theseus myth, the Minotaur is not a monster at all but a child whose family is ashamed of him for various reasons. Howard Richardson's 1965 play *The Laundry* (adapted from a French play) and Carol Dawson's 1997 novel *Meeting the Minotaur* are such adaptations of the Theseus legend. If you were writing the story of Theseus today, what might the Minotaur be like?

4. The story of Ariadne abandoned by Theseus at Naxos has inspired artists and musicians from ancient times up to contemporary times. In the opera *Ariadne auf Naxos* by Richard Strauss (1912), the composer treats the subject in the manner of *commedia dell'arte*, introducing comic aspects into the serious lament of Ariadne after Theseus leaves her behind. The role of Ariadne requires a strong and talented soprano voice. Obtain a CD of this opera from your local library and listen to the beautiful arias and duets that Ariadne sings in this most interesting opera.

5. The novelist Mary Renault wrote two novels told by Theseus in the first person, *The King Must Die* (1958) and *The Bull from the Sea* (1962). Read one or both of these novels, and discuss how Theseus presents himself. Is his self-portait similar to the impressions you received of him when you read this chapter? Why or why not?

6. In 1878 a Cretan citizen, Minos Kalokairinos, began excavation of the remains of a large, complex set of structures at Cnossus, Crete. Sir Arthur Evans, a famous British archaeologist, continued the excavation and exploration of this site from 1900 to 1931. Evans called the period in which the so-called palace was built the Minoan period after the legendary King Minos. The British School of Archeology has continued Evans' work at Cnossus down to the present day. Research to learn more about this fabulous complex of architecture, art, and artifacts, and share with your classmates. In what way does this palace appear to be "labyrinthine"?

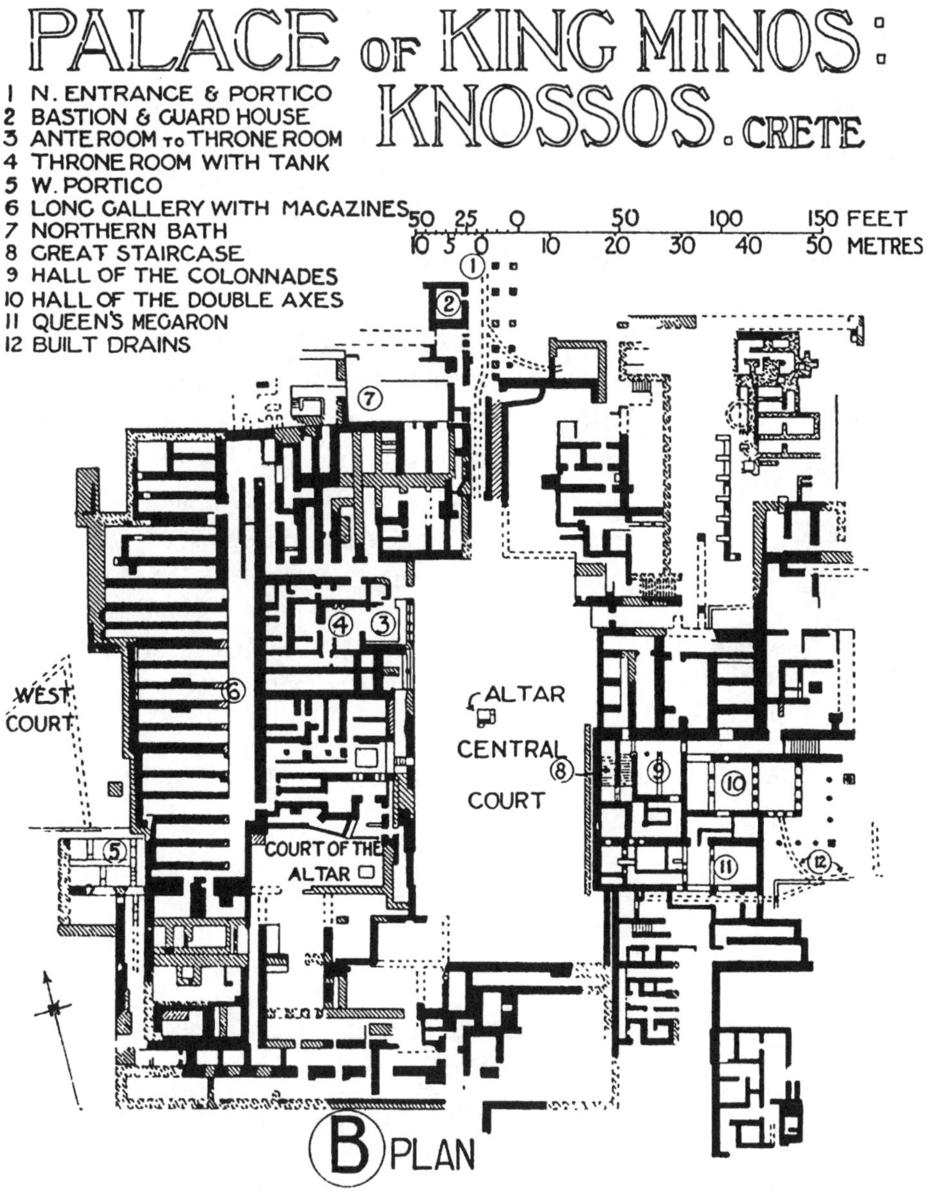

Ground plan of the palace at Cnossus, Crete

7. Theseus intended that the city of Athens serve as a refuge and sanctuary for exiles like Oedipus and others who sought his hospitality. As mentioned in the story, Theseus extended warm hospitality to exiles who could not return to their homes. The poem given below by Emma Lazarus is intended as a statement of gracious welcome to immigrants and refugees arriving in America. The words of this poem are engraved on the base of the Statue of Liberty:

The New Colossus

Not like the brazen giant of Greek fame,
With conquering limbs astride from land to land;
Here at our sea-washed, sunset gates shall stand
A mighty woman with a torch, whose flame
Is the imprisoned lightning, and her name
Mother of Exiles. From her beacon-hand
Glows world-wide welcome; her mild eyes command
The air-bridged harbor that twin cities frame.
"Keep, ancient lands, your storied pomp!" cries she
With silent lips. "Give me your tired, your poor,
Your huddled masses yearning to breathe free,
The wretched refuse of your teeming shore.
Send these, the homeless, tempest-tost to me,
I lift my lamp beside the golden door!"

Jewish Women's Archive,
"JWA - Emma Lazarus - The New Colossus,"
http://www.libertystatepark.com/emma.htm

a. Write an advertising slogan or short poem that Theseus could use to proclaim this idea of hospitality and refuge in the city of Athens.

b. Who is the "brazen giant of Greek fame" referred to in the first line above? Where was this statue located? Why was it one of the Seven Ancient Wonders of the World? (Hint: The statue portrays the sun-god whose son was Phaethon. It was found at the entrance to a harbor of one of the Greek islands.)

C. WORDS, WORDS, WORDS

The Daily Muse

News you can use

1. The **labyrinth** of the Theseus myth has come to mean any maze, or anything intricate and confusing, as you learned when studying Daedalus (in chapter 7), who built the labyrinth for King Minos. The adjectives **labyrinthian** and **labyrinthine** both describe anything that is complex, intricate, or winding. Pretend you are writing the title of a new mystery novel. Use any one of these three words given above to form a title that will attract readers to this novel. Write the title on the line given below:

____

Ground plan of the Labyrinth at the residence of King Henry VIII

2. A system that enforces uniformity or conformity without regard for individuality is called **procrustean** (from the robber **Procrustes**). The phrase **"procrustean bed"** is used to describe a situation in which an individual or a group of people is forced to conform to a standard determined by another's whim. Another way of thinking of this is: "One size fits all." Can you think of a time or a place in which a certain person or a group of persons has been forced to lie in a **procrustean bed**?

____

____

D. How 'Bout That?

- The labyrinth is also part of the inner ear. Look at the diagram below. How does this structure resemble a labyrinth? How did it get this name?

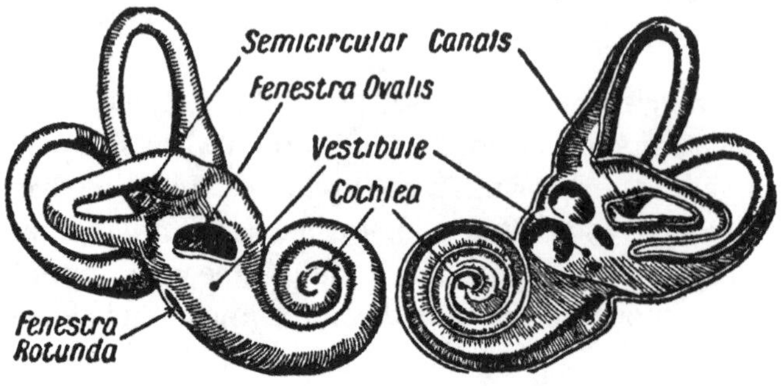

- Are there any other human body parts that have names based on Greek myths? Here's a start: The first vertebra at the top of the human spine is called the "atlas vertebra." Why is this an appropriate name?

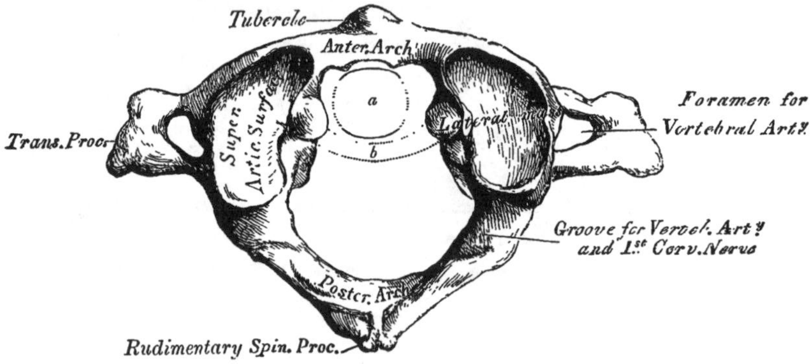

Diagram of the atlas, the first cervical vertebra in the human spine

- Did you know that there are computer programs that allow you to design your own mazes? Can you locate one of these programs and design your own labyrinth or maze? Did you know that there is a technical difference between mazes and labyrinths? Can you learn about this difference?

- Did you know that Ariadne is forever honored among the constellations in the heavens? While Theseus was in the ocean deep retrieving the ring Minos tossed into the sea as a test, the Nereid Thetis gave him an exquisite crown fashioned by the master smith, the god Hephaestus himself. He gave the crown to Ariadne, but it is not clear whether or not she wore it when she married Theseus. She did, however, wear the crown when she later married Dionysus. Dionysus was said to have been so grief-stricken upon her death that he took the crown and placed it among the stars in the sky. It is **corona borealis,** the "Northern Crown." Seven stars make up the **corona** or Crown. The brightest of the seven is called Gemma, meaning "Gem" or "Jewel," and is a magnitude 2.2 star, seventy-five light years away. To learn more about this constellation and how to view it in the night sky, visit this website: http://www.constellation-guide.com/constellation-list/corona-borealis-constellation/

- The Minotaur has lent his name to an astonishing variety of companies and services, some predictable, some less so. They include the following:
    - A publisher that specializes in mystery books
    - A character in the universe of Marvel Comics
    - A "pop culture megastore"
    - A rocket
    - A computer language
    - A series of puzzles
    - A men's fragrance

The Minotaur on a Cretan coin

- If you observe closely both the interior and exterior architecture of many buildings in the classical or neoclassical style, you might see a decorative finish in the crown molding of a ceiling or just under a roof that looks like one of these:

These are known as "Greek key" designs or frets. They are supposed to have been derived from the pattern made by the string laid down by Ariadne as she helped Theseus escape from the Labyrinth.

E. WHO'S WHO?

- For Theseus' family, see GENEALOGICAL CHART 14.

- For Europa's Minoan descendants, see GENEALOGICAL CHART 15.

Chapter Twelve

VICTIMS OF OLYMPIAN WRATH

General Sources:
Ovid *Metamorphoses*

Zeus sends forth a storm that floods all earth.

Prometheus

Literary Sources: Hesiod *Theogony* 507–616, *Works and Days* 47–105; Aeschylus *Prometheus Bound*; Catullus *Carmina* 64; Ovid *Metamorphoses* 1.7–415

Prometheus helps Deucalion and Pyrrha survive the Great Flood.

Zeus did not always show particular concern for mortals. On one occasion, he became disgusted with human wickedness and decided to drown the entire earth in a flood. Only two people escaped, Deucalion and his wife Pyrrha. They survived by building a boat. The instructions for building this boat came from a Titan who had a soft spot for humanity, the Titan Prometheus, whose name means "forethought." According to Ovid, he was the creator of the human race.

When Zeus overthrew Cronus, he assigned the gods their privileges and apportioned power to them, but made no provision for humans. Prometheus took pity on the helpless beings and gave them many gifts. He showed them how to cure illnesses with remedies from nature, and he taught them divination—how to interpret dreams and omens from the flight of birds and the entrails of animals.

Prometheus tricks Zeus to favor humans.

Prometheus also managed to trick Zeus into giving humans the best parts of slaughtered animals. He cut up a great ox and wrapped the meaty parts in the ox's stomach, so that they looked unappetizing. At the same time, he hid the bones inside a layer of fat, making them look like a prime cut. "Go ahead, Zeus, choose whichever of these you prefer!" he coaxed.

"Oh, Prometheus, you haven't divided them fairly!" exclaimed the king of the gods. He took up the portion covered in fat, and was outraged when he saw nothing but bones within. Hesiod says he had seen through the trick and made the wrong choice on purpose, to use it as an excuse to plan evils for mortals. Nevertheless, ever since then, the Greeks sacrificed the bones of animals to the gods and kept the meaty parts for themselves.

Prometheus steals fire for humankind.

"Let the humans keep their meat!" Zeus thought angrily. "I'll make sure they have no way to cook it!" He withheld fire from mortals, but Prometheus outwitted him again. He stole the fire by hiding it in a hollow stalk. When Zeus saw the fires blazing among people, he said to Prometheus, "As the price of fire, I will give men an evil that they will embrace with pleasure!"

Pandora opens the box in the presence of Epimetheus.

Zeus punishes humans with an attractive gift: a woman.

He had Hephaestus take earth and mold it into the likeness of a woman as beautiful as a goddess. Athena taught her handicrafts, and Aphrodite made her desirable and seductive. Hermes, on Zeus' orders, gave her a treacherous nature. He also gave her power to speak, and gave her a name: Pandora, or "all gifts," in tribute to what the gods had given her. She was also given a box (or a jar), which ostensibly contained bridal gifts. Zeus knew Prometheus was too clever to accept her, so he had Hermes take her to the Titan's brother, Epimetheus, whose name means "afterthought." Epimetheus forgot his brother's warning never to accept any gift from Zeus, and took her in.

Within Pandora's box lay all the troubles of the world: sickness, toil, misfortune, old age, quarrels, and many others. She lifted the lid and scattered them over the earth. The only spirit that remained within was Hope, which by order of Zeus was not allowed to emerge.

As for Prometheus, Zeus had a terrible punishment in mind. He had the Titan taken to the edge of the known world, a crag in the Caucasus Mountains, and chained up by a reluctant Hephaestus. Every day an eagle came down and ate pieces of Prometheus' liver, which regenerated during the night and healed in time for the eagle to torture him anew.

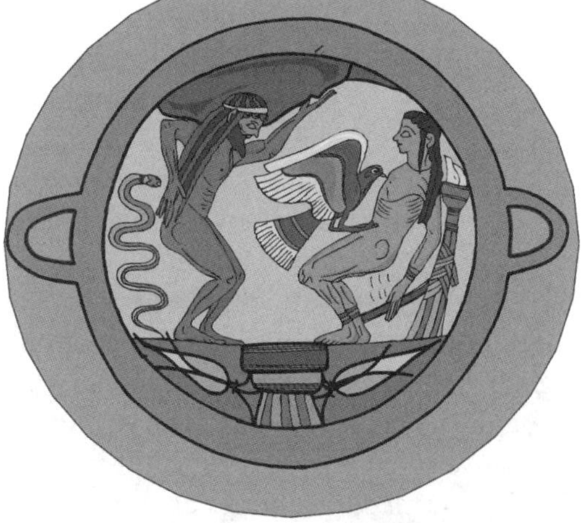

The Titan Atlas, carrying the world on his shoulders, visits his brother, Prometheus, whose liver a vulture gnaws. Representation of a Laconian black-figure cup.

Zeus allows Heracles to free Prometheus.

Zeus knew, however, that he could not keep Prometheus chained forever. Prometheus knew a very important secret: there was a goddess, Thetis, whose son was destined to become greater than his father. If Zeus married this goddess, he would be overthrown, just as he had overthrown Cronus, and Cronus had overthrown Uranus.

When Zeus failed to break Prometheus' spirit through chains and torture, he allowed Heracles to release the Titan. On Prometheus' advice, Zeus arranged for Thetis to be married to a mortal man named Peleus. They later became the parents of Achilles, the greatest of the Greeks who besieged Troy. Zeus and Prometheus were reconciled. According to the Roman poet Catullus, Prometheus even attended the wedding of Peleus and Thetis, the scars from his years of torture now faded.

The marriage scene at the top (1) of this vase is thought by some experts to depict the wedding of Thetis, seated, and Peleus, holding Thetis' hand, while Poseidon stands to the side. The scene from the back of the vase (2) is thought to show Hera dreaming of the Judgment of Paris, or Peleus and Thetis with a goddess. The cameo-glass disc (3) at the bottom was used to repair a break in the bottom of the base and shows perhaps Priam or Paris, wearing a Phrygian cap, popular among the Trojans. The Portland Vase, from the early 1st century CE, perhaps from Rome, Italy, is a famous cameo-glass vessel, made of two layers of glass, the first blue and the second white. The British Museum, London.

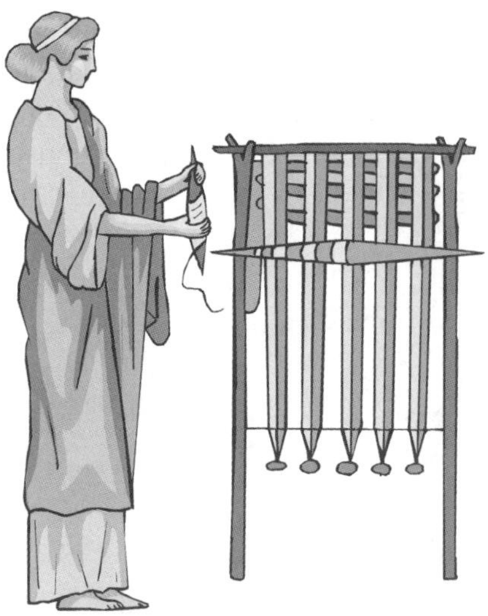

Arachne

Literary Source: Ovid *Metamorphoses* 6.1–145

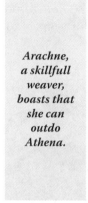

Arachne, a skillfull weaver, boasts that she can outdo Athena.

Arachne was a young woman from a small town in Lydia, a part of Asia Minor. Although her home and parentage were humble, she gained widespread fame for her skill in weaving. Even the nymphs would leave their homes along the mountains and rivers to see her weavings and to watch her work. People said, "Only Athena could have taught her!" But Arachne took offense at this, and said, "I can take on Athena! I'll compete with her, and if she wins I'll pay whatever punishment she decides!"

Hearing this, the goddess disguised herself as an old woman and came to Arachne. She said, "Take an elder's advice! Seek all the fame you want among mortals, but don't say you're better than a goddess! If you apologize to her humbly, she will forgive you."

Athena

Athena takes up Arachne's challenge to a weaving contest.

Arachne only glared at her, and retorted, "You senile old fool! Go give advice to your daughters, if you have any! I stand by what I said! Why is the goddess dodging a match with me?"

Athena replied, "She has come!" and dropped her disguise. All the women and nymphs who were there bowed down in fear, except Arachne. She blushed, but quickly recovered herself and repeated her challenge. Athena did not try to dissuade her further, and the two set up their looms and went to work. On and on their fingers flew as they wove in their many-colored threads.

Woman seated at loom

Athena depicted the gods on their thrones, surrounding a regal Zeus. In the center she wove the contest between herself and Poseidon for the privilege of being the city of Athen's patron. She showed the olive tree springing up from the earth at a blow from her spear, and the gods declaring her the winner. In the corners of the tapestry Athena wove cautionary tales of mortals who had challenged the gods and been punished. The work was framed by a border of olive leaves.

For her subject, Arachne chose the loves of the gods. She depicted Zeus transformed into a bull, a shower of gold, and many other shapes in his pursuit of mortal women; then she showed Poseidon, Apollo, Dionysus, and Cronus in similar situations. A border of flowers entwined in ivy surrounded the masterpiece.

Athena destroys Arachne's masterpiece and changes her to a spider.

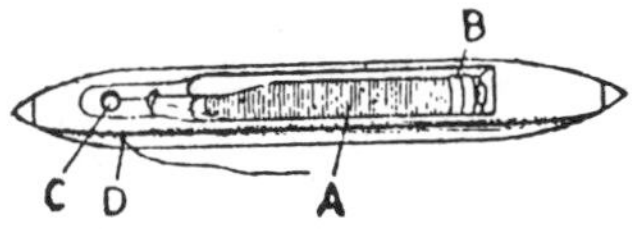

Shuttle for weaving: A, yarn; B, bobbin; C, eye through which the yarn is led; D, yarn

Even Athena had to admit that Arachne's work was as good as hers. Bitterly resenting her rival's success, the goddess tore apart Arachne's tapestry and struck the young woman in the face with her shuttle. Arachne could not bear to see her masterpiece destroyed, and fastened a noose around her neck. Athena felt stirred to mercy, and said, "You may live, but you will hang and weave forever!" She sprinkled Arachne with the juice of an herb from Hecate. At once Arachne lost her hair, nose, and ears; her head and body shrunk; her arms were now legs; most of what remained was belly, from which she still spins a thread as a spider.

Pallas Athena strikes Arachne with a shuttle as she transforms her into a spider. ***Pallas and Arachne*, 1636–1637, by Peter Paul Rubens (1577–1640), Virginia Museum of Fine Arts, Richmond, Virginia.**

Niobe, Vatican Museums, Vatican City, Italy

Niobe

Literary Source: Ovid *Metamorphoses* 6.146–312

Niobe is the proud mother of seven sons and seven daughters.

The story of Arachne's fate spread throughout Greece. Yet a woman who had known her, the queen of Thebes named Niobe, learned nothing from Arachne's misfortune. She had all blessings: her husband was a famous musician named Amphion; she claimed a distinguished list of ancestors; she had power. Yet she was the most proud of her children, seven sons and seven daughters. All would have called her the most fortunate of mothers, if she had not boasted this first. Her father was Tantalus, one of the great sinners in Hades, and she had inherited his arrogance. (See GENEALOGICAL CHART 16.)

Niobe insults the goddess Leto, who has only two children.

One day, when the women of Thebes were sacrificing to Leto, Niobe came upon them and frowned. "How silly you are to prefer gods you can't see to those you can!" she exclaimed haughtily. "Why are you worshipping Leto and not me? I have a lineage worthy of worship. My father Tantalus had the gods at his table. My grandfather on my mother's side is Atlas, and my other grandfather is Zeus himself! When my husband played his lyre, stones moved themselves to build these city walls. I am wealthy and powerful, I am as beautiful as a goddess, and I have fourteen children, whose marriages will soon make me even wealthier. How can you worship Leto, who couldn't even find a place to give birth until the island of Delos took pity on her! There she bore only *two* children! Even if something happens to some of my children, I will still have more than she does; she's practically childless! So stop these ceremonies to Leto! Go home! Take those laurel wreaths out of your hair!" The women obeyed but continued to pray to Leto in silence.

A devout worshipper

Leto asks her children, Apollo and Artemis, to punish Niobe.

Enraged at Niobe's blasphemy, Leto summoned her children and said, "Niobe is calling my divinity into doubt! If you two don't help me, my altars will be deserted! She has the nerve to call me childless! Let that word come back to haunt her!"

She would have said more, but Apollo interrupted. "We're wasting time talking when we could be punishing her!" Artemis agreed, and in an instant the twins were at the citadel of Thebes. They shot Niobe's eldest son as he was mounting his horse. The next son, seeing his brother fall, gave full rein to his horse, but Apollo's arrow overtook him and he fell beneath its legs. Two boys who were wrestling and holding each other in a tight clinch were both pierced by a single arrow, and they died in the same instant. Apollo shot the fifth as he ran towards his brothers already cold in death. The sixth was struck by an arrow behind his knee; as he was struggling to pull it out, a second arrow hit him in the neck. The youngest boy cried out in desperation, "Save me, all you gods!" Apollo felt sorry for him, but it was too late. His arrow was already on its way.

Word of the catastrophe spread throughout the city: "Niobe's seven sons are dead! And their father killed himself in grief!" Niobe's attendants tearfully told her the news, and Niobe could not believe the gods could do this to her. As she kissed her sons' corpses, she looked very different from the haughty queen who had lately ordered the women away from Leto's shrine. She lifted up her arms to the sky and cried, "I hope you're enjoying watching me grieve, Leto! Be happy with your victory! And yet it isn't really victory, is it? Even with all my losses, I still have more children than you!"

Niobe and her youngest daughter, Ufizzi Gallery, Florence, Italy

Apollo and Artemis shoot all Niobe's children.

No sooner had she spoken than Artemis' bowstring twanged. As the seven sisters stood mourning their brothers, they were shot down. At last there was only one little girl left. Niobe stretched her body and her robe over her, and cried, "Leave me my youngest one, please! One is all I ask for now!" Even as she prayed, the one for whom she was praying fell dead.

Niobe is changed to a weeping stone.

As Niobe sat surrounded by the lifeless bodies of her children and her husband, she froze in grief. Her face was colorless, her eyes fixed, her hair motionless in the breeze. Her tongue clung to the roof of her mouth; she could not move her head or limbs. She could only weep. A whirlwind carried her back to Lydia and set her on the summit of a mountain. She remained there, a weeping stone.

Meleager

Literary Source: Ovid *Metamorphoses* 8.260–546

Angered by the Calydonians, Artemis sends a boar to harass them.

Artemis, who had helped avenge her mother's honor when Niobe insulted her, showed her vengeful side again to the city of Calydon, in Aetolia. Its king had duly offered thanks for a fruitful year to all of the gods, but had omitted Artemis. In anger, Artemis sent a wild boar to ravage the land. This animal was the size of a bull, with fiery bloodshot eyes, bristles stiff as spears, teeth like an elephant's. It trampled the fertile fields of grain and the vines heavy with grapes; barns waited in vain for the year's crops. The beast ravaged the herds of cattle and sheep; dogs, shepherds, even bulls were helpless against it.

Meleager and a hound, Vatican Museums, Vatican City, Italy

Heroes Meleager, Nestor, Theseus, and Jason join the hunt for the boar.

A youth named Meleager decided to win glory by hunting down the boar. He gathered a group that included other well-known heroes, including Theseus and Jason. The group also included one female, a huntress named Atalanta. Meleager fell in love with her at first sight, and thought, "Whatever man she judges worthy of her is a lucky one!" He would have said more if the great contest were not at hand.

The hunters tracked the boar into the woods, spread out their nets, and released their dogs. The boar charged out as they readied their spears. The first casts all missed, or struck the animal without wounding it (Artemis had removed the iron from the spear-point). Several men were hurt by the boar, and would have been killed if their friends had not pulled them to safety.

Statue of a young girl, so-called Atalanta, Vatican Museums, Vatican City, Italy

A maiden hunter, Atalanta, draws first blood from the boar.

Nestor, who would later fight in the Trojan War as an old man, would have died if he had not used his spear to vault onto a tree branch. The first to draw blood was Atalanta, striking the beast under its ear. The men were embarrassed at having been bested by a woman; one of them, an Arcadian named Ancaeus, boasted, "I'll show you how men's weapons beat women's!" He lifted his weapon, a double axe, but the brute gored him first, striking him in the underbelly. He fell dead. Peirithous ran forward, raising his spear, but Theseus warned, "Keep back! Be brave at a distance! Being reckless killed Ancaeus!" Theseus then threw his own heavy spear; it was well-aimed, but blocked by a tree branch. Jason accidentally killed a fellow hunter when he shot.

Meleager's second spear throw kills the boar.

Meleager then cast two spears. The first hit the ground, but the second wounded the boar squarely in the middle of its back. It twisted around and around, spurting blood, and finally dropped dead. All raised a shout of joy and dipped their own spears into the boar's blood.

Meleager kills his uncles, who protested his sharing glory with Atalanta.

As Meleager planted a foot on the dead boar, he called out, "Let my glory be shared with you, Atalanta!" and awarded her the boar's head as a trophy. The group muttered, and Meleager's two uncles spoke out: "Put down our trophies, woman!" They took the gift from her. Meleager was infuriated, and shouted, "You can't steal another's honor!" He stabbed one of the men in the chest with his sword, and while the other was wondering what to do, Meleager stabbed him to death also.

Meleager's mother, Althaea, saw her brothers' bodies carried into the city as she was sacrificing in thanks for her son's victory. When she found out who had killed them, she lusted for revenge.

Meleager's mother kills her own son.

It so happened that when Meleager was born, the Fates had declared, "We give the boy the same life span as this log burning on the fire!" Althaea had immediately snatched the log out, dunked it in water, and kept it safely hidden in the house. Now she fetched it out and ordered a fire to be built. Several times she was on the verge of burning the log; several times she pulled back. At last her sisterly feelings overcame her mother's love. She cried, "Spirits of my brothers, receive my sacrifice!" and threw the wood into the middle of the fire, averting her eyes. The log seemed to groan as it burned, and far off Meleager felt a burning within his own body. He cried, "Lucky Ancaeus, who died fighting!" As the log burned away to ashes, Meleager's spirit departed into the air.

Meleager, dressed in the robes of a medieval monk, contemplates the decree of the Fates that the fire upon which he gazes will consume him. Illustration by Giovanni Costetti (1878–1949) for the 1903 Alinari Edition of Dante's *Purgatorio,* Canto XXV.

All of Calydon, young and old, rich and poor, men and women, plunged into mourning for the dead hero. Althaea drove a sword into her womb in remorse. At last Artemis decided that the city had suffered enough.

Actaeon

Literary Source: Ovid *Metamorphoses* 3.138–252

Actaeon

Artemis was also ruthless towards Actaeon, who committed no deliberate evil or dishonor towards her. Actaeon was a prince of Thebes, a city haunted by tragedy in the family of Cadmus. Chiron the centaur trained Actaeon to hunt. One day, he and his friends finished their morning's hunting and dispersed through the woods. Artemis had also been hunting, and came to her favorite grove of thick pine and cypress containing a crystalline natural spring within a cave. Here one nymph took the goddess' weapons, another held her robe, another tied up her hair, others removed her footwear and filled urns with water. As fate would have it, Actaeon stumbled into this cave.

Artemis

The nymphs shrieked, "A man!" They tried to surround Diana and hide her naked body, but she was too tall! She blushed deeply. Wishing she had her arrows handy, she instead threw a handful of water in Actaeon's face and exclaimed, "Now go tell people you saw me naked—if you can!"

After Actaeon accidentally sees Artemis bathing, she changes him into a stag.

At once, antlers sprouted on Actaeon's head. His neck expanded, his ears grew pointy, and his limbs changed to long slender legs. He ran away in fear, surprised at his own speed. In the water, he caught a glimpse of himself, now a handsome stag. Actaeon tried to cry, "Oh, no!" but nothing came out except a groan. Only his mind was still human as he wondered where to go now. Go home? To the woods?

Actaeon's own hounds kill him.

While he hesitated, his dogs spotted him and rushed toward him in a pack, followed closely by his companions. Eagerly, they chased him across his own former hunting grounds. He longed to call out, "It's Actaeon! It's me, your master!" Soon the fastest dogs pinned him down, and the rest tore him apart. His companions said to one another, "Too bad Actaeon's not here! Lazy fellow, he's missing a great kill!" Actaeon wished he were missing it!

***Actaeon*, 1925, by Paul Manship (1885–1966), Smithsonian American Art Museum, Washington, DC**

The gods were divided about what Artemis had done. Some thought she had been too harsh; others thought she had acted properly in defending her virtue. Only Hera did not care either way, but she was glad that a relative of Europa, Cadmus' grandson, was suffering.

Erysichthon

Literary Source: Ovid *Metamorphoses* 8.738–878

For many of the people who change shape in Ovid's stories, transformation is permanent. Others can transform multiple times, at will. Such was the daughter of a wicked man named Erysichthon. He scorned the gods, and moved the usually gentle Demeter to punish him severely.

Erysichthon scorns Demeter by cutting down an oak tree sacred to her.

There was once a giant oak, covered with ribbons and votive tablets, where the dryads, the wood nymphs, often danced. For no good reason, Erysichthon commanded his slaves to cut it down. When he saw them hesitate, he grabbed the axe himself and declared, "Even if this tree were Demeter herself, I would still make it hit the dirt!"

As he held his axe at the ready, the sacred oak groaned and shuddered. Its leaves, acorns, and branches paled as if it were a human under threat. When the axe struck the bark, blood issued forth. All were astonished, and one brave man tried to stop him. Erysichthon turned away from the tree for a moment and snarled, "Here's your reward for being so devout!" He then cut his head off.

But as Erysichthon repeatedly chopped at the trunk, a voice deep within the tree whispered, "I am a nymph of Demeter and I live in this tree. Your punishment is at hand. It will be my consolation for dying."

Demeter punishes Erysichthon by causing Famine to enter his belly.

The great tree fell at last, and the saddened dryads went to Demeter and prayed to her, "Punish Erysichthon for this crime!" The goddess nodded, and the fields shook for miles around. She devised a punishment that would have made him pitiable if his deeds had not been so unforgivable. She decided he should be tortured by Famine. Because she and Famine could never meet, she sent one of her mountain nymphs with these instructions: "Go to northernmost Scythia, where nothing ever grows. There you will find Famine. Tell her to enter the belly of this impious man and stay there!"

Demeter

Famine

The nymph journeyed in a dragon-borne chariot provided by Demeter to a mountain in the Caucasus. She found Famine scavenging for bits of grass in a field of stones. Famine was a frightful sight. Her hair was filthy and her eyes were hollow, her skin and lips were gray, her throat was rusty from disuse. So thinly stretched was her skin that you could see the internal organs underneath; her hip bones protruded and all her joints could be seen. As soon as the nymph caught sight of Famine, she gave Demeter's orders and departed at once, for she was already beginning to feel hungry.

Famine obediently went to Erysichthon's house and found him asleep, for it was night. She wrapped him in her bony arms, breathed her essence into him, and departed for her barren land once again. Even in his sleep, Erysichthon felt her effects at once: he dreamed of feasts and chewed on nothing until his teeth were worn down. He awoke to raging hunger, and sought whatever food earth or air or sea could supply. Even as he gorged himself, he cried, "I'm hungry!" He ate enough for a city or a nation; the more he ate, the hungrier he felt.

Erysichthon gorges himself.

Erysichthon's daughter disguised as a fisherman

Poseidon transforms Erysichthon's daughter into a shape-changer.

When he had spent his entire fortune on food, all that remained to him was his daughter. He sold her as a slave. She ran away from her master, and went to the seaside to pray. "Poseidon, please help me get away from this man!" Poseidon heard her prayer and transformed her into a fisherman. When her master had caught up to her, he said, "I hope you have a good day's catch, fisherman! Have you seen a girl dressed as a slave? I'm sure I saw her here, and her footprints lead straight to you!"

"Nope, no one's been on this beach 'cept fer me!" the "fisherman" answered. The master believed this and went away. The young woman changed back into her own shape and returned to her father.

After Erysichthon uses his daughter to steal food, he devours himself.

Once Erysichthon realized his daughter was able to change her appearance, he sold her off repeatedly. She used her shape-shifting powers to make her way back to him and steal food for him.

Erysichthon's misery—and his daughter's—did not end until he ended his miserable life by devouring his own body.

A. Review Exercises

1. **CHRONOLOGY COUNTS!** Place the following events in chronological order. Use the numbers 1–6, with 1 as the first event and 6 as the last event in the sequence. Write the number in the space provided.

   a. **Prometheus**

   ____ Zeus has Prometheus chained to a mountain where an eagle eats his liver.

   ____ Heracles frees Prometheus.

   ____ Zeus has the gods create Pandora.

   ____ Prometheus invites Zeus to choose between two portions of meat.

   ____ Prometheus steals fire.

   ____ Prometheus attends the wedding of Peleus and Thetis.

   b. **Niobe**

   ____ Niobe, queen of Thebes, returns to Lydia.

   ____ Apollo shoots Niobe's sons and Artemis, her daughters.

   ____ Leto calls her children, Apollo and Artemis, to her aid.

   ____ Niobe mocks the women of Thebes.

   ____ Niobe boasts of her seven sons and seven daughters.

   ____ Grief-stricken Niobe freezes into stone.

Mealeager and Atalanta at the boar hunt

c. Meleager

____ In remorse, Althaea kills herself.

____ Meleager hurls two spears.

____ Nestor vaults with his spear up to a tree branch.

____ A boar sent by Artemis ravages Calydon.

____ Meleager's uncles steal the boar's head trophy from Atalanta.

____ The Calydonian boar gores the hunter Ancaeus.

d. Erysichthon

____ One of Demeter's nymphs journeys to Scythia to find Famine.

____ The spirit of Demeter speaks from within the oak tree.

____ Poseidon transforms Erysichthon's daughter into a fisherman.

____ Erysichthon cuts down the old oak tree.

____ Erysichthon becomes obsessed by food.

____ Erysichthon consumes himself.

e. Actaeon

____ Actaeon's hounds do not recognize him, and tear him apart.

____ Actaeon and his friends enjoy a morning of hunting, then disperse.

____ Artemis splashes Actaeon with water; he transforms into a stag.

____ Actaeon accidentally catches sight of Artemis bathing.

____ Artemis finds a cave suitable for a bath; her attendants fill urns with water.

____ Actaeon catches a glimpse of himself in the water.

f. Arachne

____ Athena strikes Arachne with a shuttle.

____ Arachne is a young maiden of Lydia.

____ Arachne weaves a tapestry depicting the gods in love.

____ Athena, outraged by Arachne's impudence, transforms her into a spider.

____ Arachne, not recognizing the goddess, speaks disrespectfully to an old woman.

____ Athena sprinkles Arachne with the essence of an herb given her by Hecate.

2. **TRUE OR FALSE?** In the space provided, indicate whether each statement is true or false. Correct each false statement with the proper information.

a. ____ According to the myth of Prometheus, woman was created to be trouble.

b. ____ Someone who gives in under pressure may be said to have a promethean spirit.

c. ____ The myth of Arachne should be considered an aetiological myth.

d. ____ To the ancient Greeks, Arachne, Erisychthon, and Niobe were all victims of their own hubris.

e. ____ Meleager intentionally provoked the gods, resulting in his downfall.

f. ____ The name Althaea means "healer." It is ironic that this is Meleager's mother's name.

g. ____ Niobe was queen of Lydia.

h. ____ In the weaving contest between Athena and Arachne, Arachne wove famous human love stories and in the four corners wove cautionary tales about mortals who were punished for defying the gods.

i. ____ Someone who had an insatiable appetite could best be compared to Erysichthon's daughter.

j. ____ The goddess Famine, who embraces Erysichthon, is an example of the literary figure of personification.

k. ____ Niobe had twice the number of children as Leto.

l. ____ The story of Meleager is set in the city of Athens.

B. MUSINGS

1. A "Pandora's box" is a metaphor for troubles temporarily under control but which could be unleashed at any time with disastrous consequences. Draw your own cartoon of a "Pandora's box" being opened. You may make it a personal illustration, a political cartoon, or an illustration to a book, film, or play.

2. Discuss the punishments that the Greek and Roman gods inflicted upon mortals who dishonored them. Are they deserved? Why or why not? To what extent do these gods' actions differ from the actions of God(s) in other religious traditions?

3. Take a close look at the photo of the sculpture group *Actaeon* by Paul Manship on page 197. Paul Manship was a twentieth-century American sculptor whose work was influenced by classical mythology. Research more about Paul Manship to learn about his life, his art, and his other sculpture. Compare his art with the ancient depiction of Actaeon and Athena below. These websites will help get you started:

    - http://www.artcyclopedia.com/artists/manship_paul.html
    - http://wwar.com/masters/m/manship-paul.html

Relief sculpture of Artemis and Actaeon, metope from Temple E at Selinus, Sicily, ca. 460 BCE

C. WORDS, WORDS, WORDS

The Daily Muse

News you can use

Got arachnophobia??

The scientific name for spiders, scorpions, mites, and ticks is **arachnids,** from the same Greek word from which Arachne got her name.

Someone who has an abnormal fear of spiders has **arachnophobia.**

How many pairs of legs do **arachnids** possess? ____________________

D. HOW 'BOUT THAT?

- Both Niobe and her father, Tantalus, gave their names to the chemical elements tantalum and niobium. Tantalum is a chemical element in the periodic table. The symbol for tantalum is Ta; its atomic number is 73. A very heavy, blue-grey metal like gold or platinum, tantalum is nearly always found with niobium; at first, scientists believed them to be the same. Because of its hardness and resistance to corrosion from body fluids, tantalum is often used in the making of fine surgical equipment.

- Niobium (also known as columbium), symbolized by the letters Nb, greatly resembles tantalum in appearance, but its atomic number is 41. Niobium can be found directly above tantalum on the periodic table. When alloyed with tin or titanium, it can be used as a superconductor. It has several other industrial uses.

Research to answer the following questions:

1. What is the name of the mineral in which tantalum is found?

2. What property(ies) of this element make it similar to the mythological figure Tantalus, after whom this metal is named?

3. With what other metal(s) is tantalum frequently alloyed and why?

- Anything as filmy and delicate as a spider's web is said to be arachnoid. The arachnoid membrane is a thin, filmy membrane that is one of the layers of membranes encasing the brain and spinal cord. The same word is used to describe the insects described as arachnids above in section C.

Scorpion (arachnid)

"Althaea cried, 'Spirits of my brothers, receive my sacrifice!'"

- The log, or brand, of wood on which Meleager's life depended gave us the expression "Althaea's brand." This is any object on which someone's life or reputation depends, and by which he or she can be destroyed.

E. Who's Who?

- For the House of Atreus, see Genealogical Chart 16.

Chapter Thirteen
The House of Atreus

General Sources:
Aeschylus *Oresteia*
Sophocles *Electra*
Euripides *Iphigenia at Aulis, Electra, Iphigenia in Tauris*
Seneca *Thyestes*
Hyginus *Stories* 82–84, 86–88

Because Tantalus attempts to feed the flesh of his son, Pelops, to the gods, he is punished in the Underworld with eternal hunger and thirst.

Perhaps no family in Greek myth was as accursed as the House of Atreus, also called the House of Tantalus (see Genealogical Chart 16.) You have already read in chapter 3 the story of how Tantalus tried to feed his son Pelops to the gods. Tantalus' daughter, Niobe, inherited his arrogance, and you read her tragic tale in the previous chapter.

Pelops' abduction of Hippodamia in Poseidon's *quadriga* (a four-horse chariot). After an Attic red-figure neck amphora, ca. 410 BCE, Museo Archeologico, Arezzo, Italy.

Restored to life, Pelops competes for Hippodamia against her father Oenomaus, who dies cursing Pelops' family.

Pelops grew into a strong and handsome young man who was well liked by Poseidon. Pelops left Lydia and traveled to Greece, where he sought the hand of a beautiful princess named Hippodamia. Hippodamia's father, King Oenomaus, required all of her suitors to compete with him in a chariot race. The punishment for the losers was death. Oenomaus always won, as Ares had given him his horses. When Pelops saw the heads of the previous contenders nailed above the doors of the palace, he regretted having come, but Poseidon furnished him with horses and a chariot. To be doubly sure he would win, Pelops approached Oenomaus' charioteer Myrtilus, who secretly loved Hippodamia himself. He and Myrtilus agreed that if Pelops won the race, Myrtilus would be the first to sleep with Hippodamia. Myrtilus, therefore, removed the linchpins from Oenomaus' chariot; some say he replaced them with wax ones. As soon as Oenomaus had whipped the horses to a gallop, his chariot broke apart and the horses dragged the driver to his death. As he died, he cursed Pelops and all his family.

East pediment of the temple of Zeus, Olympia, showing Zeus at center. On the left stand Hippodamia and Pelops. On the right stand Oenomaus and his wife, Sterope, one of the daughters of Atlas. The chariot teams for each contestant stand at their sides. This temple is located in the Peloponnesus, the large peninsula named for Pelops.

Pelops kills Myrtilus, a rival charioteer, who also curses Pelops.

Returning home victorious with Hippodamia and Myrtilus, Pelops regretted the bargain he had made with Myrtilus. "This man will be a source of disgrace to me," he thought. Therefore, instead of following through with the deal, he threw the charioteer into the sea, which was named Myrtoan after him. Pelops and his family were cursed once again by Myrtilus as he drowned. But Pelops became a highly successful conqueror in Greece and took over vast amounts of land, which he named the Peloponnesus after himself.

Pelops' sons, Atreus and Thyestes, rival for Mycenae's throne; Atreus wins and banishes Thyestes.

Pelops and Hippodamia had two sons, Atreus and Thyestes. The brothers grew up to be bitter rivals for the throne of Mycenae, their native land. When the time came for them to contend for the kingship, Atreus vowed that he would sacrifice to Artemis the finest of his flocks. When he found a lamb with a golden fleece, he slaughtered the animal, but instead of sacrificing it to the goddess, he kept the fleece for himself. Thyestes, when he found out about his brother's trophy, seduced Atreus' wife and persuaded her to obtain the fleece for him without Atreus' knowledge. He then made a suggestion to the Mycenaeans. "We must let the gods decide who should rule, my brother or me. If one of us can produce a divine sign—say, the skin of a golden lamb—let him be the king." Atreus, thinking he still possessed the fleece, agreed. Imagine his outrage when Thyestes produced it instead! Atreus prayed to the gods for help, who told him to convince the Mycenaeans that they needed a more spectacular sign, such as reversing the sun in its course. When he performed this feat, aided by Zeus, the Mycenaeans proclaimed him king. He banished Thyestes from his kingdom.

Atreus plots another horrific punishment for Thyestes.

After Thyestes left Mycenae, he lived humbly in the forest, forgetting all of his cunning and ambition. But Atreus was still angry with his brother and certain that Thyestes would try to rob him of power again. He brooded, "I must do something, something that no one will admire but that no one will ever forget either! Something so bad that my brother will wish he had done it himself!"

His associate tried to warn him. "What will people think?"

"The best part of being a king is that people have to like what you do!" retorted Atreus. "Besides, what has Thyestes ever stopped at? He took my wife and kingdom! Killing him is too easy. I want him to wish he *were* dead! But how?" Then a hideous inspiration struck, prompted by the monstrous feast of his grandfather Tantalus. "What better weapon against Thyestes than Thyestes himself? I'll soon have him gobbling up his own sons!"

Atreus conveyed the message to Thyestes that he wanted to be reconciled to his brother and share the throne with him. Thyestes arrived back in Mycenae, full of misgivings. He had found happiness in his simple life and did not believe he could trust his brother. One of Thyestes' sons, ironically also named Tantalus after his great-grandfather, noticed Thyestes' distress and commented upon it: "What are you worried about? Your brother is ready to share his prize with you. Why be miserable when you can be happy?"

Thyestes' philosophical response was this: "I've learned that luxury does not make you happy. When I was in power, I never stopped being afraid. Now my house is safe without weapons. The most powerful are those who don't need power."

"What about brotherly love?" questioned Tantalus.

"Wheat will grow out of the sea before I'll believe that my brother loves me!"

"What could possibly go wrong?"

"Everything! But it's too late to turn back now. Just remember I'm the one following you!"

Atreus had been watching and listening, gloating that his prey was now approaching the trap. He greeted his brother with false warmth: "Welcome! Let me feel your embrace! Let's forget the anger of the past and nourish family love!"

Unknowingly, Thyestes feasts upon the flesh of his three sons.

Thyestes agreed, and even entrusted his three sons to Atreus as a pledge of faith. Atreus bade Thyestes replace his ragged clothing with rich robes and a crown. The citizens of Mycenae who witnessed the scene were amazed that the civil war that had wracked the city was apparently ending. Just then, however, a man burst out of the palace dazed with shock. He told a gruesome story. Atreus had dragged his three young nephews to a secret part of the palace, a dark grove watered by a murky stream of black mud. In a hideous parody of religious ritual, he tied them up and led them to the altar, singing the ritual songs and chanting prayers. He slaughtered them, one by one, starting with young Tantalus. But this was only the beginning! He cut the boys' flesh into pieces and roasted it over slow fires. Then he set it before Thyestes, who feasted on it abundantly. In horror, the sun fled from the sky, plunging the land into unnatural darkness.

Atreus was filled with savage joy as he watched his brother consuming his own sons' flesh. All that remained was to announce the truth.

Thyestes tried to raise his spirits as he ate and drank, but he could not keep the tears away. "Something bad is coming . . . or have I been wretched so long I've forgotten how to be happy? What's wrong with me?" He told Atreus, "I thank you for the feast. The only thing that could make me happier would be to share it with my children."

"Your sons are as close to you as they can be. They'll never be apart from you again," was Atreus' duplicitous reply.

"Where are they?" Thyestes cried, in pain from the abundance of food and shaken by the gathering darkness.

Atreus uncovered a platter containing Thyestes' sons' heads. "Do you recognize your sons?"

"I recognize my brother! Is this your idea of reconciliation and brotherly love? Give me their bodies so I can bury them!"

"You already have all that's left of your sons. *You've eaten them yourself!*"

Thyestes gets revenge through his son Aegisthus, who kills Atreus; Thyestes regains the throne.

"So this was what drove the day away!" Thyestes howled. He called upon all the gods above and below in rage and grief to strike down both himself and Atreus.

Thyestes immediately went to the oracle of Delphi to learn how he might avenge himself. He was told that the only way he could avenge himself was through a child born of himself and his daughter Pelopeia! Determined to have his revenge, Thyestes disguised himself and raped his daughter as she was washing her dress by a river. The son born of this rape was named Aegisthus. When Aegisthus grew up, he killed Atreus and restored Thyestes to the throne.

Atreus' sons banish Thyestes and marry Tyndareus' daughters.

Atreus' sons Agamemnon and Menelaus escaped from Mycenae when their father was killed. After several years in exile, they returned and expelled Thyestes with the help of King Tyndareus of Sparta. They also married Tyndareus' two daughters: Menelaus married Helen and Agamemnon married Clytemnestra.

Leda and Tyndareus admire their children, sitting in a swan's nest. Tyndareus does not realize that one of them, Helen, was fathered by Zeus.

Helen is the daughter of Zeus and Leda and the stepdaughter of Tyndareus.

The true father of Helen, however, was not Tyndareus, but Zeus himself! He had come to her mother, Leda, in the guise of a swan, and as a result of that union, Helen was hatched out of an egg. This was the famous Helen of Troy, whose beauty was the legendary cause of the Trojan War when she left Menelaus for the Trojan prince Paris (sometimes also called Alexander). That war will be discussed more fully in chapter 16; here we will look at the episodes that most directly affected the House of Atreus.

After Paris takes Helen, Agamemnon leads the Greeks against Troy.

Determined to avenge his brother's honor, Agamemnon assembled a great fleet of ships and prepared to sail to Troy. While they were awaiting favorable winds at the port of Aulis, however, Agamemnon shot and killed one of Artemis' favorite deer. In her anger, Artemis kept the winds from blowing. As the army grew impatient to sail, Agamemnon asked the priest Calchas for help.

"Your Majesty," replied Calchas, "the winds will not blow until you have sacrificed your first-born daughter, Iphigenia, to appease the wrath of Artemis!"

Iphigenia must be sacrificed to release winds held back by Artemis' anger.

Agamemnon was horrified. Could he bear to see his own daughter slain for the glory of the Greeks? The other leaders of the army persuaded him that he had no choice. He therefore ordered Iphigenia to be brought to Aulis, telling his wife that their daughter was to be married to Achilles, the greatest of the Greek warriors. As he waited, the horror of his plan struck him, and he tried to send a messenger to warn Iphigenia to return home. But the man was intercepted by Menelaus.

Agamemnon had been expecting Iphigenia to arrive alone. He was not pleased to see her mother Clytemnestra accompanying her!

The innocent Iphigenia at once rushed to her father and hugged him warmly and cheerfully. She had always loved him in preference to her mother. Troubled by his solemn expression, "Why do you look so sad and serious?" she asked him.

Agamemnon calls Iphigenia to Aulis pretending she is to marry Achilles.

"A king has many responsibilities, my child," he answered. He could hardly bear to embrace her, knowing what he was about to do. He sent her into the tent to prepare for her "wedding." Left alone with his wife, he told her of Achilles' illustrious family, going back to great Zeus himself.

"What about the wedding preparations?" questioned Clytemnestra.

"I have taken care of everything," the king responded uneasily. "The entire army and I will give her away."

"What about me? When you and your troops are giving away my little girl, where do I go?"

"Back home!"

Clytemnestra questions Agamemnon's plans for Iphigenia.

"No! This is not how we do things! You see to your army, I'm going to help my daughter prepare for her wedding."

After Agamemnon had returned to his army, Achilles happened to come by to speak with him. Clytemnestra emerged from the tent, prepared to welcome the man she thought was her future son-in-law. Achilles drew back shyly.

"It isn't proper for me to speak with you, ma'am," Achilles said.

"Of course it is! You *are* going to marry my daughter, after all!"

Achilles reveals to Clytemnestra his ignorance of plans to marry Iphigenia.

"Clytemnestra, what do you mean? I never sought your daughter's hand, and Agamemnon never offered it to me!"

Realizing she had been lied to, Clytemnestra knelt at Achilles' feet, begging him to help her. Achilles, upset that Agamemnon had used his name for deceit, promised to do whatever he could.

Iphigenia being carried to sacrifice. In the clouds above, Artemis rescues her by carrying her off to Tauris. Representation of Pompeiian wall painting, 70–79 BCE.

Clytemnestra and Iphigenia then confronted Agamemnon. "Haven't I been a good wife to you? You'll be away at war for a long time—what do you think will go through my mind all those years when I look at the empty places where my daughter used to sit? What kind of a homecoming do you think you will have?"

Iphigenia added, "I wish I had the musical gift of Orpheus to charm you into changing your mind! But all I have is my tears to persuade you not to kill me. Don't you remember how close we used to be, how you promised to marry me to a great man and I promised to welcome you to my house when you were old and gray?"

Iphigenia looks out to sea.

Agamemnon was touched, but he did not change his mind. Even Achilles was unable to sway the soldiers to stop pressuring Agamemnon to kill his daughter. He was prepared to fight the whole army defending Iphigenia, but suddenly the princess herself spoke up.

"I can't let Achilles risk his life for me like this. He'll be killed for nothing. I want to make this great sacrifice for my country, as all the thousands of men waiting to sail are prepared to do. Don't mourn for me, Mother—this is a great privilege, to be the benefactor of all Greece. And don't hate Father. He has no choice."

After the sacrifice of Iphigenia, Clytemnestra vows revenge.

Iphigenia departed, leaving Clytemnestra weeping inconsolably. Shortly thereafter, a messenger came, bringing report of a miracle: just as Agamemnon had been poised to slay his daughter, a cloud blanketed all. When the mist lifted, Iphigenia was nowhere to be found. In her place, a deer lay dead on the altar. Clytemnestra did not believe this, and left for home vowing revenge on Agamemnon.

Clytemnestra and her lover, Aegisthus, set a trap for Agamemnon.

While Agamemnon was away at war, Clytemnestra took Aegisthus as her lover. The two plotted to kill Agamemnon on his return and rule in his place. As the beacon fires signaling the taking of Troy spread across Argos, Clytemnestra waited, preparing her deadly net for the husband she hated. He arrived, attended by a large retinue and a new bride—Cassandra, a daughter of King Priam of Troy. She was gifted with prophetic ability but cursed because she was never believed. Clytemnestra greeted the king with a long and falsely affectionate speech, then spread out a crimson carpet for him to tread as he walked into the palace. In doing so, Clytemnestra tricked him into committing hubris, by taking for himself an honor reserved only for the gods.

As Clytemnestra lured Agamemnon into the bath where she planned to kill him, Cassandra was seized with a prophetic vision. She saw the murdered children of Thyestes carrying their own entrails in their hands, and then foresaw what lay in store for her master and herself.

Cassandra prophesies Agamemnon's murder and her own.

"I tell you, you will soon see Agamemnon dead!" she shouted to the elders who had gathered outside the palace to await Agamemnon's return.

"What man would dare plot such a thing?" they asked her.

"You misunderstand me! I see a female monster unleashed, plotting murder! The lioness will kill the lion, and then she will destroy me!"

"If you know this, why not save yourself, poor girl?"

"It's useless, my fate is sealed." She walked into the palace as the elders praised her courage. A few moments later, they heard the last cries of Agamemnon: "Aahhh! I've been hit!"

Clytemnestra emerges from the palace at Mycenae with the bloodied axe, after murdering Agamemnon.

While the elders huddled together trying to figure out what to do, Clytemnestra emerged again, spattered with Agamemnon's blood. "I did it! I threw a robe around him and struck him—once, twice, and once more in thanksgiving to Hades. His blood spurted onto me as his strength ebbed away, and it felt as refreshing as dewdrops in springtime to me!"

The elders were horrified at Clytemnestra's boasting over her slain husband, and they were even more enraged when Aegisthus entered to join his beloved in jeering at Agamemnon. "One day," they vowed, "vengeance will come upon you in turn!"

Their words were true, although Clytemnestra and Aegisthus ignored them. As much as Clytemnestra had loved Iphigenia, she was not a good mother to her other children, Electra and Orestes. (The playwright Sophocles adds another daughter named Chrysothemis.) Clytemnestra sent Orestes away to be raised by others, and she barely tolerated Electra, who dressed in sordid clothes and sheared her hair in endless mourning for her father. (According to the playwright Euripides, Clytemnestra married her off to a poor farmer whose menial labors she shared.)

Euripides, the playwright, ca. 485–406 BCE

Sent away by his mother, Orestes eventually returns.

Years after Agamemnon's murder, Orestes returned to Argos disguised as a foreign peddler, accompanied by his friend Pylades. He laid a lock of his hair on the tomb of his father as a token of mourning. Electra then came to the tomb to pray and offer sacrifice in behalf of Clytemnestra, who had been troubled by a nightmare the night before: she dreamed she gave birth to a snake, which then bit her as she tried to nurse it. She recognized the lock of hair as similar to her own, and brother and sister had a joyous reunion. (Euripides could not believe that a man's hair could be similar to a woman's, and had Electra recognize Orestes by a scar instead, which he had received helping his sister chase a pet fawn.)

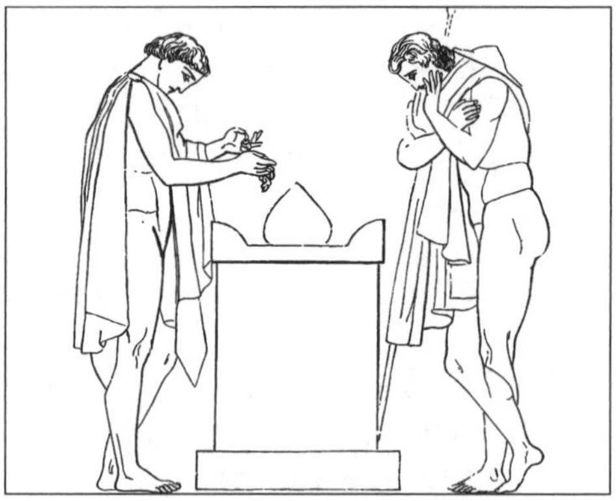
Orestes, accompanied by Pylades, lays a lock of hair on the tomb of Agamemnon as a sign of mourning.

Orestes and his sister Electra plot against Clytemnestra and Aegisthus.

The siblings then set to work plotting the deaths of their mother and her lover. They contrived a fake report of Orestes' death to lull Clytemnestra into a false sense of security. As Clytemnestra emerged from the palace to greet the "strangers," Orestes told his tale in his foreign disguise: "I'm afraid I have bad news for you, Your Majesty. Orestes is dead. It happened in a chariot race. He was neck and neck with an Athenian for the lead, but as his horses rounded the turn, he struck a column and was thrown from the chariot. He became entangled in the reins, and he was tossed up and down, until his body was such a bloody mess that not even his closest friends could recognize him. I've brought back all that's left of him in this urn, so he can be buried in his native land next to his father."

Orestes avenges Agamemnon's murder by killing Clytemnestra.

Clytemnestra pretended to be grief stricken, but her tears fooled no one. Only Orestes' old nurse, remembering the days when she had cared for him as a baby, cried for him with genuine pain. Clytemnestra invited the "strangers" in, offering them refreshment, including a hot bath. Electra remained outside to watch for Aegisthus' return. Orestes and Pylades stood behind Clytemnestra as she prepared the urn for burial. Then they struck.

"Oh my God! Help, Aegisthus! Son, pity your mother!"

"You had no pity for your son—or his father!" Electra shouted back. And to Orestes she cried, "Hit her again!"

A moment later, Orestes and Pylades emerged, their hands dripping with blood. "She's dead. She'll never taunt you again," the brother reassured his sister.

They barely had time to think about their mother's death when Electra announced, "Here comes Aegisthus! Quick, back inside!"

Aegisthus arrives, misinformed by Electra that it is Orestes who has died.

Clytemnestra's lover approached smiling and carefree, for the word of Orestes' "death" had reached him. He addressed Electra rudely:

"You there! Is this true about Orestes? I heard that some foreigners have come with news about his death."

"Yes. They have brought his body with them."

"I want to see it!"

"It's not a pretty sight."

"For once, it's a pleasure to listen to you! Bring the body out." Still in his disguise, Orestes did so.

Aegisthus gloated, "Let all the people see that anyone who challenges me will end up like this corpse! Have Clytemnestra come out here."

"She is already here," answered Orestes. "Go on, lift up the sheet."

Aegisthus uncovered the face, expecting to see Orestes. When he saw Clytemnestra instead, he knew his time had come.

After Aegisthus views Clytemnestra's murdered body, Orestes kills him.

"Get into the palace! I want you to die in the same spot where you killed Agamemnon!" Orestes commanded.

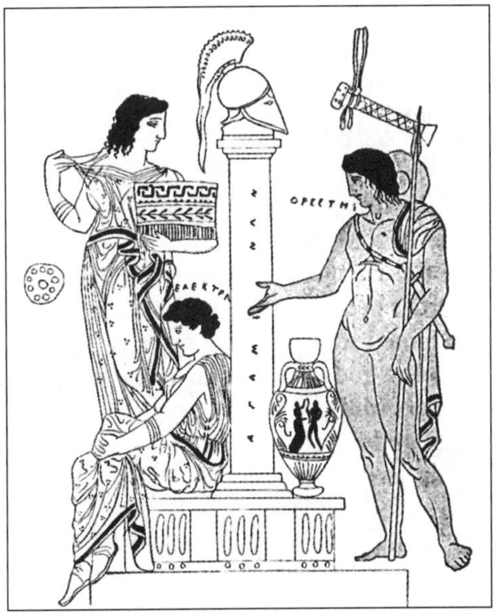

The reunion of Electra and Orestes at the tomb monument of Agamemnon

Orestes and Electra in a Hellenistic sculpture group, Museo Archeologico Nazionale, Naples, Italy

The Furies, spirits of vengeance, appear to now-remorseful Orestes.

Thus Aegisthus died. But as they gazed upon the body of their mother, remorse gripped the children. Sadly, Electra realized that she had once loved her mother. Orestes' punishment was even more terrifying, since he had done the actual killing. "Look! Old women in black, eyes dripping blood, hair like snakes, are crowding around me!" he cried. The old women were the Furies, seeking his life in return for his mother's. He fled, panic stricken.

Tormented by the Furies, Orestes flees to Delphi.

Because Apollo was the god who had commanded Orestes to take his mother's life, Orestes fled to Delphi, pursued by the Furies. There Apollo lulled the Furies to sleep, and encouraged the matricide: "I'll protect you, from nearby or far away. Do not give up, but keep on journeying until you come to Athens. When you arrive, you must clasp the ancient statue of Athena, and judges there will release you from this trouble." Orestes escaped as the ghost of Clytemnestra appeared to rouse the Furies: "Wake up! How can you let him get away and make a fool of me among the other ghosts! Look at these gashes on my body! Did I make all those sacrifices to you for nothing?"

The Furies awoke, cursing themselves for losing Orestes. Apollo ordered them from his shrine: "There is no place for you here! Go back to where heads are chopped off and eyes gouged out in the name of justice!"

The Furies pursue Orestes in a copy of a Greek vase painting.

The Furies responded, "This is our job—to hunt down those who shed kindred blood. We will not give up until we have caught Orestes."

With Apollo's help, Orestes flees to Athens to Athena's shrine.

Orestes meanwhile had arrived in Athens, where he went to Athena's shrine as Apollo had commanded. The Furies were close behind. Athena heard Orestes' prayer and came at once. Unlike Apollo, she acknowledged the Furies with respect. "Who are you, and why have you come here?"

"We have come hunting a man who killed his mother."

Athena then listened to Orestes plead his case: "My father was Agamemnon, who defeated Troy. He came home only to be murdered by my black-hearted mother. I returned from exile and cut her down—but it was Apollo who commanded me to do it, making threats against me if I refused."

The goddess declared: "This case is too difficult for anyone to judge, even me. I will select a jury of the best of my citizens, and have them hear both sides."

Athena presides over Orestes' trial; she forms a jury, the Areopagus.

At the council hall of the Areopagus assembled the world's first jury. Apollo also was there to plead for Orestes. He told the jury: "I have never made any pronouncements from Delphi that my father Zeus did not approve. This is justice at its strongest."

The Furies retorted, "So it was Zeus who ordered this man to avenge his father and disregard any honor due his mother?"

Apollo repeated the case against Clytemnestra: "A great king and a war hero was ignobly slain in his bath by a woman!"

"You say that Zeus honors a father's claims, but he himself put chains upon his own father! How do you explain that?"

"A father bound can be unbound, but there is no bringing back a dead man." Apollo then added another argument that sounds strange to us today: "A mother is not a true parent; she only takes care of the seed that the father planted in her womb. Fatherhood without a mother is possible. Look at Athena here. Zeus brought her forth by himself."

Apollo pleads Orestes' case; Athena recommends acquittal.

Athena then asked the jury's verdict. After they had voted, she announced her decision: "As Apollo has said, no mother gave me birth. Therefore I favor men in all ways, except for marrying one. If the votes are even, I favor acquitting Orestes."

The ballots were counted, and the votes were indeed even. The Furies were outraged. "Curses on you upstart gods who have trampled upon ancient laws! Our revenge will rush like wildfire over your land! You have dishonored the daughters of Night!"

Athena placates the Furies by giving them a place of honor in Athens.

Athena reasoned with them. "You were not dishonored; the votes were even. Do not hurt our land. I pledge to you a place of honor where my citizens will worship you. Give up your wrath."

The Furies repeated their cries of anger several times, but ultimately agreed to accept Athena's offer. She led them in solemn procession to their new home, where they protected Athens with their formidable power.

Euripides says that Orestes went to the Taurians' land.

According to Euripides, however, not all of the Furies relented. Half were appeased by Athena, but the other half continued to pursue Orestes. They refused to release him until he brought back to Greece the statue of Artemis from the land of the Taurians (now southern Russia). This land practiced a particularly savage form of worship to Artemis: all strangers who came there were taken to the goddess' temple and there sacrificed to her. Presiding over this cult was none other than Iphigenia, who had been saved by Artemis and taken there to serve her.

Orestes later meets but doesn't recognize Iphigenia.

When Orestes and Pylades landed there, they took refuge in a cave where they were found by shepherds, who overpowered them and brought them to the priestess. Learning that they had come from Greece, Iphigenia questioned them about people she had known there: Menelaus, Helen, Odysseus, Achilles. She worked the conversation around to her father:

Orestes reveals to Iphigenia the fate of their parents.

"Did Agamemnon survive the war?"

"Yes, but he is dead, killed by a woman's hand," Orestes answered.

"Oh no! What happened to his wife?"

"She is dead too, slain by her son in revenge for his father."

"Does he leave any children?"

"One virgin daughter, named Electra."

"Where does his son live now?"

"Nowhere and everywhere."

"He had another daughter once, didn't he? Does anyone ever talk about her?"

"Only to say that she's dead."

Iphigenia thought about what the "strangers" had told her, and an idea came to her: "Would one of you please take a letter to Argos for me? It says, among other things, that Iphigenia is alive." She selected Pylades to convey the letter, intending to sacrifice her still-unidentified brother. As she handed the paper to him, Pylades asked, "To whom should I give it?" "To my brother Orestes."

Orestes and Pylades at the court of the Taurians, with Iphigenia, as a priestess, on the steps. Pompeiian wall painting, 50 CE.

Their identities now revealed, Orestes and Iphigenia escape Tauris.

Pylades handed Orestes the letter on the spot. Brother and sister then knew all, and rejoiced at being reunited. But they still had a problem: how were they to escape from the Taurian land and certain death? Iphigenia contrived a clever plan. She told the king that because sinful men had come into the temple and polluted Artemis' statue, she needed to take it and them to the sea for purification. She added that everyone should stay within the city walls to avoid contagion. Thus they managed to reach the sea and set sail. Disaster almost struck when a tidal wave drove the ship back to shore again, but once again, Athena intervened and persuaded the king to allow the men and Iphigenia to leave. Thus the curse on the House of Atreus was ended at last.

A. REVIEW EXERCISES

1. **MULTIPLE CHOICE!** In each of the sentences below, circle the number of the answer that best answers the question or completes the statement.

a. Which of the following statements about Pelops is *not* true?

1. Pelops was the son of Thyestes.
2. Pelops was given an ivory shoulder.
3. Pelops' son was Atreus.
4. Pelops gave his name to the Peloponnesus.

b. Which deity distractedly consumed part of Pelops' shoulder?

1. Zeus
2. Artemis
3. Demeter
4. Poseidon

c. Pelops left Lydia and traveled to Greece. With whom did he fall in love?

1. Artemis
2. Hippodamia
3. Hippocrates
4. Hypsipyle

d. Which charioteer removed the linchpins from the chariot of his master, Oenomaus, causing his death and helping Pelops?

1. Atreus
2. Myrtilus
3. Aegisthus
4. Thyestes

e. Which two cursed Pelops as each was dying?

1. Oenomaus and Myrtilus
2. Oenomaus and Hippodamia
3. Myrtilus and Hippodamia
4 Myrtilus and Tantalus

f. What precious object did Atreus promise to sacrifice to the goddess Artemis, then kept for himself and broke his promise?

1. A four-horse chariot
2. A golden urn
3. A golden fleece
4. The sun

g. These two were rivals for the kingdom of Mycenae.

1. Atreus and Thyestes
2. Pelops and Oenomaus
3. Pelops and Thyestes
4. Atreus and Pelops

h. Who spoke this ironic line: "The most powerful are those who don't need power"?

1. Pelops
2. Tantalus
3. Thyestes
4. Atreus

i. Which Mycenaean ruler made a pretense of welcoming his brother home, but plotted instead the murder of his three nephews?

1. Thyestes
2. Aegisthus
3. Atreus
4. Agamemnon

j. Who was the child born of the illicit union between Thyestes and his daughter, Pelopeia, and who later killed Atreus and helped to kill his son, Agamemnon?

1. Menelaus
2. Aegisthus
3. Tyndareus
4. Tantalus

k. While preparing to sail to Troy, the Greek fleet was becalmed and unable to sail because of the displeasure of this goddess.

1. Artemis
2. Athena
3. Hera
4. Aphrodite

l. Who was the prophet who advised Agamemnon, the leader of the Greeks, that only the sacrifice of his daughter, Iphigenia, would appease the goddess' wrath?

1. Tiresias
2. Calchas
3. Oenomaus
4. Cassandra

m. Agamemnon devised a ruse to get Clytemnestra to allow Iphigenia to travel to Aulis. He told her that one of the great Greek heroes wanted to marry Iphigenia. Which hero did Agamemnon claim to be Iphigenia's intended husband?

1. Ajax
2. Atlas
3. Achilles
4. Astyanax

n. After Iphigenia had been led to the altar for sacrifice, which animal, sacred to Artemis, was found in her place, indicating that Artemis herself had intervened to save Iphigenia?

1. A hound
2. A deer
3. A pig
4. A lamb

o. Clytemnestra tricked Agamemnon into performing this action of hubris, which she said justified her killing of her husband.

1. Bringing Cassandra back with him to Mycenae
2. Walking on a red carpet into the palace
3. Sacrificing Iphigenia at Aulis
4. Stealing Briseis from Achilles

p. Which innocent person did Clytemnestra kill along with Agamemnon?

1. Orestes
2. Aegisthus
3. Electra
4. Cassandra

q. Which of these Athenian playwrights did not write about the tragedy of the House of Atreus, Agamemnon, Clytemnestra, Cassandra, Orestes, and Electra?

1. Aristophanes
2. Aeschylus
3. Sophocles
4. Euripides

r. This was the sister of Orestes who met him by surprise at the tomb of Agamemnon and who helped him plot the murder of their mother, Clytemnestra, and her lover, Aegisthus.

1. Iphigenia
2. Chrysothemis
3. Hippodamia
4. Electra

s. This token led his sister to realize that Orestes was indeed her brother.

1. A golden fleece
2. A snake
3. A bracelet
4. A lock of hair

t. Above all others, this person grieved the (false) news of the death of Orestes in a chariot race.

1. Aegisthus
2. Orestes' nurse
3. Clytemnestra
4. Pylades

u. The Erinyes, or Furies, can be taken as symbols or personification of which of the following?

1. Torture and death
2. Unremitting hunger and thirst
3. A guilty conscience
4. Hatred of one's parent(s)

v. The world's first jury, the Areopagus, was assembled in this city to hear the case against Orestes.

1. Mycenae
2. Argos
3. Delphi
4. Athens

w. Which deity served as chief judge at the trial of Orestes?

1. Apollo
2. Zeus
3. Athena
4. Hades

x. Which deity commanded Orestes to kill Clytemnestra to avenge Agamemnon's murder and later defended Orestes at the trial?

1. Zeus
2. Apollo
3. Athena
4. Hades

y. Orestes and Pylades met this woman or goddess unexpectedly in the land of the Taurians, and later, by the intervention of Athena, she escaped with them.

1. Artemis
2. Electra
3. Chrysothemis
4 Iphigenia

2. **CHRONOLOGY COUNTS!** Place the following events in chronological order. Use the numbers 1–10, with 1 as the first event and 10 as the last event in the sequence. Write the number in the space provided.

____ Cassandra warns the Mycenaean citizens that she, along with their king, is about to be murdered.

____ Clytemnestra pretends to mourn the untimely death of her son, Orestes.

____ Aegisthus uncovers the sheet from the corpse of one he thought to be Orestes.

____ Clytemnestra secretly speaks with Achilles.

____ Atreus hideously parodies sacred ritual by leading his nephews to a sacrificial altar.

____ Iphigenia, Orestes, and Pylades leave the land of the Taurians; the curse is lifted.

____ The gods curse Tantalus for the horrible outrage of offering his son as food.

____ Thyestes returns to Mycenae.

____ Agamemnon offers Iphigenia in sacrifice at Aulis for favorable winds.

____ Orestes kills Aegisthus.

B. MUSINGS

1. Archeological excavations have uncovered the remains of an elaborate royal residence or palace at the site of ancient Mycenae. It has been dated to ca. 1400–1340 BCE. Other similar palaces of what is called the "Mycenaean Period," ca. 1450–1200 BCE, have been located and excavated in the "land of Pelops," that is, the Peloponnesus, at such places as Pylos and Tiryns. (Find their location on a map.) Pictured on the next page is an architect's idea of how the palace at Mycenae might have looked, based on the archaeological evidence. This is the kind of palace that the playwrights Aeschylus, Sophocles, and Euripides might have had in mind when writing their dramas about Agamemnon, Cytemnestra, and the others!

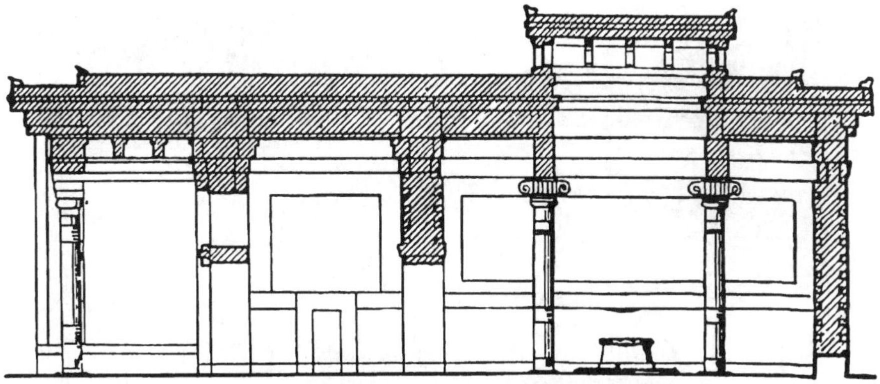

Rendering of side of palace at Mycenae

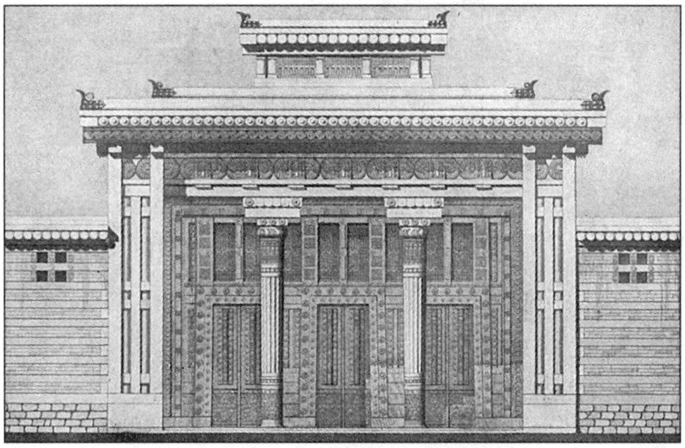

Reconstruction of front of palace at Mycenae

The palaces at Mycenae, Pylos, Tiryns, and other sites are each unique, but they all have several common features. The most striking similarity is a spacious throne room or "great hall," called a *megaron*. Like most ancient Greek houses, there are separate areas for men and women. Pictured at right, you can see a floor plan for the *megaron* at Tiryns, which can serve as a model for what the *megaron* at Mycenae might have looked like.

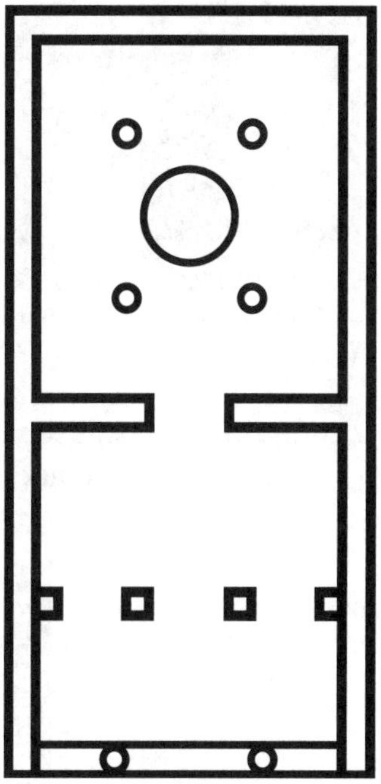

Ground plan of a *megaron* at Tiryns

The ground plan shows two circular columns standing before an open court or vestibule, which in turn is supported by four squared columns or pilasters. A person would enter the *megaron*, or throne room, through a single entrance from this vestibule. In the *megaron*, one would have seen four central columns placed around an open hearth and a raised throne placed opposite the entrance. To learn more about the *megaron* and Mycenaean palaces, go to this website:

- http://www.dartmouth.edu/~prehistory/aegean/

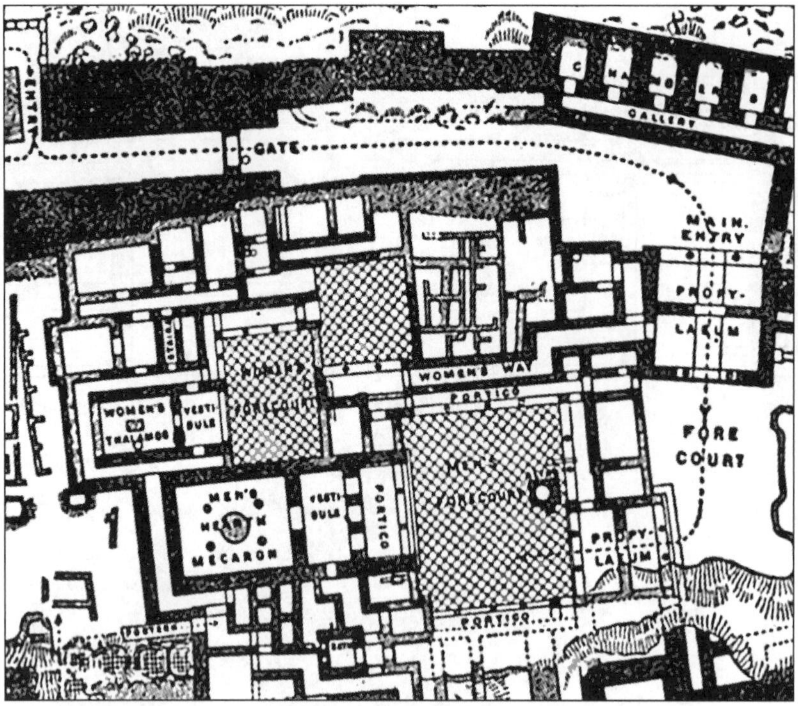

Floor plan of palace at Tiryns

Look at this detailed floor plan of the Mycenaean palace of Tiryns, very similar in many ways to the palace at Mycenae. Think about the characters in the myth related in this chapter and draw a line from each character pictured below to a room in which each might be placed.

Clytemnestra

Agamemnon and servant

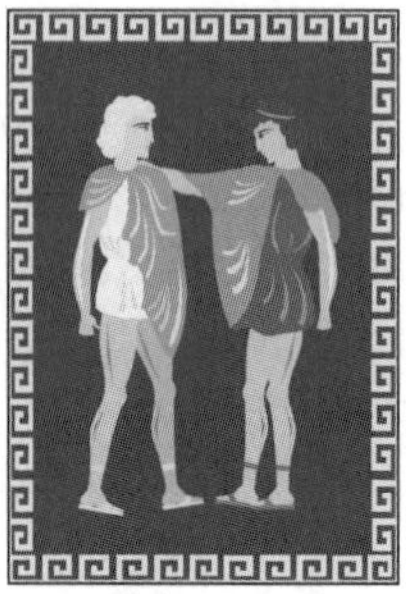

Orestes and Pylades

Electra

Cassandra

Aegisthus

2. Actors in Greek drama always wore character masks in every drama. Each mask was called a *persona.* Research more about the *personae* or masks used in ancient Greek theater. Now, create one or more of your own tragic masks of the characters in this myth and share them with your class.

3. The myths associated with the House of Atreus incorporate the lowest, most repugnant, vile, hideous crimes known to humankind including murder, rape, incest, and cannibalism. It has been thought that myths offer a socially acceptable way of expressing violent feelings, especially those directed against members of one's family. Remember how cruel Zeus and Cronus were to their own fathers! What outlets for expressing these feelings exist today?

4. For the older student: The House of Atreus has been one of the most influential myths on later literature. Below are only a few of the plays and novels it has inspired. Read one or more and comment on which aspects of the myth are changed and which remain the same. How are the characters interpreted differently by different authors?

    - Thomas Berger, *Orrie's Story* (novel, 1990)
    - Eugene O'Neill, *Mourning Becomes Electra* (play trilogy, 1931)
    - Joyce Carol Oates, *Angel of Light* (novel, 1981)
    - Jack Richardson, *The Prodigal* (play, 1960)
    - Robert Schenkkan, *The Kentucky Cycle* (play series, 1998)

C. WORDS, WORDS, WORDS

The Daily Muse

News you can use

Murder!

1. The characters in this chapter and their bloody adventures would keep a modern police **homicide** division busy for decades! As you already know, **homicide** means the murder of a human being. Use a good dictionary to look up the meanings of the two roots of this chilling word:

    homo- ______________________________

    ____

    -cide ______________________________

    ____

    What language(s) do these roots come from? ______________________________

2. Now use your prior knowledge and the information you have just looked up in the dictionary to complete the following exercise. The left-hand column is a list of nouns; the right-hand column is a list of definitions. To match each noun with its definition, put the letter of the correct definition in the space provided.

1.	____	Matricide	a.	Murder of a baby
2.	____	Patricide (or Parricide)	b.	A grass or plant killer
3.	____	Fratricide	c.	Killing of a sister
4.	____	Sororicide	d.	Murder of a mother
5.	____	Infanticide	e.	A substance that kills a fungus
6.	____	Regicide	f.	Killing a god
7.	____	Genocide	g.	A substance that kills bugs
8.	____	Herbicide	i.	A killing of a king
9.	____	Fungicide	j.	Murder of a father
10.	____	Deicide	k.	Killing of a brother
11.	____	Insecticide	l.	Murder of a race or ethnic group of people

3. In the following exercise, write the correct character name in the space provided.

Which character(s) in this chapter were guilty of matricide? ____________________

Which character(s) of regicide? ____________________

Which character(s) of fratricide? ____________________

Which of the homicide of three boys? ____________________

Which attempted homicide but did not succeed? ____________________

D. How 'Bout That?

Butterfly: ***Hypna clytemnestra***

- One of the most interesting structures to be found and excavated at the site of ancient Mycenae was the so-called Treasury of Atreus, pictured below:

Corbelled entrance to the Treasury of Atreus

Domed interior of the Treasury of Atreus

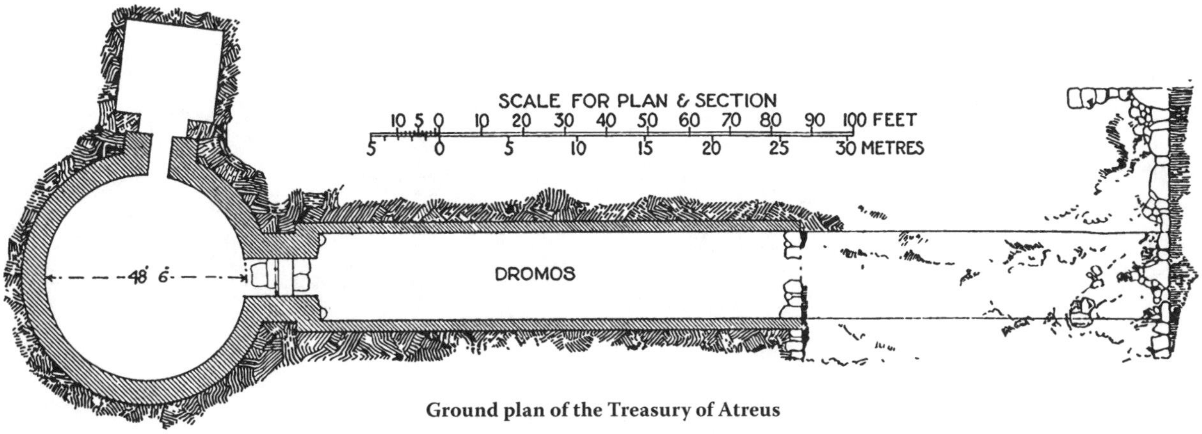

Ground plan of the Treasury of Atreus

This building is not really a treasury but a tomb, built in the shape of a beehive. Inside the entrance to the tomb, a long passage called a *dromos* leads into the circular tomb and its squared annex. Want to know more? Check out this website:

- http://www.dartmouth.edu/~prehistory/aegean/?page_id=761

E. WHO'S WHO?

- For the House of Atreus, see GENEALOGICAL CHART 16.

Chapter Fourteen

Thebes and Oedipus

General Sources:

Sophocles *Oedipus the King, Oedipus at Colonus, Antigone*

Apollodorus *Library* 3.4.1–33.7

Cadmus slays Ares' serpent-son. At left, Athena advises him. Above floats the head of Harmonia, Cadmus' future wife. Ancient vase painting.

Cadmus founds Thebes and sows the seeds of the Theban nobility after killing Ares' serpent.

Cadmus was the legendary founder of Thebes and the father of the line that led to Oedipus and his children. (See Genealogical Charts 11 and 17.) He was the brother of Europa, whose kidnapping by Zeus you read about in chapter 6. When Europa's father discovered his daughter was missing, he sent his sons to find her. After a long and fruitless search, Cadmus went to Delphi to ask whether he should continue looking or begin his own life. The oracle told him not to worry about his sister, but to make a cow his guide and follow her until she dropped dead from exhaustion. He did so, and pursued her until she lay down at the current location of the city of Thebes. Cadmus wanted to sacrifice the cow to Athena, so he sent some of his companions to fetch water from a spring sacred to Ares. A serpent, also Ares' son, guarded this spring and killed most of the men Cadmus sent. In anger, Cadmus killed the serpent and on Athena's advice, planted its teeth like seeds. Immediately, armed men sprang up. Cadmus threw rocks at them, and the armed men, thinking they were being attacked by each other, fell to fighting until most of them were killed. The five who survived became the ancestors of the Theban nobility. In return for those he killed, Cadmus spent a long time in Ares' service, but when he was released from his duties, Athena arranged for him to have the kingdom. Zeus gave him as his wife Harmonia, the daughter of Aphrodite and Ares.

Cadmus and Harmonia's four daughters suffer grievous misfortune.

Cadmus and Harmonia had several daughters: They all died tragically or suffered great misfortune. Autonoe's son was Actaeon, who was torn to pieces by his own hunting dogs after he caught Artemis (Diana) bathing (see chapter 12). Semele was the mother of Dionysus; you have already learned how she died while she was pregnant with the wine-god. After Dionysus was born, Zeus had him turned over to Ino and her husband Athamas. Hera was outraged, and sent madness to Ino and Athamas. Athamas killed one of their sons, thinking he was a deer. Ino threw their other son into a boiling cauldron, and then leaped with his corpse into the sea. (The gods took pity on them, however, and transformed them into sea deities who help sailors.) Agave was also punished with madness, you will recall, and driven to hunt down and kill her own son, Pentheus (see chapter 4).

Cadmus' great-grandson Laius orders his son killed by exposure, but the boy is rescued, adopted by the king and queen of Corinth, and named Oedipus.

Cadmus also had a son named Polydorus, of whom we know little except that he had a son named Labdacus, who had a son named Laius. Laius was married to Jocasta. An oracle told them that they should not have children, as the child would grow up to slay his father. When an infant was born to them, Laius bored through the baby's ankles with pins and gave him to a shepherd to expose. The shepherd took pity on the baby, however. He turned him over to another shepherd, who gave him to the king and queen of Corinth, Polybus and Merope, to raise as their own. They named the child Oedipus, which is Greek for "swollen foot," because of his injured ankles. He grew up to surpass his peers in strength. Out of jealousy, one of them told him he was not really his parents' son. Oedipus questioned Merope, but she avoided telling him the truth. He therefore went to Delphi to consult the oracle. The answer he received was very different from what he expected: "Do not return home, or you will kill your father and marry your mother!"

Oedipus kills an old man who attacked him with a whip while in a chariot.

Horrified, Oedipus ran away from Corinth and set out towards Thebes. His path led him to a place where three roads meet. There a driver of a horse-drawn chariot, who had one old man as a passenger, tried to push him off the road. In a rage, Oedipus struck the driver, killing him. The elderly passenger brought down his whip on Oedipus' head. A swift blow of Oedipus' staff ended his life instantly. Oedipus also killed the other attendants.

Continuing on his way, Oedipus encountered the Sphinx outside Thebes. This was a monster that perched on a cliff and asked all passing travelers the same riddle: "What walks on four legs in the morning, two in the afternoon, and three in the evening?" If they failed to answer, the Sphinx would kill them. Oedipus figured out the answer: "It is Man, who crawls on all fours as an infant, then walks on two legs, and leans on a stick to walk in old age." The defeated Sphinx threw herself off the cliff and died.

Oedipus marries the widowed queen of Thebes, Jocasta.

As a reward, the joyous Thebans granted Oedipus marriage with their queen—none other than Oedipus' own mother! They lived together happily for years and had four children: two sons, Eteocles and Polynices; and two daughters, Antigone and Ismene. However, a devastating plague struck Thebes. People succumbed by the hundreds to the devouring fever, so many that there was no more wood to build their funeral pyres. The crops stopped growing, and women stopped giving birth. In desperation, people turned to Oedipus to save them once more. The king had not been idle; he had sent his brother-in-law, Creon, to Delphi for advice from Apollo on ending the plague. The Thebans were momentarily cheered when Creon returned with his head crowned with laurel, a sign that the god had given him good news.

Oedipus encounters the Sphinx on this representation of a 5th-century, red-figure vase painting.

Laurel

Creon reveals the cause of the plague that has struck Thebes.

"Apollo says our land is impure because we are still harboring the murderer of our former king, Laius, in the city," Creon announced. "When we drive him out, the plague will end."

"I will do all I can to save the city," responded Oedipus. "Whoever killed Laius, I pray that he may suffer every evil for the rest of his wretched life. And if he happens to be one of my household, may I myself suffer the curse I just spoke! But where should I begin? Laius was killed a long time ago."

One of the Theban elders suggested, "Maybe the blind seer Tiresias can help."

"I have already sent messengers twice to him. I wonder why he has taken so long."

Oedipus consults Tiresias to learn from him who is the killer of Laius.

Just then the wise man arrived, led by a boy guide. Oedipus addressed him humbly, "Tiresias, you know about all that happens in heaven and on earth, even if you are blind. Apollo has said that release from this disease will come only when we drive out Laius' killers. If you know anything, please tell it."

"It is terrible to be wise when it does the seer no good! Let me go back home," was Tiresias' discouraging answer.

"You know and will not speak? How can you let the city rot like this?"

Tiresias reveals that Oedipus himself is the killer.

Tiresias remained silent while Oedipus continued to push him. Finally the prophet declared, "You are the killer whom you seek!"

Oedipus was outraged. "How dare you! Do you think that you can say such things because you are blind?"

"Don't taunt me with my blindness! Soon others will be directing the same remarks to you! You have eyes, but you don't see what evil you are living in! Come on, boy, take me home."

Oedipus thought that Creon had bribed Tiresias to say what he had said. He assumed Creon wanted to depose him and rule Thebes himself. Angrily he confronted his brother-in-law, who denied vigorously that he had any ambitions for the throne.

Hearing her husband and brother arguing, Jocasta emerged from the palace. "Aren't you two ashamed to be brawling out here while the city is so sick? What are you fighting about anyway?" she scolded.

Jocasta tells Oedipus that Laius was killed at a triple crossroads.

"I will tell you, Jocasta, because I respect you. Creon says that I am the murderer of Laius! He sent a phony prophet here to tell me so," responded Oedipus.

"Stop worrying about prophets and oracles! They are all useless. I know this because an oracle once came to Laius that he would die at his son's hand. It never happened; robbers killed him at a place where three roads meet. As for his poor baby, he was only three days old when Laius pierced his ankles and handed him over to be exposed on a mountain."

Jocasta's words, intended to reassure Oedipus, had the opposite effect. "Wait . . . did you say Laius was slaughtered where three highways meet?"

"That's what the rumor was."

"How long ago was this?"

"Shortly before you came to power."

"O Zeus, what have you done to me! Jocasta, tell me what Laius looked like!"

"A tall man with graying hair. He was about your size."

Oedipus realizes that in cursing Laius' killer, he has cursed himself.

"Oh, no! I think I have just called down curses on myself! Tell me one more thing: how many were with Laius when he was killed?"

"Five altogether, including a herald."

"Who told you all this?"

"One man—the only survivor—returned."

"Is he still here?"

"No. He begged me to let him be a shepherd as far as possible from the city. So I sent him away. It was the least I could do."

"Could he come back here at once?"

"Yes, but why?"

Oedipus told Jocasta the entire story of his encounter with the old man at the crossroads. He was desperate to question the former slave. Jocasta acceded to his wishes, anxious to please him.

Oedipus is relieved hearing that Polybus, his adopted father, has died.

At that moment a messenger arrived with news for Oedipus. Polybus, his adopted father, had died of natural causes in Corinth. Oedipus was sad at the loss, but relieved that he had not been responsible for Polybus' death. "Apollo's oracles are worth nothing now! And yet I'm still worried that I could somehow marry my mother Merope."

"Oh, you don't have to worry about that," the messenger answered. "She is not your real mother, and Polybus was not your real father. When you were a baby, I was working as a shepherd on Mount Cithaeron. Another shepherd found you on the mountain with your ankles pierced and handed you over to me. Then I turned you over to Polybus and Merope, who had no children of their own."

By coincidence, the shepherd who had taken the infant Oedipus to Corinth was the same one who had survived the attack on Laius and his retinue. He had now arrived at Oedipus' command, but Jocasta was afraid to let her husband continue the investigation. She had figured out everything. "May you never know who you are!" was her last word to Oedipus as she hurried into the palace.

Oedipus thought she was merely worried he would turn out to be slave born. He turned to the newly-arrived shepherd and pointed to the messenger who had brought the news about Polybus. "Have you met this man before?"

"Hard to remember . . . "

"Sure you did!" the messenger interrupted. "We both worked on Cithaeron for three years. Don't you remember giving me a child to raise as my own son? Here he is now, all grown up!"

The old servant was reluctant to speak, but Oedipus threatened him with torture. Finally he revealed all: "The baby was born of the house of Laius. It was his child, they say. Your wife can tell you for certain. She was afraid of bad oracles, that he would kill his father. I pitied him and handed him over to this man here, but it seems I only saved him to suffer something worse."

"Alas!" cried Oedipus. "At last it's all too clear. This is the last time I see the light. I married a woman I should not have married, and I killed a man I should not have killed."

Oedipus, finding Jocasta hanged, gouges out his own eyes.

Frenzied, he ran into the palace. He headed for the room he and Jocasta had shared. There he found his wife hanged by her neck, swinging to and fro. He groaned, untied the noose, and took down Jocasta's body. Then he punished himself in a hideous way: he took Jocasta's brooch off her dress and stabbed out his eyes with it!

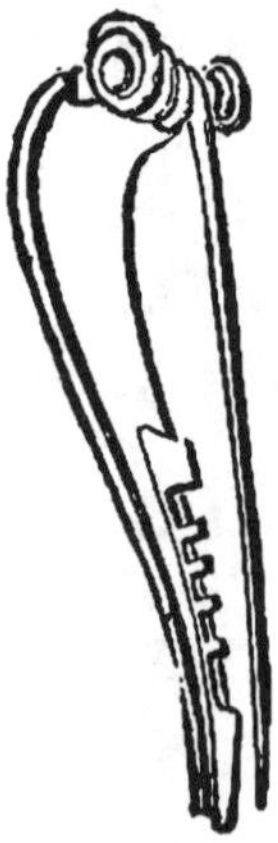

Greek brooch (*fibula*)

To those who expressed shock that he could do such a thing, he answered, "What is there in the world worth seeing for me? My children's faces? The people of my city? How can I look at my parents in the Underworld?" He then set off on his self-imposed exile from Thebes.

Oedipus and his daughter Antigone, exiles from Thebes, find refuge at Colonus.

For years Oedipus wandered as an itinerant beggar, accompanied by one or both of his daughters. One day, when he was a very old man, he and Antigone came to a suburb of Athens named Colonus. They asked a passing citizen to tell them about the place they had come to. "Get away from there at once!" the man exclaimed, shocked. "That's the grove of the Eumenides you're sitting in! It's holy ground!" Oedipus did so, but realized that his life was about to end, for Apollo had prophesied that his final resting place would be this very spot. As he prayed to the Furies, more Athenians arrived, full of curiosity about this mysterious traveler.

At that moment, Ismene entered on horseback, bearing unhappy news about her brothers. "At first they decided to leave the throne to Creon and end the curse on our house." She was referring to a prophecy that each would die at the other's hand in a fight over the throne of Thebes. "Then they decided to take turns ruling. When it was his turn to step down, Eteocles refused. So Polynices went to Argos and gathered allies to attack the city." She also added that Oedipus' grave would become a holy place, with the power to bless whatever city had it. Eteocles and Polynices were therefore determined to bring Oedipus back to Thebes, but not to allow him within the city.

Oedipus at Colonus with Antigone

"Then may the gods never end their feud! They never did anything for me, while you girls shared all my troubles and lightened my load!" exclaimed the outraged Oedipus.

Theseus, king of Athens, offers Oedipus sanctuary.

The Athenians who had gathered to see Oedipus told him what he needed to do to propitiate the dread goddesses who inhabited the nearby grove. They also pushed him to tell all the gory details of his sins in killing his father and marrying his mother. Fortunately for Oedipus, King Theseus arrived and welcomed Oedipus kindly. "I can tell from your mutilated eyes who you are and what you've suffered. I was an exile for many years too. Therefore, no stranger in adversity will find help from me lacking. Whatever you and your children need, I will provide it."

"Your generous words need no long response," answered Oedipus. "All I ask is that you bury me here in Athens, and not allow anyone to take me back to Thebes. If you do that, your city will receive a great blessing."

Theseus promised to do as Oedipus had asked, just in time, for Antigone spotted Creon approaching, attended by soldiers. "You gentlemen need not be afraid of me," he said when he had arrived. "I have only come to take Oedipus home." Turning to Oedipus, he added, "I am so sorry to see you reduced to this! Your banishment is lifted. Come back to Thebes, where you belong."

Oedipus was not fooled by Creon's false kindness. He retorted, "*Now* you feel sorry for me? Where were you years ago when I first longed to return home? When you give a man what he wants only because you want something from him, your gift is worthless."

Creon tries to force Oedipus to return to Thebes by seizing his daughters, but Theseus rescues them.

Failing to persuade Oedipus by words, Creon decided to use force. He had his soldiers drag Antigone and Ismene away. "You win. Let's see how much you enjoy your triumph with your two crutches taken away!" he sneered.

The Athenians tried to stand up to Creon's men, but they were no match for the armed troops. Theseus, however, gathered up his own soldiers and returned the young women to their father. No sooner had they joyously embraced at being reunited when Oedipus' older son, Polynices, arrived, in tears. "I don't know who is more wretched, you or I, Father," he began. "I neglected you for years and I'm sorry. But there's no changing the past. My brother has unjustly kept me from the throne that is rightfully mine. I have gathered seven leaders with their squadrons to make war on Thebes. If you give me your blessing, victory will be mine. If you refuse, I will surely die."

Ismene and Antigone surround Oedipus in *Oedipus Damning His Son, Polynices,* pen and ink copy of painting, 1883, by André Marcel Baschet (1862–1941).

Unmoved by his son's plea, Oedipus answered him bitterly. "When you held the throne that your brother now has, you drove me away and forced me to become this beggar that you now pity! If it weren't for my daughters, I would have been dead long ago! You and Eteocles are no children of mine! I curse you both and call upon Ares and the Furies to see that you each die at the hand of the other! Go back to Thebes and tell the people that this is the legacy Oedipus gives his sons!"

Antigone tried to reason with her brother. "I beg you to give up this campaign against the city!"

Polynices, refusing to end the conflict with Eteocles, leaves Oedipus.

However, Polynices would not be moved. He embraced his sisters one last time; his parting words were: "This is the last time you will see me alive. I pray you two may escape our family's curse."

As he departed, the Athenians heard rumbles of thunder. It was the gods' signal to Oedipus that the end of his life was now at hand. "Fetch Theseus!" he commanded.

When the king returned, Oedipus told him, "The gods are calling me. I will take you to the spot where my tomb is to be. Do not show it or speak of it to anyone, even my children, except for your heir. Thus the secret will pass from generation to generation, and Athens will always be safe from attacks of Thebans."

Oedipus disapears into the earth; his daughters return to Thebes.

Theseus knew that Oedipus was speaking the truth. He allowed the blind man to lead him into the mysterious grove of the Eumenides. A few moments later, Theseus returned alone. "He is gone. A messenger from heaven took him, or the earth opened to receive him. There was no thunderbolt from Zeus or whirlwind from Poseidon, no illness or pain. Be comforted that the gods were good to him in the end," he said to the weeping Antigone and Ismene.

The princesses were sorrowful at the loss of their beloved father, and even more grieved to learn that they were forbidden to see his grave. Yet they knew that he was at rest now, and they departed for Thebes to see if they could somehow prevent the war between their brothers.

Polynices and Eteocles kill each other; Creon denies burial to Polynices.

Their wishes for peace were not to be. Polynices and the other leaders, known collectively as the Seven Against Thebes, attacked the city. Eteocles led the army in the city's defense, and the brothers killed each other as Oedipus had predicted. Creon took over as king, and issued a decree that Eteocles be buried with full honors because he had died in his city's behalf. However, he refused all burial to Polynices, whom he regarded as a traitor. He added that anyone attempting to bury him would be stoned to death. This meant that the dead man's spirit could never cross the Styx, but would be doomed to wander its banks forever.

Men bear the bodies of the slain brothers, Eteocles and Polynices. Creon leads the procession. Antigone follows, leading a procession of mourning women.

Antigone thought Creon was wrong to deny Polynices the rites due the dead. She decided to defy him and bury their brother, with Ismene's help. As she confided her plan to her sister, Ismene shrank back. "We are only women! We cannot fight with men and disobey the law!" she warned.

Antigone defies Creon's decree and sprinkles Polynices' corpse with dirt as burial.

"You do what you want, but I *will* bury him, even if I have to die for it!"

Shortly afterwards, a sentry brought word to Creon. Someone had thrown several handfuls of earth on Polynices' body, enough to count as a burial and allow his spirit to cross the river of the dead. Creon was outraged at this disobedience and threatened, "Bring me the man who did this, or I'll string you up alive!"

The terrified sentry left, only to return in a brief time with Antigone. Creon was puzzled. "Why have you brought her here?"

Antigone sprinkles dust over the body of her brother Polynices.

"She was burying him! After those threats of yours, King, we went back and cleaned the dust off the body. We kept watch carefully, but suddenly a storm of dust arose from the earth. Nobody could see a thing. When it finally cleared, we saw Antigone standing over the body and mourning. She brought more dust to cover the body again. We arrested her, and she denied nothing."

Creon dismissed the sentry, and asked Antigone, "Did you know about my proclamation regarding this matter?"

"Of course. It was public."

"And yet you dared to break the law?"

"Yes. Your law is strong, but the immortal unrecorded divine laws are even stronger. I am not afraid to die, but I would have been afraid to leave my brother unburied."

Creon interrogates Antigone and accuses the innocent Ismene as well.

Creon thought she was simply being stubborn, like her father. He was especially outraged that it had been a woman who defied him. He decided that Ismene was equally guilty, and he resolved to execute both sisters. Ismene was willing to share her sister's punishment, but Antigone refused. "Save yourself; there are those who will say you did the right thing. You chose life; I chose death."

Antigone also happened to be engaged to the king's son, Haemon. Creon said to his son, "You have heard my judgment on your bride. Are you going to hate me, or obey me?"

"I am your son, Father. I always defer to your wisdom. No marriage means more to me than that," was Haemon's meek reply.

"Good. Every father prays for a dutiful son. I'm glad you aren't losing your head over this woman. She was the only one in this city to scorn my law and break it. If I can't keep order in my own family, how can I rule nations? Anyone chosen to govern must be obeyed in all things. The man who knows how to obey is the only one fit to rule when the time comes. Nothing is worse than anarchy! This is why cities fall and armies are routed. So we keep the laws and nobody gets away with breaking them, especially a woman!"

Haemon, Creon's son and Antigone's fiancé, says that the people support Antigone.

Haemon answered, "Your reasoning is good. But other people are able to reason, too, people who are afraid to give you advice because they fear your temper. I hear what they're saying in the city: 'This woman did a generous thing burying her brother; she doesn't deserve to die. She deserves to be honored.' Do not be stubborn and think that you alone are right. Look at trees in a storm—the only ones torn up by the roots are those that don't bend."

This mild response outraged Creon. "Am I, at my age, supposed to take lessons from a *boy*?"

"What does my age matter, if I am right?"

"Are you defending a criminal?"

"The city doesn't think she's a criminal."

"Is the city trying to tell me how to rule? I'm the one who gives the orders! You've been taken in by a woman!"

Realizing he could not reason with his father, Haemon left him, uttering an ominous threat as he did: "You will never see my face again!"

Creon did relent in one way: he retracted Ismene's death sentence. Yet he remained determined to destroy the brave Antigone. He ordered her imprisoned in a cave with just enough food to absolve the state of her death. As she was led away, Antigone lamented that her only marriage bed would be her tomb.

Tiresias then came to the king with news of dire omens. All the hearths and altars of the city were polluted, and the gods refused to accept any offerings. The unburied corpse of Polynices was causing the impurity. "You must correct your mistake, Creon," he advised. "What is the point of hurting someone already dead? You must yield, for your own good!"

Creon refuses to yield even to Tiresias' prophecies of disaster for Creon's own family.

Creon remained stubborn. "Why do doddering fortune-tellers always pick on me? I won't yield, even if Zeus' own eagles carry Polynices' corpse in pieces up to the heavens! I am not afraid of pollution." He added that Tiresias must be taking bribes.

"If that's what you think, then listen to this!" the blind prophet cried. "You will pay for these two—the one you condemn to living death and the dead man you deny burial—with the deaths of your own loved ones!" He departed.

This frightened Creon. "It is hard to give in, but I don't want to lose all because of stubborn pride either! Very well. I will free Antigone from her prison. I will even release her myself instead of leaving the job to others!"

Antigone, Haemon, and Creon's queen, Eurydice, all die by their own hands.

It seemed that the crisis was about to be resolved happily. But when Creon arrived at the cave where Antigone had been imprisoned, he found a horrifying sight. The young woman had hanged herself, deciding that a quick death was preferable to a lingering one. Haemon lay beside her, crying, "My love! My father took you away from me!" Creon called out to his son, "Haemon, what are you doing? What are you thinking—your eyes look so strange! Oh, my son, I'm so sorry." Haemon said nothing; he spat in his father's face. He drew his sword and lunged at his father, missing. He then turned the blade on himself and plunged it into his own side. As he died, he took Antigone in his arms for the last time.

The sons of the Seven Against Thebes sack Thebes.

When Creon's wife, Queen Eurydice, heard this dreadful news, she too committed suicide. At last Creon realized how wrong he had been, but it was too late. He had done great harm not only to his family, but to the city whose interests he had claimed to champion. The sons of the slain generals who had attacked Thebes later banded together and sacked the city.

A. Review Exercise

MULTIPLE CHOICE! In each of the sentences below, circle the letter of the answer that best answers the question or completes the statement.

1. Who was the sister of Cadmus whom he tried, in vain, to locate in Europe?
   a. Semele b. Europa
   c. Ino d. Autonoe

2. What was Cadmus compelled to do in order to found the city of Thebes?
   a. Follow a cow b. Kill a serpent
   c. Defy Ares d. All of the above

3. The armed men who fell to fighting one another on the soil of Thebes sprang from which of the following?
   a. Seeds from Demeter b. Athena's magic herbs
   c. Serpent's teeth d. Hecate's potions

4. Laius was a descendant of all of these but one.
   a. Zeus b. Cadmus
   c. Europa d. Labdacus

5. Who was the wife of Laius and queen of Thebes?
   a. Semele b. Ino
   c. Harmonia d. Jocasta

6. Who was the child of the king and queen of Thebes whose name means "swollen foot"?
   a. Creon b. Oedipus
   c. Labdacus d. Polynices

7. What was the name of the mountain where Oedipus was left by the shepherd?
   a. Cithaeron b. Olympus
   c. Parnassus d. Everest

8. What did the Sphinx do after Oedipus answered her riddle?
   a. Cursed Oedipus and his family b. Caused the plague to strike Athens
   c. Hurled herself from a cliff d. Struck Oedipus and gouged out his eyes

9. Who, though blind, identified Oedipus as Laius' killer?
   a. The shepherd from Cithaeron b. The messenger from Corinth
   c. Jocasta d. Tiresias

10. Who caused the plague suffered by the Thebans?
    a. Cadmus
    b. Creon
    c. Laius
    d. Oedipus

11. A messenger from Corinth arrived at the palace of Thebes to tell Oedipus that someone had died. Who died?
    a. Merope, Oedipus' mother
    b. Merope, Oedipus' stepmother
    c. Polybus, Oedipus' father
    d. Polybus, Oedipus' stepfather

12. Jocasta revealed to Oedipus that Laius had been killed at this place.
    a. Mount Cithaeron
    b. Thebes
    c. A triple crossroad
    d. A high cliff

13. Who discovered the hanged body of Jocasta?
    a. Oedipus, her son/husband
    b. Antigone, her daughter/granddaughter
    c. Creon, her brother
    d. Eteocles, her son/grandson

14. What instrument did Oedipus use to destroy his own eyesight?
    a. His knife
    b. Jocasta's brooch
    c. Antigone's brooch
    d. Tiresias' staff

15. Oedipus and his daughters came to this place near Athens in their exile.
    a. Eleusis
    b. Piraeus
    c. Attica
    d. Colonus

16. Which king guaranteed them sanctuary and a safe burial for Oedipus?
    a. Creon
    b. Theseus
    c. Aegeus
    d. Eteocles

17. What is another name for the Eumenides?
    a. The Fates
    b. The Graces
    c. The Furies
    d. The Seven Against Thebes

18. Who sought and was refused the blessing of his father, Oedipus, for an attempted assault against his brother now ruling over Thebes?
    a. Creon
    b. Polynices
    c. Eteocles
    d. Haemon

19. These two remained faithful to Oedipus in his exile.
    a. Antigone and Ismene
    b. Antigone and Haemon
    c. Polynices and Eteocles
    d. Antigone and Polynices

20. Which of the following statements is correct about Oedipus' final resting place in the grove of the Eumenides?
    a. It was under a sacred oak tree.
    b. It was just outside the city of Thebes.
    c. It was a secret known only to Theseus.
    d. It was a place of public veneration at Athens.

21. Who refused Antigone permission to bury her brother Polynices?
    a. Oedipus
    b. Haemon
    c. Eteocles
    d. Creon

22. What resulted from this prohibition of Polynices' burial?
    a. Haemon revolted against his father.
    b. Ismene died.
    c. Thebes was polluted.
    d. The Furies drove Creon mad.

23. Who was Antigone's betrothed, who tried gently to dissuade his father from his stubbornness?
    a. Creon
    b. Haemon
    c. Theseus
    d. Eteocles

24. This person had the unenviable task of confronting yet another king of Thebes to tell him that his hubris regarding Antigone would cause the death of his beloved family members.
    a. Creon
    b. Oedipus
    c. Tiresias
    d. Theseus

25. This king found the dead bodies of Antigone, Haemon, and Eurydice too late to correct an injustice.
    a. Oedipus
    b. Theseus
    c. Eteocles
    d. Creon

B. Musings

1. Research Greek religious practice regarding funerals and burial customs. Which types of burial customs were practiced by the ancient Greeks? Inhumation or cremation, or both? Why?

2. Why did the ancient Greeks believe that the denial of burial to a human being was a "pollution"? What are the laws and customs concerning burial in your community?

3. Both the House of Atreus and Oedipus' family suffer from a curse that brings suffering and death on both the innocent and the guilty. To what extent is the reason for the curse clear in each case?

4. What contemporary beliefs support the idea of a curse? Can you think of any other stories or movies that deal with a curse?

5. Recall the appearance of oracles in other myths. How accurate are they? What versions of oracles still exist today?

6. Oedipus differs from the other heroes about whom we have read because he defeats a monster (the Sphinx) using intelligence rather than strength or magic weapons. Look for examples of this in other myths, stories, or movies.

7. Locate the full text of the tragedies listed at the beginning of this chapter and the previous one. Act out one or more scenes from them.

8. Sophocles' play *Antigone* raises the issue of civil disobedience: whether citizens have the right to disobey laws that they consider unjust. Give some examples from other stories, fictional or historical, where this occurs. What was the outcome? Did you think that the violators in each case (and in the case of Antigone) were justified or not?

9. The play *Antigone* is often used as a means to raise discussion about contemporary issues. A 1988 play by A. R. Gurney, titled *Another Antigone,* depicts the clash between a professor and student that results when she reworks the ancient tragedy into an antinuclear protest play. Locate the play and read some scenes from it. How is the conflict in that play similar to the conflict between Antigone and Creon, and how is it different? How do the secondary characters function in each case?

10. Write a brief skit exploring a contemporary issue that uses Antigone and Creon (or characters resembling them) as characters taking opposing positions.

C. WORDS, WORDS, WORDS

The Daily Muse

News you can use

Burial customs: inhumation, cremation, interment

The myths in this chapter vividly illustrate how important and necessary it was to the ancient Greeks to carry out the proper burial rites. Here are some terms associated with burial:

- **Inhumation** refers to the practice of burying a dead body, usually within some kind of a coffin or sarcophagus, in the earth.

Look up the word **inhumation** in a good dictionary. What is the meaning of the root word

-hum- (*humus*): ______________________________

What language does ***humus*** come from? ______________________________

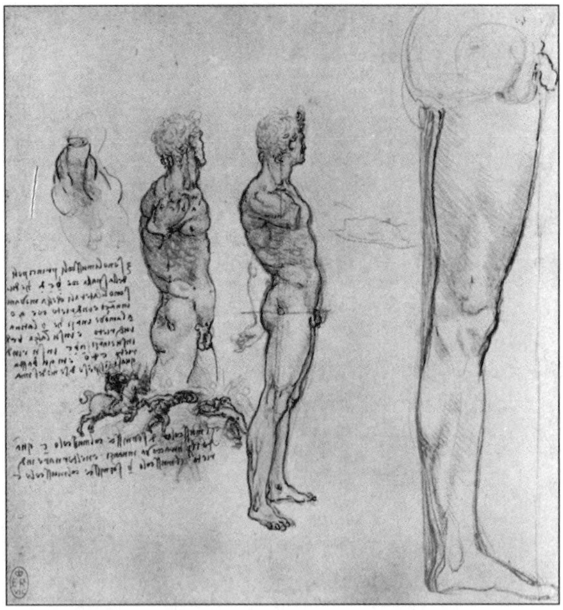

Sketches of the human figure by Leonardo Da Vinci

Ponder this: The words **inhumation** and **humus** both come from an older, Indo-European root word that also gives us the word "human," meaning an "earthly" or "earthy" being.

- **Cremation** refers to the burning of a dead body until it is consumed to ash.

Can you find the root and meaning of this word in a good English dictionary?

Root: ______________________________

Meaning: ______________________________

A collection of Roman cinerary urns that contained the ashes of cremated humans

- **Interment** refers to the placing of a deceased body in a grave in the earth.

What is the meaning of the root word **-ter-** (***terra***)? ______________________________

What language does ***terra*** come from? ______________________________

- Based on your prior knowledge and the information given above, can you match these related words and their appropriate meanings? Write the correct letter in the space provided.

1.	____	Exhume	a.	Object made from burning or firing clay
2.	____	Transhumance	b.	Moving cattle from one grazing ground toanother
3.	____	Humble	c.	To remove a dead body from a burial grave
4.	____	Ceramic	d.	An abundant natural element thought to have been formed by a primeval burning
5.	____	Carbon	e.	Lowly; acting with humility

D. HOW 'BOUT THAT?

Oedipus and psychology

Sigmund Freud, 1941

Myths are often thought to reflect the deepest concerns of the individual and society. According to the psychologist Sigmund Freud, love of mother and jealousy of father is one of the most powerful of male feelings. He referred to these feelings as the Oedipus complex, and believed these feelings were strongest between the end of a boy's third year and his fourth or fifth year. The superego, which is roughly the same as one's conscience, would then develop and prevent the boy from acting on these forbidden impulses; however, the result of acting on these impulses survives in myths, in which gods and heroes perform the acts we find socially unacceptable. The female equivalent of the Oedipus complex was named the Electra complex.

The truthfulness of Freud's theory has been often debated, and many contemporary psychologists no longer accept it. Still, the idea survives and has often been used as a springboard for humor. Woody Allen's short film *Oedipus Wrecks* in the movie *New York Stories* comically depicts a middle-aged man still struggling to resolve his relationship with his mother.

Oedipus in song

The songwriter Tom Lehrer wrote the following clever song titled "Oedipus Rex" ("Oedipus the King"):

Oedipus Rex

Tom Lehrer • 1959

From the Bible to the popular song,
There's one theme that we find right along;
Of all ideals they hail as good,
The most sublime is motherhood.

There was a man though, who it seems,
Once carried this ideal to extremes.
He loved his mother and she loved him,
And yet his story is rather grim.

There once lived a man named Oedipus Rex,
You may have heard about his odd complex.
His name appears in Freud's index
'Cause he loved his mother.

His rivals used to say quite a bit
That as a monarch he was most unfit.
But still in all they had to admit
That he loved his mother.

Yes, he loved his mother like no other,
His daughter was his sister and his son was his brother.
One thing on which you can depend is,
He sure knew who a boy's best friend is.

When he found what he had done,
He tore his eyes out, one by one.
A tragic end to a loyal son
Who loved his mother.

Duck-billed platypus

So be sweet and kind to mother,
Now and then have a chat.
Buy her candy or some flowers,
Or a brand new hat.
But maybe you had better let it go at that.

Or you may find yourself with a quite complex complex
And you may end up like Oedipus.
I'd rather marry a duck-billed platypus
Than end up like old Oedipus Rex.

Oedipus and the Sphinx in the visual arts

The story of Oedipus confronting the Sphinx and his easy answer to her confounding riddle has been a favorite topic of visual artists from the ancient Greeks onward. Find other images of Oedipus and the Sphinx and compare them to the painting at right and to the vase painting depicted earlier in this chapter.

***Oedipus and the Sphinx,* 1808, by Jean Auguste Dominique Ingres (1780–1867), Louvre, Paris**

E. Who's Who?

- For Agenor of Sidon's descendants, see Genealogical Chart 11.
- For Cadmus' descendants, the House of Thebes, and Oedipus' descendants, see Genealogical Chart 17.

Chapter Fifteen

Mortal Love and Metamorphosis

General Source:

Ovid *Metamorphoses*

Narcissus and Echo

Literary Source: Ovid *Metamorphoses* 3.344–510

Tiresias prophesies mysteriously about the lifespan of Narcissus.

Narcissus was born to a nymph named Liriope, who was the first to test the prophetic ability of the blind seer Tiresias. She wanted to know whether her son would live to old age. The prophet's answer was mysterious: "Yes, as long as he never knows himself." For a long time, the words remained unexplained, but Tiresias was proven right in the end.

Bronze statue of Narcissus (or perhaps Dionysus), Museo Archeologico Nazionale, Naples, Italy

By the age of sixteen, Narcissus was extremely handsome and much sought after. He was arrogant, however, and rejected all romantic overtures. One day, as he was hunting, a nymph named Echo spotted him. Echo had once been an eager chatterbox who distracted Hera with talk while her sister nymphs dallied with Zeus. Annoyed by Echo's babbling, Hera said, "From now on, may your talk be *very* brief!" She took away all of Echo's power to speak except to repeat the last words of others.

Echo longed to make her presence and love known to Narcissus, but she had to wait for him to speak first. Narcissus became separated from his fellow hunters. He called out, "Is anyone here?"

"Here!" answered Echo.

Narcissus looked around, startled. "Come here! Let's come together!" he cried, and received his own words back in response.

Echo reveals her love for Narcissus, embracing him.

"Let's come together!" Echo responded eagerly, and rushed out to embrace him. He had only been expressing mild curiosity about the stranger repeating his words, but she took them as a romantic invitation. As she flung her arms around his neck, Narcissus drew back in horror. "Hands off! May I die before I let you have your way with me!"

Narcissus rejects Echo, who wastes away because of her unrequited love.

Poor Echo could only respond, "I let you have your way with me," and slunk off ashamed. From then on she lived in remote caves. She wasted away from the pain of her unreturned love until there was nothing left except her voice, which can still be heard in caves and other lonely places.

***Echo and Narcissus*, ca. 1628, by Nicolas Poussin (1594–1665), Louvre, Paris**

The goddess Nemesis punishes Narcissus.

Narcissus did not escape unpunished, however. One day a lover whom he had rejected prayed to Nemesis: "May Narcissus learn what it feels like to love and not be loved in return!" The goddess heard the prayer and brought it to fulfillment. One day, Narcissus was hot and tired from hunting. He chanced upon a clear and shimmering pool. No herdsmen had ever led their flocks there; no birds or beasts had ever drunk from that cool water. As Narcissus leaned forward to drink, he was suddenly captivated by his own reflection: eyes like twin stars, wavy curls worthy of Apollo or Bacchus, smooth skin, a complexion both rosy and white. He fell madly in love. No desire for food or sleep could drag him away from that reflection.

Echo and Narcissus, **1903, by John William Waterhouse (1849–1917), Walker Art Gallery, Liverpool, UK**

He lamented to the trees, his only audience: "Has anyone ever loved more cruelly than I? There's only a little bit of water separating us!" And to the reflection he cried, "Why do you keep running away from me? It can't be my looks because all the nymphs want me! You look at me with love, when I reach out you reach back, you smile when I do and weep when I do! I even see your lips repeating my words!"

Narcissus is transformed into a flower with the same name.

Thus he kept addressing a lover that he simultaneously did and did not have. Consumed by his frustrated passion, he wasted away. Echo watched in pity as the lovely boy she had once admired grew pale and weak. Whenever he sighed, she sighed back; when he beat his breast, she imitated that sound too. As he said his last "Goodbye," she repeated, "Goodbye." Then death came to him, but as his spirit was being rowed across the Styx, he continued to stare at his reflection in the dark water. His body was never found; where it had been, there was only a flower of gold and white petals. Today, this flower, which still grows near bodies of water (profusely in spring), is called the narcissus.

Narcissus flower (daffodil)

Pyramus and Thisbe

Literary Source: Ovid *Metamorphoses* 4.55–161

Pyramus and Thisbe lived in ancient Babylon. Pyramus was the most beautiful young man in the city; Thisbe was the most beautiful young woman. They lived next door to each other and had been in love for years, but their families hated each other and kept the lovers apart. The two homes were separated by a wall with a tiny hole, unnoticed by everyone except the lovers. They used it to communicate. Often they would complain, "You nasty wall, why do you keep us apart? But we're not ungrateful; it's only because of you that we can speak to each other. If only you could let us embrace, or open up enough for us to kiss!"

Thisbe at the garden wall, from the painting by Sir Edward Burne-Jones (1833–1898)

In Babylon, young lovers Pyramus and Thisbe agree to elope.

At last they decided to run away from home and elope. They agreed to meet that night by the tomb of the ancient king, Ninus, close to which was a mulberry tree with snow-white fruit. How long that day seemed! When night finally came, Thisbe stealthily crept out of the house, her face hidden by a veil. She found Ninus' tomb and sat down under the mulberry tree, emboldened by her love. Suddenly, however, a lioness approached to drink from the nearby pool. Her mouth was stained with the blood of the cattle she had just slaughtered. By the rays of the moon, Thisbe spotted the beast, and fled for shelter to a nearby cave. As she ran, the veil she was wearing slipped off. When the lioness had finished drinking and was heading back to the woods, she chanced upon the veil and tore it up with her bloody mouth.

Arriving at the tomb, Pyramus finds Thisbe's torn and bloodied veil.

Shortly afterwards, Pyramus arrived. He grew pale when he saw the animal's footprints, and feared the worst when he saw the bloodstained veil. "One night will destroy two lovers!" he cried. "Poor Thisbe, this is my fault! I made you come to a dangerous place alone at night, and I did not arrive first! I call upon all the wild animals that live here, come and devour me too. But no, I won't just pray for death; that would be cowardly!" And with that he drew his sword and plunged it into his side. His blood spurted out like water from a burst pipe. Some of it splashed onto the white mulberries; some soaked into the tree's roots and dyed its fruit red.

Pyramus, believing Thisbe to have been killed, kills himself.

Thisbe returned to the spot, still afraid but not wishing to disappoint her lover. She was eager to tell him about the danger she had escaped. As she looked around, she thought, "This looks like the place, but didn't that tree have white fruit before?" Looking more closely, she saw blood, and then the body of her love. Flinging her arms around him, she cried, "Pyramus, what happened to you? Pyramus, answer! It's me, your own Thisbe! Please, raise up your head!" At the sound of her name, Pyramus opened his eyes, already heavy with death, and looked at her one last time.

Thisbe, finding Pyramus dead, kills herself with his sword.

When Thisbe saw her mangled veil and Pyramus' sword lying by its empty scabbard, she realized all that had happened. "Poor Pyramus, dead by your own hand because of love!" she lamented. "I have a hand strong enough to do what you did, and I feel the same love. Not even death will be able to part us! I pray that our parents will allow us to be buried together! And you, tree, may your fruit be dark forever, as a reminder of the blood of two dead lovers!" She placed the sword against her chest and fell on the weapon, still warm with Pyramus' blood.

Her final prayer touched the gods, and the fruit of the mulberry tree is now dark red when it ripens. Her plea touched the couple's parents also, who granted their children's wish to let their ashes rest in the same urn.

The Death of Thisbe, attributed to Giulio Romano (1499–1546)

Black mulberry (*Morus nigra*)

Tereus, Procne, and Philomela

Literary Source: Ovid *Metamorphoses* 6.424–674

Tereus, king of Thrace, marries Procne, daughter of the Athenian king.

Tereus was a king of Thrace who married Procne, the daughter of Pandion, king of Athens. Hera did not attend this union, nor did any other marriage gods. The Furies were the bridal attendants who led the wedding procession with torches lit from a funeral pyre. An ill-omened screech owl came to rest on the roof of the newlyweds' bedroom. All were unaware of this, however, and the couple decreed their anniversary a national holiday. Tereus and Procne were equally pleased when a son named Itys was born to them.

When the couple had been married five years, only one thing marred Procne's happiness: she missed her sister, Philomela. She asked her husband, "Please let me go visit my sister, or have her brought here. It would make me so happy to see her again!"

Tereus goes to Athens to bring Philomela to visit lonely Procne.

Tereus agreed, and he ordered a ship to take him to Athens as soon as possible. King Pandion greeted him cordially, and Tereus explained his mission. At the sight of Philomela, however, he was filled with desire for her. He begged Pandion even more urgently to let his daughter come with him, insisting, "This is what Procne wants!" He even burst into tears. The Athenian king was impressed by Tereus' concern for his wife's wishes and by Procne's devotion to her sister. He gave Philomela permission to go, but added, "Tereus, please watch over my daughter as if you were her father, and return her to me as soon as possible. She's my only comfort in my old age!" Watching father and daughter kiss each other goodbye, Tereus wished he were Pandion.

Ignoring promises to her father, Tereus rapes Philomela and leaves her in a hut.

On the journey back to Thrace, Tereus did not stop gazing at his sister-in-law. He could hardly wait for the trip to end. When it finally did, he took Philomela to a stone hut in the forest. The young woman was frightened. "Where's my sister?" she demanded.

Tereus made no answer, but brutally raped her. She screamed for help, but in vain. Then she cried, "You monster, how could you? Did my father's words mean nothing to you? Don't you care about your wife and her feelings for me? Why don't you just kill me? But I'll have my revenge, if the gods, who see all, care anything for justice! I'll tell the whole world about your crime! I'll shout it out in the marketplace!"

Fearful of being revealed, Tereus drew his sword and grabbed Philomela by the hair. She thought he was about to kill her, and she willingly offered her throat to be slit. Instead, however, the vicious tyrant cut out her tongue. When he had done that, he violated her again. Then he coolly went home to Procne, who at once asked where her sister was.

Tereus lies that Philomela died.

"Alas!" Tereus groaned and wept in pretended grief. "She died on the journey." Procne believed him and went into mourning, erecting an empty tomb and offering gifts to a ghost who was not a ghost.

Philomela weaves the truth on a tapestry sent to Procne, who frees her sister.

A year passed, and poor Philomela was still a prisoner in the closely guarded hut. But she thought of a way to communicate with her sister. She set up a crude loom and wove a tapestry that told her story. With gestures, she asked one of her sister's maids to deliver the "gift" to Procne. As the queen unrolled the weaving and read the message, she was too outraged to speak. All she could think of was plotting revenge.

During a festival of Dionysus, Procne realized her opportunity. She dressed up as a bacchant, carrying a thyrsus, wearing vine leaves in her hair, and draping a fawn's skin over her side. She led a procession of women into the forest and to Philomela's hut, her rage perfectly mimicking the frenzy inspired by the wine god. She screamed and broke down the door. Procne seized her sister, dressed her as a bacchant, and smuggled her back to the palace. Philomela was still too ashamed to look her sister in the face, but Procne declared, "No time for tears now! We need to think about vengeance! What should we do? Burn down the palace with him in it? Cut out his tongue and eyes? Inflict death by a thousand small wounds? Which will hurt him worst?"

Procne kills, cooks, and serves their child Itys to Tereus in revenge.

As Procne weighed the options, her child Itys came in. "How like your father you look!" thought Procne, now sure of what her revenge would be. He burbled, "I love you, Mommy," and her resolve weakened. But then she thought, "Why should *he* be able to talk, when my poor sister has no voice at all?" Now determined, she carried him off like a tiger dragging a fawn through the woods, until they came to an unused room deep within the palace. She plunged her sword into his side as he pleaded for his life. Then she and Philomela cut him up and cooked him.

Nightingale (*Luscinia megarhynchos*)

Hoopoe (*Upupa epops*)

Tereus turns into a hoopoe, Procne a swallow, and Philomela a nightingale.

Procne sent Tereus an invitation to a "private banquet," which she said was a special Athenian custom for husbands only, where not even servants were allowed. After he had stuffed himself with his own son's flesh, he ordered Procne, "Bring Itys here!" Unable to hide her savage pleasure, she retorted, "He's inside—inside of *you*, that is!" Philomela flung the head of the slain boy into his father's face. In horror, Tereus overturned the table and called upon the Furies for help. He drew his sword and ran after the sisters. As he pursued and they ran, the three were changed into birds. Procne became a swallow, Philomela became a nightingale; both birds bear red stains like blood on their breasts. The king became a hoopoe, a bird of prey with a crest instead of his crown and a long beak instead of his sword.

Philemon and Baucis

Literary Source: Ovid *Metamorphoses* 8.616–724

By now, you must be wondering if any love stories between mortals have happy endings! The next tale not only ends happily, it is one of our few depictions in Greek myth of love in old age.

Sometimes gods liked to roam the earth in mortal disguise, testing people's behavior towards their fellow creatures. Zeus and Hermes, disguised as travelers, once came to a town in Phrygia seeking food and shelter. They knocked on the doors of a thousand homes, and a thousand homes slammed doors in their faces.

Philemon and Baucis offer hospitality to two travelers unknown to them.

Finally they came to a humble hut, roofed with reeds from a nearby swamp. This was the home of Philemon and Baucis, two people of equal years who had been married in that hut in youth and continued to live there in old age. They made poverty light by admitting and bearing it. They cheerfully welcomed the gods, sparing no effort for their guests. They gave them a bench to sit on, which Baucis covered with a roughly woven blanket. She revived yesterday's fire, while her husband picked cabbage from the garden, and cut off a slice from an old piece of bacon hanging on a sooty rafter. They washed the disguised divinities' dirty feet with warm water in a wooden basin, and had them recline on a mattress stuffed with grass that covered a rough wooden couch. They covered the mattress with a cloth that they used only on special occasions, but which was equal to the couch in value. Baucis, trembling with age and exertion, set the table. One table leg was uneven, but she propped it up with a fragment of a broken pot. They passed the time in conversation as they waited for the food to cook.

For appetizers, Baucis served olives, pickled cherries, endive, radishes, fresh cheese, and eggs that had been lightly baked on the coals. Everything was served on earthenware, including the mixing bowl for wine and water. The cups were made of wood and patched up with wax. Then she served the cabbage flavored with pork, and finally dessert: figs, dates, plums, apples, and freshly picked grapes, accompanied by an oozing honeycomb.

***Baucis and Philemon*, 1658, by Rembrandt van Rijn (1606–1669), National Gallery of Art, Washington, DC**

When the wine jar refills itself, the old couple realizes the travelers are gods.

Baucis and Philemon realized that these were no ordinary travelers when a miracle occurred: no matter how often the bowl of mixed wine was emptied, it refilled by itself! They prayed, "Please forgive us for such a poor meal, so hastily prepared!" They decided they needed to do more, so they prepared to slaughter their only goose, the guard of their small home. The goose, however, was too swift for them. She eluded them repeatedly, and finally sought refuge with the gods, who would not allow the couple to kill her. They then revealed themselves. "We are gods. This godless town will be punished as it deserves, except for you two. Leave this hut and climb that nearby mountain with us!"

The gods turn the old couple's hut into a temple and them into priests.

The couple obeyed, leaning on walking sticks as they struggled to the summit. When they were nearly at the top, they looked back and saw that everything had been drowned in the waters of the swamp, except for their hut. They wept for their neighbors' fate, but marveled as they saw their humble home transformed. It became a magnificent temple, with marble columns replacing the wooden beams. The thatched roof turned to gold; bronze doors appeared, along with a marble courtyard!

Zeus addressed the two: "Good people, please tell us what we can do for you now." Baucis and Philemon consulted each other briefly, and then said, "We would like to be priests in your temple, and because we have lived so happily together for so long, we pray that we may die at the same time, so that neither of us has to live without the other."

Baucis and Philemon become sacred, intertwined trees.

The gods granted both of these prayers to Baucis and Philemon, whose remaining years were spent guarding the temple, until one day, as they were reminiscing about what had happened there, suddenly Baucis saw Philemon sprouting leaves, and Philemon saw Baucis do the same. As the bark covered over their faces, they said, "Goodbye, dear spouse!" They became an oak tree and a linden tree with intertwining trunks. Thereafter, their branches were covered with garlands, gifts from passersby. The two who had shown reverence and worship to the gods were revered and worshipped as gods themselves.

Orpheus and Eurydice

Literary Sources: Vergil *Georgics* 4.315–527; Ovid *Metamorphoses* 10.1–85, 11.1–43

Orpheus marries Eurydice; Eurydice dies very shortly after their wedding.

Orpheus, born in Thrace, was a son of Apollo and the Muse Calliope, and the greatest musician who ever lived. (See Genealogical Chart 1.) So beautiful were his songs that wild animals became tame and gathered around to listen. Even rocks and trees did not remain immobile but moved close to him. He was, however, unfortunate in love. At his marriage to Eurydice, the torches sputtered and produced only eye-stinging smoke, refusing to catch fire—a bad omen! Although Orpheus and his bride loved each other dearly, they did not have long to enjoy each other's company. One day, when Euryudice was strolling through the grass, she was bitten on the ankle by a snake and killed instantly. (According to Vergil, this happened while she was running away from a beekeeper named Aristaeus, who desired her.)

Orpheus plays his lyre for the people of Thrace.

Orpheus begs Hades and Persephone to restore his beloved Eurydice.

Orpheus was inconsolable. He formed a radical plan to have his wife returned to him: he decided to enter the Underworld and persuade the gods there. Passing by the shades of the dead, he came to Hades and Persephone, the rulers of the shades. Accompanied by his lyre, he pleaded his case: "Great god and goddess, I will speak the truth to you plainly. I have not come here for trivial reasons. My wife is the reason for my journey; she stepped on an adder whose venom killed her. I tried to endure it, but love overwhelmed me. Love is the supreme god in the world above, and I think that he is known even here, because he brought the two of you together. In his name, I beg you to restore Eurydice's life, which was ended far too soon. Sooner or later, we all come to you; you rule over people for a longer time than anyone. You will rule over her by right someday, when she is old; give her back to me for a short time. If you deny me this gift, then let me remain here, and you may take pleasure in the death of two."

Hermes prepares to conduct Eurydice to the Underworld as she bids farewell to Orpheus. Roman copy of a Greek relief sculpture, ca. 410 BCE. Museo Nazionale Archaeologico, Naples, Italy.

Hades and Persephone

Orpheus is permitted to take Eurydice back but without looking back.

These words, accompanied by his melodies, moved the dead so deeply that they wept. Tantalus stopped trying to reach the receding water; Ixion's wheel stood still; the birds no longer devoured Tityus' liver; the daughters of Danaus rested by their urns; Sisyphus sat on his boulder. The dog Cerberus' three mouths gaped open in wonder. Then, for the first time, even the Furies wept. Hades and Persephone decided to grant Orpheus' prayer. Eurydice was summoned from her place among the recent dead, and she came forward still limping from her recent injury. The gods allowed her to return with Orpheus, but made one stipulation: if Orpheus glanced back at her before they reached the upper world, she would be sent back to the shades.

When Orpheus looks back, Eurydice instantly recedes to the Underworld.

They ascended the steep path back to the living world, Orpheus leading and Eurydice following behind. They were almost there; Orpheus could see the daylight above him. At that moment, he could restrain himself no longer. Anxious that she would not be there and overcome by eagerness to see his wife alive once more, Orpheus looked behind him—a forgivable error, if the powers of the Underworld were able to forgive! At once a rumble was heard from the world below. Eurydice lamented, "What is this madness that has destroyed both of us, Orpheus? Look, the Fates are already calling me back; my eyes are growing dim again. I'm stretching out my arms to you, but I can't reach you any more. Goodbye, my love!"

Orpheus with the lute given to him by Apollo

Orpheus mourns Eurydice and refuses to love any other woman.

She was gone like a puff of smoke. Orpheus tried to enter the Underworld once more and fetch her back again, but the way was now closed to him. The shades did not listen to him, and Charon refused to row him across again. He sat by the banks of the river, lamenting ceaselessly. He rejected the love of all women as he sat playing his music.

Depiction of bacchantes dancing

Thracian bacchants kill Orpheus.

One day, the women of Thrace in a bacchic frenzy observed him from the summit of a hill. "There he is!" one of them cried. "That's the man who scorns us!" She threw her lance towards his mouth; it struck him but did not hurt him because it was wreathed in leaves. Another one threw a stone, but it was so overwhelmed by his lovely music that it fell at the poet's feet, as if begging forgiveness for trying to harm him. The women's rage increased, but their weapons continued to fly in vain, tamed by the enchantment of his song. At last the sounds of the flutes, the horns, the drums, and the bacchants' clapping and howling drowned out his music. The stones grew red with the poet's blood as the frenzied women savagely drove off the animals and birds that had been listening to him. They attacked him with their *thyrsi,* with branches broken off the trees, with rocks, and with their bare hands. They tore his body to pieces and flung his head and lyre into the river.

Orpheus is reunited with Eurydice for eternity in the Elysian Fields.

Thus Orpheus went back once more to the Underworld, this time as a shade. He searched the Elysian Fields until he found Eurydice, and passionately threw his arms around her. There they were together for eternity. Sometimes they walked side by side; sometimes she ran ahead and he followed; sometimes he preceded and she went behind. Now there was no longer any danger for Orpheus when he looked behind him at Eurydice.

Orpheus playing his lyre. Fresco in the Casa Orfeo, Pompeii, Italy.

***Pygmalion and the Image: the Heart Desires,* 1868, by Sir Edward Burne–Jones (1833-1898)**

Pygmalion and his statue

Literary Source: Ovid *Metamorphoses* 10.238–297

Pygmalion was a sculptor from Cyprus, who had become disgusted by the immoral women he saw around him. He withdrew from all feminine company and remained a bachelor. During that time he carved an ivory statue. It was an artistic masterpiece, with a beauty greater than any living woman's. It looked so true to life that you would think it could move and was remaining still only because of modesty. Pygmalion promptly fell in love with it. He touched it repeatedly, as if unwilling to admit it was only a statue and not alive. He kissed it, imagining it kissing back; he caressed it, but gently, fearing to bruise it. He tried to win its affection by giving it presents, small ones at first, such as seashells, pet birds, and all sorts of flowers. Later he bought it more expensive things: bracelets, earrings, and clothes. At night he placed it on a bed with a purple covering and placed soft pillows under its head, as if it could feel them.

Pygmalion and the statue

When the next festival of Aphrodite arrived, all Cyprus turned out to celebrate. Pygmalion also attended. He placed his gift on the altar and prayed timidly: "If you in heaven can grant us what we want, I beg, let me have as my wife . . . " he wanted to say, "the maiden of ivory," but did not dare. Instead he finished his prayer, " . . . a woman like the maiden of ivory." Venus heard his prayer, and knew what he really wanted. The flames of the altar leaped up high three times—a good omen!

Aphrodite answers Pygmalion's prayers by bringing the statue to life.

Once home, Pygmalion lay down on the couch and began kissing his statue once more. Was it his imagination, or was the ivory growing warm? He caressed it again, and once again the statue seemed to grow soft, yielding to his touch. She was alive! He could feel her veins pulsing under his fingers. Timidly she opened her eyes and looked on the light of day and her beloved at the same moment. Pygmalion offered his prayers of thanks to Aphrodite, who attended the wedding that she had made possible.

(Ovid never gives the statue a name; later sources have named her Galatea.)

Pen and ink representation of the marble statue Pygmalion and Galatea, 1763, by Etienne Maurice Falconet (1716–1791), Walters Art Gallery, Baltimore, Maryland.

Atalanta and Hippomenes

Literary Source: Ovid *Metamorphoses* 10.560–707

Atalanta forces her suitors to race with her; the penalty for losing is death.

There once was a young woman named Atalanta (not the same one who had participated in the Calydonian Boar Hunt and accompanied the Argonauts), who could run faster than any man. She did not want to marry, for an oracle had once warned her against husbands. Because she was so beautiful, however, many men desired her. She tried to discourage them by setting out cruel terms for her hand in marriage: "Any man who can defeat me in a foot race may marry me, but the penalty for losing is death!"

Hippomenes offers to race against Atalanta; she reluctantly agrees.

Such was her beauty that many men took up the challenge even so. One spectator of these races was a young man named Hippomenes. He said to himself, "Why are men so foolhardy, taking such a risk just for a bride?" Then he saw Atalanta and exclaimed, "I take back what I said! I had no idea what a superb trophy they were racing for!" He decided, "Nothing risked, nothing gained!" and prayed no man would prove faster as he watched Atalanta darting past him. When the race was over and the unhappy losers were led away to death, Hippomenes approached the winner and addressed her, "Why do you settle for easy victory by running against these slowpokes? Contend with me! If you lose, you lose to someone worthy; I am the grandson of Poseidon himself. If you win, you will be famous for defeating Hippomenes."

Atalanta and Hippomenes **by Guido Reni (1575–1642), Museo Nazionale di Capodimonte, Naples, Italy**

As he spoke, Atalanta was torn. "Do I want to win the race against this man or not?" she thought. "What god put him up to this? His courage and youth touch my heart even more than his beauty—though his beauty *could* touch my heart! Oh, flee while you still can, stranger; any other woman would be happy to marry you! But why do I care about *you*, when so many others have died? Let him learn the hard way, then! But he shouldn't have to die just because he wants to marry me! I wish you would either give up or be just a little bit faster! Poor Hippomenes! You deserve to live, and if the Fates weren't so harsh, you would be the husband I would choose!"

Aphrodite assists Hippomenes in winning the race by means of a trick.

Such were her thoughts; she had fallen in love without realizing it. As all the people clamored for the race to begin, Hippomenes prayed to the love goddess: "Aphrodite, I pray that you may be present at my undertaking, and help these fires of love that you have ignited." The goddess heard, and had a plan for helping him. She happened to be returning from a field in Cyprus famous for its wealth, which had a tree that produced golden apples. She showed herself to Hippomenes alone, gave him three apples from this tree, and told him how to use them to advantage.

The runners crouched at the starting line and took off at the sound of the horn. They ran so fast you would think they could run over the sea without wetting their feet, or dash across stalks of wheat without bending one. The crowd cheered for the young man: "Go for it, go for it, run, Hippomenes! Don't hold back! Win!" It was hard to say whether these words pleased him or Atalanta more; for a while she hung back, and then reluctantly sped ahead of him. Hippomenes was already panting and the finish line seemed far off. He dropped one of the apples. The sight of the radiant fruit amazed Atalanta, who turned to pick it up. As Hippomenes sped past her, the crowd roared its pleasure. Atalanta swiftly caught up and passed him once more; he dropped a second apple. Once more she retrieved it and caught up. As the finish line loomed ahead with the two neck and neck, Hippomenes flung the last apple to the far side of the field with all his strength. Atalanta was reluctant to run after it, but the goddess forced her to fetch it and made it extra heavy besides. Hippomenes won!

Atalanta's Race, 1876, by Sir Edward John Poynter (1836–1918). This oil painting hung in the billiard room of Wortley Hall, South Yorkshire, UK, until it was accidentally destroyed during the occupation of the building by Allied forces during World War II.

Aphrodite punishes Hippomenes and Atalanta for their forgetful ingratitude, and Cybele transforms them into yoked lions.

There was, however, an unhappy sequel to his victory. Hippomenes failed to thank Aphrodite for helping him. In her anger, she resolved to make an example of him and his new bride. They were deep in the forest when they passed a temple of Cybele, the eastern mother-goddess. Atalanta and Hippomenes decided to go in and rest. Aphrodite caused them to become possessed by uncontrollable lust. Cybele was outraged at the forbidden act performed within her shrine, and she was ready to kill the pair on the spot. However, she decided that was too light a punishment and she transformed the couple into lions. Thereafter, they were a terror to all others, but slaves to the goddess. She placed yokes on their necks and forced them to draw her chariot.

Bronze statuette of Cybele (Meter), holding a tambourine and driving a chariot drawn by lions (the transformed couple of Atalanta and Hippomenes), 2nd century CE, found near the Metroön Temple in the Athenian Agora. Metropolitan Museum of Art, New York, New York.

Seated statue of Cybele crowned. Roman copy of earlier Greek original. Museo Nazionale Archeologico, Naples, Italy.

Cybele was the most important goddess, the "Great Mother," of Asia Minor. Her cult spread through Greece and the western Mediterranean. She came to be identified with both Rhea (the mother of Zeus) and Demeter in Greece and with Ceres in Rome and Spain.

Ceyx and Alcyone

Literary Source: Ovid *Metamorphoses* 11.410–748

Ceyx, a king in Thessaly, wanted to take a sea voyage to consult a far-off oracle of Apollo. When he told his wife Alcyone his plans, she grew pale and burst into tears. She pleaded with him: "Don't you love me any more? Why this sudden desire for a long trip? Sea travel is so dangerous! I've seen pieces of broken ships on shore! But if you are determined to go, take me with you at least. If there are storms, let's face them together!"

He was moved by her lament, but wished neither to cancel his journey nor to let Alcyone share in its dangers. He said all he could to comfort her, and promised, "If the Fates allow, I will be back before two months are up."

His promise momentarily consoled her, but she became frightened all over again when his ship was brought down to the water's edge. She watched from the shore until his ship had completely receded from sight. Then she went to their room and wept again, missing him already.

Ancient Greek sailors in a ship

Her fears were justified. When Ceyx's journey was almost at its midpoint, as night fell, the waves began to whiten and gale force winds arose. The ship's captain had no idea what to do as the surging waves resounded and the thunder crashed. The billows were high as mountains. The sides of the ship gave out enormous crashes, like the towers of a city being assaulted by battering rams. Nine successive waves battered the hull; the tenth broke it apart. As the relentless waters rushed into the craft, the panic-stricken sailors moaned, begged for death, prayed to heaven in vain, and called the names of their loved ones left behind. Ceyx thought of Alcyone; he longed to see her once more, but was glad she was not there. A whirlwind destroyed the mast, and one final wave plunged the ship to the bottom of the sea. Most of the men were drowned, but a few still clung to pieces of wreckage, including Ceyx. His wife's name was on his lips as he floated, and he prayed that his body would be washed ashore where she could find it and lay it in a tomb. He swam as long as he could, but finally a giant swell of black water buried him beneath the waves.

Alcyone prays to Hera for her husband's safe homecoming.

Meanwhile, Alcyone was unaware of this disaster. She had already laid out Ceyx's clothes for his return, and chosen what she would wear as well. She burned incense to all the divinities, especially Hera, praying for a homecoming that would never be.

Hera could not bear to hear these prayers for someone already dead. She sent Iris to deliver a message to the god Sleep. "Tell him to send a likeness of the late Ceyx to Alcyone in her sleep, so that she may learn the truth."

Morpheus appears to Alcyone to tell her the sad news of Ceyx' drowning.

The messenger obeyed, and hastened to Sleep's realm, a place forbidden to the sun, totally dark and silent. There were no crowing roosters or barking watchdogs, not even branches rustling in the wind. This god's home was a cave, around which grew poppies and other sleep-inducing herbs. Doors were forbidden because of the possibility of noisy hinges creaking. Sleep lay on a platform in the middle of a cave on a soft bed made of ebony wood, covered by a dark sheet. Around him were the empty shapes of dreams that could imitate any form. Iris' bright robes lit up the cave as she entered. With difficulty, the drowsy god raised himself on one elbow and asked Iris why she had come. The messenger replied, "Sleep, order an image of Ceyx to go to Alcyone and tell her about the shipwreck that killed him. These are Hera's orders." Having delivered her message, Iris departed at once, already feeling sleepy.

Sleep roused his son Morpheus, who was most skillful at impersonating other people's appearance and speech. (Other children of Sleep specialized in imitating animals or plants or landscapes.) He told Morpheus what to do, and then went back to bed.

Morpheus assumed the form of Ceyx in his drowned state, naked and pale, his hair streaming with water. Weeping, he leaned over Alcyone's bed, and addressed her: "My poor Alcyone, do you recognize me, or has my appearance changed in death? Your prayers went unanswered; I am dead. The winds and the waves battered my ship until it broke apart; I called your name until I drowned. This is the truth. Put on your mourning clothes and do not let me go to the Underworld without lament."

The dead body of Ceyx floats on the sea.

Alcyone called out, "Wait! Take me with you!" Awakened by her cries, the servants rushed in with a lamp. When they asked why she was so distressed, she answered, "I just saw my husband's ghost, naked and dripping wet! He's dead! I knew he never should have left! If I go on living now, I am crueler than the sea."

At dawn, she returned to the sad place on the shore where they had parted. As she thought back to their parting, she noticed a body floating on the water. "Poor man, whoever you are! And poor wife, if you have one!" she thought. When the waves washed the body close enough to shore to be recognized, she saw who it was. "My dearest husband! This was not the homecoming you promised me!"

The gods transform Ceyx and Alcyone into halcyon birds.

There was a breakwater along the shore. Alcyone threw herself from it, and suddenly she was flying! She gave out shrill cries that sounded like the laments of a mourner, and kissed her husband's cold cheek with her hard beak. The gods had mercy on Ceyx, and restored him to life as a bird. As birds, Ceyx and Alcyone remain faithful to each other and raise their young. For seven days in winter, the sea grows calm as Alcyone sits on her nest. These days are known as halcyon days.

European kingfisher (halcyon)

A. Review Exercises

1. **MATCHING!** Match the statement or question in the right-hand column with the correct word from the left-hand column. Write the letter in the space provided.

1.	____	Alcyone	a.	This king of Thrace married Procne.
2.	____	Narcissus	b.	He and his wife welcomed disguised gods.
3.	____	Atalanta	c.	He was drowned at sea.
4.	____	Morpheus	d.	This goddess punished Narcissus.
5.	____	Orpheus	e.	Along with her husband, she became a lion.
6.	____	Hippomenes	f.	He fell in love with his statue.
7.	____	Eurydice	g.	She spoke through a wall to her beloved.
8.	____	Tereus	h.	She dreamed of her dead husband.
9.	____	Echo	i.	This god could impersonate others.
10.	____	Philemon	j.	He is a son of Apollo and a Muse.
11.	____	Pygmalion	k.	Her love for Narcissus was unrequited.
12.	____	Pyramus	l.	She was reunited with her beloved in the Elysian Fields.
13.	____	Ceyx	m.	He fell in love with his own reflection.
14.	____	Thisbe	n.	This Babylonian youth met his beloved at the tomb of King Ninus.
15.	____	Nemesis	o.	He won his wife in a foot race, but was transformed into a lion for offending Cybele.

2. **UNITE THESE LOVERS!** Draw a line linking the correct male character to his female beloved.

Pyramus	Eurydice
Pygmalion	Baucis
Ceyx	Atalanta
Philemon	Thisbe
Orpheus	Galatea
Hippomenes	Alcyone

3. **HOLY METAMORPHOSES!** Match the items from nature (tree, flower, bird, etc.) listed in the left-hand column to the mythological characters with whom they are associated in the right-hand column. Write the correct letter in the space provided.

1.	____	Linden	a.	Atalanta and Hippomenes
2.	____	Lions	b.	Philomela
3.	____	Hoopoe	c.	Alcyone
4.	____	Kingfisher (halcyon)	d.	Pygmalion's statue
5.	____	Daffodil	e.	Philemon
6.	____	Mulberry	f.	Pyramus' blood
7.	____	Oak	g.	Narcissus
8.	____	Human being	h.	Baucis
9.	____	Nightingale	i.	Tereus

B. MUSINGS

1. The story of Pygmalion and his statue has inspired many writers, many of whom wrote during the twentieth century. The Irish playwright George Bernard Shaw wrote a very well-known play, *Pygmalion*, which tells the story of an upper-class English professor of phonetics who finds a London Cockney flower-girl upon whom he conducts an experiment: he transforms her into a lady. The play, which opened in London in 1914, about the same time as the beginning of World War I, raised some timely and important questions. Among these questions were: How would it feel for a young woman to be taken from her home and familiar surroundings by an older, educated, and well-to-do man and to have every aspect of her life altered, from her speech patterns, to the clothing she wears, to the activities and occupations she engages in? How do you think the statue-woman, carved and willed into life by Pygmalion, might have thought and felt when she came to life in Pygmalion's studio? Write a short monologue or soliloquy to be spoken by the statue-woman as she comes to life, and perform it for your class.

2. Read the play *Pygmalion* by Shaw. List some other questions raised by Shaw in this work and discuss these with your class.

George Bernard Shaw (1856–1950)

3. Shaw's play *Pygmalion* was adapted in 1956 and transformed into a Broadway hit musical, *My Fair Lady*, by Frederick Loewe and Alan Jay Lerner. The role of the professor was played by Rex Harrison, and the Cockney flower-girl by Julie Andrews. A few years later, the Hollywood director George Cukor made a smash-hit film of *My Fair Lady* starring Rex Harrison and Audrey Hepburn in the leading roles. Another film that has a similar theme of transformation and metamorphosis is *Educating Rita* (1983), directed by Lewis Gilbert

and starring Michael Caine and Julie Walters. Watch a recording of either or both these movies and discuss how they are rooted in the myth of Pygmalion. What social and moral issues do these films raise?

4. The story of Pyramus and Thisbe is said to be the oldest love story in the world. It is a story that has appeared and reappeared in various forms thoughout the history of literature. Perhaps the most famous reworking of this myth in English is told in the play *Romeo and Juliet* by William Shakespeare. Interestingly, Shakespeare also wrote a parody of the story of Pyramus and Thisbe in a play within the play *A Midsummer Night's Dream.* Many scholars think that both plays were written by Shakespeare about the same time. Write a page comparing or contrasting the stories of Pyramus and Thisbe and Romeo and Juliet.

5. Another American musical, *West Side Story,* 1957, by Leonard Bernstein, Stephen Sondheim, Jerome Robbins, and Arthur Laurents, explores the same territory as the love story of Pyramus and Thisbe. View the 1961 film version of this musical.

6. American author Louisa May Alcott wrote her best-known novel for young readers, *Little Women,* in 1868. The story of Pyramus and Thisbe clearly influences her depiction of Jo, the heroine. Jo sends messages through the garden wall of the boy living next door, Theodore Laurence ("Laurie"), with whom she eventually falls in love, but does not marry. Can you think of other stories influenced by the sad tale of Pyramus and Thisbe?

C. Words, Words, Words

The Daily Muse

News you can use

Hey, kids! Take a look at these words from words you've met in Ovid's *Metamorphoses.*

Narcissism

Would it be a compliment to identify someone as **narcissistic**? Why or why not?

____

How would you, in your own words, describe **narcissism**? Can you think of a film role in which the actor acts in a **narcissistic** manner?

____

____

Halcyon days

Like Alcyone and Ceyx in their happiest moments of enjoying life, have you experienced any care-free, fun-filled times in *your* life that you would describe as **halcyon days**? In the space below, describe these days and why they were **halcyon**:

D. How 'Bout That?

Politics, cartoons, and mythology

Political cartoon, 1860. The vice president of the U.S., John C. Breckinridge, is attired as Thisbe. The president at that time, James Buchanan, is the wall personified that separates the lovers. The orator and Illinois senator Stephen Douglas is dressed as Pyramus, who says, "O wicked wall through whom I see no bliss" (*A Midsummer Night's Dream*, act 5, scene 1, line 182). Douglas and Breckinridge came in second and third to Abraham Lincoln's first place victory in the election of 1860. This cartoon refers to Buchanan's opposition to the mutual belief of Douglas (a northern Democrat) and Breckinridge (a southern Democrat) that free elections in the states themselves should determine whether a state like Kansas should be admitted to the Union as a slave or free state. Buchanan believed that Congress only should make such a decision. Buchanan worked to block Douglas' election and helped to squash a possible movement by Breckenridge to throw his support to Douglas.

Draw a political cartoon, using a mythological figure to represent at least one of the characters depicted in your cartoon. Share with your class.

The most beautiful plaza in Madrid is the Plaza de Cibeles, at the center of which is the Cibeles Fountain, 1777–1782, designed by Ventura Rodriguez. The statue of Cybele shows the goddess driving her lion-yoked chariot. This statue and its fountain have become the meeting place for the fans of the Real Madrid soccer (football) team whenever the team enjoys a big victory.

Philomela

The English poet Matthew Arnold (1822–1888) wrote the following poem after hearing the song of a nightingale:

Philomela • 1853

Hark! ah, the nightingale—
The tawny-throated!
Hark, from that moonlit cedar what a burst!
What triumph! hark!—what pain!

O wanderer from a Grecian shore,
Still, after many years, in distant lands,
Still nourishing in thy bewilder'd brain
That wild, unquench'd, deep-sunken, old-world pain—

Say, will it never heal?
And can this fragrant lawn
With its cool trees, and night,
And the sweet, tranquil Thames,
And moonshine, and the dew,
To thy rack'd heart and brain
Afford no balm?

Orfeo

Two accomplished composers have written operas about the poignant story of the young Orpheus and his bride, Eurydice: Claudio Monteverdi wrote *Orfeo* in 1607; the opera *Orfeo ed Euridice* was composed by Christoph Willibald von Gluck in 1762 and is the better known of the two pieces. Obtain a CD of the latter opera by Gluck and listen to the stunning aria sung by the tenor taking the part of Orpheus, "Che faró senza Euridice?" ("What will I do without Eurydice?").

A modern version of Atalanta's story

As you've probably noticed from your reading here and in other places, there are sometimes more than one, even several, version(s) of the various myths. Even in antiquity, various writers may have felt the need to alter a myth to suit their purposes, for political and other reasons. Here is a relatively recent version of the Atalanta myth. What do you think the author was trying to accomplish in this version?

"Atalanta" by Betty Miles, from *Free to Be . . . You and Me* (Running Press, 1974)

Once upon a time, not long ago, there lived a princess named Atalanta, who could run as fast as the wind.

She was so bright, and so clever, and could build things and fix things so wonderfully, that many young men wished to marry her.

"What shall I do?" said Atalanta's father, who was a powerful king. "So many young men want to marry you, and I don't know how to choose."

"You don't have to choose, Father," Atalanta said. "I will choose. And I'm not sure that I will choose to marry anyone at all."

"Of course you will," said the king. "Everybody gets married. It is what people do."

"But," Atalanta told him, with a toss of her head, "I intend to go out and see the world. When I come home, perhaps I will marry and perhaps I will not."

The king did not like this at all. He was a very ordinary king; that is, he was powerful and used to having his own way. So he did not answer Atalanta, but simply told her, "I have decided how to choose the young man you will marry. I will hold a great race, and the winner—the swiftest, fleetest young man of all—will win the right to marry you."

Now Atalanta was a clever girl as well as a swift runner. She saw that she might win both the argument and the race—provided that she herself could run in the race too. "Very well," she said. "But you must let me race along with the others. If I am not the winner, I will accept the wishes of the young man who is."

The king agreed to this. He was pleased; he would have his way, marry off his daughter, and enjoy a fine day of racing as well. So he directed his messengers to travel throughout the kingdom announcing the race with its wonderful prize: the chance to marry the bright Atalanta.

• •

As the day of the race grew nearer, young men began to crowd into the town. Each was sure he could win the prize, except for one; that was Young John, who lived in the town. He saw Atalanta day by day as she bought nails and wood to make a pigeon house, or chose parts for her telescope, or laughed with her friends. Young John saw the princess only from a distance, but near enough to know how bright and clever she was. He wished very much to race with her, to win, and to earn the right to talk with her and become her friend.

"For surely," he said to himself, "it is not right for Atalanta's father to give her away to the winner of the race. Atalanta herself must choose the person she wants to marry, or whether she wishes to marry at all. Still, if I could only win the race, I would be free to speak to her, and to ask for her friendship."

• •

At last, the day of the race arrived.

Trumpets sounded in the early morning, and the young men gathered at the edge of the field, along with Atalanta herself, the prize they sought. The king and his friends sat in soft chairs, and the townspeople stood along the course.

• •

And now a bugle sounded, a flag was dropped, and the runners were off!

The crowds cheered as the young men and Atalanta began to race across the field. At first they ran as a group, but Atalanta soon pulled ahead, with three of the young men close after her. As they neared the halfway point, one young man put on a great burst of speed and seemed to pull ahead for an instant, but then he gasped and fell back. Atalanta shot on.

Soon another young man, tense with the effort, drew near to Atalanta. He reached out as though to touch her sleeve, stumbled for an instant, and lost speed. Atalanta smiled as she ran on. I have almost won, she thought.

But then another young man came near. This was Young John, running like the wind, as steadily and swiftly as Atalanta herself. Atalanta felt his closeness, and in a sudden burst she dashed ahead.

Young John might have given up at this, but he never stopped running. Nothing at all, thought he, will keep me from winning the chance to speak with Atalanta. And on he ran, swift as the wind, until he ran as her equal, side by side with her, toward the golden ribbon that marked the race's end. Atalanta raced even faster to pull ahead, but Young John was a strong match for her. Smiling with the pleasure of the race, Atalanta and Young John reached the finish line together, and together they broke through the golden ribbon.

Trumpets blew. The crowd shouted and leaped about. The king rose. "Who is that young man?" he asked.

"It is Young John from the town," the people told him.

"Very well. Young John," said the king, as John and Atalanta stood before him, exhausted and jubilant from their efforts, "You have not won the race, but you have come closer to winning than any man here. And so I give you the prize that was promised—the right to marry my daughter."

Young John smiled at Atalanta, and she smiled back. "Thank you, sir," said John to the king, "but I could not possibly marry your daughter unless she wished to marry me. I have run this race for the chance to talk with Atalanta, and, if she is willing, I am ready to claim my prize."

Atalanta laughed with pleasure. "And I," she said to John, "could not possibly marry before I have seen the world. But I would like nothing better than to spend the afternoon with you."

Then the two of them sat and talked on the grassy field, as the crowds went away. They ate bread and cheese and purple plums. Atalanta told John about her telescopes and her pigeons, and John told Atalanta about his globes and his studies of geography. At the end of the day, they were friends.

On the next day, John sailed off to discover new lands. And Atalanta set off to visit the great cities.

By this time, each of them has had wonderful adventures, and seen marvelous sights. Perhaps some day they will be married, and perhaps they will not. In any case, they are friends. And it is certain that they are both living happily ever after.

Questions

1. What aspects of the story did the author omit, and which did she add? Why do you think she made these changes?

2. Imagine you are writing a children's book based on one of the myths in this chapter. Rewrite the story, with appropriate illustrations.

E. WHO'S WHO?

- For Orpheus' ancestry and family, see GENEALOGICAL CHART 1.

Chapter 16

THE HOUSE OF TROY AND THE TROJAN WAR

General Sources:

Homer *Iliad*
Sophocles *Philoctetes*
Euripides *The Trojan Women, Hecuba*
Apollodorus *Library* 3.12, *Epitome* 3–5
Vergil *Aeneid* 2
Hyginus *Fabulae* 91, 95, 96, 102, 103
Ovid *Metamorphoses* 12–13
Seneca *The Trojan Women*
Lucian *The Judgment of the Goddesses*

Troy is also called Ilium after Ilus, son of Tros, founder of Troy.

The land of Troy (sometimes called the Troad) was named for its legendary founder, a man named Tros. Although we generally use Troy as the name of a city, the proper name of the city is Ilion or Ilium, so called after a son of Tros named Ilus. Homer's epic the *Iliad* receives its title from this name for the city. Ilus was responsible for bringing a statue known as the Palladium to the city; this statue would later play an important role in the Trojan War. The Palladium received its name from a playmate of Athena named Pallas. One day, Pallas and Athena were practicing the arts of war. When Pallas was about to land a blow, Zeus protected Athena by placing his aegis in the way, causing Pallas to look upward. Athena then landed a blow that killed Pallas. In her friend's memory, Athena built a statue of Pallas holding the aegis which had caused her death. Zeus dropped the statue from the sky outside the tent of Ilus, who took it up and established it within a temple of Athena.

Odysseus carries off the sacred Palladium from the temple of Athena at Troy near the end of the Trojan War.

Troy's royal family: King Priam, Queen Hecuba, sons Hector and Paris, and many other children

At the time of the Trojan War, the king of Troy was Priam, and his wife was Hecuba. Their first son was Hector, who would grow up to be the greatest of Trojan warriors. (See GENEALOGICAL CHART 18.) When their second child was about to be born, Hecuba had a dream in which she gave birth to a torch, whose fire spread throughout the whole city and burned it down. An interpreter of dreams told them that the birth of the child would mean destruction for the city, and advised that the child be exposed. Priam gave the infant to a servant, who did not kill the boy but raised him as his own and named him Paris. Paris grew up to be handsome and strong, and he acquired the further name of Alexander, which is Greek for "man who protects," because it was his job to protect flocks of sheep. He also acquired a wife, the nymph Oenone.

Paris and Oenone

The judgment of Paris at the wedding of Peleus and Thetis

One day, this deceptively humble shepherd was asked to be the judge of a most unusual beauty contest. At the wedding of Achilles' future parents, Peleus and Thetis, all the gods were guests except one: Eris, the goddess of quarrels. "If we invite her," the gods thought, "the bride and groom and all the guests will be arguing before the ceremony is over!" The unpopular goddess had a scheme, however. She went to the garden of the Hesperides, plucked one of the golden apples from the tree, and inscribed "For the Fairest" on it. Immediately, Hera, Athena, and Aphrodite began quarrelling over it. They asked Zeus to decide which one should receive it.

"I refuse to judge because I love you all the same," the king of the gods answered. "Besides, if I pick one, the other two will be angry with me. I'll send you to a young Trojan man of royal blood, who will make the decision. Hermes will take you to him."

The goddesses assented. On their way, they questioned Hermes about their prospective judge. "Is he married?" Aphrodite asked.

"He is, but she's just a country girl, and he doesn't seem that thrilled with her."

"Does he care about success in war and yearn for glory?" questioned Athena.

"I'm not sure, but he seems to be a typical young man; he probably does."

When they reached their destination, Hera whispered cattily to Aphrodite, "Why don't *you* lead the way here? You're familiar with the place, as you come here to visit Anchises."

The Judgment of Paris. At center, Paris is seated, and Hermes is pointing to Paris with his *caduceus*. Hera sits to the left of Hermes. Aphrodite and Eros are to the right of Paris. At lower left, Athena is at her temple with the Palladium.

Aphrodite ignored Hera's sarcasm, for they were now standing before Paris. Hermes explained why they were there. Paris was intimidated by the formidable trio of beauties before him, and requested the opportunity to look over each one separately.

As Hera came to the fore, Paris thought what a worthy bride for Zeus was this queen in her royal splendor. "If you judge me the most beautiful, Paris," she told him, "you shall be the master of all Asia."

Paris resolved to judge on the basis of beauty alone, and not to be bribed. He looked at Athena next. "Choose me, Paris," she said, "and I will be at your side in battle always. You will become a mighty and undefeated warrior."

"My land is at peace, so I have no use for war. But don't worry, Athena, I'll judge you fairly. It's time for Aphrodite to appear now."

For choosing Aphrodite as winner, Paris will receive the world's most beautiful woman.

The love goddess had waited patiently because she was sure of her victory. "Here I am, Paris, have a good look," she said seductively. "You're quite good-looking yourself! Why do you live here in the mountains where your beauty goes to waste? You shouldn't be married to a peasant, but to a woman from a sophisticated city like Sparta. The queen there, Helen, is as beautiful as I am, and I know she would leave everything to go with you if she saw you!" Paris was hesitant when he learned Helen was married, but Aphrodite promised to see to everything. He awarded the apple to her.

Venus Crouching. Roman copy of Greek original, Museo Nazionale Romano (Terme di Diocleziano), Rome, Italy.

Despite the unpropitious start to their wedding, disrupted by quarreling goddesses, Peleus and Thetis had a loving marriage. When their son, Achilles, was born, his mother dipped him in the River Styx to make him invulnerable. (See GENEALOGICAL CHART 19.) However, since she was holding on to his heel, this one spot was not protected by the water. Ever since, a fatal weakness has been called an Achilles' heel.

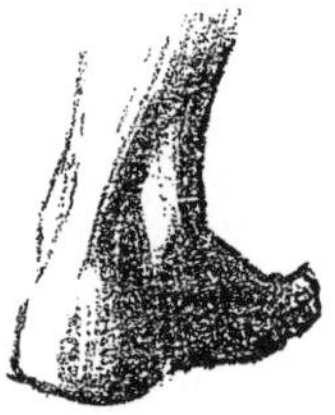

Achilles' heel

Some time after this, Paris was reunited with his parents. Priam's servant had come to fetch a bull for the games that were to be held in honor of the king's dead son (that is, for Paris himself). Paris went to the games and defeated all. When one of the angry losers (ironically, a brother of Paris) drew his sword at Paris, the prophetic Cassandra, a sister of theirs, recognized who he was. Priam acknowledged his long-lost son and welcomed him into the palace.

While Menelaus is away, Paris and Helen fall in love and elope to Troy.

Aphrodite then put her scheme into action. She arranged for Paris to sail to Sparta, where Menelaus and Helen hospitably welcomed him. Shortly thereafter, Menelaus had to leave to attend his grandfather's funeral, but he left Helen with Paris. Aphrodite caused Helen to fall in love with the handsome young guest, and she abandoned her husband and home to sail away with him.

When Helen and Menelaus had married, all of the leading warriors of Greece had sworn an oath to fight anyone who tried to take her away from her husband. Agamemnon therefore began marshalling them to pursue the runaways, but two warriors—ironically, epic heroes both—tried ruses to avoid going to war.

Thetis hides Achilles to prevent his going to war, but Odysseus finds him.

Because Achilles' mother, Thetis, knew that her son would die pursuing glory in Troy, she sent him to the island of Scyrus, ruled by King Lycomedes. The king had Achilles dress in women's clothing, and hid him among his daughters. They named him "Pyrrha," from the Greek word for fire, because of the color of his hair. Two Greek generals, Odysseus and Diomedes, knew that Achilles was there, and came to the palace to persuade him to fight. They could not find him, however—so cleverly did he blend in with the young women! But the wily Odysseus had an idea. He set out feminine gifts, but included a shield and spear among them. He then had a trumpeter sound the call to arms. Achilles, thinking the island was being attacked, threw off his female disguise and grabbed the weapons. He had no choice but to sail away, not knowing that a son would soon be born to him, named Neoptolemus. We will hear more of his deeds later.

Diomedes, left, and Odysseus, right, discover Achilles hiding among the women at the court of Lycomedes of Scyrus. At right background, Thetis lifts her veil.

Odysseus himself had tried to escape going to war by feigning madness.

Odysseus himself had earlier tried a different tactic to evade the war. He had received an oracle that he would be away from home for twenty years, and would return home destitute and bereft of all his men. He therefore pretended to be insane. When the embassy came for him, he put on a felt hat, yoked a horse and a bull together to a plow, and proceeded to plow the beach. A man even wilier than he, Palamedes, realized that he was faking, and placed Odysseus' infant son Telemachus in the path of the plow. When Odysseus swerved to avoid hurting the child, all realized that he was sane.

The Greeks abandon snake-bitten Philoctetes at Lemnos.

Odysseus plowing the beach

We have already read of the sacrifice of Agamemnon's daughter, Iphigenia, so that the army could sail. Trouble dogged them on their trip. When they landed on the island of Lemnos, a leader named Philoctetes was bitten on the foot by a serpent. Hera had sent this snake because of a grudge she bore against the man, who you may recall had lit the funeral pyre of the dying Heracles. The wound refused to heal, and the Greeks found it impossible to sacrifice and pray with Philoctetes' ill-omened cries continually interrupting them. They therefore made a cruel decision: they abandoned the sick man on the island.

The tragedy of the Greek soldier, Protesilaus, and his beloved, Laodamia

Tragedy struck again as soon as they landed in the Troad. The Greeks had received an oracle that the first man off the ships would be the first casualty. All held back except Protesilaus, whose name ironically means "first of the people." He was instantly killed by Hector. This man happened to be newly wed, and the gods took pity on him and his wife, Laodamia. They restored the young man to life for three hours so that he could have some time with his bride. When he died a second time, Laodamia could not endure the grief, and built a golden statue of her late husband. Her father could not bear to see her talking to and caressing this statue, so he had the object burned. Laodamia leaped into the fire, and was reunited with her husband in death.

Agamemnon takes Chryseis; plague falls on the Greeks; Calchas reveals Apollo's anger.

For nine years the war dragged on, with neither side gaining the advantage. In the tenth year of the war, Achilles and Agamemnon had a great quarrel, which forms the subject of Homer's *Iliad*. The quarrel arose because Agamemnon happened to have as one of his prizes Chryseis, the daughter of Apollo's priest Chryses. The priest had come to Agamemnon with gifts to ransom his daughter back, but the Greek leader had scorned him. In anger, therefore, Chryses prayed to Apollo, who punished the army by sending a plague upon them. For nine days, men and animals sickened and died; on the tenth, Achilles summoned an assembly. He addressed the king: "Agamemnon, I fear all our fighting all these years will be in vain. We need to ask a prophet why Apollo is so angry with us and what we can do to appease him."

Chryseis, Agamemnon's war prize

The priest Calchas responded: "Achilles, I can explain Apollo's anger, but promise you will protect me, because what I am about to say will enrage a very powerful man." Achilles gave his word, and the prophet continued: "Apollo is angry because Agamemnon spurned his priest and refused to return Chryseis. This plague will not end until we return the girl without ransom."

Agamemnon was furious with the priest, and declared, "You always enjoy giving prophecies that mean misery for me, Calchas! I don't want to return this girl. I like her better than my own wife Clytemnestra! But I have to keep my people safe, so I will give her back. But I need to have another prize at once. It's a disgrace for me to be the only man of the Argives without one!"

Achilles replied, "Most honored Agamemnon . . . greediest of men! All the prizes have already been distributed. But we will pay you back three and four times over if Zeus allows us to take Troy someday."

Agamemnon returns Chryseis and takes Briseis, Achilles' war prize.

This did not satisfy Agamemnon. He retorted, "You're not going to cheat me, Achilles! Do you think you can enjoy your own prize, Briseis, while I sit empty-handed? I'm taking her, to show you who's the leader here, and to make an example for the next man who tries to challenge me!"

Achilles glared at him. "Shameless! How do you expect us to fight your enemies and obey you? The Trojans never did *me* any harm! We all followed you to fight for your honor and Menelaus'! And now you threaten to take my prize that I fought long and hard for! I've had enough! Why should I stay here to enrich you? I'm going back to Phthia!"

"Fine, go home!" Agamemnon shouted back. "I don't need you! But I'm still taking your Briseis!"

Achilles was ready to draw his sword and cut down Agamemnon on the spot, but Athena came to his side at that moment. "Hera told me to come to you, because she loves both you and Agamemnon. Let your sword be. One day Agamemnon will pay you back threefold for his insults to you now. Obey Hera and me!"

Achilles in deference to the goddess abstained from physical force, but continued to lash Agamemnon with insults. He concluded by vowing, "Someday, I swear, you will wish you had me here, when hordes of your men are being cut down by Hector!" And he left, accompanied by his friend Patroclus and the rest of his men, the Myrmidons. He called for his mother, Thetis, who appeared at once, and told her all that had happened. He begged her to go to Zeus and tell him to give victories to the Trojans, so that Agamemnon would feel keenly the absence of his greatest warrior.

Achilles and Briseis, **1803, by Bertel Thorvaldsen (1770–1844), representation of relief sculpture, Thorvaldsens Museum, Copenhagen, Denmark**

Because of Achilles' anger, Thetis asks Zeus to favor the Trojans.

Thetis flew off to Olympus, and knelt at the feet of Zeus. "Father Zeus," she entreated, "if I have ever honored you, honor my son Achilles, who is doomed not to live long." She told him what Achilles wanted.

Zeus was troubled. "This will start a quarrel between Hera and me. She always accuses me of favoring the Trojans too much as it is! But I will give you what you want."

He nodded his head, and all Olympus shook as he did so. Then she returned to the depths of the sea as he went back to his own halls and took his place in the assembly of the gods. Hera, however, was fully aware of what had taken place. She lit into her husband at once: "So, which god was scheming with you this time? You love to do things behind my back! You never tell me anything!"

Zeus answered sharply, "Hera, do not try to know all my thoughts. When the time is right, trust me, you'll be the first to know. But if I choose to make plans apart from the other gods, do not pry!"

Hera replied, "Sir, what are you saying? *Me,* pry? But I'm very much afraid that Thetis has been talking to you, and that you agreed to exalt Achilles and slaughter vast numbers of Greeks!"

"And just what are you going to do about it, Hera? Sit down and be quiet! If you don't obey me, all the gods here will not be able to protect you if I lay my invincible hands on you!"

Hera reluctantly obeyed. Hephaestus handed her a goblet of wine, and said, "Patience, Mother! I don't want to see you hurt when I can't do anything to help you! Last time I did, my father grabbed me by the foot and threw me off Olympus! I fell all day until I landed at Lemnos nearly dead, and the mortals there had to take care of me!"

Hera accepted the cup and smiled at her son. He poured out some nectar for the other gods as well, and they all laughed at his awkwardness. Happiness was restored, and the gods feasted and enjoyed the melodies of Apollo and the Muses.

Zeus sends to Agamemnon a false dream of imminent victory.

That night, however, Zeus began to put his plan into action to help Thetis and Achilles. He sent Agamemnon a false dream, commanding him to attack Troy full force at once, for he would receive certain victory. When Agamemnon awoke, he reported the dream to his fellow chieftains, who marshaled the troops for battle. When they were assembled, however, Agamemnon decided to test their loyalty, and told them the opposite of what he wanted them to do: "Men, Zeus told me nearly ten years ago that I would bring down the walls of Troy. Now I see he was deceiving me. Nine years have passed and victory is nowhere in sight. So I order you all to prepare to sail home to our beloved fatherland!"

Agamemnon perversely tests his soldiers' loyalty with a false order, but Odysseus countermands it at Athena's urging.

The soldiers at once charged towards the ships, ready to depart, chaotic as fields of wheat in a hurricane. They might have set out if Athena had not run down to Odysseus and urged him on: "What is going on? You can't give up now! Hold the men back; don't let them sail!"

Odysseus hastened to obey. When he saw a man of rank, he used persuasion; when he saw a common soldier, he hit him with the scepter and scolded him. He had the whole army re-assembled, when a common soldier named Thersites, the ugliest man in the army and a notorious rabble-rouser, spoke up: "What do you want now, Agamemnon? More gold? More women? Is this what we're fighting for? We're going home! Let's see how long you last without us! If Achilles had more nerve, your insult to him would have been the last one!"

Odysseus ordered him to be quiet and sit down, bringing down his scepter across the heckler's neck and shoulders. The rest of the army prepared themselves for battle. Agamemnon offered a ritual sacrifice and prayed to Zeus for victory. Zeus accepted the sacrifice but, remembering his promise to Thetis, did not answer Agamemnon's prayer.

Paris, after Hector rebukes him, offers to fight Menelaus in one-to-one combat.

As the Greek army charged, Paris sprang to the front line ready for battle but shrank back as soon as he saw Menelaus leaping down from his chariot and heading for him, eager as a hungry lion that happens to spot a stag or wild goat. Hector, the mightiest warrior among the Trojans, rebuked his brother: "Paris, you womanizer! I wish you had never been born! The Greeks must be roaring with laughter at you, all good looks and no heart for fighting! Pity that we Trojans were too cowardly to stone you to death a long time ago!"

Paris replied, "Hector, your criticism is fair. But if you really want me to fight Menelaus one on one, I will."

Hector was glad to hear his brother take up the challenge, and advanced between the two armies. Agamemnon ordered his troops to hold their fire while Hector stated the terms of the duel. There would be a truce, Paris and Menelaus would take the field in single combat, and the winner would take Helen with all her wealth. Menelaus agreed, and the two armies exulted, thinking this would be the end of the war. Iris came to Helen in the likeness of one of Hector's sisters, and told her the exciting news that two champions were about to duel for her. Helen's heart was filled with longing for the husband and city she had left behind, and she hurried to a lookout post along the city gates, eyes filled with tears.

Menelaus and Paris armed themselves for the fight. Hector placed lots in a helmet to see who would cast the first weapon, and Paris' lot leaped out. He threw his long spear, and the shaft hit the center of Menelaus' shield but did not pierce it. Menelaus prayed, "Lord Zeus, grant me revenge against this man who wronged me!" and cast. His spear struck Paris' shield in the center also, and worked its way through his breastplate, but the Trojan swerved before it could inflict a mortal wound.

As Menelaus is about to kill Paris, Aphrodite spirits him away.

Menelaus then drew his sword and brought it down on the ridge of Paris' helmet. The blade shattered into pieces, and Menelaus cried out in frustration, "Father Zeus, no god is more deadly than you! I thought I had him, but I didn't even touch him!" He grabbed Paris by the crest of his helmet, swung him around, and was trying to drag him towards the Greeks' battle line.

The helmet strap was strangling Paris, and Menelaus would have killed him, but Aphrodite broke the strap, leaving Menelaus holding an empty helmet! The enraged Spartan spun it around and sent it flying among the Greeks, who hurried to retrieve it, and went after Paris with his spear once again. But Aphrodite had taken him away, wrapped him in mist, and set him down safely in his and Helen's bedroom. She, in the guise of an old woman, then told Helen to go to him.

By now Helen was weary of Paris, but she was too afraid of the goddess to disobey. She berated her lover, "If only you had been brought down by my ex-husband! For years, you used to boast that you were the better fighter! Why not go back and challenge him again? But no—he would probably impale you!"

Paris replied, "True, Menelaus won today, but I'll get him next time. Let's go to bed now—I'm more in love with you than I was the day I took you away from Sparta!"

They went; meanwhile, Menelaus was still stalking up and down the lines of men, looking for Paris. Agamemnon cried, "Trojans! Menelaus has won the duel! You must surrender Helen with all her treasure at once!" The Greeks shouted assent.

Athena incites Pandarus to wound Menelaus, whom Machaon then cures.

Zeus was prepared to let the war end there, but Hera and Athena insisted that the Trojans had to be punished further. He reluctantly yielded to them, since it was fated for Troy to fall. The goddesses schemed to make the Trojans break the truce. Athena went to a Trojan archer named Pandarus, disguised as one of his comrades. "Come on, Pandarus, here's your chance for glory!" she said. "Do you have the nerve to take a shot at Menelaus? Think of how much fame you will receive among the Trojans, especially Paris! Imagine the gifts he'll give you when Menelaus dies!" She persuaded him. He strung his bow as the other Trojans hid him, and shot. The arrow went through Menelaus' belt and grazed his flesh. Agamemnon was frightened at the sight of his brother bleeding, but Menelaus assured him that the wound was not serious. Machaon, the son of Asclepius and one of the army's doctors, quickly healed him.

Diomedes, a Greek strongman, injures Aeneas, a Trojan hero.

Because the truce was now broken, the Trojans and Greeks fought with renewed eagerness. Many were killed in the subsequent battle, including Pandarus, who received an arrow to the face. Athena granted special strength and daring to Diomedes. He went after Aeneas, who was second only to Hector in glory among the Trojans. (His story will be told in chapter 18.) Diomedes lifted a huge boulder and struck Aeneas in the side.

Diomedes, aided by Athena, wounds the war-god Ares.

He sank down and the world went black; he would have died there if his mother Aphrodite had not been watching out for him. She lifted him up, but Diomedes, knowing she was not a fighter, thrust his spear at her soft wrist. Apollo gathered up Aeneas and took him to safety covered in dark mist; Iris led Aphrodite away from the battlefield. Aphrodite's mother, Dione, healed her wound, while Leto and Artemis took care of Aeneas. Ares then entered the fray, and Athena urged Diomedes, "With my help, you can take on Ares! He's a liar; he just now promised Hera and me that he would support the Greeks, and there he is leading the Trojan charge!" The goddess took the place of Diomedes' charioteer, and they drove straight for the war god. Diomedes yelled his war cry and lunged with his spear, which Athena drove deep into Ares' belly. The immortal gave a yell as loud as ten thousand men, and soared back to Mount Olympus. He complained to Zeus, "Why don't you ever say no to that murderous daughter of yours? First she had Diomedes go after Aphrodite, and then she had him attack *me*! Lucky I'm so fast on my feet, or I would have been among those corpses down there!"

Zeus was not sympathetic. "Don't whine to me! You're just like your mother, out of control! You're my son too, though, and I won't let you suffer. But if you were anyone else's, I would have sent you to Tartarus long ago." He healed the war-god, who then took his place among the other Olympians.

Hector asks Hecuba to pray to Athena to spare the Trojans.

As the fighting raged on, Hector was ordered to return to Troy to instruct his mother Hecuba to gather the other older women, take the best robe from the royal halls, and offer it as a gift to Athena. When he found her in an inner courtyard of the palace, she took him by the hand and offered him wine, but he refused. He told her, "Not now; it would make me lose my nerve to fight. And I can't make a drink-offering to Zeus, blood-spattered like this. *You* are the one who needs to pray now. You and the other women must go to Athena's temple with your richest robe, and pray to the goddess to hold Diomedes back from our city!" His mother did as he wished, but the goddess refused to hear the women's prayers.

Hector then went to Paris' room, where he found his brother polishing his battle gear. He was disgusted, and said, "What are you doing here while men are dying for you! Get moving!"

Hector chances upon Paris and Helen; he declines their hospitality.

Paris said, "Hector, you're right; Helen here was just telling me the same thing. Wait until I put on my armor—or go on ahead; I'll catch up with you."

Helen said, "Hector, I wish some whirlwind had swept me off to the mountains or drowned me in the sea the day I was born! But since the gods ordained these things, I wish I were the wife of a better man! Come rest beside me for awhile, since you fight the hardest, Hector, for Paris and me."

Hector replied, "No, thank you, Helen, I'm anxious to return to the fight, but I want to visit my own wife and child first."

He found his wife Andromache standing by one of the watch-towers of the city. A female servant was carrying their toddler Astyanax. Andromache greeted her husband tearfully: "Dear Hector, your courage will be the death of you! Have pity on your little son, and on me! I have lost my mother, and my father and seven brothers were killed by Achilles."

Hector bids his wife, Andromache, and son, Astyanax, farewell.

Hector answered, "My dear, all these things trouble me too. I hate to think about you taken away by some Greek to serve in his household. But I could never face the men and women of Troy if I hung back from the fighting." He reached out to his little boy, but the child shrank back, crying in fear at his father's armor with its helmet of bronze and horsehair crest. His parents laughed, troubled though they were. Hector removed his helmet, took Astyanax in his arms, and prayed: "Zeus and all other gods, grant that this boy may become strong and brave and rule Troy one day, and that those seeing him returning from battle may say, 'He is even greater than his father!'"

Hector says goodbye to Andromache and Astyanax.

The combat between Hector and Ajax ends in a draw.

Hector and Paris returned to battle. Hector challenged any man of the Greeks to single combat, and the lot fell to the huge Ajax, second in greatness only to Achilles. Hector threw his spear and struck Ajax's shield; the weapon pierced six layers but was stopped by the seventh. Ajax's spear tore through Hector's breastplate, but the Trojan swerved aside and avoided death. Both grabbed their lances and attacked each other like a pair of lions or boars. Hector stabbed at Ajax's buckler but did not pierce it; Ajax's thrust went through Hector's shield and grazed his neck, drawing blood. Hector did not give up; he tossed a boulder at Ajax that hit the center of the immense man's shield. Ajax then seized an even larger boulder, and knocked Hector flat on his back. Apollo picked him up, and the two would have continued to fight with their swords if heralds of Zeus and both armies had not stopped the fight. "You are both great fighters, and Zeus loves you both. Night is coming; best to stop." The two warriors exchanged weapons as a pledge of mutual respect. Then they went back to their comrades, each exulting in victory.

Hector and Ajax in combat

With the near-defeat of the Greeks, Agamemnon suggests they give up.

Zeus had not forgotten his promise to Thetis. He demanded that the rest of the gods not interfere with the fighting. Then he took out the golden scales of destiny and placed lots in each pan. The Greeks' side sank down towards death. The next day, the Trojans fought their way close to the Greeks' ships. The army was panic-stricken, and Agamemnon was in despair. He stood before the troops in tears, and proposed—seriously, this time—that they abandon the war and return home.

Nestor urges Agamemnon to apologize and ask Achilles to return to battle.

Nestor, an elderly warrior and wise counselor, had a better idea: Agamemnon should apologize to Achilles, grant him an abundance of gifts, including Briseis, and urge him to return to battle. Agamemnon agreed, and sent three men as an embassy to Achilles: Odysseus, Ajax, and Phoenix, an old friend and tutor of Achilles.

Ajax, Odysseus, and Phoenix visit Achilles in his tent to apologize.

When they arrived at Achilles' tent, the great warrior immediately had Patroclus prepare a meal for them. When they had eaten and drunk their fill, Phoenix nodded silently to Odysseus, who delivered Agamemnon's message: "Achilles, we thank you for this wonderful feast. But we're facing disaster now. The Trojans have pitched camp right by our ships, and there's no stopping Hector. I am afraid we are all going to die in Troy. Come back to us while there's still time, and let your anger go! Agamemnon will give you much if you do: twenty cauldrons, a dozen stallions, seven women, plus Briseis, whom he promises he did not touch. If the gods allow us to take Troy, you can have all the gold and bronze you want, plus twenty Trojan women of your choice. Then, if we make it home, Agamemnon will let you marry one of his daughters and give you a magnificent dowry of seven cities. All this if you will just end your anger! But if you still hate Agamemnon, think of the rest of us, and think of the glory you will win if you kill Hector now! You are the only one of us who can."

Still furious, Achilles at first refuses to yield.

Achilles responded: "Odysseus, I hate like the gates of death the man who says one thing and hides another in his heart. Agamemnon will not win me over. I've fought and suffered hardship for years in this war, and for what? So that I could enrich Agamemnon and see him parcel out bits and pieces to the others? Then he had the nerve to steal from me, the best of the Greeks, the woman I love. Let him keep her! Since I stopped fighting, he's had to erect a rampart, and he still can't stop Hector! Tomorrow I will load up my ships and sail home. Agamemnon can die for all I care! He couldn't make up for the way he hurt me even if he gave me ten or twenty times as much. I don't need his daughters; there are plenty of Greek women who would make fine wives to me. No wealth is worth my life. Material goods can be replaced, but once a man's life is gone, no trade brings it back. My mother, Thetis, once told me that I have the choice of two fates: If I besiege Troy, I will never return home, but I will have eternal glory. If I sail home, my glory will be gone, but my life will be long. I advise the rest to do the same: sail home now!"

The ambassadors were shocked at his words. Phoenix finally spoke up: "Achilles, listen to me, since your father trusted me to raise you. This stubbornness is wrong! Even the gods can be bent by prayer, and they are much more powerful than we. No one blames you for being angry, but Agamemnon is humbling himself, offering you much, and sending the army's leading warriors to plead with you. A day may come when you will be forced to fight without receiving these gifts, and then your glory will be much less."

Even Achilles' old tutor, Phoenix, fails to persuade him.

Achilles answered firmly, "Phoenix, I do not need honors like that. You should not be degrading yourself speaking for Agamemnon like this! Ajax and Odysseus can take my message back. You spend the night here, and tomorrow we will decide whether we stay in Troy or sail home."

Ajax stood up and declared, "Come on, Odysseus, let's go back. We won't get what we came for, I see. Achilles has a heart of iron; he doesn't care about any of the men here who honored him."

The embassy to the seated Achilles, Ajax at far left, Odysseus leaning on his spear, and Phoenix, on the right, resting on his walking stick. Representation of Attic red-figure vase painting.

This stung Achilles, who retorted, "Ajax, I'm not disagreeing with you. But I can't forgive Agamemnon for his arrogance and the way he humiliated me in front of the army, as if I were nobody! I will not arm for war again until Hector tries to burn my own ship!"

After Hector sets fire to the Greek ships, Patroclus rebukes Achilles.

The men returned with the discouraging news to Agamemnon. But Diomedes rallied the king's and the men's spirits to continue the fight. Despite his and the others' courage and strength, however, the Greeks continued to lose. Agamemnon, Odysseus, and Diomedes were all wounded in the subsequent fighting. When Hector set fire to the Greeks' ships, Achilles' friend Patroclus could stand by no longer. He scolded Achilles, "You must have been born from the rocks, not from Thetis. How can you not defend your fellow soldiers? But if you are still determined not to fight, give me your armor and let me go into battle in your place."

Achilles was still angry with Agamemnon, but he agreed to do as Patroclus requested. However, he cautioned, "As soon as you have driven the enemy back from the ships, come back. Do not try to take Troy, or one of the gods who loves the Trojans may intervene."

Patroclus takes the field and kills many Trojans until he is stopped by Apollo and slain by Hector.

Patroclus took the field with the Myrmidons, Achilles' troops who were fresh and eager to fight. The Trojans, believing that Achilles had returned, panicked and retreated. Patroclus killed many men, including Zeus' own son Sarpedon. Forgetting Achilles' warning, he charged at the gates of Troy three times before Apollo pushed him back: "It is not fated for you to take Troy, or even for Achilles, a greater man than you!" the god cried. As Patroclus drew back, Apollo disguised himself as one of Hector's allies and said, "Hector, why are you holding back? Head straight for Patroclus, and Apollo might give you glory!" Hector did so, and Patroclus killed Hector's charioteer. As the Trojans and Greeks each fought to drag away the driver's corpse, Patroclus charged three times, and each time killed three men. Then, at the fourth assault, the end of Patroclus' life drew near. Apollo slammed his hand against the warrior's shoulders and back, and his eyes were dizzied by the blow. The spear in his hand was shattered, and Apollo wrenched his breastplate off. One of the Trojans speared him between the shoulder blades, and then Hector stabbed him through. The Greeks groaned to see him fall, as Hector boasted over him: "Patroclus, I suppose you thought you would bring the city down, you fool! But I drove you off! Achilles couldn't save you! I bet he told you not to come back until you had killed me, and you listened to him!"

Gasping for breath, Patroclus said, "You can boast all you want. It was Apollo who really killed me. But your own death is not far off. Achilles . . . "

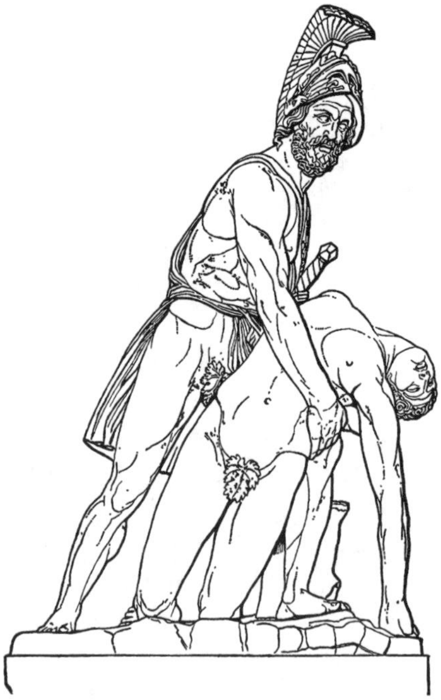

Menelaus carrying Patroclus from the field at Troy

Hector taunted the now-dead Patroclus, "Why are you predicting my death? Who knows, maybe *I'll* kill *Achilles*!" He stripped Achilles' armor off Patroclus and kept it as a trophy, but Menelaus and Ajax rushed over and defended Patroclus' body from being dragged off by the Trojans. Another soldier brought the bad news to Achilles, who had been watching from his ships and wondering why the Greeks were again being routed.

After Patroclus is killed, the grief-stricken Achilles blames himself.

Achilles in grief took handfuls of earth and poured them over his face and clothes, tore his hair, and groaned loudly. He was so distraught that those around him grabbed his hands, fearing he would kill himself on the spot. Thetis heard him from the depths of the sea, and she and her sister nymphs mourned with him. Then she came to Achilles and let him tell what had happened, although she already knew. "I sat here by the ships, useless, while my dearest friend died, because I was angry with Agamemnon! But I will put that behind me and go kill Hector. I accept my death when Zeus wills it. But now let me go to win glory!"

Thetis answered, "Very well, son. But your armor is in the hands of Hector. I will go to Hephaestus and have him fashion you a new set."

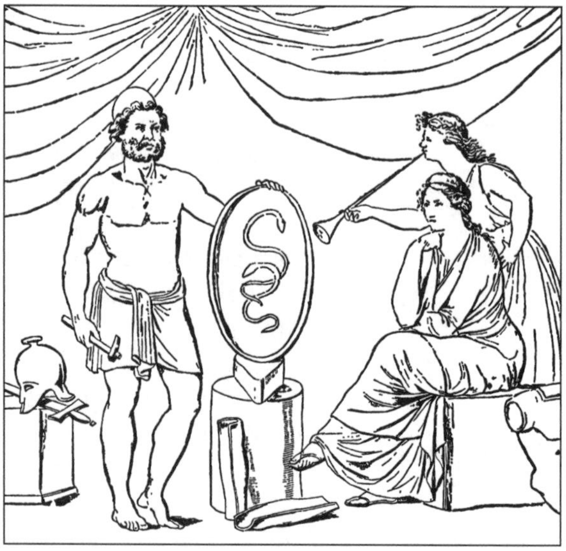

Hephaestus makes new armor for Achilles while Thetis, at right, waits.

As she set off towards Olympus, Iris came down sent by Hera, and advised Achilles to stand at the trench and show himself to the Trojans. So formidable was the sight of Achilles, even unarmed, and so terrible was his war cry that the Trojans were panic-stricken.

Hephaestus fashions a new set of armor for Achilles.

Hephaestus made splendid armor for Achilles. The shield had carvings representing earth, sea, and sky; populous cities; fields; vineyards; and forests full of animals. The breastplate was brighter than fire, the helmet golden, and the greaves of gleaming tin.

His parents, not wanting Hector to die, discourage him from returning to battle.

Achilles armed himself with the fire-god's gifts and returned to battle, sending the Trojans to flight like frightened deer. Hector alone took his stand before the gates. His parents were afraid for him as they saw Achilles dashing towards Troy. "Oh, Hector!" old Priam pleaded. "Don't stand there, come inside the walls! Pity me, an old man! I've seen so many of my sons killed and my daughters dragged away. I know what lies in store for me. Some enemy will cut me down, and the dogs I bred myself to guard my halls will lap my blood. A young man slain in war still looks noble, but there's nothing more shameful than an old man mutilated by dogs." Hecuba bared her breast, and added, "I beg you by this, if you ever were comforted by it as a baby, do not go forth against Achilles! Your wife and I will not be able to mourn you on your deathbed; Achilles will leave your body to be eaten by the animals!" So they wept, but they were not able to change Hector's mind.

King Priam sits on the walls of Troy observing the contest between Hector and Achilles.

Standing alone outside the walls, however, Hector began to have second thoughts. "Is there still time to get inside the walls? No, the others will call me a coward. . . . I could promise Achilles to give back Helen and all her treasures, and let the Greeks loot our citadel. . . . What am I saying? No, he'll show no mercy. Better to face him in battle, and let Zeus give the victory however he will." As Achilles closed in on him, Hector's nerve failed. He fled in fear, and Achilles chased him around the city walls. Zeus took pity on him, and said to the other gods, "I feel bad for Hector. He sacrificed much to me over the years. Do the rest of you think I should save him now, or allow Achilles to take his life?"

Athena retorted, "Father, what are you thinking? His doom was sealed long ago."

"Don't worry, Athena, I wasn't serious. Go, do what you want to."

The battle goddess swept down from Olympus ready to fight. Achilles pursued Hector relentlessly; he would have caught him long ago, but Apollo, helping Hector for the last time, put strength in his legs. When the warriors began their fourth run around the walls, Zeus held out his golden scales and placed the lots of Achilles and Hector in them. Hector's lot sank down low, and Apollo left him.

Athena stood beside Achilles and said, "Now you and I will win! Stand here and catch your breath, while I go and persuade Hector to take a stand against you." She went over to the Trojan disguised as his brother Deiphobus. "Come on, Hector," said the disguised goddess. "Let's beat back Achilles together!"

Hector was heartened, thinking his brother was with him. He said, "I won't run from you anymore, Achilles. Prepare to kill or be killed! I swear that if I defeat you, I won't mutilate your body, and I'll give it back to your allies for burial. Promise that you will do the same for me."

Achilles was in no mood to swear a pact with Hector. He snarled, "Wolves and lambs don't make treaties; neither can we. I wish I could cut off your flesh and eat it raw! Now you'll pay for all the grief you brought me!"

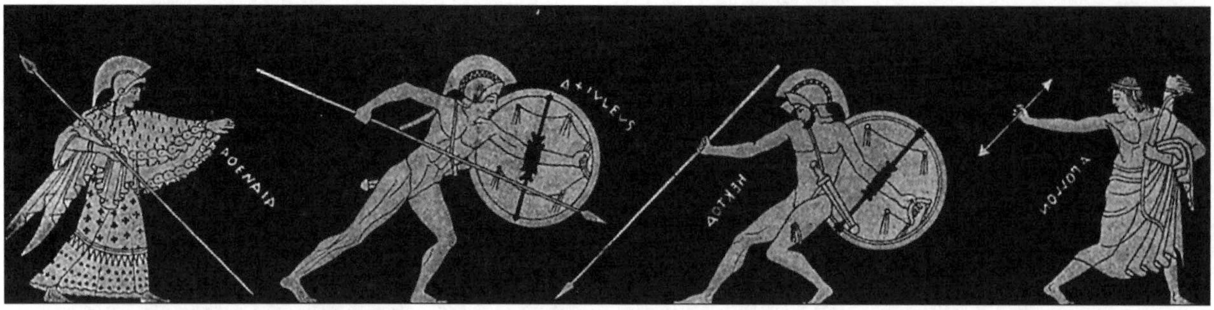

The battle between Achilles, aided by Athena at left, and Hector, guided by Apollo at right. Attic vase painting, 490 BCE.

He threw his spear, but Hector dodged it. Athena was there, however, and returned the missile to Achilles, unseen by Hector. The Trojan exclaimed, "You missed! You were all talk, after all! Now prepare to dodge *my* spear!" The weapon struck Achilles' shield, but bounced off harmlessly. Hector seethed at the wasted shot, and called out, "Deiphobus! My lance!" But Deiphobus was not beside him. Hector realized then that he was doomed. He resolved to die fighting, and charged at Achilles with his sword. Achilles charged too, looking for a vulnerable spot. He found it, and pierced through Hector's neck. "Hector, I'm sure you thought you were safe when you stripped off Patroclus' armor! But a stronger man was waiting at the ships! Now Patroclus will be buried with honor, and the dogs and birds will maul you!" With his last breath, Hector begged once more to let his body be returned to his friends. He also predicted, "Beware . . . Paris and Apollo will kill you too. . . ."

Achilles kills Hector and drags his corpse around the walls of Troy.

Not satisfied to have killed Hector, Achilles pierced his feet, knotted straps of hide through them, and tied them to his chariot. He then dragged the body around the walls of Troy as those within the walls watched and loudly lamented.

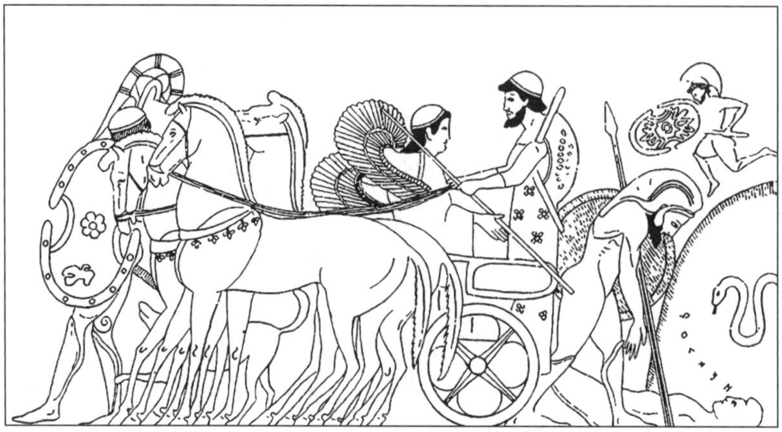

Achilles dragging the corpse of the fallen Hector at the back of his chariot. Representation of Greek vase painting.

That night, Patroclus' ghost came to Achilles in a dream. "Achilles, have you forgotten me? You need to bury me; the other ghosts keep me off and won't let me cross the Styx. Our time together on earth is over. One last request: let our ashes rest in the same urn."

Achilles kills Hector and drags his corpse around the walls of Troy.

Achilles said, "I will do all you say. But come closer, and let me hold you one more time!" He tried to embrace his dead friend, but the ghost slipped away like a wisp of smoke. The next day, the Greeks laid Patroclus to rest amid a variety of funeral games. Achilles' grief was still unappeased, however, and that night he was sleepless. He continued to dishonor Hector's body, dragging it around his comrade's tomb. Zeus had had enough, and he said to Thetis, "Go and tell your son that the gods are angry with him, and he needs to return Hector's body to the Trojans." To Iris he said, "Have Priam go to Achilles tonight, alone, and ransom his son. Tell him Hermes will guide him." The two goddesses set off on their separate missions. Zeus also removed any sign of mutilation from Hector's body, so that his father would not become enraged at Achilles.

Priam comes to Achilles asking for the body of his son Hector. Representation of Attic red-figure vase painting.

When Priam arrived at Achilles' tent, he knelt at the Greek warrior's feet. "Achilles, I beg you, think of your own father, who is as old as I am. I once had a multitude of sons, but most are dead now. I come now to ransom my first and greatest son. Have pity on me. I do what no man has ever done: kiss the hands that killed my great Hector."

Achilles was overcome by thoughts of his own father and by grief for Patroclus. The two wept together, and Achilles felt a bond with this old man who had suffered so much. He ordered Hector's body washed and anointed, and laid it on Priam's wagon himself. The king then hurried back to Troy, although Achilles invited him to eat and stay the night in his tent. The Greeks and Trojans had a brief truce to bury their dead.

Paris wounds Achilles in his vulnerable heel and kills him.

Homer's *Iliad* concludes with the funeral of Hector, but the war did not end there. The Greeks suffered two serious losses shortly after the war resumed. Apollo came down to Paris, who was shooting his arrows haphazardly, and said, "Why do you waste your ammunition on nobodies? Take aim at Achilles and avenge the deaths of your brothers!" Paris did so, and Apollo guided the arrow to Achilles' one vulnerable spot: his heel. That was the first time since the death of Hector that Priam had cause to celebrate!

Achilles mourns the death of his friend, Patroclus, as Thetis, left with shield, and her accompanying Nereids mourn as well.

Odysseus inherits Achilles' armor; Ajax goes mad.

No sooner was Achilles' body burned to ashes and laid to rest with Patroclus' than the two greatest surviving heroes, Odysseus and Ajax, quarreled over which of them should receive Achilles' glorious armor. Each presented his case to the Greeks; Ajax pointed out all of his achievements in battle, but he was no match for Odysseus' eloquence. The armor was awarded to Odysseus. That night, Ajax lost his wits, possibly because of Athena's anger (he had once refused her help in battle). He killed a flock of sheep, believing they were the Greek soldiers, and brought back one particularly hefty ram to his tent to torture, mistaking it for his rival. Coming to his senses again and realizing what he had done, he decided he could not continue to live in such disgrace. He fell upon his sword. Ironically, it was the one Hector had given him after their duel.

The Greeks then learned they could not take Troy without the bow of Heracles, which Philoctetes possessed. He had spent the past ten years on Lemnos alone, his wound still unhealed and painful. Odysseus was dispatched to fetch him, along with Achilles' young son Neoptolemus, also known as Pyrrhus, and a group of sailors. Understandably, Philoctetes was embittered against the Greeks, especially Odysseus, whom he blamed for persuading the rest to abandon him. Upon their arrival on Lemnos, Odysseus explained that Philoctetes would never agree to go with them to Troy; he needed to be tricked. "Tell him that you have a grudge against the Greeks too, and you're sailing home now. Say that nasty Odysseus refused to let you have your father's armor and claimed it for himself. Insult me all you want, I won't care. Offer to take him back to Greece with you. Of course, he'll really be going to Troy."

Neoptolemus hated the thought of deceiving this sick and lonely man. "I don't think this is what my father would have done!" he complained.

"You have the rest of your life to be honest! Be cunning just this once!" retorted Odysseus.

Neoptolemus urges Philoctetes to come to Troy with them.

Neoptolemus reluctantly agreed as Odysseus hid nearby. When Philoctetes entered, clad in rags and limping horribly, Neoptolemus was seized with pity but played his role as Odysseus had instructed. He persuaded Philoctetes to leave with him, and they were on their way to the ship, but suddenly Philoctetes was seized with an attack of violent pain. "AAAhhh!" he screamed as the pangs racked his body. "Take the bow . . . keep it safe until this attack passes. . . . I'll fall asleep when it does. Don't leave me!"

"I promise!" Neoptolemus exclaimed as Philoctetes handed over the bow and sank into sleep, exhausted.

"All right, now's your chance! Sneak off with the bow before he wakes up!" the accompanying sailors advised.

Neoptolemus hesitated, long enough for Philoctetes to wake up and express joy at finding the young man still beside him with the precious bow. Neoptolemus was too overcome by conscience to continue the charade further. "Oh, Philoctetes! I have to confess to you, I haven't come to take you home, I've come to take you to Troy!" And he explained all.

Philoctetes was outraged by this deception. "How can you do this to me when I trusted you? I know this isn't your real nature! Please, give me back my bow!"

"Don't!" exclaimed Odysseus, suddenly reappearing. "If you won't come with us, Philoctetes, we can take Troy without you. We have the bow; that's all we need. Goodbye, enjoy your island!" And he shoved Neoptolemus off to the ship.

"Alas for me!" groaned Philoctetes. "I'm really helpless now! I'm going to be the prey of all those birds and animals that I used to hunt!"

He was ready to throw himself off the rocks and end his life when Neoptolemus returned with the bow, closely pursued by an angry Odysseus. "Take it back, Philoctetes. This time there's no trick. Are you sure you refuse to come with us? If you relent, you'll be cured of your wound and you'll win glory."

"I still refuse. Why should I help men who let me waste ten years of my life in pain?"

"Very well. I'll take you back to Greece as I said I would before. No, Odysseus, my mind is made up."

Heracles' spirit appears to Philoctetes, urging him to go to Troy.

The young man and the ill soldier were about to depart together, when the spirit of Heracles appeared. "Do what they want, Philoctetes. It is Zeus' will for you to go to Troy. You remember how much I suffered, and how I was rewarded in the end. You will be, too."

"I will do it out of love for you, my dearest friend Heracles," responded Philoctetes.

At Troy, Philoctetes' wound was healed by Machaon, guided by his father Asclepius. No sooner was he well again than he shot Paris. The wounded Trojan went back to his first love, the nymph Oenone, who had once promised to heal him if he needed it. Angry with him because he had deserted her for Helen, however, she now withheld her skills, and Paris died.

The Trojan horse

The Trojans find the wooden horse left by the Greeks.

Still, victory through combat eluded the Greeks. Athena advised them to win the war by trickery. They built a horse, big as a mountain, and concealed their best warriors in it. The rest hid on the island of Tenedos offshore. Rumors circulated that the horse was an offering to Athena for the Greeks' safe return home. The Trojans could hardly believe their good fortune when they saw no trace of the enemy! Some gazed at the "offering" to Athena and marveled at its huge size. People were uncertain of what to do. Some favored bringing it within the walls; others more wisely suggested burning it or throwing it into the sea or cutting holes in it and exposing its secrets.

Laocoon warns against it.

The priest Laocoon, watching all this, ran forward and scolded the Trojans: "You fools! Do you really believe that the Greeks have sailed away? Either there are Greeks in here, or there is some other trick. Whatever it is, I fear the Greeks, even bearing gifts." With these words, he flung a spear at the horse's side. There was a groan from within. In another moment, the Trojans would have dismantled the horse. At that moment, however, there was a sudden outcry, and some Trojan shepherds appeared dragging a man with his hands tied behind his back.

Sinon, left by the Greeks as a decoy, urges bringing the horse into the city.

"Oh me!" he cried. "First the Greeks try to kill me, and now the Trojans want to!"

The Trojans felt pity for this "prisoner," who had actually been planted by the Greeks for the Trojans to capture and interrogate. They asked him who he was.

"My name is Sinon," he said. "My dearest friend and kinsman was Palamedes. Odysseus hated Palamedes, who had once outwitted him, and Odysseus had him framed as a traitor. He planted Trojan gold in Palamedes' tent, accused him of taking bribes, and had him put to death." (Odysseus had in fact set up Palamedes in this way.) "Because I was closer to Palamedes than anyone, Odysseus kept looking for an excuse to kill me too. Now the Greeks had long ago wanted to sail back home, but rough seas kept them from doing so. They sent a man to find out from the oracle what the problem was. The answer he brought back chilled us all: 'Apollo says that you had to sacrifice someone to come here, and you will have to sacrifice someone to go home.' Odysseus persuaded the priest Calchas that 'someone' meant me! While they were preparing the sacred rites, I escaped and hid until your shepherds found me. Please, have mercy!"

Priam ordered Sinon's hands unbound. "We will accept you as one of us," the king declared. "But tell us truthfully, what is the purpose of this horse?"

Laocoon and his sons, Vatican Museums, Vatican City, Italy

"I will tell you. But first, promise me you will give me asylum."

The king gave his word. "The Greeks have always relied on Athena's help. But after Odysseus and Diomedes stole her statue, the Palladium, from the temple in Troy, she turned against us. The priest told us we had to build this horse as an offering to appease her. If you violate it, destruction will surely come upon your city. But if you bring it within your walls, victory will be yours."

Laocoon and his sons are strangled by sea serpents.

Cassandra warns the Trojans not to allow the horse within the walls.

The Trojans were convinced, especially in view of what happened next. Two immense sea serpents came from the direction of Tenedos and slithered onto the land. They headed straight for Laocoon and his two sons, ensnared them in massive coils, and bit them to death. Terrified that this had happened because the priest had thrown a spear at the horse, the Trojans hesitated no longer. They placed wheels under the massive structure and wheeled it into the city. It became stuck four times on the threshold and the armor rattled within, but at last it was brought inside and taken to Athena's citadel. The prophetic Cassandra cried out a warning, but she was ignored. On the last day of their city's life, the Trojans celebrated and decked the gods' shrines with flowers.

Sinon opens the horse to let the Greeks out into the city.

When night came and the Trojans all staggered home to bed, the Greeks who had been hiding on Tenedos sailed to shore, and Sinon undid the bolts of the horse. The hidden soldiers rushed out into a city buried in wine and sleep, killed the guards taken unawares first, and then opened the gates to admit the rest of the army.

Cassandra

Troy became a chaos of fires and slaughter. Cassandra was dragged away from Athena's temple by Ajax son of Oileus (sometimes called the Lesser Ajax, to distinguish him from the massive soldier of the same name). As the Greeks, led by Neoptolemus, invaded the palace, Hecuba and the other women took refuge on a great altar there. Priam wanted to die defending his city. He buckled his long-unused armor onto his trembling frame and took up his sword. Hecuba protested, "Are you mad? There is nothing you can do. Not even Hector, if he were alive, could help us now. Come take refuge here with us."

Just then Neoptolemus appeared, chasing one of Priam's sons named Polites, who was already seriously wounded. Polites barely reached the altar when he collapsed and died. Priam cried out to Neoptolemus, "May the gods give you what you deserve for making an old father witness his son's death! You're no son of Achilles! He had respect for suppliants when he gave me back my son Hector's body and let me return safely to my city." With these words, Priam feebly threw his spear. It reached the center of Neoptolemus' shield and stuck there, useless.

Neoptolemus kills Priam himself.

Neoptolemus sneered, "Soon you'll be seeing my father yourself! Remember to tell him how bad his son is! Now die!" He dragged Priam to the altar through the pool of his son's blood. Clutching Priam's hair in his left hand, he raised the sword with his right and buried it in the king's side. Thus Priam died, the king who had once been the ruler of great lands.

The Greeks distribute Hecuba and Andromache as war prizes.

No one suffered more in the defeat of Troy than Queen Hecuba. All her sons were killed in battle except her youngest, Polydorus, who was too young to fight. His parents had smuggled him out of the city to take refuge with the king of Thrace. The queen and the other women were rounded up and taken to a detention camp outside Troy, where they awaited word about who would take them as slaves and concubines. When a herald came announcing the news, Hecuba was distressed to learn that she had been assigned to the ruthless and cunning Odysseus. She was even more horrified at the thought of the chaste Cassandra in the hands of Agamemnon, but her priestess daughter consoled her: "Agamemnon will die ignobly as he deserves. Our men were fortunate to die in their homeland, lamented by their own people, and their glory will endure forever."

Pyrrhus (Neoptolemus) grasps Polyxena with one hand as he prepares to cut her throat. Queen Hecuba pleads for the life of her youngest daughter. Polites, Polyxena' s brother, lies dead at their feet. *The Abduction of Polyxena,* 1866, by Pio Fedi (1816–1892), Loggia di Lanzi, Florence, Italy.

Neoptolemus also kills the royal children.

Andromache then learned of her wretched fate: she was to marry Neoptolemus, the son of the man who had killed her husband! But worse was to come. Achilles' ghost had appeared at his tomb, ranting, "Are you Greeks going to sail home with your women and forget all about me? I will not let you leave until you sacrifice to me!" The sacrifice he wanted was Priam and Hecuba's youngest daughter, Polyxena. The Greeks had also decided that Hector and Andromache's son Astyanax could not be permitted to live, lest he grow up to avenge his father and the other Trojans. Soldiers came to take the two young people away. Each died bravely. As Neoptolemus prepared to sacrifice Polyxena, she cried out, "Son of Achilles, untie me. I die of my own free will." He unbound her hands, and she said, "See, I bare my throat for you to strike." She even fell dead in a dignified way. Astyanax also embraced his death; according to the philosopher/playwright Seneca, he did not wait for the Greeks to throw him off the wall but rushed ahead and jumped. Nor was Polydorus saved as his parents had hoped. The treacherous king of Thrace who was supposed to be shielding him killed him for his gold.

Hecuba is turned into a dog en route to Greece; only Aeneas escapes burning Troy.

All these sorrows were too much for Hecuba. On the voyage to Greece, she was metamorphosed into a dog. The only adult male of fighting age to escape from Troy alive was Aeneas, whose journeys we will read about in chapter 18.

A. Review Exercises

1. **MATCHING!** The left-hand column is a list of leaders' names. The right-hand column lists the city or territory each leader ruled. Match each leader with the correct place name. Write the letter in the space provided.

1.	____	Nestor	a.	Mycenae
2.	____	Achilles	b.	Ithaca
3.	____	Odysseus	c.	Scyrus
4.	____	Priam	d.	Sparta
5.	____	Menelaus	e.	Pylos
6.	____	Lycomedes	f.	Phthia
7.	____	Diomedes	g.	Salamis
8.	____	Agamemnon	h.	Troy
9.	____	Ajax son of Telamon	i.	Argos

2. **WHOSE SIDE?** Below is a list of most of the gods/goddesses who played a role in the Trojan War. Circle the names of those who sided with the Greeks. Underline the names of those who fought for the Trojans. Draw a square around those who were neutral or played no role.

Zeus	**Hera**	**Apollo**	**Artemis**	**Aphrodite**	**Demeter**
Athena	**Iris**	**Hephaestus**	**Ares**	**Thetis**	**Poseidon**

3. **MULTIPLE CHOICE!** For each sentence below, circle the number of the answer that best answers the question or completes the statement.

a. What is another name Homer uses for "Troy" that gives its name to the great epic about the Trojan War?

1. Thrace
2. Phrygia
3. Ilium
4. Lydia

b. Whose marriage provided the setting for the Judgment of Paris?

1. Zeus and Hera
2. Aphrodite and Hephaestus
3. Peleus and Thetis
4. Poseidon and Amphitrite

c. Who wasn't invited to this wedding?

1. Apollo
2. Hebe
3. Eris
4. Eileithyia

d. Oenone the shepherdess was the wife of which of these sons of Priam and Hecuba?

1. Hector
2. Helenus
3. Polites
4. Paris

e. Which young woman was the war prize who was reluctantly given over to Agamemnon by Achilles?

1. Chryseis
2. Cassandra
3. Briseis
4. Polyxena

f. After Thetis dipped the infant Achilles into this river of invulnerability, Achilles could be wounded only in the heel by which she grasped him. Which river was this?

1. Styx
2. Lethe
3. Phlegethon
4. Scamander

g. The theme of Homer's *Iliad* is concerned with which aspect of Achilles' character and temperament?

1. Self-pity
2. Wrath
3. Sorrow
4. Athletic prowess

h. In the contest between Menelaus and Paris, which of the following was the outcome?

1. Paris wounded Menelaus.
2. Menelaus seized and held Paris as his prisoner.
3. Paris was spirited away by Aphrodite.
4. Paris ran from the battlefield to Helen.

i. Which Greek hero did Hector not fight against?

1. Ajax
2. Menelaus
3. Achilles
4. Patroclus

j. Which of these fighters wore Achilles' armor into battle?

1. Ajax
2. Agamemnon
3. Diomedes
4. Patroclus

k. Which of these prophets had the unhappy task of informing Agamemnon of two very difficult problems: the necessary sacrifice of Iphigenia and the necessary return of Chryseis to her father, Chryses?

1. Tiresias
2. Calchas
3. Laocoon
4. Nestor

l. Which god was outraged over Agamemnon's seizure of Chryseis?

1. Zeus
2. Ares
3. Apollo
4. Hephaestus

m. Which god, when wounded by a spear wielded by both Diomedes and Athena, bellowed like an army of ten thousand men, his cries heard from Troy all the way across the Aegean Sea to Olympus itself?

1. Hephaestus
2. Poseidon
3. Ares
4. Apollo

n. Which deity sought out Hephaestus to ask him to make new armor for Achilles?

1. Thetis
2. Athena
3. Poseidon
4. Hermes

o. Why could Hector himself not offer sacrifice to Athena at her temple before he went to battle against Achilles?

1. Paris and Helen detained him.
2. He disdained the goddess who was helping Odysseus and the Greeks.
3. He was blood-spattered from battle and therefore polluted.
4. He was embarrassed with his appearance after combat.

p. Whom did Hector ask to offer sacrifice to Athena in his place?

1. His sister, Cassandra
2. His wife, Andromache
3. His sister-in-law, Helen
4. His mother, Hecuba

q. Who feared the crested helmet of Hector, forcing Hector to remove it before the battle?

1. Andromache
2. Helen
3. Hecuba
4. Astyanax

r. In the midst of the battle, Hector found the courage to face Achilles for the last time because he believed that one of his brothers had come to his aid and was at his side. In reality it was a deity in disguise. Which deity was disguised as which of Hector's brothers?

1. Aphrodite as Paris
2. Apollo as Helenus
3. Athena as Deiphobus
4. Ares as Polites

s. Who came to Achilles to beg for the corpse of Hector that had been dragged three times around the city of Troy by the conquering chariot?

1. Priam
2. Hecuba
3. Polites
4. Polydorus

t. Which of these Trojans warned against admitting the wooden horse, the gift of the Greeks, into the city?

1. Hecuba
2. Priam
3. Laocoon
4. Polyxena

u. Which of these Greeks was left behind to convince the Trojans that the wooden horse was a gift and was admitted to the city, only later to open the gates of Troy that night?

1. Odysseus
2. Calchas
3. Philoctetes
4. Sinon

v. Who fatally wounded the Greek hero Achilles?

1. Paris
2. Helenus
3. Hector
4. Polites

w. Which man, bitten by a snake before the beginning of the war, had been abandoned by the Greeks on the island of Lemnos because of the stench of his festering wound?

1. Philoctetes
2. Neoptolemus
3. Sinon
4. Heracles

x. In a prophecy, the Greeks learned that they would have to obtain the bow of Heracles in order for them to win the war. Who had been given this bow and later killed Paris while using it?

1. Neoptolemus
2. Philoctetes
3. Odysseus
4. Thersites

y. What was the fate of Cassandra, the priestess whose prophecies were not believed?

1. She married Neoptolemus.
2. She became Agamemnon's war prize.
3. She died with her family at Troy.
4. She escaped with Aeneas.

B. MUSINGS

1. The poet Homer never mentions the term "Achilles' heel" in his descriptions of Achilles' vulnerability. The story that his heel was the point of Achilles' vulnerability first appears many centuries after Homer wrote the *Iliad* in a poem by the Roman writer Statius in the first century CE. What do you believe Achilles' real weakness (fatal flaw) to have been? Write a short essay defending your belief.

2. Of all the human characters described in this chapter, which one do you feel acted in the most moral manner? Who was the most immoral, according to your beliefs? Write a short essay describing the reasons for your answers to these two questions.

3. What does the intervention and behavior of the gods in the Trojan War say to you about Greek religion and religious belief in the gods? Write a short paragraph in a thoughtful reaction/reflection about this question.

C. WORDS, WORDS, WORDS

The Daily Muse

News you can use

The names of several characters and features of the Trojan War have become a colorful part of our English language. Here are just a few:

As a noun, a **hector** is a bully or a braggart. As a verb, to **hector** is to harass someone by putting personal pressure on him or her. Do you think these are appropriate to Homer's **Hector**? Why or why not?

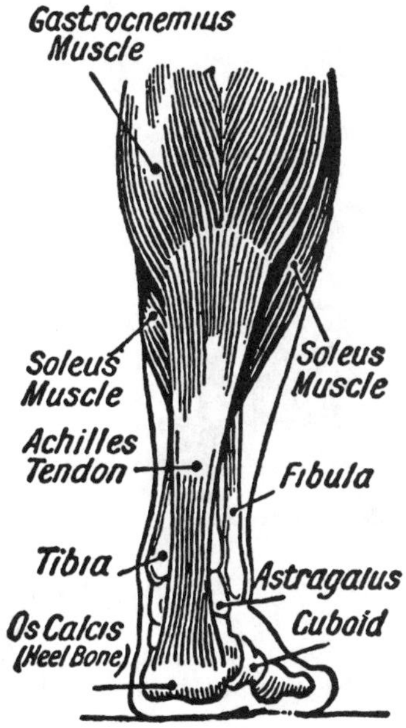

The **Achilles' tendon**, shown in the drawing, joins the heel bone to the calf muscle in the leg.

Achilles' heel, as we have seen, is a common metaphor for a weakness or vulnerability.

What do you think is the **Achilles' heel** of the security of the United States?

____

Think of a politician or government leader. Does this person have an **Achilles' heel?** What is it?

____

Cassandra was the Trojan priestess of Apollo, daughter of Priam and Hecuba, whose fate it was that others would never believe or take seriously her prophecies. In our language, a **Cassandra** is someone whose words or predictions are disregarded or disbelieved. Can you think of any other historical figure who could be described as a **Cassandra**? Explain your choice.

____

____

In the context of computers, a **Trojan horse** is a program that appears to be legitimate software but that is actually harmful when opened. Have you ever experienced a **Trojan horse** that entered your computer? What happened?

____

____

D. How 'Bout That?

Ouch! My Achilles' heel!

The term "Achilles' heel" was first used by a Dutch anatomist, Philip Verheyden, in 1693 when he dissected *his own amputated leg*![1]

1 *Online Etymology Dictionary,* see "Achilles tendon," http://www.etymonline.com/index.php?allowed_in_frame=0&search=Achilles+tendon&searchmode=none (accessed March 7, 2015).

The face that launched a thousand ships

You may have heard the phrase "a face that launched a thousand ships" used to describe Helen. The origin of the phrase is a sixteenth-century play, *Doctor Faustus*, by Christopher Marlowe. Here is the full speech. How many mythological allusions can you spot?

Was this the face that launched a thousand ships?
And burnt the topless towers of Ilium?
Sweet Helen, make me immortal with a kiss:
Her lips suck forth my soul, see where it flies!
Come Helen, come, give me my soul again.
Here will I dwell, for heaven is in these lips.
And all is dross that is not Helena.
I will be Paris, and for love of thee,
Instead of Troy shall Wertenberg be sack'd;
And I will combat with weak Menelaus,
And wear thy colours on my plumed crest;
Yea I will wound Achilles in the heel,
And then return to Helen for a kiss.
O thou art fairer than the evening air,
Clad in the beauty of a thousand stars:
Brighter art thou than flaming Jupiter,
When he appeared to hapless Semele;
More lovely than the monarch of the sky
In wanton Arethusa's azur'd arms;
And none but thou shalt be my paramour.

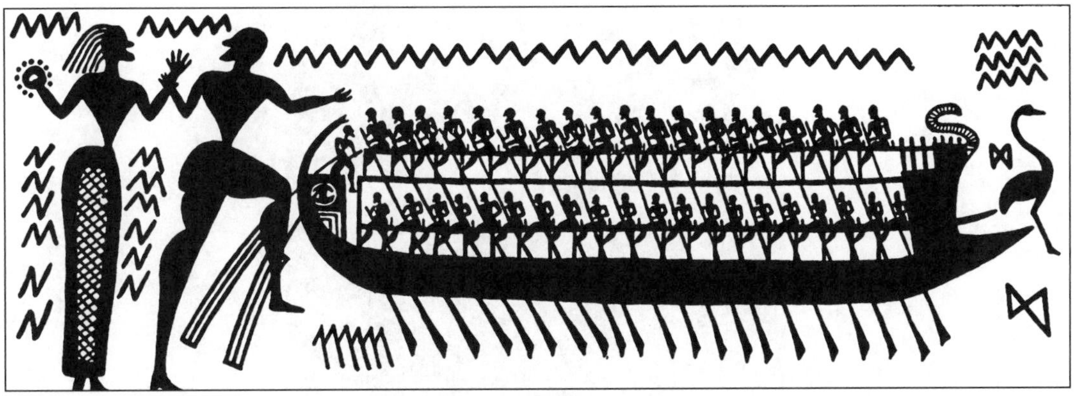

Note the shape of the ship (a bireme of two banks of rowers), the way the waves in the water are represented, and the silhouette figures of Helen, Paris, and the rowers.

Who is Helen of Troy today?

Find a picture of a contemporary woman who you think best represents a modern day Helen. Paste it here:

Trojan War characters in art

The black and white representation of the painting pictured below shows Hector bidding farewell to Andromache. What event contemporary with this painting might have influenced de Chirico to paint this subject?

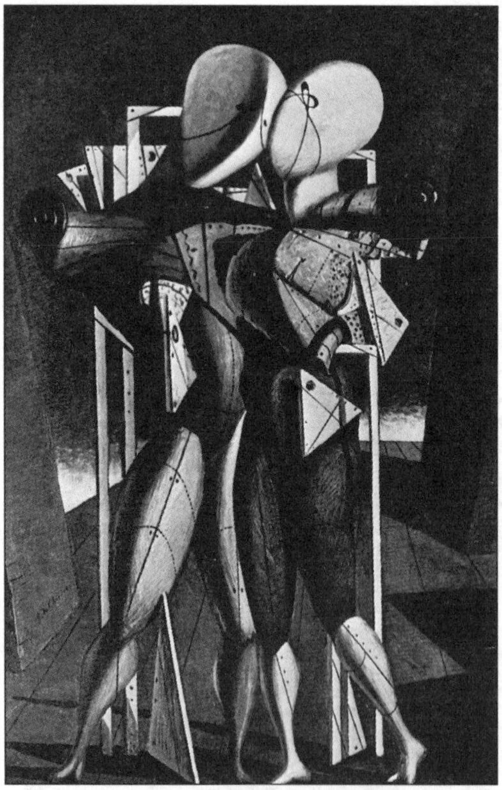

***Hector and Andromache*, 1916, by Giorgio de Chirico (1888–1978), a "Metaphysical" painter, Coll. Mattidi (private collection), Milan, Rome**

Ajax the hero

Here is a newspaper and magazine advertisement for a product that was a predecessor of the staple machines that we use today. Its inventors apparently bestowed the name "Ajax" because they wanted to convey the idea that it was a strong machine that would not give out easily when binding a large sheaf of papers. Find other products that are named for the great Greek hero Ajax and list them below. If you can find one, tape or paste an Ajax product label or advertisement in the space below.

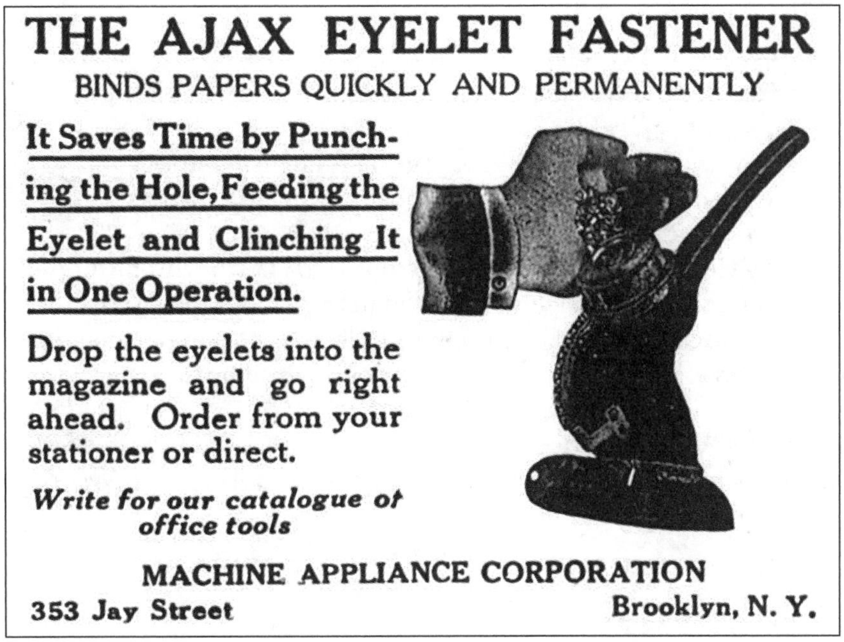

Hector Protector

The stupendously courageous figure of Hector, the protector of the city of Troy, has inspired many poets, writers, and artists throughout history. An old English nursery rhyme you may know goes like this:

> Hector Protector was dressed all in green;
> Hector Protector was sent to the Queen.
> The Queen did not like him,
> Nor more did the King;
> So Hector Protector was sent back again.

Scholars who study the meanings behind our old English nursery rhymes think that the "Hector" referred to in this poem is Richard Plantagenet, Duke of York (1411–1460), whose relative was the weak, and perhaps mentally unstable, King Henry VI. Duke Richard attempted to take the throne himself, claiming that he was protecting England from this ineffective king and his ambitious queen. Hector Protector/Richard was dressed all in green because he had been sent to Ireland as a young man and fled back to Ireland again after he was dismissed from his role as Protector of England by the Queen, Margaret of Anjou.[2]

Celebrated children's author Maurice Sendak provided a creative illustrated version of this Hector Protector story in one of his earliest books, *Hector Protector and As I Went Over the Water* (first published in 1965 and revised in 1993).

E. WHO'S WHO?

- For the House of Troy and Priam's descendants, see GENEALOGICAL CHART 18.
- For Achilles' family see GENEALOGICAL CHART 19.

2 Keith Dockray, interview by Ivan Howlett, *BBC Radio Four: Making History,* BBC, July 5, 2005. Ivan Howlett, of BBC Radio Four, interviews Keith Dockray, a historian of fifteenth-century England, formerly of Huddersfield University, about the origins of the nursery rhyme "Hector Protector." One can read a précis of this interview at http://www.bbc.co.uk/radio4/history/making_history/making_history_20050705.shtml. For the origins and history of Hector Protector, see http://www.rhymes.org.uk/a28-hector-protector.htm.

Chapter Seventeen
Odysseus

General Source:
Homer *Odyssey*

Odysseus' character is **polytropos.**

Like Heracles and Helen, Odysseus is a character that appears in various incarnations throughout Western literature. He has been depicted in a number of ways—from epic hero to stage villain, from an exceptional man to the common man. In Homer's epics, a common epithet for him is *polytropos,* or "man of many turns." This means that he is never at a loss for an idea in a difficult situation. As we saw in the previous chapter, some of Odysseus' schemes make him seem dishonest or cruel. Homer depicts him most favorably—strong, intelligent, passionate, and eloquent.

Statue of Odysseus, Roman copy of a 3rd-century BCE original from Pergamum

Telemachus' Search for Information and Odysseus' Arrival at Phaeacia

In the Homeric epic named for him, Odysseus does not appear until the fourth book (books being a rough equivalent of chapters in modern novels). The first four books feature the travels of his son Telemachus, on a quest for information about his father, who has been gone for more than ten years. (See Genealogical Chart 20.)

During Odysseus' absence, Penelope weaves a shroud for Laertes by day and unravels it at night, so as to stall her harassing suitors.

Because Odysseus had been away from his home of Ithaca for so long, hordes of suitors had taken up residence in his palace, seeking to marry his wife Penelope. She remained faithful to Odysseus, repeatedly refusing the suitors' requests. As one of her stalling tactics, she told them she would marry them after she had completed weaving a funeral shroud for her elderly father-in-law, Laertes. She wove busily all day, only to unravel her handiwork at night. A treacherous female slave discovered her trick, and then told the suitors. They forced Penelope to finish the task, but she still did not choose one of them and remarry.

A Possible Route for the Voyage of Odysseus from Troy to Ithaca

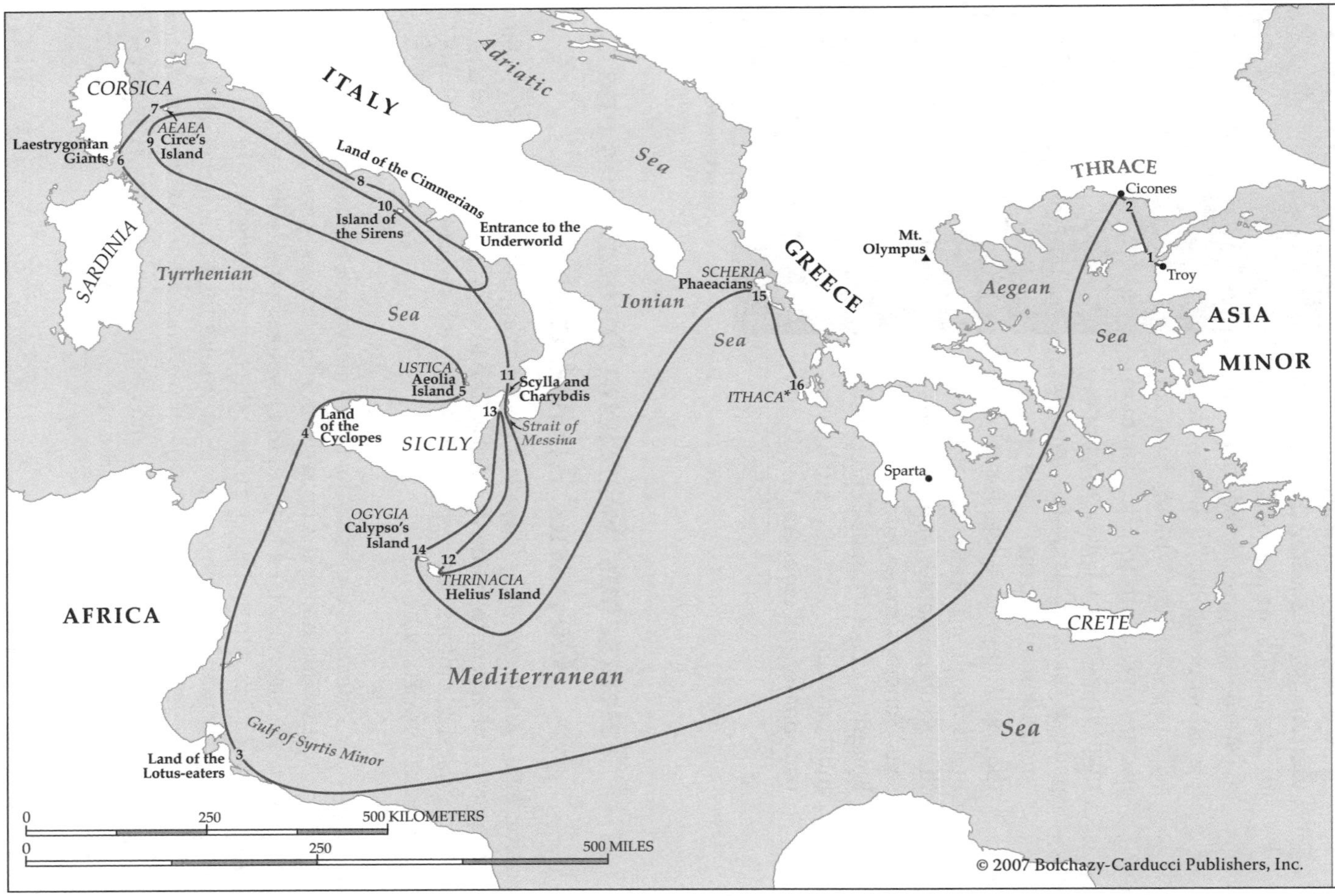

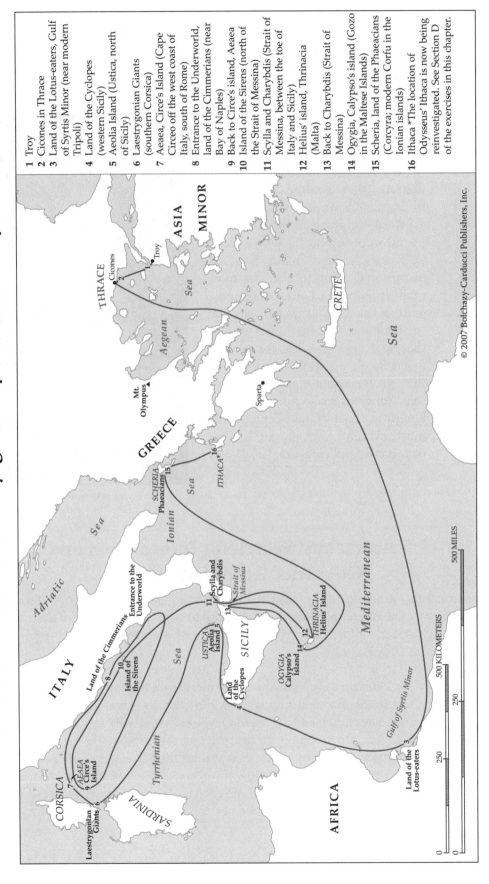

1 Troy
2 Cicones in Thrace
3 Land of the Lotus-eaters, Gulf of Syrtis Minor (near modern Tripoli)
4 Land of the Cyclopes (western Sicily)
5 Aeolia Island (Ustica, north of Sicily)
6 Laestrygonian Giants (southern Corsica)
7 Aeaea, Circe's Island (Cape Circeo off the west coast of Italy, south of Rome)
8 Entrance to the Underworld, land of the Cimmerians (near Bay of Naples)
9 Back to Circe's island, Aeaea
10 Island of the Sirens (north of the Strait of Messina)
11 Scylla and Charybdis (Strait of Messina, between the toe of Italy and Sicily)
12 Helius' island, Thrinacia (Malta)
13 Back to Charybdis (Strait of Messina)
14 Ogygia, Calypso's island (Gozo in the Maltese Islands)
15 Scheria, land of the Phaeacians (Corcyra; modern Corfu in the Ionian islands)
16 Ithaca *The location of Odysseus' Ithaca is now being reinvestigated. See Section D of the exercises in this chapter.

Athena helps Odysseus' son, Telemachus, oppose the overbearing suitors.

Telemachus was helpless to stand up against so many unwanted suitors. Athena looked down upon him and decided to help him. She took the form of a man named Mentes, and appeared at Odysseus' palace while the suitors were in the midst of one of their drunken feasts. Telemachus greeted the guest, apologizing for the chaos, and offered "him" food and drink. Then he said, "Please tell me who you are and what brings you to Ithaca."

Telemachus and Penelope

Athena answered, "My name is Mentes, and I'm on a trading voyage. Your father and mine were friends. I thought he might have come home. I can see he hasn't, but that doesn't mean he won't!"

Telemachus responded, "Thank you for your encouragement, but I'm afraid my father may be dead."

Athena uges Telemachus to voyage to Pylos and Sparta to get news of his father.

Athena said, "You need to go on a voyage to find out for certain. Go first to Pylos and seek information from Nestor, then to Sparta to question Menelaus, as he was the last to reach home. If you learn that he is still alive, you can wait for his return. But if he's dead, you can hold funerary rites for him and marry off your mother to one of the suitors."

Telemachus follows Mentor in his quest to find his father, Odysseus.

With no news of Odysseus, Nestor of Pylos reveals Agamemnon's fate.

Telemachus decided to take her advice and set sail the next day, accompanied by an older man named Mentor. The suitors, disturbed by his sudden show of initiative, decided to kill Telemachus on his return. From old Nestor, Telemachus learned that Athena had become angry with the Greeks and let them die on their return voyages because the lesser Ajax had violated Cassandra. Nestor had lost track of Odysseus after their paths diverged on their journeys. He could give Telemachus no further information about his father, but he did tell him about the fate of Agamemnon, slain by his wife, and how he had been avenged by Orestes.

Menelaus tells Telemachus that Odysseus is alive but Calypso's captive.

At the palace of Menelaus, now reunited with Helen, Telemachus heard more of how brave and smart Odysseus had been. Helen recalled a time when Odysseus came into Troy disguised as a beggar, looking for information. Menelaus recollected that when the men were inside the Trojan Horse, Helen walked around the horse calling out to the men inside imitating the voices of their wives, but Odysseus clamped his hands over the mouth of any man tempted to call back. Menelaus also talked about his own travels. On the voyage home, he was marooned in Egypt, where he had received information from the shape-shifter Proteus about several of his comrades, including Odysseus: "He is being kept captive by a nymph named Calypso. He sits looking out to sea, weeping from homesickness." Telemachus sailed for home the next day, cheered at the knowledge that his father was still alive.

Menelaus

Meanwhile, the gods were discussing Odysseus. "Father Zeus," Athena said, "it is not right that a great ruler like Odysseus should languish far from his kingdom. He has no way to escape from the clutches of Calypso, while his wife's suitors are plotting to murder his son."

Zeus agreed with her. He sent Hermes to Calypso's island to tell her that it was time to let Odysseus go. She complained a bit: "You gods are so hard-hearted! It's all very well for a god to have a mortal woman as a lover, but as soon as a goddess does the same with a mortal man, you're all outraged! But I know I can't defy Zeus."

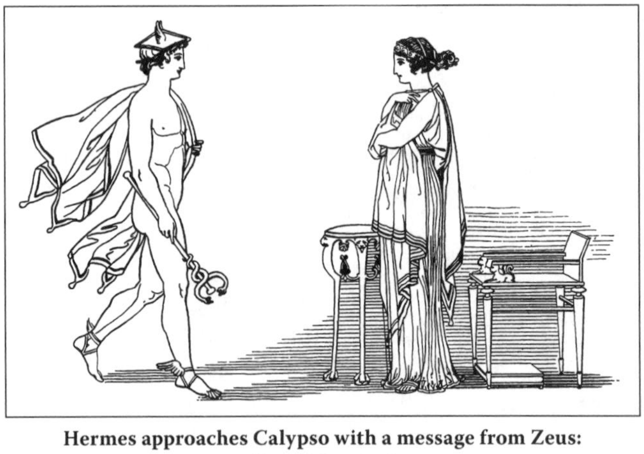

Hermes approaches Calypso with a message from Zeus: Free Odysseus!

Calypso provides Odysseus with a raft and supplies to sail to Phaeacia.

The nymph went to Odysseus, who was sitting on the beach staring longingly at the sea. She told him, "My poor Odysseus, I realize that you want to leave. Come and I will show you trees to cut for a raft, and I will give you food and clothing to send you on your journey. Sail to the shore of the Phaeacians. They will receive you as a god and take you the rest of the way home."

Odysseus gladly obeyed, and in a few days he was ready to depart. Sadly, Calypso watched him sail away. For seventeen days his voyage went smoothly, but when Poseidon spotted his raft approaching the Phaeacians' land, the sea-god was angry. He had a grudge against Odysseus, for reasons that will soon become plain. He caused a storm to rise up, wrecking the raft. Odysseus lamented, "How blessed those were who fell to the Trojans in the war! If only I could have died there instead of drowning here!" And he sank beneath the sea, dragged down by his clothing. Ino, the sea nymph who had once been Cadmus' daughter, felt pity for him. "Odysseus, strip off your clothing and swim for your life. Here, tie my scarf around your waist. It will keep you safe until you reach the Phaeacians' shore. When you arrive, throw it back."

Angry Poseidon blows up a storm against Odysseus' fleet.

The sea-goddess Ino helps shipwrecked Odysseus swim safely to shore.

Odysseus made it to shore with this divine aid, and he returned the goddess' gift to her. He then staggered inland to take shelter under a pile of leaves and fell asleep, exhausted.

Early next morning, Athena went to the princess Nausicaa of Phaeacia, and spoke to her in a dream. "Nausicaa, you lazy girl! Why are you sleeping when the family laundry needs to be done? Ask your father to give you mules and a coach to take the clothes down to the water."

Athena appears to Nausicaa in a dream.

At the seashore, Nausicaa and her friends are startled to see a naked Odysseus!

The princess did as instructed, and soon she was on her way, accompanied by her maids. Her mother had packed her a picnic lunch. When the young women had washed the clothes and eaten, they began to play ball. Athena caused Nausicaa's throw to land near the bushes where Odysseus was sleeping. Their shouts woke him up, and he thought, "What type of people live here, civil or hostile? I had better go and see for myself." He broke off a branch to hide his nakedness, and ventured forth. The girls shrieked at his wild appearance, but Athena put courage in Nausicaa's heart and the princess stood her ground.

Odysseus addressed her: "Princess, are you a mortal or a goddess? You must be Artemis! Or if you are a mortal, how lucky your parents are, and how lucky the man who will marry you! I want to clasp your knees and beg for your help, but I don't want to frighten you. I have been cast up by the sea, and I know no one here. I don't even know where I am."

Nausicaa takes Odysseus to her parents, King Alcinous and Queen Arete.

The princess answered, "We all have to endure the troubles sent by Zeus! But I can take you to my father's house. This is the land of the Phaeacians, my name is Nausicaa, and my father is Alcinous, the king here." She had the maids feed him with the remains of their picnic, and they showed him a place to bathe and gave him a clean tunic. When he had cleaned himself and dressed, Athena endowed him with special beauty. Nausicaa looked at him admiringly, and said, "Now let us go to the palace. Stranger, walk with my maids beside the chariot. I am sorry that you cannot ride with me, or people will gossip. When you arrive, make your appeal to my mother first."

Odysseus fastens the tunic given to him by Nausicaa, the princess of Phaeacia.

He did as the princess instructed. Falling at the knees of the queen, he begged, "Arete, I have come to ask help from you, your husband, and your people. I need help in reaching my homeland, which I have missed for far too long." Arete did not respond at once, but Alcinous announced, "Tomorrow we will summon an assembly and entertain our guest fittingly. We will then make all the necessary arrangements to send him home, and guard him against any dangers. Who knows, he may be one of the immortals in disguise, sent to test us."

Odysseus follows Nausicaa and her friends returning to the palace of Phaeacia.

The queen was a bit more skeptical. She questioned, "Stranger, who are you and where do you come from? And who gave you those clothes?"

Odysseus answered, "I have sailed from the island of Calypso, where I landed after being shipwrecked. The goddess received me well, and even offered to make me immortal so that I could live forever with her. But I only wanted to go home to my wife." Odysseus then told how he had come to their island and been helped by their daughter.

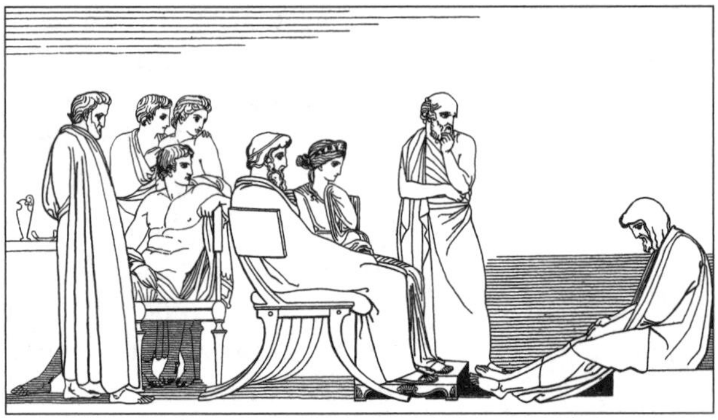

Odysseus presents himself to Alcinous and Arete, the king and queen of Phaeacia.

The next morning, Alcinous summoned the people and held a banquet, as he had promised to do. After the feast, he summoned a musician named Demodocus, a man from whom the Muses had taken eyesight but given the gift of song to compensate. The singer told the amusing tale of Ares and Aphrodite, and how Aphrodite's husband Hephaestus had ensnared the two lovers in a net and placed them on display for the other gods to ridicule. When the singer began to sing of Troy, however, Odysseus was overcome by memories and began to weep. Alcinous, noticing this, gently told the singer to stop. Then he asked, "Stranger, you have not told us your name yet. Did you lose a loved one in the Trojan War?"

Demodocus chants the tale of the Trojan War as Odysseus begins to weep.

A banquet is held and Odysseus is asked to recount his previous travails.

Odysseus then revealed his name and consented to tell the tale of his adventures.

The Travels of Odysseus

After Odysseus and his companions left the Trojan shores, unfavorable winds blew them to the land of the Cicones, where they sacked the city, slaughtering the men and taking the women as slaves. As the men drank on the shores of the land in celebration, the Cicones had time to gather their neighbors to help them repel the invaders. The Greeks were routed, losing many of their bravest men in the process.

The Lotus-eaters drug Odysseus' men.

For the following nine days, they were victims of continual storms at sea. At last, they landed where the Lotus-eaters live. Odysseus sent out a small scouting party while the others rested on the shore. They met the Lotus-eaters, who meant them no harm, and had them eat of their land's diet. The lotus was a strange fruit that took all of people's cares away from them. At once, Odysseus' men forgot all about home and were content to stay there forever, eating the sweet fruit. When Odysseus found them, they refused to leave; they wept and fought to remain. Odysseus had to tie them up and keep them below deck, and he forbade any of his other men to touch the fruit. They sailed away as fast as possible.

The land of the Cyclopes

When they next put to shore, they did not realize they had reached the land of the Cyclopes. These were a lawless people who had no assemblies or legal codes but lived in caves, every household looking out for itself. Odysseus set out with a small group of men to explore the island, curious about the sort of people who lived there. He happened to take along with him a goatskin of especially strong wine, given to him by a priest of Apollo.

Cyclops

The men found a cave and entered; the owner was not at home. The cave was well stocked with cheeses, and nearby were full milking pails. Odysseus' companions suggested, "Let's take the food with us and go!" Odysseus felt a foreboding about the place, but was curious to see whether the resident of the cave would bestow gifts upon him in accordance with the traditions of hospitality. Little did Odysseus realize just how rude a host he would be!

Odysseus offers Polyphemus a cup of wine.

At the island of the Cyclopes, Odysseus and his men eat Polyphemus' food.

Odysseus and his men were eating from the stock of cheeses when in walked Polyphemus, a giant with one eye. He drove his sheep and goats into the cave and closed the entrance with a vast boulder. After he milked his animals, he noticed the intruders. "Who are you and where did you come from?" he bellowed. "Are you pirates, or traders looking for easy money?"

Odysseus was disturbed by his rudeness, but answered calmly. "We are Greeks on our way home from sacking Troy. Contrary winds forced us here, and we're at your mercy. We hope that you will treat us as the laws of Zeus' hospitality command."

The Cyclops imprisons the Greeks in his cave and eats six of them.

"Zeus—ha! We don't care about Zeus here! We're stronger than he is!" And with that, Polyphemus grabbed two of Odysseus' men and dashed their brains out against the floor of the cave. He ate them and washed down their flesh with a bowl of milk. Then he fell asleep. Odysseus was ready to kill him on the spot, but thought better of it: "If we kill him, we'll still be trapped in this cave, since we can't move away the boulder!"

The next morning, Polyphemus seized two more men and ate them for breakfast, then set out to the hills with his flocks, rolling the boulder over the cave's entrance once more. Odysseus prayed to Athena to inspire him with an idea, and she did. Spotting the giant's club at a corner of the cave, Odysseus had his men sharpen its end to a point.

That night, the one-eyed giant returned and devoured two more men. Odysseus stepped forward with a bowl full of the strong wine he had brought with him. "Cyclops," he said, "would you like a cup of wine to wash down that human flesh you've just eaten?"

The Cyclops gets drunk on wine, and Odysseus tells him his name is "No-Man."

The monster grabbed the cup and drained it. "More! Gimme more a' thish good wine, 'n tell me yer name 'n I'll give ya a gift!" Odysseus filled the bowl again, and the Cyclops drank it greedily and then gulped down three more bowlfuls. Odysseus said, "You asked me my name. It's No-Man. Now, what about that gift you promised me?"

"No-Man, huh? OK, No-Man. I'll eat ya last. Thash my gift!" His great head lolled on his chest, and he fell asleep.

Odysseus and the men blind the one-eyed monster with a sharpened stake.

Odysseus whispered to his men to bring the sharpened stake. They thrust the point into the fire and watched carefully until it was red-hot. Then they lifted it, took aim, and rammed it straight into the monster's eye.

Odysseus blinds Polyphemus, the Cyclops.

"OWWW!" Polyphemus' bellows of pain brought neighbors running to his cave.

"What is it, Polyphemus?" they asked. "Why are you screaming in the middle of the night? Who's hurt you?"

When he is asked who hurt him, the Cyclops cries, "No-Man hurt me!"

"It's No-Man! No-Man hurt me!"

"If no man hurt you, then it must be some sickness from Zeus. Nothin' we can do! You should pray to your father Poseidon!" They left.

Odysseus and the men, tied to the underbellies of sheep, escape.

The next morning, the blinded Polyphemus sat at the entrance of his cave to catch any of the men who smuggled themselves out. He also felt the backs of his animals, thinking that they would try to ride out on them. Odysseus, however, had thought of this. He yoked the beasts together in threes and tied his men beneath the belly of the ones in the middle. For himself, he chose the largest ram and curled up under it. His ram was the last one out of the cave. Polyphemus noticed this, and commented, "Why are you last one out today, old man? Usually you lead the way. Maybe you're feeling sad because of your master's pain? I wish you could talk and tell me where No-Man is! I'd soon grab him and dash his brains against the rocks!"

As Polyphemus drove the ram out the door, Odysseus and his men quickly gathered up the sheep and drove them towards the ship. There, they hastily told the tale to the men who had been left behind. There was no time to grieve; they loaded up the ship and cast off. But as the shore receded, Odysseus called out, "Cyclops! Did you think it was a coward you were keeping in your cave? What happened to you is the judgment of Zeus!"

The Cyclops Polyphemus checks his rams, yoked in a threesome, as they leave his cave.

In a rage, the monster roared and picked up a rock and threw it in the direction of the voice. It made a wave that nearly capsized the ship. The men warned, "Quiet, Odysseus, don't provoke him again! He nearly sank us!"

Odysseus ignored them and roared, "Cyclops! If anyone asks who put your eye out, tell them it was Odysseus, son of Laertes, king of Ithaca!"

Poseidon

The Cyclops cried out in frustration, "The prophets warned me about you! But I thought you'd be some strong man, not a nasty little trickster! Come on back, and I'll give you gifts, real ones this time, I promise! I'll tell my father Poseidon to bring you home safely! Maybe he can heal my eye."

Out of range by now, Odysseus shouted back, "He'll never give you your eyesight back!"

Tricked by Odysseus, Cyclops asks Poseidon to curse Odysseus.

The Cyclops prayed, "Father Poseidon! I pray that Odysseus, son of Laertes, king of Ithaca, will never see home again! But if it's fated for him to return, I pray that he'll arrive late with everything lost and that he'll face more trouble at home!" He threw another boulder into the sea, but Odysseus was long gone. Poseidon granted his son's prayer, however.

Odysseus visits Aeolus, Lord of the Winds, at Aeolia.

The voyagers came next to Aeolia, the island of Aeolus, ruler of the winds. Aeolus, along with his children, welcomed Odysseus and crew hospitably. Then he asked how he could help them.

After Aeolus, king of the winds, gives Odysseus a bag of winds, an insubordinate sailor opens it, unleashing a sea storm.

The ruler agreed to help. He fetched a leather bag and tied in it all the winds except the one needed to blow them gently home. For nine days and nights, they sailed safely, and on the tenth, the shoreline of Ithaca was in sight. Worn out from guiding the ship and guarding the bag of winds, Odysseus decided to take a nap. Seeing his captain asleep, a troublemaker in the crew said to the others, "I bet there's gold in that bag there, and our fearless leader is goin' to take it all! How come we do all the work and he gets all the glory? I say we open the bag and divvy up the loot!" No one stopped him, and he slid the bag open. The winds burst out and blew the ship far from Ithaca, tossing it about on the waves like an empty bottle. Odysseus awoke at the roaring of the winds and the cries of the men. Realizing what had happened, he briefly considered throwing himself overboard. The winds blew the ship back to Aeolus, but Odysseus had little hope that he could ask the king for help a second time.

Aeolus, furious, refuses to help Odysseus again

He was right. "Get out of here!" Aeolus shouted. "I don't know what god you angered, but there is no man on earth more damned than you! You wouldn't be here now if the gods didn't hate you!" And so he drove them from the island.

The Laestrygonians destroy all but one ship and devour many of Odysseus' men.

They wandered aimlessly for six days and six nights. On the seventh day, they landed at the country of the Laestrygonians. Odysseus sent out a small scouting party. They came upon a young woman drawing water from a stream, and asked her where they might find the king and queen. She pointed out a house a short distance away. When they entered, they were greeted by a monstrously huge woman with wild hair and teeth the size of javelins. They disliked her instantly! She called for her husband, Antiphates, who promptly grabbed the smallest of the men and devoured him on the spot. Terrified, the survivors fought their way out of the palace, closely pursued by the immense queen. They barely made it back to the ships as a pack of giants thundered after them. As the ships retreated, Laestrygonians hurled boulders at the ships, smashing almost all. They speared the thrashing men like fish and cooked them on the beach. Odysseus' ship was the only one to escape.

The Laestrygonian giants Antiphates and his wife attack Odysseus' men and smash all the ships but one.

Odysseus and the surviving crew members land on a mysterious island.

The next time they reached land, they stayed on the beach for two days, resting and grieving for the companions they had lost. On the third day, Odysseus rose and climbed a hill, searching for evidence of habitation. He found none except for a bit of smoke rising from the center of the island. The men were reluctant to venture forth to investigate it, remembering what had happened at the hands of the Laestrygonians and the Cyclopes. One man, Eurylochus, was particularly vocal. "What do you want to do, Odysseus, get more of us killed?" he demanded.

Odysseus divides his crew into two groups for safety and a search of the island.

Odysseus decided to divide the crew into two parties, one led by himself and the other by Eurylochus, to placate him. They drew lots to see which group would go exploring, and Eurylochus' was selected to go.

Eurylochus returns saying that Circe enchanted the men and changed them to swine.

The group followed a path to the center of the island until they came upon a house. Wolves and lions surrounded it, and when the men approached, the beasts wagged their tails and licked the men's faces. They heard a woman singing within. Hearing their voices, she came out to greet them. Eurylochus warned the others, "Don't go in! It could be a trap!" They ignored him, leaving him to wait outdoors, and sat down to a feast. When they had finished, Circe—that was the woman's name—touched them with a wand of hazelwood and turned them into pigs! Then she drove them into the pigsties.

Circe transforms Odysseus' men into pigs.

Eurylochus rushed back and told Odysseus everything that had happened. Odysseus demanded, "Take me there!" but Eurylochus cried, "No! There's no telling what she'll do to me. You're a fool if you tempt fate that way!"

Hermes gives Odysseus an herb to preserve him from Circe's spells.

"All right, Eurylochus, you wait here and rest. I'll go alone." Odysseus set out, and when he had almost reached the house, a handsome youth appeared before him—the god Hermes in disguise. "Where are you going? You want to save your men, right? You can't do it, not without help." Hermes handed Odysseus a small plant. "This is an herb the gods call 'moly.' It will keep you safe from Circe's magic if she enchants your food and drink. Then, when she tries to use her wand on you, pull out your sword. She will back down and invite you to share her bed. Do not refuse her, but make her promise to do you no harm."

Circe offers Odysseus some wine.

Odysseus took the herb and went into the witch's house. She had him sit on a fine couch and poured him a drink of wine. When he finished, she struck him with the wand and said, "Go, join your companions in the pigsties!" He drew his sword and held its point to her throat. Astonished, she exclaimed, "What—who are you? No one has ever escaped my spells before! Ah, you must be the clever Odysseus. Hermes told me you would land here. Come, share my bed!"

Odysseus retorted, "Circe, how can you suggest that after you turn my friends into pigs! I would be happy to make love to you, but first you must promise not to work any of your magic spells against me."

She promised, and the two spent the night lovemaking. But the next morning, Odysseus refused to eat the breakfast Circe set out for him. She asked him what was wrong.

Odysseus forces Circe to remove the spell from the swine and restore his men.

"Circe," he answered, "I can't eat knowing my friends are outside in the pigsties! You must remove your spell from them." She consented, and changed the men back to human form, looking even younger and more handsome than before. Then she suggested, "Odysseus, go back to the rest of your men and have them beach the ship here and fix it. They're all welcome to stay with me."

The men left behind were delighted that their comrades were all right. They gladly accepted Circe's invitation, except Eurylochus, who complained, "She'll turn us into animals! Don't you remember the Cyclopes?" Eventually, however, he too went along.

After Odysseus and his men stay for an entire year with Circe, she allows them to leave, telling Odysseus to consult Tiresias in the Underworld.

They stayed there for a year, enjoying the witch's hospitality. Then they became eager to journey homewards again. Odysseus said to Circe, "We've had a wonderful time here. But it is time for us to move on. Please help us to return home."

She answered, "If that is what you want, I will not force you to stay. But before you can continue your journey home, you have to make another journey—to the Underworld. There you must question the ghost of Tiresias about the way to your island. Of all the ghosts, he is the only one Persephone allowed to keep his wits; the others are insubstantial shades."

Odysseus was disheartened, and asked, "How do I get there? No living man has ever returned from that journey."

Circe said, "Boreas, the North Wind, will speed you there. You will land near a grove sacred to Persephone. Cast anchor here and go to where the rivers Pyriphlegethon and Styx pour their waters into the Acheron River. Here, dig a trench and pour out offerings to the dead: milk and honey, wine, and water. Sacrifice a black ram to Tiresias, and then another ram and a black ewe, catching their blood in your trench. The ghosts will come forward at the smell of the blood. Hold them off and do not let them drink of the blood until you have questioned Tiresias."

Boreas, the North Wind

Odysseus lands at the Underworld's entrance and makes ritual sacrifices.

The voyagers reluctantly set out until they had come to the edge of the world, the land of the Cimmerians, a place of continual darkness. Here they landed, and Odysseus walked along the shore with a couple of companions and the black animals until they came to the place Circe had described. He made the required sacrifices and waited as the souls of the dead crowded around the edge of the bloody pit. To his surprise, he recognized the youngest of his companions there, a man named Elpenor. He asked, "How did you get here, Elpenor, ahead of our ship?"

"Alas!" the young man sighed. "Last night, I had too much to drink, and went up to the roof to sleep it off in the cool night air. When I heard you all getting ready to leave this morning, I got up still half asleep, missed my footing on the ladder, and fell off the roof and broke my neck. When you go back to Circe's island, burn my body along with my weapons, bury me on the shore, and place my oar on my grave."

Tiresias warns Odysseus to expect more dangers and not to eat Helius' cattle.

Odysseus promised. Tears came to his eyes as he saw the ghost of his mother, Anticleia, who had been alive when he left Ithaca. Yet he kept her away from the blood along with the rest, allowing only Tiresias' shade to approach. The dead seer drank thirstily, and then spoke: "Odysseus, your homecoming will not be sweet. Poseidon hates you because you blinded his son, the Cyclops Polyphemus. When you reach the island of Thrinacia, the island of Helius the sun-god, none of you must eat his cattle. If you do, your ship and entire crew will be destroyed. You will reach home alone in a foreign ship, to find men eating your goods and demanding that your wife choose a new husband. After you kill them, you must sail away again to a far land. When you arrive there, take your oar upon your shoulder and travel inland until you find a people who know nothing about the sea. When someone there asks you why you carry a winnowing fan upon your shoulder, plant the oar, make a sacrifice to Poseidon, and return home. There you will spend the rest of your life at ease. Death will be very gentle to you, and it will come late."

Helius in his fiery chariot

Odysseus was saddened to learn what he would have to endure before Poseidon's wrath against him ended, but he was curious about his mother. "Why doesn't my mother recognize me? How can I speak with her?"

Tiresias answered, "If you wish to speak with any of the ghosts, you must allow them to drink the blood. Otherwise, they will slip back into the darkness." And the seer's spirit turned away and departed.

Odysseus held back the other ghosts and allowed his mother's to approach the pit. When she had drunk the blood, she recognized her son, and said, "My son, how did you come here when you're still alive? Did you make your way here from Troy? Have you not been home yet?"

Odysseus encounters Tiresias in the Underworld, relief sculpture.

Odysseus speaks with his mother, who has died during his absence.

He answered tearfully, "Mother, I was ordered to come here to consult Tiresias before I could sail home. But how did *you* come to be here? Did Artemis shoot you with her silver arrows? What about my father and son? And Penelope . . . is she still waiting for me, or does someone else have my lands and my wife now?"

Anticleia responded soothingly: "Yes, Penelope is still faithful, although things are becoming more difficult for her and your son as time passes. Your father is still alive, but he stays on the farm living in poverty, and no longer goes to the city. As for me . . . no, it wasn't Artemis who killed me, or any other sickness. It was longing for you that took my life away."

At these words, Odysseus tried three times to embrace his mother, but each time her ghost slipped through his arms. "Son," she said, "this is the way it is when life has left the body. You need to return to the living world and tell your wife what you have seen in this place."

Before he did, however, Odysseus saw the ghosts of several Greek commanders. Agamemnon's shade came forth, drank the blood, and tried to reach out to Odysseus. The Ithacan was shocked to see his former leader reduced to this, and cried, "Agamemnon! Did Poseidon wreck your ship? Did a hostile tribe kill you? Were you slaughtered invading another city?"

Odysseus meets Agamemnon, killed by his wife, Clytemnestra, and Aegisthus.

Agamemnon's spirit groaned. "None of those! I was killed by my cousin Aegisthus and my murderous wife! She's disgraced all women with her evil deed! I'm warning you, Odysseus, don't trust your own wife too much, although she's probably a better person than Clytemnestra."

Odysseus also saw Achilles' ghost. "Odysseus, why are you here?" the spirit of the greatest warrior asked.

"I have come to consult with Tiresias about my homecoming. Bad luck and the gods' anger have kept me wandering all these years. I envy you, Achilles. You were the most honored among us when you were alive, and you still hold power among the dead."

Achilles glared at him. "Don't tell me about my glorious death, Odysseus. I would rather be a peasant's hired hand than the greatest of the dead. But tell me about my son. Did he go to Troy and have a part in the fall of the city?"

Odysseus meets the shades of fallen Greek warriors in the Underworld.

Seeing Achilles, Odysseus tells him about his son Neoptolemus.

"You can be proud of him, Achilles. He was always in the front lines. When we were hidden in the wooden horse, many men wept and trembled, but not him. He couldn't wait to jump out and fight! He killed many men that night, including Priam."

Achilles strode away, happy at this news about Neoptolemus. Other dead souls crowded around, begging for news of their loved ones left behind. Only the ghost of the huge Ajax stood apart; he was still angry at Odysseus because of Achilles' armor.

The greater Ajax refuses to talk with Odysseus because of an old grudge.

"Ajax, are you still blaming me? A curse on those weapons for causing us to lose you! We still mourn you as much as we mourned Achilles. Come closer and listen to me!" But Ajax's ghost ignored him and went to join the rest of the dead.

Odysseus saw the ghosts of many other men and women, including Heracles. By now, so many souls were crowding around that he feared Persephone would send up the Gorgon or some other monster. He and his men hastened back to their ship and returned to Circe's island. There they gave Elpenor the burial Odysseus had promised, and had a last banquet with Circe. She gave them advice about the voyage ahead.

"You will come to the Sirens, whose song is so enchanting it causes a man to forget home and family and stay with them until he starves to death. Plug up the ears of your men with wax before you sail past. But if you insist on hearing their songs yourself, have the men bind you hand and foot to the mast, and not free you until you are well past the island. After that, you must sail between two cliffs. On one there lives the dreaded Scylla, a loathsome creature with six barking dog heads, each of which has three sets of teeth. No ship can sail past her without losing a man to each of those heads. Below the other rock is Charybdis, which gulps down the seawater and spews it back up again three times a day. Any ship she sucks in is doomed. Better to give up six of your men to Scylla than lose all to Charybdis. Don't think you can fight her, either; you'll only lose more men." Circe also repeated the warning Tiresias had given about Thrinacia and the cattle of Helius.

Odysseus, tied to the mast, listens to the songs of the Sirens as his men sail past their island.

After burying Elpenor, Odysseus and the crew encounter the Sirens, whom Odysseus, tied to the ship's mast, manages to evade.

They set out. Odysseus followed the witch's advice on passing the Sirens safely; he stopped up his men's ears and made them tie him to the mast. As the ship approached the Sirens' rock, which was surrounded by the bones of earlier sailors, the creatures took up their song. Melodiously, they promised Odysseus greater knowledge and tales of his own adventures. He frantically called out for the men to pause, but they did not cease rowing and did not release him until they were well out of earshot of the music.

The sea monster Scylla devours six of Odysseus' men in her whirlpool.

The men grew apprehensive as they heard raging surf and breakers crashing against rocks up ahead. Odysseus encouraged them, not mentioning the horrors to come: "We've been through worse than this! Remember the Cyclopes? Soon this will be behind us too. Steer clear of the foaming water and draw close to the high cliff." Despite Circe's attempt to discourage him from fighting, Odysseus put on his armor and seized two lances. He tried to catch a glimpse of Scylla before she could attack, but it was no use. He could only watch helplessly as the creature snatched six men off the ship; their futile cries of "Odysseus!" rang in his ears as the craft pulled away.

Odysseus fights with the monstrous Scylla.

Odysseus' exhausted crew demands that they rest at Thrinacia.

They soon drew near the island of Thrinacia, where they could already hear the mooing of the sun-god's cattle. Remembering the warnings of Tiresias and Circe, Odysseus wanted to avoid tempting fate and steer past the island. But Eurylochus complained, "Your heart is as hard as iron, Odysseus. We need a rest, and night is approaching. I say we spend the night there and start out fresh tomorrow morning." The others applauded him, and Odysseus reluctantly gave in, fearing a mutiny. "Very well," he said, "but everyone must solemnly promise that you will not kill a single animal on the island. They belong to the sun-god, and if we harm them, we are doomed."

The men gave their word. That night, however, the weather changed, and the seas turned violent. For a month, they were unable to sail. The food Circe had given them ran out, and the men turned to fishing. Feeling their morale sink, Odysseus went inland to a secluded spot and prayed to the gods that they would be allowed to leave the island safely. Sleep overtook him there.

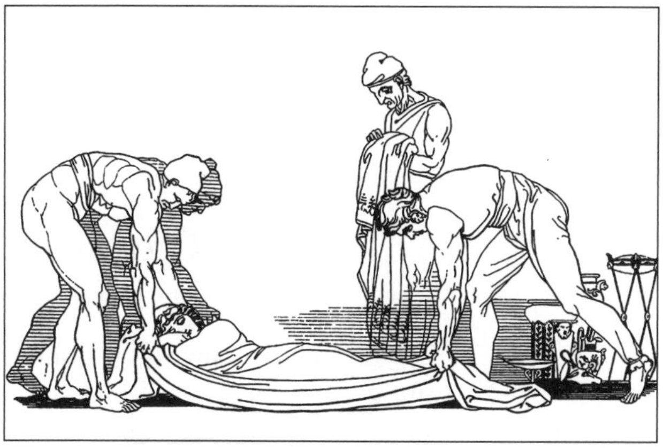

Sleep overtakes Odysseus, and his men make him comfortable.

When Odysseus falls asleep, his crew eats Helius' cattle.

While Odysseus slept, Eurylochus gathered the men and spoke: "Friends, there's no death worse than starvation. We can see the cattle, but we have only Odysseus' word that killing them will mean disaster. What if he's wrong? I say we round them up and slaughter them, and when we get home we'll build a temple to the sun-god to thank him. Even if Odysseus is right, I'd rather have a quick death at sea than a slow one here. What do you say?"

They were persuaded, and they butchered some of the cattle and cooked them. On his way back to his men, Odysseus smelled the meat roasting, and cried out, "Zeus and all gods! How could you let me fall asleep and have my men do this?"

Furious, Helius calls upon Zeus to drown all the men, except Odysseus.

The sun-god had already learned what had happened. "Zeus!" he prayed. "Punish these men of Odysseus, who have killed my precious cattle! If you do not avenge me, I will go down to Hades, and I will never shine on the living again!" The king of the gods vowed to strike down the ship as soon as it put to sea. He sent evil portents to the men: the hides of the slain cattle began to crawl about, and the meat that was cooking bellowed as if in pain. Yet, the men continued to feast for six days. On the seventh, the sea finally became calm again and they sailed off. Almost immediately, however, the sky darkened again and the ship was buffeted by winds. Then one of Zeus' thunderbolts struck it, and the men were all washed overboard except Odysseus. He drifted back towards Charybdis, and the remains of the ship were sucked under. Odysseus barely escaped by clutching a fig tree hanging over Charybdis' mouth. He clung to it until his mast and keel were spewed back up, and he dropped back onto them and drifted away. For nine days he floated there; on the tenth, he washed up onto Ogygia, the home of Calypso, where he remained for seven years.

Odysseus clings to the battered remains of his ship after it has passed by Charybdis. He clings to the mast for nine days until he reaches Ogygia.

Odysseus' Return to Ithaca and Revenge on the Suitors

The Phaeacians row Odysseus to Ithaca.

The Phaeacians were fascinated by Odysseus' tale. They gave him abundant guest-gifts, and had a ship ready for him the next day. As soon as he climbed aboard, he lay down on the deck and slept as the Phaeacian men rowed. He was still asleep as they landed on Ithaca; the men carried him ashore and laid him down and stowed his gifts carefully out of sight. On their voyage back to their land, however, Poseidon turned their ship to stone as a warning to others who give hospitality to those in disfavor with a god.

Odysseus awoke, not realizing where he was. He worried that he had been tricked. Athena came to him disguised as a shepherd, and he asked, "Where am I?"

She told him, "Everyone knows this place! It's Ithaca, of course, well-known throughout the Mediterranean."

On Ithaca, Odysseus meets a shepherd, Athena in disguise.

The traveler was pleased to be home, but he was cautious as always. He told the disguised goddess a lying tale about being a Cretan in exile who had stowed away on a merchant ship and been left behind accidentally. She smiled and said, "Oh, Odysseus, how I love your clever ways! You always want to use subterfuge to find out what you want! Let me tell you, first, that your wife is still faithful to you. But we need to make plans to eliminate these suitors who are encroaching on your home. First, I need to disguise you as a beggar. Second, you must go to your swineherd and take shelter with him; he's stayed loyal to you and your family. Third, I'll go to Sparta and bring Telemachus home." With that, Athena touched Odysseus on the forehead. His skin wrinkled and his hair turned gray. The goddess changed his clothing into shabby rags and draped a moth-eaten wallet over his back. A well-used walking stick completed the disguise.

Eumaeus, Odysseus' loyal swineherd, welcomes the disguised beggar.

Odysseus made his way to the hut of the swineherd named Eumaeus. As he approached, a pack of hounds came rushing out at him, baying loudly. Eumaeus rushed to the door, drove off the animals with stones, and helped his guest into the hut. "Are you all right? Those beasts almost killed you, and that would have been more grief for me! It's bad enough I have to raise pigs for those freeloaders in the palace. I wish my master Odysseus would come home!"

"Don't worry. I have it on very reliable sources that he will return soon."

"I hope so, but don't go raising false hope in my mistress! She's had enough of that."

Odysseus was encouraged by Eumaeus' loyalty. Eumaeus then fed him a simple meal. Odysseus did not reveal himself, however; he repeated his tale of being an exile from Crete.

Odysseus, standing, meets the swineherd Eumaeus: "Eumaeus, O my swineherd!"

Telemachus returns home from Sparta.

The next day, Telemachus returned from Sparta. He went first to the hut of the swineherd, who greeted him joyfully. When Eumaeus went to the palace to tell Penelope that her son was home, Athena watched him leave. She signaled to Odysseus, unseen by Telemachus, that it was now time to reveal himself to his son. She transformed him back to his usual handsome appearance. Telemachus said, astonished, "I don't know who you are, but you look so different now. You must be one of the gods sent to test our hospitality."

Odysseus answered, "Why do you call me one of the gods? I am the father that you have missed all these years." He wept and kissed his son.

Telemachus drew back. "No . . . you're some demon sent to trick me. How else could you be an old man one minute and godlike the next?"

"There is no trickery here, Telemachus. The change in me is Athena's doing. Believe it! I have returned after twenty years."

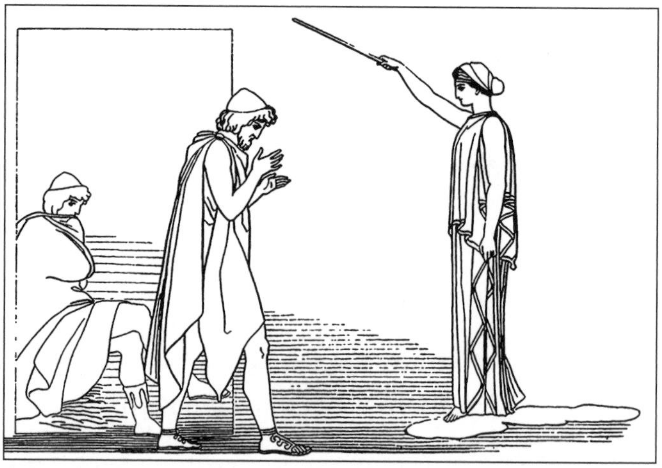

Athena restores Odysseus to his kingly appearance in the presence of Telemachus.

Odysseus reveals his true identity to Telemachus.

Telemachus threw his arms around his father, and they wept together. At last Odysseus said, "Enough tears! We need to talk about these suitors. How many are there?"

"There are over a hundred, plus a couple of servants helping them. I'm worried that if we attack them, they'll kill us."

Odysseus tells Telemachus Athena's plan to drive out the suitors, and that Telemachus must conceal that Odysseus has returned.

"We have Athena on our side! Now listen: go back to the palace. The swineherd will bring me along later, looking like a poor old beggar. If the suitors insult me, tell them to have mercy but do not show anger. Also, when you see the signal from me, round up all the weapons in the hall and hide them. If anyone asks why, say you want to keep them from being damaged by the smoke. Above all, *do not tell anyone I have returned*, not even your mother. We need to figure out whom we can trust."

Odysseus' faithful old dog Argus recognizes his master and dies.

Telemachus agreed. On their trip to the palace, they met Odysseus' cowherd Philoetius. When the two herdsmen and the disguised Odysseus arrived, Odysseus' old dog Argus recognized his master's voice and pricked up his ears. He had been a fine hunting dog once; now he lay flea-bitten and forgotten on the garbage heap in the yard. He wagged his tail feebly and tried to crawl to Odysseus' side, but he was too weak. He died after this last glimpse of his master.

Odysseus and Argus

Eumaeus informs Penelope that a beggar with news of Odysseus has arrived.

Inside the palace, most of the suitors were horribly rude to Odysseus, abusing him and throwing things at him, but a few gave him scraps of food. Odysseus gave his silent signal to Telemachus to hide the weapons. Eumaeus told Penelope that he had brought a man claiming to have news of Odysseus.

"Bring him to me. If only Odysseus himself would return! He'd soon get rid of those suitors!"

At these words there was a loud sneeze from Telemachus downstairs. Penelope laughed and said, "Did you hear how my son sneezed at my words? It's an omen!"

Eumaeus obeyed and fetched Odysseus. Sitting opposite his wife for the first time in twenty years, Odysseus once more told his story about being a man from Crete. He claimed to have hosted Odysseus there.

Penelope decided to test him. "Can you describe what he looked like, what clothes he was wearing, and what men were with him?"

"It was a long time ago, but let me think . . . he was wearing a purple cloak with a golden brooch. It showed a hound hunting a stag. He had a man with him, a bit older than himself, named Eurybates."

Penelope recognized the description of the cloak and the brooch. She wept and said, "I believe you *have* seen him. I gave him those clothes myself. But I don't believe I'll ever see him again."

Odysseus was touched by her tears. He said, "Don't cry. Odysseus will be here soon, I promise it!"

Penelope and Odysseus converse.

Penelope listens to the beggar's description of Odysseus and offers him hospitality.

Penelope sighed and said, "I hope you are right. This house has certainly fallen on hard times! But we can still offer you proper hospitality." And she ordered her maids to come and wash the "beggar's" feet.

Odysseus protested, "I have been through too much to accept these comforts. I don't want my feet washed, unless you happen to have an old, wise servant who has suffered as much as we have."

"Of all the strangers who have come and gone, none has pleased me as much as you! I do have such a servant: Odysseus' old nurse, Eurycleia." She summoned the elderly woman, and said, "Come, Eurycleia, wash your master's . . . acquaintance's feet."

Eurycleia washes the feet of Odysseus as Telemachus and Penelope watch. Remains of a terracotta relief plaque.

Odysseus orders Eurycleia not to reveal his identity yet.

Eurycleia obeyed. She too felt drawn to this mysterious man who reminded her of her departed master. As she fetched the water and basin, Odysseus was suddenly alarmed. He remembered an old scar he had from a wound made by a boar on his first hunting trip! He tried to draw his rags over it, but he was not fast enough. Eurycleia saw it and dropped his foot. It struck the basin and the water slopped over the floor. "*Yes! You are Odysseus!*" she exclaimed. She looked over at Penelope, who had been fortuitously distracted by Athena.

Odysseus pressed his hand over the old nurse's mouth and whispered, "Nurse, do you want to ruin me? Be quiet! I warn you, I'll kill you if you give me away!"

"Calm down! Of course I won't give you away! I'll even tell you which of the female slaves have stayed loyal to you and which are helping the suitors."

Penelope tells the beggar her dream; it foretells Odysseus' killing of the suitors.

She finished washing his feet. Penelope then said, "I have one more question for you, stranger. I had a dream that I saw a flock of geese. Then an eagle swooped down and broke all their necks. He perched upon a beam and said, 'This is no ordinary dream. I am your husband and I have returned from my journeys to kill the suitors.' What do you think that means?"

Odysseus responded, "The meaning seems obvious. Odysseus has returned and will take his vengeance."

Penelope's plan is that the contest winner will use Odysseus' bow to shoot an arrow through twelve axe-heads.

"I hope you're right. But there are two gates of dreams: the gate of horn and the gate of ivory. Those that come through the gate of horn are true, but those that come through the gate of ivory only deceive the dreamer. I wish I knew where this dream came from! If it's true, my son and I will be so happy! But I have a plan to test the suitors: I will set up twelve axe-heads in a row. If a man can string the bow of Odysseus and shoot an arrow through all twelve, I will marry him and leave this home so full of fond memories."

"My queen, this is a good idea. Let the contest take place tomorrow. I have a feeling that Odysseus might show up."

Penelope retrieves Odysseus' bow. The suitors feast in the background.

That night, Odysseus was restless as he thought of the next day. But Athena was present to reassure him. The next morning, Penelope went to the store room and took down Odysseus' bow. She wept at the memories it brought back, but dried her tears and faced the suitors resolutely. "Listen carefully, everyone! This is the day you've waited for. Anyone who can string this bow and shoot an arrow through those axe-heads that Eumaeus is setting up may have me as his bride."

Telemachus added, "Yes, enough delays!" Just to test his own strength, he made several attempts to string the bow. He barely managed to budge it on his fourth attempt, when Odysseus shook his head to signal him to stop. "I give up!" he said. "I guess I don't have my father's strength. Maybe one of you can do better."

Another man tried and failed. The suitors decided, "It needs greasing." They addressed the goatherd who was friendly to them, "Melanthius, go get a lump of tallow from the storehouse."

As the suitors buttered the bow, Odysseus motioned the cowherd and swineherd outside. "Tell me," he said, "if Odysseus were to return, would you fight with him or with the suitors?"

They agreed, "I wish he would come! I'd give those guys in there what's coming to them!"

Revealing his true identity to the swineherd and cowherd, Odysseus enlists their help against the suitors.

"Well then, here I am!" Odysseus announced. "I'm delighted that the two of you prayed for my return. I'll reward you if Zeus helps me regain my household. If you need further proof, here is the wound I received from the boar's tusk long ago."

They examined the scar, then wept for joy and embraced their returned master. "Enough!" exclaimed Odysseus after a while. Now follow me back into the hall, separately, and wait for my signal."

Odysseus tests the bow.

Back inside the hall, the suitors were still unable to string the bow. They decided to try again tomorrow. Then Odysseus said, "You're right, maybe tomorrow Apollo will give you the power to string it. But I'd like to try it myself, just to see if I still have the strength I used to."

Not surprisingly, the suitors sneered at him. "You're drunk! Stay out of respectable men's business, you loser!"

Penelope spoke up: "Are you worried about your reputations if he defeats you? You have no reputation to lose, the way you've behaved here! If he succeeds, I'll give him some new clothes and a ship to sail wherever he wants to."

The suitors taunt the beggar; Telemachus asks Penelope to leave the hall.

Telemachus added, "The bow is mine until Odysseus comes home, and if I choose to allow the stranger a shot, I will. Mother, you should go back to your loom upstairs, and leave this contest to the men."

She was amazed at her son's sudden tone of authority, but departed as instructed. Odysseus then gave the signal for Eumaeus to hand him the bow and for Philoetius to lock down the hall. He turned the instrument carefully in his hands, checking for worm damage. The suitors mocked him, saying, "Hah, big expert! Wonder if he has one like it at home?" They stopped laughing when he effortlessly bent the bow and a loud thunderclap from Zeus resounded through the hall. Odysseus picked up an arrow and sent the shaft through the axe-heads.

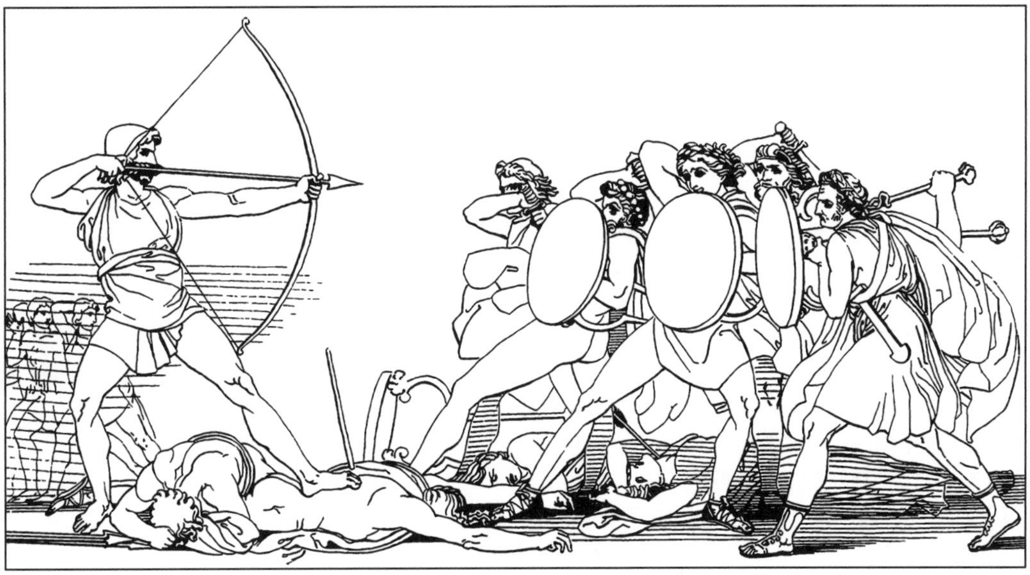

Odysseus takes aim at the suitors.

Odysseus wins the contest; with Telemachus' and the herdsmen's help, he kills the suitors.

"Well, Telemachus, the stranger didn't make a fool of himself after all, did he?" he shouted triumphantly. "The game is over, men!" He took aim at the suitors' ringleader, who was unsuspectingly sipping at a cup of wine, and brought him down with a single shot. Uproar followed and the other suitors frantically looked around for weapons, but there were none. They tried to plead with Odysseus. "You've killed the guilty man. There's no reason to kill the rest of us. Let us leave and we'll bring you an abundance of treasures tomorrow." But Odysseus did not listen; he, Telemachus, Eumaeus, and Philoetius slaughtered all the suitors. The male and female servants who had been disloyal were slain also, but the herald and minstrel were spared.

In her excitement, Eurycleia shouts that Odysseus has returned.

Eurycleia rushed upstairs to tell the news to her mistress, who had fallen asleep, thanks to Athena. "Odysseus is back! And he's killed all those arrogant fools!"

Penelope was skeptical. "Dear nurse, the gods have addled your mind! I wish it were true, but it can't be. Some god must have killed the suitors, but I think Odysseus is dead."

Eurycleia stubbornly insisted, and Penelope at last came downstairs to see for herself. She saw what Eurycleia had described, but was uncertain whether to run to the man and kiss him or stay aloof and question him some more. Telemachus could not believe her behavior: "Mother, how can you be so hard-hearted? Don't you love him any more? What kind of woman just sits there when her husband comes home after twenty years' absence?"

"Be patient, Telemachus. Your mother needs time to accept this," Odysseus said calmly.

Penelope turned to the nurse, and said, "Eurycleia, have the great bed moved out of our room and make it ready for him to sleep here."

Odysseus' description of their marriage bed assures Penelope that he is indeed Odysseus.

This upset Odysseus. "Who moved that bed?" he demanded. "It has a stump of an olive tree for a leg, and it's rooted to the ground!"

At this, Penelope's heart pounded and her knees grew weak. This was it—the secret she had been waiting for! She ran to Odysseus and hugged him.

The reunion of Odysseus and Penelope

That night, they told each other the stories of what they had endured during their long separation. The next day, Odysseus revealed himself to his elderly father, Laertes. The suitors' fathers formed a small uprising, but Athena stopped them with Zeus' thunderbolts and restored peace.

Odysseus' Later History

Literary Source: Apollodorus *Epitome* 7

Odysseus travels.

Post-Homeric stories of Odysseus and Penelope are curious; the two behave in ways that seem out of character after the *Odyssey*. Odysseus traveled once again, as Tiresias had told him in the Underworld that he would. He went to the land of the Thesprotians and at last propitiated Poseidon through the sacrifices that Tiresias had instructed. The queen of the Thesprotians, named Callidice, offered him the throne if he would remain with her. He did, and they had a son named Polypoetes. When Callidice died, he left the throne to his son and returned to Ithaca, where he discovered that Penelope had borne him another son named Poliporthes.

Odysseus' son Telegonus

Circe had also had a child by Odysseus, named Telegonus. Arriving at the island of Ithaca, he plundered some of Odysseus' cattle. When Odysseus came to rescue them, Telegonus killed him. When Telegonus learned what he had done, he wept bitterly, but later married Penelope in the land of Circe. Telemachus married Circe.

There are myths in which Penelope did not stay faithful to Odysseus, but married one of the suitors. In Arcadia, where the horned god Pan was widely worshipped, there was a tradition that Penelope was his mother. Others say that she married a suitor named Amphinomus, who in the *Odyssey* is depicted as the most gentlemanly of the lot, and that Odysseus killed her! Neoptolemus judged Odysseus and sent him into exile, where he remarried and died at an extremely advanced age.

Pan

A. Review Exercises

1. **CHRONOLOGY COUNTS!** Place the following events in chronological order. Use the numbers 1–6, with 1 as the first event and 6 as the last event in the sequence. Write the number in the space provided.

   a. **Phaeacia**

   ____ The bard Demodocus begins to chant tales of the Trojan War.

   ____ Nausicaa loans Odysseus a tunic.

   ____ Nausicaa and her friends meet the shipwrecked stranger, Odysseus.

   ____ Nausicaa drives home in her chariot with Odysseus following.

   ____ Odysseus tells the story of his travels.

   ____ Queen Arete and King Alcinous welcome Odysseus.

   b. **Isle of the Cyclopes**

   ____ Odysseus tells Polyphemus his name is "No-Man."

   ____ Odysseus offers Polyphemus cups of wine.

   ____ Polyphemus eats two of Odysseus' men.

   ____ Odysseus and his men yoke the rams in groups of three.

   ____ Polyphemus hurls an immense boulder at Odysseus' ship.

   ____ Odysseus blinds Polyphemus.

   c. **Circe's Court**

   ____ Elpenor falls off the roof of Circe's palace.

   ____ Eurylochus leads a search party.

   ____ Odysseus holds a knife to Circe's throat.

   ____ Circe turns some of the men into pigs.

   ____ Odysseus and his men decide to stay with Circe.

   ____ Odysseus and Eurylochus switch leadership roles.

d. The Underworld

____ Odysseus tries to embrace his mother three times.

____ Anticleia drinks the blood of the sacrifice.

____ Odysseus meets Achilles, who wishes he were a peasant and still alive.

____ Tiresias reveals the course of Odysseus' remaining voyage and homecoming.

____ Odysseus has a surprise meeting with young Elpenor.

____ Odysseus sacrifices black animals and gathers their blood.

e. The Homecoming to Ithaca

____ Odysseus strings his bow and shoots straight through twelve aligned axe-heads.

____ Eurycleia recognizes Odysseus by the scar on his leg caused by a boar-tusk.

____ Odysseus goes to the hut of his swineherd, Eumaeus.

____ Athena disguises Odysseus as a beggar.

____ Argus greets his master, then passes away.

____ Odysseus reveals his identity to Telemachus.

2. **MATCHING!** Match the phrase in the right-hand column with the correct name from the left-hand column. Write the letter in the space provided.

1.	____	Mentor	a.	Odysseus' father, for whom Penelope wove a shroud
2.	____	Circe	b.	One who kept Odysseus until Hermes ordered his release
3.	____	Tiresias	c.	One who rejected Odysseus' apology in the Underworld
4.	____	Polyphemus	d.	Odysseus' faithful hound
5.	____	Elpenor	e.	Cowherd who swore loyalty to Odysseus
6.	____	Eurylochus	f.	King of the Laestrygonians
7.	____	Antiphates	g.	Odysseus' mother, whom he met in the Underworld
8.	____	Ajax	h.	Older man who served as Telemachus' guide
9.	____	Eurycleia	i.	One who warned Odysseus away from the cattle of Helius

10. ____	Anticleia	j.	One who prophesied Odysseus' encounter with the Sirens
11. ____	Laertes	k.	One who could not resist the wiles and cleverness of "No-Man"
12. ____	Argus	l.	One whom Odysseus buried on the island of Circe
13. ____	Calypso	m.	One who was sworn to silence after recognizing Odysseus' scar
14. ____	Philoetius	n.	One who sought Odysseus at the court of Menelaus and Helen
15. ____	Telemachus	o.	One who convinced the sailors to eat the cattle of Helius

B. Musings

1. The ancient Greeks admired "*Odysseus Polytropos*" for his clever ruses, his keen intelligence, and his ability to extricate himself from unbelievably harrowing predicaments. Now that you have read about the exploits of Odysseus during the Trojan War and during his sea voyage home, what do you think about Odysseus' character? Write a brief essay explaining your position using examples from both this chapter and the previous chapter to illustrate your beliefs.

2. Just by reading the retelling of the Odyssey in this chapter, you can gather a good bit of information about what it was like to be the wife of a noble Greek in ancient times. Describe the life Penelope leads. Is there anything that attracts you to her character? What aspects of her situation do you find hard to comprehend in today's society?

3. One of the themes of the *Odyssey* could be "There's no place like home!" Do you think that it was in Odysseus' nature to be a man of adventure or was he as much a "homebody" who wanted only to return home as he said he did?

4. The movie industry has attempted, mostly unsuccessfully, to capture the *Odyssey* on film. Most recently, Hollywood released a made-for-TV movie, *The Odyssey* (1997), starring Armand Assante, Geraldine Chaplin, and Irene Pappas. Like most of the previous movies about Odysseus/Ulysses, the special effects are clunky and often downright hilarious when they are supposed to be scary. The film *O Brother, Where Art Thou* (2000), starring George Clooney, is inspired by the tale of Homer's *Odyssey*. In it, three members of a chain gang, including Clooney's character, Ulysses Everett McGill, break away and have a humorous series of misadventures and encounters with weird characters on their quest to return home. View one or both of these films (with parental permission, of course) and discuss how they follow or diverge from Homer's version.

C. WORDS, WORDS, WORDS

The Daily Muse
News you can use

- Now you know that an **odyssey** is a long journey or a quest. Describe an adventure you have had that you think of as your personal **odyssey**.

- Did you also know that a **mentor** is a person who serves as a guide? Even a minor character can lend his or her name to our vocabulary, as we have seen. **Mentor**, who accompanies Telemachus, has come to mean "a trusted counselor or guide."

Can you think of any other person, whether in literature or in a film, who has served in the role of **mentor** to another? Give the name of the literary work or film below, and describe how that person **mentored** another:

D. HOW 'BOUT THAT?

- The ongoing Odysseus Unbound Project is investigating if the true site of Odysseus' Ithaca is on the Paliki peninsula of Kephallenia, due west of the modern island of Ithaki. (See http://www.odysseus-unbound.org/press.html for more information.)

- Odysseus is a tool designed for testing the security of web applications.

- There have been international conferences on freight transportation and logistics called "Odysseus."

Ulysses/Odysseus in poetry

As mentioned at the outset of the chapter, the character of Odysseus has been used in various ways by many authors. Here is a poem by Alfred, Lord Tennyson titled "Ulysses." (It was quoted on the final episode of the television show *Frasier*!) How is the Homeric hero depicted here?

Ulysses • 1842

It little profits that an idle king,
By this still hearth, among these barren crags,
Match'd with an aged wife, I mete and dole
Unequal laws unto a savage race,
That hoard, and sleep, and feed, and know not me.

I cannot rest from travel: I will drink
Life to the lees: all times I have enjoy'd
Greatly, have suffer'd greatly, both with those
That loved me, and alone; on shore, and when
Thro' scudding drifts the rainy Hyades
Vext the dim sea: I am become a name;
For always roaming with a hungry heart
Much have I seen and known; cities of men
And manners, climates, councils, governments,
Myself not least, but honour'd of them all;
And drunk delight of battle with my peers,
Far on the ringing plains of windy Troy.

I am a part of all that I have met;
Yet all experience is an arch wherethro'
Gleams that untravell'd world, whose margin fades
For ever and for ever when I move.
How dull it is to pause, to make an end,
To rust unburnish'd, not to shine in use!
As tho' to breathe were life. Life piled on life
Were all too little, and of one to me
Little remains: but every hour is saved
From that eternal silence, something more,
A bringer of new things; and vile it were
For some three suns to store and hoard myself,
And this gray spirit yearning in desire
To follow knowledge like a sinking star,
Beyond the utmost bound of human thought.

This is my son, mine own Telemachus,
To whom I leave the sceptre and the isle—
Well-loved of me, discerning to fulfil
This labour, by slow prudence to make mild
A rugged people, and thro' soft degrees
Subdue them to the useful and the good.
Most blameless is he, centred in the sphere
Of common duties, decent not to fail
In offices of tenderness, and pay
Meet adoration to my household gods,
When I am gone. He works his work, I mine.

There lies the port; the vessel puffs her sail:
There gloom the dark broad seas. My mariners,
Souls that have toil'd, and wrought, and thought with me—
That ever with a frolic welcome took
The thunder and the sunshine, and opposed
Free hearts, free foreheads—you and I are old;
Old age hath yet his honour and his toil;
Death closes all: but something ere the end,
Some work of noble note, may yet be done,
Not unbecoming men that strove with Gods.
The lights begin to twinkle from the rocks:
The long day wanes: the slow moon climbs: the deep
Moans round with many voices. Come, my friends,
'Tis not too late to seek a newer world.
Push off, and sitting well in order smite
The sounding furrows; for my purpose holds
To sail beyond the sunset, and the baths
Of all the western stars, until I die.
It may be that the gulfs will wash us down:
It may be we shall touch the Happy Isles,
And see the great Achilles, whom we knew.
Tho' much is taken, much abides; and tho'
We are not now that strength which in old days
Moved earth and heaven; that which we are, we are;
One equal temper of heroic hearts,
Made weak by time and fate, but strong in will
To strive, to seek, to find, and not to yield.

Odysseus, at home in Ithaca, regards the constellations in the night sky.

Politics, cartoons, and Ulysses

It was probably inevitable that Ulysses S. Grant, the Civil War Commander of the Union Army and later twice President of the United States, would be compared to his namesake, Homer's Ulysses. Here are two cartoons, both entitled "The Return of Ulysses."

Tenniel's 1872 cartoon, appearing after Grant's reelection, congratulates America, personified by the young woman in Native American dress. Nast's cartoon honors Grant, who had completed a lengthy world tour to meet foreign leaders after he left office. Grant returned to America in 1879 on the steamship "City of Tokio," (see the boat's name in the cartoon). The scroll on the ground welcomes Grant, implying that American dissatisfaction with his presidency has been forgiven. Rather than Medusa's head, Athena's aegis bears a map of Europe and a picture of the land of the rising sun, Japan.

***The Return of Ulysses*, 1872, by Sir John Tenniel (1820–1914). Tenniel was the chief cartoonist for the English publication *Punch* as well as a book illustrator.**

The Return of Ulysses*, 1879, by Thomas Nast (1840–1902), first published in *Harper's Weekly

How does each cartoonist reveal his feelings about Grant in the details of each drawing?

Can you identify the various figures that are represented in each of these cartoons?

E. Who's Who?

- For Odysseus' family, see GENEALOGICAL CHART 20.

Chapter Eighteen
Aeneas

General Sources:
Vergil *Aeneid*
Ovid *Fasti* 3.545–656

The Aeneid tells the story of Aeneas, a Trojan hero.

Aeneas is a relatively minor character in Homer's *Iliad*, but he is the protagonist in the great epic by the Roman poet Vergil. Many famous Romans, including Julius Caesar, claimed to be descended from Aeneas through his mother Venus. (See Genealogical Chart 18.) Throughout the following narrative, notice the numerous parallels between Aeneas' adventures and those of Homer's heroes. You'll also notice that Vergil, a Roman, is using Latin names for the deities, compared to the Greek names Homer used.

With Aeneas, Vergil created a new type of hero. Aeneas achieves glory not through defeat of monsters, valor in battle, or cleverness, but through his willingness to make personal sacrifices in fulfillment of a plan of the gods that extends far beyond his lifetime. He reaped little personal benefit from his deeds. As Vergil said in the first lines of the poem, "*Tantae molis erat Romanam condere gentem*" (Such a great task it was to found the Roman race).

19th-century woodcut of Publius Vergilius Maro

Juno asks Aeolus to loose the winds against Aeneas and his crew.

The *Aeneid* begins with Aeneas in the seventh year of his journey from Troy to Italy. The goddess Juno held a grudge against him, and wanted to keep him from reaching Italy (also known as Hesperia) as long as possible. She still hated all Trojans because of Paris' judgment against her. She was also worried because she knew that a race descended from Trojan blood was destined to destroy her most beloved city, Carthage. She brooded, "Here I am, the queen of the gods, and I cannot keep those hated Trojans from Italy! Who will worship me now, if I don't punish the people I loathe!"

Juno, who held a grudge against Aeneas

Aeolus, lord of the winds, depicted in illuminated manuscript letter, 15th century

She went to Aeolus, the ruler of the winds, and asked for help in her plan: "Aeolus, Jupiter has given you the power to control the winds, so I have a request of you. Send a storm and submerge the ships of those people hateful to me! If you do this, I will give you Deiopeia, a nymph of surpassing beauty, to be your lawful wife."

A Possible Route of Aeneas

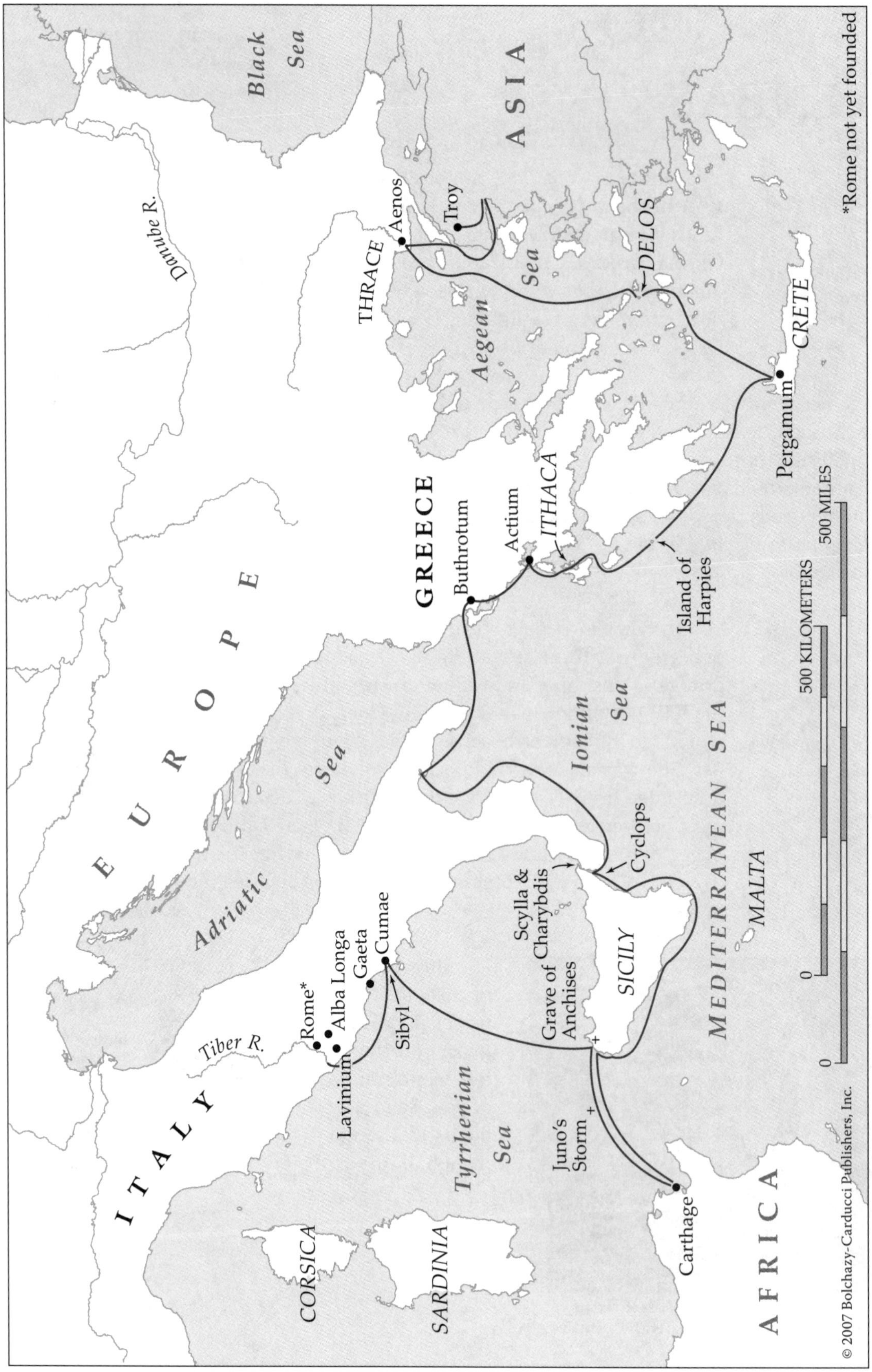

Aeolus answered, "You command, I obey. I have power only because of you and Jupiter." And he struck the mountain in which the winds were imprisoned. At once, the winds rushed out upon the sea with their squalls. Ropes creaked, men shouted, and the sky was blotted out by dark clouds. Thunder crashed and lightning flashed. Aeneas' limbs went weak, and he held his hands up to heaven and cried, "How lucky those men were who died in Troy! I wish Diomedes had killed me there, where Hector and so many other brave men are buried!" Even as he prayed, the storm raged on. Neptune heard the commotion from the depths of the sea, and he surfaced to look upon the mischief of his sister Juno. He scolded the winds, "How dare you raise these storms without my divine authority? Go back and tell your king he can swagger around his island all he wants, but to leave the sea alone!"

Neptune

Neptune orders the winds to return to Aeolus' island.

The winds obeyed, and Neptune calmed the waters and scattered the clouds. Triton and the nymphs gave a hand to the ships that had become stuck on cliffs and sandbars. Satisfied that order was restored, Neptune skimmed his chariot over the now calm sea.

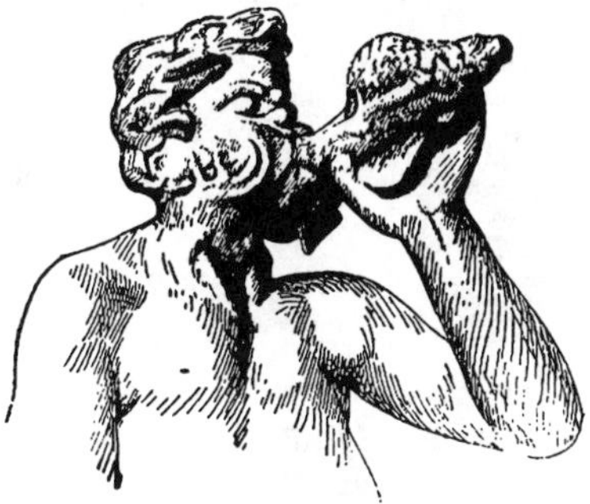

Triton

Aeneas' fleet reaches an unknown shore.

Aeneas and his men, exhausted, headed for the closest shore. They found a peaceful natural harbor, disembarked, built a fire, and dried the grain that had not been lost in the storm. Aeneas climbed a rock to look for the ships that were still missing. He could not see them, but he did see a herd of deer wandering along the shore. He shot seven, first the leaders and then some of the rest, and carried them back to his men with the help of his faithful companion, Achates. He encouraged the crew: "Friends, we have been through worse than this. Gather your courage once again. Perhaps someday it will be pleasant to remember even these things." He kept his own doubts and fears to himself.

Venus implores Jupiter to help Aeneas.

While the men were butchering and cooking the deer Aeneas had killed, Venus went to her father, Jupiter, her lovely eyes filled with tears. "Great king, what has my son Aeneas done to anger you? Didn't you promise that the Romans would arise from his stock, and rule over land and sea? What has changed your mind? Is this the way you reward the virtuous?"

Jupiter foretells a glorious destiny for Aeneas and his descendants.

The heavenly ruler smiled. "Don't worry, Venus, nothing has changed my mind. Your son will wage war in Italy and unite the people there under his rule. His reign will last three years, and then his son Ascanius, also known as Iulus, will rule for thirty years and transfer the power to the city of Alba Longa. Here the descendants of Hector's people will reign three hundred years, until a priestess, pregnant with the offspring of Mars, will give birth to twin sons. Then Romulus will build a city that he will name after himself, and its power will have no end. Even Juno will give up her anger and cherish its people. As the years pass, these people will enslave the lands of Achilles and Agamemnon, and there will be born a great Caesar, who will become a star in the sky at his death. Then there will be everlasting peace."

Jupiter sends Mercury to Carthage to prepare Dido for Aeneas' arrival.

Thus spoke Jupiter, and he sent down his son Mercury to make Carthage (for that was where the Trojans had landed) and its queen, Dido, hospitable to Aeneas.

Mercury prepares to carry out Jupiter's directions.

Venus, disguised as a huntress, meets Aeneas near Carthage.

The next morning, Aeneas set out with Achates to explore the land. Walking towards a city, they encountered Venus, in disguise as a young huntress. She called out to them first: "Hello, there! Have you seen any of my sisters around here?"

Awestruck, Aeneas replied, "No, we haven't seen any of your sisters, miss—but how should I address you? You look like a goddess—maybe Diana, or one of the nymphs? You don't seem to be a mortal."

Venus tells how Sychaeus, Dido's husband, was killed by her brother, Pygmalion.

Venus kept up her playacting. "Oh, I'm no goddess. All of us Tyrian girls dress like this to hunt. This is the city of Carthage, which people from Tyre settled. The queen is Dido, and she's been through a lot. Once she was married to a wealthy man named Sychaeus, and the two were deeply in love. But the kingdom of Tyre was ruled by her evil brother Pygmalion [not the same man as the sculptor of Galatea]. Blinded by lust for his brother-in-law's gold, he ambushed and killed the man at an altar. He concealed the crime and lied to his sister about her husband's absence. But one night, Sychaeus' ghost came to Dido in her sleep. He showed her his wounds and told her what had happened. He urged her to escape with all haste, and he showed her where all of his treasure was buried. She gathered followers, who also hated the tyrannical Pygmalion, and sailed away with the gold Pygmalion had killed for. They bought this land when they arrived and built the city you now see. Now, tell me who you are."

Aeneas answered, "It will take all day to tell the story of my troubles. I am Aeneas, and we have come from Troy. I am carrying the household gods, the Penates, brought from Troy. My lineage is from Jupiter himself, and I left my homeland with twenty ships as my goddess mother led the way. Now I have only seven, and I'm a helpless stranger in an unknown land."

Venus directs Aeneas to go to Queen Dido.

Venus said sympathetically, "Whoever you are, I do not think the gods hate you. Proceed along this road, and you will come to the queen's door. I can tell you that your missing comrades and ships are all right. Look, there are twelve swans in formation. An eagle was just chasing them, but they escaped him and are landing safely."

As she turned away from him, a smell of ambrosia came from her hair and her short tunic became a billowing dress. Aeneas recognized his goddess mother and cried, "Why do you mock me with disguises? Why can't I ever see you face to face as you really are?"

Venus brings armor for Aeneas.

Aeneas and his friend Achates observe the rising walls of Carthage.

He and Achates then headed for the city, but Venus wrapped them in a thick mist so that they could travel unseen. They admiringly watched the building going on, and Aeneas remarked, "Lucky people! *Their* walls are already rising!" They came to a wooded grove, in the center of which was a temple of Juno. Here they entered to wait for the queen.

The temple walls were decorated with murals of scenes from the Trojan War. Aeneas wept to recall those terrible events, and said, "Is there any place on earth that does not know our misfortunes? Look, there's Priam! These people recognize great deeds and shed tears for human affairs."

Dido with Cupid, wall fresco from Pompeii

Aeneas then sees Dido in the new temple to Juno.

As Aeneas gazed in wonder at the paintings, Queen Dido entered, attended by a band of warriors. She took her place and was assigning tasks and dispensing justice when a group of the shipwrecked Trojans arrived. The oldest of them addressed her: "Have mercy upon us, O queen. We are survivors of the Trojan War, and our leader was Aeneas, known far and wide for his goodness. We have not come to harm you or your people. We ask only to repair our battered ships and continue on our voyage."

The queen answered, "Have no fear. Everybody knows about the Trojans and Aeneas. I will give you whatever you need for your journey, or let you stay here if you prefer."

Aeneas, his appearance enhanced by Venus, stands before Queen Dido.

Venus dissolved the concealing cloud and endowed Aeneas with special beauty as he stood before the queen. He said, "May the gods reward your kindness towards us, Queen Dido! I will sing your praises wherever I journey!" He and his men had a joyous reunion, and Dido repeated her promise to assist them, adding, "I have suffered myself, and I am learning to help other sufferers."

Aeneas meets Dido.

Venus exchanges Cupid and Ascanius; Dido takes the child into her lap and urges Aeneas to tell the story of the fall of Troy.

The queen ordered a banquet for her new guests. But Venus, fearing that Juno might work some mischief, had a plan of her own. She sent Aeneas' son Ascanius to sleep and replaced him with Cupid in disguise. As Dido took the adorable little boy on her lap, Cupid filled her with passion for Aeneas. At the end of the banquet, she requested, "Please tell your hosts about the treachery of the Greeks and about your own wanderings!"

Aeneas said, "You are asking me to relive unspeakable grief, and the hour is late. But if you have such desire to learn of Troy's fall, I will tell you."

Hector appears to Aeneas and orders him to escape from Troy.

He described how the Trojans had been tricked into admitting the wooden horse into their city and how the priest Laocoon had tried in vain to stop them. While the Greeks were slaughtering sentries and admitting their comrades into Troy, Aeneas was fast asleep. Hector's ghost came to warn him, looking as bloody and mutilated as he had been when Achilles dragged his body around the walls. Confused, Aeneas asked, "Hector, savior of Troy! What has kept you away from us for so long? And how were you so horribly wounded?"

Hector ignored the futile questions, and said with a groan, "Aeneas, you must escape. The enemy has taken over Troy. You have done enough for your country and Priam. If Troy were meant to be saved, I would have saved it. Take the household gods and look for a new city to establish them."

Aeneas and his comrades witness Priam being killed by Neoptolemus.

After he awoke, Aeneas climbed onto the roof of his house and saw the truth of his dream. All around him, houses were in flames; the noise of trumpets and shouts of people reached to heaven. Still, his first thought was to put on his armor and rush into battle. As his fellows gathered around, Aeneas rallied them: "The gods have deserted us, but if you're all determined, let's go down fighting!" And they rushed into the thick of fighting, slaughtering madly all the way. They fought their way to Priam's palace, where Aeneas, watching from the roof, saw the old king fall by the hand of Neoptolemus.

Neoptolemus kills King Priam.

Priam reminded Aeneas of his own elderly father, Anchises. Aeneas looked around and saw he was alone; those who had accompanied him had fallen away. He began making his way home, defeated. He spotted Helen by the flames' light, crouching within the temple of Vesta. Overcome with rage, he rushed at her, preparing to kill her, but suddenly Venus appeared before him. "Son, what is this madness? Have you forgotten your father and son and your wife Creusa? They would have died long ago if I hadn't protected them. The fall of Troy is not Helen's fault, or Paris' either. The gods are the ones destroying the city. See, I will clear your vision and enable you to see them." And Aeneas saw Neptune tearing up the foundations with his great trident, and Juno at the gates rallying the Greeks, and Minerva sitting on top of the citadel with her Gorgon-adorned shield.

Aeneas thought no more of fighting. When he finally reached home, his only concern was to take his family away safely. Anchises, however, resisted. "I am too old. If the gods had wanted to preserve my life, they would have preserved my city. I have been useless ever since Jupiter's thunderbolt disabled me. Leave me here."

Two omens convince the reluctant Anchises to leave Troy with Aeneas.

Aeneas, Ascanius, and Creusa all pleaded with him, but he remained determined. Suddenly a miracle occurred: a flame surrounded the head of Ascanius, but did not harm him. Anchises cried out, "Jupiter, if you answer prayers, if our devotion to you means anything, please help us and confirm this omen!" In answer, a peal of thunder rang out, and a shooting star streaked through the sky. At last Anchises was convinced to escape. "Wherever you lead, my son, I will follow."

Aeneas' wife, Creusa, disappears as they flee burning Troy.

Aeneas gave his father the ancestral gods to carry and lifted him up onto his own shoulders. He took his small son by the hand and led him along. Creusa followed a few steps behind. Aeneas, who had proceeded through Troy fearlessly when he was alone, now started at every noise. Suddenly he thought he heard the sound of marching feet behind him, and Anchises exclaimed, "Run!" Aeneas rushed off blindly, and did not stop until he was at the sanctuary of Ceres outside the city. He made a horrifying discovery as he looked around: Creusa was missing! Aeneas left all the others behind, put on his armor again, and set off in frantic search of her. He retraced his steps through the city, which was now eerily silent, and returned to his house, thinking it was just possible she had returned there. The house was all in flames. He returned to Priam's palace and went to the shrine of Juno, where the Greeks were already piling up the treasures of Troy. Long lines of frightened women and children stood around. In desperation, he cried out, "Creusa! Creusa!" He continued to rush about, when suddenly her phantom appeared, larger than she had been in life.

Creusa's ghost appears to Aeneas and directs him to go on without her.

She comforted him with these words: "Beloved, why are you grieving so? What happened was the will of the gods, and it was not in their plan for me to accompany you away from here. You must go on a long voyage until you reach the land of Hesperia. There you will find a new kingdom and a new bride. Do not cry for your Creusa! I will never have to go with any Greek as a slave, but will serve the Great Mother of the Gods here. Goodbye! Take care of our son."

Aeneas tried to embrace her, but she vanished like smoke through his arms. By now the night was over. Aeneas rejoined the weary band of refugees that had gathered, lifted his father onto his shoulders once more, and set out.

The Trojan prince Polydorus tells Aeneas to flee from Thrace.

The refugees came to Thrace first. The city had ancient ties with Troy, so Aeneas began to erect walls there. But a horrifying thing happened when he began hewing at one particular tree: it began to bleed! Then it spoke: "Aeneas, why are you tearing my poor body? I am no ordinary tree. I am Polydorus, Priam and Hecuba's youngest son, treacherously slain for my gold. Get away from this evil country!"

The oracle at Delos prophesies: Go to the land of your ancestors.

The Trojans gave Polydorus a second burial and hastened away. They headed for Delos, the small island sacred to Apollo, to seek advice about their destination. The word was: "The land of your ancestors will be the land to receive you, and from there your descendants will rule the whole world."

Anchises interprets the message as a direction to go to Crete, but the Penates appear, ordering Aeneas to sail to Hesperia (Italy).

Anchises decided, "Our ancestor Teucer founded his kingdom in Crete before Ilium was a city. So our destiny must lie there!" They went to Crete and were settling in, plowing fields, and building new homes. Suddenly, however, a plague set in. Many died, and the fields grew barren. Anchises suggested consulting the oracle of Apollo again. That night the Penates, which Aeneas had rescued from Troy, appeared to the hero in his sleep and spoke: "This is not where Apollo commanded you to settle. There is a place which the Greeks call Hesperia, and which the natives call Italy. Here is our true home, not Crete."

Illustration of the Harpies by Armando Spadini (1833–1925), created for the Alinari Edition (Florence, 1902–1903) of Dante Alighieri's *La Divina Commedia.*

Astonished by the vision, Aeneas woke and made appropriate sacrifices. The surviving Trojans set out the next morning towards their proper course. However, a huge storm at sea blew them about on a blind course for three days and three nights. On the fourth day, they landed at the first shore they could find, which happened to be the Strophades, the land of the Harpies. They killed several of the animals they found grazing on the shore and prepared to feast upon them, when the loathsome bird-women swooped down and snatched the food away, leaving their foul stench behind. The men tried to fight back, but the Harpies were invulnerable. Their leader, Celaeno, screeched out: "Are you attacking us, Trojans? Hear the prophecy which I bring from Jupiter and Apollo: You will reach Italy, but you will not be allowed to build your city until famine comes upon you, and you will eat your tables in your hunger!"

At Buthrotum Aeneas meets Helenus, Priam's son.

The men were disheartened, but set sail once again. In due course, they came to the city of Buthrotum. Here they heard an unbelievable rumor: Helenus, a son of Priam, was king there! Walking from the harbor, Aeneas saw Hector's widow Andromache, who was now married to Helenus. Andromache grew faint at the sight of Aeneas, but at last was able to ask: "Are you really here? Are you still alive, or are we in the land of the dead? If we are dead, where is Hector?"

Aeneas answered, "I am alive. Believe it. But tell me about yourself. Are you still married to Neoptolemus?"

Andromache told him that she had had another child by Neoptolemus, but that her second husband had then left her for Helen's daughter Hermione and married her off to Helenus. Neoptolemus had then been slain by Orestes, who wanted Hermione for himself. Some of Neoptolemus' kingdom had passed into the possession of Helenus, who used it to erect a little Troy. It contained a replica of the fallen city's citadel and a small stream that he named Xanthus after a river in Troy.

Helenus prophesies a long voyage and an omen of a sow and her piglets.

Aeneas was anxious to question Helenus, who was a seer, about the future, especially about the dire prophecy of the Harpy. "It will be a long voyage," the seer proclaimed, "but the auspices are favorable. When you reach Italy, look for a white sow nursing thirty white piglets near a lonely river. Here will be the settlement preordained for you. As for what the Harpy said, do not be afraid, for the Fates will find a way. When you approach Sicily, beware of Scylla and Charybdis. After you leave Sicily and arrive in Cumae, consult the Sibyl there. She will tell you more about the wars to come. Now go and carry on the greatness of Troy!"

Avoiding Scylla and Charybdis, the crew drifts close to Cyclops' isle.

The voyagers headed towards Sicily, careful to follow the instructions of Helenus and veer away from Scylla and Charybdis. However, they drifted towards the land of the Cyclopes. As they landed, a man ran towards them, ragged, filthy, and half dead from hunger. He shuddered when he saw their Trojan clothing, but made his plea anyway: "I beg you, Trojans, by all the gods, take me away from here! Anyplace! I admit I was one of the Greeks who attacked your country. Go ahead and kill me, if you hate me for it. I'd rather die at the hands of men than monsters!"

Scylla and Charybdis off the coast of Sicily

The Trojans asked, "Who are you and what happened to you?"

He explained, "I'm from Ithaca, one of the companions of Odysseus. My name is Achaemenides. They left me behind in their haste to escape from Polyphemus. I've been here three months, hiding out in the woods and living on herbs and berries, running away from the Cyclopes."

He had scarcely finished speaking when the Trojans saw Polyphemus lumbering towards the shore. Although he was blind and feeling his way with the trunk of a pine tree, he was still a terrifying sight. He scooped up the sea water and washed out the hollow of his eye, which was still bleeding. The Trojans scrambled aboard their ship, taking the fugitive with them. The blind giant turned in the direction of the voices, but the ships were out of his reach. He bellowed loudly, causing the land to shake and the waves to tremble. At once his fellows came running and began throwing boulders at the ships. The men rowed even faster, and were soon safe, though close to Scylla and Charybdis. They steered away from the twin dangers and rowed on.

Aeneas' tale ends with Anchises' death.

In the town of Drepanum on the island of Sicily, Aeneas faced his greatest sorrow yet. His father Anchises died, a loss predicted to Aeneas neither by the Harpy nor Helenus. The saddened group departed from Sicily, and the storm sent by Juno led them to Carthage. Here Aeneas' tale to Dido ended.

Dido confesses love of Aeneas to her sister Anna, who encourages the romance.

By now, Dido had fallen deeply in love with Aeneas. As the next day dawned, she confided in her sister Anna: "Oh, Anna, what a man this is! What a great warrior! He must be descended from the gods! And did you hear how much suffering he has been through? If I were not so resolved never to marry again after the death of poor Sychaeus, I admit I could be tempted. I feel the old flames stirring. May the earth open up and swallow me, may Jupiter blast me with his thunderbolt, before I break my vow to remain loyal to Sychaeus! My heart is in the grave with him!" And she wept copiously.

Anna replied sympathetically, "Dearest sister, are you determined to waste your youth in mourning and never know the joys of love and children? Do you think the dead care? You have plenty of suitors from the people around us, and you've ignored them all. Remember that enemies surround us and that our brother is still a threat! I think it was by Juno's design that this man came to us now. How glorious Carthage will become if you have his help! Make your prayers and sacrifices to the gods, and think of reasons to keep the guest here. The seas are stormy and his ships are damaged."

Dido, offering sacrifices, searches for favorable omens about her love for Aeneas.

With these words, Anna overcame Dido's doubts. Dido made all of the ritual sacrifices, and stared at the animals' entrails searching for favorable signs. She was like a wounded deer in her lovesickness. Often she took Aeneas through the city, showing off its wealth. She held more banquets and asked Aeneas to tell his adventures again and again. After they parted, she lay on the couch where Aeneas had just been. She also spent much time with Ascanius, marveling at his resemblance to his father. All the building in Carthage stopped.

Juno deceitfully asks Venus' help in uniting the Carthaginians and Trojans, but Venus, suspicious, tells her to consult Jupiter.

Juno, realizing what had happened, spoke to Venus: "What a great triumph for you and your boy, two immortals against one woman! Now that you have what you want and Dido is passionately in love, why don't we work together and make one people of the Carthaginians and Trojans?"

Venus recognized Juno's motives, and she replied craftily, "This is a wonderful idea, and it would be insane to work against you. Just one problem—I don't know if Jupiter and the Fates will allow it. But you are Jupiter's wife, and I'm sure you know how to approach him. Go ahead, and I'll follow."

Juno lays a plan to trap Dido and Aeneas.

"Then hear what my plans are. Tomorrow, Aeneas and Dido are going on a hunting trip. I will send a great storm in the middle of it. When everyone scatters, Dido and Aeneas will take refuge in the same cave. I will be present and, if you agree, I will join them in everlasting marriage." Venus nodded in assent, all the time secretly laughing at Juno.

Forced to find shelter in a cave, Aeneas and Dido consummate their love.

The next morning, the men and beasts left the gates of Carthage in a colorful parade. Dido led them, wearing an elaborately woven purple cloak and carrying a golden quiver. Aeneas, riding beside the queen, was as splendid as Apollo. They climbed into the mountains and chased the deer and wild goats from their hiding places. Suddenly thunder began to rumble and was shortly followed by a downpour of hail. Dido and Aeneas rushed into a cave together. Earth gave the signal first, and Juno was present as matron of honor. Fires flashed and the nymphs of the mountain shrieked. This was the beginning of Dido's sufferings and her downfall. From this day on, she had no more thought for her reputation, and covered her guilt by calling it marriage.

The evil goddess Rumor spreads the news about Dido and Aeneas.

The goddess Rumor did not take long to spread the news. This was the last of the daughters of Earth, sent to plague people. Small and timid at first, she expanded rapidly until she reached the sky. She was covered in swift wings, and under each wing there was an all-seeing eye, an ever-eavesdropping ear, and a never-silent tongue. She flew beneath earth and sky, chattering in the night, and never sleeping. She loved to spread news all around, mixing truth and fiction, and before long all of the surrounding nations had heard about Dido and Aeneas.

Iarbas, Dido's former suitor, is outraged about Dido's liaison with Aeneas.

The word came to Iarbas, one of the suitors whom Dido had rejected. He was the son of Jupiter and a nymph, and to his father he had erected a hundred altars that were always draped in garlands and streaming with the blood of sacrifices. Enraged, he demanded, "Father Jupiter, do you see all this, or do we worship you in vain? I gave this woman the land to build her city, and she takes in this Trojan, with his perfumed hair and his unmanly ways!"

Jupiter sends Mercury to remind Aeneas his destiny lies in Italy, not Carthage.

Jupiter did not ignore his son. He sent down Mercury to remind Aeneas of his destiny. As the messenger god touched down in Carthage, he saw Aeneas helping Dido erect her city's buildings, wearing a jewel-encrusted sword and a rich purple and gold cloak given to him by the Carthaginian queen. Mercury delivered Jupiter's word: "Have you forgotten your destiny? The ruler of the gods himself sent me to remind you! If you don't care about yourself, think of Ascanius' inheritance. You owe him a kingdom in Italy."

Aeneas was dumbstruck by Mercury's words. He knew he needed to leave, but how to break the news to Dido? He decided to have his men prepare the fleet and tell no one, while he waited for the appropriate moment to talk with the queen. The men willingly made preparations, delighted to be moving on at last.

Aeneas secretly prepares to leave, but Dido confronts him.

Dido was not deceived. Rumor had already told her of her beloved's plans to depart. Wild as a bacchant, she rushed to Aeneas and cried, "Traitor, did you think you could leave in secret? Does our love mean nothing to you? Why are you in such a hurry to sail in these stormy seas? Are you running away from *me*? I beg you, by the marriage we have made, do not abandon me like this! There are enemies all around me, and my own people have turned against me. My reputation is gone." She concluded piteously, "If only I had a little Aeneas playing in my palace! I might not feel so alone then."

Aeneas tells Dido that Destiny demands that he must leave to seek Italy.

Aeneas was deeply touched, but he remembered Jupiter's warnings. Choosing his words carefully, he said: "Dido, I know you have done many kind things for me, and I will never deny that I owe you much. I never intended to deceive you or leave without telling you. But neither did I offer you marriage. If Fate allowed me to live as I wanted, Troy would still be standing, and I would have built a new citadel there. But now Apollo commands me to seek Italy. Every night, my father appears to me and warns me in my dreams. The messenger of the gods himself has told me I must leave. Do not aggrieve both of us with your complaints. I am not seeking Italy of my own will."

Wild with grief, Dido accuses Aeneas of cruelty.

Dido was not appeased. "You are not human! You were born from the rocks and nursed by tigers! I took you in and this is how you repay me! Go, then, seek your Italy. But I hope the day will come when your ship hits the rocks and you die calling my name!" She broke off and rushed away. Aeneas longed to follow her and say more, but he returned to the ships and prepared to carry out Jupiter's orders.

Dido goes mad and plans her death.

Dido made a last appeal through her sister Anna, but Aeneas was deaf to her pleas. At the same time, weird omens terrified her. When she made drink offerings, the milk went black and the wine turned to blood. She thought she heard her husband's ghost calling her, and a screech owl on the roof cried mournfully. When she slept, she had nightmares of wandering alone on desolate roads, pursued by a now-evil Aeneas. She resolved to die, but kept her designs from her sister. She put on a cheerful face, and said, "Anna, I have finally thought of a way out of this madness. A priestess taught me a spell to cure lovesickness. Go build a pyre in the courtyard of the palace, and place everything that I have of the traitor's on it. Don't forget the marriage bed that was my undoing. I want to wipe out everything that reminds me of the man, and this is the way the priestess said to do it."

Dido swears eternal enmity between the Carthaginians and Aeneas' descendants.

As soon as the pyre was built, Dido placed on the bed an effigy of Aeneas and all the things he had left behind. Mercury, seeing that Aeneas was still in Carthage, came down and warned him a second time. While he sailed away, Dido uttered a curse: "O heavenly sun and Juno and Hecate and avenging Furies, hear me! If that man must reach Italy, let him face war there and see his people dying! Let him not enjoy his rule for long, but die early! May there always be hatred between his people and mine, and let an avenger arise from my ashes!"

Dido sent Sychaeus' old nurse to fetch Anna. Then she climbed the pyre and took up the sword that Aeneas had given her. She lay down on the bed and spoke her last words: "I have lived the life that Fortune allowed to me. I have founded a great city and avenged my husband's death. I would have been happy if the Trojans' ships had never reached these shores."

Atop her own funeral pyre, Dido falls upon Aeneas' sword.

Then Dido fell upon the sword. Her attendants screamed as blood pooled around her. Rumor rushed wildly through the city once more. Anna heard the shouts, and plunged through the crowd in terror. She cried out to Dido, "Is *this* what you were planning all along? Why didn't you let me die with you instead of having me build your own funeral pyre?" She clutched Dido's body, sobbing as she tried to stop the bleeding with her own clothes. Dido opened her heavy eyes and groaned at being still alive. Three times she tried to raise herself; three times she fell back.

Juno pitied Dido as she struggled to die, and sent down Iris to release Dido's spirit. The rainbow goddess flew down on her saffron wings, and consecrating a lock of Dido's hair to the gods of the Underworld, she said, "I now free you from your body!" With these words, all the warmth went out of Dido's body, and her spirit passed into the winds.

Aeneas sails away as Dido expires.

As the Trojans sailed away, their minds were filled with dark foreboding when they saw the flames arising from Carthage. They were now in mid-ocean with no land in sight, when another storm arose. The helmsman Palinurus said, "I wouldn't risk sailing for Italy in this storm if Jupiter himself guided us! I suggest we return to Sicily and wait it out." Aeneas agreed. He was glad to revisit the land where his father was buried; he knew there was a Trojan there named Acestes who would receive them kindly. Because it had been a year since the death of Anchises, the Trojan men celebrated funeral games in his honor.

Juno sends Iris in disguise to incite the Trojan women to burn the ships.

Juno still schemed against Aeneas, however. She saw the Trojan women sitting apart on the beach, lamenting for Anchises and complaining of the hard voyages past and future. She sent down Iris in the guise of an elderly Trojan woman named Beroe. The disguised messenger addressed the company of women: "Why couldn't we have died at the hands of the Greeks in Troy? We have been traveling for seven years in search of Italy. How much more hardship will we have to endure? It's too much. Why don't we settle here? I saw Cassandra in a dream telling me, 'This is your home. This is the new Troy.' Look, here are four altars of Neptune! Be daring!" And she snatched up a torch and threw it with all her might at the ships.

The other women were uncertain whether or not to do likewise. Another old woman named Pyrgo cried out, "This is not Beroe! I just left Beroe; she's sick and unhappy that she couldn't come and pay respects to Anchises! Look at her bearing—this is a goddess!" At the sight of the rainbow that appeared when Iris returned to the sky, the women were overwhelmed by madness. They grabbed torches and fired the ships.

Aeneas asks for help from Jupiter, who sends rain to quench the ships' fires.

Aeneas encourages the elderly and sick to stay in Sicily.

Anchises, in a dream, tells Aeneas to visit the Underworld.

At the sight of the flames, Ascanius came running, followed by Aeneas and the other men. "What are you doing? Why are you burning your own future?" he shouted. The women fled in shame, their senses restored. But the ships continued to burn. Aeneas prayed, "Father Jupiter, grant that our fleet may escape from the flames! Or strike us all down with your thunderbolt right now!" The supreme god at once sent down a torrential rain, quenching the fires. The ships were saved, but Aeneas was more uncertain than ever. An elderly companion named Nautes advised, "Hand over to Acestes all those people who do not wish to continue the journey—the old men and women and those who have no stomach for danger. Let them have their city here, and the rest will continue on to Italy." While Aeneas was pondering whether to take this advice, the form of Anchises came down from the sky. "Dearest son, I come to you by the command of Jupiter. Follow Nautes' advice. Take only the bravest with you, for you have wars to face in Italy. But first, you must come to the Underworld and meet with me. I am in Elysium. The Sibyl of Cumae will show you the way, and you will learn of your descendants. But now the sun is beginning to rise, and I must depart."

The Trojans remained in Sicily nine days more, and then made their departure amid many tearful farewells. Venus, watching them, asked Neptune, "Why does Juno persist in this terrible rage, unchanged by time and prayers? You saw the storm she created, and now she drove the Trojan women to do wrong. I beg you to give them a safe crossing from this point on!"

Neptune assures Venus that only one life will be lost enroute to Avernus in Italy.

Neptune answered, "Have no fear. He will arrive safely in Italy in the harbor of Avernus. Only one man will be lost, only one life given for many."

When it was nearly midnight, and all the men were sleeping except Palinurus the helmsman, the god Sleep came to him in the disguise of a comrade. "Palinurus, the wind is carrying the ship along nicely. This is a time for sleep. Why don't you rest a while, and I'll steer for you?"

Palinurus answered drowsily, "No . . . I know a calm sea can fool a man, and I'm not going to desert my post."

The Trojan helmsman, Palinurus, overcome by sleep, is washed overboard.

The god took a branch dripping with the waters of Lethe and Styx and shook it over Palinurus. The helmsman struggled to stay awake, but at last he let go of the tiller. The god washed him overboard as he called in vain to his fellows. Aeneas sensed that he was adrift, and he woke and seized control of the ship. He wept that Palinurus had trusted a calm sea and clear sky.

At Cumae, Aeneas meets Sibyl, the priestess of Apollo.

At length, they landed in Cumae, and headed directly for the temple of Apollo on its acropolis. As Aeneas was admiring the carvings on the temple doors, the Sibyl Deiphobe came to him and said, "This is no time to sightsee, Aeneas! You should be making your sacrifices!" He did, and she led him into the lofty temple, which had a hundred openings from which the words of the Sibyl resounded. "The god is near!" she cried, feeling Apollo take possession of her. "Make your prayers, Aeneas!"

Representation of the Cumaean Sibyl, a detail of the ceiling fresco in the Sistine Chapel (1510) by Michelangelo Buonarroti (1475–1564), the Vatican Palace, Vatican City, Italy

Aeneas prayed, "Apollo, you have always stood by the Trojans and pitied their suffering. I beg that their labors end now."

The Sibyl prophesies wars, further dangers, and a bride for Aeneas.

The priestess, speaking with the god's voice, responded: "You have survived the perils of the sea, but greater ones remain on land. I see wars, horrible wars, ahead. You will find another Greek camp, and another Achilles born of a goddess. Another foreign bride will cause grief. And Juno will never be far away. But face these dangers boldly, and you will receive unexpected help from a Greek city."

"None of these things come as a shock to me," said Aeneas. "I have one other prayer: show me the way through the Underworld to my dear father."

The Sibyl directs Aeneas to find a golden bough in order to enter the Underworld.

"The descent to the Underworld is easy," was the reply. "But to return . . . that is the task. A few especially dear to Jupiter or distinguished in virtue have succeeded. If you are determined to do it, you must find the golden bough hidden in a dark grove. Proserpina demands it as an offering to her. If you are called by the Fates, the branch will easily break off in your hand; if not, no effort will succeed. There is also a comrade of yours who is polluting the fleet with his death. You must bury him. If you do these things, you will be allowed to cross the Styx and return."

After Misenus is drowned, Aeneas finds the golden bough while collecting timber for the funeral pyre.

Aeneas left the temple sorrowfully, wondering which man he had lost now. When he came to the shore, he came upon the body of his trumpeter, Misenus. This man had been blowing into a seashell and had been foolish enough to challenge the sea-gods to a trumpeting contest. Triton at once sent up a tidal wave and drowned him.

The tearful Trojans set out to gather wood to build his funeral pyre. As they worked, Aeneas prayed, "If only the golden bough would show itself now!" At once, two doves, the birds of Venus, came down and settled on the grass in front of him. "Be my guides now, please, and show me where the golden bough is! And you, my goddess mother, do not fail me!" he begged. The birds took off and settled near the top of a tree that gave forth a golden glitter amid the green. Aeneas instantly seized the branch, which resisted a bit but then came off in his hand.

After Aeneas did this, he and the others carried out the funerary rites for Misenus. Aeneas raised a great mound and placed on top of it the trumpeter's weapons, the oars he rowed with, and the musical instrument he played.

At Lake Avernus, the Sibyl leads Aeneas into the Underworld.

Now it was time to begin the descent to the Underworld. They entered through a huge deep cave near a dark lake named Avernus, which is Greek for "birdless" because no birds ever flew over it. Around the entrance crowded all sorts of sinister phantoms: Grief, Old Age, Revenge, Disease, Fear, and Hunger, among others. Monsters rushed forward also: Gorgons, Harpies, triple-bodied Geryon, the Chimera, and more. Aeneas drew his sword in fear, but the Sibyl assured him they were only disembodied spirits.

They came to the Styx and approached the boat of Charon. On the banks of the river, Aeneas saw his helmsman Palinurus, who had actually managed to swim to shore after falling overboard but had been killed by the natives there. The Sibyl consoled him for his death by telling him there would be a consecrated mound raised on the place where he died.

A drawing of Geryon, 1902, by Alberto Zardo (1876–1959) in the Alinari Edition (Florence, 1902–1903) of Dante Alighieri's *La Divina Commedia*

When Charon saw Aeneas and the Sibyl preparing to enter his boat, he called out, "Hold it right there! No living people allowed here! When I let Theseus and Peirithous in, they tried to carry off my mistress, and Hercules stole Cerberus!"

When the Sibyl shows the golden bough to Charon, he agrees to ferry them across the Styx.

The Sibyl answered, "Aeneas has no such violent schemes. His devotion has led him here to see his father in the Elysian Fields. Look, he has the golden bough."

The Sibyl feeds some drugged cake to Cerberus, Hades' three-headed hound.

No further words were needed. Charon marveled at the sign, turned his boat, and allowed Aeneas and the Sibyl to enter. The boat groaned and filled with water under Aeneas' living weight, but the ferryman was able to row them across. When Cerberus snarled at them and tried to block their way, the Sibyl fed him pieces of cake soaked with sleeping drugs.

As Aeneas entered the Underworld, he heard weeping and lamentation. In the Plains of Mourning were people dead before their time: infants, the wrongfully executed, and the suicides. Wandering among them was Dido, with her wound still fresh. Aeneas could barely discern her; she was as faint as the crescent moon behind clouds. He spoke words of love to her: "Dido! So it was true after all that you took your own life! Was I the cause? I swear to you, it was the gods' commands that drove me from your land, the same commands that brought me here. I never meant to hurt you so! Wait, don't leave!" Dido made no reply but kept her glare fixed upon the ground, then rushed away to rejoin Sychaeus in the shadows of the wood. Aeneas stared after her tearfully, pitying her misfortune.

Next they came to the fields set aside for brave warriors. Aeneas groaned to see all the fallen Trojans there who crowded around him and tried to learn why he had come. When the ghosts of the Greek leaders saw him, they were seized with panic and tried to raise a war cry, but only the faintest squeak came from their mouths. Then Aeneas saw one man who presented a shocking sight, his whole face and body mutilated. His nose and ears had been chopped off. This was Deiphobus, the son of Priam who had married Helen after Paris's death. Aeneas asked, "Who could have done such a thing to you?"

Deiphobus lamented, "It was Helen's doing, the traitor! After the Greeks invaded the city, she pretended to lead the Trojan women in the worship of Bacchus, then signaled to the Greeks from the top of the citadel with her torch! She removed my sword and armor while I was sleeping, and she led Menelaus right to me! You can guess the rest. But why are *you* here?"

The Sibyl interrupted, "Aeneas, we're wasting time. This is where the road forks. The left path leads to Tartarus; we won't be going there. The right path will take us to Elysium."

In the Elysian Fields, Anchises joyfully greets his son, Aeneas.

They came at last to the paradise. The plains were bathed in glowing light, and the blessed had their own sun and stars. Some were holding athletic contests; some danced and sang to the lyre of Orpheus; others cared for their favorite horses. There were priests and true prophets and others who had made the world better through their skills. Deep in a green valley was Anchises. Seeing Aeneas, he rushed to him joyfully, and exclaimed, "I knew you would come! I was so afraid the Carthaginians would do you harm, but I never doubted your devotion."

Aeneas answered, "It was my vision of you that kept me going and brought me here. Give me your right hand, Father, do not avoid my embrace." He tried three times to clasp his father, but the phantom repeatedly slipped through his hands.

Anchises allows Aeneas to see a vision of the future great leaders of Rome.

After Aeneas caught sight of the people lined up by the River Lethe, preparing to drink the waters of forgetfulness and begin a new life, Anchises showed him a vision to fire up his spirit for the labors ahead: the great Romans of the future. He concluded: "Others will shape bronze and marble into human likenesses more artistically. Others will plead cases better and will trace the courses of the stars more skillfully. But your task, O Roman, will be to govern the peoples of the world in your empire, to spare the defeated and to crush the proud."

Aeneas and the Sibyl return to the upper world through a Gate of Ivory.

Anchises then sent Aeneas and the Sibyl to the upper world through the Gate of Ivory. On their journey towards their destined site, Aeneas had to bury one more person: his elderly nurse, who had not remained behind with the other women in Sicily but had accompanied her former charge.

Latinus postpones his daughter Lavinia's marriage to the Rutulian Prince Turnus.

Aeneas and his men sailed north and finally landed at the Tiber River in Latium, a land ruled by King Latinus. Latinus had one daughter named Lavinia, the woman Aeneas was destined to marry. Latinus' queen was named Amata. She longed to see her daughter married to Prince Turnus, of a local tribe named the Rutulians, but contrary omens troubled her. A swarm of bees settled on a tree sacred to Apollo, which a prophet said foretold an invading army. More mysteriously, while Lavinia was standing by her father at the altar, her long hair suddenly caught on fire but did not burn her. Latinus consulted the oracle of his father Faunus, which said, "My son, do not give your daughter in marriage to a Latin. Marry her to a stranger, whose race will reach the stars in glory."

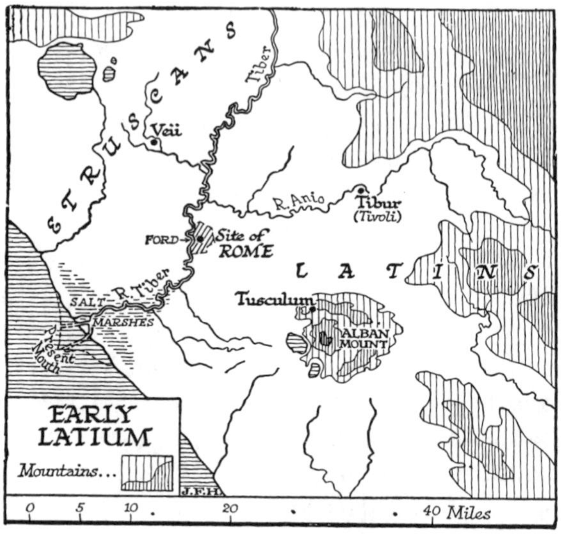

Latium

The first meal that Aeneas and his crew had in Italy consisted of flat wheat crusts heaped with the local fruits. When the fruits proved too scanty to be satisfying, the men devoured the flat quarters of bread. Suddenly Ascanius exclaimed, "Look, we're eating our tables!" Aeneas realized that this was the fulfillment of the Harpy's prophecy. The next day, he sent a delegation of men to Latinus, while he began the task of constructing the new city's walls.

Unable to change Destiny, Juno plans wars between the Italians and the Trojans.

Latinus received them courteously, but Juno was not about to allow a peaceful union of the peoples. She fumed, "Why couldn't those wretched Trojans accept defeat when their city was in flames? They must think my divine powers are exhausted! If I can't stop them with the help of the gods above, I'll go to the gods below! I know I can't stop Aeneas from marrying Lavinia and establishing his kingdom, but I can see to it that Lavinia's dowry will be the blood of Italians and Trojans!"

Juno enlists the Fury Allecto to sow discord in the mind of Queen Amata.

Once more, Juno went to another divinity for help, this time the Fury Allecto. This was a creature loathed even in the Underworld by her own father, Pluto, and by her sisters, with a thousand fearful shapes and hair crawling with black serpents. "Here is a task you will enjoy," Juno told her. "See to it that Aeneas and his men do not win over Latinus. You know how to set the most loving people against each other, so use all your means to shatter this peace. Make the young men eager to go to war!"

Allecto went straight to the chamber of Amata, who was already seething with disappointment at the loss of the wedding with Turnus. The Fury took one of the snakes from her hair and flung it at the queen. Amata did not feel its coils as it became a great necklace of twisted gold around her neck. Yet its effect on her was instant. Before the venom fully possessed her, she tried to persuade Latinus to change his mind. "How can you turn your daughter over to these exiles? What about your pledge to Turnus? Do you hold these foreigners in higher regard than your own people?" When the king stood firm, the queen became completely mad. She raced through the city in frenzy, like a spinning top lashed in children's games. She pretended to be possessed by Bacchus, and hid her daughter in the woods. "Ho, Bacchus! Only you are worthy of her!" she cried. The other women were touched by the same passion, and also took to the woods in maenads' clothing. The heavens rang with the wailing of the women.

A Fury

Allecto goads Turnus to fury; he takes up arms against the Trojans.

The Fury also visited Turnus in his sleep. She transformed herself into an aged priestess of Juno, and spoke to the Rutulian prince: "Are you going to stand by and let the king give your beloved to another man? Fight, Turnus! Juno herself sent me to tell you this!"

Turnus laughed at her. "I know that a fleet has arrived here, but Juno has not forgotten us. It's senility making you afraid about nothing. Go back to your own duties, and leave war to men."

Blazing with anger, Allecto resumed her true form. Her eyes flashed fire and the snakes on her head stood up as she declared, "Senile, am I? Look! I bring war and death!" With these words, she flung a burning torch at the prince. He awoke in terror, on fire with lust for war, and stirred up the Rutulians to arms.

Ascanius wounds a pet stag; in the confusion, both Trojans and Latins are killed.

The Fury made one more stop before returning to the Underworld. She spotted Ascanius hunting on the shore and sent madness into his hounds. They gave chase to a stag that was a pet of the royal herdsman's children. Fired by love of glory, Ascanius shot the stag, which staggered home moaning. The shepherd's daughter raised a cry for help, and the country people came running, armed with stakes and clubs. Allecto took advantage of the opportunity. Perched on the farm's roof, she sounded the war trumpet. The Trojans streamed out to help Ascanius; in the ensuing melee several were killed, including a son of the shepherd.

Caught between Amata's outrage and Faunus' prophecies, Latinus withdraws from the conflict.

While a crowd of herdsmen carried the bodies of the slain to Latinus, Turnus continued to stir up fear: "The Trojans are going to become part of our kingdom! Latin blood will be tainted by these filthy foreigners!" Amata and the other women added their cries to the chaos. Helpless under the blows of fate, Latinus shut himself in his palace and gave no commands.

Turnus assembles the tribes of Italy for war, including the Etruscans.

Led by Turnus, the Italians now assembled for war. First to come was Mezentius, an Etruscan who had been deposed from power because of his tyrannical rule and scorn of the gods. With him was his son Lausus, second in beauty only to Turnus, a young man who deserved a better father. The sons of Hercules and Neptune led other companies. Greeks who had fought in the Trojan War were also there, eager to fight against Trojans once more. Lastly there came the warrior maiden Camilla. Her father had been driven from his throne by his people, and he escaped, holding his infant daughter while an angry mob pursued them. He tied her to a spear and threw her across a river, vowing to dedicate her to Diana if she survived. She had grown up as a follower of the hunter-goddess, scorning womanly arts, and turning her hand to war instead.

In Aeneas' dream, Father Tiber reveals that the white sow and piglets will be found the next day.

This turn of events deeply troubled Aeneas. He lay tossing and turning for a long time that night before finally falling asleep. In his sleep, Father Tiber came to him, wearing a blue-green cloak and with reeds shading his hair. The river-god said, "This is where you were destined to be. Do not let this war intimidate you. When you wake, you will find a white sow with a litter of thirty white piglets lying under a tree, the sign the gods foretold. You must also go to King Evander of the Arcadians, who rules the city of Pallentium near here. Make a treaty with his people."

After finding the sow, Aeneas visits King Evander and his son, Pallas, in Pallantium.

When Aeneas awoke, he found the sow that the god had described. The Tiber River was also unusually calm, and Aeneas and his men immediately began their journey to Pallentium. When they arrived, Evander was performing sacrifices for the yearly rites in honor of Hercules. First to see the Trojans was Evander's young son Pallas, who rushed out with a spear to confront the strangers alone. He called out, "Who are you, from where? Do you come in peace or war?" Aeneas held out the olive branch of peace and explained their mission. Evander had known Anchises, and greeted them joyfully. He explained the reason for their honors to Hercules, who had defeated the monster Cacus in their land long ago. He added, "Hercules entered my humble home back then, and I hope you too will not scorn my poor accommodations."

Hercules and Cacus, 1534, a statue by Baccio Bandinelli (1488–1560), Florence, Italy

Venus asks Vulcan to create armor for Aeneas; Vulcan adorns the shield with scenes of Rome.

While Aeneas rested in Evander's hut on a bed of leaves covered with a bear skin, Venus went to Vulcan and asked him to create a suit of armor for her son. The fire-god crafted a fire-spurting helmet, a sharp sword and spear, a breastplate of blood-red bronze, and greaves of electron and gold. His greatest masterpiece, however, was the shield, which was richly carved with scenes from the future of Rome.

Venus brings armor for Aeneas.

To Aeneas, the elderly Evander entrusts his young son, Pallas, to learn the warrior arts.

Before Aeneas went back to Latium, bearing the gifts of Vulcan, Evander gave him charge of Pallas: "I wish I still had my old fighting strength to go with you. Take my son with you to learn the arts of war under your leadership. I pray to live long enough to see him come home again. But I hope I die before I receive bad news of him, my only source of joy, born to me late in life."

Turnus attacks the Trojans, killing many.

While Aeneas was away, Turnus had managed to reach the Trojans' ships and was about to set them on fire, when they metamorphosed into nymphs. Jupiter had long ago decided that they would survive in this form when their task of carrying Aeneas to Italy was complete. Turnus took this as an omen in his favor: "The Trojans are trapped here! There's no escape for them! We can defeat them, and we won't have to hide inside a wooden horse either!" Supported by Juno, he slaughtered Trojans and did not withdraw until Jupiter commanded Juno to stop interfering. Turnus leaped into the Tiber in full armor and swam back to his comrades.

The flash of Aeneas' shield as he returns with Pallas heartens the dispirited Trojans.

As Aeneas sailed back along the Tiber, accompanied by Pallas and many new allies, the nymphs who had been his ships came up alongside his boat and encouraged him. He saw his allies hard pressed, and he lifted up his new shield and made it flash. This signal heartened the Trojans and their allies; they fought with renewed strength.

When Pallas saw the Arcadians retreating, he fired them up. "Remember your bravery in the past! Fight for me as you fought for my father! They're only men like you, not gods!" Pallas bore the brunt of the fighting for the Trojans and their allies, Lausus for the Italians. They were nearly the same age and equally noble, but each was destined to fall at the hands of a stronger enemy.

Juturna, a nymph who was a sister of Turnus, advised her brother to take Lausus' place. He charged into the fighting, and called out, "Move aside! No one attacks Pallas but me! I only wish his father were here to watch me kill him!" Unafraid, Pallas retorted, "Don't threaten me. I'll win glory either way today, either by stripping your dead body or by dying a hero's death." Pallas made the first attack, hoping that fortune would help the underdog. He prayed to Hercules, "My father gave you hospitality and friendship once. Be with me as I fight Turnus, and let my face be the last thing he sees!" Hercules wept for Pallas' fate and his own helplessness, but Jupiter consoled him: "Everyone has his allotted day. Many brave men fell at Troy, including my own son, but the glory of their deeds lives on. Turnus' dying day is near also."

Pallas' spear pierced through Turnus' shield and grazed his skin, but did not harm him. Turnus gloated, "Now see if my own shot is better!" It penetrated the layers of Pallas' shield and tore through his chest. "Arcadians, tell Evander that I am sending him back the son he deserves! He's welcome to any comfort he finds in building his son a tomb!" boasted Turnus. He planted his foot on Pallas' body in his eagerness to strip off the young man's belt and take it as a trophy.

Afraid for Turnus, Juno makes a phantom Aeneas, who leads Turnus away from the real Aeneas.

Aeneas heard of the calamity, and he charged forth with the force of a hundred-handed fire-breathing monster. Juno was afraid for Turnus, and she crafted a phantom Aeneas with the power to speak, copying his weapons perfectly. The fake Aeneas brandished his weapons and shouted challenges to Turnus, who threw his spear at long range. The phantom turned and ran. Turnus chased it, shouting, "Where are you running, Aeneas? Don't leave! Your marriage is all arranged!" He pursued the apparition onto a ship, whose moorings Juno cut. The phantom vanished and the ship brought Turnus back to his home town, as he shouted in frustration all the way.

Mezentius took the place of Turnus on the battlefield, cutting down multitudes of Trojans and their allies. Aeneas picked him out from the crowds and charged towards him, but the exiled tyrant stood his ground. He cried, "I'll strip off that thief's armor and give it to you, Lausus!" He threw his spear, but it missed Aeneas and struck another man. Then Aeneas cast, striking Mezentius in the side, but it was not a mortal blow. Lausus groaned to see his father in distress, and threw himself between Mezentius and Aeneas. Aeneas warned, "Why are you in a hurry to die, and why do you take on more than you can handle?" Lausus, maddened with rage, did not listen. Aeneas drove his sword through the young man's body, burying it to the hilt. Seeing Lausus die, Aeneas thought of his love for his own father, and he sighed deeply.

By the bank of the Tiber, Mezentius was washing his wounds. He heard the wailing from far off, and knew the truth. When his son's body was brought back to him, he cried, "How could I love life so much that I let my son die for me! My crimes have tarnished his name. But I am still alive, and I can still fight!"

Although slowed by his wound, he mounted his horse and charged into battle once again. He addressed his horse as he rode: "You and I have lived a long time. Today we will either avenge Lausus by carrying back the head of Aeneas, or we will fall together. With your courage, I don't think you'd want to serve anyone else!" He galloped into battle, shouting the name of Aeneas. Confronting him, Mezentius cried, "Nothing frightens me now. I came here to die. But first I have *this* for you!" He threw spears repeatedly at Aeneas, hitting the Trojan's shield but inflicting no wound. At last Aeneas threw his spear, catching Mezentius' horse between the temples. It reared up and threw the rider, then fell on top of him, pinning him down. His last words were, "I know people all around hate me. Protect me from their wrath and let me be buried with my son."

After the Italic tribes and the Trojans bury their dead, the warrior maiden Camilla is killed.

Aeneas set up a trophy to Mars on the spot where Mezentius fell, and there was a truce between the Trojans and Italians to bury their dead. Aeneas saw to the burial of Pallas. In the renewed fight that ensued, Camilla fought bravely and died.

Latinus and Amata try to convince Turnus to surrender to the Trojans; Turnus refuses.

Latinus and Amata, seeing the tide of battle turning against the Italians, tried to persuade Turnus into giving up the fight. Their pleas only made him more infuriated and determined. The next day, Latinus and Aeneas made a treaty. Aeneas swore that if victory fell to Turnus, the Trojans would withdraw to the city of Evander and never again make war on the Italians. But if his side proved victorious, the Italians and Trojans would rule the land together as equals. Latinus agreed. Yet it seemed to the Italians that the contest was uneven, and they were disturbed as they saw how pallid and immature their champion Turnus looked.

Juno interfered once more. She went to Juturna and said, "Do whatever you can to save your brother from death, or stir up war once again and make useless this treaty they have struck." Juturna sent an omen: an eagle swooped down and seized a swan from the waves, whereupon the other birds attacked him until he let his prey drop. The Italians were heartened by this, and the fight was renewed.

Aeneas leaves the battlefield to tend to his wounded leg; Turnus kills many Trojans.

In the ensuing chaos, an arrow flew and struck Aeneas in the leg as he was trying to restore order. No one claimed credit for it; whether a human or a god sent it will never be known. When Turnus saw Aeneas leaving the field, his spirits soared and he cut down many a hero. He was the equal of Mars accompanied by his retinue of Fear, Ambushes, and Angers.

Venus heals Aeneas' wound; Aeneas returns to the field.

His comrades helped Aeneas, limping and leaning on his spear, back to camp. The Trojans, including a grieving Ascanius, stood around anxiously. Their doctor, who had been taught his art by Apollo himself, labored to dislodge the shaft, but he could not budge it. It was Venus who brought her son the necessary remedy. She picked some dittany, an herb with strong healing powers, and mixed it along with some ambrosia in the water that the doctor was using to wash Aeneas' wound. At once, the bleeding stopped, the arrow came out, and Aeneas was completely well. The doctor shouted, "Bring the warrior his arms, quickly! This healing was no human work, but the touch of a god!" Aeneas, hungry for battle, took up his weapons again.

Dittany
(*Cunila origanoides*)

A doctor attends wounded Aeneas, with Venus and Ascanius on either side, 1st-century CE Pompeiian fresco, Museo Archeologico Nazionale, Naples, Italy.

Juturna guides Turnus away from Aeneas.

Now the Rutulians were in retreat as they saw Aeneas advancing. He did not cut down any of the men who fled from him, but searched for Turnus only. Juturna, determined to preserve her brother from the final confrontation as long as possible, disguised herself as Turnus' charioteer and repeatedly steered her brother clear of Aeneas. When a furtive shot from another Rutulian sheared off the plumes from Aeneas' helmet, his anger rose. Calling upon Jupiter to witness the breaking of the treaty, he plunged into the middle of the foe and was inspired by Mars in his slaughter.

Venus then inspired Aeneas to attack Latinus' city. He cried to his troops, "I'm not waiting for Turnus to decide he's ready to meet me! This city is the cause of the war! Bring your torches, men, and we'll enforce the treaty with fire!"

Queen Amata, thinking Turnus dead, hangs herself.

As Amata saw the enemy approaching the city, the fire burning the buildings, and Turnus nowhere in sight, she thought the Rutulian leader had been killed. Her mind was deranged with grief, and she cried, "It's all my fault! I caused all this evil!" She hanged herself in desperation. Her daughter was the first to tear her hair and cheeks in grief, lamentations rang through the palace, and Latinus poured dirt over his hair in mourning for his wife and his city.

Turnus noticed the shouts of terror coming from the city, and wondered, "Why this clamor?" His disguised sister ignored his misgivings, and said, "Come on, this way! Let's go after these Trojans! Others can defend the city."

Turnus resists Juturna's efforts to shield him from Aeneas.

Her brother was not fooled. "I recognized your doings some time ago, Juturna. Why are you here? Fate is too strong to fight. I'm ready to face Aeneas and not to run away from him."

In the heavens, Jupiter spotted Juno watching the battle from an icy cloud, and said to her, "My dear wife, where will it end? You know what Aeneas' destiny is. The time has come for you to end your grudge. You have inflicted enough sorrow, and I forbid you to go any further."

Ordered to end her grudge against Aeneas, Juno asks that the Latin language and customs prevail.

Juno replied, "I know your will, and I have already abandoned Turnus. I will not stand in the way of Aeneas and Lavinia's marriage. But when the two races are united, I beg you not to make the Latins change their name or to adopt Trojan customs or language. Troy is dead; let it remain so."

The heavenly king said, "I grant you this. The Italians will keep their language and their ancient ways. The people who will arise from this union will be second to none in paying you honor." Juno departed from the cloud, rejoicing.

Jupiter orders Juturna to cease helping Turnus.

Jupiter then sent an omen to warn Juturna to withdraw. He sent down a Fury, which flew again and again in Turnus' face, screeching and beating his shield with her wings. Juturna, seeing it from far off, lamented, "There's nothing I can do for you now, Turnus! I wish the gods hadn't given me immortality, so that I could join you in death!" Covering her head in a blue-green veil, the goddess returned to the depths of her own river.

After Turnus hurls a boulder at Aeneas in vain, Aeneas brings Turnus down with his spear.

At last, Turnus and Aeneas stood face to face. Turnus looked around and saw a huge boulder; he picked it up and threw it with all his might at Aeneas. But he was like a man in a nightmare where we try to speak or move and cannot. The throw fell short. Then Turnus knew definitely that he was alone with his doom upon him, and he trembled. As he faltered, Aeneas cast his spear and brought down Turnus. The Rutulians gave a groan that echoed through the mountains.

"I have deserved this. Do what you must, but remember your father Anchises and take pity on my own father. Give me, or my body, back to my people. You win, everybody saw me defeated and pleading. Lavinia is yours. Do not take your anger any further," the wounded warrior begged.

After seeing Pallas' belt worn as spoils around Turnus' waist, Aeneas kills Turnus.

Aeneas hesitated, and was on the point of sparing Turnus' life, when he suddenly caught sight of Pallas's belt, which Turnus was wearing. Enraged, he cried, "Do you think you can escape wearing my dear friend's spoils? This blow is for Pallas!" He plunged the sword deep into his enemy's breast, and Turnus' spirit flew resentfully to the world below.

Aeneas marries Lavinia, princess of the Latins; their son is Aeneas Silvius.

Here the *Aeneid* ends, but we know from indications within the epic and other sources what happened next. Aeneas married Lavinia, who gave him another son named Aeneas Silvius. (See Genealogical Chart 22.)

Meantime, at Carthage, Iarbas, former suitor to Dido, sacks the city and assumes leadership.

The poet Ovid tells an amusing sequel in Book 3 of his poem *Fasti* ("Holidays"), lines 545–656. According to him, after Dido's suicide, her rejected suitor Iarbas did sack the city of Carthage and take over the palace. "At last, I'm in Dido's bedroom!" he gloated.

Aeneas meets Dido's sister, Anna, who has escaped from their brother, Pygmalion.

Anna, whose evil brother Pygmalion was still after her, then took to the sea. After many perils, including a dangerous storm, she landed in Italy. There she came upon Aeneas, who happened to be walking on the beach with Achates. Aeneas wondered whether to run off, but he apologized to Anna for causing her sister's death: "I swear to you, it was the gods who were angry about my delay in Carthage and forced me to leave. I had no idea your sister would kill herself. But you are welcome in my house because I owe much to you and your sister." Anna agreed to accompany him home, and when they arrived there, Aeneas said to Lavinia, "This woman is from Carthage, and a shipwreck drove her here. I hope that you will love her like a sister."

Anna of Carthage is transformed into a Roman deity, Anna Perenna.

Lavinia thought this was the woman whom Aeneas had loved in Carthage. She pretended to be agreeable, but secretly plotted to kill Anna. That night as Anna slept, Dido's ghost came to her and warned, "Get out of this house! Don't hesitate!" Anna rushed out through an open window. She fled until she came to the closest stream, where the river-god Numicius received her in his waves. She was transformed into a deity the Romans called Anna Perenna, whose rites they celebrated every year.

The death and deification of Aeneas

Aeneas ruled for three years only. When he died, Venus received him into the heavens, as Jupiter had promised she would. The Romans believed he set the precedent for others of their people who would be deified, including Julius Caesar and the Emperor Augustus.

Julius Caesar (100–44 BCE)

Augustus Caesar, a.k.a. Octavian (63 BCE–14 CE)

A. Review Exercises

1. **WHO'S WHO?** In the list of names that follows, circle the names of Aeneas' Trojan family, friends, companions, and allies. Underline the names of those who opposed Aeneas and his companions.

Juno	**Lausus**	**Menelaus**	**Helenus**	**Anchises**
Achates	**Juturna**	**Creusa**	**Turnus**	**Evander**
Ascanius	**Mezentius**	**Camilla**	**Venus**	**Celaeno**

2. **GEOGRAPHY, BY GOLLY!** The left-hand column is a list of places Aeneas visited in his travels. The right-hand column contains descriptions of these places. Match the place name with its proper description; write the correct letter in the space provided.

1. ____	Carthage	a.	The home of the Sibyl Deiphobe
2. ____	Alba Longa	b.	Underworld residence of fallen warriors
3. ____	Strophades	c.	Site of Anchises' funeral games and Trojan colony
4. ____	Elysium	d.	Where the Oracle of Apollo is located
5. ____	Tyre	e.	The location of the entrance to the Underworld
6. ____	Hesperia	f.	New home of Helenus and Andromache
7. ____	Drepanum	g.	Land of the Harpies
8. ____	Cumae	h.	Place where Aeneas' descendants would rule 300 years until the founding of Rome
9. ____	Crete	i.	Resting place of the Just and the Good
10. ____	Avernus	j.	Phoenician colony in North Africa
11. ____	Buthrotum	k.	A city of Phoenicia (Lebanon)
12. ____	Thrace	l.	First landing place for the Trojans; Polydorus' resting place
13. ____	Delos	m.	City located in Asia Minor, home of Aeneas
14. ____	Fields of Mourning	n.	Where the Trojans suffer plague and the Penates say, "Leave this place"
15. ____	Troy	o.	Italy

3. **MULTIPLE CHOICE!** For each sentence below, circle the number of the item that best answers the question or completes the statement.

a. Why didn't Aeneas realize that the Greeks had entered Troy by means of the wooden horse?

1. He was sleeping. 2. He had sailed away to Tenedos.
3. He was hiding. 4. His men had abandoned him.

b. The hatred of this god or goddess drove the Trojans in all their wanderings.

1. Jupiter 2. Juno
3. Venus 4. Juturna

c. Who was Aeneas' faithful helmsman, killed just before the Trojans reached Italy?

1. Palinurus 2. Ascanius
3. Achates 4. Anchises

d. From whom did Dido and her sister, Anna, flee from Phoenician Tyre to escape?

1. Dido's husband, Sychaeus 2. Their brother, Pygmalion
3. Their father 4. Dido's suitor, Iarbas

e. Disguised as a Tyrian, which deity appeared to Aeneas on the shore of Northern Africa to urge him to go to Carthage?

1. Jupiter 2. Venus
3. Mercury 4. Juno

f. Dido enjoyed the company of this child of Aeneas and encouraged him to sit on her lap.

1. Iulus 2. Achates
3. Anchises 4. Misenus

g. As Aeneas and his family escaped from Troy, they lost this family member in the chaos of the burning city.

1. Ascanius 2. Anchises
3. Creusa 4. Helenus

h. At Delos, Aeneas received the prophecy that he should seek his ancestral home. To where did Aeneas mistakenly think he should sail?

1. Carthage 2. Crete
3. Sicily 4. Athens

i. Who was Dido's deceased Phoenician husband?

1. Pygmalion
2. Sychaeus
3. Belus
4. Iarbas

j. Who, in madness, set fire to the Trojan ships?

1. Dido
2. Beroe
3. Creusa
4. Anna

k. Who was Aeneas' chief rival among his Italian opponents?

1. Pallas
2. Latinus
3. Turnus
4. Evander

l. This Greek leader of the Arcadians in Italy allied himself and his son to Aeneas.

1. Evander
2. Lausus
3. Mezentius
4. Faunus

m. Who was Camilla?

1. The daughter of Latinus and Amata
2. A warrior queen of the Volscians, one of the Italian allies
3. Queen of Carthage
4. A Trojan princess

n. This god convinced Juturna, the sister of Turnus, to yield to Fate and quit helping Turnus to escape.

1. Jupiter
2. Mercury
3. Apollo
4. Mars

o. With what event does Vergil's *Aeneid* close?

1. The wedding of Peleus and Thetis
2. The suicide of Dido
3. The death of Turnus at the hand of Aeneas
4. The Trojans' giving their name to the land they conquer

p. What does Anchises in the Underworld say will be Rome's greatest contribution to the world?

1. Sculpture
2. Government
3. Pleading cases
4. Astronomy

q. Which daughter of the king of the Latins did Aeneas marry?

1. Anna
2. Lavinia
3. Camilla
4. Juturna

r. In some versions of the myth, Anna Perenna (the Roman goddess of the new year) is identified with whom?

1. The sister of Dido
2. The wife of Aeneas
3. The mother of Lavinia
4. The sister of Turnus

s. Who authored the *Aeneid?*

1. Horace
2. Vergil
3. Apollonius
4. Ovid

t. Which phrase best describes Aeneas?

1. Crafty and clever
2. Loyal and devoted to fulfilling the gods' plans
3. Single-minded, Mars-like warrior
4. Egocentric dandy

B. Musings

1. Like Homer in the *Iliad* and *Odyssey,* Vergil invoked the Muse in the opening lines of his epic poem, the *Aeneid.* Obtain copies of the invocations from these three epic poems. What is similar? What is different?

2. Ancient writers spoke of the enormous power Vergil's poetry held over his listeners. In the painting at right, the artist, Ingres, captures the impact of the *Aeneid* on the family of the Emperor Augustus (27 BCE–14 CE). In this painting, Augustus, with his wife Livia gazing on, gently supports his sister, Octavia, who has fainted. She collapsed after hearing Vergil read the lines: "You will be Marcellus. . . ." (*Aeneid* 6.884ff.). For Octavia, the mention of the name "Marcellus" conjures the memory of her beloved, recently deceased only son, Marcellus. In this highly dramatic moment of the *Aeneid,* Vergil mythologizes Marcellus as he mythologizes other famous Romans like Julius Caesar.

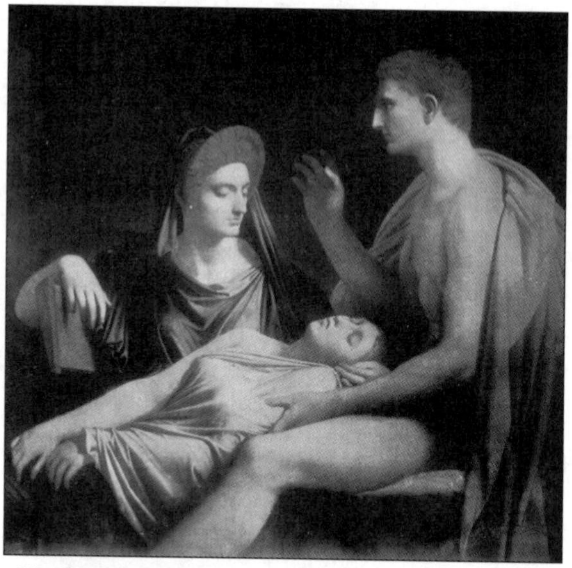

***Virgil Reading the Aeneid to Augustus, Octavia and Livia* (circa 1812) by Jean Auguste Dominique Ingres (1780–1867), Musee des Beaux-Arts, Brussels, Belgium. Note that the poet, Vergil, does not appear in the painting.**

a. Who was this young man, Marcellus, anyway? Research the life of Marcus Claudius Marcellus (42–23 BCE) and report back to your class on what you learned.

b. This dramatic reading of the *Aeneid* was only one of several classical and/or mythological subjects painted by Jean Auguste Dominique Ingres. Look online or in an art history book to find another of this artist's works with a subject from classical myth.

3. The English composer Henry Purcell wrote an opera, *Dido and Aeneas,* which was first performed in or about 1689. Not only is it one of the earliest operas written in English, but it is probably one of the best ever written in English. It is based on the love story of Dido and Aeneas, but Purcell introduces some significant changes. Read a summary of this opera and listen to the magnificent final aria, "Dido's Lament."

4. Hector Berlioz wrote an opera in six acts called *Les Troyens* (1863). This opera (written in French) tells the story of Aeneas and the Trojans. It opens with the introduction of the wooden horse, continues with the Trojans' escape from Troy, and concludes with Aeneas' arrival at Carthage and Dido's suicide. Note the first name of the composer! Do you think his name might have influenced his choice of topics in writing this piece? Research the life of Berlioz and see whether you can find an answer. Listen to the music of the "Trojan March" from part 2, act 1. The music was written in a minor key to accompany the Trojans' entrance, with Ascanius leading the way, to the court of Dido.

5. To a Roman reading or listening to the *Aeneid,* the idea of Aeneas falling in love with a Carthaginian queen would have seemed shocking in light of Roman history. Explain this.

6. Aeneas had a goddess mother and a mortal father. Can you think of another hero who shared a similar parentage?

7. Many phrases from Vergil's *Aeneid* have become famous; some of these phrases are listed below. The numbers in parentheses indicate the book and line in the *Aeneid* where the phrase is located. Choose a phrase and complete one or more of the following activities:

   a. Write the phrase on a poster. Include an illustration showing either the context of the phrase within the *Aeneid* or some other situation you think applies.

   b. Adopt one of the phrases as your personal motto. Design a shield or seal featuring the phrase. Include other information about you that shows why you chose it.

   c. Write a short story illustrating the truth or falsehood of the phrase.

   The phrases:

   Arma virumque cano (1.1): I sing of arms and a man

   Auri sacra fames (3.57): Accursed hunger for gold

   Dux femina facti (1.364): A woman [was] the leader of the deed

   Fama volat (8.554): Rumor flies

   Haec olim meminisse iuvabit (1.203): It will give pleasure to remember these things someday

   Imperium sine fine (1.279): Rule without end

   Non ignara mali, miseris succurrere disco (1.630): Not unacquainted with evils, I learn to help the unhappy

   Pendent opera interrupta (4.88): Jobs interrupted are left hanging

   Possunt quia posse videntur (5.281): They can because they think they can

Sunt lacrimae rerum (1.462): There are tears for things

Timeo Danaos et dona ferentes (2.49): I fear Greeks, even bearing gifts (sometimes translated as "Beware of Greeks bearing gifts")

Una salus victis nullam sperare salutem (2.354): The one hope for the conquered [is] to hope for no safety (cf. the line in the song "Me and Bobby McGee" about what freedom means)

C. WORDS, WORDS, WORDS

The Daily Muse

News you can use

Dux, the leader!

Aeneas was the ***dux*** (Latin for "leader") of the Trojans. Vergil tells us that Dido was also a ***dux*** (***Dux*** *femina facti,* "A woman was leader of the deed") of the Carthaginians. The Latin word ***dux*** is rooted in yet another old-time Indo-European word, *deuk-*, which means "to lead."

What English word do you know that comes from ***dux*** and means "a high-ranking noble," whose powers are just below that of a king? ________________________________

This word ***dux*** (***-du-, -duc-, -duct***) lies at the root of quite literally hundreds of English words like "produce," "introduction," and "subdue." These words, derived from a Latin root, are called *derivative* words.

In the spaces below, list at least ten derivative words that have the forms ***du, duc,*** or ***duct*** as a root. Identify the part of speech of each word you have listed (noun, verb, adjective, or adverb). Compare your list with lists made by your classmates.

Derivative Words	Part of Speech
1.	
2.	
3.	
4.	
5.	
6.	
7.	
8.	
9.	
10.	

D. How 'Bout That?

Aeneas and the Internet

Did you know that "Aeneas" is the name of an Internet telephone service provider? The establishment's web page offers this as an explanation for the choice of name: "Like our services crossing great distances to bring people together in communication, Vergil's Aeneas is a model of leadership not limited by geographic boundaries. His worthiness of his people's trust acts as a model of our dedication to our customers and our responsibility to those we serve." To learn more, visit: www.aeneas.net/about.shtml.

Anna Perenna

The feast of the Roman deity, Anna Perenna, the personification of the New Year, was celebrated on the Ides of March, March 15. The Romans worshipped her in a sacred grove near the Via Flaminia. Anna Perenna is often identified with Anna, Dido's sister.

E. Who's Who?

- For the House of Troy and Priam's descendants, see Genealogical Chart 18.
- For Romulus' ancestry and family, and the chronology of the kings of Rome, see Genealogical Chart 22.

Chapter Nineteen
THE KINGS OF ROME

General Source:

Livy *Ab Urbe Condita* 1

Livy, early Rome's historian, never lets the facts get in the way of a good story.

The stories about Rome's founding are a mix of myth and history. Livy, the Roman historian who tells them, stated in the preface to his work that his chief purpose was to depict good role models for contemporary youth to imitate, and bad ones for them to avoid. He therefore was more interested in telling a good story than sticking to "facts" as we understand them. We may compare him in some ways to Parson Weems, who told the story of George Washington as a child admitting to cutting down a prized cherry tree. The lesson that one should tell the truth is more important than whether young Washington ever did such a deed.

Rhea Silvia gives birth to twins, Romulus and Remus, fathered by Mars.

After Aeneas' son Ascanius founded Alba Longa in Italy, his descendants ruled peacefully for three hundred years. After many generations, however, violence broke out between two brothers, Numitor and Amulius. Amulius drove his older brother off the throne and killed Numitor's son. He made Numitor's daughter, Rhea Silvia, a Vestal Virgin so that she would not bear children who would overthrow him. She nevertheless became pregnant by the god Mars, and gave birth to twin sons named Romulus and Remus. (See GENEALOGICAL CHART 22.) Amulius ordered the priestess to be imprisoned and the infants to be drowned in the Tiber River. By chance the river had overflowed its banks, making approach impossible to the place where the current was strongest. Those who had been ordered to expose the infants left the basket containing them on the riverbank, hoping they would drown anyway. A she-wolf heard their crying and came to them. While she gently nursed them, a shepherd named Faustulus came upon the scene and took the babies back to his wife Larentia to raise.

Representation of portrait bust of the Roman historian Livy

When the boys grew up, they embarked upon a Robin Hood–like pursuit: they attacked robbers laden with loot and distributed the goods among the shepherds. One time, the robbers fought back and captured Remus. They first took him to Amulius, but because the brothers had been poaching on Numitor's land, Remus was handed over to his great-uncle.

Representation of the bronze Capitoline Wolf, Musei Capitolini, Rome, Italy

Faustulus had long suspected that the two children he was raising were of royal blood, and he told Romulus his suspicions. When Numitor learned that his prisoner had a twin, he compared Remus' age with the number of years that had lapsed since the infants had been exposed. When the truth came out, the brothers formed two separate groups and surrounded Amulius on all sides. He was killed in the resultant coup, and Numitor was restored to the throne of Alba Longa.

Italy in the Time of the Kings

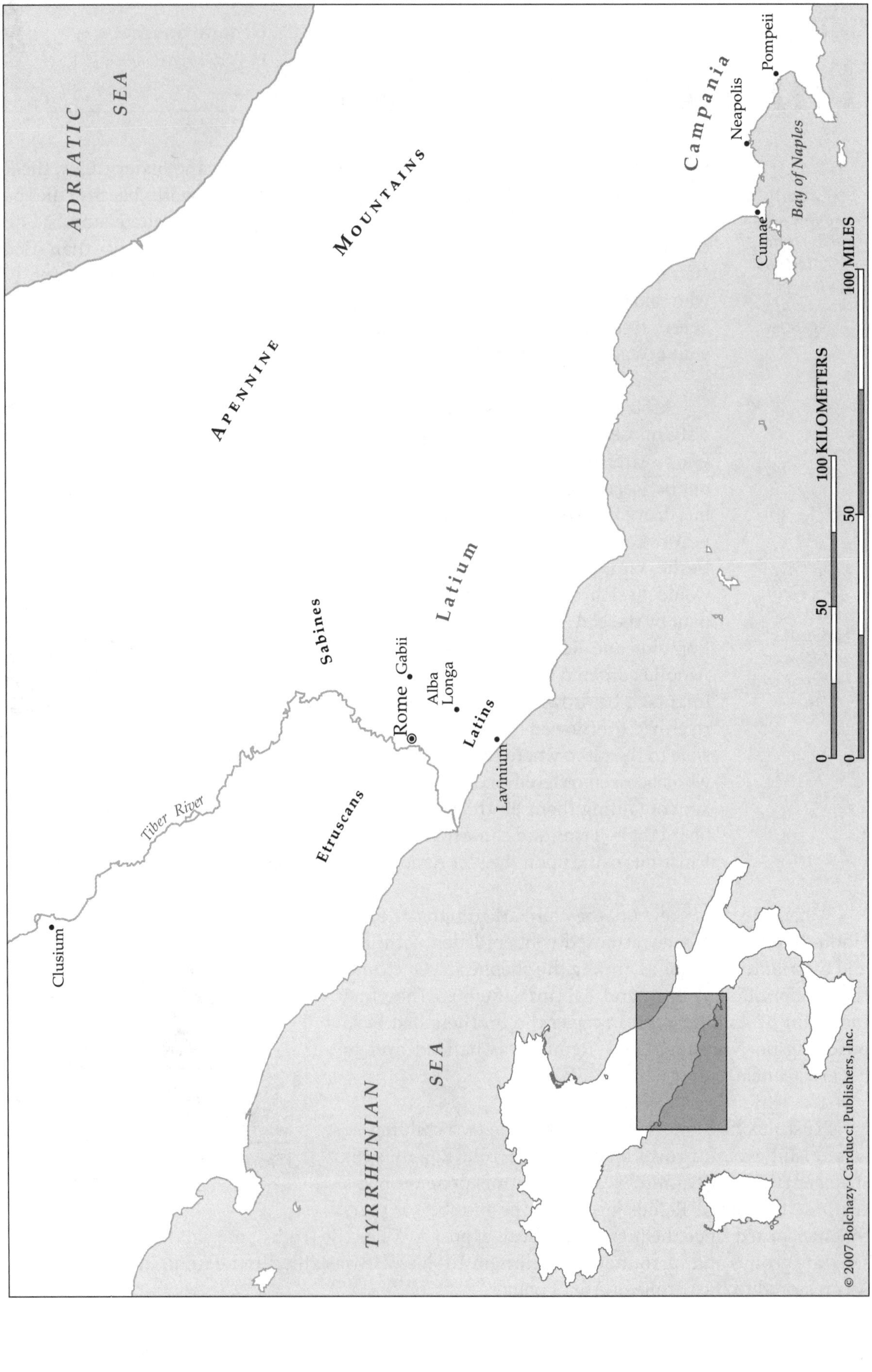

Romulus establishes the city Rome on the Palatine Hill.

Romulus and Remus now wished to establish a city on the spot where they had been exposed. The desire for kingly supremacy followed them like a family curse, however, and they decided to compete for the throne by using bird omens. Romulus stood watch on the Palatine Hill and Remus on the Aventine Hill. Remus was the first to see an omen, six vultures flying overhead. After this had been reported to the people, Romulus saw twelve vultures flying over him. A fight broke out between the brothers' bands of supporters, and Remus was killed in the melee. Another story is that after Romulus took control he began to build up the city's walls. Remus said, "Ha! Do you think those walls can keep anyone out?" and leaped over them. Romulus killed him and declared, "Let the same thing happen to anyone else who breaches my walls!"

Origins of the senate and the patricians

The new city, now called Rome in honor of Romulus, attracted a motley group of men who were eager for a fresh start in life in a place where there was no distinction between slaves and free people. Romulus established laws, adopted royal paraphernalia, and selected a group of wise elders to advise him. These were called senators, from the Latin word for "old man" (*senex*). They were also called *patres*, or "fathers," and their descendants were called patricians. One thing was lacking, however: women. The city would not last for more than one generation if the men did not find brides soon. Romulus sent embassies to all of the neighboring cities to seek women, but the ambassadors were rebuffed everywhere.

Roman senators wore purple-bordered togas and red shoes.

Romulus invites the neighboring Sabines to Rome for the festival of Neptune.

The king had a scheme. He established festival games in honor of Neptune, issued invitations to the neighboring cities, and made preparations for all the pageantry that he could. Many attended, including those from the nearby nation of the Sabines. The visitors were amazed at how much the city had grown in such a short time. All were absorbed in Romulus' games, when suddenly, at a prearranged signal from the king, soldiers rushed forth and seized the women, both married and unmarried.

Pen and ink reproduction of *The Sabine Women*, 1799, by Jacques Louis David (1748–1825), Louvre, Paris

Rome: the Seven Hills and the Tiber River

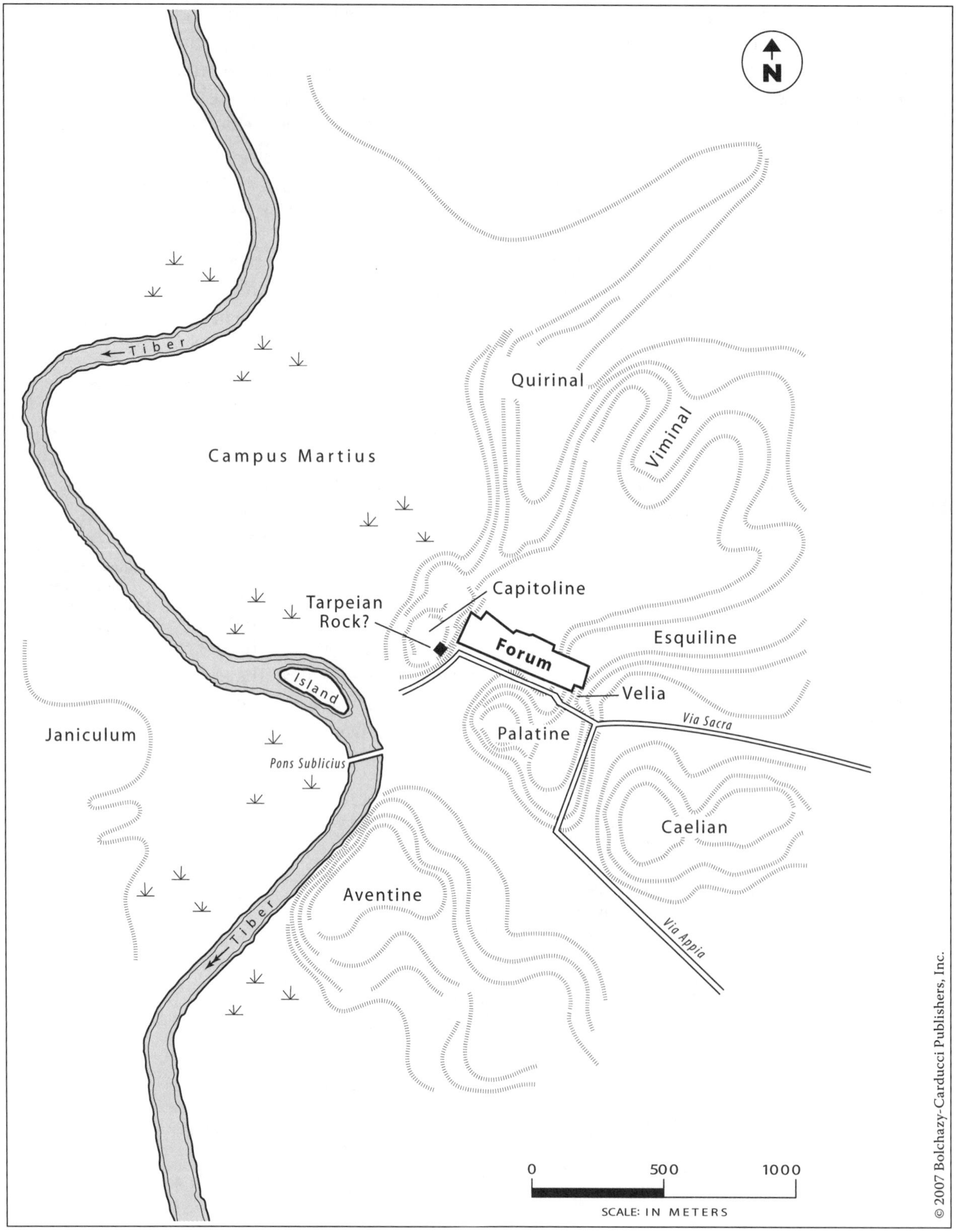

(Map adapted from Peter J. Aicher, *Rome Alive: A Source-Guide to the Ancient City,* Volume I.
© 2006 Bolchazy-Carducci Publishers, Inc.)

The Romans seize the Sabine women and make them their wives.

The outraged Sabines protested that the Romans had violated the sacred laws of hospitality. They went home to prepare for war. However, Romulus spoke words of reassurance to the abducted women: "Those to blame for what happened to you are your parents, who refused to intermarry with us. Nevertheless, you will all enjoy full rights as wives and, in time, as mothers. Do not be angry, but give your hearts to the men who have you now. In time, affection will replace resentment. Your husbands will be especially kind to you and will do their best to fill the void left by your loss of parents and country." The husbands added their own words of entreaty, and in time they won the women over.

Tarpeia betrays Rome to the Sabines and is hurled from the citadel.

The parents were still angry, however. The communities flocked from all sides to the king of the Sabines, Titus Tatius, and went to war on Rome. They used subterfuge as well as military force. Tatius approached a young woman named Tarpeia, the daughter of the citadel's commander. He asked for her help in taking the citadel.

"If I do," she said flirtatiously, greedily eyeing the soldiers' golden bracelets, "will you give me what you have on your left arms?" The Sabines agreed, and she admitted them into the city. "Now, how about my reward?" she asked.

Roman Tarpeia bargains with Titus Tatius (helmeted) and other Sabine warriors.

"Here it is!" they cried, and crushed her to death under their shields, which they carried on their left arms. They threw her body over the cliff, where the Romans executed criminals ever after. It would be known as the Tarpeian Rock.

Romulus promises to build a temple to Jupiter on the Capitoline Hill.

Seeing that the Sabines had taken control of the citadel, Romulus prayed: "Jupiter, you sent your sign to me on this hill. Stop the enemy from seizing it! I promise you a temple on this site, to remind posterity that the city was saved with your help!" Then, as if he sensed that his prayer had been heard, he cried, "Romans! Jupiter commands us to renew the fight on this spot!" The Romans rallied and were gaining the upper hand, when the women intervened, rushing into the thick of battle. "Stop!" they shouted. "We have family we love on both sides of this war. Don't kill each other on our account! Kill us instead! We'd rather die than be widows and orphans!" Their appeal moved both leaders, who made a treaty on the spot. Romulus and Titus Tatius agreed to share the kingship, and they ruled harmoniously until Tatius was killed during another war.

Romulus shares power with the Sabine leader, Titus Tatius.

After his death, Romulus is deified by the Romans as Quirinus.

Romulus continued to lead his nation in war and peace for many years. His passing was mysterious. One day, while he was reviewing his troops, a sudden storm arose with mighty claps of thunder, and enveloped him in a dense cloud. When the storm passed, the king's throne was empty, and Romulus was never seen on earth again. (See GENEALOGICAL CHART 23.) Onlookers proclaimed Romulus' divinity; thereafter, the Romans worshipped him as a god named Quirinus. The Romans sometimes referred to themselves as Quirites, the sons of Romulus.

The Sabine Numa Pompilius becomes Rome's second king.

A column capitol from the Ducal Palace arcade in Venice, early 15th century CE, depicting an anachronistic Numa Pompilius with Egeria, building a church. Numa evidently was considered one of the "virtuous Roman pagans."

It was uncertain who would hold the power after Romulus. A man in a Sabine town, Numa Pompilius, was famous for his justice and piety. Romans were reluctant to choose a Sabine man, yet could see no reason to oppose his kingship. The rightness of his appointment was confirmed by augury. An augur stood with Numa in the middle of a field, and prayed, "Father Jupiter, if it is heaven's will that Numa become king of Rome, send us indisputable signs within the bounds of this field." Livy does not say what signs the augur was looking for, only that he received them and that Numa was declared king.

Numa's wife, the nymph Egeria, advises him about religious practices.

After he received the power in this way, Numa determined to reform Roman justice, law, and religion. He made the temple of Janus an indicator of peace and war: the temple's gates were open during wartime and closed during peacetime. Numa believed that continual warfare brutalizes the soul, so he made treaties of alliance with Rome's neighboring peoples. He realized that people who had previously been orderly through fear of their neighbors might become rebellious in peace. Therefore, he sought to make them well behaved through fear of the gods. He made it known that his wife was a goddess named Egeria, who gave him advice when he visited her in a grotto supplied by a fountain of ever-flowing water.

Numa also reformed the calendar, dividing the year into twelve months according to the phases of the moon. His calendar included days on which one could not conduct public business. He instituted various priesthoods as well. The Romans became so devout that their neighbors considered it sacrilege to attack such religious people, and left them alone. Numa died after forty-three years of peaceful rule.

Numa Pompilius meets Egeria at her grotto.

Tullus Hostilius becomes the third king of Rome.

The next king, Tullus Hostilius, was the grandson of a man who had bravely defended the citadel under Romulus. He was even more combative than Romulus, and decided that the Romans had become weak during the years of Numa's reign. It so happened that the Romans and the nearby Albans (of Alba Longa) had been conducting cattle raids on each other's territory. Each city sent envoys to the other at almost the same time. Tullus had instructed his men to carry out their mission quickly, knowing that the Albans would refuse and he could thus declare war in good conscience. At the same time, he conducted his own business with the Alban ambassadors at a slow pace. While the Albans were enjoying a banquet with the king, the Roman ambassadors demanded satisfaction. When they did not receive it, they declared war upon the Albans. Tullus said to his Alban guests, "Tell your king that the king of Rome has the gods on his side! They saw who rejected whose overtures of peace! The guilty ones will be defeated in this war!"

Both sides then made preparation for what was virtually a civil war, as both peoples were descended from the Trojans whom Aeneas had brought to the land of Italy. After the armies had assembled, the Albans' leader Mettius Fufetius made a proposal to Tullus: "Your official position for starting this war is that we broke our treaty with you. But let's be honest: the desire to dominate one another is the real reason we're here. Let me remind you, however, that the Etruscans are threatening both of us. We will suffer losses fighting each other, and then the Etruscans will defeat us both. Is there a way we can settle this power struggle without massive losses and bloodshed?"

The Roman Horatii triplet brothers fight the Alban Curiatii triplets.

Tullus agreed. It happened that each side had triplet brothers, the Horatii (on the Roman side) and the Curiatii (on the Alban). The leaders agreed that these six would fight it out, and the winner's nation would rule the loser's. The champions took up their arms, and the remaining soldiers settled down to watch. They were all nervous, knowing that the fate of their nation depended upon the skill and courage of so few.

The last surviving Roman brother, Horatius, prevails over the Curiatii.

Both sides fought fiercely. Two of the Romans were killed first, but not before they had wounded all three Albans. The Albans cheered and the Romans despaired, as their only surviving man was now surrounded and outnumbered. However, Horatius was not injured, and he had a plan. He knew he could not defeat three at once, but that he could fight them individually. He therefore took to flight to separate them, knowing that they would be hampered by their wounds. As he looked behind him, he saw two far off and one closing in on him. He turned and attacked ferociously, as the Romans loudly encouraged him. Their cheers gave him strength to fell the second man. Now it was one against one, but they were not on equal terms; the Roman was still unhurt and the Alban was not. Horatius cried, "I killed the first two for my brothers. This one is for Rome!" He buried his sword in the last Alban's throat, and stripped the corpse.

Reproduction of *The Oath of the Horatii*, ca. 1784, by Jacques Louis David (1748–1825), Louvre, Paris

The Romans returned to the city in triumph, with Horatius at the front bearing the three men's spoils. He was met at the city gate by his sister, who had been engaged to one of the Curiatii. When she saw her brother wearing her fiancé's military cloak, which she herself had made, she immediately began wailing and calling the dead man's name.

Horatius slays his sister, Horatia, who weeps at the sight of the military cloak of her fiancé, Curiatius.

Her weeping enraged the hot-tempered Horatius, coming as it did in the moment of his triumph. He drew his sword and stabbed her in the heart, crying out, "Go to your beloved, as you don't care about your brothers or me or your country! Let this happen to any Roman woman who mourns an enemy!"

Although the senators and people admired Horatius' courage on the battlefield, they were shocked at his action. He was arrested and taken to the king for justice. However, Tullus was reluctant to convict him because it was repugnant to him and would be unpopular with the people. In accordance with the law, he therefore appointed a two-man board to judge Horatius. They felt that they had no choice but to find him guilty, but as his hands were being bound, Tullus prompted him to ask for an appeal. The appeal was taken before the people, who were greatly influenced by the eloquence of the defendant's father, who said, "A short time ago I was the proud father of a large family. Now I beg you not to take away my one remaining child." He embraced the young man and pointed to the spoils of the Curiatii. "Do you really want to hang a man you have just honored? Could you beat to death the liberator of the city? The enemies themselves would shudder at the sight!" The people acquitted Horatius out of respect for his courage and his father's grief.

Peace with Alba Longa did not last long. Mettius' countrymen were displeased that he had allowed the outcome of the war to be in the hands of a few, so Mettius incited neighboring states to attack Rome. When one of these states broke into open revolt against Rome, Tullus summoned Mettius and his army from Alba and marched out against them. After he defeated them, Tullus announced, "It was Mettius who broke the treaty and instigated the war. I intend to single him out as an example to anyone who contemplates such a breach of faith in the future." He had two four-horse teams of chariots brought forward. Mettius was tied to each of the chariots, which were sent off in opposite directions. All averted their eyes from the hideous sight, and that was the last time the Romans used such a primitive punishment.

Tullus orders the evacuation and destruction of Alba Longa.

Tullus ordered all of the Albans evacuated and transplanted to Rome, while the legions leveled the city. The refugees stood on their doorsteps, asking their neighbors, "What do we do now?" Or they wandered aimlessly through houses that were theirs for the last time. At last they filed sadly from their homes, passing the temples where they had once worshipped, leaving their gods behind like prisoners of war. When the Albans had gone, the Romans pulled down all the buildings. They destroyed in one hour what it had taken four hundred years to build.

Tullus defeats the Sabines but antagonizes the gods, who demand sacrifices.

Pestilence strikes the Roman army, and a Jovian thunderbolt kills Tullus.

Tullus next fought and defeated the Sabines. Yet there were signs of the gods' displeasure. It was reported that stones had rained from the sky on Mount Alba. The Romans did not believe this, and sent out a delegation to investigate. The delegates witnessed for themselves the stones falling and piling up in drifts. They also heard, or thought they heard, a voice from the sky saying, "Albans, you have abandoned your ancestors' religious customs! Romans, you must perform sacrifices for nine days!" Both peoples hastened to honor the gods, but not much later a pestilence struck. At first, Tullus refused to abandon his warlike ways, believing that the soldiers would recover more quickly in active service than at home. Then he himself was stricken, and for the first time in his life he became religious. People began to say, "This never would have happened under King Numa! The only release from this sickness is the pardon of the gods!" Tullus began to consult Numa's writings privately, and he discovered certain secret sacrifices to Jupiter. He hid himself away to perform them, but because he did them incorrectly, Jupiter not only refused to grant the king's prayers, he blasted him with a thunderbolt. The king and palace were destroyed together.

Ancus Marcius, Numa's grandson, becomes Rome's fourth king.

The fourth king was Ancus Marcius, a grandson of Numa Pompilius. He was well aware of his grandfather's reputation, and he realized that the previous reign had gone wrong because of neglect of religion. However, he also had Romulus' fighting spirit, and realized that the times needed a king who was more like Tullus than Numa. Adding to the religious ceremonies Numa had instituted for peacetime, Ancus devised ritual procedures for declaring and waging war. If the Romans felt they had been wronged by another nation, an envoy would go to the borders of that nation, and call out, "Hear me, Jupiter and Faith! I speak for the Roman people. . . ." he would then name his demands, and conclude, "If my demands are unjust, may I never see my native land again!" He would repeat this when he crossed the border, when he met the first inhabitant, when he entered the city gates, and when he entered the marketplace. If restitution did not come within thirty-three days, he said again, "Hear me, Jupiter and all gods! I call you to witness that these people are unjust!" He then returned to Rome and consulted with the king and senators about whether to go to war. If they decided to do so, a priest would carry a spear to the offending nation, declare war in the presence of at least three men of military age, and throw the spear into their territory.

Ancus annexes more land and local towns, increasing Rome's size and population.

Ancus took over several other surrounding towns and relocated their people to Rome. He settled them on various hills in the city, and also annexed the Janiculum Hill as a stronghold. He built the first wooden bridge across the Tiber River to connect this hill with the rest of the city. To curb the growing lawlessness brought on by the increased population, he established Rome's first prison in the center of the city overlooking the Forum. He also extended Rome's boundaries, and founded Rome's seaport Ostia at the mouth of the Tiber.

Lucumo and his wife, Tanaquil, leave Etruria to seek a new situation at Rome.

During the reign of Ancus, a wealthy and energetic man named Lucumo migrated to Rome. He had not been able to achieve high public standing in his native Etruscan city of Tarquinii, a situation that was not pleasing to him or his wife, a high-born lady named Tanaquil. She could not bear the thought of losing status through her marriage, and she was determined to see him elevated to high office. Realizing that the foreign-born could rise in Rome through their merit, they packed their belongings and headed for Rome. When they had reached the Janiculum, an eagle suddenly swooped down. With one motion, it snatched off the cap that Lucumo was wearing, flew screaming over the wagon, and then placed the cap deftly back on his head. Like many Etruscan women, Tanaquil was skilled in the interpretation of omens. She excitedly embraced her husband, declaring, "This means something great is in store for you! The eagle is the bird of Jupiter, and it crowned you!"

Lucumo changes his name to L. Tarquinius Priscus and serves as tutor to Ancus' sons.

Lucumo changed his name to Lucius Tarquinius Priscus. Very soon, influential Romans were familiar with the newcomer, who made many friends through his agreeable ways, hospitality, and generosity. He gradually made himself useful to Ancus and was eventually placed in charge of tutoring the king's sons.

When Ancus Marcius dies, Priscus seizes power, becoming the fifth king.

When Ancus died after twenty-four years of reign, Priscus embarked upon a scheme to seize the throne. He sent Ancus' sons on a hunting expedition, and then began campaigning among the people. "I am not seeking anything unusual," he pointed out. "Foreigners have ruled Rome before. Titus Tatius was not only a foreigner, he was once an enemy! Numa Pompilius knew nothing about this city before he was chosen king! I came to Rome as soon as I was of age, and I have served the city since then. I have learned your laws and religious customs under the best of teachers, King Ancus Marcius himself! I have done as much for the king as anyone, and I have been comparable to him in serving others."

Priscus was overwhelmingly chosen king. To confirm his power, he elevated a hundred men of lesser families to the senate; they were grateful to him for their election and supported him in all things. Apart from the excessive ambition he showed to achieve power, he was a good king. He fought successful wars with the Sabines and the ancient Latins. He was also a builder; he erected a stone wall around the city, and he constructed sewers that drained off into the Tiber.

Priscus and Tanaquil raise a poor Roman boy, Servius Tullius, in their household.

A miraculous event occurred in the palace during his reign. The head of a slave boy named Servius Tullius burst into flame as he lay sleeping. Naturally, all those who saw this made an uproar, bringing the king and queen to the scene. The servants wanted to fetch water, but Tanaquil cried, "Wait! Quiet, everyone! Don't disturb him, but let him wake up by himself." Unaware of the fuss around him, the child awoke and the flames went away.

Servius Tullius is betrothed to the daughter of Tarquinius Priscus.

Tanaquil took her husband aside and said, "This is no ordinary boy being raised in such humble circumstances in our house! He is destined to rule one day. We should educate him as a prince." From then on, Servius was raised as their own son, even though he was the child of slaves. Priscus could find none of the Roman youth to compare with Servius, and he betrothed his own daughter to him.

The sons of Ancus Marcius murder Tarquinius Priscus in his residence.

By the thirty-eighth year of Priscus' reign, Servius was highly regarded not only by the king but by the senators and common people. The sons of Ancus Marcius, however, had long been resentful that a foreigner such as Priscus had taken a position they saw as their own. When it looked as though a slave-born man would succeed Priscus instead of them, their sense of outrage became too much and they planned revenge. Because they were more angry with Priscus than Servius, their plot was directed against the king. They conscripted two unruly shepherds who staged a loud fight in the forecourt of the palace. Both bellowed for the king at the top of their lungs, and the king ordered them inside so that he could hear their case. At first they continued to abuse each other, shouting at the same time, but when one of the king's attendants commanded, "One at a time!" they quieted down. As one was presenting his case and Priscus listened attentively, the other crept up behind the king and brought down an axe on his head. They fled, leaving the axe buried in Priscus' head. The king's attendants seized the pair immediately.

Tanaquil conceals the murder and encourages Servius to seize power.

During the commotion, Tanaquil ordered the palace to be sealed off and any witnesses sent home. She made preparations for treating the king's wound as if he were still alive and could recover. At the same time, she summoned Servius and told him, "Do not allow your father-in-law to be unavenged or your mother-in-law to be ridiculed by her enemies. The throne is yours, if you have courage! Don't let it pass to those who let others do their dirty work for them! Obey the will of the gods, who long ago encircled your head with fire. Don't think of your humble origin, think of the kind of man you are now! If your mind is too confused to make plans right now, follow mine!"

Noisy crowds gathered around the palace and could no longer be ignored. Tanaquil addressed them from an upstairs window: "Be hopeful! The king has a concussion and a surface wound, but he has regained consciousness and should be able to appear before you very soon. In the meantime, Servius Tullius will be taking over the royal duties."

Priscus' death is revealed; Servius is approved king by the senate without popular election, and marries his daughters, both named Tullia, to Tarquinius' sons, Arruns and Lucius.

Servius made an appearance wearing the royal robes. He took his seat on the throne and made certain decisions, but pretended he needed to consult with Priscus on others. Priscus' death was concealed for days, while Servius' position on the throne was strengthened. Then at last, Tanaquil allowed those in the palace to begin the ritual lament, announcing the death of Priscus. Servius thus became the first of the kings to rule without being elected by the people, although the senate approved of him. The sons of Ancus went into exile after they learned that their hired assassins had been caught and the king was supposedly still alive. In order to avoid the kind of hostility that had killed Priscus, Servius married off his two daughters (both named Tullia) to the two sons of Priscus: Arruns and Lucius.

Servius gained popularity with the people after successful wars against several surrounding states. Domestically, he established the first census, a means of counting the citizens of Rome and how much property each owned. He annexed more hills to the city to house the ever-increasing population. Servius heard that a temple of Diana had been built in Ephesus as a cooperative effort by the people of Asia Minor, so he had a similar one built in Rome in conjunction with members of the Latin nobility. He won favor with the common people by dividing up land captured from the enemy among them. Belatedly, Servius asked for their formal consent to his rule, and he received it with more unanimity than any of his predecessors.

His downfall came from within his own household. One of his sons-in-law, the ambitious Lucius Tarquinius, wanted the throne for himself and saw his opportunity when he saw that the senators did not wholly approve of Servius' land distribution. Lucius Tarquinius gained their favor by denouncing the king on the senate floor. His brother, Arruns, was a very gentle sort of man. It happened that Servius' two daughers were also of opposite character. The good Tullia was married to the evil Lucius; the bad Tullia was married to the good Arruns. The bad Tullia was unhappy that her husband (Arruns) lacked fire and ambition. She therefore turned to his brother (Lucius), telling him that he was a real man and true son of a king. She also ridiculed her sister for being married to such a fine specimen of manhood and for lacking the backbone to support his plans. The two ruthless people were drawn to each other. The evil Tullia kept denouncing her sister and her husband to Lucius, saying, "We're both being stifled in our marriages to these spineless people! We would have been better off unmarried than married to such unsuitable partners!" In time, she induced Lucius to kill his wife while she herself killed her husband Arruns, and they married each other.

Once she was married to Lucius, she kept badgering him, reminding him that his father had not just hoped for the throne, but had grabbed it. She added, "If you are the man I think you are, I salute you as husband and king. If not, then I'm even worse off than before, because my husband is not just a coward but a criminal. Why don't you act? Think of your royal blood! If you keep on disappointing everyone's hopes, then you should stop acting like a prince of the royal family and just slink back to the Tarquinii!" She goaded him with taunts like this, but was equally hard on herself. "How is it that Tanaquil, a foreign woman, could make *two* men kings but I can't make any headway with one? And I'm of royal blood!" she thought.

Driven by both his own and his wife's ambition, Lucius sought favor wherever he could, especially among the senators of lesser families whom his father had supported. Finally, he was ready to make his move. He entered the Forum with a band of armed men and took the king's seat at the entrance to the senate house. He then ordered a herald to summon the senators to the presence of King Tarquinius. The senators assembled, some because he had told them to be there, others because they feared their absence would be noted and would get them in trouble. All believed that Servius was doomed. Lucius Tarquinius attacked Servius: "He was a slave born of a slave! After my father's shameful murder, he seized the throne without observing any of the proper procedures! His throne was the gift of a woman! When he was king, he championed the dregs of society from which he himself had come. In his hatred for the nobility of others, he took the land that should have been theirs and gave it to trash! All the burdens that used to be shared are now shouldered only by the nation's leaders! He created the census to make the rich an object of jealousy!"

While he was haranguing the senators in this way, Servius burst into the senate chamber. "What is the meaning of this, Lucius? How dare you summon the senate and sit in my place?"

Lucius Tarquinius seizes power and throws Servius down the steps; Tullia drives her carriage over the corpse.

Lucius retorted, "I'm in my father's seat, and I have a better claim to it than you! You've lorded it over your betters long enough!" By now the senate chamber was very crowded, and the supporters of each man began fighting one another. Lucius then made his boldest move. He seized Servius around the waist, carried him out of the chamber, and flung him down the stairs. He then returned to the chamber and ordered the senators to sit back down. Servius managed to rise. Assisted by his bodyguards, he began heading back to the palace. But Lucius sent men after him and cut him down. Tullia rode into the forum on a wagon and called out, "Hail, King Lucius Tarquinius!" Lucius ordered her, "Go back home, it's dangerous here!" She did so, but on the way home, she ran over her father's body in the road with her wagon and spattered herself with his blood. This street was known as Crime Street ever after.

Lucius Tarquinius Superbus is Rome's seventh king.

The death of Servius after forty-four years of rule marked the end of just rule by kings in Rome. Lucius Tarquinius proved such an arrogant ruler that he was given the name Superbus, Latin for "the proud." He forbade the burial of his predecessor, justifying this by saying that Romulus had never received burial either. He killed off senators who had favored Servius. Because he was so unpopular, he surrounded himself with an armed guard all the time. He had many people arrested on false charges, and tried them in a court where he alone was judge and jury. In this way, he was able to execute, exile, and fine people whom he disliked or whose money he wanted. Instead of consulting with the senate on all matters, he deliberated only with his personal friends.

Tarquinius Superbus reluctantly purchases the Sibylline books.

One example of his poor judgment was not recorded in Livy, but in the early Christian writers. This occurred when the Sibyl of Cumae visited him bearing nine books, which she said contained many important prophecies. She named a high price for them, but Tarquinius Superbus refused her. She burned three volumes, then returned and offered to sell him the remaining six at the same price she had demanded for nine. Tarquinius Superbus told her, "You're crazy!" She burned an additional three and offered him the last three for the same price as the original nine. Tarquinius Superbus finally capitulated and obtained the three books for the price of nine. These became known as the Sibylline Books and were often consulted by the Romans for guidance on the future.

Tarquinius Superbus rejects the Sibyl.

Tarquinius proves the validity of the name "Superbus" by arrogant treatment of both Romans and their allies.

Tarquinius Superbus gained influence with the Latins, but he used the same underhanded tactics to obtain their support that he had used at home. On one occasion, he arranged a meeting with the Latins. He kept them waiting all day and arrived only a little before sunset. People grumbled about his absence, and one man named Turnus Herdonius was particularly vocal: "No wonder they call him Tarquinius the Proud! What could be more arrogant than the way he's treated us today! He summoned us here and then he stays away! He's trying to see how much abuse we're willing to take, because he wants control of us. Look at how he treats his own people! Why should we hope for better treatment? I say we all go back home and treat this meeting with the same contempt as the man who called it!"

Tarquinius Superbus appeared as Herdonius spoke. All fell silent, and the king explained his absence by saying that he had been obligated to act as a mediator between father and son and the case had taken all day.

Herdonius called out, "How could that take all day? Father-and-son disputes are simple: the son obeys the father or else!"

Tarquinius Superbus was very angered by this, but he did not reveal his emotions. He told the Latins that the meeting would be postponed until the following day, and then at once began to plot Herdonius' death. He bribed one of Herdonius' slaves to look the other way while he planted a bunch of swords in the man's tent. A little before dawn, Tarquinius Superbus summoned the other leaders of the Latins, pretending that he had made a shocking discovery. He said, "Divine providence was at work in my delay yesterday, and it saved both you and me! Herdonius is plotting to kill us and take over the nation of the Latins! You heard his belligerent remarks yesterday—he was angry because he wasn't able to carry out his plan! He will show up at the meeting today with a gang of armed men. If you don't believe me, go look at his tent—there's a stash of swords in it!" The Latins believed Tarquinius Superbus; they went to Herdonius' tent and found the weapons. Without giving the man a chance to explain, they threw him in a nearby river and buried him under a pile of stones.

Although skillful in war, Tarquinius Superbus frequently resorts to trickery.

Tarquinius Superbus had his strengths as well as his faults; he was quite accomplished in warfare, although this too was tainted by his deceptions. He went to war with a neighboring city, Gabii, which took longer than expected. When open attack was unsuccessful, he tried another tactic. He pretended to abandon the war in order to focus on domestic projects like a new temple. Then he sent his son Sextus into Gabii, ostensibly as a deserter. Sextus told the Gabians, "My father has finally turned his famous arrogance against his own family! He wants to kill us, just as he killed the senators! I don't think there's any safe haven for me anywhere except among his enemies! Don't think he's given up the war, either; you're not safe! He'll attack you by surprise at the first opportunity! If there's no place for suppliants like me here, I'll just keep traveling all through Latium until I find people who are willing to protect a son from an evil father. Maybe some of them will have the spirit to take up arms against the world's most arrogant king and warlike people."

The people of Gabii were sympathetic to him. "It was inevitable," they said, "that a man who made war on citizens and allies would eventually turn on his own family. You are welcome here, and with your help we should be able to defeat Rome."

Tarquinius uses his son, Sextus, who pretends to be a deserter from Rome, to defeat Gabii.

From then on, Sextus was a part of all the councils of state. He kept pushing the Gabians to reopen the war, and he went out with the soldiers himself. So well did he accomplish his missions that he was chosen as commander-in-chief. In the clashes between Romans and Gabians, the Gabians won more often than not. The soldiers loved him for his willingness to share their dangers and divide his loot with them.

When Sextus decided the time was right, he sent a confidant to Rome to ask the king what he should do now that all of Gabii was in his hands. Tarquinius said nothing; he simply strolled around his garden and lopped off the heads of the tallest flowers with his staff. The messenger grew tired of asking questions and receiving no response; he returned to Sextus and complained, "The king wouldn't say a word! He just cut off the heads of flowers!" Sextus, however, knew what his father's message was: "Kill the leaders of Gabii!" He used his own father's tactics to accomplish this, putting some to death on trumped-up charges and secretly killing those he could not frame. He offered others the option of exile. By redistributing the property of the slain and the exiled, he was able to maintain his own popularity with the people. In this way, Gabii passed into Roman hands without a fight.

Tarquinius completes the temple of Capitoline Jupiter and Rome's great sewer system, the Cloaca Maxima.

After taking over Gabii, Tarquinius turned his attention back to his building projects. He completed the great temple of Jupiter on the Capitoline Hill and constructed the Cloaca Maxima, the great sewer of Rome. In the midst of his activities, however, an omen frightened him: a serpent darted out from behind a wooden column. He sent two of his sons, Titus and Arruns, to the oracle of Delphi to find out what this meant. Their cousin Lucius Junius Brutus accompanied them. This young man's last name meant "stupid," because he pretended to be dull-witted to protect himself from his uncle's schemes. He made an offering to Apollo that symbolized himself: a staff of gold hidden inside a staff of wood.

Tarquin's sons consult the Delphic oracle to learn which of them will become king.

While the sons of Tarquinius were at Delphi, they decided it would be a good idea to ask the oracle who would rule Rome next. The oracle's response was typically cryptic: "Whoever of you first kisses his mother shall have the supreme power in Rome next." Arruns and Titus decided to tell their brother Sextus nothing about this, in order to eliminate him as a possible candidate. They drew lots to decide which of them would kiss their mother as soon as they returned to Rome. Brutus, however, interpreted the oracle differently. Pretending to stumble, he fell to the ground and kissed the earth, the mother of all.

When the princes returned to Rome, they found the city at war again because Tarquinius needed to replenish the funds he had spent on his building projects. While Sextus Tarquinius was in his tent with some of the other officers, including his cousin Tarquinius Collatinus, the men began debating whose wife was the best. Each praised his own wife extravagantly; when the discussion grew heated, they decided, "Why argue? Let's ride back to town and see what the ladies are doing when they aren't expecting us!" They did so, and found all the wives enjoying themselves. When they arrived at Collatinus' hometown of Collatia, they found his wife Lucretia hard at work. Although it was late at night, Lucretia was still spinning by candlelight, surrounded by her maids. She happily welcomed her husband and graciously invited the others with him to enter.

Sextus Tarquinius rapes his cousin's wife, Lucretia, an exemplar of a Roman matron's virtue.

Sextus was filled with desire by her beauty and goodness. A few days later, without Collatinus' knowledge, he returned to that house with a single companion. Suspecting nothing, Lucretia gave her guests hospitality and allowed them to stay the night. That night, he came to her bedroom with a sword in hand. "Quiet, Lucretia! It's Sextus Tarquinius. Make a sound and I'll kill you!" He confessed his feelings to her, but she would not yield, even at the cost of her life. Finally he threatened to place the naked body of a dead slave next to her corpse. Only then did she reluctantly submit.

After disclosing to her husband and father Sextus' crime against her, Lucretia kills herself.

After Sextus left the house, pleased with himself, Lucretia sent a message to her father and husband to come with one trusted companion each, because a terrible thing had happened. She wept when they arrived, and when they asked, "Are you all right?" she answered, "Not at all! Collatinus, another man has been in your bed, but only my body was violated, not my soul. Pledge that Sextus Tarquinius, who did this to me, will not go unpunished!" Although she had done nothing wrong, she believed that her virtue had been destroyed. She took a dagger she had hidden in her clothing and stabbed herself to death.

Lucius Junius Brutus, cousin of Collatinus, swears vengeance.

Brutus had accompanied Collatinus, and he pulled the dagger from Lucretia's body. Holding it up, he declared, "By this blood, which was pure before Sextus Tarquinius defiled it, I swear that I will drive Lucius Tarquinius Superbus and all his children out of Rome any way I can, and I will never allow anyone else to be king of Rome!" He then handed the dagger to the other three men present, who were astonished at the change in him. They took the same oath.

The men carried Lucretia's body from the house to the forum of Collatia, gathering a crowd as they went. They told the people what Sextus had done, and all were scandalized and outraged. Brutus rebuked them, "What good are your tears and complaints? Act like men and Romans! Fight against those who committed this crime!" The most daring young men rushed to take up arms, and the rest followed their lead. Brutus left a garrison in Collatia to prevent anyone's notifying the royal family that a revolt was brewing. He then led the rest of the rebels to Rome. People were as appalled there as they had been in Collatia. Brutus made a speech recounting all the crimes of the Tarquins, from the murder of Servius Tullius to Sextus' final outrage. He added that free men had been forced to do slave labor in the king's building projects. He ordered the exile of the king, together with wife and children. Tullia fled from her home, reviled by all. When word of the uprising reached the king in camp, he tried to return to Rome, but found the gates barred against him. In the camp, Brutus was hailed as a liberator and Titus and Arruns were driven away. They joined their father in exile in Etruria. Sextus fled to Gabii where he had once held power, but the citizens, intent on settling old scores, killed him.

Engraving of *The Death of Lucretia*, 1511–1512, after Raphael, by Marcantonio Raimondi (1480–1527), Museum of Fine Arts, Boston, Massachusetts

Brutus and Collatinus establish a republic at Rome and become the first consuls.

After 244 years of rule by kings, Rome became a republic. Lucius Junius Brutus and Lucius Tarquinius Collatinus were its first consuls; they functioned as copresidents.

In his attempt to regain the throne, the exiled Tarquinius Superbus asked his allies to attack Rome. In the subsequent fighting, several Roman men and women distinguished themselves. Here are the stories of three: Horatius Cocles, Gaius Mucius, and Cloelia.

Lars Porsenna, the Etruscan king of Clusium, marches on Rome.

One of the ex-monarch Tarquinius' most powerful allies was Lars Porsenna, the king of Clusium, an Etruscan state. The allies argued, "If kings do not defend their thrones, the highborn will soon find themselves on the same level as the lowly. Although it is the finest form of government, monarchy will become a thing of the past." Porsenna believed in monarchy also, and thought it would be good to have an Etruscan monarch in Rome. The senate was terrified when Porsenna and his army marched on the city, not only because he was a powerful enemy but because they feared the common people would be willing to surrender their liberty for peace. Both country and city folk took shelter within Rome's walls.

A Roman warrior, Horatius Cocles, defends a wooden bridge that spans the Tiber River.

The city was generally well protected by its walls and by the Tiber River, but a wooden bridge across the Tiber offered the enemy a path into Rome. The Etruscans might have invaded Rome in this way if a man named Horatius Cocles had not been guarding the bridge. He was stationed at the bridge when the Clusians seized Janiculum Hill. As the enemies charged over the hill, Horatius' comrades began to desert in panic. Horatius grabbed one man after another and shouted, "By all the gods, don't abandon your post! If the enemies cross the bridge, they'll be all over the Palatine and Capitoline! Break the bridge! Use whatever you have—fire, steel! I'll hold off the enemy!"

After holding off Porsenna and the Etruscans, Horatius leaps into the Tiber and escapes.

He stood at the entrance to the bridge, astonishing the Etruscans with his boldness. Two Roman men, Spurius Larcius and Titus Herminius, stood by Horatius. When only a small part of the bridge was left standing and those cutting it down cried out, "Get back! Get back!" he urged the two to flee to safety also. He glared defiantly at the Etruscan soldiers, taunting them, "You're all slaves to arrogant kings! You don't care about your own freedom, so you come to attack other people's!" They all threw their weapons at him, but the spears stuck in his shield. Horatius stood firm. The crash of the bridge breaking and the cheers of the Romans stopped the enemies in their tracks. Horatius cried out, "Father Tiber, I pray you, please receive this armed soldier in your waters!" He leaped into the river in full armor and, as the Etruscans' arrows bombarded him, he swam safely to his comrades on the other shore.

Another Roman, Gaius Mucius, attempts to assassinate Lars Porsenna.

After this, Porsenna abandoned his plan to take the city by storm. He decided to blockade the city instead to starve the Romans into submission. As grain grew scarce and prices skyrocketed, a young man named Gaius Mucius had a plan. He took it to the senate, not wishing to act without their permission. "Senators, I wish to enter the enemy camp, not to plunder, but to do . . . something greater." The senators granted his request, and he departed with a sword hidden in his clothing.

He managed to sneak into the camp, intending to assassinate Porsenna. There was only one problem: he did not know Porsenna by sight! It was payday, and a great crowd gathered around the king's secretary who was handing out their salaries. He was dressed very much like the king, so Mucius reasoned, "This man is well dressed, all the soldiers are crowding around him, and so he must be Porsenna!" He could not ask if that actually was the king without giving himself away, so he took the chance and stabbed the secretary to death. The king's bodyguards seized him at once and dragged him before Porsenna. Even though he was outnumbered, the others were more afraid of him than he was of them. He declared, "I am Gaius Mucius, a Roman citizen. I came here as an enemy to kill an enemy, and I'm not afraid to kill or die. There are many like me back in Rome, so if you want to continue this war, you should worry not only about open combat but about secret assassins!"

Angry and afraid, Porsenna tried intimidating Mucius. "Throw him into the fire, unless he explains these threats!" he commanded.

Mucius thrusts his right hand into a fire, proving his bravery and determination.

"Do you think those who seek glory care what happens to their bodies?" roared Mucius. "Look!" He thrust his right hand into the fire and held it there as though he felt no pain.

The king was dumbstruck. He ordered Mucius pulled back from the flames, and said, "You've done more harm to yourself than to me. If you were one of my countrymen, I would hail you as a hero. As you are not, I will release you unharmed."

Mucius responded, "Because you value courage so highly, I will tell you what my threats meant. Three hundred of our finest men have vowed to ambush you as I did. It was only by the luck of the draw that I came first. The others will keep on trying until one of them succeeds."

To honor Mucius' heroism, the senate gives him the cognomen of Scaevola, "Lefty."

Because of Mucius' action, Porsenna makes peace with Rome.

After Mucius returned to Rome, the senate awarded him the name of Scaevola, which means "Lefty," because he had burned off his right hand. They also awarded him a large tract of land. Mucius' courage gave Porsenna incentive to seek peace, as he dreaded the thought of 299 more assassins! He and his soldiers withdrew from the Janiculum, and the Romans demanded an exchange of hostages as pledges that the peace would be kept.

Mucius thrusts his hand into the fire to the astonishment of Lars Porsenna.

Cloelia, one of the hostages exchanged with Porsenna, swims across the Tiber to Rome, but the Romans return her to Porsenna, who, in turn, releases her unharmed.

One of these hostages was a young woman named Cloelia, who showed that females were capable of heroism as well as males. Because the camp was not far from the Tiber River, she and the other girls slipped past the guards and swam across the river as the enemy's weapons rained down on them. They all reached Rome safely. When the king learned of this, he was angry at first and demanded Cloelia's return; he was not much concerned about the others. At the same time, he realized that she had shown as much courage as Cocles and Mucius. He announced, "If this hostage is not returned, I will consider our agreement broken. But if she is given back, I will restore her to the Romans unharmed." Both sides kept their word. The Romans sent Cloelia back to Porsenna's camp, and he not only released her but allowed her to take a group of the remaining hostages with her. After the peace was re-established, the Romans honored Cloelia's courage by erecting a statue of a young woman on a horse at the head of the Sacred Way, the main road running through the Forum. As for the Tarquins, they went back into exile and did not try to seek royal power in Rome again.

A. Review Exercise

MULTIPLE CHOICE! For each sentence below, circle the letter of the answer that best answers the question or completes the statement.

1. How many men served as kings of Rome?

   a. Two
   b. Seven
   c. Ten
   d. Twelve

2. Who were the real parents of Romulus and Remus?

   a. Aeneas and Lavinia
   b. Faustulus and Larentia
   c. Rhea Silvia and Mars
   d. Anna Perenna and Turnus

3. Which of these hills was the first to be settled in the foundation laid by Romulus?

   a. Caelian
   b. Janiculum
   c. Palatine
   d. Aventine

4. In what position did the original Roman senators appointed by King Romulus serve?

   a. Military leaders
   b. Royal advisors
   c. Religious leaders
   d. Philosophers

5. Lacking women for wives, the Romans forcibly took wives from this people during the kingship of Romulus.

   a. Latins
   b. Albans
   c. Sabines
   d. Etruscans

6. In early times, the Romans sometimes referred to themselves by this name associated with Romulus.

   a. Oscans
   b. Gabians
   c. Quirites
   d. Homines

7. The Romans despised this woman because she betrayed Rome to the enemy.

   a. Tarpeia
   b. Camilla
   c. Tanaquil
   d. Lavinia

8. The second king, Numa Pompilius, sought the advice of this nymph in her grotto just outside the city. He is later said to have married her.

   a. Larentia
   b. Tarpeia
   c. Egeria
   d. Lucretia

9. Numa established the practice of opening the temple of this two-faced god in times of war and closing it in peacetime.

   a. Mars
   b. Quirinus
   c. Janus
   d. Jupiter

10. During the reign of Numa, what did the Romans become known for?

    a. Their devotion to the gods and religious practices
    b. Their disregard of religious practice and attention to war
    c. Their building program
    d. Their greed

11. The third king of Rome, Tullus Hostilius, and his Alban counterpart, Mettius Fufetius, agreed to do which of the following?

    a. Hand over the keys of Alba Longa to the king of Rome
    b. Allow the Horatii brothers to fight the Curiatii brothers
    c. Meet at the spring of Egeria
    d. Throw criminals from the Tarpeian rock

12. What happened to Horatia, the sister of the Horatii brothers?

    a. She married Curiatius.
    b. She ran away from Rome.
    c. Her brother killed her because she wept when she saw the dead Curiatii.
    d. Curiatius killed her because she wept when she saw her dead brothers.

13. Rome's fourth king, Ancus Marcius, established the seaport of Rome at the mouth of the Tiber River. What was the name of this seaport?

    a. Rome
    b. Ostia
    c. Alba Longa
    d. Gabii

14. The fifth king of Rome and his wife, Tanaquil, came from this Italic tribe.

    a. Etruscans
    b. Sabines
    c. Latins
    d. Gabians

15. What was the name of the slave child whose head was not consumed by fire, and who became the sixth king of Rome?

    a. Tarquinius
    b. Brutus
    c. Collatinus
    d. Servius Tullius

16. The seventh king of Rome, Lucius Tarquinius, was given the uncomplimentary name "Superbus" because of which attribute?

    a. Arrogance
    b. Defiance
    c. Greed
    d. Sloth

17. In whose presence did Tarquinius Superbus declare himself to be king and kill his predecessor, Tullius?

    a. The citizens of Gabii
    b. The Roman senators
    c. The Roman *plebes* (the people)
    d. The citizens of Alba Longa

18. Which of these events did not cause the Roman citizens to rise up against Tarquinius Superbus?

    a. His refusal to allow the burial of Servius Tullius
    b. His son's attack upon Lucretia
    c. The building of the Temple of Jupiter on the Capitoline Hill
    d. His treatment of the town and citizens of Gabii

19. This man, a nephew of Tarquinius Superbus, led the Roman uprising against his uncle and later served as one of the two first consuls of Rome.

    a. Mettius Fufetius
    b. Lucius Junius Brutus
    c. Sextus Tarquinius
    d. Arruns

20. The husband of Lucretius, this man was another relative of Tarquinius who also served as one of Rome's first consuls.

    a. Sextus Tarquinius
    b. Tarquinius Collatinus
    c. Tarquinius Priscus
    d. Arruns

21. This Roman warrior successfully kept the Etruscans from entering Rome by defending, then destroying the bridge across the Tiber River.

    a. Lars Porsenna
    b. Lucius Junius Brutus
    c. Horatius Cocles
    d. None of the above

22. What did Mucius Scaevola do to demonstrate his opposition to the Etruscan king and keep him out of Rome?

    a. He sneaked into the Etruscan camp.
    b. He killed the secretary of Lars Porsenna.
    c. He thrust his right hand into the fire in the presence of Lars Porsenna.
    d. All of the above

23. After Mucius' successful mission against Lars Porsenna was accomplished, the Romans and Etruscans exchanged these as guarantors that neither side would break the peace and declare war.

    a. Horses
    b. Handshakes
    c. Hostages
    d. Kings

24. This young Roman woman escaped from Lars Porsenna by swimming across the Tiber, leading a group of fellow female hostages.
    a. Lucretia
    b. Tanaquil
    c. Cloelia
    d. Tullia

25. What was the fate of Lucius Tarquinius Superbus?
    a. He was hanged.
    b. He drowned in the Tiber River.
    c. He was exiled.
    d. He was sent as a hostage to the Etruscans.

B. Musings

1. The first king of Rome was named Romulus. The first emperor of Rome was Augustus. The last emperor of Rome, 475–476 CE, was a young boy named Romulus Augustus (or "Romulus Augustulus"). What happened to this young emperor? Research to learn more.

2. To the Romans, Lucretia was a hero. She killed herself in protest against having been dishonored. By modern standards, Lucretia was certainly innocent of crime or dishonor, but modern society finds the idea of her suicide repugnant because it is a waste of innocent human life; Lucretia did nothing wrong.
    - Do you think that Roman ideas about honor are more like our ideas of honor or more unlike our ideas?
    - Do Americans have a sense of honor in the same way as did the Romans?
    - Do you believe Lucretia had a better or alternative course of action?
    - How could Lucretia's family and friends reach out to help her and punish Sextus Tarquinius?
    - How would you rewrite the ending to Lucretia's story?

3. Compare the role of Sextus Tarquinius in Gabii in this chapter with that of Sinon in the previous chapter. What do their actions tell us about Roman morality?

4. In Livy's preface to his work on Roman history (the first book of which formed the basis for this chapter), Livy stated that his purpose was to give his readers, particularly young ones, role models to adopt and bad examples to avoid.
    - Which of the characters in this chapter could still serve as role models today?
    - Which ones illustrate the differences between the ancient Romans' values and modern values?

C. Words, Words, Words

The Daily Muse

News you can use

Rex and tyrant

You've just finished reading the story of the seven kings of Rome. Each had the Latin title ***rex***. In chapter 14, you read the story of Oedipus. The Athenian dramatist Sophocles wrote a play about him called, in Greek, *Oidipous Tyrannos,* which is given in Latin as *Oedipus Rex.* Both mean, more or less, "Oedipus the King."

A Roman king

To the Greeks, a **tyrant** was someone who had made himself king by use of force. Therefore, he usually would not have been a hereditary ruler like Agamemnon or Menelaus. However, to the ancient Greek way of thinking, to be a **tyrant** did not necessarily mean that the ruler was cruel, arrogant, or ruthless.

Rex takes the form of **-reg-**, meaning "rule" or "direct" in derivative words such as **regal, regulation**, **regent**, and **regime**.

How would you describe the difference between a "king" and a "**tyrant**" in English?

____

Why do you suppose that **Rex** is such a popular name for dogs?

____

What is the meaning behind the name ***Tyrannosaurus rex*** that includes *both* words?

____

MATCHING! Match the word in the left-hand column with the correct phrase from the right-hand column. Write the letter in the space provided.

1.	____	Interregnum	a.	Not according to rule, accepted order, or general practice
2.	____	Tyranny	b.	Acting like a tyrant, despotic
3.	____	Regulation	c.	A rule
4.	____	Regime	d.	A grouping in the military
5.	____	Tyrannize	e.	One who rules in place of a king or queen, usually in the case of a youthful or ill sovereign
6.	____	Irregular	f.	A leaderless time between the reigns of two monarchs
7.	____	Regimen	g.	An administration of government or pattern of living
8.	____	Tyrannical	h.	To oppress or rule despotically
9.	____	Regiment	i.	Rule by a single absolute leader who holds all power
10.	____	Region	j.	A large area or district
11.	____	Regent	k.	Rule by government or a system of exercise and diet

D. How 'Bout That?

Calling all Trekkies!

Trekkies, that is, fans of the old TV series *Star Trek*, already know that Romulus and Remus are twin homeworlds of similar size, like Earth and Venus. To learn more about the fates of *Star Trek*'s Romulus and Remus, check out the film *Nemesis* (Paramount Pictures, 2002).

Wild things!

The legend of Romulus and Remus is only one of many stories, real and fictional, of feral children, or children raised by animals. Check out the series *Raised Wild* shown on the Animal Planet television network in 2012. To read more, see http://listverse.com/2008/03/07/10-modern-cases-of-feral-children/

See also the book *Savage Girls and Wild Boys: A History of Feral Children* by Michael Newton (Macmillan, 2004).

Remus

If you have read the Harry Potter books, describe why the name Remus Lupin is so appropriate to the character.

Shakespeare and Brutus

Read Shakespeare's *Julius Caesar* in its entirety (or at least the first three acts). Pay particular attention to the following speech of Cassius, in which he tries to turn Marcus Brutus, a descendant of the Lucius Junius Brutus in the chapter, against Julius Caesar. What role does his famous ancestor play in convincing Marcus Brutus to join the conspiracy to assassinate Caesar?

Cassius:
Why, man, he doth bestride the narrow world
Like a Colossus, and we petty men
Walk under his huge legs and peep about
To find ourselves dishonorable graves.
Men at some time are masters of their fates:
The fault, dear Brutus, is not in our stars,
But in ourselves, that we are underlings.
Brutus and Caesar: what should be in that 'Caesar'?
Why should that name be sounded more than yours?
Write them together, yours is as fair a name;
Sound them, it doth become the mouth as well;
Weigh them, it is as heavy; conjure with 'em,

Marcus Junius Brutus

Brutus will start a spirit as soon as Caesar.
Now, in the names of all the gods at once,
Upon what meat doth this our Caesar feed,
That he is grown so great? Age, thou art shamed!
Rome, thou hast lost the breed of noble bloods!
When went there by an age, since the great flood,
But it was famed with more than with one man?
When could they say till now, that talk'd of Rome,
That her wide walls encompass'd but one man?
Now is it Rome indeed and room enough,
When there is in it but one only man.
O, you and I have heard our fathers say,
There was a Brutus once that would have brook'd
The eternal devil to keep his state in Rome
As easily as a king.

Gaius Cassius Longinus

E. WHO'S WHO?

- For Romulus' ancestry and family, and the chronology of the kings of Rome, see GENEALOGICAL CHART 22.
- For the family of the kings of Rome and the first consuls, see GENEALOGICAL CHART 23.

Appendix A

Deities Chart

GOD OR GODDESS	PARENTS	DOMINION	FAVORITE PLACE(S)	SYMBOLS	ARCHETYPE (PERSONALITY CHARACTERISTICS)
Zeus (Jupiter, Jove)	Cronus and Rhea	Sky, weather, especially thunderstorms and winds	Olympus, Dodona, Crete	Thunderbolt, eagle, aegis (goatskin shield), oak tree	Ambitious, decisive, competitive; "networker"
Hera (Juno)	Cronus and Rhea	Marriage, fertility	Argos	Crown, scepter, cow, peacock, pomegranate	Traditional, marriage-minded; fierce opponent of any threat to family
Poseidon (Neptune)	Cronus and Rhea	Sea, earthquakes, horses	Sounion	Trident (three-pronged spear), horse	Emotionally intense, impulsive; can be angry and vengeful and troubled by sense of inferiority
Demeter (Ceres)	Cronus and Rhea	Crops, motherhood	Eleusis	Stalk of wheat, torch	Motherly, nurturing, deeply spiritual
Persephone (Proserpina)	Zeus and Demeter	The Underworld	Eleusis	Torches, sheaf of grain	Compliant, girlish
Hades (Pluto)	Cronus and Rhea	The Underworld	The Underworld	Magical helmet of invisibility, bident (2-pronged staff), chariot	Dark, secret, imaginative; can become depressed
Hestia (Vesta)	Cronus and Rhea	The home	Rome (as Vesta)	Hearth fire	Home-loving, unassuming
Athena (Minerva)	Zeus (and Metis)	The arts and crafts, wisdom, training, taming horses	Athens	Helmet, spear and shield, aegis decorated with the head of the Gorgon Medusa, thunderbolt, owl, olive tree	Intelligent, creative; identifies with males
Apollo (Apollo, Phoebus Apollo)	Zeus and Leto	Music, poetry, healing, the woods, medicine, grazing animals, herds	Delphi, Parnassus, Delos	Sun, silver or golden bow/arrows, laurel tree, dolphin	Artistic, rational, orderly; "favorite son"; can be arrogant
Artemis (Diana)	Zeus and Leto	Hunters and hunting, young children, youth	Woods and forests	Moon, silver bow, deer, stag, dog	Athletic, fond of nature and animals, close to other females; can be violent
Aphrodite (Venus)	Zeus and Dione (according to Homer) or born from Cronus' severed member (according to Hesiod)	Love and beauty	Cyprus, Corinth, Cythera	Rose, dove	Emotionally open, appreciative of beauty and luxury; can be vain

Hermes (Mercury)	Zeus and Maia	Liars, thieves, travelers, merchants and commerce; domesticated herds (cattle, sheep), dogs, boars, lions; weights and measures, pipers; guiding dead souls in transit to the Underworld	Roads	*Caduceus* or wand, winged sandals, winged traveler's helmet (*petasus*), lyre, syrinx (shepherd's pipes)	Mischievous, fun-loving, communicative with all; trickster
Ares (Mars)	Zeus and Hera	War	Thebes, Thrace	Helmet, sword, shield, spear	Angry and violent, intensely competitive
Hephaestus (Vulcan)	Zeus and Hera, or Hera alone	Smithing and crafts of the forge, metalworkers, artisans	Lemnos, Mount Etna in Sicily, other volcanoes in the Mediterranean region	Hammer and anvil	Earthy, gentle, creative, kindly, even when mocked or wounded
Dionysus (Bacchus, Liber)	Zeus and Semele	The vine, wine	Asia Minor, Thebes	Wine cup; vine leaves; thyrsus (a staff topped with a pine cone); many wild animals, especially panther, lion, tiger, leopard, dolphin, and snake	Moody, mystical, friendly to women, passionate; may develop substance abuse problems

Literary Sources:

Zeus: Hesiod *Theogony* 886*ff.*
Hera: Homer *Iliad* 15.18–22
Poseidon: Homer *Odyssey* 4.365*ff.*, Ovid *Metamorphoses* 6.75*ff.*
Demeter and Persephone: *Homeric Hymn to Demeter* (2)
Hades: *Odyssey* 11, Apollodorus 1.5.1–3, Vergil *Aeneid* 6
Hestia: *Homeric Hymn to Aphrodite* (2)
Athena: Hesiod *Theogony* 886–898, *Homeric Hymn to Athena* (28)
Apollo and Artemis: Hesiod *Theogony* 12, *Homeric Hymns to Apollo* (3) and *to Artemis* (27)
Aphrodite: *Homeric Hymns to Aphrodite* 5, 6; Homer *Iliad*
Hermes: Hesiod *Theogony* 935–940, *Homeric Hymn to Hermes* (4)
Ares: Homer *Iliad* 5; Hesiod *Theogony* 921–923, 934–937
Hephaestus: Homer *Iliad* 1, Hesiod *Theogony* 927–929
Dionysus: *Homeric Hymn to Dionysus* (7), Euripides *Bacchae*, Ovid *Metamorphoses* 3.256–315

Appendix B
Genealogical Charts

1. The Muses (and Ancestry of Orpheus)

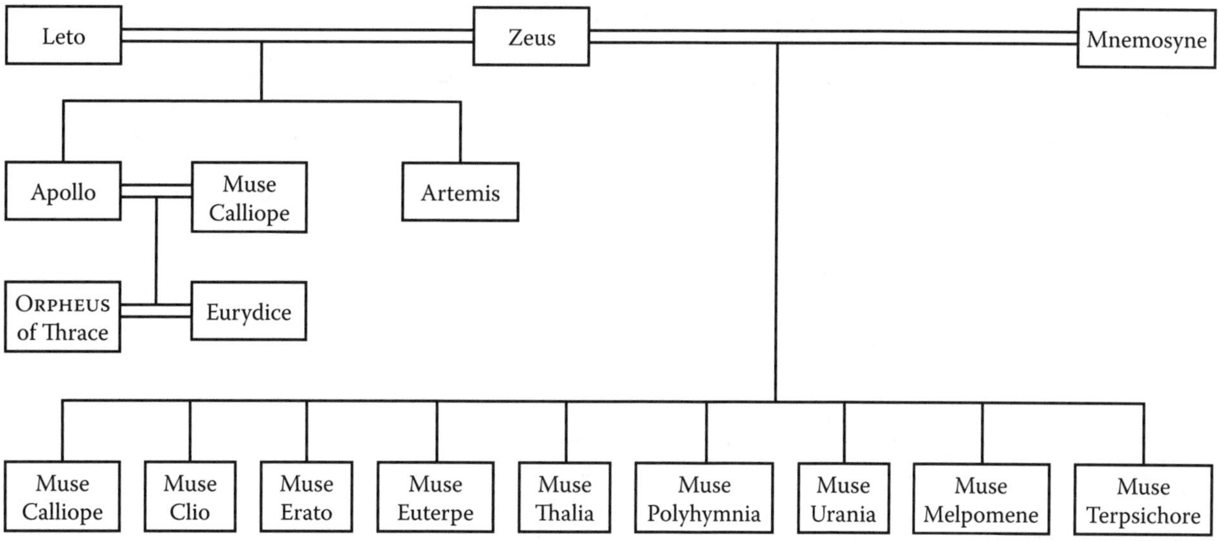

2. Descendants of Chaos

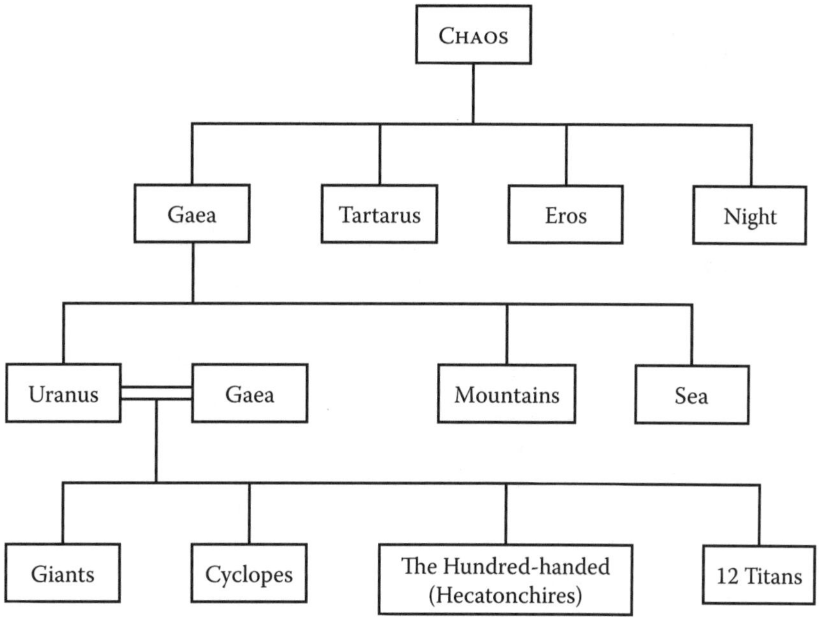

3. Descendants of Uranus and Gaea

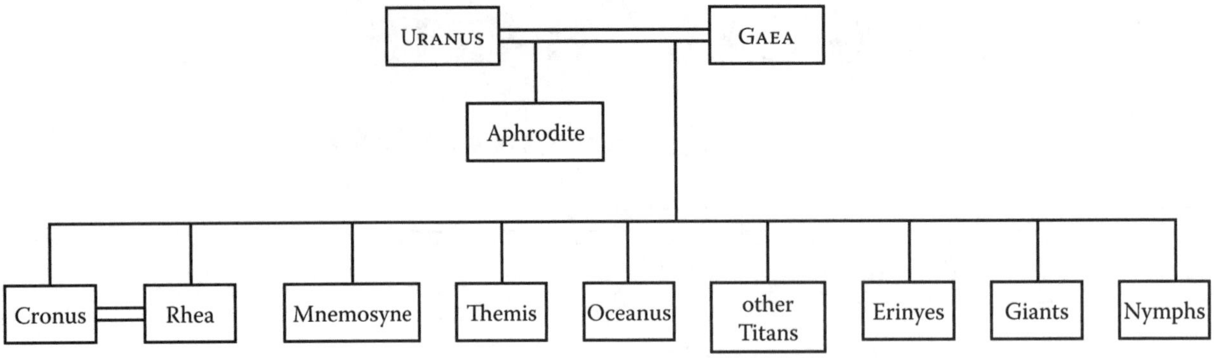

4. Descendants of Cronus and Rhea

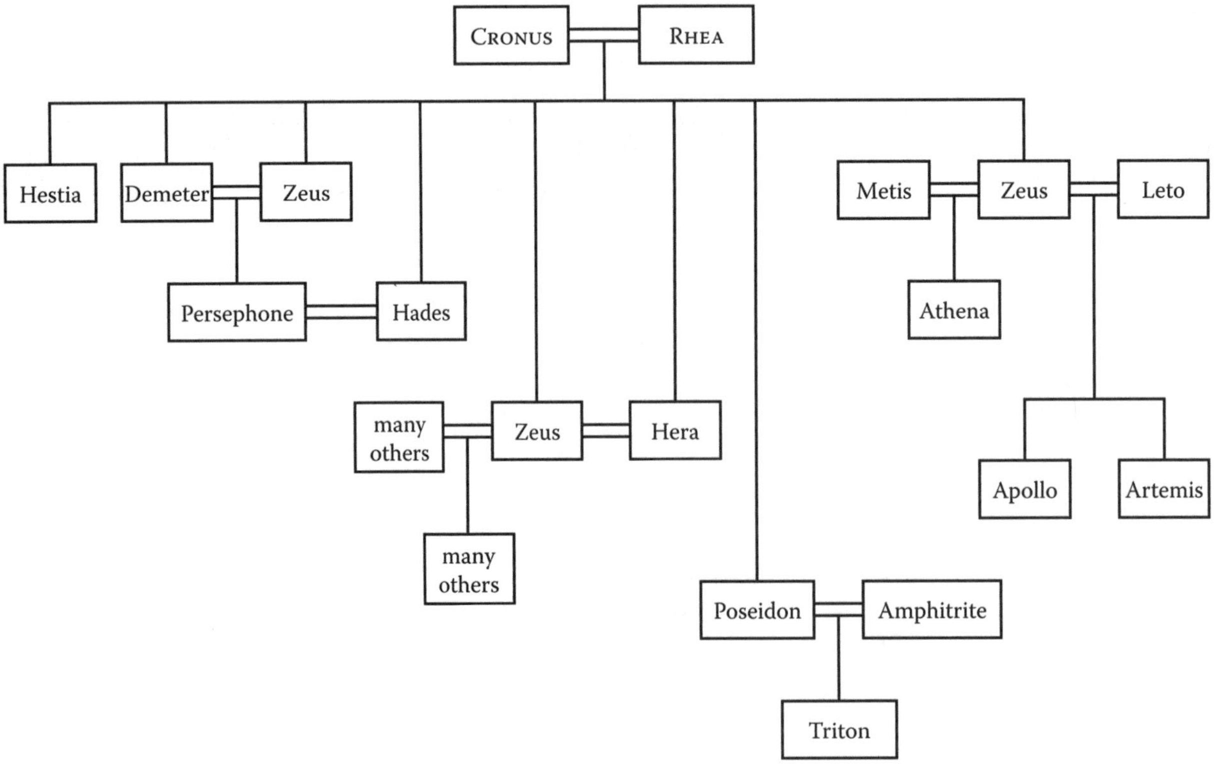

5. Wives and Descendants of Zeus

Some of His Divine Wives, Lovers, and Children

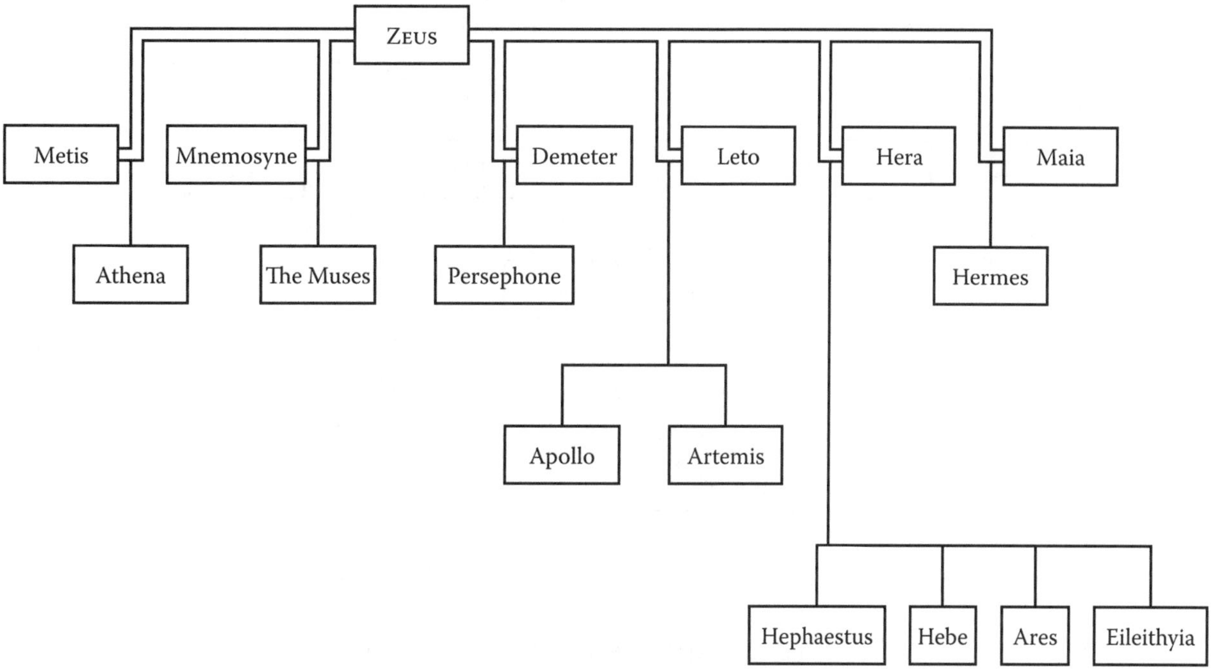

Some of His Human Lovers, and Their Children

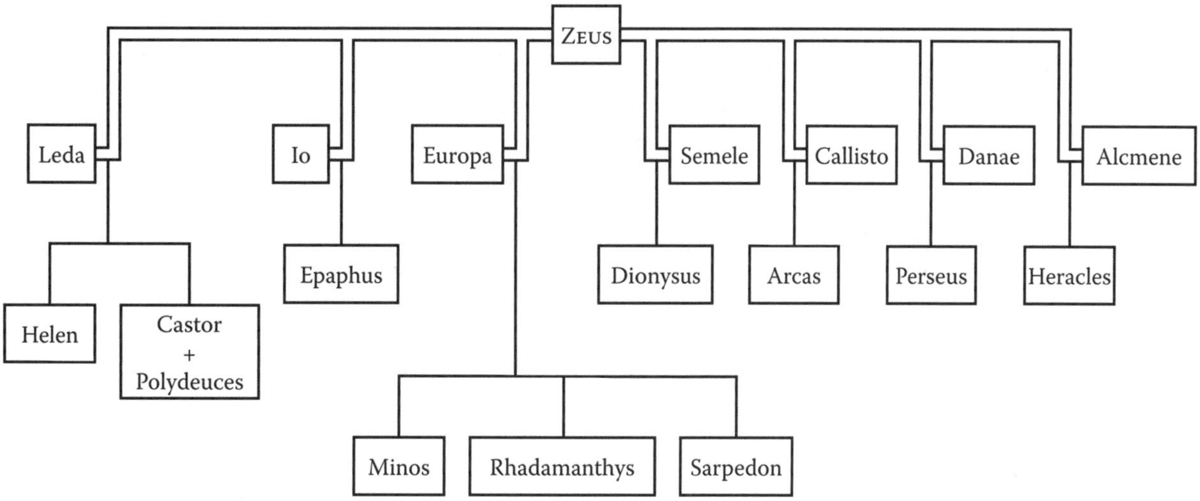

6. Ancestry and Select Descendants of Apollo

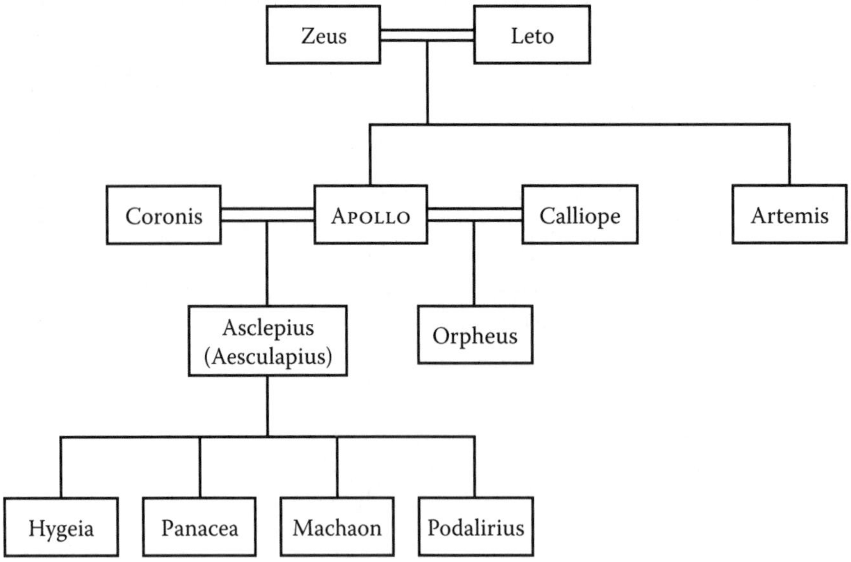

7. Descendants of Nyx (Night)

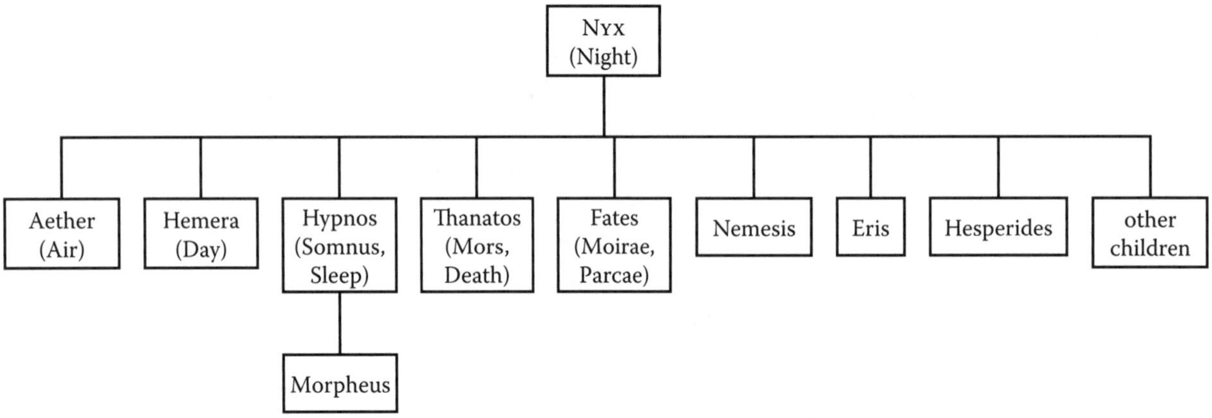

8. Descendants of Gaea and Pontus

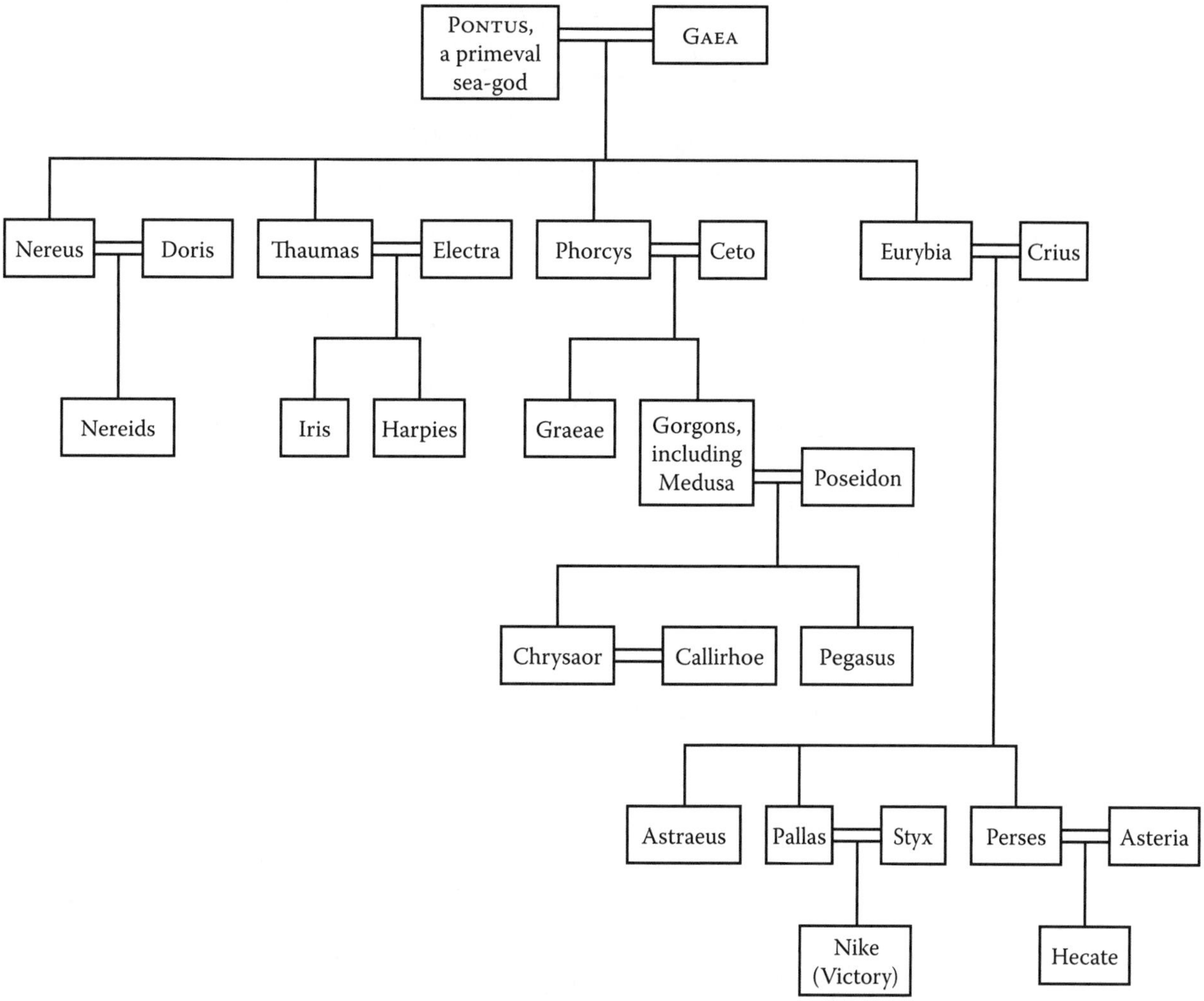

9. Descendants of Hyperion the Titan

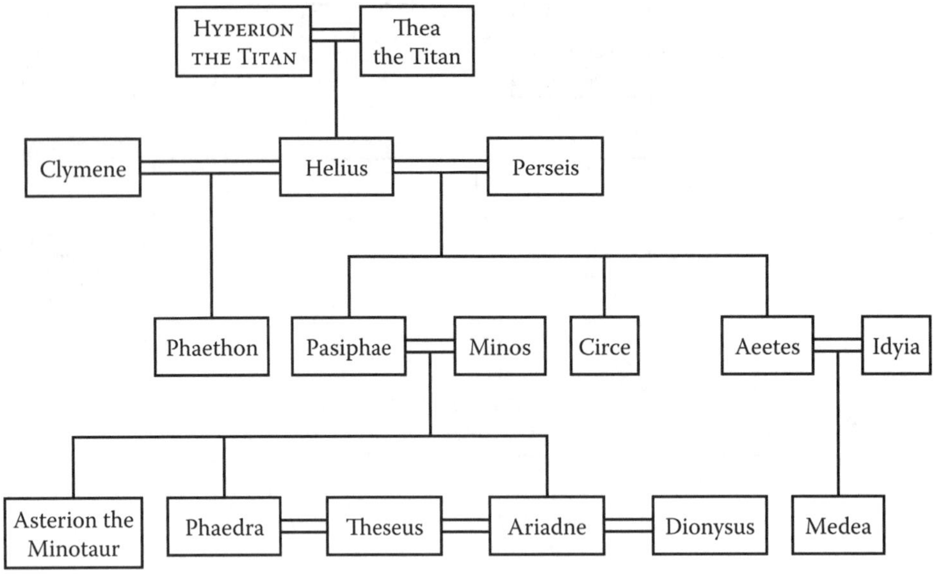

10. Ancestry of Phaethon

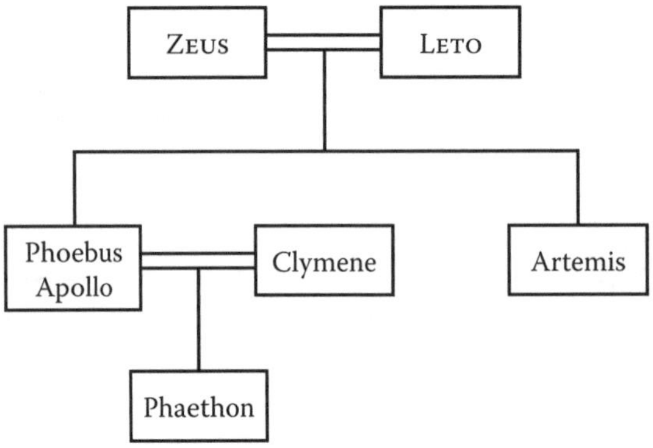

11. Descendants of Agenor of Sidon
(including Cadmus, Europa, Minos, and Oedipus)

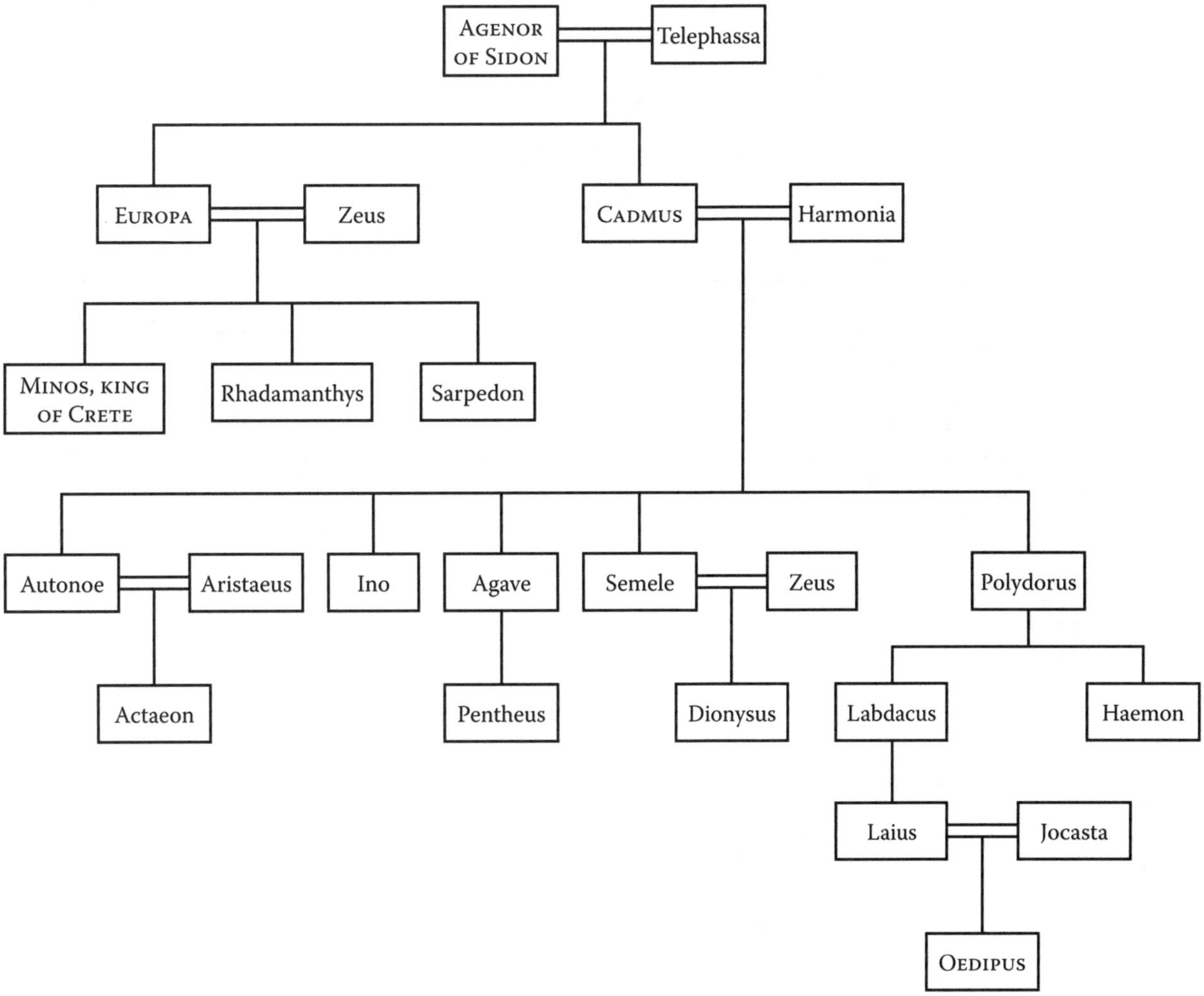

12. Descendants of Zeus and Danae
(including Perseus and Heracles)

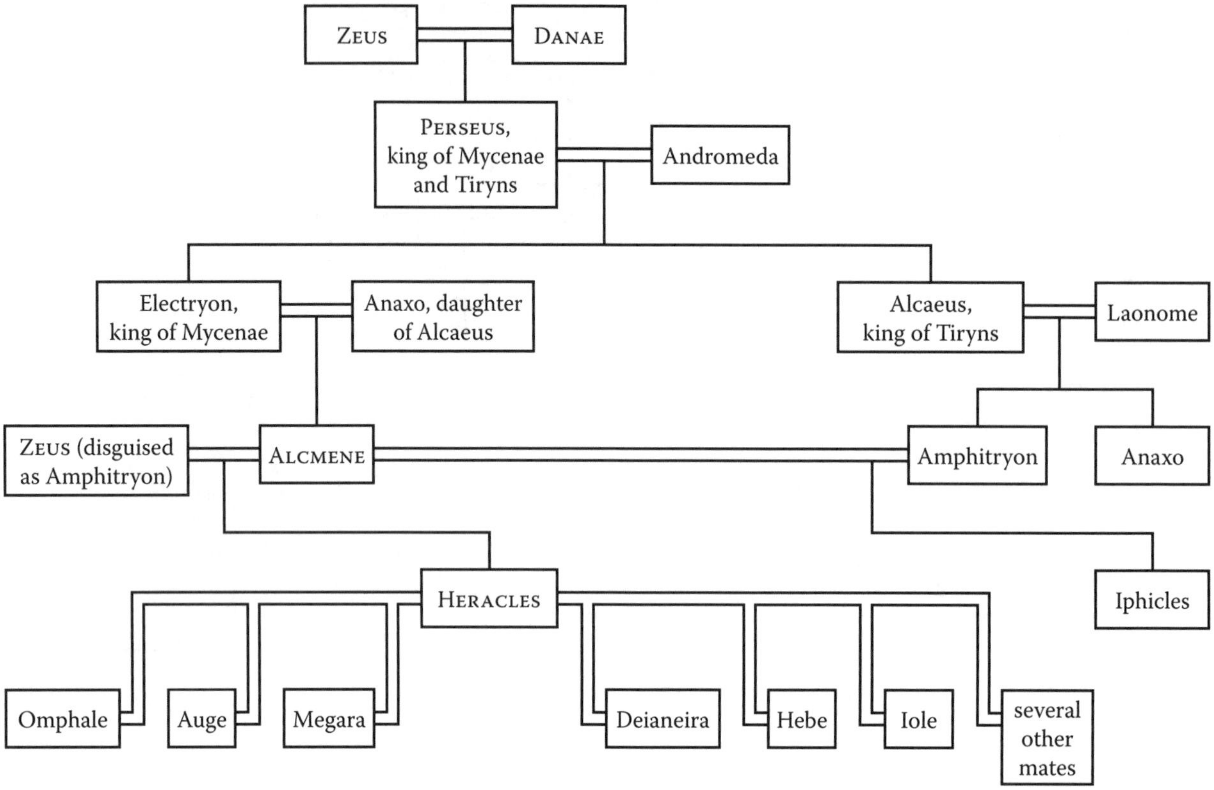

13. Family of Jason

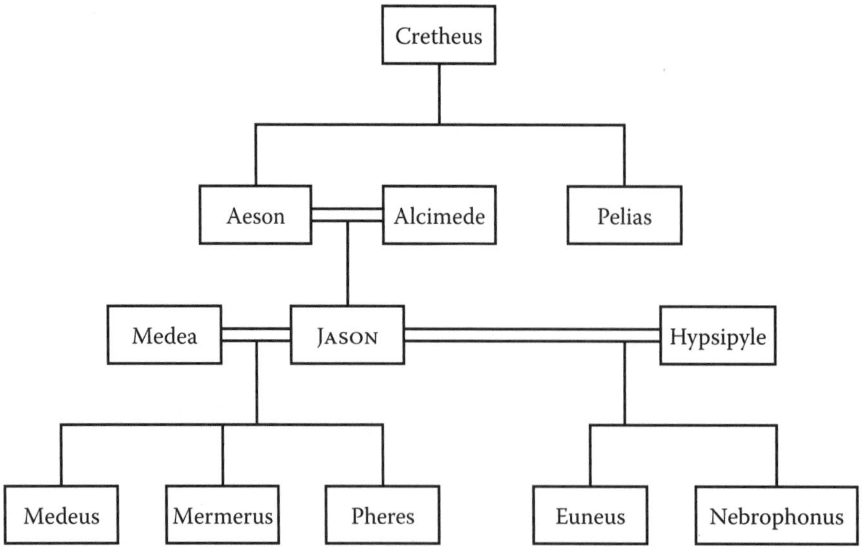

14. Family of Theseus

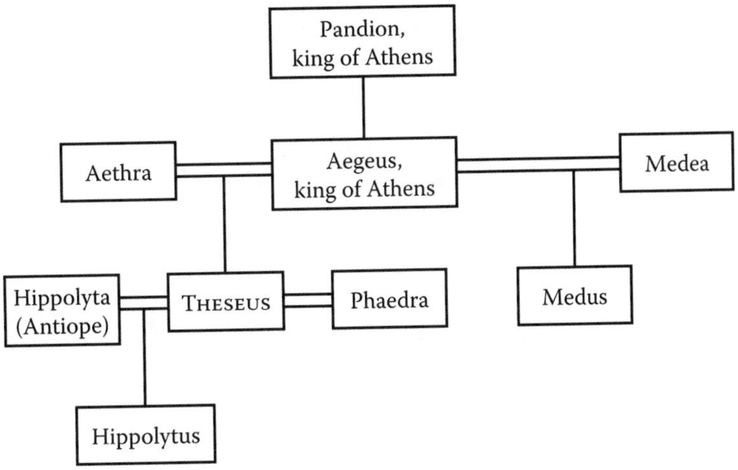

15. Minoan Descendants of Europa

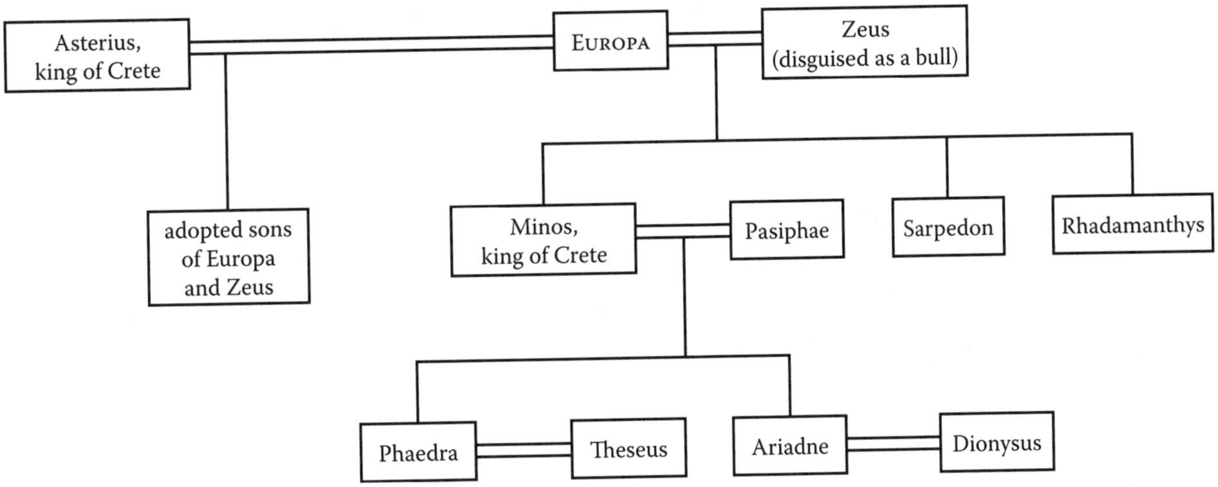

16. House of Atreus

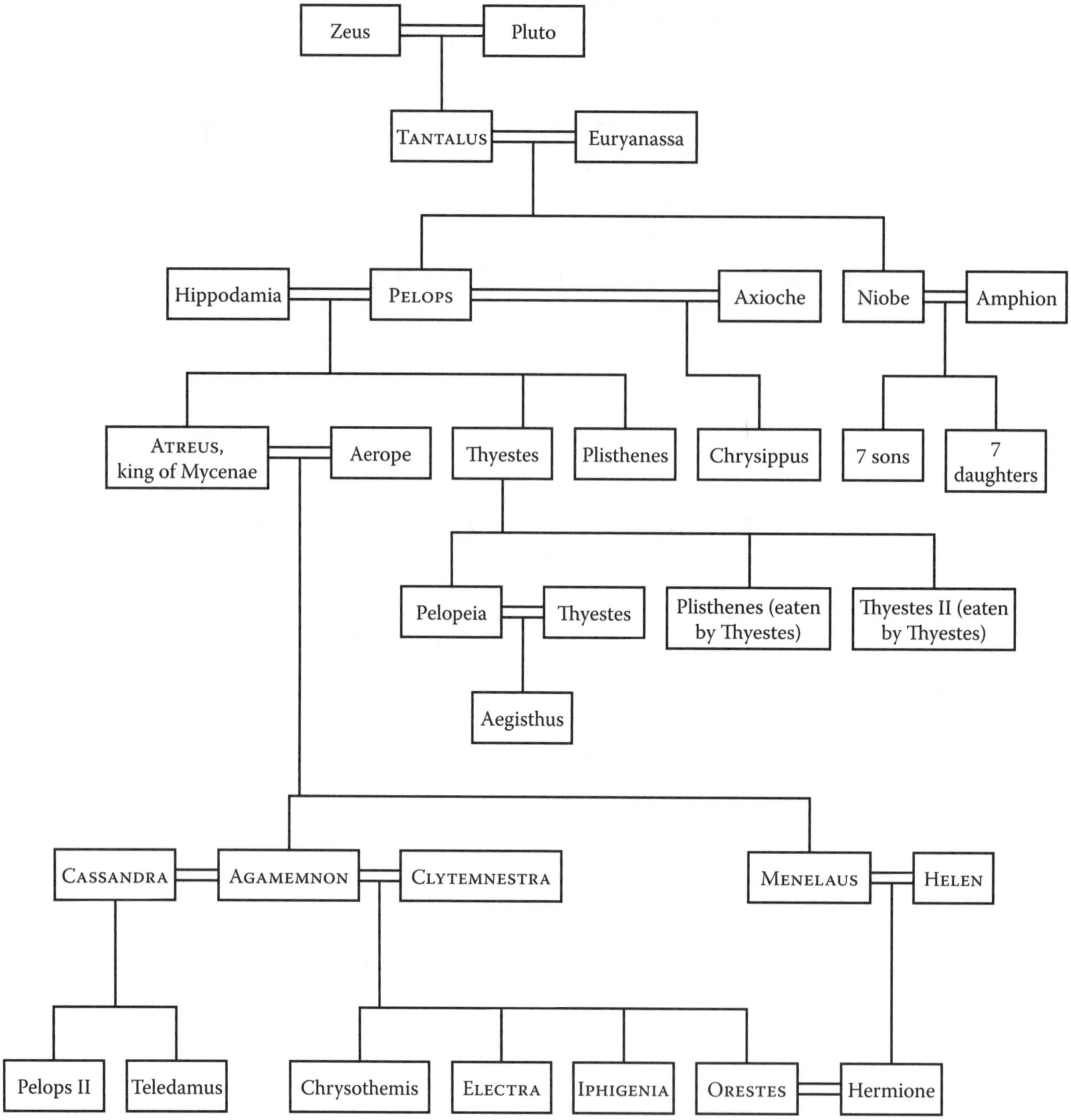

17. Descendants of Cadmus, House of Thebes, and Descendants of Oedipus

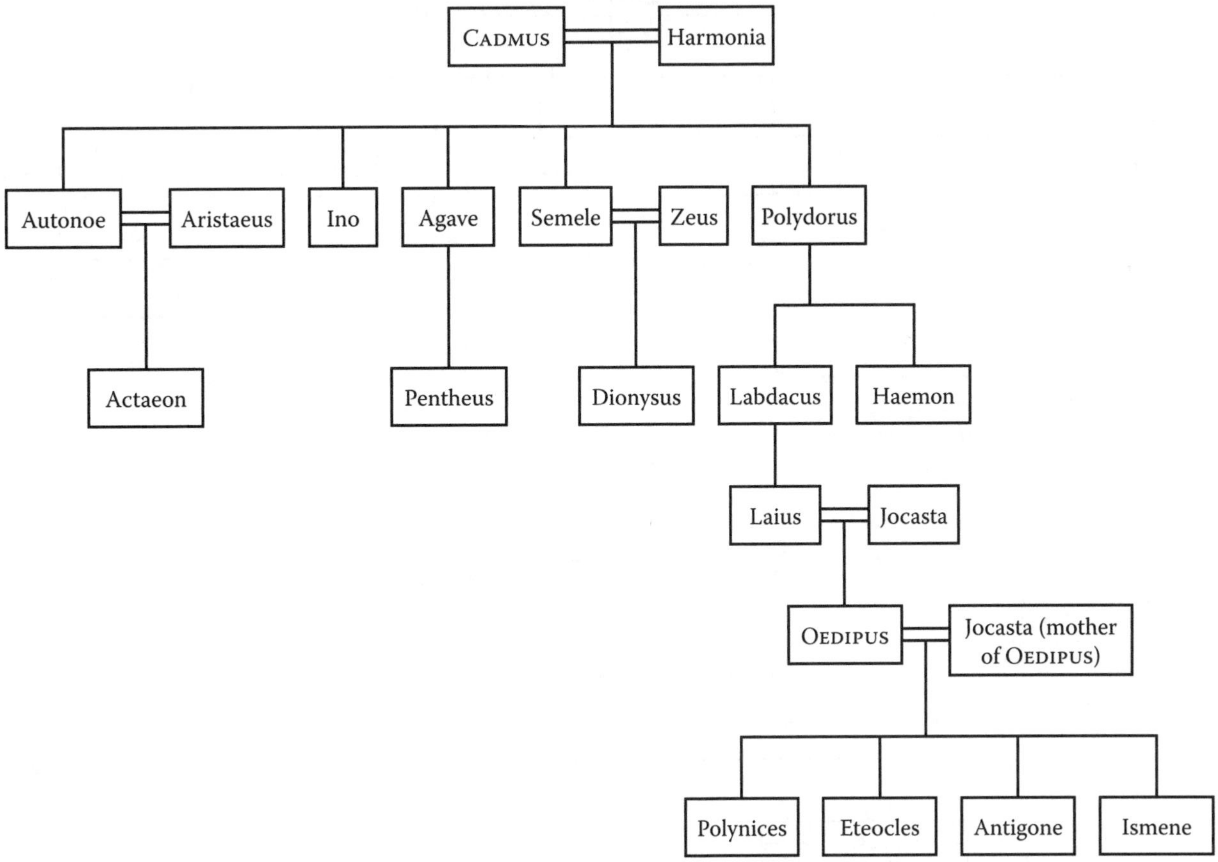

18. House of Troy: Descendants of Priam

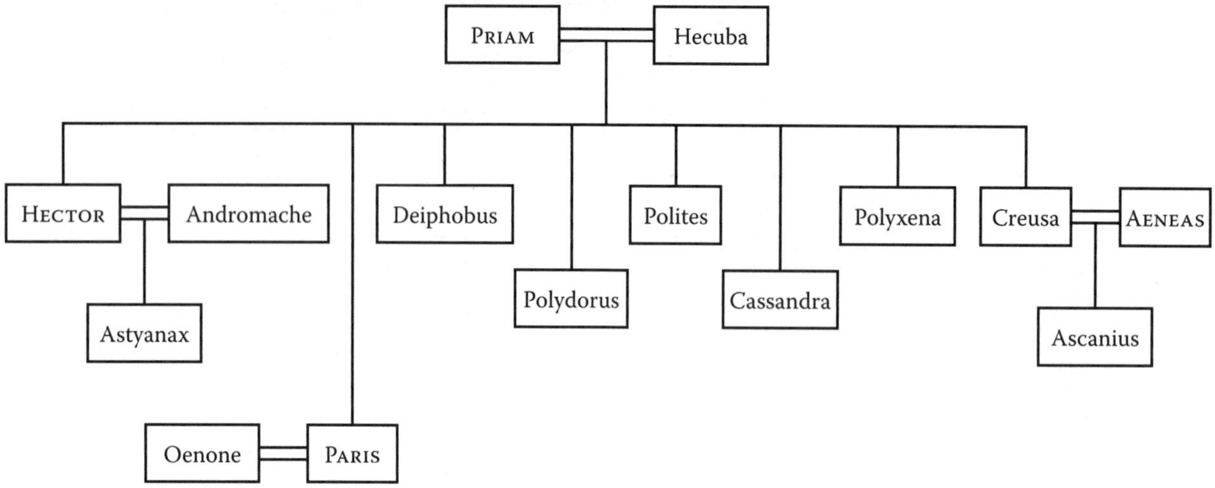

19. Family of Achilles

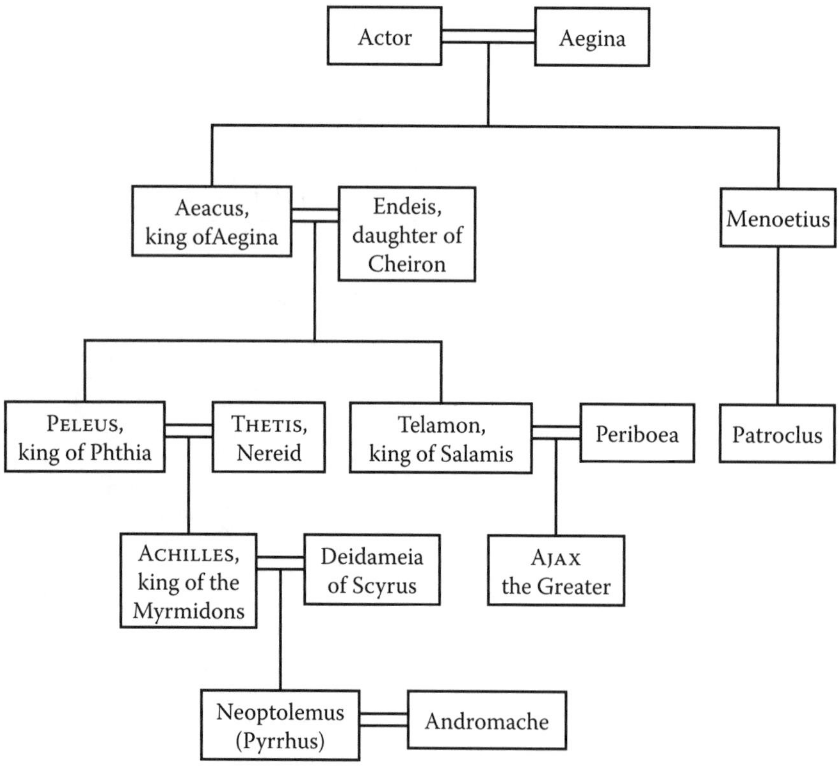

20. Family of Odysseus (Ulysses)

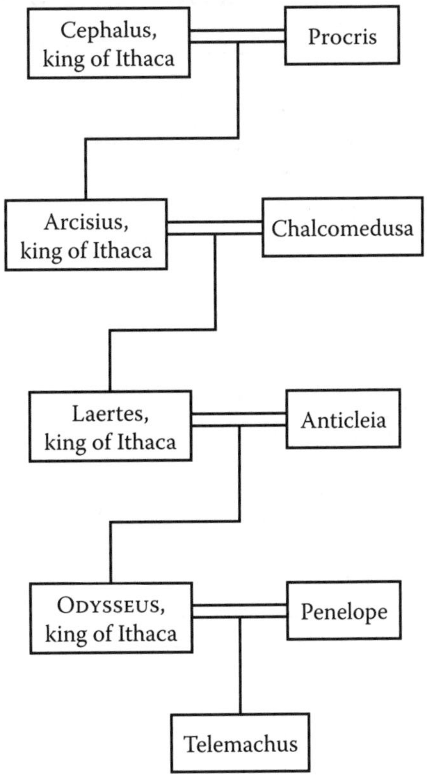

21. Family of Heracles (Hercules)

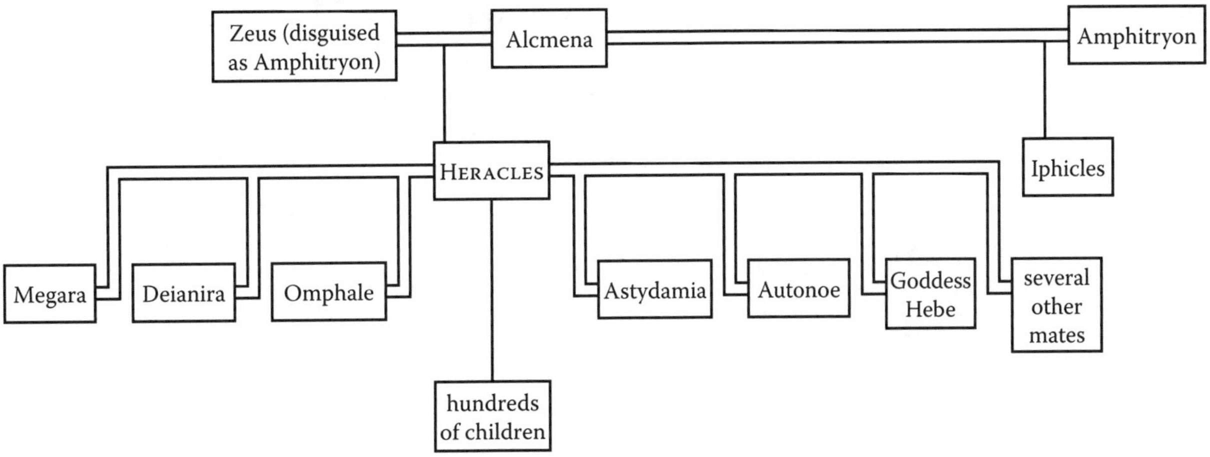

22. Ancestry and Family of Romulus; Kings of Rome

Ancestry and Family of Romulus

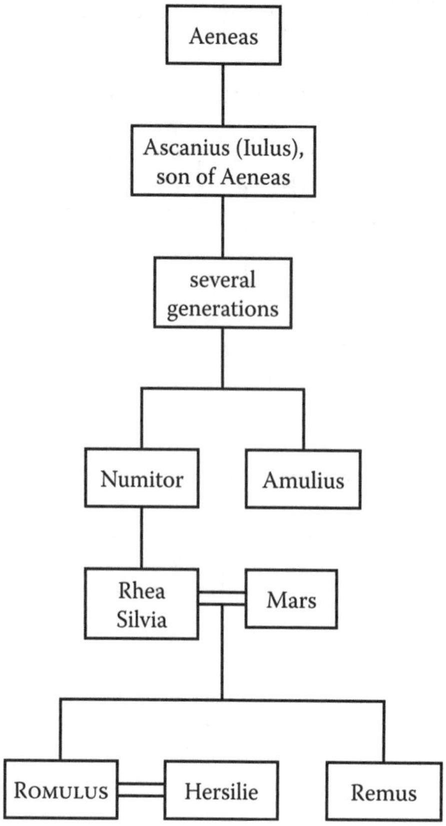

The Kings of Rome

Romulus, 753–715 BCE
Numa Pompilius, 715–673 BCE
Tullus Hostilius, 673–642 BCE
Ancus Marcius, 642–617 BCE
Tarquinius Priscus, 616–579 BCE
Servius Tullius, 578–535 BCE
Tarquinius Superbus, 534–509 BCE

23. Sabine, Latin, and Etruscan Kings of Rome and the First Consuls

The Sabine Kings

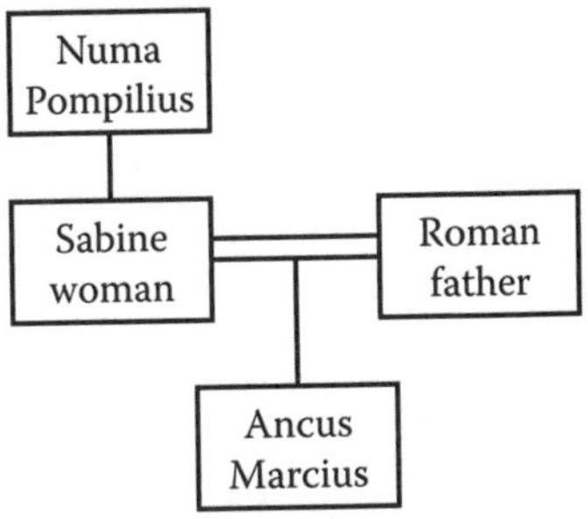

Etruscan Kings of Rome and the First Consuls

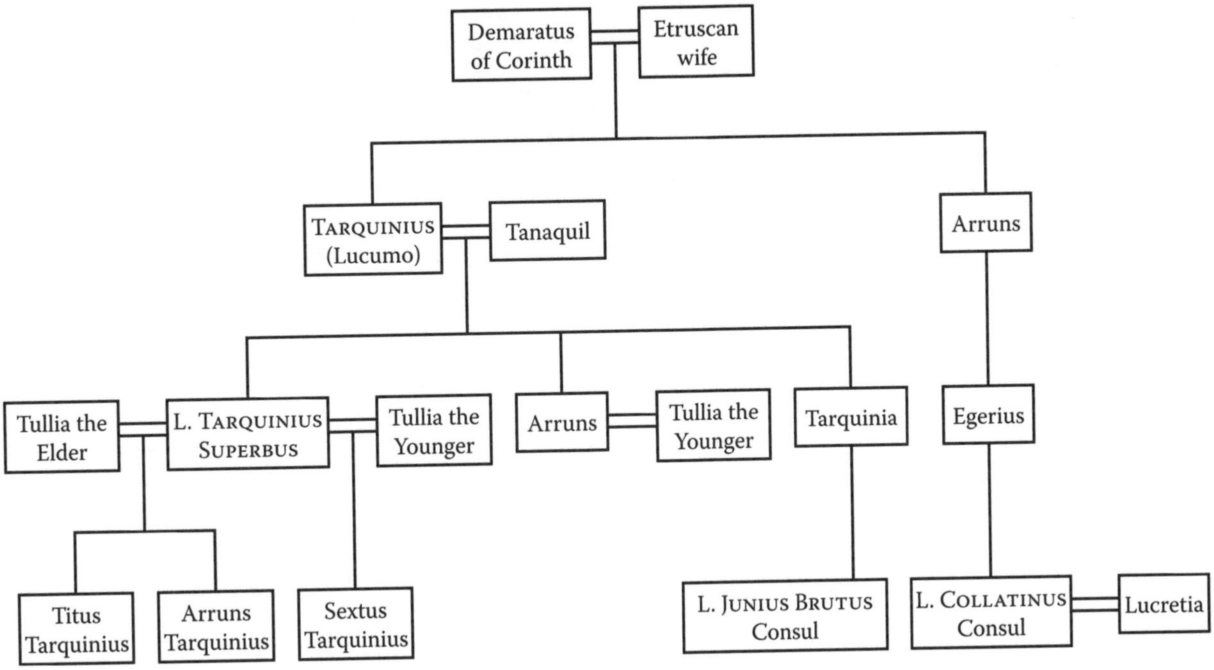

Appendix C
Chapter-by-Chapter Glossary of Names and Pronunciation Guide

The following lists are intended to help students and teachers identify the primary and secondary characters mentioned in these stories. The primary characters' names should be learned; the others may be learned if one is especially interested in mythology or planning to compete in mythology tournaments. An asterisk denotes a name that has appeared on a list from a previous chapter. The lists are arranged chapter-by-chapter as a tool to help the student review material presented in each chapter.

The pronunciation guide marks vowels short and long according to standard dictionary pronunciations. Unmarked vowels before "r" use a characteristically different pronunciation (ar, er, or, ur). Pronunications vary, and when the teacher prefers a different pronunciation, it can easily be substituted for or given in addition to the sounds given here.

Chapter 1

The student should be familiar with the concept of a Muse; many teachers will likely regard memorization of the specific names below as optional.

Calliope: kə - lī′ ə - pē
Clio: klē′ ō
Erato: ĕr′ ə - tō
Euterpe: ū - ter′ pē
Hesiod: hē′ sĭ - əd
Melpomene: mĕl - pŏm′ ĭ - nē
Polyhymnia: pŏl - ĭ – hĭm′ nē - ə
Terpsichore: terp - sĭk′ ə - rē
Thalia: thă′ lē - ə
Thamyris: thăm′ ĭ - rĭs
Urania: ū - rā′ nē - ə

Chapter 2

Primary Names:

Aphrodite: ăf - rō - dī′ tē
Cronus: krō′ nəs
Cyclopes: sī - klō′ pēz
Delphi: dĕl′ fē
Demeter: dē - mē′ ter
Erinyes: ĕ - rĭn′ ĭ - ēz
Gaea: jē′ ə
Hades: hā′ dēz
Hera: hē′ rə
Hestia: hĕs′ tē - ə
nymphs: nĭmfs
Ovid: ŏv′ ĭd
Poseidon: pə - sī′ dŏn
Rhea: rē′ ə
Saturn: săt′ ern
Uranus: ū′ rə - nəs
Zeus: zūs

Secondary Names:

Amalthea: ăm - ăl - thē′ ə
Briareos: brĭ - ĕr′ ē - ŏs
Chaos: kā′ ŏs
Cottus: kŏt′ təs
Gyes: gī′ ēs

Iapetus: ē - ăp′ ə - təs
Mnemosyne* nē - mŏs′ ĭ - nē
Oceanus: ō - sē′ ə - nəs
Themis: thē′ mĭs

Chapter 3

Primary names:

For pronunciation of Zeus, Poseidon, Hades, Demeter, Hera, and Hestia, see the list for chapter 2.

Acropolis: ə - krŏp′ ə - lĭs
Apollo: ə - pŏl′ ō
Artemis: ar′ tə - mĭs
Athena: ə - thē′ nə
Cerberus: ser′ bə - rəs
Ceres: sē′ rēz
Charon: kĕr′ ŏn
Eleusis: ĕ - lū′ sĭs
Elysian (ĭ - lĭzh′ ən) Fields
Ixion: ĭk - zī′ ŏn
Jove: jōv
Juno: jū′ nō
Jupiter: jū′ pĭ - ter
Leto: lē′ tō
Metis: mē′ tĭs
Neptune: nĕp′ tūn
Olympus: ō - lĭm′ pəs
Persephone: per - sĕf′ ə - nē
Pluto: plū′ tō
Proserpina: prō - ser′ pĭ - nə
Proteus: prō′ tĭ - əs
Sisyphus: sĭs′ ĭ - fəs
Styx: stĭks
Tantalus: tăn′ tə - ləs
Tartarus: tar′ tə - rəs
Vesta: vĕs′ tə

Secondary names:

Amphitrite: ăm - fĭ - trī′ tē
Argos: ar′ gŏs
Celeus: sē′ lĭ - əs
Crete: krēt
Danaus: dăn′ ā - əs
Demophon: dĕ′ mŏ - fŏn
Dodona: dō - dō′ nə
Doso: dō′ sō
Hecate: hĕk′ - ə - tē
Helius: hē′ lĭ - əs
Iambe: ī - ăm′ bē
Lethe: lē′ thē
Metaneira: mĕt - ə - nē′ rə
Odysseus: ō - dĭs′ ĭ - əs
Orpheus: ōr′ fĭ - əs
Pelops: pē′ lŏps
Polyphemus: pŏl - ĭ - fē′ məs
Sounion: sū′ nē - ŏn
Thoricus: thō′ rĭ - kəs
Triptolemus: trĭp - tŏl′ ə - məs
Triton: trī′ tŏn

Chapter 4

Primary names:

Acropolis* ə - krŏp′ ə - lĭs
Agave: ə - gā′ vē
Aphrodite* ăf - rō - dī′ tē
Apollo* ə - pŏl′ ō
Ares: ĕr′ ēz
Artemis* ar′ tə - mĭs
Athena* ə - thē′ nə
bacchantes: bə - kănt′ ēz
Bacchus: băk′ əs
Cupid: kū′ pĭd
Delphi* dĕl′ fē
Dionysus: dī - ō - nī′ səs
Eros: ĕr′ ŏs
Hephaestus: hə - fēs′ təs
Hermes: her′ mēz
Leto* lē′ tō
Liber: lē′ ber
maenads: mē′ nădz
Mars: marz
Mercury: mer′ kū - rē
Metis* mē′ tĭs
Parthenon: par′ thə - nŏn

Pentheus: pěn′ thĭ - əs
Phoebus: fē′ bəs
Semele: sěm′ ə - lē
Thebes: thēbz
Venus: vē′ nəs
Vulcan: vul′ kăn

Secondary names:

Aegean (ē - jē′ ən) Sea
Atlas: ăt′ ləs
Cadmus: kăd′ məs
Cithaeron: sĭ - thē′ rŏn
Corinth: kor′ ĭnth
Cyllene: sĭ - lē′ nē
Cyprus: sī′ prəs
Cythera: sĭ - thē′ rə
Delos: dē′ lŏs
Demodocus: dě - mŏd′ ə - kəs
Diomedes: dī - ō - mē′ dēz
Dione: dē - ō′ nē
Eileithyia: ē - lē - thĭ′ yə
Etna: ět′ nə
Eurynome: ū - rĭn′ ə - mē
Hebe: hē′ bē
Lemnos: lěm′ nŏs
Maia: mī′ ə
Parnassus: par - năs′ əs
Pieria: pī - ĭr′ - ē - ə
Pythia: pĭth′ ē - ə
Pytho: pī′ thō
Themis* thē′ mĭs
Thetis: thē′ tĭs
Thrace: thrās

Chapter 5

Primary names:

Aesculapius: ēs - kū - lā′ pē - əs
Asclepius: ăs - klē′ pē - əs
Aurora: ə - rōr′ ə
Eos: ē′ ŏs
Eris: ě′ rĭs
Hypnos: hĭp′ nŏs
Iris: ī′ rĭs
Janus: jā′ nəs
Luna: lū′ nə
Mors: morz
Nemesis: něm′ ə - sĭs
Nike: nī′ kē
Pan: păn
Selene: sē - lē′ nē
Somnus: sŏm′ nəs
Syrinx: sĭr′ ĭngks
Thanatos: thăn′ ə - tŏs
Tithonus: tĭ - thō′ nəs

Secondary names:

Aeetes: ē - ē′ tēz
Aquila: ăk′ wĭ - lə
Augeas: au - jē/ əs
Circe: ser′ sē
Coronis: kə - rō′ nĭs
Eileithyia* ē - lē - thĭ′ yə
Endymion: ěn - dĭm′ ē - ŏn
Ganymede: gă - nĭ - mē′ dē
Hebe* hē′ bē
Hecate* hěk′ - ə - tē
Helius* hē′ lĭ - əs
Hygeia: hĭ - jē′ ə
Medea: mə - dē′ ə
Morpheus: mor′ fĭ - əs
Panacea: păn - ə - sē′ ə
Pasiphae: pə - sĭf′ ē
Phaethon: fā′ ə - thŏn
Rhodes: rōdz
Sol: sŏl

Chapter 6

Primary names:

The names of the gods are in the lists for chapters 3 and 4.

Adonis: ə - dŏn′ əs
Anchises: ăn - kī′ sēz
Arcas: ar′ kəs

Argus: ar′ gəs
Callisto: kə - lĭs′ tō
Daphne: dăf′ nē
Io: ī′ ō
Psyche: sī′ kē

Secondary names:
Aeneas: ē - nē′ əs
Arcadia: ar - kā′ dē - ə
Argos* ar′ gŏs
Cerberus* ser′ bə - rəs
Charon* kĕr′ ŏn
Epaphus ĕp′ ə - fəs
Erinyes* ĕ - rĭn′ ĭ - ēz
Inachus: ĭn′ ə - kəs
Parnassus* par - năs′ əs
Peneus: pĕ - nē′ əs
Phrygia: frĭj′ ē - ə
Python: pī′ thŏn
Zephyr: zĕf′ er
Gorgon, Gorgons: gor′ gən, gor′ gənz
Hippocrene: hĭ - pŏ - krē′ nē
Hippolochus: hĭ - pŏl′ ə - kəs
Iobates: ī - ŏb′ ə - tēz
Isander: ī - săn′ der
Labyrinth: lăb′ ə - rĭnth
Laodamia: lā - ō - də - mē′ ə
Lucifer: lū′ sĭ - fer
Lycia: lĭsh′ ē - ə
Medusa: mə - dū′ sə
Minos: mī′ nŏs
Mycenae: mī - sē′ nē
naiads: nī′ ădz
Philonoe: fĭl - ŏn′ ō - ē
Proteus* prō′ tĭ - əs
Sisyphus* sĭs′ ĭ - fəs
Stheneboea: sthĕn - ə - bē′ - ə
Tartarus* tar′ tə - rəs
Tiryns: tĭr′ ĭnz
Typhon: tī′ fŏn

Chapter 7

Primary names:
Bellerophon: bĕ - lĕr′ ə - fŏn
Chimera: kī - mē′ rə
Daedalus: dēd′ ə - ləs
Helius* hē′ lē - əs
Icarus: ĭk′ ə - rəs
Pegasus: pĕg′ ə - səs
Phaethon* fā′ ə - thŏn
Phoebus* fē′ bəs

Secondary names:
Amazons: ăm′ ə - zŏnz
Anatolia: ăn - ə - tō′ lē - ə
Anteia: ăn - tē′ ə
Aurora* ə - rōr′ ə
Clymene: klĭm - mē′ nē
Corinth* kor′ ĭnth
Echidna: ē - kĭd′ nə
Epaphus* ĕp′ ə - fəs
Glaucus: glau′ kəs

Chapter 8

Primary names:
Andromeda: ăn - drŏm′ ə - də
Danae: dăn′ ā - ē
Gorgon, Gorgons: gor′ gən, gor′ gənz
Medusa* mə - dū′ sə
Perseus: per′ sĭ - əs

Secondary names:
Acrisius: ə - krĭs′ ē - əs
Cassiopeia: kăs - ĭ - ō - pē′ ə
Cepheus: sē′ fĭ - əs
Cetus: sē′ təs
Dictys: dĭk′ tĭs
Graeae: grē′ ē
Hippocrene* hĭ - pŏ - krē′ nē
Hyperboreans: hī - per - bō′ rĭ - ənz
Larisa: lə - rĭs′ ə
Mycenae* mī - sē′ nē
Nereids: nē′ rĭ - ĭdz
Pegasus* pĕg′ ə - səs

Phineus: fĭn′ ĭ - əs
Polydectes: pŏl - ĭ - dĕk′ tēz
Seriphos: sĕr′ ĭ - fəs
Simonides: sĭ - mŏn′ ĭ - dēz
Thessaly: thĕs′ ə - lē

Chapter 9

Primary names:

Alcmena: ălk - mē′ nə
Amphitryon: ăm - fi′ trē - ŏn
Deianira: dē - yə - nī′ rə
Eurystheus: ū - rĭs′ thĭ - əs
Heracles: hĕr′ ə - klēz
Hercules: her′ kū - lēz

Secondary names:

Admetus: ăd - mē′ təs
Alcestis: ăl - sĕs′ tĭs
Amazons* ăm′ ə - zŏnz
Antaeus: ăn - tē′ əs
Atlas: ăt′ ləs
Augean: au - jē′ ən
Cacus: kā′ kəs
Cerberus* ser′ bə - rəs
Cerynean: ser - ĭ - nē′ ən
Diomedes* dī - ō - mē′ dēz
Eileithyia* ē - lē - thĭ′ yə
Erymanthian: ĕr - ĭ - măn′ thē - ən
Erythia: ĕr - ĭ - thē′ - ə
Eurytus: ū′ rĭ - təs
Geryon: gĕr′ ē - ŏn
Hebe* hē′ bē
Hesperides: hĕs - pĕr′ ĭ - dēz
Hippolyta: hĭ - pŏl′ ĭ - tə
Hydra: hī′ drə
Hyllus: hĭ′ ləs
Hyperboreans* hī - per - bō′ rĭ - ənz
Iole: ī′ ə - lē
Iphicles: ĭf′ ĭ - klēz
Iphitus: ĭf′ ĭ - təs
Ladon: lā′ dŏn
Laomedon: lā - ŏm′ ə - dŏn
Lernaean: ler - nē′ ən
Libya: lĭb′ ĭ - ə
Linus: lī′ nəs
Marathon: mĕr - ə - thŏn
Megara: mĕg′ ə - rə
Meleager: mĕl - ē - ā′ jər
Nemean: nē - mē′ ən
Nereus: nē′ rĭ - əs
Nessus: nĕs′ əs
Oeta: ē′ tə
Omphale: ŏm′ fə - lē
Peloponnese: pĕl - ə - pə - nēz′ (or Peloponnesus: pĕl - ə - pə - nē′ səs)
Philoctetes: fĭl - ŏk - tē′ - tēz
Priam: prē′ əm
Stymphalian: stĭm - fā′ lē - ən
Theseus: thē′ sĭ - əs
Tiresias: tī - rē′ sē - əs
Tiryns* tĭr′ ĭnz
Trachis: trā′ kĭs
Xenophon: zĕn′ ə - fən

Chapter 10

Primary names:

Argo: ar′ gō
Colchis: kŏl′ kĭs
Jason: jā′ sən
Medea* mə - dē′ ə
Pelias: pē′ lē - əs

Secondary names:

Absyrtus: ăb - ser′ təs
Aegeus: ē′ jĭ - əs
Aeson: ē′ sŏn
Aeetes: ē - ē′ tēz
Bithynia: bĭ - thĭn′ ē - ə
Calais: kăl′ ā - is
Castor: kăs′ ter
Chalciope: kăl - kī′ ō - pē
Charybdis: kə - rĭb′ dĭs

Chiron: kī′ rŏn
Circe* ser′ sē
Corinth* kor′ ĭnth
Creon: krē′ ŏn
Cyzicus: sĭz′ - ĭ - kəs
Danube: dăn′ yūb
Euxine: ūk′ sĭn
Glauce: glau′sē
Harpies: har′ pēz
Helle: hĕl′ ē
Hellespont: hĕl′ əs - pŏnt
Heracles* hĕr′ ə - klēz
Hylas: hī′ ləs
Hypsipyle: hĭp - sĭp′ ĭ - lē
Lemnos: lĕm′ nŏs
Lynceus: lĭn′ sĭ - əs
Oileus: ō′ ē - lūs
Orpheus* ōr′ fĭ - əs
Peleus: pē′ lĭ - əs
Phaeacians: fē - ā′ shĭ - ənz
Phineus: fĭn′ ĭ - əs
Phrixus: frĭk′ səs
Pollux: pŏl′ əks
Scylla: sĭl′ ə
Symplegades: sĭm - plĕg′ ə - dēz
Talus: tā′ ləs
Telamon: tĕl′ ə - mŏn
Thrace* thrās
Zetes: zē′ tēz

Chapter 11

Primary names:

Aegeus* ē′ jĭ - əs
Ariadne: ĕr - ĭ - ăd′ nē
Minos* mē′ nŏs
Minotaur: mĭn′ ə - taur
Theseus* thē′ sĭ - əs

Secondary names:

Aethra: ē′ thrə
Androgeus: ăn - drŏ′ jĭ - əs
Antiope: ăn - tē′ ə - pē
Bacchylides: bə - kĭl′ ə - dēz
Catullus: kə - təl′ əs
Cimon: sē′ mŏn
Corynetes: kor - ĭ - nē′ tēz
Crommyonian: krŏm - ĭ - ō′ nē - ən
Hecale: hĕk′ ə - lē
Helen: hĕl′ ən
Heracles* hĕr′ ə - klēz
Hippolyta* hĭ - pŏl′ ĭ - tə
Hippolytus: hĭ - pŏl′ ĭ - təs
Isthmian: ĭsth′ mē - ən
Jason* jā′ sən
Labyrinth* lăb′ ə - rĭnth
Lapiths: lăp′ ĭthz
Lycomedes: lī - kō - mē′ dēz
Medea* mə - dē′ ə
Naxos: năk′ sŏs
Oedipus: ĕd′ ĭ - pəs
Pasiphae* pə - sĭf′ ē
Peirithous: pī - rĭth′ ō - əs
Periphetes: pĕr - ĭ - fē′ tēz
Phaea: fē′ ə
Phaedra: fē′ drə
Procrustes: prō - krəs′ tēz
Sciron: skē′ rŏn
Scyrus: skī′ rəs
Sinis: sē′ nĭs
Troezen: trē′ zən

Chapter 12

Primary names:

Actaeon: ăk - tē′ ŏn
Althaea: ăl - thē′ ə
Arachne: ə - răk′ nē
Epimetheus: ĕp - ĭ - mē′ thĭ - əs
Erysichthon: ĕr - ĭ - sĭk′ thŏn
Meleager* mĕl - ē - ā′ jər
Niobe: nī′ ə - bē
Pandora: păn - dō′ rə
Prometheus: prō - mē′ thĭ - əs

Secondary names:

Amphion: ăm - fē′ ŏn
Ancaeus: ăn - sē′ əs
Atalanta: ăt - ə - lăn′ tə
Catullus* kə - təl′ əs
Caucasus: kau′ kə - səs
Chiron* kī′ rŏn
Deucalion: dū - kā′ lĭ - ŏn
Leto* lē′ tō
Lydia: lĭd′ ē - ə
Nestor: nĕs′ tor
Peirithous* pī - rĭth′ ō - əs
Peleus* pē′ lĭ - əs
Pyrrha: pĭr′ ə
Thebes* thēbz
Theseus* thē′ sĭ - əs
Thetis* thē′ tĭs

Chapter 13

Primary names:

Aegisthus: ē - jĭs′ thəs
Agamemnon: ăg - ə - mĕm′ nŏn
Atreus: ā′ trĭ - əs
Cassandra: kə - săn′ drə
Clytemnestra: klī - təm - nĕs′ trə
Electra: ē - lĕk′ trə
Helen* hĕl′ ən
Iphigenia: ĭf - ĭ - jə - nē′ ə
Menelaus: mĕn - ə - lā′ əs
Orestes: ō - rĕs′ tēz
Paris: pĕr′ ĭs (or Alexander: ăl - ĕk - zăn′ der)
Pelops* pē′ lŏps
Thyestes: thī - ĕs′ tēz

Secondary names:

Achilles: ə - kĭl′ ēz
Areopagus: ĕr - ē - ŏp′ ə - gəs
Aulis: au′ lĭs
Calchas: kăl′ kəs
Chrysothemis: krĭ - sŏth′ ĭ - mĭs
Euripides: ū - rĭp′ - ĭ - dēz
Hippodamia: hĭp - ə - də - mē′ ə
Leda: lē′ də
Mycenae* mī - sē′ nē
Myrtilus: mer′ tĭ - ləs
Myrtoan: mer - tō′ ən
Oenomaus: ē - nŏm′ ā - əs
Pelopia: pĕ - lō - pē′ - ə
Peloponnesus: pĕl - ə - pə - nē′ səs (or Peloponnese* pĕl - ə - pə - nēz′)
Pylades: pĭl′ ə - dēz
Tantalus* tăn′ tə - ləs
Taurians: tau′ rĭ - ənz
Tyndareus: tĭn - dar′ ĭ - əs

Chapter 14

Primary names:

Antigone: ăn - tĭg′ ə - nē
Cadmus* kăd′ məs
Colonus: kə - lō′ nəs
Creon* krē′ ŏn
Eteocles: ē - tē′ ō - klēz
Ismene: ĭs - mē′ nē
Jocasta: jō - kăs′ tə
Laius: lī′ əs
Oedipus* ēd′ ĭ - pəs
Polynices: pŏl - ĭ - nē′ sēz
Thebes* thēbz
Tiresias* tī - rē′ sē - əs

Secondary names:

Agave* ə - gā′ vē
Athamas: ăth′ ə - məs
Autonoe: au - tŏn - ō′ ē
Cithaeron* sĭ - thē′ rŏn
Eumenides: ū - mĕn′ ĭ - dēz
Eurydice: ū - rĭd′ - i - sē
Haemon: hē′ mŏn
Harmonia: har - mō′ nē - ə
Ino: ī′ nō
Merope: mĕr′ ō - pē
Polybus: pŏl′ ĭ - bəs

Semele* sĕm′ ə - lē
Sphinx: sfinks
Theseus* thē′ sĭ - əs

Chapter 15

Primary names:

Alcyone: ăl - sī′ ə - nē
Atalanta* ăt - ə - lăn′ tə
Baucis: bau′ kĭs
Ceyx: sē′ ĭks
Echo: ĕk′ ō
Eurydice: ū - rĭd′ - i - sē (not the same Eurydice as Creon's wife, chapter 14)
Galatea: găl - ə - tē′ ə
Hippomenes: hĭ - pŏm′ ə - nēz
Narcissus: nar - sĭs′ əs
Orpheus* ōr′ fĭ - əs
Philemon: fĭl - ē′ mŏn
Philomela: fĭl - ō - mē′ lə
Procne: prŏk′ nē
Pygmalion: pĭg - mā′ lĭ - ŏn
Pyramus: pĭr′ ə - məs
Tereus: tē′ rĭ - əs
Thisbe: thĭz′ bē

Secondary names:

For the names associated with the Underworld, see the list for chapter 3.

Aristaeus: ĕr - ĭs - tē′ əs
Calliope* kə - lī′ ə - pē
Cybele: sĭb′ ĭ - lē
Cyprus* sī′ prəs
Itys: ĭt′ ĭs
Liriope: lē - rē′ ō - pē
Morpheus* mor′ fĭ - əs
Nemesis* nĕm′ ə - sĭs
Pandion: păn - dē′ ŏn
Phrygia* frĭj′ ē - ə
Thrace* thrās

Chapter 16

Primary names:

Achilles* ə - kĭl′ ēz
Ajax: ā′ jăks
Agamemnon* ăg - ə - mĕm′ nŏn
Alexander* ăl - ĕk - zăn′ der (or Paris: pĕr′ ĭs)
Cassandra* kə - săn′ drə
Diomedes* dī - ō - mē′ dēz
Hector: hĕk′ ter
Hecuba: hĕk′ ū - bə
Helen* hĕl′ ən
Ilium: ĭl′ ĭ - əm
Menelaus* mĕn - ə - lā′ əs
Neoptolemus: nē - ŏp - tŏl′ ə - məs
Odysseus* ō - dĭs′ ĭ - əs
Paris* pĕr′ ĭs (or Alexander: ăl - ĕk - zăn′ der)
Patroclus: pə - trō - kləs
Priam* prē′ əm
Troad: trō′ ăd

Secondary names:

Aeneas* ē - nē′ əs
Andromache: ăn - drŏm′ ə - kē
Astyanax: ăs - tī′ ə - năks
Briseis: brē - sē′ ĭs
Calchas* kăl′ kəs
Chryseis: krī - sē′ ĭs
Chryses: krī′ sēz
Deiphobus: dē - ĭf′ ə - bəs
Eris* ĕ′ rĭs
Ilus: ē′ ləs
Laocoon: lā - ŏk′ ō - ŏn
Laodamia* lā - ō - də - mē′ ə
Lemnos* lĕm′ nŏs
Lycomedes* lī - kō - mē′ dēz
Machaon: mə - kā′ ŏn
Myrmidons: mer′ mĭ - dŏnz
Nestor* nĕs′ tor
Oenone: ē - nō′ nē
Palamedes: păl - ə - mē - dēz
Palladium: pə - lā - dĭ - əm

Pallas: păl′ əs
Pandarus: păn′ də - rəs
Peleus* pē′ lĭ - əs
Philoctetes* fĭl - ŏk - tē′ - tēz
Phoenix: fē′ nĭks
Phthia: thē′ ə
Polites: pə - lē′ tēz
Polydorus: pŏl - ĭ - dō′ rəs
Polyxena: pō - lĭk′ sə - nə
Protesilaus: prō - tĕs - ĭ - lā′ əs
Sarpedon: sar - pē′ dŏn
Scyrus* skē′ rəs
Sinon: sē′ nŏn
Telemachus: tə - lĕm′ ə - kəs
Tenedos: tĕn′ ə - dŏs
Thersites: ther - sē′ tēz
Thetis* thē′ tĭs

Chapter 17

Primary names:

Ithaca: ĭth′ ə - kə
Odysseus* ō - dĭs′ ĭ - əs
Penelope: pə - nĕl′ ə - pē
Telemachus* tə - lĕm′ ə - kəs

Secondary names:

Achilles* ə - kĭl′ ēz
Aeolia: ē - ō′ lē - ə
Aeolus: ē′ ō - ləs
Agamemnon* ăg - ə - mĕm′ nŏn
Ajax* ā′ jăks
Alcinous: ăl - sĭn′ ō - əs
Amphinomus: ăm - fĭn′ ə - məs
Anticleia: ăn - tĭ - klē′ ə
Antiphates: ăn - tĭf′ ə - tēz
Arete: ə - rē′ tē
Argus: ar′ gəs (not the same Argus as in chapter 6)
Callidice: kə - lĭd′ ĭ - sē
Calypso: kə - lĭp′ sō
Charybdis* kə - rĭb′ dĭs
Cicones: sĭ - kō′ nēz
Cimmerians: sĭ - mĭr′ ē - ənz
Circe* ser′ sē
Cyclopes* sī - klō′ pēz
Demodocus: dĕ - mŏd′ ə - kəs
Elpenor: ĕl - pē′ nor
Eumaeus: ū - mē′ əs
Eurycleia: ū - rĭ - klē - ə
Eurylochus: ū - rĭl′ ə - kəs
Helius* hē′ lĭ - əs
Ino* ī′ nō
Laertes: lā - ĕr′ tēz
Laestrygonians: lēs - trĭ - gō′ nē - ənz
Melanthus: mə - lăn′ thəs
Menelaus* mĕn - ə - lā′ əs
Mentes: mĕn′ tēz
Mentor: mĕn′ tor
Nausicaa: nau - sĭk′ ə - ə
Neoptolemus* nē - ŏp - tŏl′ ə - məs
Nestor* nĕs′ tor
Ogygia: ō - gĭ′ jē - ə
Phaeacia: fē - ā′ shē - ə
Phaeacians: fē - ā′ shē - ənz
Philoetius: fĭl - ē′ shĭ - əs
Poliporthes: pŏl - ĭ′ por - thēz
Polyphemus* pŏl - ĭ - fē′ məs
Polypoetes: pŏ - lĭ- pē′ tēz
Pylus: pī′ ləs
Scylla* sĭl′ ə
Sirens: sī′ rənz
Sparta: spar′ tə
Telegonus: tĕ - lĕg′ - ə - nəs
Thesprotians: thĕs - prō′ shē - ənz
Thrinacia: thrĭ - nā′ shē - ə
Tiresias* tī - rē′ sē - əs

Chapter 18

Primary names:

Aeneas* ē - nē′ əs
Anchises* ăn - kī′ sēz
Anna: ăn′ ə

Ascanius: ăs - kā′ nĭ - əs
Carthage: kar′ thĭj
Dido: dī′ dō
Hesperia: hĕs - pĭr′ ē - ə
Iulus: ū′ ləs
Turnus: ter′ nəs

Secondary names:

For the names associated with the Underworld, see the list for chapter 3.

Acestes: ə - kĕs′ tēz
Achaemenides: ăk - ə - mĕn′ ə - dēz
Achates: ə - kā′ tēz
Aeneas Silvius: ē - nē′ əs sĭl′ vē - əs
Aeolus* ē′ ō - ləs
Alba Longa: ăl′ bə lŏng′ gə
Allecto: ə - lĕk′ tō
Amata: ə - mā′ tə
Andromache* ăn - drŏm′ ə - kē
Anna Perenna: ăn′ ə per - ĕn′ nə
Avernus: ə - ver′ nəs
Beroe: bĕ - rō′ ē
Buthrotum: bū - thrō′ təm
Camilla: kə - mĭl′ lə
Celaeno: sĕ - lē′ nō
Crete* krēt
Creusa: krē - ū′ sə
Cumae: kū′ mē
Deiphobe: dē - ĭf′ ō - bē
Deiphobus: dē - ĭf′ ō - bəs
Delos* dē′ lŏs
Drepanum: drə pā′ nəm
Evander: ə - văn′ der
Faunus: faw′ nəs
Harpies* har′ pēz
Hector: hĕk′ ter
Helen: hĕl′ ən
Helenus: hĕl′ ə - nəs
Iarbas: ē - ar′ bəs
Juturna: jū - tern′ ə
Laocoon* lā - ŏk′ ō - ŏn
Latinus: lə - tē′ nəs
Latium: lā′ shĭ - əm
Lausus: lau′ səs
Lavinia: lə - vĭn′ ē - ə
Mezentius: mə - zĕn′ tĭ - əs
Misenus: mī - sē′ nəs
Nautes: nau′ tēz
Neoptolemus* nē - ŏp - tŏl′ ə - məs
Numicius: nū - mĭk′ ĭ - əs
Palinurus: păl - ĭ - nū′ - rəs
Pallantium: pə - lăn′ tĭ - əm
Pallas: păl′ əs
Penates: pə - nā′ tēz
Polydorus: pŏl - ĭ - dō′ rəs
Priam* prē′ əm
Pygmalion: pĭg - mā′ lĭ - ŏn (not the same Pygmalion as the sculptor, chapter 15)
Pyrgo: pĭr′gō
Romulus: rŏm′ ū - ləs
Rutulians: rū - tū′ lĭ - ənz
Sibyl: sĭb′ əl
Strophades: strŏf′ ə - dēz
Sychaeus: sĭ - kē′ əs
Thrace* thrās
Tiber: tī′ ber
Tyre: tīr
Vergil: ver′ jĭl

Chapter 19

Primary names:

Amulius: ə - mū′ lĭ - əs
Ancus Marcius: ăng′ kəs mar′ shĭ - əs
Cloelia: klō - ē′ lē - ə
Gaius Mucius: gī′ əs mū′ shĭ - əs
Horatius Cocles: hō - rā′ shĭ - əs kō′ klēz
Lars Porsenna: lars por′ sĕn - nə
Lucius Junius Brutus: lū′ shĭ - əs jū′ nĭ - əs brū′ təs
Lucius Tarquinius Priscus: lū′ shĭ - əs tar - kwĭn′ ĭ - əs prĭs′ kəs
Lucius Tarquinius Superbus: lū′ shĭ - əs tar - kwĭn′ ĭ - əs sū - pĕr′ bəs

Lucretia: lū - krē′ shē - ə
Lucumo: lū - kū′ mō
Numa Pompilius: nū′ mə pŏm - pĭl′ ĭ - əs
Numitor: nū′ mĭ - tor
Remus: rē′ məs
Romulus* rŏm′ ū - ləs
Scaevola: skē - vō′ lə
Servius Tullius: ser′ vĭ - əs tŭl′ lĭ - əs
Tanaquil: tăn′ ə - kwĭl
Tarquinius Collatinus: tar - kwĭn′ ĭ - əs kŏl - ə - tē′ nəs
Tullia: tŭl′ lĭ - ə
Tullus Hostilius: tŭl′ əs hŏs - tĭl′ ĭ - əs

Secondary names:

Arruns: ĕr′ ənz
Aventine (ăv′ ən - tīn) Hill
Cloaca Maxima: klō - ā′ kə măx′ ĭ - mə
Clusium: klūs′ ĭ - əm
Collatia: kŏl - ā′ - shē - ə
Curiatii: kū - rĭ - ā′ shĭ - ē
Egeria: ē - jĭr′ ē - ə
Faustulus: faus′ tū - ləs
Gabii: gā′ bi -ē
Horatii: hō - rā′ shĭ - ē; singular, Horatius: hō - rā′ shĭ - əs
Janiculum (jə - nĭk′ ū - ləm) Hill
Janus* jā′ nəs
Larentia: lə - rĕn′ tē - ə
Mettius Fufetius: mĕt′ ĭ - əs fū - fē′ tĭ - əs
Ostia: ŏs′ tē - ə
Palatine (păl′ ə - tīn) Hill
Quirinus: kwĭ - rī ′ nəs
Rhea Silvia: rē′ ə sĭl′ vē - ə
Sabines: sā′ bīnz
Sextus: sĕks′ təs
Sibyl* sĭb′ əl
Sibylline (sĭb′ əl - līn) Books
Spurius Larcius: sper′ ĭ - əs lark′ ĭ - əs
Tarpeia: tar - pē′ ə
Tarquinii: tar - kwĭn′ ĭ - ē
Titus: tī′ təs
Titus Tatius: tī′ təs tā′ shĭ - əs
Titus Herminius: tī′ təs her - mĭn′ ĭ - əs
Turnus Herdonius: ter′ nəs her - dō′ nĭ - əs

Bibliography

Primary Sources

Anthology of Classical Myth: Primary Sources in Translation. Ed. and trans. Stephen M. Trzaskoma, R. Scott Smith, and Stephen Brunet. Indianapolis, IN: Hackett Publishing Company, 2004.

Apollodorus. *The Library.* Volumes I and II. Trans. Sir James George Fraser. Loeb Classical Library. Cambridge, MA: Harvard University Press, 1995 and 1996.

Campbell, David A. *Greek Lyric Poetry.* New York: St. Martin's Press, 1967.

Edmonds, J. M. *Greek Bucolic Poets: Theocritus, Bion, Moschus.* Loeb Classical Library. Cambridge, MA: Harvard University Press, 1960.

The Epic of Gilgamesh. Second edition. Trans. Danny P. Jackson. Wauconda, IL: Bolchazy-Carducci Publishers, 1997.

Hesiod, et al. *Hesiod, Homeric Hymns, Epic Cycle, Homerica.* Trans. Hugh G. Evelyn-White. 2nd rev. edition. Loeb Classical Library. Cambridge, MA: Harvard University Press, 2002.

Hesiod. *Theogony.* Trans. Norman O. Brown. Indianapolis, IN: Bobbs-Merrill Company, Inc., 1953.

Homer. *The Iliad.* Trans. Richmond Lattimore. Chicago: University of Chicago Press, 1961.

Homer. *The Odyssey.* Trans. Robert Fitzgerald. New York: Doubleday & Co., 1963.

Lattimore, Richmond, trans. *Greek Lyrics.* 2nd edition. Chicago: University of Chicago Press, 1975.

Lang, Andrew. *Theocritus, Bion and Moschus Rendered into English Prose.* Whitefish, MT: Kessinger Publishing Co., 2005.

Ovid. *Metamorphoses,* Books I–VIII. 3rd edition. Trans. Frank Justus Miller; rev. G. P. Goold. Loeb Classical Library. Cambridge, MA: Harvard University Press, 1999.

Ovid. *Metamorphoses.* Trans. Rolfe Humphries. Bloomington: Indiana University Press, 1974.

Stanford, W. B., ed. *ΟΜΗΡΟΥ ΟΔΥΣΣΕΙΑ, The Odyssey of Homer.* 2 volumes. 2nd edition. London: Macmillan, Ltd., 1959.

Secondary Sources

Abrams, M. H. *A Glossary of Literary Terms.* 7th edition. Fort Worth, TX: HarcourtBrace College Publishers, 1999.

D'Aulaire, Ingri, and Edgar Parin D'Aulaire. *D'Aulaire's Book of Greek Myths.* New York: Doubleday, 1962.

Grimal, Pierre. *The Dictionary of Classical Mythology.* Trans. A. R. Maxwell-Hyslop. Malden, MA: Blackwell Publishers, 1996.

Guerber, H. A. *The Myths of Greece and Rome.* New York: Dover Publications, 1993.

Hamilton, Edith. *Mythology.* New York: New American Library, 1969.

Harris, Stephen L., and Gloria Platzner. *Classical Mythology: Images and Insights.* 3rd edition. Mountain View, CA: Mayfield Publishing Company, 2001.

Holman, C. Hugh. *A Handbook of Literature.* 4th edition. Indianapolis, IN: Bobbs-Merrill Educational Publishing, 1980.

James, Vanessa. *The Genealogy of Greek Mythology.* New York: Melcher Media, Inc., 2003.

Jollife, H. R. *Tales from the Greek Drama.* Wauconda, IL: Bolchazy-Carducci Publishers, 1984.

Kirkwood, G. M. *A Short Guide to Classical Mythology.* Wauconda, IL: Bolchazy-Carducci Publishers, 2003.

Mayerson, Philip. *Classical Mythology in Literature, Art and Music.* Scott, Foresman and Company, 1975.

Morford, Mark P. O., and Robert J. Lenardon. *Classical Mythology.* 2nd edition. New York and London: Longman, 1977.

Rose, H. J. *A Handbook of Greek Mythology.* New York: E. P. Dutton and Co., Inc., 1959.

Rosenberg, Donna, and Sorelle Baker. *Mythology and You.* Skokie, IL: National Textbook Company, 1981.

Resources for Teachers: General

Children's Books on Ancient Greek and Roman Mythology: An Annotated Bibliography. Compiled by Antoinette Brazouski and Mary J. Klatt. Westport, CT: Greenwood Press, 1984.

Buller, J. L. "What Becomes a Legend Most?" *Classical Outlook* 78.4 (2001), 145–49. A comparison of the ancient oral mythic tradition with the modern Internet-driven phenomenon of the urban legend.

Buxton, Richard. *The Complete World of Greek Mythology.* London: Thames and Hudson, 2004.

Cornelius, Geoffrey. *The Starlore Handbook.* San Francisco: Chronicle Books, 1997. A guide to all the heavenly bodies with names drawn from myths.

Grant, Michael, and John Hazel. *Who's Who in Classical Mythology.* New York: Routledge, 2002. Detailed entries on all the ancient gods and heroes, by two prominent classical scholars.

Veyne, Paul. *Did the Greeks Believe in Their Myths?* Trans. Paula Wissing. Chicago: University of Chicago Press, 1988. An in-depth answer to the perennial student question, by a professor of Roman history.

Resources for Teachers: Theories of Myth

Below are some resources on theories of myth. Those wishing to explore this complex topic in greater depth are advised to start with John Peradotto's *Classical Mythology: An Annotated Bibliographical Survey* (American Philological Association, 1977), and with Eric Csapo's *Theories of Mythology* (London: Blackwell, 2005).

Anthropological Approaches to Myth

Beye, Charles R. *Ancient Epic Poetry.* Expanded reprint edition. Wauconda, IL: Bolchazy-Carducci Publishers, 2006.

Bolchazy, Ladislaus J. *Hospitality in Antiquity.* Rev. edition. Chicago: Ares Publishers, 1995. Origins of ethical and religious concepts; various stages of xenophobic and theoxenic hospitality; archetypes of "Emmanuel" (God with us).

Bultmann, R. *Jesus Christ and Mythology.* New York: Scribner's, 1958.

Dodds, E. R. *The Greeks and the Irrational.* Berkeley: University of California Press, 1951. A pioneering work that pointed out the prominence of violence and madness in Greek culture and myth and served as a counterpoint to earlier scholarship that depicted the Greeks as supremely rational beings.

Foley, Helene P. *The Homeric Hymn to Demeter.* Princeton, NJ: Princeton University Press, 1993.

Fontenrose, Joseph. *Python: A Study of the Delphic Myth and Its Origins.* Berkeley: University of California Press, 1959. A study of the ritual origins of combat myths.

Frazer, Sir James George. *The Golden Bough: A Study in Magic and Religion* (originally published 1890, but also available online at http://www.bartleby.com/196/). A monumental work that claims the heart of all religions is the legend of a solar god wedded to an earth-goddess, ritually slain in his earthly incarnation as a priest-king, and miraculously resurrected.

Gaster, T. *Myth, Legend and Customs in the Old Testament.* New York: Harper & Row, 1969.

Harrison, Jane. *Prolegomena to the Study of Greek Religion.* New York: World, 1957; originally published 1922; and *Themis: a Study of the Social Origins of Greek Religion.* New York: World, 1962; originally published 1927. Harrison belonged to the "Cambridge School" of myth, which held that myth is the spoken counterpart to rituals performed.

Heidel, A. *The Gilgamesh Epic and Old Testament Parallels.* Chicago: University of Chicago Press, 1967.

Heidel, A. *The Babylonian Genesis.* Chicago: University of Chicago, 1963.

Meagher, Robert E. *The Meaning of Helen.* Wauconda, IL: Bolchazy-Carducci Publishers, 2001.

Raglan, Lord. *The Hero.* New York: Random House, 1956; originally published 1936. Another very influential work on the ritual theory of myth.

Sowa, Cora A. *Traditional Themes and the Homeric Hymns.* Wauconda, IL: Bolchazy-Carducci Publishers, 1984.

Myth and Psychology

Boden, Jean Shinoda. *Goddesses in Everywoman: A New Psychology of Women.* New York: Harper and Row, 1984. A Jungian psychologist analyzes the archetype of each Greek goddess as she manifests herself through the female life cycle.

———. *Gods in Everyman: A New Psychology of Men's Lives and Loves.* New York: Harper and Row, 1989. A companion book to *Goddesses in Everywoman* discussing the Greek gods as manifested in men's personalities.

Campbell, Joseph. *The Hero With a Thousand Faces.* Princeton, NJ: Princeton University Press, 1949. A seminal work that outlines the author's theory of the "monomyth" at the heart of all cultures' myths. George Lucas has admitted the influence of this book on his *Star Wars* saga.

Freud, Sigmund. *The Interpretation of Dreams.* New York: Oxford University Press, 1999. A discussion of the symbolism in both myths and dreams which includes the pioneering psychoanalyst's discussion of Oedipus.

Jung, Carl et al. *Man and His Symbols.* New York: Dell, 1968. A good lay person's introduction to Jung and his theory of archetypes.

Mullahy, Patrick. *Oedipus: Myth and Complex.* New York: Grove Press, 1955. A survey of psychological theories of myth, with particular attention to the importance of the Oedipus myth in the thought of the pioneering psychoanalysts of the twentieth century.

Structural Approaches to Myth

Lévi-Strauss, Claude. "The Structural Study of Myth." In Thomas Sebeok's *Myth: A Symposium.* Bloomington, IN: University of Indiana Press, 1965. An introduction to this important theorist's belief that the function of myth is to mediate between opposites.

———. *The Raw and the Cooked.* Trans. J. and D. Weightman. New York: Harper and Row, 1969. A further development of the idea of myth as mediator, especially between nature and culture.

Propp, Vladimir. *The Morphology of the Folktale.* Trans. L. Scott. Rev. and ed. L.A. Wagner. Austin, TX: University of Texas Press, 1968. A work that greatly influenced Lévi-Strauss in its analysis of the recurrent motifs in folk tales.

Vernant, Jean-Pierre. *Myth and Society in Ancient Greece.* Trans. J. Lloyd. New York: Zone Books, 1988. Another important author of structural interpretations of myth, who focused more directly upon the historical culture of ancient Greece than Lévi-Strauss did.

Zeitlin, Froma I. "The Dynamics of Misogyny: Myth and Mythmaking in the *Oresteia.*" *Arethusa* 11.1–2 (1978), 149–84. A discussion of the role of male/female opposites in Aeschylus' trilogy and how they are resolved via the subordination of matriarchy to patriarchy.

Post-structuralism

Csapo, Eric. *Theories of Mythology.* Malden, MA: Blackwell, 2005. Useful as a bibliography, the chapter on "Ideology" includes a Marxist analysis of the myth of Heracles.

Detienne, Marcel. *The Gardens of Adonis.* Trans. J. Lloyd. Princeton, NJ: Princeton University Press, 1994. An unveiling of a number of "codes" in the system of Greek thought, as demonstrated via the myths of Demeter, Adonis, Prometheus, and others.

Eagleton, Terry. *Literary Theory.* 2nd edition. Minneapolis: University of Minnesota Press, 1996. A guide to many of the thinkers mentioned in this bibliography.

Post-classical Adaptations of Classical Myths

Berger, Pamela. *The Goddess Obscured: Transformations of the Grain Protectress from Goddess to Saint.* Boston: Beacon, 1985.

Galinsky, G. Karl. *The Herakles Theme: The Adaptations of the Hero in Literature from Homer to the Twentieth Century.* Oxford: B. Blackwell, 1972.

Komar, Kathleen L. *Reclaiming Klytemnestra: Revenge or Reconciliation.* Urbana: University of Illinois Press, 2003.

Moddelmog, Debra A. *Readers and Mythic Signs: The Oedipus Myth in Twentieth-Century Fiction.* Carbondale: Southern Illinois University Press, 1993.

Panofsky, Dora, and Erwin Panofsky. *Pandora's Box: The Changing Aspects of a Mythical Symbol.* 3rd edition. Princeton, NJ: Princeton University Press, 1991.

Pratt, Annis. *Dancing with Goddesses: Archetypes, Poetry, and Empowerment.* Bloomington: Indiana University Press, 1994.

Stanford, W. B. *The Ulysses Theme: A Study in the Adaptibility of a Traditional Hero.* Oxford: B. Blackwell, 1963.

Suzuki, Mihoko. *Metamorphoses of Helen: Authority, Difference, and the Epic.* Ithaca: Cornell University Press, 1989.

Yarnall, Judith. *Transformations of Circe: The History of an Enchantress.* Urbana: University of Illinois Press, 1994.

Resources for Students

Asimov, Isaac. *Words from the Myths.* Boston: Houghton Mifflin, 1961. Reading level: 5th–7th grade. Some of the science is dated, but the author remains a charming storyteller in explaining how many everyday and scientific words are derived from ancient myths.

Barber, Antonia. *Apollo and Daphne.* Los Angeles, CA: J. Paul Getty Museum, 1998. Reading level: 8th–9th grade. Fifteen Greek and Roman myths are retold for young readers. The myths are illustrated with details of paintings by artists such as Botticelli, Raphael, Titian, Rembrandt, Poussin, and Burne-Jones.

Bierlein, J. F. *Parallel Myths.* New York: Ballantine Books, 1994. Reading level: 10th–11th grade. A useful resource for comparative mythology, broken down by broad categories, i.e., creation stories, hero myths, journeys to the Underworld.

Bulfinch's Mythology. Ed. and comm. Richard Martin. New York: HarperCollins Publishers, 1991. Reading level: 8th grade (stories), 11th grade (commentary). A classic of its kind, this book originating in 1855 has been introducing the general (and often very young) reader to ancient myth for generations. The story of Thomas Bulfinch, told in the introduction, is worth reading also.

Frenkel, Emily. *Aeneas: Vergil's Epic Retold for Young Readers.* Illus. Simon Weller. Bristol Classical Press, 1991. Reading level: 8th–9th grade. The great Roman epic is adapted for mature middle school students and high school students.

Graves, Robert. *Greek Myths.* Condensed and illus. edition. Ed. John Buchanan Brown. London: Cassell, 1984. Reading Level: 9th–12th grades. Fiction. Excellent photos of classical masterpieces illustrate Graves' stories.

Graves, Robert. *The Greek Myths, Complete Edition.* London: Penguin, 1993.

Green, Roger Lancelyn. *Tales of the Greek Heroes.* London: Puffin Classics of Penguin Books, 2002. Reading Level: 4th–6th grade. Fiction. Nineteen stories of Greek heroes including Prometheus, Heracles, Theseus, Perseus, Jason, Meleager, and Atalanta.

Guerber, H. A. *Myths of Greece and Rome.* Mineola, NY: Dover Publications Inc., 1993; orig. published 1907. Reading level: 10th–11th grade. The print is somewhat old-fashioned, but the writing is simple and graphic. It is illustrated with 64 halftones by such masters as Michelangelo, Raphael, Titian, Rubens, Canova, and Bernini.

Harris, John. *Strong Stuff: Herakles and His Labors.* Art by Gary Baseman. Los Angeles, CA: J. Paul Getty Museum, 2005. Reading level: 6th–8th grade. A recap of the most famous deeds of the world's first superhero, narrated and illustrated with humor.

———. *Greece! Rome! Monsters!* Art by Calef Brown. Los Angeles, CA: J. Paul Getty Museum, 2002. Reading level: 6th–8th grade. This book presents twenty of the best-known mythical monsters in updated form (e.g., a blue centaur heads out to a disco). Also includes a pronunciation guide and a pop quiz.

Khanduri, Kamini. *Tales of the Trojan War.* Illus. Jeff Anderson. New York: Usborne Publishing, Ltd, 1998. Reading Level: 4th–7th grade. Fiction. Nine pivotal tales of the Trojan War, rather grimly illustrated, from the Judgment of Paris to the Wooden Horse. Includes a Who's Who with a pronunciation guide and a guide to "Important Places."

Lister, Robin. *The Odyssey.* Illus. Alan Baker. New York: Kinfisher, 1994. Reading Level: 5th–7th grade. Fiction. A beautifully illustrated retelling of the saga in seventeen chapters.

McCarty, Nick. *The Iliad.* Illus. Victor Ambrus. New York: Kingfisher, 2000. Reading level: 5th–7th grade. Homer's great epic of the Trojan war is adapted for young readers.

McLean, Mollie, and Anne Wiseman. *Adventures of the Greek Heroes.* Boston: Houghton Mifflin Co., 1989. Reading Level: 4th–6th grade. Fiction. Six sections on these heroes: Hercules, Perseus, Theseus, Orpheus, Meleager, Jason and Argonauts.

Martell, Hazel Mary. *Myths and Civilization of the Ancient Greeks.* New York: Peter Bedrick Books, 1998. Reading level: 7th–8th grades. This book contains a selection of important myths and each is supplemented by historical or cultural nonfiction. The myths are carefully chosen to contain reference to important aspects of the civilization.

Osborne, Mary Pope. *Favorite Greek Myths.* Illus. Troy Howell. New York: Scholastic, 1988. Reading level: 4th–7th. Fiction. Twelve stories, most adapted from Ovid's *Metamorphoses* and Apuleius: e.g., Ceres and Proserpine, King Midas, Echo and Narcissus, Cupid and Psyche. Luminously illustrated but no pronunciation guide.

Russell, William F. *Classic Myths to Read Aloud: The Great Stories of Greek and Roman Mythology.* New York: Three Rivers Press, 1992. Reading Level: 1st–7th grade. Fiction. This collection of myths is designed to be read aloud, preferably by candlelight or flashlight. Wonderful for rainy days.

Sutcliffe, Rosemary. *Black Ships Before Troy.* Illus. Alan Lee. London: Delacorte Press, 2004. Reading Level: 5th–7th grade. Fiction. Kate Greenaway Award Winner for illustrations, 1993. Authentically detailed illustrations in this retelling of the *Iliad* by an acclaimed novelist. Includes a pronunciation guide.

Thistle, Louise. *Dramatizing Greek Mythology.* Lyme, NH: Smith and Kraus, 2002. Reading level: 9th grade. The book contains five Greek myths in play form designed to give everyone in a class of up to thirty-five students a significant role. Each myth includes a play script, writing and art lessons, story questions for critical thinking, and action pictures.

Credits

The following credits acknowledge material used by permission.

p. 104, ch. 6, NASA photo of Jupiter and moons from National Aeronautics and Space Administration.

p. 128, ch. 8, 'Eve Meets Medusa': © Michelene Wandor. In 'Gardens of Eden Revisited', Five Leaves Publications, 1999. Her website is http://www.mwandor.co.uk/.

p. 175, ch. 11, translation of Catullus *Poem 64* lines 149–55, reprinted by permission of the publisher from John Godwin, ed. and trans., *Catullus Poems 61–68* (Aris and Phillips 1996).

pp. 245–246, ch.14. "Oedipus Rex" by Tom Lehrer. ©1959 Tom Lehrer. Used by permission.

pp. 272–274, ch.15. "Atalanta" by Betty Miles, from *Free to Be . . . You and Me* (Running Press 1974).

Index

For the more important gods and heroes, the page numbers of the main discussion are in boldface type. Page numbers with "i" refer to illustrations. For persons and gods such as Odysseus and Zeus who appear in large numbers of illustrations, there are subcategories "illustrations of." The numerous definitions (e.g., aetiological, allegory) and etymologies (e.g., arachnid, titanic) are grouped under Definitions and Etymologies, respectively.

A

Absyrtus, 162
Acestes, 355–356
Achaemenides, 352
Achates, 345–347, 368
Acheron, 321
Achilles, 54, 191, 211–212, 278, 280–283
  in the *Aeneid,* 345, 348, 357
  in the *Iliad,* 278, 280–284, 286–294, 298–299
    illustrations, 280, 283, 289, 292–294
  in the *Odyssey,* 323–324
Achilles' heel, 280
Acrisius, 123, 123i, 126
Acropolis, 22, 41, 115
Actaeon, 197–198, 197i, 230
Admetus, 139–140, 139i
Adonis, 95, 104i
Aeetes, 72, 158, 159–162
Aegeus, 165–166, 171–172, 171i, 176
  Aegean Sea named for, 176
aegis (goatskin shield), 20, 39, 65i, 73
Aegisthus, 210, 213–216, 224i
Aeneas, 46, 377, 383
  in the *Aeneid,* **343–368,** 347–348i, 355i, 363i, 366i
  in the *Iliad,* 285–286, 299
  phantom of, 364
Aeneas Silvius, 367
Aeolia, 318
Aeolus, 318–319, 318i, 343–345, 343i
Aeschylus
  Oresteia, 207
  Prometheus Bound, 189
Aesculapius. *See* Asclepius
Aeson, 153, 164
Aethra, 171, 171i, 177
Aetolia, 195
Agamemnon, 210–213, 213, 217, 224i
  in the *Aeneid,* 345, 350–351, 353–354, 357, 360, 365
  in the *Odyssey,* 311, 323
  in the Trojan War, 280–282, 284–285, 288–290, 298
Agave, 56–58, 58i, 230
  plant named after, 66i
Agenor, 97–98
Ajax (the Greater, son of Telamon)
  in the *Iliad,* 287–290, 287i, 289i, 294
  in the *Odyssey,* 324
  in popular culture, 307, 307i
Ajax (the Lesser, son of Oileus), 297, 311
Alba Longa, 377, 383, 385
Albans, 383–385
Alcestis, 139–140, 139i, 164
Alcinous, 314–315, 314i
Alcmena, 135
Alcyone, 264–266
Alexander. *See* Paris
Allecto, 360–361
Alphaeus, 48

Althaea, 196
Amalthea, 11
Amata, 360–362, 365–366
Amazons, 114, 140, 140i, 158, 176
ambrosia, 11, 25, 43, 91, 346, 365
  modern recipe for, 14
Amphinomus, 334
Amphion, 193
Amphitrite, 22, 163i, 173, 174i
Amphitryon, 135
Amulius, 377
Amycus, 156
Anatolia, 113
Ancaeus, 196
Anchises, 278, 349–350, 352, 355–356, 359–360, 362, 367
  and Aeneas, 97i
  and Aphrodite, 96–97
Ancus Marcius, 386–388
Androgeus, 173
Andromache, 286, 287i, 298, 351
  in modern art, 306i
Andromeda, 125–127, 126i
  constellation, 132–133, 132i
  galaxy, 133
anemone, 95, 95i
animals, and Dionysus, 55
Anna, 352–355, 368
Anna Perenna, 368
Antaeus, 141, 141i
Anteia, 112i, 113
Anticleia, 322–323
Antigone, 231, 234–237i, **234–239**
Antiope, 176
Antiphates, 319, 319i
Aphrodite (Venus), 10, 20, **46,** 46i, 70i, 90, 91, 98, 279i
  and Aeneas, 96–97
  in the *Aeneid,* 33, 343, 345–346, 348–349, 353, 356, 358, 365–366, 368
    illustrations of, 347, 363, 366
  and Anchises, 96–97, 96i
  in astronomy, 67–68
  and Atalanta and Hippomenes, 262–263
  birth of, 9, 10i
  and Hippolytus, 177–178
  and Jason, 158–159, 165
  in the Judgment of Paris, 278–279, 279i
  lovers of
    Adonis, 95, 104i
    Ares, 52–53, 315
  in the *Odyssey,* 315
  and Pandora, 190
  in popular culture, 67–68
  and Psyche, 86
  and Pygmalion, 261
  in the Trojan War, 278–280, 285–286
Apollo (Phoebus, Phoebus Apollo), 20, 31, 40i, **42–45,** 42i, 44i, 45i, 56i, 69
  in the *Aeneid,* 350–351, 353–354, 357, 360, 365
  also named Phoebus, 43
  on Arachne's tapestry, 192
  and Daphne, 92–93, 92i
  and Heracles, 142
  and Hermes, 47–50
  in the *Iliad,* 292i
  lyre of, 259i
  and the Muses, 1i, 2
  and Niobe, 194
  in the *Odyssey,* 315, 332
  and Oedipus, 234
  oracles of, 88
  and Orestes, 216–217
  and Orpheus, 257
  and Phineus, 156
  and popular culture, 77
  in Rome, 391
  in the Trojan War, 281–283, 286–287, 289–293, 296
Apollodorus, *Library,* 73, 123, 135, 229, 277, 334
Apollonius Rhodius, *Argonautica,* 153
apotheosis
  of Aeneas, Julius Caesar, and Augustus Caesar, 368
  of Heracles, 144, 144i
apples, golden, 46, 141, 262, 278
Apuleius, *Metamorphoses,* 86–91
Aquarius, 71
Aquila (constellation), 71
Arachne, 192–193, 192i, 193i

Arcadia, 73, 334
Arcadians, 362, 364
Arcas, 94–95
Areopagus, 217
Ares (Mars), 29, 40i, **52–53,** 52i, 53i, 69–70, 140, 207
  in the *Aeneid,* 345, 365–366
  and Aphrodite, 72
  bronze-footed bulls of, 160
  and Cadmus, 229
  in the *Odyssey,* 315
  in Roman history, 377
  serpent son of, 229, 229i
  in the Trojan War, 286
Arete, 314, 314i
Argives, 282
Argo (constellation), 169
Argo (ship), 155, 155i, 158
speaking plank of, 162
Argonauts, 153, 155, 157–163, 157i, 163i
Argos (city), 21, 83, 213–214, 218
Argus (builder of the Argo), 155, 160
Argus (dog), 328, 329i
Argus (monster), 51, 84–85, 84i
Ariadne, 161, 174–175, 175i, 177, 186
  in astronomy, 186
Aries (constellation), 169
Aristaeus, 257
arrows, lead and gold, 92
Artemis (Diana), **42–45,** 42i, 44i, 45i, 46, 69, 92, 96, 162
  and Actaeon, 197–198, 197i, 230
  in the *Aeneid,* 346, 362
  and Agamemnon, 211
  and Atreus, 208
  and Callisto, 93–94, 93i, 94i
  and Heracles, 138, 138i
  and Hippolytus, 177–178
  in the history of Rome, 388
  and Iphigenia, 212i, 218
  and Meleager, 195–196
  and Niobe, 194–195
  in the *Odyssey,* 313, 323
  and Selene, 74
  temple of, in Rome, 388
  in the Trojan War, 286
arts and crafts, 39
Ascanius (Iulus), 97i, 377
  in the *Aeneid,* 345, 348–349, 353–354, 356, 360–361, 365, 366i
Asclepius (Aesculapius), 69, 69i, 285, 296
Asia, 98
Asia Minor, 192
aster (Greek word for "star"), 129
astronomy, muse of, 3
Astyanax, 286–287, 287i, 298–299
Atalanta (Hippomenes' beloved), 261–263, 262i, 263i
  in modern fiction, 272–274
Atalanta (Meleager's beloved), 195–196, 195i, 201i
Athamas, 230
Athena (Minerva), **39–41,** 46, 52, 96, 115
  in the *Aeneid,* 349
  and Arachne, 192–193
  and Cadmus, 229, 229i
  and Heracles, 138, 144
  in the *Iliad,* 292i
  illustrations, 39–41, 65, 70, 159
  and Iphigenia, 219
  and Jason, 155, 158–159
  in the Judgment of Paris, 278–279, 279i
  and Nike, 73
  in the *Odyssey,* 311–314, 313i, 316, 327–328, 328i, 330–331, 333–334
  and Orestes, 216–218
  and Pandora, 190
  and Perseus, 124–126
  in the Trojan War, 277–279, 282, 284–286, 291–292, 294, 296–297
Athens, 41, 112, 166, 171–172, 176, 216, 234–236
Atlas, 111, 126, 141, 141i, 190i, 194
Atlas Mountains, 126
Atreus, 208–210
Attica, 112, 177
Augean Stables, 138
Augeas, 72, 138
augurs and augury, 382

Augustus Caesar, 345, 368, 368i, 372, 372i
Aulis, 211
Aurora. *See* Eos
Autonoe, 230
Aventine Hill, 379
Avernus, 358
axe, Clytemnestra's, 213i

B

Babylon, 252
bacchantes, 56, 259i
Bacchus. *See* Dionysus
Bacchylides, 173
Baucis, 255–257, 256i
bed, Odysseus', 333–334
Bellerophon, 112–114, 112i, 114i
  ship named after, 118, 118i
Belt of Hippolyta, 140
Berlioz, Hector, 373
Beroe, 356
bident (2-pronged staff), 28
Bithynia, 156
Black (Euxine) Sea, 153, 156
blacksmithing, and Hephaestus, 54
boars
  Adonis', 95
  Calydonian, 195–196
  Erymanthian, 138, 138i
Boreas, 321, 321i
bow, 42, 45
  of Heracles and Philoctetes, 294
  of Odysseus, 331–333, 331i, 332i
Briareus, 9
Briseis, 282, 283i
Bronze Age, 11
Brutus, Lucius Junius, 391–393, 402
Brutus, Marcus Junius, 402, 402i
bull
  Hippolytus', 178
  Zeus as, 98–99
Buthrotum, 351

C

Cacus, 140, 362, 362i
Cadmus, 55, 60, 97, 197–198, 229–230, 229i, 313
caduceus (wand), 47, 51, 69
Calais, 155, 157–158
Calchas, 211, 282, 296
calendar reform, 383
Callidice, 334
Calliope, 3, 257
calliope (musical instrument), 8
Callisto, 93–95, 93i, 94i
Calydon, 195–196
Calypso, 51, 312–314, 312i, 326
Camilla, 362, 365
Cancer, the crab, 109, 109i, 151
cannibalism in myth, 30, 225, 255, 316
cap of invisibility, 28, 125
Capitoline Hill, 394
Capitoline Wolf, 377i
Carina (constellation), 169
Carthage, 343, 346–347, 352–355, 368
Cassandra, 213, 224i, 280, 297–298, 297i, 311, 356
Cassiopeia, 125–126, 125i
  chair of, 132
  constellation, 130i, 132, 132i
Cassius (Gaius Cassius Longinus), 402, 402i
Castor, 155, 163i
Cattle of Geryon, 140
Catullus, 189
  quoted, 175
Caucasus, 190, 199
Celaeno, 351
Celestial M, Celestial W, 132
Celeus, 24–25
census, first at Rome, 388
centaurs, 176, 176i
Cepheus, 126
  constellation, 132
Cerberus, 29, 141, 141i, 258, 358–359
Cerynean Deer, 138

Cetus, 125–126
  constellation, 132
Ceyx, 264–266, 265
Chalciope, 160
Chaos, 9, 11
Charon, 28, 28i, 259, 358–359
Charybdis, 163, 324–326, 326i, 351–352, 352i
Chimera, 113–114, 113i, 358
  as computer name, 122
Chiron, 153, 153i, 197
Choice of Hercules, 136–137, 148
Chronus (Time), 13
Chryseis, 281–282, 282i
Chryses, 281
Chrysothemis, 214
Cicones, 315
Cimmerians, 321
Cimon, 178
Circe, 72, 162, 162i, 320–322, 320i, 324–325, 334
Cithaeron, Mount, 58, 233
Cius, 156
Claros, 92
Clashing Rocks (Symplegades), 158
Clio, 3
  in popular culture, 9
Cloaca Maxima, 391
Cloelia, 395
club, Heracles', 137
Clymene, 107–108
Clytemnestra, 210–217, 213i, 224i, 282
  ghost of, 216
Cnossus, 182
Coeus, 43
coin, for burial, 28
Colchis, 153, 158, 162
Collatia, 392–393
Colonus, 234
Colossus of Rhodes, 72
  compared to Statue of Liberty, 183–184
comedy, muse of, 3
constellations, listed, 169
consuls, first at Rome, 393
Copernicus, 112
coral, and Medusa, 126
Corinth, 46, 112, 165, 230, 233
cornu copiae (horn of plenty), 11, 11i
corona borealis (constellation), 186
Coronis, 69
Corynetes, 172
Cottus, 9
cow, 48
  followed by Cadmus, 229
  Hera's animal, 21
"cow-eyed," epithet, 21
Crane Dance, 175
Creon (king of Corinth), 165
Creon (king of Thebes), 231–232, 235–239, 236i
Cretan Bull, 138, 138i, 173i
Crete, 10, 12, 20, 24, 99, 115, 163, 172–173, 174, 350
  Odysseus claims to be from, 327, 329
Creusa, 349–350
Crime Street, 389
Crommyonian sow (Phaea), 172
Cronus (Saturn), 9–11, 9i, 17, 20–23, 31, 40, 46, 99, 189
  on Arachne's tapestry, 192
  children of, 19
  confused with Chronus (Time), 13
crossroads, and Hecate, 71
crow, 69
crown, Helius', 108
Cumae, 351, 357
Curiatii, 383–385
Cybele (Great Mother of the gods), 263–264, 263i
  in the *Aeneid,* 350
  modern statue of, in Madrid, 271i
Cyclopean walls, 17, 17i
Cyclopes, 9, 11, 17, 20, 315–318, 325, 352
  Polyphemus, 315i, 316–318, 317i, 318i, 322
Cyllene, Mount, 47, 48
Cyprus, 46, 59, 96, 260
Cythera, 46
Cyzicus (city and king), 155

D

Daedalus, 115–116, 115i, 116i, 121i, 173
  in popular culture, 121–122
Danae, 123–124, 123i
Danaids (daughters of Danaus), 30, 258
Danaus, 30
dance, muse of, 3
Daphne, 92–93, 92i
Dawn (goddess). *See* Eos
Day, 9
Death, 29
  and Alcestis, 139–140
Definitions
  aetiological, 27
  allegory, 41, 91
  antihero, 167
  apotheosis, 144
  apotropaic, 126
  carbon, 244
  ceramic, 244
  charter myth, 27
  colloquialism, 103
  cremation, 243–244
  epiphany, 59
  epithet, 20, 36
  exhume, 244
  hubris, 114
  humble, 244
  humus, 243–244
  inhumation, 243–244
  interment, 243–244
  invocation, 1
  irony, 15
  matronymic, 30
  megaron, 223
  metamorphosis, 102
  metaphor, 147
  patronymic, 30
  personification, 2
  polytropos, 309
  transhumance, 244
  triclinium, 5
Deianira, 141, 143, 143i
Deiphobe, 357
Deiphobus, 291–292, 359
Delos, 42–43, 175, 194, 350
Delphi, 11, 42–43, 92, 171
Delphic oracle, 86, 123, 136, 142, 173, 178, 210, 216, 229–231, 391–392
Demeter (Ceres), 10, 19–20, **23–27,** 23i, 25i, 26i, 30, 71, 90, 112
  and Erysichthon, 198–199, 198i
  identified with Cybele, 264
  and the Parthenon, 38
  temple of, 25
Demodocus, 53, 315, 315i
Demophon, 25, 27
Deucalion, 189
Diana. *See* Artemis
Dictys, 124, 126
Dido, 346–348, 347i, 348i, 352–355, 355i, 359, 368
Dido and Aeneas (Purcell), 373
Diomedes, 52, 280, 285–286, 289, 297, 345
  and the Trojan War, 280, 280i
Dione, 46, 286
  plant named after, 66i
Dionysus (Bacchus, Liber), **55–60,** 55i, 56i, 58i, 59i, 359, 361
  on Arachne's tapestry, 192
  and Ariadne, 174–175, 175i
  and Pentheus, 230
dittany, 365, 365i
Doctor Faustus (Marlowe), 305
Dodona, 20
Doso, 24
dove, 46
Draco (the Dragon), 151
dragon, guarding the Golden Fleece, 162
Drepanum, 352
dromos, 227
dryads, 198
dust, as burial rite, 237

E

eagles, 20, 49, 331
  Prometheus', 190
  Zeus', 71, 71i
Earth (goddess), 39, 111, 353
  as mother of all, 392

earthquakes, 22
"earthshaker," epithet, 22
Echidna, 113
Echo, 249–251, 250i, 251i
Egeria, 382, 382i, 383i
Egypt, 59, 85, 312
Eileithyia (Ilythia), 40i, 52, 69, 135
Electra, 214–216, 215i, 218, 224i
Electra complex, 245
Eleusinian Mysteries, 27, 34
Eleusis, 23–24, 34
Elis, 138
Elpenor, 321–322, 324
Elysian Fields, 29, 260, 358
Elysium, 356, 359
Endymion, 74, 74i
Eos (Aurora, Dawn), 70, 70i, 74, 110
Epaphus, 85, 97, 107
  as Horus, 85i
epic poetry, muse of, 3
Epimetheus, 190, 190i
Erato, 3
Erinyes (Furies), 9–10, 163, 177i, 218, 355, 361i. *See also* Eumenides
  and Io, 85
  pursue Orestes, 216, 216i
Eris (Strife), 70, 70i, 278
Eros (Cupid, Love), 9–10, 46, 46i, 70i, 95, 98
  and Apollo, 92
  and Ariadne, 174–175
  and Danae, 123i
  and Dido, 348
  and Jason, 159–160
  at the Judgment of Paris, 279i
  and Psyche, 86–92, 86i, 89i, 91i
Erymanthian Boar, 138, 138i
Erymanthus, 138
Erysichthon, 198–199, 199i
Erythia, 140
Eteocles, 231, 234–236, 236i
Etna, Mount, 54
Etruscans, 362, 383, 386, 393–394
Etymologies
  Achilles' heel, 303–304
  Achilles' tendon, 303
  aegis, 65
  Althaea's brand, 205
  Amazon, 148
  amuse, 6
  arachnid, 204–205
  arachnoid, 205
  arachnophobia, 204
  argonaut (mollusc), 169
  asterism, 130
  asteroid, astrology, astronomy, 129
  astronaut, 168
  atlas vertebra, 186
  Augean Stables, 148
  bemused, 7
  a Cassandra, 304
  chimera, 120
  chronic, chronicle, 14
  chronological, 13
  chronology, chronometer, 13–14
  constellation, 130
  cosmonaut, 168
  crony, 14
  Cyclopean, 17
  deicide, 226
  fratricide, 226
  fungicide, 226
  galaxy, 130
  genocide, 226
  halcyon days, 270
  hector (verb), 303
  herbicide, 226
  herculean, "a Hercules," 149
  homicide, 225
  hydra-headed, 147
  hygiene, 79
  hypnosis, 79–80
  infanticide, 226
  insecticide, 226
  insomnia, 79–80
  iridescent, 79
  January, 72
  jovial, 65
  labyrinth (part of inner ear), 186
  labyrinthian, labyrinthine, 185

labyrinthine, 120, 120i
leonine, 119, 119i
lethal, 35
lethargic, 35
lunacy, 78
lunatic, 79
martial, 65
matricide, 226
mentor, 338
metamorphoses, metempsychosis, 103
Minoan, 182
morphine, 72, 79
mortal, 79
muse (verb), 7
museum, music, 6
narcissism, narcissistic, 269
nausea, nautical, nautilus, 168
nebula, 130
nemesis, 79, 82
niobium, 204
odyssey, 338
Pandora's box, 204
panic, 73, 79
patrician, 379
patricide, 226
phaeton, 121, 121i
plutocrat, 65–66
procrustean, 185
protean, 35
psyched, psychiatry, psychology, 103
regal, regent, regime, regulation, 400
regicide, 226
senator, 379
shirt of Nessus, 148
somnambulist, 79–80
somnolent, 79–80
sororicide, 226
stygian, 35
syringe, 79
tantalizing, 35
tantalum, 204
titanium, 15
Trojan horse (computer program), 304
Tyrannosaurus rex
tyrant, 400
uranium, 15
volcano, 65
vulcanize, 65

Eumaeus, 327, 327i, 329, 331–333
Eumenides (Furies), 234, 236
Euripides, 214, 214i, 218
  Alcestis, 135
  Bacchae, 55–58
  Hippolytus, 177–178
  Iphigenia at Aulis, 207
  Iphigenia in Tauris, 207
  Medea, 153, 168
Europa, 97–99, 98i, 198, 229
Europe, named for Europa, 99
Euryale, 125
Eurybates, 330
Eurycleia, 330, 330i, 333
Eurydice (wife of Creon), 239
Eurydice (wife of Orpheus), 257–260, 258i
Eurylochus, 319–321, 325
Eurynome, 54
Eurystheus, 127, 136–142
Eurytus, 142–143
Euterpe, 3
Euxine (Black) Sea, 153, 156
Evander, 362–365
Eve and Medusa, English poem on, 128

F

Famine (goddess), 198–199, 199i
Fates, 20, 25, 196
Father Time, 11
Faunus, 360
Faustulus, 377
fibula (brooch), 234i
fire
  made by rubbing sticks together, 48
  theft of, 190
flute and wind instruments, muse of, 3
Forum, Roman, 386, 389
Free to Be . . . You and Me (Miles), 272–274
Freud, Sigmund, 245, 245i
Furies. *See* Erinyes

G

Gabii, 391, 393
gadfly, and Io, 85
Gaea (Earth), 9, 11, 23, 39, 40, 99
Galatea, 261, 261i
Galileo, 112
Games
  Isthmian, 176
  Olympian, 44
  Pythian, 44
Ganymede, 71, 71i, 159
Gate of Horn, 331
Gate of Ivory, 331, 360
geese, 256, 331
Geryon, 140, 358, 358i
Giants, 9
Glauce, 165
Glaucus, 112
Golden Age, 11
golden bough, 358
Golden Fleece, 153, 153i, 155, 158–162, 162i
Gorgons, 39, 41i, 124–125, 324, 358
  names of, 125
Graces, 20, 96
Graeae, "Gray Ones," 124–125
grain, 23
  sorted by Psyche, 90
Great Bear (constellation), 95
"Greek key" designs, 187, 187i
Gyes, 9

H

Hades (Pluto), 10, 19, 23–24, 26, **28–30,** 28i, 29i, 141, 177, 213, 258i, 360
  and Persephone, 24i, 26i, 28
Haemon, 237–239
halcyon (kingfisher), 266, 266i
Happiness (goddess), 136–137
Harmonia, 229–230, 229i
Harpies, 156–158, 157i, 351–352, 351i, 352, 358, 360
hearth, 31
Hebe, 52, 71, 71i, 144i
Hecate, 23, 71, 71i, 160–161, 161i, 355
Hector, 293i
  in the *Aeneid,* 345, 348–349, 351
  in the *Iliad,* 278, 281–282, 284–294, 287i, 292i, 298
  in modern art, 306i
  in nursery rhyme, 308
Hecuba, 278, 286, 291, 297–298, 298i
Helen of Troy, 73, 155
  in the *Aeneid,* 349, 351, 359
  in Marlowe's *Doctor Faustus,* 305
  in the *Odyssey,* 309, 312
  in the Trojan War, 177, 210, 280, 284, 286, 291, 296, 305i
Helenus, 351–352
Helicon, 1, 125
Helius (Sol, Phoebus), 23–24, 53, 72, 72i, 74, 107–112, 108i, 109i, 140, 322i, 325
  cattle of, 324–325
Helle, 153
Hellespont, 153
Hephaestus (Vulcan), 30i, 40, 53, **54,** 54i, 110, 140
  in the *Aeneid,* 363
  in the *Iliad,* 283, 290
  in the *Odyssey,* 315
  and Pandora, 190
  and Prometheus, 190
  in the Trojan War, 283, 290i
Hera (Juno), 10, 19, **21,** 21i, 30, 52, 69, 70i, 90, 98, 166, 198, 343i
  in the *Aeneid,* 343, 345, 347–350, 352–353, 355–357, 360–361, 363–365, 367
  and Alcyone, 265
  and Apollo and Artemis, 42–43
  Echo and, 249
  and Hephaestus, 54
  and Heracles, 135, 139, 144i
  and Jason, 155, 158–159, 161
  in the Judgment of Paris, 278–279, 279i
  in the Trojan War, 281– 283, 285–286, 290, 294

and Zeus' lovers
Callisto, 93–94
Io, 83–85
Semele, 55
Heracles (Hercules), 127, 135–144, 165
in the *Aeneid,* 358, 362, 364
on the Argo, 155, 156
and Cacus, 362i
Choice of, 136–137, 148
constellation, 151
and the Hydra, 113
illustrations of, 137–139, 141–142
and Philoctetes, 281, 295
Pillars of, 140
in popular culture, 146, 149
and Prometheus, 191
and Theseus, 171–172, 173, 176
Hercules beetle, 150, 150i
Hercules' club (shrub), 150–151, 150i
Herdonius, Turnus, 390–391
Hermes (Mercury), 26, 28–29, 30i, 40i, **47–51,** 47i, 51i, 69, 70i, 90–91, 98
in the *Aeneid,* 346, 346i, 354–355
and Argus, 84i, 85
and Eurydice, 258i
in the *Iliad,* 278–279, 293
and the Judgment of Paris, 278, 279i
in the *Odyssey,* 312, 312i, 320
and Pan, 73
and Pandora, 190
and Perseus, 124–126
and Philemon and Baucis, 255–257
and shepherd's pipes, 85
Herminius, Titus, 394
Hermione, 351
Hesiod, 2, 5, 189
and Hecate, 71
Theogony, 1–2, 9–11, 20, 40–42, 52–53, 54, 113, 189
Works and Days, 70, 189
Hesione, 140
Hesperia, 343, 350
Hesperides, 141, 163, 278
Hestia (Vesta), 10, 19, **31,** 31i, 46
in popular culture, 37
Hippocrene
Boeotian, 125
Corinthian, 114
Hippodamia, 207–208, 207i, 208i
Hippolochus, 114
Hippolyta, 140, 176
Hippolytus, 176–178, 177i, 178i
Hippomenes, 261–263, 262i, 263i
history, muse of, 3
Homer, 2, 5
Iliad, 2, 21, 52–54, 72, 112–113, 281, 343
Odyssey, 2, 22, 28, 334
Homeric Hymns
2. to Demeter, 23–27
3. to Apollo, 42–44
4. to Hermes, 47–50
5. to Aphrodite, 31, 46, 96–97
7. to Dionysus, 55, 58–60
19. to Pan, 73
27. to Artemis, 42, 44
28. to Athena, 39–40
hoopoe, 255, 255i
Horace, *Odes,* 123, 177
Horatia, 384–385
Horatii, 383–385
oath of, 384i
Horatius Cocles, 393–395
horses
of Diomedes, 139
of Helius, 108–110, 108i, 109i, 110i
as Poseidon's animal, 22
Hours, 108, 110
House of Atreus, 207–219
curse on, 207–208, 219
modern plays and novels about, 225
House of Tantalus, 207
hubris, 114, 125
Hundred-handed Ones, 9, 11
hunting, goddess of, 43
Hydra, Lernaean, 113, 137, 137i
constellation, 151
Hygeia, 69, 69i
Hyginus, *Stories,* 207

Hylas, 156, 156i
Hyllus, 143, 143i
hymns, sacred, muse of, 3
Hyperboreans, 59, 125, 138
Hypnos (Somnus), 72, 72i, 80
Hypsipyle, 155

I

Iambe, 24–25
Iapetus, 9
Iarbas, 353, 368
Icaria, 116
Icarus, 115–116, 115i, 116i
Ida, Mount, 96
Iliad. *See* Homer, *Iliad*
Ilium/Ilion, 277
Ilus, 277
Ilythia. *See* Eileithyia
Inachus, 83–84, 107
Indo-European, 129
Ino, 230, 313
invocation, 1, 5
Io, 83–85, 83i, 84i, 97, 123
  as Isis, 85i
Iobates, 113–114
Iolaus, 137
Iolcus, 153, 155, 164
Iole, 142–143
Iphicles, 135
Iphigenia, 211–212, 212i, 214, 218–219, 218i, 281
Iphitus, 142
Iris, 72, 265, 284, 286, 290, 355–356
iris (flower), 72i
Iron Age, 11
Isander, 114
Isis, 85
Ismene, 231, 235–238, 235i
Ister (Danube), 162
Isthmian Games, 176
Italy, 140
Ithaca, 309, 311, 318–319, 322–323, 326–327, 334, 352
Itys, 255
Iulus, 345. *See also* Ascanius
Ixion, 29i, 30, 30i, 258

J

Janiculum (hill), 386, 394–395
Janus, 72, 72i
Jason, 153–166, 153i, 166i, 195
  in popular culture, 167
Jocasta, 230–234
Jove. *See* Zeus
Judgment of Paris, 70, 70i, 278–279, 279i, 343
Julius Caesar, 343, 368, 368i
Julius Caesar (Shakespeare), 402
Jupiter. *See* Zeus
jury, first, 217
Juturna, 364–367

K

kingfisher (halcyon), 266, 266i
"Know thyself," 64

L

Labdacus, 230
Labors of Heracles, listed, 137–141
Labyrinth, 115, 173–175, 183i
labyrinth (maze), 185, 185i
Ladon, 141
Laertes, 309, 318, 334
Laestrygonians, 319, 319i
Laius, 230–233
Laocoon, 296–297, 297i, 348
Laodamia, 114, 281
Laomedon, 140
Lapiths, 176, 176i
Larcius, Spurius, 394
Larentia, 377
Larisa, 126

Lars Porsenna. *See* Porsenna, Lars
Latins, 361, 367, 387, 390–391
Latinus, 360–362, 365–366
Latium, 360, 363, 391
  map of, 360i
laurel, 45, 102, 231i
  Apollo and, 42, 93
  Daphne and, 93
Lausus, 362, 364–365
Lavinia, 360, 367–368
Leda, 210, 210i
Lemnos, 54, 155, 281, 283
Leo, 109i
Leo (constellation), 151
Leonardo da Vinci, 244
Lernaean Hydra, 137, 137i
Les Troyens (Berlioz), 373
Lethe, River, 29, 357
Leto, 20, 42, 96, 194
Liber. *See* Dionysus
Libya, 141
Linus, 136
lion
  Atalanta and Hippomenes transformed into, 263
  Dionysus as, 59
  and Thisbe, 252
Lion Gate (Mycenae), 17
lion skin, Heracles', 137
Liriope, 249
Little Bear (constellation), 95
Little Women (Alcott), 269
Livia, 372, 372i
Livy, 377, 377i
looms and weaving, 192i, 193i
Lotus-eaters, 315
love, goddess of, 46
Lucifer, the morning star, 110
Lucretia, 392–393, 393i
Lucumo. *See* Tarquinius Priscus
Lycia, 113
Lycomedes, 178, 280, 280i
Lydia, 142, 192, 195, 207
Lynceus, 155
lyre, 45, 47, 47i, 50–51
  Anchises and, 96
  Apollo and, 92
  muse of, 3
lyric poetry, muse of, 3

M

Macbeth (Shakespeare), 71
Macedonia, 19
Machaon, 285, 296
maenads, 56, 57i, 175i
Maia, 47, 49
Marathon
  Battle of, 178
  Plain of, 138
Marlowe, Christopher, 305
marriage, 21
Medea, 72, 159–162, 164–166, 172
  illustrations of, 162–164
medicine, Apollo and, 42, 92
Medusa, 39, 124–126
  English poem on, 128
  illustrations of, 41, 70, 124–126, 128
  jellyfish, 133
Megara, 136
Melanthius, 331
Meleager, 141, 143, 195–196, 195i, 196i, 201i
Melpomene, 3
Menelaus, 210
  in the *Aeneid,* 359
  in the *Iliad,* 280, 282, 284–285, 290, 290i
  in the *Odyssey,* 311–312, 312i
Mentes, 311
Mentor, 311, 311i
Mercury. *See* Hermes
Merope, 230, 233
metalworking, and Hephaestus, 54
Metaneira, 24–25
Metis, 20, 39–41
  as Common Sense, 40
Mettius Fufetius, 383, 385

Mezentius, 362, 364–365
Minerva. *See* Athena
Minos, 99, 115, 173
Minotaur, 115, 173–174, 174i
  in popular culture, 187
Misenus, 358
Mnemosyne, 2, 5, 9
moly, 320
moon, goddess of, 42
Morpheus, 72, 265
Moschus, *Europa,* 98
Mucius Scaevola, Gaius, 393–395, 395i
  reason for his name, 395
mulberry, 252–253, 253i
The Muses, **1–3,** 1i, 3i, 20, 125, 315
  listed, 3
  in popular culture, 4–5
music, god of, 42
My Fair Lady, 268
Mycenae, 17, 17i, 112, 127, 208–209, 222, 227
  palace at, 222, 223i
Mycenaean Period, 222
Myrmidons, 282, 289
Myrtilus, 207–208
Myrtoan Sea, 208

N

Naiads, 111
Napoleon Bonaparte, 118, 118i
Narcissus, 249–251, 249i, 250i, 251i
narcissus (flower), 251, 251i
Nausicaa, 313–314, 313i, 314i
Nautes, 356
Naxos, 174–175, 175i
nectar, 11, 43, 71, 283
Nemean Lion, 137, 137i, 172
  as constellation, 151
Nemesis, 73, 73i, 250
  in modern culture, 82
Neoptolemus (Pyrrhus), 280, 294–295, 297–299, 298i, 323–324, 334, 349–350, 349i
Nereids, 98, 174i, 294i
Nereus, 141
Nessus, 143, 143i
Nestor, 196, 288, 311
Night, 9
  daughters of (Erinyes), 217
nightingale, 255, 255i
Nike (Victory), 41i, 73, 73i, 81, 81i
Nile, 85, 111
Ninus, 252
Niobe, 193–195, 193i, 194i, 207
No-Man, 316–317
North Star (Polaris), 132
North Wind (god), 155
"Nothing in excess," 64
Numa Pompilius, 382–383, 382i, 383i, 385–387
Numicius, 368
Numitor, 377
nymphs, 9, 56, 94, 96–97, 156, 156i, 353
  Aeneas' ships transformed into, 363–364

O

O Brother, Where Art Thou? (movie), 337
oak, 20
Oceanus, 9, 20
Octavia, 372, 372i
Odysseus (Ulysses), 309i, 341i
  in the *Aeneid,* 352
  in modern poetry, 339–340
  in the *Odyssey,* 22, **309–334,** 323
    illustrations, 163, 314–318, 320, 324–334
  in the Trojan War, 277, 280–281, 284, 288–289, 294–298
    illustrations, 277, 280–281, 289
Odyssey. See Homer, *Odyssey*
The Odyssey (movie), 337
Oedipus, 176, 229, **230–236**
  grave of, 234
  illustrations, 231, 234–235, 246
  in popular culture, 245–246
Oedipus complex, 245
Oenomaus, 207, 208i
Oenone, 278, 278i, 296
Oeta, 144

Ogygia, 326
Oileus, 155
olive tree, 22, 138
Olympian Games, 44
  Heracles and, 138
Olympus, Mount, 19i, *passim*
Omphale, 142–143
Orestes, 214–219, 218–219, 351
  illustrations of, 214– 216, 218, 224
Orpheus, 28, 155, 163, 163i, 212, 257–260, 359
  illustrations of, 257–260
  in opera, 272
Ostia, 386
Ovid
  Fasti, 368
  Metamorphoses, passim

P

Palamedes, 296
Palatine Hill, 379, 394
Palinurus, 355–358
Palladium, 277, 277i, 279i, 297
Pallas (epithet of Athena), 39–40. *See also* Athena
Pallas (playmate of Athena), 277
Pallas (son of Evander), 362–365, 367
  swordbelt of, 367
Pallentium, 362
Pan, 73, 73i, 334, 334i
Panacea, 69
Pandarus, 285
Pandion, 253–254
Pandora, 190, 190i
panpipes, 73
Paris (Alexander), 46, 210, 278–279, 280, 349, 359
  in the *Iliad,* 278–280, 284–287, 292–293, 296
  illustrations of, 70, 278–279, 305
Parnassus, 42–43, 92
Parthenon, 38, 41
parthenos, "virgin," title of Athena, 41
Pasiphae, 72, 173, 173i, 174
Patara, 92
Patroclus, 282, 288–290, 290i, 292–294, 294i
peacock, 21, 70i, 85, 85i
Pegasus, 112i, 114, 114i, 125
Peirithous, 176–177, 177i, 196, 358
Peleus, 155, 192, 278, 280
Pelias, 153, 155, 159, 164
  daughters of, 164, 164i, 165
Pelopeia, 210
Peloponnesus (or Peloponnese) 112, 137, 208
Pelops, 30, 207–208, 207i, 208i
Penates, 346, 350
Penelope, 309, 311i, 323, 327, 329–334, 330–331i, 334i
Pentheus, 56–58, 58i, 230
peplos, 38, 41
Periphetes, 172
Persephone (Proserpina), 20, **23–27,** 29, 30, 71, 72, 91, 112, 162, 177, 321, 357
  illustrations of, 23, 24, 26, 29, 141
  and Orpheus, 258, 258i
  and the Parthenon, 38
Perseus, 123–127, 123i, 125i, 126i, 135
  constellation, 132, 132i
Persia, 41
Persian Wars, 41, 178
persona (mask), 224
personification, 2, 5
petasus, 47, 51i
Phaea (Crommyonian sow), 172
Phaeacians, 163, 312–314, 326
Phaedra, 177–178, 177i
Phaethon, 72, 107–112, 110i, 111i
Phidias, 38
Philemon, 255–257, 256i
Philoctetes, 144, 281, 294–296
Philoetius, 328, 331–333
Philomela, 253–255
  in English verse, 271
Philonoë, 114
Phineus, 126
Phineus (blind seer), 156–158
Phocis, 43
Phoebus. *See* Apollo; Helius

Phoenicia, 97
Phoenix, 288–289, 289i
Phrixus, 153, 155
Phrygia, 96–97
Phthia, 282
Pieria, 2, 48
Pillars of Heracles, 140
Pindar
  Nemean Odes, 135
  Olympian Odes, 114
  Pythian Odes, 123–127, 153
plague, at Thebes, 231
Plains of Mourning, 359
Plautus, *Amphitryon,* 135
Pleasure (goddess), 91
Pluto. *See* Hades
Po, River, 111
poetry, god of, 42
Polaris (the North Star), 132
Poliporthes, 334
Polites, 298, 298i
Polybus, 230, 233
Polydectes, 124, 126
Polydeuces (Pollux), 155–156, 163i
Polydorus, 230, 298, 350
Polyhymnia, 3
Polynices, 231, 234–238, 235i, 236i, 237i
Polyphemus, 22, 352
Polypoetes, 334
Polyxena, 298–299, 298i
pomegranate, 21, 21i, 26
pontus, 153
Porsenna, Lars, 395i
Poseidon (Neptune), 10, 19, **22,** 31, 43, 98, 111, 140, 173
  in the *Aeneid,* 345, 349, 356, 362
  and Andromeda, 125–126
  on Athena's and Arachne's tapestries, 192
  and Bellerophon, 112, 114
  and Cassiopeia, 132
  chariot of, 207i
  and Erysichthon's daughter, 199
  in the history of Rome, 379
  illustrations of, 22, 163, 174, 344
  in the *Odyssey,* 313, 313i, 317–318, 322–323, 326, 334
  and Pelops, 207
  and Theseus, 171, 178
Priam, 140, 213
  in the *Aeneid,* 347, 349–351, 349i, 359
  in the *Odyssey,* 324
  in the Trojan War, 278, 280, 291, 291i, 293, 293i, 297–298
Prince of Robbers (Hermes), 50
prison, first in Rome, 386
Procne, 253–255
Procrustes, 172
Proetus, 112–113, 112i
"Promethean charm," 160
Prometheus, 40, 158, 158i, 189–191, 189i, 190i
prophecy, Apollo and, 92
Propontis, 155
Protesilaus, 281
Proteus, 22, 312
Psyche, 86–92, 86i, 87i, 89i, 91i
  etymology of, 103
Puppis (constellation), 169
Purcell, Henry, 373
Pygmalion (brother of Dido), 346, 368
Pygmalion (sculptor), 260–261, 260i, 261i
  in modern literature and art, 268–269
Pygmalion (Shaw), 268
Pylades, 214–215, 214i, 218–219, 218i, 224i
Pylos, 222, 311
Pyramus, 252–253
  in a modern political cartoon, 270i
Pyrgo, 356
Pyriphlegethon, 321
Pyrrha, 189, 280
Pyrrhus. *See* Neoptolemus
Pythia, 44
Pythian Games, 44
Pytho (Delphi), 49
Python, 43, 92
Pyxis (constellation), 169

Q

Quirinus, 382
Quirites, 382

R

rainbow, 72
Recipes
  ambrosia, 14
  gorgonzola tortellini, 133
Remus, 377, 379
Rhadamanthys, 99
Rhea, 9–10, 9i, 17, 20–23, 26, 31
  children of, 19
  identified with Cybele and Demeter (Ceres), 264
Rhea Silvia, 377
Rhodes, 72
Rhone, 111
Romans
  and Heracles (Hercules), 140
  mission of, 359
Rome
  future of, 363
  and Hestia, 31
Romulus, 377, 379, 381–383, 386, 389
  in popular culture, 401
Rumor, 353
Rutulians, 360–361, 366–367

S

Sabine Women, 379i
Sabines, 379–381, 381i
sacrifice, Greek, 189
Sagittarius, 109i
Samothrace, 73
sandals, winged, 125
Sarpedon, 99, 289
Satan, 28
satyrs, 56i, 175i
Scaevola. *See* Mucius Scaevola
scar, recognition by, 214, 330
Sciron, 172
Scorpio, 109i
Scylla, 163, 163i, 324–325, 325i, 351–352, 352i
Scyrus, 178, 280
Scythia, 198
sea monster
  and Andromeda, 126, 126i
  and Hesione, 140
seagull, 90
seals, Poseidon's, 22
seasons, 11, 108
Selene (Luna, Moon), 74, 74i
Semele, 55–56, 56i, 60, 230
Seneca, 299
  Thyestes, 207
Seriphus, 124, 126
Servius Tullius, 387–389, 393
Seven against Thebes, 236
sewer, first in Rome, 387
Shakespeare
  Julius Caesar, 402
  Macbeth, 71
  A Midsummer Night's Dream, 269
  Romeo and Juliet, 269
Shaw, George Bernard, 268–269
ships, ancient, 264i, 305i
Sibyl, Cumaean, 351, 356, 357i, 358, 390, 390i
Sibylline Books, 390
Sicily, 54, 351–352
sickle, 9
Sidon, 97–98
Silver Age, 11
Simonides, *Poems,* 124
Sinis, 172, 172i
Sinon, 296–297
Sirens, 163, 163i, 324, 324i
Sisyphus, 29, 29i, 112, 258
Sky. *See* Uranus
Sleep, 162, 265, 356–357
snake, 69
Sol. *See* Helius

Solymi, 114
Sophocles
  Antigone, 229, 243
  Electra, 207
  Oedipus at Colonus, 229
  Oedipus the King, 229
  Trachiniae, 135
soul, Psyche as, 91
Sounion, 22
Sparta, 112, 280, 311, 327
The Sphinx, 230, 231i, 246i
spider, 193
Spurius Larcius, 394
stella (Latin word for "star"), 129
Sterope, 208i
Stheno, 125
Sthenoboea, 113
Strophades, 351
Stymphalian Birds, 138
Styx, River, 20, 28i, 55, 158, 236, 280, 321, 357–358
suitors of Penelope, 309, 311, 326–334, 333i
Sun. *See* Helius (Phoebus)
sun, and Apollo, 42
sunrise, aetiology of, 112
superego, 245
Sychaeus, 346, 352, 355, 359
Symplegades (Clashing Rocks), 158
Syrinx (nymph), 73
syrinx (shepherd's pipes), 47, 50–51, 50i, 73i

T

Talus, 115, 163, 163i
Tanaquil, 386–389
Tantalus, 29i, 30, 30i, 193–194, 207–208, 258
Tantalus junior, 209
Tarpeia, 381, 381i
Tarpeian rock, 381
Tarquinii (city), 386
Tarquinius, Arruns (brother of Superbus), 388
Tarquinius, Arruns (son of Superbus), 391–393
Tarquinius, Sextus (son of Superbus), 391–393
Tarquinius, Titus (son of Superbus), 391–393
Tarquinius Collatinus, Lucius, 392–393
Tarquinius Priscus, Lucius (Lucumo), 386–389
Tarquinius Superbus, Lucius, 388–393, 390i
  reason for name Superbus, 389
Tarquins (the whole family), 393, 395
Tartarus, 9, 20, 29, 29i, 50, 113
Tauris and the Taurians, 218, 218i, 219
Taurus, 109i
Telamon, 155
Telegonus, 334
Telemachus, 281, 309, 311–312, 311i, 327–334, 328i, 330i
Telephassa, 97
Tempe, 83
Tenedos, 92, 297
Tennyson, Alfred Lord, 339–340
Tereus, 253–255
Terpsichore, 3
  in popular culture, 9
Teucer, 350
Thalia, 3
Thamyris, 2
Thanatos (Mors), 72
"the maiden," epithet, 23
Thebes, 52, 56–58, 135–136, 193–194, 197, 229–231, 235–236, 239
Themis, 9, 43
Theocritus, *Idylls,* 135
Thersites, 284
Theseus, 138, 141, 161, **171–178,** 171i, 172i, 174i, 195–196, 358
  modern musical about, 182
  and Oedipus, 234–236
  in popular culture, 182
Thesprotians, 334
Thessaloniki, 19
Thessaly, 19, 83, 126, 264
Thetis, 54, 186, 190–191
  in the Trojan War, 278, 280, 280i, 282–284, 288, 290, 290i, 293, 294i

Thisbe, 252–253, 252i, 253i
in a modern political cartoon, 270i
Thrace, 52, 139, 156, 253, 257, 298–299, 350
women of, 259
Thrinacia, 324
thunderbolt, Zeus', 20, 97, 111, 144
Thyestes, 208–210, 213
thyrsus, 57i, 58i, 259
Tiber, 111
Tiber (god), 362, 394
Tiber (river), 360, 362–364, 377, 386–387, 394–395
bridge across, 386
Time, Father, 11
Tiresias, 135, 136i, 231–232, 238, 249, 321–322, 322i, 325, 334
Tiryns, 112, 142
megaron at, 223i
palace at, 222–223, 224i
Titans, 20, 41–42
in astronomy, 16
listed, 9
in popular culture, 16
Tithonus, 70
Titus Herminius, 394
Titus Tatius, 381–382, 381i
Tityus, 258
tortoise, 47
Trachis, 143–144
tragedy, muse of, 3
Treasury of Atreus, 227, 227i
trident, 22
Triptolemus, 26i, 27
Triton(s), 22, 98, 99i, 174i, 345, 345i, 358
triumph, laurel leaves and, 93
Troad, 277, 281
Troezen, 171
Trojan Horse, 296–297, 296i, 363
Trojan War, 46, 52, 70, 210, **277–299**
painted on Dido's temple, 347
as subject of song, 315
Trojans, 96
Tros, 277
Troy, 140, 211, 217
fall of, 213
walls of, 291i
Tullia (evil sister), 388–389, 393
Tullia (good sister), 388
Tullus Hostilius, 383
Turnus, 360–367
Turnus Herdonius. *See* Herdonius
turtle, Sciron's pet, 172
Tyndareus, 210, 210i
Typhon, 113, 113i
Tyre, Tyrians, 346

U

Ulysses. *See* Odysseus
Ulysses (Tennyson), 339–340
Underworld, 20, 23–27, 28–30, 47, 86, 90, 113, 141, 177, 321, 323i, 356–357
Orpheus and Eurydice in, 258–260
Urania, 3
Uranus (Sky), 9–10, 40
urns, cinerary, 244i
Ursa Major and *Minor* (constellations), 95

V

Vela (constellation), 169
Venus. *See* Aphrodite
Vergil (Publius Vergilius Maro), 343, 343i, 372, 372i
Aeneid, 135, 343
quotations from, 343, 373–374
Georgics, 257
Vesta. *See* Hestia
Vestal Virgins, 31, 31i, 377
Vice (goddess), 136–137
Virtue (goddess), 144
volcanoes, and Hephaestus, 54
Vulcan. *See* Hephaestus
vulture, Prometheus', 190i

W

weather, and Zeus, 41
weaving and looms, 192i, 193i
  used to send a message, 254
West Side Story, 269
winds, bag of, 319
winged sandals, 125
winnowing fan, in Odysseus' future, 322

X

Xanthus, 351
Xenophon, 136, 136i
  Memorabilia, 135

Z

Zephyr, 87– 89
Zetes, 155, 157–158
Zeus (Jupiter, Jove), 19, **20,** 20i, 31, 43, 86, 91, 92, 159, 173, 208i
  in the *Aeneid,* 343, 345–346, 349, 352–357, 363–364, 366–368
  and Anchises, 97
  on Athena's and Arachne's tapestries, 192
  birth of, 10–11
  children of
    Aphrodite, 46
    Asclepius, 69
    Athena, 39–41, 40i
    Dionysus, 60
    Helen of Troy, 210
    Hephaestus, 54
    Heracles, 135, 142, 144, 144i
    Hermes, 50
  and Demeter, 23–24, 25
  eagle of, 90
  Echo and, 249
  fish named after, 66i
  in the history of Rome, 382, 385–386, 391
  and Jason, 161
  and the Judgment of Paris, 278–279
  lovers of
    Callisto, 93–95
    Danae, 123, 123i
    Europa, 97–99, 98i, 229
    Io, 83–85, 83i, 107, 123
  and the Muses, 2
  and Niobe, 194
  in the *Odyssey,* 312, 314, 316–318, 326, 332, 334
  and Phaethon, 111
  and Philemon and Baucis, 255–257
  and Phineus, 156–158
  and Prometheus, 189–191, 189i
  temple of, at Olympia, 208i
  and Thyestes, 208
  in the Trojan War, 277–279, 282–291, 293, 295

Classical Mythology and Epics

A Short Guide to Classical Mythology
G. M. Kirkwood

120 pp. (1959, Reprint 2003) Paperback, ISBN 978-0-86516-309-6

On Unbelievable Tales
Palaephatus Peri Apiston

Jacob Stern, ed., trans.

vii + 167 pp. (1996)
Paperback ISBN 978-0-86516-320-1 • Hardbound, ISBN 978-0-86516-310-2

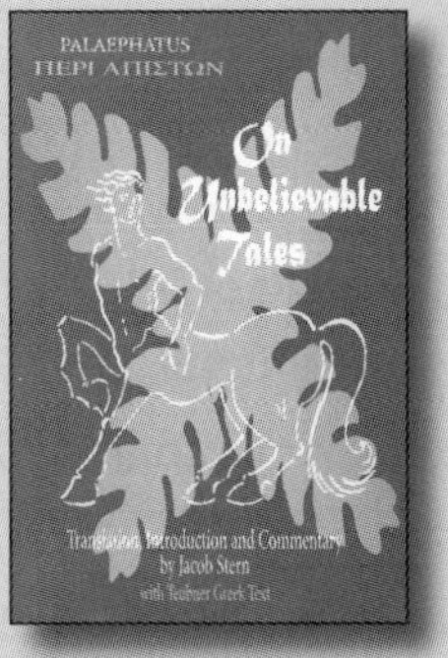

Vergil's *Aeneid*: *Hero • War • Humanity*
G. B. Cobbold, translator

— Novelistic Translation with Reader Aids —

xviii + 366 pp., 91 illustrations + 1 map (2005) 5" x 7 ¾" Paperback
ISBN 978-0-86516-596-0

Tales from the Greek Drama
H. R. Jolliffe

xi + 311 pp. (1962, Reprint 1984) Paperback ISBN 978-0-86516-013-2

The Epic of Gilgamesh, 2nd edition
Verse rendition by Danny P. Jackson, Introduction by Robert D. Biggs, Illustrations by Thom Kapheim, Interpretive essay by James G. Keenan

Student Edition: B&W illustrations, 115 pp. (1997, Reprint 2000) Paperback
ISBN 978-0-86516-352-2

Ancient Epic Poetry: *Homer, Apollonius, Virgil; With a Chapter on the Gilgamesh Poems*
Charles Rowan Beye

x + 318 pp. (2006, Expanded Reprint of the 1993 Cornell University edition)
6" x 9" Paperback,ISBN 978-0-86516-607-3

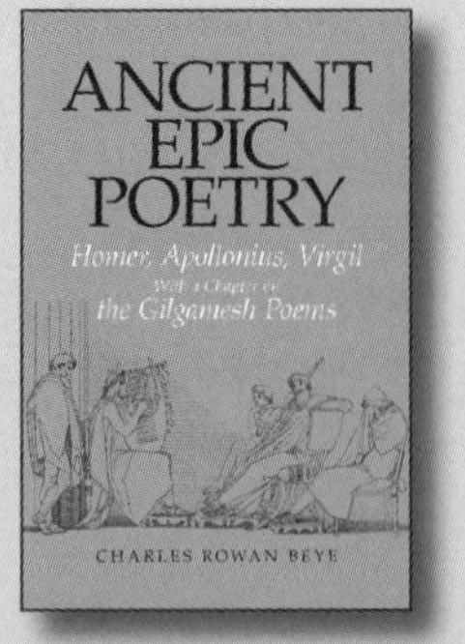

Latina Mythica
Bonnie A. Catto; Illustrations by Christopher J. White

xiv + 202 pp. (2006) 6" x 9" Paperback, ISBN 978-0-86516-599-1

Latina Mythica II: *Troia Capta*
Bonnie A. Catto

xv + 241 pp. (2015) 6" x 9" Paperback, ISBN 978-0-86516-825-1

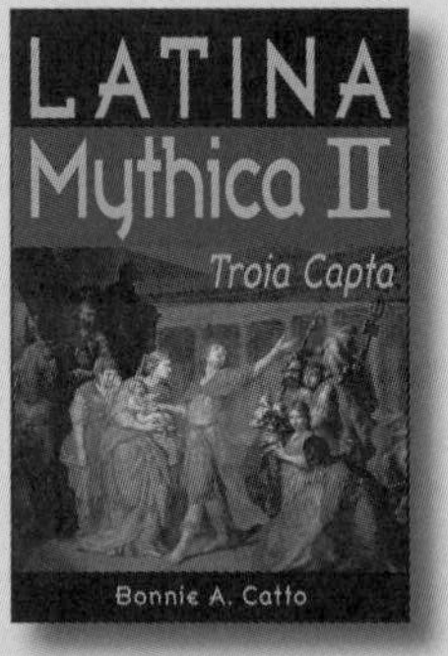

Visit our website for more information on these and our other titles, including in-depth descriptions, reviews, and more.

www.BOLCHAZY.com

Bolchazy-Carducci Publishers, Inc.
www.BOLCHAZY.com